# Windows 3.1 SECRETS Testimonials

# *Windows 3 SECRETS* Testimonials

# INFO WORLD

# Windows
# GIZMOS

## by Brian and Margie Livingston

**IDG**
**BOOKS**

IDG Books Worldwide, Inc.
An International Data Group Company

CALIFORNIA ◆ INDIANA ◆ MASSACHUSETTS

**Windows GIZMOS**
Published by
**IDG Books Worldwide, Inc.**
An International Data Group Company
155 Bovet Road, Suite 610
San Mateo, CA 94402

Library of Congress Catalog Card No.: 92-74307

ISBN 1-878058-66-5

Printed in the United States of America

10 9 8 7 6 5 4 3 2 1

Distributed in the United States by IDG Books Worldwide, Inc.

Distributed in Canada by Macmillan of Canada, a Division of Canada Publishing Corporation; by Woodslane Pty. Ltd. in Australia and New Zealand; and by Computer Bookshops in the U.K. and Ireland.

For information on translations and availability in other countries, contact Marc Jeffrey Mikulich, Foreign Rights Manager, at IDG Books Worldwide. Fax: 415-358-1260.

For sales inquiries and special prices for bulk quantities, write to the address above or call IDG Books Worldwide at 415-312-0650.

# Acknowledgment

The publisher would like to give special thanks to Patrick J. McGovern, without whom this book would not have been possible.

# About IDG Books Worldwide

Welcome to the world of IDG Books Worldwide.

IDG Books Worldwide, Inc., is a division of International Data Group (IDG), the world's largest publisher of computer-related information and the leading global provider of information services on information technology. IDG publishes over 185 computer publications in 60 countries. Thirty million people read one or more IDG publications each month.

If you use personal computers, IDG Books is committed to publishing quality books that meet your needs. We rely on our extensive network of publications, including such leading periodicals as *InfoWorld, PC World, Computerworld, Macworld, Publish, Network World,* and *SunWorld,* to help us make informed and timely decisions in creating useful computer books that meet your needs.

Every IDG book strives to bring extra value and skill-building instruction to the reader. Our books are written by experts, with the backing of IDG periodicals, and with careful thought devoted to issues such as audience, interior design, use of icons, and illustrations. Our editorial staff is a careful mix of high-tech journalists and experienced book people. Our close contact with the makers of computer products helps ensure accuracy and thorough coverage. Our heavy use of personal computers at every step in production means we can deliver books in the most timely manner.

We are delivering books of high quality at competitive prices on topics customers want. At IDG, we believe in quality, and we have been delivering quality for over 25 years. You'll find no better book on a subject than an IDG book.

John Kilcullen
President and CEO
IDG Books Worldwide, Inc.

IDG Books Worldwide, Inc. is a division of International Data Group. The officers are Patrick J. McGovern, Founder and Board Chairman; Walter Boyd, President; Robert A. Farmer, Vice Chairman. International Data Group's publications include: **ARGENTINA's** Computerworld Argentina, InfoWorld Argentina; **ASIA's** Computerworld Hong Kong, PC World Hong Kong, Computerworld Southeast Asia, PC World Singapore, Computerworld Malaysia, PC World Malaysia; **AUSTRALIA's** Computerworld Australia, Australian PC World, Australian Macworld; **AUSTRIA's** Computerwelt Oesterreich, PC Test; **BRAZIL's** DataNews, Mundo IBM, Mundo Unix, PC World, Publish; **BULGARIA's** Computerworld Bulgaria, Ediworld, PC World Express; **CANADA's** ComputerData, Direct Access, Graduate Computerworld, InfoCanada, Network World Canada; **CHILE's** Computerworld, Informatica; **COLUMBIA's** Computerworld Columbia; **CZECHOSLOVAKIA's** Computerworld Czechoslovakia, PC World Czechoslovakia; **DENMARK's** CAD/CAM WORLD, Communications World, Computerworld Danmark, Computerworld Focus, Computerworld Uddannelse, LAN World, Lotus World, Macintosh Produktkatalog, Macworld Danmark, PC World Danmark, PC World Produktguide, Windows World; **EQUADOR's** PC World; **EGYPT's** PC World Middle East; **FINLAND's** Mikro PC, Tietoviikko, Tietoverkko; **FRANCE's** Distributique, GOLDEN MAC, InfoPC, Languages & Systems, Le Guide du Monde Informatique, Le Monde Informatique, Telecoms & Reseaux; **GERMANY's** Computerwoche, Computerwoche Focus, Computerwoche Extra, Computerwoche Karriere, edv aspekte, Information Management, Macwelt, Netzwelt, PC Welt, PC Woche, Publish, Unit; **HUNGARY's** Computerworld SZT, PC World; **INDIA's** Computers & Communications; **ISRAEL's** Computerworld Israel, PC World Israel; **ITALY's** Computerworld Italia, Lotus Magazine, Macworld Italia, Networking Italia, PC World Italia; **JAPAN's** Computerworld Japan, Macworld Japan, SunWorld Japan; **KOREA's** Computerworld Korea, Macworld Korea, PC World Korea; **MEXICO's** Compu Edicion, Compu Manufactura, Computacion/Punto de Venta, Computerworld Mexico, MacWorld, Mundo Unix, PC World, Windows; **THE NETHERLANDS'** Computer! Totaal, LAN Magazine, Lotus World, MacWorld Magazine; **NEW ZEALAND's** Computerworld New Zealand, New Zealand PC World; **NIGERIA's** PC World Africa; **NORWAY's** Conputerworld Norge, C/world, Lotusworld Norge, Macworld Norge, Networld, PC World Ekspress, PC World Norge, PC World's Product Guide, Publish World, Student Guiden, Unix World, Windowsworld, IDG Direct Response; **PERU's** PC World; **PEOPLES REPUBLIC OF CHINA's** China Computerworld, PC World China, Electronics International; **IDG HIGH TECH** Newproductworld, Consumer Electronics New Product World; **PHILLIPPINES'** Computerworld, PC World; **POLAND's** Computerworld Poland, PC World/Komputer; **ROMANIA's** InfoClub Magazine; **RUSSIA's** Computerworld-Moscow, Networks, PC World; **SOUTH AFRICA's** Computing S.A.; **SPAIN's** Amiga World, Autoedicion, Communicaciones World, Computerworld Espana, Macworld Espana, Network World, PC World Espana, Publish, Sunworld; **SWEDEN's** Attack, CAD/CAM World, ComputerSweden, Corporate Computing, Lokala Natverk/LAN, Lotus World, MAC&PC, Macworld, Mikrodatorn, PC World, Publishing & Design (CAP), DataIngenjoren, Maxi Data, Windows World; **SWITZERLAND's** Computerworld Schweiz, Corporate Computing, Macworld Schweiz, PC & Workstation; **TAIWAN's** Computerworld Taiwan, Global Computer Express, PC World Taiwan; **THAILAND's** Thai Computerworld; **TURKEY's** Computerworld Monitor, Macworld Turkiye, PC World Turkiye; **UNITED KINGDOM's** Lotus Magazine, Macworld, Sunworld; **UNITED STATES'** AmigaWorld, Cable in the Classroom, CIO, Computerworld, DOS Resource Guide, Electronic News, Federal Computer Week, GamePro, inCider/A+, IDG Books, InfoWorld, InfoWorld Direct, Macworld, Multimedia World, Network World, NeXTWORLD, PC Games, PC World, PC Letter, Publish, RUN, SunWorld, SWATPro; **VENEZUELA's** Computerworld Venezuela, MicroComputerworld Venezuela; **YUGOSLAVIA's** Moj Mikro.

 This book is printed on recycled paper and can be recycled.

# About the Authors

Brian Livingston is the Window Manager columnist for *InfoWorld,* the Optimizing Windows columnist for *Windows Magazine,* and a contributor to other publications. He is the author of *Windows 3.1 SECRETS* (published by IDG Books Worldwide, 1992) and *Windows 3.0 SECRETS* (published by IDG Books Worldwide, 1992), which have more than a quarter million copies in print in 15 languages. He was a recipient of the 1991 Award for Technical Excellence from the Microcomputer Managers Association.

Margie Livingston is the Graphic Options columnist for *Windows Style Magazine.* She is a computer art director and writer who formerly worked for the New York headquarters of the Ogilvy & Mather and Deutsch Inc. advertising agencies, where her clients included AT&T International, Singer, Dove, General Foods, and others.

# Credits

**President and CEO**
John J. Kilcullen

**Vice-President and Publisher**
David Solomon

**Managing Editor**
Mary Bednarek

**Acquisitions Editor**
Terrie Lynn Solomon

**Project Editor**
Sandy Blackthorn

**Editor**
Alice Martina Smith

**Technical Reviewer**
Linda Slovick

**Production Director**
Lana J. Olson

**Editorial Assistant**
Megg Bonar

**Text Preparation**
Mary Ann Cordova
Dana Bryant Sadoff

**Proofreader**
Charles A. Hutchinson

**Indexer**
Joan Dickey

**Book Design and Production**
Peppy White
Francette M. Ytsma
Tracy Strub
*(University Graphics, Palo Alto, California)*

# Contents at a Glance

**Read This First** ...................................................1
*Information to help you get the most out of this book*

**Address Manager** ..............................................22
*Print your own database, on lists and labels*

**The Barry Press Utilities** ...............................66
*Switch your printer, match text files, and more*

**Checkers** ...........................................................90
*The classic hop-over game, kings and all*

**ClipMate** ...........................................................96
*Save and manage all your Clipboard text*

**Code Breaker** ..................................................128
*A challenging puzzle that changes every time*

**DirNotes for Windows** ...................................132
*Break DOS's eight-character filename limit*

**Disk Copy for Windows** .................................138
*Make perfect disk copies simply and easily*

**Exclaim** ...........................................................148
*Replace your DOS sessions with this powerful toolbox*

**File Garbage Can for Windows** ............................. **166**
*Delete files securely with drag and drop*

**GrpIcon 2.0** ....................................................... **172**
*Customize your Program Manager group windows*

**Hearts for Windows** ........................................... **190**
*A cutthroat game where rudeness may pay off*

**Hyperoid** .......................................................... **198**
*Blast your way through this exciting space game*

**IconCalc** ........................................................... **204**
*A complete calculator, no bigger than an icon*

**Jewel Thief** ....................................................... **214**
*A game of wits with jewels and guards*

**MathGraf** .......................................................... **222**
*Graphs even the toughest equations for you*

**Mega Edit** .......................................................... **234**
*Edit any text file without Notepad's limitations*

**μLathe (MicroLathe)** ......................................... **260**
*Draw any line and watch a 3D model take shape*

**Mile Bones** ........................................................ **274**
*Beat your opponent to the finish line and win*

**Money Smith** ..................................................... **284**
*A full-blown home or business bookkeeping system*

**Parents** .................................................. 338
*Track your lineage and preserve your family tree*

**PixFolio** ................................................ 348
*Manage your picture library in any graphics format*

**Recipe Maker** ...................................... 384
*Compute your menu plans and shopping lists*

**RS232 Serial Monitor** .......................... 396
*Catch modem problems fast*

**SideBar Lite** ........................................ 400
*The fastest replacement for Program Manager*

**Super Resource Monitor** ..................... 428
*Manage your memory resources*

**Widget** ................................................. 436
*Track your computer's CPU workload*

**WinClock** ............................................. 444
*Set alarms and never miss another appointment*

**WinEZ** .................................................. 462
*The best drop-down menu system for Windows*

**WinKey** ................................................ 476
*Control your Shift, Caps Lock, and Num Lock keys*

**WinPoker** ............................................. 486
*Your own video poker game that never quits*

**xiv**

**WinStart** .................................................................**496**
*Start up in any Windows mode*

**ZiPaper** ...................................................................**498**
*Rotate your wallpaper for a fresh look*

**ZIP Tools for Windows**.........................................**510**
*File compression and decompression in Windows*

**Index**.......................................................................**568**

**Complete Installation Instructions
for the Windows GIZMOS Diskettes** ......................**586**

# Table of Contents

## Read This First ............................................. 1

How To Use This Book .............................................................................. 1
What You Find in This Book ....................................................................... 2
Quick Installation Instructions ................................................................. 2
For New Windows Users: The Least You Need To Know about DOS ............. 3
For New Windows Users: How To Put an Application on the Path ................. 4
For New Windows Users: How To Load an Application at Start-Up ................. 5
How Commands Are Explained .................................................................. 6
Giving You Our Best ................................................................................. 8
How You Can Benefit from Freeware and Shareware ................................... 8
    Freeware: Programs at no cost .......................................................... 9
    Shareware: Fully functional free trial software .................................... 9
    Crippleware: Programs that do little or nothing ................................ 11
Shareware Registration from Outside the U.S. ......................................... 11
The Association of Shareware Professionals .............................................. 12
    Why have shareware registration notices? ........................................ 12
    The ASP ombudsman program ....................................................... 12
General License Agreement ..................................................................... 13
Technical Requirements .......................................................................... 13
Technical Support .................................................................................. 14
Direct Technical Support through CompuServe ........................................ 14
Preventing Viruses ................................................................................. 15
The Windows Series ............................................................................... 16
    Programs found in Windows 3.1 SECRETS ....................................... 17
    Programs found in Windows GIZMOS ............................................. 19

## Address Manager .................................................. 22

Overview ............................................................................................... 23
Getting Started ...................................................................................... 24
    How to get up to speed quickly with Address Manager ...................... 24
    Word for Windows macros ............................................................. 26
User Interface ........................................................................................ 26
Control Bar ............................................................................................ 28
Keyboard ............................................................................................... 29

Menu Commands ........................................................................30
    File.....................................................................................30
    Edit....................................................................................34
    Dialer! ...............................................................................36
    View ..................................................................................36
    Lists ..................................................................................37
    Help...................................................................................39
                           40
Designing Custom View Templates ........................................42
Printing Dot-Matrix Labels ....................................................42
    Printing to Avery dot-matrix labels ................................42
    Printing to dot-matrix labels (non-Avery) .....................43
    Printing multiple dot-matrix labels for the same name ....43
    Notes on printing dot-matrix labels ...............................44
Printing Laser-Printer Labels .................................................46
Printing Envelopes .................................................................47
Settings ...................................................................................49
International Support ..............................................................50
Smart Dialer Settings .............................................................51
Special Lists ............................................................................53
Importing Data into Address Manager ..................................53
Common Questions ................................................................55
Hints and Tips ........................................................................57
HP LaserJet III Information ...................................................57
Registration ............................................................................58
Legal Matters .........................................................................58
Update Policy .........................................................................60
On-Line Support .....................................................................60
Association of Shareware  Professionals Ombudsman Statement ....60
Software License .....................................................................63
Wilson WindowWare Products ...............................................65
Ordering Information .............................................................

# The Barry Press Utilities ...............................66

Installation ...........................................................................67
Applet ...................................................................................68
CalPop — A Simple Calendar for Microsoft Windows .......69
Flipper — Simple Printer-Orientation Control for Microsoft Windows ..........70
Portland (PORTRAIT.EXE and LANDSCAP.EXE) — Direct Printer-Orientation
Control for  Microsoft Windows .........................................71
Holder for Windows ............................................................72
    Command-line parameters ............................................72
    Using Holder in the Windows StartUp group ...............72
    System menu commands ...............................................73

Match — Text Comparison for Microsoft Windows and DOS..........76
  Summary of operation ................................76
  Match keyboard shortcuts ...........................77
  Matching algorithm .................................79
  File menu commands .................................80
  Search menu commands ...............................81
  Options menu commands .............................83
  Help menu ..........................................85
Runner — A Simple Command Line for Microsoft Windows ........85
  Use Alternate Shell ...............................86
  Run Minimized .....................................86
  Menu ..............................................86
Time — Yet Another Digital Clock for Microsoft Windows .......86
Registration ...........................................88
Source Code Availability ...............................89
Disclaimer .............................................89

# Checkers ..................90

Game Instructions ......................................91
  Noncapturing move ..................................92
  Capturing move .....................................92
  Crowning ...........................................92
Moving the Pieces ......................................93
  Mouse instructions .................................93
  Keyboard instructions ..............................93
  Captures ...........................................93
  The computer's turn ................................93
The Menus ..............................................94
  The Setup menu .....................................94
  The Level menu .....................................94
Contributions and Source Code ..........................95

# ClipMate ..................96

Installation Notes .....................................97
  Using special filenames for data ...................97
  Looking at files ClipMate creates ..................98
Overview ...............................................98
Buttons of the Main Window .............................99
  Visual cues ........................................99
  Checking and graying ...............................99

Layout — Full Layout versus Brief Layout ...................................................... 100
How to change layouts ................................................................ 101
Limitations of Brief Layout ......................................................... 102
Magnify Window ................................................................................ 102
To open the Magnify window ....................................................... 102
To close the Magnify window ....................................................... 103
Editing ................................................................................... 103
The buttons ............................................................................ 103
Editor hot keys ....................................................................... 104
Power hints ............................................................................ 104
Clip Items ........................................................................................ 105
Clip Item Lists ................................................................................. 105
The Recyclable List ................................................................. 105
The Safe List .......................................................................... 106
Using the Main Window Buttons ........................................................ 106
Delete button .......................................................................... 106
Print button ............................................................................ 107
Glue button ............................................................................. 107
Magnify button ........................................................................ 108
Copy to Safe List button ........................................................... 108
Activate Recyclable List button .................................................. 109
Activate Safe List button ........................................................... 109
Clip Item Selection List combo box ............................................. 109
Multiple Selection List button and dialog box ............................... 111
Configuration button and dialog box ........................................... 112
About button and dialog box ...................................................... 115
Menus .............................................................................................. 116
File menu ............................................................................... 116
Edit menu ............................................................................... 117
View menu .............................................................................. 117
CLIPMATE.INI .................................................................................. 118
Additional Settings ........................................................................... 119
Known problems ...................................................................... 119
Bug reports ............................................................................. 119
Distribution Files .............................................................................. 120
Deinstallation .................................................................................. 120
Registering ClipMate .......................................................................... 121
How much does it cost? ............................................................. 121
What does it get you? ............................................................... 121
Bonus programs for registered users ........................................... 122
License Agreement ............................................................................ 123
How To Register ............................................................................... 123
Ordering directly from Thornton Software Solutions ....................... 123
Foreign registrations ................................................................ 124
Ordering through CompuServe .................................................... 125
Ordering from Software Excitement! ............................................ 125

# Code Breaker ...................................................**128**

Playing Code Breaker ........................................................................129

# DirNotes for Windows...............................................**132**

Description ........................................................................................134
The DirNotes Menus .........................................................................135
Program Structure ............................................................................136
    Start-up ........................................................................................136
    Main WndProc ............................................................................136
    Wakeup ........................................................................................136
    FillListBox ...................................................................................137
    CopyComments ...........................................................................137
    NewDir ........................................................................................137

# Disk Copy for Windows...................................**138**

Overview ...........................................................................................138
Command Line Syntax ......................................................................139
    Options ........................................................................................139
    Exit values ...................................................................................140
Disk Copy Dialog Box .......................................................................140
    Icon ..............................................................................................141
    Pause ............................................................................................141
    Verbose ........................................................................................141
    Verify ...........................................................................................142
    Format Mode ...............................................................................142
    OK button ....................................................................................142
    Cancel button ..............................................................................142
    Execute button ............................................................................142
    Abort menu item .........................................................................143
Keyboard Shortcuts...........................................................................143
Temporary File Location ...................................................................143
Recommended Usage ........................................................................143
Installing the Program Manager Group Window ............................143
Why Register? ....................................................................................145

# Exclaim ........................................ 148

Overview ........................................................... 150
How To Start Exclaim ........................................ 150
Exclaim Files and Uninstall ............................... 151
Exclaim (!.EXE) Quick Reference Card ............... 151
!.INI .................................................................. 154
Running External Applications .......................... 154
Keeping a Batch File Window Open ................... 155
Running DOS Commands in a Separate Window ... 155
Pipes and Redirection ........................................ 156
Virus Protection ............................................... 156
Command Reference .......................................... 156
    ATTRIB .......................................................... 156
    CALL ............................................................... 157
    CDD ................................................................ 157
    COLOR ............................................................ 158
    DISPLAY ......................................................... 158
    ECHO .............................................................. 159
    IF *condition* THEN ... ENDIF .......................... 159
    MOVE .............................................................. 160
    PROFILE .......................................................... 160
    PROMPT .......................................................... 161
    REN and RENAME ........................................... 161
    RETURN .......................................................... 162
    TASK ............................................................... 162
Registration ...................................................... 162
    Why register? .................................................. 162
    Shareware notice and disclaimer ..................... 163
    Order form ...................................................... 163

# File Garbage Can for Windows .............. 166

Overview ........................................................... 168
Options ............................................................. 168
    Confirm Delete (turned on by default) ............. 168
    Secure Delete (turned on by default) ............... 168
Command Line Options ...................................... 169
Shareware ......................................................... 169
    *Caveat emptor* (Let the buyer beware) ........... 169
    *Cetera desunt* (The rest is missing) ............... 169
    Order form ...................................................... 170

# GrpIcon 2.0 .............................................. 172

Overview ................................................................................................ 173
Starting GrpIcon ................................................................................... 173
Using GrpIcon 2.0 ................................................................................ 174
   Modifying options .......................................................................... 174
   Changing start-up configurations ............................................... 174
   Changing the Group Properties menu fonts ............................... 174
   Changing the Group Properties menu icon size ........................ 175
   On-line Help ................................................................................... 175
   Registration .................................................................................... 175
   GO .................................................................................................... 175
Customizing Program Manager Groups ............................................. 175
   Assigning group icons .................................................................. 175
   Setting wallpaper backgrounds ................................................... 178
   Changing background colors in group windows ....................... 179
Looking at the Inner-City Software Icon Library ............................. 181
Registering GrpIcon .............................................................................. 182
   How to register .............................................................................. 182
   GrpIcon 2.0 registration form ...................................................... 183
   About Inner-City Software ............................................................ 183
   Who we are ..................................................................................... 183
      Other Inner-City Software product offerings ..................... 184
   Product catalog .............................................................................. 184
   Mailing list ..................................................................................... 184
   Inner-City Software's mission and how U can help ................... 184
   Credits ............................................................................................. 185
   Acknowledgments and thanks ..................................................... 186
Software License ................................................................................... 187
Glossary of Terms ................................................................................. 188

# Hearts for Windows ....................................... 190

Brief Description of Hearts ................................................................. 191
Game Play .............................................................................................. 191
Game Options and Menu Items .......................................................... 192
How To Run Hearts for Windows ...................................................... 195
The Author of Hearts ........................................................................... 196
Registration ........................................................................................... 196
Future Directions ................................................................................. 197
   Registration Form .......................................................................... 197

# Hyperoid ............................................198

Hello and Welcome to Hyperoid Version 1.1 ..................198
The Controls ...................................................199
Rules ...........................................................200
HYPEROID.INI .................................................200
Virtual Key Codes ............................................202
Hit the Stars! .................................................203
Legal Junk .....................................................203

# IconCalc ...........................................204

Introduction ...................................................205
Requirements for Running IconCalc ..........................205
Entering Numbers .............................................206
Moving IconCalc ..............................................207
Closing IconCalc ..............................................207
Understanding IconCalc Options .............................207
    Help ......................................................207
    Preferences ............................................207
    About .....................................................208
Getting Help ...................................................209
How To Contact the Shareware Author ......................209
How To Pay for and Register IconCalc .......................209
    Registration form ......................................210
    Thanks! ..................................................212
    Other products by the same author ..................212
    Disclaimer ..............................................212

# Jewel Thief .......................................214

How To Play .....................................................215
History and Humor .............................................215
Program Contents ..............................................216
Author Information .............................................216
Shareware .......................................................217
    Some definitions .......................................217
    The shareware concept ................................218
Trial Use License ...............................................220
Ombudsman Statement .........................................220
Warranty Information ..........................................220
    Jewel Thief Order Form ..............................219

# MathGraf ...................................................222

Running MathGraf ..................................................................................223
The File Menu .......................................................................................224
  New, Open, Save, and Save As ......................................................224
  About ..............................................................................................224
The Edit Menu ......................................................................................224
  Copy ................................................................................................224
The View Menu .....................................................................................224
  Coordinates ....................................................................................224
  Zoom ...............................................................................................224
  Wider ..............................................................................................225
  Origin ..............................................................................................225
The Function Menu (How To Define Your Own Math Functions) .............225
The Plot Menu .......................................................................................227
  Redraw ............................................................................................227
  Interval ...........................................................................................228
  Options ...........................................................................................229
The Help Menu ......................................................................................229
Printing .................................................................................................230
Installation Notes .................................................................................230
  License key .....................................................................................230
  Updates ...........................................................................................231
  Copyrights and warranty ...............................................................231
  Suggestions and bug reports .........................................................231
  Registration Form ..........................................................................232

# Mega Edit ...............................................234

Overview ...............................................................................................235
Editing Multiple Files ...........................................................................236
Split Window Features ..........................................................................236
Keyboard Commands .............................................................................238
  Navigation ......................................................................................238
  General functions ...........................................................................238
  Extend highlighted selection .........................................................238
  Accelerator keys (menu shortcut keys) ..........................................238
File Menu Commands .............................................................................239
  New ..................................................................................................239
  Open... .............................................................................................240
  Save (F2) ..........................................................................................241
  Save As... ..........................................................................................241

Save All ...................................................................................................241
Close ......................................................................................................241
Close All ................................................................................................241
Include File... ........................................................................................242
Export/Convert .....................................................................................242
Run DOS Shell (F12) .............................................................................242
Exit (Alt+F4) ..........................................................................................243
Edit Menu Commands ...............................................................................243
Cut (Shift+Delete) .................................................................................243
Copy (Ctrl+Insert) .................................................................................244
Paste (Shift+Insert) ...............................................................................244
Clear (Ctrl+Delete) ...............................................................................244
Selecting Text .............................................................................................244
Selecting with the mouse .....................................................................244
Selecting with the keyboard ................................................................245
Selecting with the scroll bar ................................................................245
Search Menu Commands ...........................................................................246
Find .......................................................................................................246
Again (F3) ..............................................................................................247
Replace ..................................................................................................247
Goto .......................................................................................................248
Window Menu Commands ..........................................................................248
Split Window (Ctrl+S) ...........................................................................248
Unsplit Window (Ctrl+X) ......................................................................248
Switch Pane (Ctrl+W) ...........................................................................248
Options Menu Commands ..........................................................................249
Word Wrap On/Off ................................................................................249
Set Tab ...................................................................................................249
Colors ....................................................................................................249
Change Font ..........................................................................................250
Enlarge Font ..........................................................................................250
Reduce Font ..........................................................................................251
Preferences ...........................................................................................251
Print Menu Command ................................................................................252
Print File (Ctrl+P) .................................................................................252
Mega Edit Files ...........................................................................................253
Troubleshooting ..........................................................................................253
Tips on Using Mega Edit .............................................................................254
Registration ................................................................................................255
Benefits of registration .........................................................................255
How to register .....................................................................................256
Product registration form .....................................................................258
Disclaimer of Warranty ..............................................................................259

# μLathe (MicroLathe)............................................260

Overview ........................................................................260
Procedures ....................................................................261
    Creating a 3D object .............................................261
    Viewing a 3D object ..............................................262
    Using the μLathe Control Panel ...........................263
File Menu Commands ..................................................264
    New ........................................................................264
    Open .......................................................................264
    Save ........................................................................264
    Save As ...................................................................264
    Save Image .............................................................264
    Save Sequence .......................................................265
    Exit .........................................................................266
Edit Menu Commands .................................................266
    Undo .......................................................................266
    Copy ........................................................................266
    Clear .......................................................................267
    Grid .........................................................................267
    Light Source ...........................................................267
    Repaint ...................................................................268
View Menu Commands .................................................268
    Lathe .......................................................................268
    3D ...........................................................................268
    Control Panel .........................................................268
MiniMovie 1.5.1 ...........................................................269
    Creating movies .....................................................269
    Starting MiniMovie .................................................270
    Notes .......................................................................270
    MiniMovie controls ...............................................271
Registration Information ..............................................271

# Mile Bones ......................................................274

Overview ........................................................................274
The Cards......................................................................275
    Mileage cards .........................................................275
    Hazard cards (also called "dirt") ...........................275
    Remedy cards .........................................................276
    Safeties ...................................................................276
    *Coup Fourré* ........................................................276

How do the cards relate to each other? ........................................................ 277
How many of each card are there? ............................................................... 278
Playing the Game ................................................................................................ 278
Where can a card be played? ....................................................................... 280
When can a card be played? ........................................................................ 280
What is an extension? ................................................................................... 281
End of game ................................................................................................... 282
High Score table ........................................................................................... 282
Tips on Playing Mile Bones Version 2.1 ......................................................... 282
Registration ........................................................................................................ 283

# Money Smith ...................................................284

Introduction to Money Smith ............................................................................ 284
Why use Money Smith? ................................................................................ 284
About the documentation ............................................................................. 285
About Money Smith ...................................................................................... 285
Help ................................................................................................................. 286
Step 1: Starting Money Smith .......................................................................... 286
Licensing window ......................................................................................... 286
Exiting Money Smith .................................................................................... 287
Step 2: Using Money Smith Files ...................................................................... 287
For the beginner ............................................................................................ 287
Creating a new Money Smith file ................................................................ 287
Saving a Money Smith file ........................................................................... 287
Opening an existing file ............................................................................... 288
Using passwords ........................................................................................... 288
Copying, backing up, and saving as another name ................................... 288
Step 3: Learning Interactive Windows ............................................................ 288
About Interactive Windows ......................................................................... 289
A summary of interactive fields .................................................................. 289
Investment report fields .............................................................................. 289
Other interactive functions ......................................................................... 290
Interactive graphs ........................................................................................ 290
Step 4: Setting Up Your Accounts .................................................................... 290
Using Account view ...................................................................................... 290
For the beginner ............................................................................................ 291
Adding accounts ........................................................................................... 291
Editing accounts ........................................................................................... 292
Deleting accounts ......................................................................................... 292
Limitations .................................................................................................... 292
Step 5: Entering Transactions .......................................................................... 293
Thinking transactions .................................................................................. 293
Transaction view .......................................................................................... 293
Current Register report ................................................................................ 293

Account Reconciliation report ................................................................294
Dates ..................................................................................................294
Adding transactions ..........................................................................294
Using smart-number fields and the calculator ..............................296
Making up accounts on the fly ........................................................296
Performing recurring transactions on the fly ...............................296
Performing split transactions ..........................................................297
Editing transactions ..........................................................................297
Deleting transactions ........................................................................298
Printing transactions ........................................................................298
Limitations ........................................................................................298
Step 6: Using Money Smith Reports ....................................................298
Using reports ....................................................................................299
Assessing your financial position ..................................................299
Setting the report/graph title ..........................................................300
Limitations ........................................................................................301
Step 7: Using Money Smith Graphs......................................................302
Using graphs ....................................................................................302
Setting the report/graph title ..........................................................302
Limitations ........................................................................................304
Printing Basics ........................................................................................304
What can I print? ..............................................................................304
General printing tips ........................................................................304
Printing windows ..............................................................................304
Adjusting print options ....................................................................304
Printing graphs ................................................................................305
Ordering checks ................................................................................305
Printing tractor-fed checks ..............................................................306
Printing laser checks ........................................................................306
Setting Up Recurring Transactions ......................................................306
What's a recurring transaction? ......................................................306
Creating recurring transactions the easy way ...............................307
Editing recurring transactions ........................................................308
Running recurring transactions ......................................................308
Running memorized transactions....................................................308
Mixing transaction periods: nonstandard frequencies .................309
Limitations ........................................................................................309
Defining Account Categories ................................................................309
What's an account category? ............................................................309
Creating categories the easy way (on the fly)...............................309
Editing categories ............................................................................310
Viewing category data ......................................................................310
Looking at sample applications ......................................................310
Limitations ........................................................................................310
Understanding Investment Accounts ....................................................311
What's an investment account? ........................................................311
Establishing an investment account ...............................................311
Looking at investment records ........................................................311

Filling in an investment history record ........................................................311
Editing history records ................................................................................312
Deleting investment history records ...........................................................312
Viewing history records ..............................................................................312
Removing investments from an account .....................................................312
Using another way to edit investments ......................................................312
Using the investment reminder service ......................................................313
Limitations ...................................................................................................313
Performing End-of-Year Processing ................................................................313
Why roll out transactions? ..........................................................................313
What really happens? ...................................................................................313
Running the end-of-year process ...............................................................314
Looking at Examples Using Money Smith .......................................................314
Sample files .................................................................................................314
Homeowners and renters ............................................................................314
Real property: to add or not to add? ..........................................................315
Tracking a small business ...........................................................................315
Using BUSINESS.ACT for your business .....................................................316
Tracking real estate .....................................................................................317
Using the Money Smith Financial Calculator .................................................317
Using financial functions .............................................................................318
Performing compound financial calculations .............................................318
Using the smart-number entry fields .........................................................319
Using the Infix Algebra command ..............................................................320
Using the Postfix Algebra command ..........................................................320
Using the Present Value (PV) function .......................................................321
Using the Present Value of an Annuity (PVA) function ..............................321
Using the Present Value of a Perpetuity (PVP) function ...........................323
Using the Present Loan Payment (PMT) function ......................................324
Using the Future Value (FV) function .........................................................324
Using the Future Value of an Annuity (FVA) function ...............................325
Using the Investment Required for a Future Value (INV) function ..........325
Using the Effective Annual Interest (EffI) function ...................................326
Using the Internal Rate of Return (IRR) function ......................................327
Using the Internal Rate of Return for an Annuity (IRRA) function ..........328
Using the ACRS Depreciation (ACRS) function .........................................328
Licensing Terms ..............................................................................................329
Obtaining registered licensed versions ......................................................329
License ..........................................................................................................330
Definition of shareware ..............................................................................330
Registering ...................................................................................................330
Benefits of registration ...............................................................................331
Phone-ordering services .............................................................................331
CompuServe electronic mall .......................................................................332
Direct international registration ..................................................................332
Eurosoft Registration Service in foreign currency ....................................332

Registration form for Version 2.0 .................................................333
License agreement .........................................................................334
Single-user license .......................................................................334
Notice .............................................................................................334
Limited warranty for registered users ......................................335
Limitation of liability ..................................................................335
Assign to successor clause .........................................................335
General terms ...............................................................................335
Acknowledgments ........................................................................336

# Parents ..................................................338

Introduction ...................................................................................338
Getting Started ..............................................................................339
The Individual Work Sheet .........................................................340
   Menu selections for the Individual Work Sheet ................340
   Pushbutton actions for the Individual Work Sheet ...........341
The Immediate Family Tree .........................................................342
   Menu selections for the Immediate Family Tree ..............343
Special Features .............................................................................345
   Drag and drop .........................................................................345
   Clipboard .................................................................................345
   Printing .....................................................................................345
Exiting .............................................................................................346
Registration ....................................................................................346

# PixFolio ...............................................348

Overview .........................................................................................349
Understanding Catalogs and Their Uses ...................................350
Creating a Catalog ........................................................................350
   Using the Select Catalog dialog box ..................................351
   Changing catalog attributes .................................................352
   Deleting a catalog ..................................................................352
Cataloging an Image .....................................................................352
   Cataloging manually ..............................................................352
   Cataloging with the Catalog Build function ......................354
   Maintaining catalog information .........................................355
Viewing Images .............................................................................360
Looking at Supported Formats ....................................................360
   Color resolution formats .......................................................362
   Thumbnail view .......................................................................362

Editing Images ............................................................................... 366
    Cropping or trimming an image ................................................. 366
    Expanding an image .................................................................. 366
    Resizing an image ...................................................................... 367
    Rotating and flipping an image .................................................. 368
    Using Clipboard operations ....................................................... 368
    Using palette operations ............................................................ 368
Creating a New Image .................................................................... 369
Saving Images ................................................................................ 371
    Format conversions .................................................................... 371
    Color resolution ......................................................................... 371
    Dithering .................................................................................... 372
Printing .......................................................................................... 372
    Selecting a printer ..................................................................... 372
    Printing images .......................................................................... 374
    Printing catalog entries .............................................................. 375
Using the Options Menu ................................................................. 375
    Display Warnings ....................................................................... 375
    Center Image .............................................................................. 376
    DIB to Screen ............................................................................. 376
    Auto Dither ................................................................................ 376
    Verify Catalog ............................................................................ 377
    Fix TIFF ..................................................................................... 377
    Background Color ....................................................................... 377
Setting the Play Rate ...................................................................... 378
Setting Default Options .................................................................. 378
    Default Catalog .......................................................................... 378
    Default Extensions ..................................................................... 378
    Default Directory ....................................................................... 379
    Center Image .............................................................................. 379
    DIB to Screen ............................................................................. 379
    Solid Background ....................................................................... 379
    Fix TIFF ..................................................................................... 379
    Display Warnings ....................................................................... 379
    Auto Dither ................................................................................ 379
Using Removable Media .................................................................. 380
Understanding Profile Options ....................................................... 381
Disclaimer Agreement .................................................................... 381
Registration Form ........................................................................... 382

# Recipe Maker ...................................................... 384

Introduction ................................................................................... 386
Getting Started ............................................................................... 386

What Are Lists? .................................................................................387
    List window actions ....................................................................387
    Measurements List .....................................................................388
    Item Group List ..........................................................................389
    Ingredients List ..........................................................................389
Recipe and Instruction Cards .........................................................389
Weekly Plan and Shopping List ......................................................391
What If ..............................................................................................392
Special Features ..............................................................................394
    Drag and drop.............................................................................394
    Clipboard ...................................................................................394
    Exiting .......................................................................................394
    Registration ...............................................................................395

# RS232 Serial Monitor ......................................396

Description .......................................................................................397
Principle ...........................................................................................397
Distribution......................................................................................399

# SideBar Lite ................................................400

Overview ..........................................................................................401
    The SideBar Lite concept ...........................................................401
    The anatomy of SideBar Lite ......................................................401
    Organizing your Windows desktop .............................................401
    Organizing and opening your applications .................................402
    Boosting Windows performance .................................................402
    Requirements ............................................................................402
    The SideBar Lite files .................................................................403
    Opening SideBar Lite .................................................................403
SideBar Lite Notes ...........................................................................403
    System box.................................................................................404
    Title bar .....................................................................................404
    Arrange buttons .........................................................................404
    Command line ............................................................................404
    View Titles .................................................................................404
    SideBar view ..............................................................................405
    Disk view ...................................................................................405
The Main Menu ................................................................................405
    View ...........................................................................................406
    Iconbar .......................................................................................406

Applications ............................................................................................406
Work With ..............................................................................................406
Preferences ............................................................................................406
About SideBar Lite ..................................................................................407
Close .......................................................................................................407
Shutdown ...............................................................................................407
The View Menu ..............................................................................................407
Refresh ...................................................................................................408
The Iconbar Menu .........................................................................................408
Views ......................................................................................................409
Fonts .......................................................................................................409
Left/Right Side of Screen .......................................................................409
Include Active Tasks ...............................................................................410
Keep on Top ...........................................................................................410
Show Status Bar ......................................................................................410
The Applications Menu .................................................................................410
The Work With Panel .....................................................................................410
Placing an object on SideBar Lite ..........................................................412
Removing an object from SideBar Lite ...................................................413
Changing the description of an object on SideBar Lite ...........................413
The Preferences Panel ...................................................................................414
SideBar Lite directory .............................................................................414
Replace task manager ............................................................................415
Start as Windows shell ...........................................................................415
Minimize upon opening object ...............................................................415
Confirm when closing SideBar Lite and Confirm when shutting down
system .....................................................................................................415
Font selection .........................................................................................415
Cancel .....................................................................................................416
Save .........................................................................................................416
The Command Line .......................................................................................416
SideBar Lite and the Mouse .........................................................................417
SideBar Lite and the Keyboard ....................................................................419
Key Terms .......................................................................................................420
SideBar Lite Tips ...........................................................................................421
Using the Include Active Tasks option ...................................................421
Turning off Include Active Tasks before running  Microsoft tutorials .....421
Limiting the drives shown on Sidebar Lite .............................................422
Creating and removing directories with SideBar Lite .............................422
Registration Information ...............................................................................422
Thank you ...............................................................................................423
Intensely simple ......................................................................................423
SideBar versus SideBar Lite ....................................................................424
Ordering SideBar or SideBar Lite ...........................................................424
Be a part of the dream ............................................................................425
Paper Software and the environment .....................................................425
Things you should know ..........................................................................426
Registration Form ...................................................................................427

# Super Resource Monitor .................................428

Overview .................................................................................429
The Main Window ..................................................................429
 What are Free System Resources? .......................................430
 GDI Heap, User Heap, and Current Task Heap .......................430
Configuring Meter Colors and Alarms ....................................430
Configuring the Time and Free Memory Windows .....................432
The About Button ...................................................................432
The Close Button ...................................................................433
The Options Button ................................................................433
 Sample Every x Second .......................................................433
 Compact Every x Second ......................................................434
 The Compact Memory check box ...........................................434
 The Keep Monitor In Front check box .....................................435
SmartPad for Windows ............................................................435

# Widget .........................................................436

Introduction ...........................................................................438
How Metz Widget Works .........................................................438
The File Menu .........................................................................438
 Pause command .................................................................438
 Clear Window command .......................................................438
 Reset File command ............................................................439
 Preferences command .........................................................439
The Preferences Dialog Box ....................................................439
 Window check box ...............................................................439
 File check box ....................................................................440
 Filename box ......................................................................440
 Time interval box ................................................................440
 User box ............................................................................440
 Hide window check box ........................................................440
 Pause on startup check box ..................................................440
Other Programs from Metz Software .........................................441
 Metz File F/X .....................................................................441
 Metz Task Manager .............................................................441
 Metz Desktop Manager .........................................................441
 Metz Desktop Navigator .......................................................441
 Metz Phones ......................................................................442
 Metz Dialer ........................................................................442
 Metz Lock ..........................................................................442
 Metz Runner .......................................................................442
 Metz Time ..........................................................................442
 Metz Freemem ...................................................................442
For More Information ..............................................................442

## 11:27 WinClock ..................................................444

Introduction ...............................................................445
Using the WinClock Options .......................................446
   Help ....................................................................446
   Set Time/Date ......................................................446
   Alarms .................................................................447
   Enhanced alarms ..................................................449
   Timers .................................................................450
   Hourly Beep .........................................................451
   Preferences ..........................................................452
   About ..................................................................455
Getting Help ...............................................................455
Displaying or Hiding the System Box .........................455
Cascading or Tiling with WinClock ............................455
   Cascading ............................................................456
   Tiling ..................................................................456
Moving WinClock .......................................................456
Closing WinClock .......................................................456
Using the WinClock Files ............................................456
How To Contact the Shareware Author ......................457
How To Pay For and Register WinClock ......................457
   Thanks! ...............................................................458
   Other products by the same author .......................458
Error Messages and Solutions .....................................460
Disclaimer .................................................................460
   Registration Form ................................................461

## WinEZ ..........................................................462

Introduction ...............................................................463
Overview ...................................................................464
Installing and Getting Started .....................................465
Features .....................................................................465
   The Fast Path icon (left icon) ................................465
   The Task Switch icon (right icon) ..........................466
   Run dialog box facility ..........................................467
Setting WinEZ's Options ............................................467
   Switching behavior ...............................................468
   Fast Path icon actions ..........................................469
   WinEZ icon position .............................................469
Using WinEZ with Norton Desktop ............................469
General WinEZ Notes and Information ........................470
Disk Contents ............................................................471

Licensing and Distribution ............................................................ 472
   ASP .......................................................................................... 473
   Trademarks ............................................................................. 473
   Limited warranty ................................................................... 473
Registration and Order Information .......................................... 473
   How do I register? ................................................................ 474
   WinEZ registration form ...................................................... 475

# WinKey ................................................................ 476

Overview ........................................................................................ 477
Installation .................................................................................... 478
   How to run WinKey one time only ..................................... 478
   How to run WinKey every time you start Windows .......... 478
Disabling WinKey ......................................................................... 479
Deinstallation ............................................................................... 479
Settings .......................................................................................... 479
   The WinKey icon ................................................................... 481
   Owner information ............................................................... 482
   Let's hear from you! .............................................................. 482
The WinKey Files .......................................................................... 482
Registration Information .............................................................. 483
   How to register ..................................................................... 483
   Technical support .................................................................. 483
   Disclaimer .............................................................................. 484
   Registration form ................................................................. 484

# WinPoker ............................................................ 486

Overview of Video Poker ............................................................. 486
Playing the Game .......................................................................... 487
   Playing the game using a mouse ........................................ 488
   Playing the game using the keyboard ............................... 488
The Winning Hands of Video Poker ........................................... 489
Video Poker Strategy .................................................................... 490
The Menu Commands ................................................................... 490
   Game ....................................................................................... 490
   Options .................................................................................... 491
   Bet ........................................................................................... 492
   Deal ......................................................................................... 493
The WinPoker Files ....................................................................... 493
Miscellaneous Information ........................................................... 493

Registration Information .................................................................494
   The fine print ............................................................................494
   A special thanks to. . ...............................................................494
   WinPoker Registration Form ....................................................495

# WinStart .......................................................496

Overview ......................................................................................496
   Installation ...............................................................................497
   Program notes ..........................................................................497

# ZiPaper ........................................................498

Introduction and a Quick Tour ....................................................499
Installation ..................................................................................499
   Requirements for running ZiPaper ..........................................499
   Preparing wallpaper files .........................................................500
Advanced Options .......................................................................501
   Setup Screen: /S .....................................................................501
   Configurations: /1, /2, /3, and /4 ...........................................503
   Tiling options: /W, /W /T, and /W /C .......................................503
   File Selection: /F, /F?, and /F=filename.BMP ...........................504
   Not Random: /NR .....................................................................505
Life with ZiPaper .........................................................................505
Installing Over Older Versions ....................................................506
   Users of ZiPaper Version 1.3a, 1.3, 1.2a, 1.2 ........................506
   Users of ZiPaper Version 1.1 ..................................................506
   Users of ZiPaper Version 1.0 ..................................................506
If You Have Problems ..................................................................507
The Association of Shareware Professionals Ombudsman Information ......507
How To Pay For and Register ZiPaper .........................................507
   ZiPaper V1.3c Registration Form ............................................508

# ZIP Tools for Windows ..................................510

Welcome ......................................................................................511
   Using this documentation ........................................................512
Preface.........................................................................................513
Acknowledgments and Legal Notices ..........................................514
Fundamental Concepts ...............................................................515
   Shareware distribution.............................................................515
   File compression and archives ...............................................515
   Archive and compression formats: a history ...........................517

Getting Started ................................................................................518
    FlashPoint ZIP/ZIPX (FPZIP.EXE and FPZIPX.EXE) ............................518
    FlashPoint WIZiper (WIZ.EXE) ...........................................................519
    Packing list .........................................................................................519
    Installing FlashPoint ZIP Tools ..........................................................520
Using FlashPoint Development's WIZiper (WIZ.EXE) ...........................522
    What is WIZiper? ...............................................................................522
    Windows, dialog panels, and controls ............................................522
Using Windows Drag-and-Drop Functions ............................................538
    Dropping ZIP files ..............................................................................539
    Dropping non-ZIP files ......................................................................540
Using FlashPoint ZIP (FPZIP.EXE) .......................................................540
    Command line format .......................................................................540
    Command line parameters and switches .......................................541
    The Setup dialog panel .....................................................................546
Using FlashPoint ZIPX (FPZIPX.EXE) ..................................................549
    Command line format .......................................................................549
    Command line parameters and switches .......................................549
    The Setup dialog panel .....................................................................553
Getting More Help .................................................................................555
Registered User Support and Feedback................................................556
How To Register and Get License Applications ...................................557
    License fees .......................................................................................557
    Required deposits — quantity and purchase orders .....................557
    Fees and charges are subject to change ........................................558
Order Information ..................................................................................558
    Prepaid (non-credit card) orders ....................................................558
    Site license orders ............................................................................559
    Credit-card, telephone, fax, and modem orders ............................559
    Purchase orders and billing .............................................................560
    International orders ...........................................................................561
License and Agreements .......................................................................561
    FlashPoint Development license agreement ...................................562
Order Form ............................................................................................564
Site License Agreement .........................................................................565

**Index** .................................................................**568**

**Complete Installation Instructions
for the Windows GIZMOS Diskettes............586**

# Read This First

W elcome to *Windows GIZMOS!* We have spent countless hours evaluating literally hundreds of software programs to bring you this book — the best Windows freeware and shareware.

Reading this chapter will help you get the most out of the programs in this book in the least possible time.

This book features 33 of the very best programs available free or for a nominal registration from independent Windows programmers. *Windows GIZMOS* is designed to complement *Windows 3.1 SECRETS,* a book of undocumented Windows features written by Brian Livingston and published by IDG Books Worldwide. *Windows 3.1 SECRETS* features 44 freeware and shareware programs for Windows. It is not necessary, however, for you to buy that book to use the programs featured in this one.

At the time, we thought that *Windows 3.1 SECRETS* encompassed the best Windows shareware there would ever be. But we were wrong: A flood of great programs was just beginning! Without taking anything away from the programs found in *Windows 3.1 SECRETS,* we think you'll agree that the programs in *Windows GIZMOS* are even more mature, powerful, and fun to use.

## How To Use This Book

If you are a new user of Windows, three sections in the next few pages are included to help you: "The Least You Need To Know about DOS," "How To Put an Application on the Path," and "How To Load an Application at Start-Up." Read these sections to understand some of the instructions in the chapters that follow.

If you have used Windows for several months or years, simply skip the three "new user" sections in this chapter if you already understand these topics.

# What You Find in This Book _____

We have taken great pains to bring you not only the best Windows freeware and shareware, but also the best publication on the subject:

♦ *Windows GIZMOS* packs onto four high-density disks (more than almost any other computer book!) *every single program* described in the text.

♦ Each program is fully documented in the text, complete with our advice, including illustrations and graphics to help you get the most out of each application, tool, or game.

Since the publication of *Windows 3.1 SECRETS,* we have seen imitations with lofty claims. One such book was mostly composed of paragraphs *about* shareware programs with an invitation to obtain most of them from a pay-by-the-hour service. Another book placed on its accompanying disks only *six* of the programs described in its text.

We will never shortchange our readers. You find on the disks included with this book *every* program described in the text, with full documentation and contact information for the authors (for those programs that provide registration and technical support).

# Quick Installation Instructions _____

To install any of the programs on the *Windows GIZMOS* disks, follow these steps:

1. Insert Disk 1 into the appropriate disk drive (drive A: or drive B:).

2. From the Windows Program Manager, pull down the File menu and then click Run.

3. In the dialog box that appears, type **A:\WSETUP** if you're using drive A: or **B:\WSETUP** if you're using drive B:.

That's it! The WSETUP program enables you to select those programs you want to install. When you click the Install button, WSETUP prompts you to change disks when necessary.

For more details, refer to the Complete Installation Instructions on the page facing the disks inside the cover of this book.

# For New Windows Users:
# The Least You Need To Know about DOS

If you are a DOS beginner or are starting to use Windows after working on another graphical environment (such as a Macintosh), this section is for you.

Windows does not protect you from the way DOS stores information on the
disk drives. You can see exactly where everything is stored on the drives and
organize it as you like. It's sometimes said that DOS is hard to learn. But, if you
know a few terms, you can use the Windows File Manager (or a similar program) to do everything you need.

**Disk drives.** Most PCs have two or more disk drives for storing information.
These drives are identified by the letters A through Z, followed by a colon (:).
The first *floppy disk drive* in the PC is drive A:. The second disk drive — if you
have one — is drive B:. The first *hard drive* is drive C:, and so on.

**Subdividing a disk.** Drives are subdivided into *directories,* also called *folders.*
Directories make it easier for you to find your documents than if everything was
stored in one huge list. For example, if you often write memos, you might create
a directory called MEMOS. You can create a subdirectory called BOSS for memos
to your boss, one called MAILROOM for memos to the mailroom, and so on.

The *backslash* is a special character in DOS; it indicates your level in a drive's
directory structure. The directory C:\MEMOS\BOSS has two backslashes in it,
indicating that you are two levels down from drive C:'s main directory, called
the *root directory.* The root directory of drive C: is indicated by a backslash with
no directory name after it, such as C:\. All other directories *branch* off this main
directory. This is the reason that all the directories on a drive are collectively
called a *tree.* In Windows, the File Manager initially shows you the directory tree
of the current drive, from which you can choose to display any folder.

**Storing documents in files.** All documents must be given names. Each document is called a *file,* and DOS allows each *filename* to have from one to eight
characters, followed by a period, followed by zero to three more characters
called the filename's *extension.* Names like MYFILE.DOC and README.TXT are
legitimate DOS filenames.

A filename can contain any letter or number, plus any of the punctuation marks
found on the keyboard number keys, 0 – 9 (except the asterisk). Extensions
indicate what type of information is in each file. The extension DOC probably
means a document created by a specific word processor; the extension TXT
probably means a plain text file that any text-editing program like Windows
Notepad can read. Most programs require that you type only the first eight
letters when naming a file; the program automatically adds the proper extension for you.

# For New Windows Users:
# How To Put an Application on the Path_____

When you start a program such as Windows Notepad, Windows looks for a file called NOTEPAD.EXE in a list of directories called the *path*.

Some of the applications found on the *Windows GIZMOS* disks require that you place their directory on the path if they are to work properly. Fortunately, this is a simple procedure.

The directories on the path are usually determined by a line in the C:\AUTOEXEC.BAT file. The PC reads this file every time you reboot.

You can add a directory to the path by opening C:\AUTOEXEC.BAT with Windows Notepad. If Windows isn't running, and you have DOS 5.0 or later, you can type **EDIT C:\AUTOEXEC.BAT** at a DOS prompt to edit the file. (Don't open AUTOEXEC.BAT in a word processor; this action can make the file unreadable.) After you open the file, you should see a line similar to the following:

    path=c:\windows;c:\dos;c:\;c:\bat

This line indicates that four directories are on the path: the Windows directory, DOS, the root directory, and a directory containing batch files. Windows and DOS must be on the path if they are to run properly. The root directory should also be on the path to help applications find COMMAND.COM and other programs that may be located there.

If you want to add a directory, such as C:\ZIPTOOLS (ZIP Tools for Windows) to the path, add a semicolon and the name of the directory to the end of the path statement. After you add this directory to the path, the line shown earlier looks as follows:

    path=c:\windows;c:\dos;c:\;c:\bat;c:\ziptools

You must save your changes and reboot the PC for this new path statement to take effect.

You must make sure that the PATH= statement does not exceed 127 characters (including the word PATH and the equals sign). DOS ignores information in the PATH= statement after the first 127 characters, which can cause strange behavior. If the path statement gets too long, you may have to take some directories off the path or make the directory names shorter.

# For New Windows Users:
# How To Load an Application at Start-Up _____

You may want to have several of the programs found on the *Windows GIZMOS* disks load themselves automatically every time you start Windows. This also is a simple process.

### In Windows 3.1 and later:

The Windows 3.1 Program Manager usually has a group window called StartUp. Any icons placed in this group are automatically loaded every time Windows starts.

To copy an icon from another Program Manager group window into the StartUp group window, hold the Ctrl key while using the mouse to drag the desired icon into the StartUp window. This action makes a duplicate copy of the icon in the StartUp group window. Dragging an icon without holding the Ctrl key *moves* the icon permanently.

After placing the icon in the StartUp group window, click it once to select it and then click File Properties from the Program Manager menu. The Properties dialog box that appears gives you several options. You can start the application *minimized* (as an icon at the bottom of the screen) or *normal* (in a window). You can also change the command line that starts the application or select a different icon. The files PROGMAN.EXE and MORICONS.DLL contain numerous icons from which you can choose.

### In Windows 3.0 and later:

Windows 3.0 does not support a StartUp group in its Program Manager. To load a program automatically, you must add its name to either the LOAD= or RUN= line in the WIN.INI file.

You can open WIN.INI in Windows Notepad or DOS 5.0's Edit program. (Don't use a word processor.) You should see lines near the top of the file that look like this:

```
[windows]
load=
run=
```

You add the programs you want to run as icons to the LOAD= line. Add the programs you want to run in normal-sized windows to the RUN= line. For example, to load IconCalc and MegaEdit as icons, and Super Resource Monitor in a normal window, find their full filenames and add them to the LOAD= and RUN= lines as follows:

```
[windows]
load=c:\iconcalc\iconcalc.exe c:\megaedit\megaedit.exe
run=c:\superrm\superrm.exe
```

Remember that the LOAD= and RUN= lines can be no more than 127 characters in length, including the words *load* and *run* and the equals sign. Windows ignores characters after the first 127.

If you run out of space, you can delete the extension EXE from the LOAD= and RUN= lines, like this:

```
[windows]
load=c:\iconcalc\iconcalc c:\megaedit\megaedit
run=c:\superrm\superrm
```

To save even more space, rename the directories to shorter names (and make sure that you adjust any settings in the program to use the new names, if necessary). Or place the directories on the path and then leave out the directories and use only the application names, as follows:

```
[windows]
load=iconcalc.exe megaedit.exe
run=superrm.exe
```

In Windows 3.1 and later, you can start programs in the StartUp group of Program Manager, as well as in the LOAD= and RUN= lines. The programs listed in WIN.INI load *before* the programs in the StartUp group.

One curious thing about the LOAD= and RUN= lines is that placing an application here does not override the way the application itself insists on starting up. IconCalc, for example, runs only as an icon. It has no normal-sized window. Placing ICONCALC.EXE on the RUN= line, therefore, loads IconCalc as an icon anyway. In the same way, Super Resource Monitor runs only as a window and cannot be minimized into an icon. Placing SUPERRM.EXE on the LOAD= line does not load Super Resource Monitor as an icon.

# How Commands Are Explained _____

Several programs enable you to configure them by typing options on a command line. To start a program by typing a command line, you can click File Run in either the Program Manager or File Manager. (Many other Windows programs also support a File Run dialog box.) Type the command and then click OK to run the command.

When we show a command in this book, we place it on a separate line or lines for clarity, or we emphasize it in the text of a paragraph. Commands are presented as follows:

✦ Parts you must type exactly as shown appear in CAPITAL letters.

✦ Parts you may change appear in lowercase letters.

✦ Parts that are placeholders for other information appear in *italics.*

✦ Parts that are optional appear in curly braces {like this}.

For example, you can start Word for Windows in a directory like C:\DOCS with the command WINWORD, followed by a filename and (optionally) the parameter /M. This command line is shown as follows:

c:\docs\WINWORD *filename* {/M}

In the preceding line, *c:\docs* appears in lowercase because you can change this example to any directory name you want. *WINWORD* appears in capital letters because you must type it exactly as it appears. *Filename* appears in italics because you do not type the word but instead substitute any legitimate name. And */M* appears in uppercase and curly braces because, if you use this parameter, you must use the letter *M* and not some other letter.

When such a command appears embedded in the text of a paragraph, instead of on a separate line, capital letters appear in small caps: c:\docs\WINWORD *filename* {/M}. This setup helps the reader's eye flow smoothly over sections that contain many capital letters and avoids the "flashing" effect that would occur if many lines on the page contained full capital letters.

Whenever you see the term *filename,* you can substitute any full-length filename specification acceptable to DOS. For example, the following are all legitimate substitutes for *filename:*

MYFILE.TXT
C:\DOCS\MYFILE.TXT
\DOCS\MYFILE.TXT

Your location in the DOS directory structure determines which form of the filename is appropriate in a particular command line.

In this book, keys on the keyboard are indicated by their labels on the key caps. Examples of these keys include Enter, Tab, Shift, Alt, Ctrl (Control), and Esc (Escape). When we say "press Enter," you know not to type the letters *e, n, t, e,* and *r*; just press the Enter key once.

If one of the shift keys (Shift, Alt, or Ctrl) must be *held down* at the same time you also press another key, the two keys are shown together, separated by a plus sign. For example, *press Ctrl+A* means to press and hold the Ctrl key, press the A key, and then release both keys. *Press Ctrl+Shift+A* means to press and hold both the Ctrl and Shift keys as you press A.

If you are supposed to *let up* on a key *before* pressing another one, those keys are separated by commas. For example, you can press Alt, F, O to run a program's File Open dialog box. The sequence Alt, F, O activates the main menu, pulls down the File menu, and chooses the Open item.

Most Windows users these days have a mouse, although it is possible for you to run almost all Windows commands by using the keyboard. To avoid describing every procedure twice (once for mouse users and once for keyboard users), we use the phrase *click*. In this book, for example, *Click File Open* means you can use a mouse to click File and then click Open; it also means you can press the keys on the keyboard that represent the words File and Open.

# Giving You Our Best _____

We have added our comments to each chapter covering the *Windows GIZMOS* programs. In addition to selecting the best Windows freeware and shareware, we want you to know how the programs work for us and any tips we can pass along.

Each chapter starts with a section in *italics*. In this introductory section, we describe what we like about the program that earned it its place in this book. At the end of this section, we define the type of program, what version of Windows it requires (and other requirements it may have), whether the program is freeware or shareware, the program's technical support (if any), and whether there are similar programs in this book or in *Windows 3.1 SECRETS*.

These comments are followed by detailed instructions for using the program, which we've based closely on the on-line documentation provided by the programs' authors. In certain cases, we've added comments or illustrations to the on-line documentation to make it clearer for you. The program's author, of course, remains the final authority on what his or her program does and how it works, in case there is any discrepancy between what we've written and how a program actually acts.

# How You Can Benefit from Freeware and Shareware _____

Because many people are not familiar with the concepts of freeware and shareware, it's important to clarify these little-known forms of software marketing.

# Freeware: Programs at no cost

*Freeware programs* are programs that have no registration fee. You can use them and copy them to as many other computers as you like without ever paying for a license to use them.

Freeware programs are usually circulated by their authors with little or no technical support. These programs, because of their simplicity, almost never require technical support, fortunately. Freeware programs include some quite useful tools and some very enjoyable games, so their simplicity is not necessarily a limitation.

There are two kinds of freeware programs: *free, public-domain* programs and *free, copyrighted* programs.

Public-domain programs are programs to which the author has released all claims. Other people can sell the program or modify it and put their names on it as their own. These programs are often simple utilities and implementations of math algorithms that the author does not want to support or upgrade in the future. None of the programs on the *Windows GIZMOS* disks is a public-domain program, as far as we know.

Free, copyrighted programs are programs to which the author retains all rights. Although the program's author charges nothing for the program and permits others to circulate the program, no one may sell or alter the program without the author's permission. All the freeware on the *Windows GIZMOS* disks is copyrighted.

You may distribute and use free, copyrighted programs on as many computers as you like without ever paying a fee. But you may not sell such programs or bundle them with a product that is for sale without permission from the authors of the programs. We are authorized by these authors to distribute their programs.

# Shareware: Fully functional free trial software

*Shareware programs* are 100 percent fully functional programs distributed by authors who want to call attention to the registered versions of the same programs. Shareware programs often are backed with technical support, frequent upgrades that have new features, and customized versions for users with special requests. Shareware authors usually provide these services only to users who register and obtain a license for a nominal fee.

We think that the concept of shareware is one of the most important distribution techniques available to both program authors and software users. We are paid-up, registered users of all the shareware programs in *Windows GIZMOS* and have specific permission from all the shareware authors to distribute their programs with this book.

Shareware programs are copyrighted, commercial programs. The only difference between shareware programs and their opposites — retail programs sold through retail channels — is that you have the opportunity to try shareware programs before you invest any money in them.

Compare this with retail programs. Most retail programs cost from $100 to $500. As soon as you take a retail program out of a store, you usually cannot get any kind of a refund — even if the program doesn't do what it said on the box or won't run on your kind of PC.

Most software programmers would face great difficulty launching a retail product. It is often estimated that a company has to have at least $1 million — preferably more like $5 million — to pay for the advertising, marketing, packaging, and other expenses required to launch a successful shrink-wrapped product.

Because of the high overhead of the retail channel, even the simplest program — with one disk and a thin manual — can seldom be sold for less than a list price of about $39.95.

Shareware authors, in contrast, *encourage* you to share their programs with as many of your friends and coworkers as you like. This is their main marketing and advertising method. Because shareware authors spend little or nothing on advertising, fancy buildings, and other overhead, they can pass this savings along to you. Most shareware authors' registration fee is less than $39.95 — often as low as $5, $10, or $15.

And what do you get for your registration fee? Depending on the conditions stated by the on-line documentation for each program, you receive the following items and services:

♦ At the very least, a permanent license to use the program on your PC.

♦ In most cases, the ability to upgrade to a future version of the program, with features that may significantly enhance the version you have.

♦ Technical support if you have questions or configuration problems regarding your particular type of PC. Technical support is usually provided by an electronic-mail system (in which case you receive a response directly from the authors in a few hours), by regular mail, or, in some cases, by telephone.

♦ Sometimes, a printed manual with more detail or better illustrations than can be provided with the shareware version. If you register multiple copies for your company, you get enough printed material for each of your staff.

♦ In a few cases, a disk that contains a registered version of the program along with other "bonus" shareware programs not otherwise listed.

♦ In all cases, the registration of shareware encourages the development of new Windows shareware programs. Some new shareware program could be the next Windows "killer app."

As registered users of each of the shareware programs in this book, we can truly say that the extras we have received after registering the programs constantly surprise and impress us. Shareware programs are the world's greatest software bargain.

## Crippleware: Programs that do little or nothing

Some people say, "Why should I register for shareware programs I already have?" Or "Why do shareware programs sometimes remind me to register?"

Registering shareware programs encourages the development of more shareware. *Not* registering frustrates programmers into distributing useless programs that do little or nothing (these programs are called *crippleware*).

Crippleware programs are limited in some essential way that makes them useless, unless you buy what is essentially a retail version of the program. Crippleware programs sometimes cannot save any information, cannot print more than one page, or cannot print at all. Some crippleware programs disable themselves or expire after a certain date. Other programs do nothing but display a series of screens that advertise a retail program. This last type of program is even less valuable than crippleware and is usually called a *rolling demo.*

*Windows GIZMOS* does not include, to our knowledge, any crippleware programs. All shareware programs we support are 100 percent fully functional. This gives you the opportunity to try all aspects of the program thoroughly before making a commitment to use a certain program.

The existence of shareware programs benefits us all. And the more we register, the more benefits we gain.

# Shareware Registration from Outside the U.S.

Most of the shareware vendors in this book request payment in U.S. funds, drawn on a U.S. bank. The reason is that U.S. banks charge large fees, sometimes more than the registration fee for a shareware package, to accept non-U.S. checks. If you are outside the U.S. and want to register a shareware package with a U.S. author, you can use Postal International Money Orders. They are available at most post offices around the world and are accepted without a fee by all U.S. post offices and many U.S. banks. If you are in Europe, do not send Eurochecks, which are not accepted by U.S. banks.

# The Association of Shareware Professionals __

Because shareware has grown into an important distribution method for software programmers, many of them have banded together into the Association of Shareware Professionals. This group promotes shareware and encourages high standards of shareware programming, including no-crippling policies intended to enhance the value of shareware.

If you are a software author, the ASP may help you find distribution channels for your program. Membership fees are very reasonable and should not prevent even casual programmers from joining. For more information, write the Executive Director, Association of Shareware Professionals, 545 Grover Road, Muskegon, MI 49442-9427 or send a message to CompuServe ID number 72050,1433.

We are pleased to support the ASP by contributing a portion of the royalties from *Windows GIZMOS* and *Windows 3.1 SECRETS* to the ASP to further the shareware concept.

## Why have shareware registration notices?

All shareware programs have some kind of pop-up window that lets you know how to contact the author and register the program. Some programs display this window after you click Help About or some other menu choice; other programs display it automatically when you exit or start the program.

The ASP specifically allows this type of reminder notice. The notice does not cripple a program in any way; rather, it provides the user with the address of the shareware author and an incentive to register.

We view these reminders like the appeals you sometimes hear on user-supported radio and television. Although they are slightly annoying, the stations could not continue to broadcast without the membership fees they receive. Similarly, shareware authors cannot continue to distribute their programs without the registration fees *they* receive. Reminder notices — which disappear totally after you register a package — are a slight irritation but are well justified by the full functionality (no crippling) you get in a true shareware package.

## The ASP Ombudsman program

To resolve any questions about the role of shareware, registrations, licenses, and so on, the ASP established an Ombudsman to hear all parties. Not all the shareware authors who have programs on the disks in this book are members of the ASP. If you have a support problem with an author who is a member of the ASP, and you cannot settle the problem directly with that author, the Ombudsman may find a remedy. Remember that you cannot expect technical support for any program unless you are a registered user of that program.

As the Association's literature describes it, "ASP wants to make sure that the shareware concept works for you. If you are unable to resolve a shareware-related problem with an ASP member by contacting the member directly, ASP may be able to help. The ASP Ombudsman can help you resolve a dispute or problem with an ASP member but does not provide technical support for members' products. Please write to the ASP Ombudsman at P.O. Box 5786, Bellevue, WA 98006 or send a CompuServe message via Easyplex to ASP Ombudsman, 70007,3536."

# General License Agreement

Each of the shareware programs on the accompanying disks has its own license agreement and terms. These are printed in the chapter describing each program or in a text file included with the program on the disks. For more information, contact the ASP at the address given earlier for a copy of its General License Agreement, which suggests individual and site license terms for shareware authors and users.

The programs featured in this book are supplied as is. Brian and Margie Livingston and IDG Books Worldwide, Inc., individually and together disclaim all warranties, expressed or implied, including, without limitation, the warranties of merchantability and of fitness for any particular purpose; they assume no liability for damages, direct or consequential, which may result from the use of the programs or reliance on the documentation.

The selection and organization of the software on the *Windows GIZMOS* disks, and the information file that installs the software, are copyrighted by the authors of this book. The *Windows GIZMOS* disks may not be sold, or bundled with a product or service that is sold, without permission from the authors.

# Technical Requirements

When a program featured in this book states that it "requires Windows 3.0 or later," you should always assume that it requires the standard or enhanced mode of Windows. *Real mode,* which exists only in Windows 3.0, is not suitable for running many of today's programs. Most of the programs featured in this book do not run at all in real mode.

Although many programs say that 1MB of memory is required, most of them (along with other Windows programs) run much better with 2MB to 4MB of memory. Memory prices are currently low, and adding more memory is usually the best way to get better performance from Windows.

# Technical Support _____

*All Windows programs have bugs.* This includes all retail Windows software as well as all shareware featured in *Windows GIZMOS.* Every program, no matter how simple, has some unexpected behavior or another. This is just the nature of software; the bugs are usually fixed in the release of a newer version of the program.

Because each of the programs featured in *Windows GIZMOS* is unique and complex, Brian and Margie Livingston and IDG Books Worldwide cannot provide any technical support for these programs.

The shareware authors represented in this book all provide technical support by one means or another. Each chapter describes how to contact the author, how to register, and how to obtain technical support. If you cannot resolve a problem by reading the documentation, the author of that program may be able to help. By buying this book, you *did not license the shareware programs;* you only purchased the right to a free trial of each of the programs. Shareware authors usually cannot provide technical support except to registered users.

If a program is listed as freeware, it probably has no technical support. In this case, if a program does not work on your particular PC configuration, you probably cannot obtain technical support for it.

# Direct Technical Support
# through CompuServe _____

The fastest and best method to obtain technical support is usually to contact the shareware author directly, using the CompuServe Information Service (CIS). This electronic-mail service should be the first choice for anyone who has a modem attached to his or her PC.

Most shareware authors have an electronic-mail address on CompuServe. These ID numbers are printed at the end of each chapter, if the shareware author has one.

The advantages of CompuServe for technical support are several:

♦ An electronic-mail message can be delivered almost immediately, as opposed to a telephone call that usually results in a busy signal or leads to a voice-message system at most big software companies.

♦ Electronic mail enables the shareware author to send you tips to help diagnose a problem, bug fixes, or new versions right to your modem.

♦ CompuServe can be less expensive than telephone calls, especially if you prepare a plain-text message in Notepad and transmit it to CompuServe at the fastest rate of your modem.

♦ CompuServe is available from most countries in the world and can handle a virtually unlimited number of messages 24 hours a day.

To start using CompuServe, call 800-848-8990 in the U.S., Puerto Rico, and the U.S. Virgin Islands; call 614-457-8650 outside these areas. Or write to CompuServe, Customer Service, P.O. Box 20212, 5000 Arlington Centre Blvd., Columbus, OH 43220. CompuServe currently offers a flat monthly rate, which includes more electronic-mail messages than most people are likely to send. There is also a per-minute rate at which you are charged only for the time you are actually on-line.

CompuServe provides you with a telephone number that you call from your PC and modem. CompuServe instructs you how to set up your communications software (usually 7 data bits, even parity, and 1 stop bit — often abbreviated 7E1 in computer literature). You can use the Terminal program included with Windows for all communications with CompuServe, or you can use a variety of other packages. In Terminal, you establish the communications parameters by clicking Settings Communications and then File Save to save your settings.

After you log on to CompuServe, type **GO CIS:MAIL** at any prompt to access the electronic-mail service. Depending on your class of service, you may be able to shorten this to **GO MAIL.** At that point, type your message and then send it to the CompuServe ID number listed in the documentation for the program. Most shareware authors check and respond to their electronic-mail messages once or more each business day.

Electronic mail has advantages for everyone. It's faster than regular mail (even overnight courier) and easier to respond to (no envelopes to tear open). If you have a modem and you haven't tried an electronic-mail service, do look into it.

# Preventing Viruses

Computer viruses are small programs that copy themselves into other programs and clog up or erase parts of your hard disk. Professionals who have studied viruses have found that the most common way a computer gets infected is by traveling salespeople who use the same disk to demonstrate programs in different companies. Another common cause of the spread of viruses is passing around an unprotected disk to several friends, exposing the disk to viruses that may be present on one of the PCs.

The disks that accompany *Windows GIZMOS* have been tested by the latest version of virus-scanning programs from McAfee Associates and found to be free of viruses. You can ensure that these disks remain virus-free by keeping a write-protect tab on each disk before inserting it into a drive. Viruses cannot get into a disk if the disk is protected by a write-protect tab. Additionally, the programs on the *Windows GIZMOS* disks are stored in a compressed form, which is resistant to virus infection.

Shareware programs are generally less prone to viruses than other programs. The reason is that shareware authors are aware of viruses and control access to their programs so that viruses cannot get in. Additionally, shareware programs are handled by far fewer people before release (usually only one person) than retail programs. Retail programs may pass from hand to hand among dozens of people in a large software company before being released to the public. By this means, viruses have found their way into retail software packages from vendors of spreadsheets, networks, and many other packages.

If you want to guard against viruses from disks or other channels, you should obtain the Virus Scan utilities from McAfee Associates. These shareware utilities, as described in *Windows 3.1 SECRETS,* may be obtained directly from McAfee Associates. A registered version of Scan can be obtained for $25 plus $9 for a disk and shipping from McAfee Associates, 1900 Wyatt Dr., Suite 8, Santa Clara, CA 95054-1529. You can also call 408-988-3832 or Fax to 408-970-9727. Shareware versions of Scan and other McAfee utilities (Clean-Up, Vshield, and others) are also available for downloading from the McAfee Associates bulletin board system. Call 408-988-4004 with your modem set to 8 data bits, no parity, and 1 stop bit. Registration entitles you to free upgrades from the bulletin board for one year. McAfee Associates also has numerous distribution agents in countries around the world.

# The Windows Series _____

You can look at the freeware and shareware in *Windows GIZMOS* and *Windows 3.1 SECRETS* as part of a complementary series of books. No program in *Windows GIZMOS* depends on *Windows 3.1 SECRETS.* Nor do you need *Windows 3.1 SECRETS* to enjoy any of the programs in *Windows GIZMOS.* But you may find just the tool or game you seek in *Windows 3.1 SECRETS* if it isn't in *Windows GIZMOS.*

For your convenience in finding the perfect program, we present here two lists, broken into categories, of all the freeware and shareware programs in *Windows 3.1 SECRETS* and *Windows GIZMOS*.

# Programs found in *Windows 3.1 SECRETS*

### Use This First

Viruscan and Clean-Up — Virus detectors and removers

### File and Program Management

Desktop Navigator — Replaces the Windows File Manager

File Commander — Add your own drop-down menus to Windows 3.1's File Manager

Launch — Starts applications with a click

RecRun — Runs Recorder macros automatically

RunProg — Runs programs in any size window

Task Manager — Top-rated Windows Task List replacement

### Graphics

Icon Manager — Icon editor with hundreds of icons

MetaPlay — Displays Windows graphics metafiles

Paint Shop — Converts and manipulates graphics files

WinGIF — Converts graphics to Windows formats

### Text Editing and Searching

Hunter — Full-text search and retrieval

WinEdit — A much better Notepad

WinPost — On-screen sticky notes

### Database Application

WindBase — Customizable, easy-to-use Windows database

### Communications

ComReset — Sets communications ports for Windows

Unicom — A great Windows communications program

**Games**

| Chess | Graphical chess for Windows |
| Klotz | A better Tetris-like game |
| Lander | A challenging moon-landing game |
| Puzzle | A tile game with DDE support |

**Utilities**

| Big Cursor | Make your mouse pointer more visible |
| BizWiz | A Windows version of the famous HP-12C financial calculator |
| ClockMan | Sets alarms and schedules events |
| EDOS | Enhances DOS sessions |
| SnagIt | Prints the screen or any portion of it |
| Superload | Loads applications and configures them |
| Trash Can | Drag files to delete them |
| Whiskers | Redefines your mouse buttons |
| WinBatch | The Windows graphical batch language |
| WinCLI | A DOS-like command-line interpreter |
| WinExit | A way to exit Windows quickly |
| Windows Unarchive | Decompresses ZIP and ARJ files within Windows |
| WordBasic Macros | Macros, ANSI characters, and shortcut keys |
| W.BAT | A batch file for Windows |

**Visual Basic Programs**

| Graphic Viewer | Displays files in different graphics formats |
| PrintClip | Sends text in the Clipboard to the printer |
| Simon | A game of sound and color |
| X World Clock | Supports any time zone in the world |

# Programs found in *Windows GIZMOS*

### Applications

| | |
|---|---|
| Address Manager | Print your own database on lists and labels |
| MathGraf | Graphs even the toughest equations for you |
| Mega Edit | Edit any text file without Notepad's limitations |
| μLathe | Draw any line and watch a 3D model take shape |
| Money Smith | A full-blown home or business bookkeeping system |
| Parents | Track your lineage and preserve your family tree |
| Recipe Maker | Compute your menu plans and shopping lists |

### File and Program Management

| | |
|---|---|
| File Garbage Can for Windows | Delete files securely with drag and drop |
| SideBar Lite | The fastest replacement for Program Manager |
| WinEZ | The best drop-down menu system for Windows |

### Games

| | |
|---|---|
| Checkers | The classic hop-over game, kings and all |
| Code Breaker | A challenging puzzle that changes every time |
| Hearts for Windows | A cutthroat game where rudeness may pay off |
| Hyperoid | Blast your way through this exciting space game |
| Jewel Thief | A game of wits with jewels and guards |
| Mile Bones | Beat your opponent to the finish line and win |
| WinPoker | Your own video poker game that never quits |

### Tools

| | |
|---|---|
| Barry Press Utilities | Switch your printer, match text files, and more |
| ClipMate ✗ can't use | Save and manage your Clipboard text |
| DirNotes for Windows | Break the DOS eight-character filename limit |
| Disk Copy for Windows | Make perfect disk copies simply and easily |
| Exclaim | Replace your DOS sessions with this powerful toolbox |

| | |
|---|---|
| Group Icon | Customize your Program Manager group windows |
| IconCalc | A complete calculator, no bigger than an icon |
| PixFolio | Manage your picture library in any graphics format |
| RS232 Serial Monitor | Catch modem problems fast |
| Super Resource Monitor | Manage your memory resources |
| Widget | Track your computer's CPU workload |
| WinClock | Set alarms and never miss another appointment |
| WinKey | Control the Shift, Caps Lock, and Num Lock keys |
| WinStart | Start up in any Windows mode |
| ZiPaper | Rotate your wallpaper for a fresh look |
| ZIP Tools for Windows | File compression and decompression in Windows |

# Address Manager

## Copyright © by Wilson WindowWare

*Everyone needs a good Windows program to keep track of addresses and phone numbers. Wilson WindowWare's Address Manager may be just the program for you.*

*The program comes already set up for you to click File New and then start typing addresses for your business associates and friends. It prints addresses on plain paper or labels and enables you to insert addresses and phone numbers into Microsoft Word for Windows or Wilson WindowWare's Reminder program (useful if you're supposed to call someone at a certain time, for example). Address Manager is unusual among Windows programs in that it automatically saves every name you type; you never have to remember to save the file.*

*If you want a special layout or format that Address Manager doesn't provide, you can design your own form by dragging the mouse in a special dialog box included for that purpose. Address Manager welcomes customization.*

| | |
|---|---|
| **Type of Program:** | Database |
| **Requires:** | Windows 3.0 or later |
| **Registration:** | Use the form at the end of this chapter to register with the shareware author. |
| **Technical Support:** | Wilson WindowWare provides registered users with technical support by way of telephone, fax, and CompuServe. |
| **Similar Shareware:** | WindBase, a database program featured in *Windows 3.1 SECRETS,* published by IDG Books Worldwide, can be customized to accept addresses, but it is not already set up for address storage and printing, as Address Manager is. |

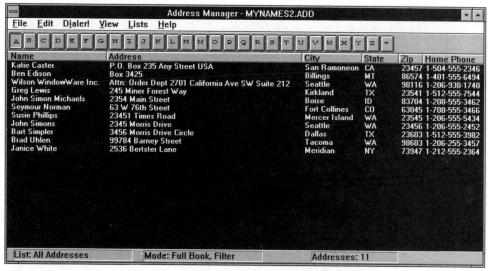

**Address Manager keeps track of addresses and phone numbers in a database format.**

# Overview

Address Manager is a full-featured Windows application designed to manage your address book. Address Manager includes the following features:

◆ Supports up to 8,000 entries per address book.

◆ Prints labels to dot-matrix or laser printers. Templates are provided for commonly used Avery laser labels. See "Printing Dot-Matrix Labels" or "Printing Laser-Printer Labels."

◆ Prints envelopes to laser printers. See "Printing Envelopes."

◆ Prints address information to Rolodex cards.

◆ Use Address Manager to print lists of the addresses you entered. Print the addresses in a single column, in two columns, or on a single line left to right. All printers supported by the Windows operating environment are also supported by Address Manager.

◆ Full support for international languages. See "International Support."

◆ Fully customizable View Forms. Use the provided forms or create your own forms for viewing data. See "Designing Custom View Templates."

◆ Address Manager supports up to 32 User-Defined Lists. A *User-Defined List* is a list that you define to store addresses. Lists are a subset of the names in a file. For example, within a single data file, you may have a list of business clients, a list of friends, and a list of local businesses. See "Special Lists."

♦ Support for all the typical database functions — for example, Add/Modify/ Delete names. Also, there is a Search function and the capacity for you to sort your data a number of ways (by First Name, Last Name; Last Name, First Name; City; ZIP; or State).

♦ Telephone Dialer. Address Manager will dial the phone for you, provided that you have your modem on COM1, COM2, COM3, or COM4.

♦ Three ways are available for you to view your data. The Full Book mode displays the Name, Address, City, State, ZIP, and Home, Work, or Facsimile phone number for each address. The Quick Look mode displays only the name and phone number information. The All Important Dates view displays His Birthday, Her Birthday, and an Anniversary date.

♦ Import names and addresses from a comma- or tab-delimited file. See "Importing Data into Address Manager." Or choose to export the data in Address Manager to a comma- or tab-delimited file. You can also copy your names and addresses to any other Windows application via the Windows Clipboard.

♦ Customizable fonts and colors. Any available font may be selected for displaying the data.

♦ Support for the Windows Dynamic Data Exchange, or DDE. Included with Address Manager are Word for Windows macros to import addresses into your documents.

# Getting Started

## How to get up to speed quickly with Address Manager

If this is your first time to run the Address Manager program, select New from the File menu to open a new file for storing addresses. After you select New, a dialog box will appear, prompting you for the name of the data file. You can type any valid filename for your address book (DOS limits you to eight characters for the filename and three characters for the extension). The ADD file extension is automatically added to your filename. If you enter **ADDRBOOK** as the name for your address book, for example, then the filename is ADDRBOOK.ADD. When you use the File Open command, *.ADD* is entered into the filename box by default, making it easy for you to locate your data file if it was saved with an ADD extension.

After you have specified a name for your new address book, you are immediately placed in the Add mode. Because this is the first time you are running Address Manager, each field in the Edit Box dialog box is labeled with the information that you should enter into the edit boxes. This information is only displayed when there are no entries in your address book. Delete the label text (such as First Name) and begin entering names. Each name you enter will be added to your address book.

The title bar for the dialog box, Edit Box-Add Names to All Addresses, indicates that the dialog box is for adding names to the All Addresses list.

Choose the More... button to indicate the following additional information for a name:

His Birthday

Her Birthday

Anniversary

Comments

The text entered into the Comments edit box will be word-wrapped automatically. A maximum of 256 characters can be entered into the Comments box. When entering dates for the other options in the dialog box, use one of the following formats: 3/4/78 or 3-4-78. If you are running Reminder, a personal information manager available from Wilson WindowWare, Inc., a button labeled To Reminder will appear. When pressed, this button will automatically enter

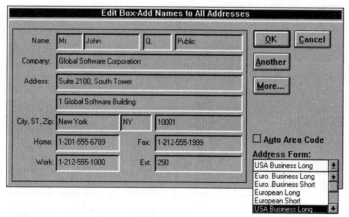

**Adding names to the All Addresses list is as easy as typing information in the data boxes.**

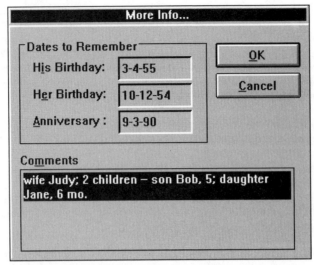

You can even add birthday and anniversary dates and up to 256 characters of comments.

the birthday and anniversary information into Reminder. When the address information is complete, choose the Another button to add the name and bring up another blank dialog box, or choose OK to add the name and return to the Address Manager list window.

## Word for Windows macros

Word for Windows users can run the provided WordBASIC macros to import address information from Address Manager into a Word for Windows document. Simply type a name into a Word for Windows document and run the InsertAddress macro to bring in the address information. If you are using Word for Windows 1.x, refer to the MACRO.DOC file for instructions on how to add and use this macro. If you are using Word for Windows 2.0, refer to the MACRO2.DOC file for installation and macro-usage information.

## User Interface

This is a quick discussion of how to use Address Manager. There are really only a couple of things to keep in mind in order to use this program efficiently. The main display window shows you the addresses in an extended selection list box, which means that you can highlight one or more names at a time. Hold the Ctrl key and click with the mouse to select discontinuous items or hold the Shift key to select a range. Any combination of names can be highlighted. Most menu selections will "act on" the highlighted names. For example, suppose that you just had a huge fight with all your in-laws. In a moment of rage, you decide to delete them from your address list. Choose Delete Highlighted Names from the Edit menu to permanently delete the highlighted names.

To modify or view the address information for a name, double-click the name with the mouse or press the Enter key to bring up the Edit Box - Modify/Delete dialog box with the information for the selected name. This box gives you the opportunity to change any information about the selected name.

When you're viewing your data, there are three column-heading layouts to choose from:

> Full Book
>
> Quick Look
>
> All Important Dates

Full Book displays the Name, Address, City, State, ZIP, and choice of Home, Work, or Fax telephone numbers. *Note:* The type of phone number (Home, Work, or Fax) is indicated in the Settings dialog box (choose Settings... from the File menu).

Quick Look displays the Name and Phone Number (Home, Work, or Fax).

All Important Dates displays the Name, His and Her Birthdays, and an Anniversary date.

When viewing your data, click any of the lettered buttons below the menu bar. If you are in Page mode, indicated on the status bar, you will see only those names for the selected letter. If the status bar along the bottom of the window indicates that you are in Filter mode, all names from the selected letter to the

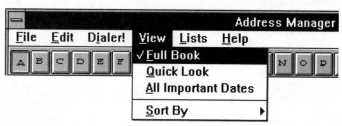

The View menu gives you three column-heading layouts to choose from.

| List: All Addresses | Mode: Full Book, Filter | Addresses: 11 |

**The status bar at the bottom of the screen tells you what options are in use for the Address Manager program (List, Mode, and Addresses).**

end of the alphabet will be displayed in the window. Refer to the "Control Bar" section for more information on the Page and Filter modes.

To determine what options are in use for the Address Manager program, look at the status bar at the bottom of the Address Manager screen.

List:        User List Name or All Addresses

Mode:        Full Book, Quick Look, or View Dates; and Filter or Page

Addresses:        The number of addresses in the active list or all addresses in the file

# Control Bar _____

The Control Bar enables you to quickly point and click to get to different areas of your address book. In addition to the Full Book, Quick Look, and View Important Dates modes, Address Manager has two other modes for displaying your data. These modes are referred to as the Page mode and Filter mode.

Use the * button (just after the Z button) to toggle between Page mode and Filter mode.

Page mode shows you a single page of your book, such as all the names for the letter *B*.

Filter mode shows you all the names from the letter that is pressed on the Control Bar to the end of the alphabet. For example, if you have the C button pressed and are in Filter mode, the first name displayed will be the first name in your book that begins with a *C*. All other names through the end of the alphabet will follow thereafter.

**The Control Bar near the top of the screen lets you click on buttons to move to different parts of the address book.**

If you are in Page mode (as indicated in the status bar), pressing the A button will display all the names in the list that begin with the letter *A*. Note that the names displayed will depend on the selected sort mode. For example, if you are sorting by First Name, Last Name, pressing the A button will display entries in the list whose *first* names begin with an *A*.

To change the sort mode, choose Sort By from the View menu. There are five Sort options to choose from:

Last Name, First Name

First Name, Last Name

City

State

ZIP Code

# Keyboard

The following keyboard shortcuts are useful in Address Manager:

| | |
|---|---|
| + or Insert key | Adds a new address |
| – or Delete key | Deletes currently selected address(es) |
| Enter key | Brings up the Edit/Modify dialog box for the currently selected address |
| Up and down arrows | Recalls the last three Cities and Last Names entered into the City or Last Names edit fields in the Add or Edit/Modify dialog box |
| F1 key | Accesses Address Manager Help |
| F5 key | Invokes the telephone Dialer |
| F6 key | Selects all names in the Address Manager window |

# Menu Commands _____

Following is the main menu bar for the Address Manager window:

File    Edit    Dialer!    View    Lists    Help

The underlined character indicates the Alt key combination for keyboard usage; for example, press Alt+F to activate the File menu without the use of a mouse. Choosing the Dialer! menu activates the Address Manager Dialer (no other items are under the Dialer! menu).

Each of these menu items is described in detail in the following sections.

## File

### New...

Choose New... from the File menu to start a new data file. Typically, you will not use this item a great deal because it is possible to keep several types of names and addresses in a single file. Within this file, you can create User-Defined Lists that represent different logical groups (for example, Christmas Lists, Friends, Family, Business Contacts, and so on). If you do decide to create a new data file, the filename can be any valid DOS filename. Address Manager will automatically add ADD as the file extension.

### Open...

Choose Open... to open a data file that already exists on disk. When you choose Open... from the File menu, the current file is automatically saved before the new data file is opened. Only one file may be open at a time (opening a second file will close and save the first file).

### Save As...

Choose Save As... to save your current data to a different filename. This feature is most useful for making backup copies of your Address Manager data files (for example, save a copy of MYNAMES.ADD to BACKUP.ADD). Do not use the Save As... command to save your data to the current file. Address Manager will automatically save your data as you enter names and before you exit the program.

### Merge...

Choose Merge... to copy the highlighted addresses to another Address Manager file. Select the name or names to copy and choose Merge from the File menu. From the dialog box that appears, select a filename to merge the names to and choose the OK button. The selected names will be merged to the selected file and will also still appear in the original file.

## Settings...

Choosing Settings... from the File menu enables you to configure the Address Manager program.

## Smart Dialer Settings...

If you will be using the Dialer function of Address Manager, you will want to select this option to give the Dialer some "brains." Refer to the "Settings" topic for more information on the options in the Smart Dialer Settings dialog box.

## Import...

Choose Import... to add data from a tab- or comma-delimited text file to your existing Address Manager file. Within the Import File dialog box, select the filename, the field delimiter (comma or tab), and the default Address Form for the names and addresses.

## Export...

Choose Export... to copy the highlighted names to a tab- or comma-delimited text file. All information will be copied, including birthdays and comments. Enter a filename with an extension (for example, EXPORT.TXT) and choose from a comma- or tab-delimited text file.

## Windows Printer Setup...

Choose Windows Printer Setup... to configure options within the active Windows printer driver. Select the appropriate printer and choose the OK button to access the Windows printer setup dialog box. If you select from the list a printer driver that is not active, then the following error message will appear: Unable to access printer driver. To change a printer driver to an active status, you will need to go through the Windows Control Panel.

## Select Printer...

Prior to printing from Address Manager, choose Select Printer... to indicate your printer selection. All printers that are currently set up on your system are in the list box labeled Reports. Select the appropriate printer before printing. If you do not select a printer, Address Manager will use the default printer as set up through the Windows Control Panel.

## Print➤

### Rolodex Cards

Choose this menu selection if you want to print your selected addresses to
Rolodex cards. From the resulting dialog box, you will be able to specify the
dimensions of the cards you are using. The Lines Per Label field represents the
size of the *entire* Rolodex card (default of 13 for the Courier font). Typically,
several lines at the top of the Rolodex card will not be suitable for printing text.
Enter the number of lines suitable for printing in the Printable Lines field (default of 10 for the Courier font). The entire address will be printed. You also
have the option of including any or none of the following fields:

His Birthday

Her Birthday

Anniversary

Comments

These fields will be printed in the preceding order, following the address information. (To control which address fields print, set Print Fields for the Form in
the Custom Form Designer.) Note that if you select *all* the optional fields, there
may not be enough room on the card for every field. If this is the case, Address
Manager will notify you when a card is missing some fields. Rolodex cards will
print in the default or internal printer font (which is usually Courier).

### Dot Matrix Labels

Choose this menu selection to print labels to a dot-matrix printer. From the
resulting dialog box, you will be able to choose from a list of Avery labels or
specify the dimensions of the labels in the numerous edit boxes (horizontal
distance is measured in characters; vertical distance is measured in lines). Dot-
matrix labels will print in the default or internal printer font (which is usually
Courier).

### Laser Labels

If you have a laser printer and Avery labels (or labels with similar dimensions),
you can use Address Manager to print your names and addresses to labels. Any
font and point size may be selected for each line of the label.

### Print List

This selection will print the data as it appears in the main window of Address
Manager. If you have not selected a printer using File Select Printer, Address
Manager will use the default printer as set up in the Windows Control Panel.
This menu option prints the names in the active list, regardless of which names
are highlighted.

### Print Preview

Before choosing Print List, choose the Print Preview option to view a sample
printout of your address list.

### Print Single Column

This option enables you to print the contents of the main Address Manager window in a single-column fashion. This means that instead of printing the names left to right on a single line, this option will print the data similar to how labels are printed:

Name
Address
City, State ZIP

Name
Address
City, State ZIP

As with the Print List option, this menu selection will print the entire list, regardless of which names are highlighted.

### Print Double Column

The Print Double Column selection enables you to print your addresses in two columns:

| | |
|---|---|
| Name | Name |
| Address | Address |
| City, State ZIP | City, State ZIP |

### Envelopes

Choose Print➤ Envelopes to print manually fed envelopes to a laser printer. Select a name for the envelope from the names in the main Address Manager window and choose File Print➤ Envelopes.

## Fonts

Select this menu option to change the display font used in the main Address Manager window. Any screen font that is available to the system can be selected. Attributes such as italics and boldface can also be set. Changes to the screen font will be remembered for the next session of Address Manager.

## Colors

Address Manager enables you to customize the screen colors that are used throughout the program. You can specify the background color that is used in the main Address Manager windows (Listbox), as well as the display text (Listbox Text) and the color of the highlighted display text (Selected Text). The colors for the "slider" (the column headings) can also be set through the Slider Bar and Slider Bar Text options. Color changes that are set in the Colors dialog box are saved and will be remembered for the next session of Address Manager.

### Exit

Choose Exit from the File menu to end your Address Manager session (your data is automatically saved).

## Edit

### Modify/Delete...

Select a name to view/modify and select Modify/Delete... from the Edit menu or press the Enter key. The Modify/Delete edit box will appear with the information for the currently selected name. You may change or add to the information in the dialog box. To change the data about a person, type the new information into the edit fields and then choose the OK button. You can also permanently delete a name from your file by using the Delete button. Choose the Next button to view the information for the next name in the list or the Prev button to view the previous name information.

### Add

Use this menu option to add a new name to your address book. If you are adding several names at a time, use the Another button in the resulting edit box to continue adding names. Choose the OK button when you have added the final entry. When entering the Last Name or City, use the up- and down-arrow keys to recall the last three entries. Doing so helps reduce the number of times you will have to type the same last name or city.

When you tab to an empty phone field, Address Manager will insert the local area code for you if the Auto Area Code box is checked.

### Copy

Choose Copy to place the selected names in the Address Manager window into the Windows Clipboard. The information will be tab-delimited and can then be pasted into any other Windows application. Only 640 names can be copied to the Clipboard at a time.

### Set Address Form...

Use this selection to assign a new address form to one or more addresses. This item is useful when you're changing the address View Form for a group of names. Simply select the names and choose this menu item. A dialog box will appear with a listing of the available address forms. The View Form for an individual name and address can also be changed in the Modify/Delete edit box.

## Search...

Use this menu selection to find any name in your address book. You can either search the currently selected list or search all names in the data file. Specify the search criteria field (for example, Name Fields) to tell Address Manager which fields to search through. Type the text string you are looking for in the Search For: field.

For example, if you want to find all the people in your data file who live in Washington state, do the following:

1. Type **WA** in the Search For edit box.

2. Specify the State field as your search criteria (mark the State field with an *X*).

3. Choose All Names for the Search option at the bottom of the dialog box.

4. Choose the Find button to start the search.

Address Manager will search through your data file for those that have *WA* in the State field. Those names that meet this criteria will be displayed in a dialog box, along with their home telephone number. To view additional information about a name resulting from the search, choose the name and press Enter or choose the OK button. The Edit Box - Modify/Delete dialog box will appear with the complete information for the selected name. Choose the Cancel button to exit the Found Strings dialog box and return to the main Address Manager window.

## Delete Highlighted Names

This menu selection will permanently delete the highlighted names from your data file. Prior to deleting the names, Address Manager will ask you whether you are sure that you want to delete the highlighted names. Choose Yes if you want to have the selected name(s) deleted. If you want to delete the name from a User List only, choose Delete from User List... from the Lists menu.

## Save Heading Columns

When viewing your data, you can adjust the column widths by clicking and dragging the column boundaries (the line between two column headings) on the slider bar. Doing so enables you to format the columns as far apart or as close as you like. If you want Address Manager to remember these column heading widths for the next session, you need to select Save Heading Columns from the Edit menu. The heading columns can be saved separately for the Quick Look and Full Book modes. This menu item will be grayed out if Best Fit Columns is specified in the File Settings dialog box.

## Dialer!

The Dialer item is for people with modems. This feature enables you to let Address Manager dial the phone. To use this feature, highlight/select a single name in the main window and click Dialer! or press F5 from the keyboard. This action will bring up the Dialer with the phone number of the selected name listed in the Phone # edit box. Now click the Dial button and wait for the connection to be made. When the connection is made, pick up the telephone receiver and wait for someone to answer your call.

If no name is highlighted or more than one name is highlighted, the dialer dialog box will appear with no phone number inserted. In this case, you can either type a phone number into the Phone # edit box or use the mouse to insert the number by clicking the number buttons.

## View

### Full Book

When the Full Book mode is active (as indicated by a check beside the Full Book menu selection as well as the status bar statement Mode: Full Book), the following column headings will appear: Name, Address, City, State, ZIP, and one of three phone number fields (Home, Work, or Fax). To indicate which type of phone number to display, choose Settings... from the File menu and select Home, Work, or Fax. If you have not used the Full Book mode before or do not have Best Fit Columns selected in File Settings, you may need to adjust the column width. To adjust the column width, click the mouse on the line between the column

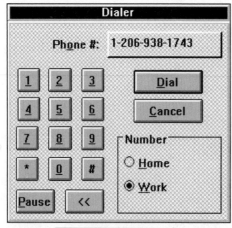

Select a single name in the main Address Manager window and click on the Dialer! menu option to display the Dialer.

headings and drag the mouse to adjust the column width. Be sure to select Save Heading Columns from the Edit menu so that the next time you enter Full Book mode, Address Manager will preset the column widths as you like them.

## Quick Look

The Quick Look mode displays only the Name and Phone number information, omitting the address information from the display. The phone number is the phone number type as indicated in the File Settings dialog box.

## All Important Dates

The All Important Dates mode displays the Name, His and Her Birthday dates, and an Anniversary date. This information is entered into the More Info dialog box along with comment information. To edit or add to this information, double-click the name in the main window or choose Edit/Modify... from the Edit menu. Now choose the More... button to add or view existing information for the selected name.

## Sort By

To change the sort mode for your data, choose Sort By from the View menu. There are five Sort options to choose from:

**Last Name, First Name**
Anderson, Bixbee, Collins . . .

**First Name, Last Name**
Anne, Beth, Charlie . . .

**City**
Anchorage, Boise, Cle Elum . . .

**State**
Alaska, California, Florida . . .

**ZIP Code**
09821, 13421, 22033 . . .

# Lists

## Create User List...

Choose Create User List... when you want to create a new list to store names. For example, you may want to create a User List to store the names of those people whom you sent Christmas cards this year. Type a name for the new User List and choose the New button to create the list. This action will only create the list. To add names to a list, see Add to User List, which follows shortly.

## Delete User List...

Just as you can create User Lists, you can delete User Lists. Choosing Delete User List... will bring up a dialog box with the names of all your current Lists. Select the User List name that you want to delete and choose the Delete button. When might this option be necessary? Well, suppose that all of a sudden you decide that you really don't care who your friends are, and so you don't need a special list for them. Selecting this option will enable you to delete a User List such as Friends. Note that any names that were on the list are *not* actually deleted from the file but rather removed from the User-Defined List. If you want to permanently delete names from your address book, choose Delete Highlighted Names from the Edit menu.

## Edit User List Names...

Use the Edit User List Names... option to change the name assigned to a list you previously created. For example, suppose that you previously created a list named *Chrstmas List* and later noticed the typo in the word *Christmas*. Instead of creating a new list named *Christmas List* and then moving all the names to the new list, you can simply edit the name of the list to correctly read *Christmas List*. Select the name to edit from the list of User List names, change the name in the edit box, and choose the Change button.

## Add to User List...

The Add to User List... option enables you to add names to a list that already exists in your data file. This option saves you from rekeying data when creating lists of names. To copy names to a list, do the following:

1. Choose All Addresses from the List menu to view all addresses in your file.

2. Highlight those names you will want to add to the User List.

3. Choose Add to User List... from the Lists menu.

4. Select the User List name from the resulting list box of names.

5. Choose the Add button to add the names to the selected list.

6. From the Lists menu, choose Group 1➤ User List Name to view the names.

## Delete from User List...

This menu item works in much the same way as Add to User List... but enables you to remove names from a User-Defined List. This item will not delete names from the file but will simply remove the highlighted names from the specified

List. For example, if a person on your Clients list is no longer a business client, you can select that name and choose Delete from User List.... In the resulting dialog box, choose the Clients list and choose the Delete button.

### All Addresses

Choose this menu option to display all the names in your data file regardless of assigned User List.

### Group 1

If you have created User-Defined Lists, the names will pop out to the right of Group 1. Selecting a User List displays only those names that you have added to the list. A second group called Group 2 will be added when more than eight lists are under Group 1.

## Help

### Index

This selection displays an Index of the Address Manager on-line help information.

### Overview

This selection displays overview information for Address Manager.

### Keyboard

This selection displays the keyboard controls for Address Manager.

### Commands

This selection displays information about the Address Manager menu commands.

### Help on Help

This selection activates the Microsoft Windows Index to Using Help.

### About Address

This selection displays the Address Manager About dialog box.

# Designing Custom View Templates _____

Custom View Forms enable you to design your own way of viewing and printing addresses. The Edit/Modify dialog box (choose Modify/Delete... from the Edit menu or double-click a name in your address book) will display information as defined by the Custom View Forms. The available forms are listed in the list box labeled Address Form. Choose one of the forms from the list box, and the dialog box will update to the layout of the new Custom View Form. Different forms can be used for different names and addresses. For example, you can use a business form such as USA Business Long for your business contacts in the United States and the European Short form for your friends in Europe.

A number of forms are provided with Address Manager, and you also can design your own. To create a new form or modify an existing form, choose Design Custom View Forms... from the File menu. This action brings up the Custom View Form Designer and the last form you edited. To load a different form, choose Load Form... from the File menu.

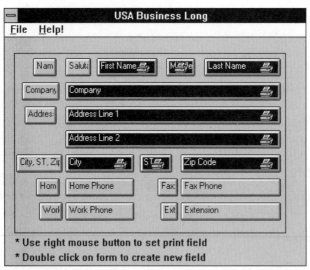

The USA Business Long form changes the layout when you view or print addresses.

To create/add a new field to a form, double-click the left mouse button on the form where you want the new field to appear. A form can have any of the following fields:

Salutation

First Name

Middle Name

Last Name

Company

Address 1

Address 2

Address 3

City

State

ZIP

Home Phone

Work Phone

Extension

Fax Phone

In addition to field names, you can add up to 20 text fields. A *text field* is static text that will appear on the final form. You may want to identify some of your fields so that it is obvious which data should be entered. For example, before the Fax Phone field, you may want to include a text field that reads *Fax:*.

After double-clicking the form with the left mouse button, choose a field name; if you are defining a text field, select the Text option and type the text for the field in the edit box. The new field will be positioned on the form at the point where you double-clicked the mouse.

To adjust the length of the fields, position your mouse cursor near the right or left edge of the field and click and drag the mouse. The fields have a fixed height and can only be sized horizontally.

To change the placement or position of the field on the form, position your mouse over the field so that the cursor changes to a hand and click and drag the field to a new position on the form.

To delete a field from the form, position your mouse over the field so that the cursor changes to a hand and press the Del or Delete key on your keyboard.

After you create a form, the form name will be added to the list of available forms to choose from when you're adding/editing names in your address book.

In addition to using the Custom Forms to control the layout for your on-screen fields, you also can use the Custom Forms when printing addresses to an envelope or a label. The order and position of the fields on the form are used to determine how the address will be printed. To indicate which fields you want to have printed, mark the fields on the form as *print fields*. To do this procedure, position the mouse cursor over a field and click the right mouse button. The field will turn red, and a printer icon will be displayed on the right edge of the field, indicating that this field should be printed when you're printing an address that uses this form.

For example, the European Forms that are included with Address Manager specify ZIP, State, City for the last address line. When an address that uses a European Form is printed to a label, it is printed in the same order as the field's display (ZIP, State, City). The print-field option is a *toggle*; click the right mouse button again to remove or add the print-field option.

# Printing Dot-Matrix Labels

To print labels to a dot-matrix printer, choose Print➤ Dot Matrix Labels... from the File menu. The resulting dialog box has many options to help you navigate the address to the appropriate position on the label.

## Printing to Avery dot-matrix labels

If you are using Avery labels, simply choose the Template name that corresponds to the number on the Avery box of labels (for example, Avery 4144). When a template is selected, the appropriate values are placed into the edit boxes for you. Choose Print Labels to print labels for the names you selected in the main Address Manager window.

## Printing to dot-matrix labels (non-Avery)

The Dot Matrix Labels dialog box contains many options for controlling the placement of the address information on the label:

**Lines Per Label:** The height of the label measured by the number of lines. Typically, there are 6 lines per inch, so if your labels were an inch tall, the number of lines would be 6 (1.5-inch high labels would be 9 lines).

**Labels Across:** The number of labels left to right. This value is usually 1 for single-column labels, 2 for double-column labels, or 3 for three-column labels.

**Lines Between Labels:** The vertical spacing between each label, again measured in lines. The number of lines between each label is usually 1.

**Width of label in chars:** The horizontal width of the labels measured in characters. To calculate the number of characters, measure the width of the labels with a ruler and convert inches to characters. Typically, there are 10 characters per inch, so a 3.5-inch wide label would be 35 characters wide.

**Distance between labels in chars:** The horizontal distance between the columns of labels. Usually, this distance is fairly minimal — perhaps 1 to 5 characters at most.

## Printing multiple dot-matrix labels for the same name

In order to print multiple copies of each name selected in the main Address Manager window, indicate the number of copies of each label in the Dot Matrix Labels dialog box:

1. Select the names for printing labels in the main Address Manager window. Select as few as a single name or as many as you want.

2. Choose Print➤ Dot Matrix Labels from the File menu.

3. In the edit box labeled Copies of each label, indicate the number of labels you want to print for each of the selected names. For example, you may want to print an entire page of a single name/address (for example, Copies of each label = 16) or two labels for each name/address selected.

4. Choose the Print Labels button.

## Notes on printing dot-matrix labels

Only the names that are highlighted in the main Address Manager window will be printed. If you want to print a label for all the names in the active window, press F6 to select all the names prior to printing labels.

Information printed to the label will be the contents of the Print Fields for the selected View Form. To change the Print Fields for a form, do the following:

1. Choose Design Custom View Forms from the File menu.

2. Choose Load Form from the File menu of the Custom Form Designer and choose the form to edit.

3. Position your cursor over a field and click the right mouse button to toggle the Print Field status on or off.

Dot-matrix labels will print in the default internal font for the printer (usually a monospaced font, such as Courier).

# Printing Laser-Printer Labels

If you have a laser printer and Avery labels, Address Manager enables you to easily print labels. Any font and point size may be selected for each line of the label. For example, the name can be printed in Arial 12, and the other address lines can be printed in the Times New Roman 10-point font.

To access the Laser Label configuration screen, select the names you want to print labels for and choose Print➤ Laser Labels... from the File menu.

When you enter the Laser Label Settings dialog box, Address Manager will default to the Avery 5160 label template. A pictorial representation of this template is shown in the window to the right of the dialog box. If you choose a different label type (say, Avery 5161), then the display on the right will be updated to show you the general layout of the selected label template. One of the labels will have the text START displayed. This is the indicator for which label you want Address Manager to begin printing first. This is useful if you only print a few labels at a time and want to feed the same sheet through the printer the next time you print labels. To change the START label for Address Manager, click the mouse on the address label you want to have Address Manager print first. Or choose the Set Start button to move the focus to the graphic window. You can now use the arrow keys to specify the starting label.

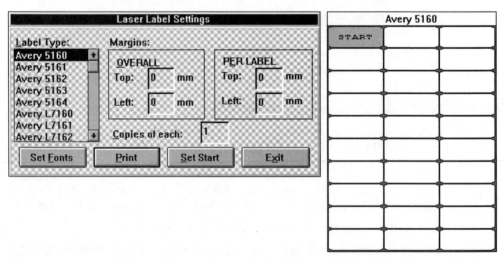

When you print to laser-printer labels, you select the Avery label type you are using and then specify where on that sheet of labels you want to start printing.

In the Laser Label Settings dialog box on the left, you can specify attributes for the labels, including margins and copies of each label. To set a font for a field or address line, do the following:

1. Choose the Set Fonts... button.

2. Below Set font for, choose the address line to change and then select a font name, style, and size.

3. Choose the Apply button to apply the font to the selected address line (Address line 1, for example).

4. Repeat steps 2 and 3 for each of the address lines.

5. Choose the OK button to return to the Laser Label Settings dialog box.

These font selections will be remembered the next time you bring up Address Manager. The templates are set up to work properly with the Avery laser-printer labels, but you may still want or need to fine-tune the margin settings. The Margins box enables you to change the overall margins for the page or for the individual labels. Indicate adjustments to the Top and Left margins in millimeters (mm).

Finally, the Copies of each edit box enables you to specify the number of copies you want for name(s) selected in the main Address Manager window. If you want a page of labels for each of the selected names, you might type **30** for the copies of each. If you need to send each of the selected names two pieces of mail, you might type **2** for the number of copies. Choose the Print button to begin the print job. Address Manager will print a label (or multiple labels if Copies of each is set greater than 1) for each name that was highlighted/selected prior to when you entered the Laser Label Settings dialog box.

*Note:* If you have labels with the same dimensions as the Avery templates that are provided, you can still use the laser label feature of Address Manager. The dimensions for the current templates are as follows:

| | |
|---|---|
| Avery 5160 | $1" \times 2 \frac{5}{8}"$ |
| Avery 5161 | $1" \times 4"$ |
| Avery 5162 | $1 \frac{1}{3}" \times 4"$ |
| Avery 5163 | $2" \times 4"$ |
| Avery 5164 | $3 \frac{1}{2}" \times 4"$ |

# Printing Envelopes _____

The envelope-printing facility of Address Manager is designed to print manually fed envelopes on a laser printer. Templates are provided for the following sizes of envelopes:

Envelope 9

Envelope 10

Envelope 11

Envelope 12

Envelope DL

Envelope C5

Monarch

To print manually fed envelopes to a laser printer, do the following:

1. In the main Address Manager window, select a single name or multiple names for which you want to print envelopes.

2. Choose Print➢ Envelopes from the File menu.

3. Choose the Envelope Size that you will be printing to. Envelope 10 (4⅛" by 9½") is the standard business-size envelope in the United States.

4. Type your return address in the upper left in the Return Address Info box.

   If you have selected a single name for which to print an envelope, the address information for this name will appear in the Send to Address Info box. If you have selected multiple names for envelopes, the first selected name will appear in the Send to Address Info box.

   *Note:* The address displayed in the Send to Address Info box cannot be edited in the Print Envelopes dialog box.

5. Choose the Set Fonts... button to specify the fonts for both the Send To and Return addresses. A font dialog box will appear in which you can specify the font name, style, and size for a given address line. Choose the Apply button to record the font setting for the selected address line. When you have specified the fonts for both the Send To and Return addresses, choose the OK button. Note that each envelope supports its own font information. This way, you can have one font style for your business envelopes and another for your personal envelopes.

6. Choose the Print this One button to print a single envelope with the address information as displayed in the Print Envelopes dialog box. If you have multiple names selected, you can choose either Print this One or Print All.

If you have more than one name selected in the main Address Manager window, use the Next and Previous buttons to thumb through the names that you selected in the main window.

**Copies:** This indicates the number of copies (envelopes) you want to print for each name selected.

*Notes:* Your return address information is associated with the envelope size. So you can enter a business address for a business-size envelope and your home address for another size envelope. Choose to save changes when exiting the Print Envelope dialog box, and your return address will be remembered for the next session. Envelope feeders are not currently supported. If your laser printer does not feed envelopes through the middle of the paper tray, read the following discussion.

The templates have default positioning values that are based on the assumption that the manual envelope feeder pulls the envelopes through the middle of the paper tray. If your laser printer pulls envelopes aligned with the top or bottom portion on the paper tray, the Left and Top millimeter values will need to be adjusted. Both the Return and Send address text have edit boxes for the Left and Top positions.

To determine what values to place in these edit boxes, you must place an envelope on top of an 8.5-by-11-inch piece of paper. The envelope should be placed in relation to how the manual feeder pulls the envelope. So, if your envelope feeder is aligned with the bottom of an 8.5-by-11 sheet of paper, you align the envelope at the bottom of the 8.5-by-11-inch paper. Now measure with a ruler from the top portion of the 8.5-by-11-inch page to where you want the return address to print on the envelope. Determine the number of millimeters this is from the top of the 8.5-by-11-inch page and to the left of the 8.5-by-11-inch page. Apply the same concept for determining the millimeter values for the send address. All of this is necessary because the millimeter values are measured from the edge of a normal sheet of paper and not from the edge of the envelope.

# Settings

The following information details the options in the File Settings and Smart Dialer Settings dialog boxes (both are located under the File menu).

**Disable Label Warning:** Disable Label Warning disables the warning that Address Manager posts just before printing dot-matrix labels. When you're printing dot-matrix labels, the warning reminds you to make sure that no other

```
┌─────────────────────────────────────────────────┐
│                    Settings                        │
├─────────────────────────────────────────────────┤
│  ☐ Disable Label Warning    ┌─Display Phone──────┐│
│                             │  ◉ Home Phone       ││
│  ☐ Show Last Name First     │                     ││
│                             │  ○ Work Phone       ││
│  ☒ Best Fit Columns         │                     ││
│                             │  ○ Fax Phone        ││
│  Local area code:  │212│    └─────────────────────┘│
│                                                    │
│  ┌─Modem Settings──────────────────────────────┐  │
│  │  Prefix: │    │   Init. String: │ATDT│        │  │
│  │                                               │  │
│  │  COM Port:          Baud Rate:                │  │
│  │  │COM1      │▼│     │2400           │▼│         │  │
│  └───────────────────────────────────────────────┘  │
│                                                    │
│  Language:                                         │
│  │English        │▼│      │ OK │  │ Cancel │       │
│  │English           │                               │
│  │French            │                               │
│  │                  │                               │
└─────────────────────────────────────────────────┘
```

**Use the Settings dialog box to change assump-tions and defaults for the Address Manager.**

applications are printing. (See "Common Questions" for an explanation of why this error occurs.) If you get tired of seeing this warning box each time you go to print dot-matrix labels, you can disable it by using this option.

**Show Last Name First:** Show Last Name First is an option for changing the way the names are displayed. By default, the names are shown in the order First, Middle, Last. Mark the Show Last Name First option to reverse the order that the names are displayed.

**Best Fit Columns:** Best Fit Columns is an option that, when selected, tells Address Manager to automatically adjust the column widths to best fit the data that is currently being displayed. When this option is selected, the Save Heading Columns menu item is grayed under the Edit menu.

**Local Area Code:** Local Area Code is where you need to enter the area code from which you will be dialing. Doing so is necessary so that the Smart Dialer can strip off an area code if the number you are dialing is within your local area code. For example, if your local area code is 206, Address Manager will strip off the area code whenever dialing a phone number with the 206 prefix.

**Display Phone:** The group of radio buttons in the Display Phone box enables you to choose which phone number you want to view when viewing your data in the Full Book or Quick Look view of Address Manager. Full Book mode displays the Name, Address, City, State, ZIP, and choice of Home, Work, or Fax telephone numbers. Choose from Home, Work, or Fax.

**Modem Settings:** Use the box labeled Prefix to specify any prefix number you need to dial before dialing the phone number. This option is useful if you are in an office where you need to dial 9 for an outside line. By entering 9 as a prefix, 9 will automatically be added to any phone number you choose to dial with the Dialer. Select the communications port that your modem is connected to (COM1 through COM4) and choose the baud rate for your modem. Finally, specify the modem initialization string. The default is ATDT and should be used when you're dialing from a Touch-Tone phone. ATDP can be used for dialing from a pulse phone.

# International Support

The drop-down Language box in the Settings dialog box indicates the current language for Address Manager. Address Manager is designed to support *any* language in the world (excluding the double-byte character set languages, such as Japanese). Several languages are shipped with Address Manager, including English, French, and German. To change the language representation of the program, simply select Settings... from the File menu. In the dialog box that appears, there will be a list of languages to choose from. Select the desired language and choose OK. The program will automatically switch to the new language!

To add support for your own language, follow these simple steps:

1. Open the STRINGS.USA text file (included with Address Manager) into your favorite text editor.

2. Translate the strings to your language.

3. Open the ADDRESS.LNG text file from your Address Manager program directory. Under the [Settings] section, add your language to the AvailableLanguages line. For example, if you are adding support for Spanish, you add Spanish as follows:

```
[Settings]
AvailableLanguages=English,Spanish
```

Note that the languages must be separated by a comma.

4. At the bottom of the ADDRESS.LNG file, create a new section that has the exact name you added to the AvailableLanguages line (in this example, the entry would be [Spanish]).

5. Copy your translated strings and paste them into the ADDRESS.LNG file under this new section.

Now, when you run Address Manager again, your newly supported language will be listed in the Languages entry of the Settings dialog box. When creating support for your own language, try to keep the length of each string to approximately the same length as the English equivalent or shorter.

## Smart Dialer Settings

When entering phone-number information about the people in your address book, it is recommended that you enter complete phone information (for example, 1-206-555-1212). Including the area code allows the Smart Dialer to strip off area codes appropriately. Address Manager keeps track of your local area code, as specified in the File Settings dialog box. Typically, if the number you are dialing has the same area code as your local area code, the Smart Dialer will strip off the 1-206 portion. However, sometimes you may be dialing an intrastate number that is actually a long-distance call. These numbers don't require the area code but still require the 1-. Using the Smart Dialer Settings dialog box will enable you to tell Address Manager which 3-digit prefixes require a 1-.

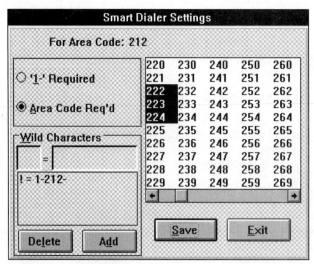

Use the Smart Dialer Settings dialog box to specify when to use an area code and when 1- is required.

To indicate the numbers that require a 1-, choose the numbers from the list box by clicking the numbers with the mouse. When the appropriate numbers are selected, choose the Save button to save the selections.

You may soon need to include an area code when dialing phone numbers in your same state. The reason is that the phone companies are running out of area codes in certain geographic areas, such as California. For example, currently a call from Seattle to Tacoma requires the 206 area code. Even though Tacoma uses the same area code as Seattle and is only 40 miles away, a 206 is required when you're calling Tacoma. In the Smart Dialer Settings dialog box, you can indicate which 3-digit prefixes within your state require an area code. To indicate the numbers that require an area code, choose the Area Code Req'd option and then the area-code numbers from the list box (click the numbers with the mouse to select). When the appropriate numbers are selected, choose the Save button to save the selections.

The area code that is listed at the top of the dialog box (For Area Code: *XXX*) is the area code that has been set in the Settings dialog box. If you travel a lot and will be dialing from many different area codes, you can create Smart Dialer settings for any number of area codes you choose. To do this, just make sure that when you go to a different area code, you change the area code in the File Settings dialog box.

The Wild Characters option in the Smart Dialer Settings dialog box enables you to indicate a special character as a place holder for a series of characters. For example, you can define the ! character to represent the number 234. Then, when you're entering a phone number and you need to enter 234, you can just type the wild character !. If you then select the name and choose the Dialer! menu option, the ! character in the phone number is changed to 234.

# Special Lists

Address Manager enables you to create up to 32 User-Defined Lists. These lists are essentially logical subsets of the All Addresses list. For example, you may want to create a list of all your friends and another list of all your family members. When you create a User List, the name you supply will be appended to the Lists menu (under Group 1). Selecting a list name will show you only those names that are on the specified list (only your family's or only your friends' names).

To create a User List such as Friends or Family, choose Create User List... from the Lists menu. In the resulting dialog box, type a name for the list (for example, Family, Friends, or Business). Choose the New button to create the User List.

After you have created a User List, you will want to put some people's names and addresses on the list. If you want to add a name that is currently not in your data file, choose Add... from the Edit menu and type in the data. If you have previously typed in the name, follow these steps to add a name to a User List:

1. Choose All Addresses from the Lists menu to view all names in your data file.

2. Locate and highlight the names you want to have in your new User List (to select multiple names, press the Ctrl key in combination with selecting the names with the mouse).

3. Choose Add to User List... from the Lists menu.

4. In the resulting dialog box, select the list you want the names added to and choose the Add button.

5. From the Lists menu, choose Group 1➤ *list name* (for example, Friends), and you will see that the names have been added to the list.

*Note:* The status bar at the bottom of the Address Manager screen indicates which list is on the screen: List: All Addresses or List: Friends.

Deleting names from User Lists works much the same way as adding names with Add to User List. To remove names from a User List, select Delete from User List... from the Lists menu. This option will *not* delete the names from your address file but will remove the highlighted names from the list you specify. If you mean to remove the name from the data file entirely, choose Delete Highlighted Names from the Edit menu.

*Note:* If you tell Address Manager to delete a name from a User-Defined List and the name is not in the User List, Address Manager will simply ignore this directive.

Refer to the "Hints and Tips" section for step-by-step instructions on copying and moving names from one list to another. To display all the names and addresses in your data file, choose All Addresses from the Lists menu. The status bar will be updated to indicate List: All Addresses. If you have created User-Defined Lists, the names will pop out from Group 1 under the Lists menu. Selecting a User-Defined List name from the Lists menu will display only those names that you have put on the list. A second group called Group 2 will be added when more than eight lists are under Group 1. Again, look at the status bar to determine which list you are viewing.

# Importing Data into Address Manager _____

If you have name and address data in another program, it is possible for you to export the data to a text file and read the data into Address Manager. The fields in the exported text file can be either comma- or tab-delimited.

There are 19 fields (18 commas or tabs per record) in the Address Manager input file format:

Mr.[TAB]David[TAB]A.[TAB]Slim[TAB]Phillips Oil[TAB]1234 Main Street[TAB][TAB][TAB]Boise[TAB]ID[TAB] 83704[TAB]208-555-1212[TAB][TAB][TAB]208-555-1213[TAB]06/07/66[TAB][TAB][TAB]College buddy from class of 90

If your data file meets the preceding format specification, follow these steps to import it into Address Manager:

1. Open an existing file or create a new file for the imported data.

2. Choose Import... from the File menu.

3. Select the file name to import and the type of field separator used in the text file (comma or tab).

4. Each address will initially need to use the same default View Form. Select a Form from the list box of Address Forms.

5. Choose OK to start the import process. Just below the Comma option button is an indicator of the number of records imported (Total Imported: *X*). The Import File dialog box will remain on-screen until all the records are imported and sorted.

# Common Questions _____

**Q: I don't see a Save option anywhere on the menu. How do I make sure that my data is saved?**

**A:** Address Manager will automatically save your data for you anytime you make changes. This way, if there is a power failure or your system crashes for some reason, you will not lose any data.

**Q: When I go to print dot-matrix labels, I get a warning telling me to make sure that no other Windows applications are printing. I thought that if I was using the Windows Print Manager, I didn't need to worry about printing from different applications at the same time. What's going on here?**

**A:** This warning appears because labels are printed directly to LPT1. If another application is printing at the time, unpredictable results will surely follow!

## Address Manager Input File Specifications

| Field # | Description | Length |
|---------|-------------|--------|
| 1. | Salutation | 15 |
| 2. | First name | 20 |
| 3. | Middle name | 20 |
| 4. | Last name | 20 |
| 5. | Company | 30 |
| 6. | Address line 1 | 40 |
| 7. | Address line 2 | 40 |
| 8. | Address line 3 | 40 |
| 9. | City | 20 |
| 10. | State | 20 |
| 11. | ZIP code | 10 |
| 12. | Home phone | 30 |
| 13. | Work phone | 30 |
| 14. | Work extension | 4 |
| 15. | FAX number | 30 |
| 16. | His birthday | 8 |
| 17. | Her birthday | 8 |
| 18. | Anniversary | 8 |
| 19. | Comments | 255 |

The reason labels are sent directly to LPT1 is that Windows 3.0 automatically forces a form feed after a certain number of lines have been printed. Because labels are continuous, you would have to waste 3 or 4 labels each time Windows decided to do a form feed. This is only an issue for dot-matrix printers. This warning can be turned off in the File Settings dialog box.

**Q: How do I move an address from one list to another?**

**A:** To do this, you should select the name(s) that you want to be moved. Then select Lists/Add to User List...; when the dialog box comes up, select the list you want the names moved to and click Add. Now select Lists/Delete from User List... and select the list you want the names removed from.

**Q: How can I change the font for the lists I print?**

**A:** Address Manager assumes that the font for printed lists will be Courier. There is no support in this version for selecting different fonts for printed lists.

Q: **What if I don't have Avery labels?**

A: Address Manager comes with several templates that are predefined to work with Avery laser labels. If you have labels with the same dimensions as the Avery templates that are provided, you can still use the laser labeler. The dimensions for the current templates are as follows:

| | |
|---|---|
| Avery 5160 | 1" × 2 ⅝" |
| Avery 5161 | 1" × 4" |
| Avery 5162 | 1 ⅓" × 4" |
| Avery 5163 | 2" × 4" |
| Avery 5164 | 3 ½" × 4" |

Q: **The top line of my laser-printer label is printing too high. How can I center the information on the label or move it down?**

A: To make minor adjustments to where the text is printed on laser labels, use the Margins box in the Select Label Fonts dialog box (choose File Print➤ Laser Labels to access this dialog box). Adjustments can be made to the overall label sheet or to each individual label (values are entered in millimeters).

Q: **I change all the column widths by using the slider and can't select Save Heading Columns. Why?**

A: If Save Heading Columns is grayed out, deselect the Best Fit Columns box in the File Settings dialog box.

# Hints and Tips

The best way to use Address Manager is to keep one file with all your data in it. Because it is possible to create your own User-Defined Lists, it is less efficient to have one file for your business addresses, one file for your personal addresses, one file for your Christmas-card recipients, and so on. Instead, just maintain one file and create User-Defined Lists.

Use the Save As... menu item from the File menu to create a backup copy of your address book. If your address file is named NAMES.ADD, choose Save As and type **BACKUP.ADD** for the backup copy. Choose OK to save to the new filename. Then choose Open... from the File menu and open your original data file, NAMES.ADD, and continue working with the file. Address Manager automatically saves your address files when you exit the program or add/edit address-book information.

To the right of the alphabetic buttons is a * button. This asterisk toggles you between two viewing modes (Page and Filter). If you are in Page mode and the A button is pressed, then only the names from the current list that begin with the letter *A* will be displayed. For example, if you are sorting by Last Name, First Name, you see all the people in the current list whose last names begin with *A*. Clicking the * button again puts you in Filter mode. If you're in this mode and the D button is pressed, the first name in the list will be the first person whose last name begins with *D*, with all names from D through Z following thereafter.

The status bar along the bottom of the Address Manager window indicates whether you are in the Page or Filter mode (Mode: Quick Look, Filter).

There are two options for controlling the column widths. One option automatically adjusts the widths of the columns and is called Best Fit Columns (indicated in File/Settings...). The second option enables you to manually set the column widths by adjusting the widths of the column headings with the mouse. Choose Save Heading Columns... from the Edit menu to save the current column width settings. You can set the column headings manually for the Quick, Full Book, and All Important Dates modes. The next time you load Address Manager, the saved settings will be used for the column widths. *Note:* The Save Heading Columns menu item is grayed when the Best Fit Columns box is checked in the File Settings dialog box.

When you're entering a slew of names and addresses, use the up- and down-arrow keys to help minimize the number of keystrokes you type. For the Last Name field and the City field, Address Manager will remember the last three entries. This way, you don't have to type **Seattle** for *all* your friends who live in Seattle. Instead, use the arrow keys when your cursor is in the City field to cycle through the last three city names entered.

Use different View Forms for different addresses. If you are entering a personal address, use the USA Short Form rather than one of the business forms. When you're editing your address information, the available View Forms are listed in the list box labeled Address Form. You can use different View Forms for different addresses. Address Manager remembers which View Form is assigned to which address.

Use the Custom View Form Designer to make changes to the existing forms or to design new ones altogether. Choose Design Custom View Form from the File menu to access the Form Designer.

If you need to copy names and addresses to another Windows application, simply choose the names to copy and choose Copy from the Edit menu. Switch to the other application (such as Excel) and choose Paste from the Edit menu.

Look at the status bar at the bottom of the Address Manager window for information on which list is active, the viewing mode, and the number of addresses in the list.

List:        User List Name or All Addresses

Mode:        Full Book, Quick Look, or View Dates; and Filter or Page

Addresses:   The number of addresses in the active list (User-Defined List or All Addresses)

# HP LaserJet III Information

Due to problems with the HPPCL5A.DRV printer driver distributed with Windows 3.1, Address Manager is only capable of printing envelopes to the HP LaserJet III printer *if it is your Windows default printer.*

If you need to print envelopes and require that the LaserJet III *not* be your default printer, you may want to try the driver for the HP LaserJet Series II, which a lot of people are having a good deal of success with.

# Registration

Unlicensed copies of Wilson WindowWare products are 100 percent fully functional. We make them this way so that you can have a real look at them and then decide whether they fit your needs. Our entire business depends on your honesty. If you use it, we expect you to pay for it. We believe that if we treat you right, you will treat us right.

Unlicensed copies of our products do have a pesky registration reminder screen that pops up whenever you start the program. This shouldn't really affect your evaluation of our software.

We're sure that after you see the incredible quality of our software, you will dig out your credit card, pick up the phone, call the nice people at our 800 number, and register the software.

When you pay for the shareware you like, you are voting with your pocketbook and will encourage us to bring you more of the same kinds of products. Pay for what you like, and *voilà!* more of what you like will almost magically be developed.

# Legal Matters

Of course, the usual disclaimers still apply. We are not responsible for anything at all. Nothing. Even if we are held responsible, the limit of our liability is the licensing fees you paid. The full text of our license agreement is presented later in this chapter and is in the README2.TXT file.

# Update Policy

It is the policy of Wilson WindowWare to protect faithful customers and to derive the majority of its income via sales to new customers instead of continually attempting to extract more funds from existing customers. Of course, we must at least cover our costs, or we could not stay in business bringing you new and updated software.

Wilson WindowWare frequently updates its products. There are various kinds of updates, including major updates, minor updates, and bug-fix updates.

Minor and bug-fix updates for our shareware products are free — subject only to our reasonable shipping and handling charges for disks. Because we are not in the disk-selling business, you may find that shareware vendors specializing in disk sales can easily sell disks cheaper than we can. On the other hand, we *always* have the most recent versions of our software.

Our shipping and handling charges for update disks are as follows:

> $10.00 United States and Canada for the first product
>
> $ 5.00 United States and Canada for each additional product
>
> $ 9.50 surcharge for shipping outside of the United States and Canada

If you obtain a minor or bug-fix update from CompuServe or another on-line service, a BBS, a shareware disk vendor, or another source, there is no charge from us (of course, you will have to pay the on-line service fees, disk vendors fees, or at least your phone bill for downloading from a BBS). In addition, you may use a single disk to update any number of copies of a product.

The policy and pricing for major shareware updates vary. Depending on the nature of the upgrade, length of time since the previous major upgrade, desirability of new features added, extent of revisions to the printed manuals (if any), work involved, and possible price changes for new users, we may or may not charge fees. Because it is difficult to determine what the cost of future major updates will be, and because we do not want to commit ourselves to the uncertainty of the future, we have provided information on the cost of major past updates here so that you can see our track record and possibly feel reassured about the future:

**Command Post first released: May 1988**

| | |
|---|---|
| 1.0 through 6.*x* | Free |
| < 6.*x* to 7.*x* | $18.50 (included a new manual) |
| 7.0 to 7.2+ | Free |

**WinBatch first released: January 1991**

| | |
|---|---|
| 1.0 to 3.3+ | Free |

**File Commander first released: May 1992**

| | |
|---|---|
| 1.0 | No major updates so far |

**WinCheck first released: October 1990**

| | |
|---|---|
| 1.0 through 2.*x* | Free |
| < 2.*x* to 3.0 | Free (new manual and disk — $10) |
| 3.0 through 3.0+ | Free |

**Address Manager first released: July 1991**

| | |
|---|---|
| 1.0 to 1.1b | Free |
| 1.1b to 2.0+ | Free (new manual and disk — $10) |

**Windows Reminder first released: July 1991**

| | |
|---|---|
| 1.0 to 1.3+ | No major updates so far |

**WinEdit first released: November 1990**

| | |
|---|---|
| 1.0 to 1.3+ | No major updates so far |

| | |
|---|---|
| **Free** | In the preceding list, *Free* means that the update costs the same as a minor update; if you want us to send you a disk, there is only our standard shipping and handling charges for disks. |
| + | In the preceding list, a + indicates current versions. |

# On-Line Support _____

Wilson WindowWare has on-line support!

The home of all Wilson WindowWare is on CompuServe, in the WINAPA forum, in the Wilson WindowWare section (#15 currently). Also, the latest and greatest downloads are available from DL15 of the WINAPA forum. The Wilson WindowWare section of the WINAPA forum is checked on a daily basis, and all questions will be responded to.

The Fidonet Windows echo is also checked on a fairly regular basis. We only look at the titles of the messages. If you want to leave a message for us, be sure that one of the following words is in the title:

WINDOWWARE WILSON BATCH CMDPOST COMMANDER WINBATCH WIL

Registered users may also call our BBS for the latest versions of our products: (206) 935-5198 USR HST D/S V.42bis 9600+ 8N1

# Association of Shareware Professionals Ombudsman Statement _____

Wilson WindowWare, the producer of Wilson WindowWare software, is a member of the Association of Shareware Professionals (ASP). ASP wants to make sure that the shareware principle works for you. If you are unable to resolve a shareware-related problem with an ASP member by contacting the member directly, ASP may be able to help. The ASP Ombudsman can help you resolve a dispute or problem with an ASP member but does not provide technical support for members' products. Please write to the ASP Ombudsman at 545 Grover Road, Muskegon, MI 49442 or send a CompuServe message via easyplex to ASP Ombudsman 70007,3536.

# Software License _____

Wilson WindowWare software is not and has never been public-domain software, nor is it free software.

Nonlicensed users are granted a limited license to use our software on a 21-day trial basis for the purpose of determining whether the software is suitable for their needs. Any use of our software, except for the initial 21-day trial, requires registration. The use of unlicensed copies of our software, outside of the initial 21-day trial, by any person, business, corporation, government agency, or any other entity is strictly prohibited.

A single-user license permits a user to use one copy of the licensed software product only on a single computer. Licensed users may use the program on different computers but may not use the program on more than one computer at the same time.

No one may modify or patch any of our executable files in any way, including but not limited to decompiling, disassembling, or otherwise reverse-engineering our software programs.

A limited license is granted to copy and distribute our shareware software only for the trial use of others, subject to the above limitations and also the following:

1. The software must be copied in unmodified form, complete with the file containing this license information.

2. The full machine-readable documentation must be included with each copy.

3. Our software may not be distributed in conjunction with any other product without a specific license to do so from Wilson WindowWare.

4. No fee, charge, or other compensation may be requested or accepted, except as authorized below:

   A. Operators of electronic bulletin board systems (sysops) may make our products available for downloading only as long as the above conditions are met. An overall or time-dependent charge for the use of the bulletin board system is permitted as long as there is not a specific charge for the download of our software.

   B. Vendors of user-supported or shareware software approved by the ASP may distribute our products, subject to the above conditions, without specific permission. Nonapproved vendors may distribute our products only after obtaining written permission from Wilson WindowWare. Such permission is usually granted. Please write for details (enclose your catalog). Vendors may charge a disk-duplication and handling fee, which, when pro-rated to each individual product, may not exceed eight dollars.

   C. Nonprofit user groups may distribute copies of our products to their members, subject to the above conditions, without specific permission. Nonprofit groups may collect a disk-duplication fee not to exceed five dollars.

## LIMITED WARRANTY

Wilson WindowWare guarantees your satisfaction with this product for a period of 90 days from the date of original purchase. If you are unsatisfied with the product within that time period, return the package in saleable condition to the place of purchase for a full refund.

Wilson WindowWare warrants that all disks provided are free from defects in material and workmanship, assuming normal use, for a period of 90 days from the date of purchase.

Wilson WindowWare warrants that the program will perform in substantial compliance with the documentation supplied with the software product. If a significant defect in the product is found, the purchaser may return the product for a refund. In no event will such a refund exceed the purchase price of the product.

EXCEPT AS PROVIDED ABOVE, WILSON WINDOWWARE DISCLAIMS ALL WARRANTIES, EITHER EXPRESS OR IMPLIED, INCLUDING, BUT NOT LIMITED TO, IMPLIED WARRANTIES OF MERCHANTABILITY AND FITNESS FOR A PARTICULAR PURPOSE, WITH RESPECT TO THE PRODUCT. SHOULD THE PROGRAM PROVE DEFECTIVE, THE PURCHASER ASSUMES THE RISK OF PAYING THE ENTIRE COST OF ALL NECESSARY SERVICING, REPAIR, OR CORRECTION AND ANY INCIDENTAL OR CONSEQUENTIAL DAMAGES. IN NO EVENT WILL WILSON WINDOWWARE BE LIABLE FOR ANY DAMAGES WHATSOEVER (INCLUDING WITHOUT LIMITATION DAMAGES FOR LOSS OF BUSINESS PROFITS, BUSINESS INTERRUPTION, LOSS OF BUSINESS INFORMATION, AND THE LIKE) ARISING OUT OF THE USE OR THE INABILITY TO USE THIS PRODUCT EVEN IF WILSON WINDOWWARE HAS BEEN ADVISED OF THE POSSIBILITY OF SUCH DAMAGES.

Use of this product for any period of time constitutes your acceptance of this agreement and subjects you to its contents.

## U.S. GOVERNMENT RESTRICTED RIGHTS

Use, duplication, or disclosure by the Government is subject to restrictions as set forth in subdivision (b)(3)(ii) of the Rights in Technical Data and Computer Software clause at 252.227-7013. Contractor/manufacturer is Wilson WindowWare, 2701 California Ave. SW /Suite 212/ Seattle, WA 98116.

## TRADEMARKS

Microsoft and MS-DOS are registered trademarks of Microsoft Corporation.
Windows is a trademark of Microsoft Corporation.
File Commander is a trademark of Wilson WindowWare, Inc.
Command Post is a trademark of Wilson WindowWare, Inc.
WinBatch is a trademark of Wilson WindowWare, Inc.

WinCheck is a trademark of Wilson WindowWare, Inc.
Reminder is a trademark of Wilson WindowWare, Inc.
Address Manager is a trademark of Wilson WindowWare, Inc.
WinEdit is a trademark of Wilson WindowWare, Inc.

# Wilson WindowWare Products

Our great line of Windows products includes the following:

**Address Manager**   Tracks addresses, phone numbers, comments, and important dates. Includes dialer and label printer. Supports DDE. $39.95

**Command Post**   A powerful text-based shell for Windows. Programmable menus, built-in batch language, file viewer, and more. $49.95

**File Commander**   Allows addition of programmable menu items to the Windows 3.1 File Manager. Make File Manager into a super-powerful shell. $49.95

**Reminder**   Personal schedule manager. Keeps track of to-do lists, sets alarms (which can launch apps), and prints reports. Supports DDE. $59.95

**WinCheck**   Your personal finance manager for Windows. Manages checking, savings, cash, and credit-card accounts. Features galore! Supports DDE. Custom Reports. $69.99

**WinEdit**   Power programming for the Windows environment. Full-featured editor or simple file browser. Super-high-speed, super-powerful. Batch language supported. $59.95

**WinBatch**   Write your own Windows batch files! Dialog boxes, automatic program control, and powerful data manipulation let you control Windows. A must for the power user. $69.95

**WinBatch COMPILER!**   *Not a shareware product.* The WinBatch compiler can compile WinBatch batch files into stand-alone EXE files that may be distributed on a royalty-free basis. Great for networks and corporate gurus. Compile your WBT files and then hand them out like candy. $395.00

## Wilson WindowWare Order Form

Name: _____

Company: _____

Address: _____

_____

City: _____ State: _____ ZIP: _____

Phone: ( _____ ) _____ Country: _____

____ Address Manager(s)　　@ $39.95:　　_____.____

____ Command Post(s)　　@ $49.95:　　_____.____

____ File Commander(s)　　@ $49.95:　　_____.____

____ Reminder(s)　　@ $59.95:　　_____.____

____ WinBatch(s)　　@ $69.95:　　_____.____

____ WinCheck(s)　　@ $69.99:　　_____.____

____ WinEdit(s)　　@ $59.95:　　_____.____

____ WinBatch Compiler　　@$395.00:　　_____.____ *call*

____ Foreign air shipping (except Canada)
　　　　　　　　@ $9.50:　　_____.____

　　　　　　　　Total:　　_____.____

Please enclose a check payable to Wilson WindowWare. Or you may use Access, Amex, Visa, MasterCharge, or EuroCard. For credit cards, please enter the information below:

Card #:__ __ __ __ - __ __ __ __ - __ __ __ __ - __ __ __ __

Expiration date: ____ /____

Signature: _____

Send to:　　**Wilson WindowWare, Inc.**
　　　　　　2701 California Ave. SW #212
　　　　　　Seattle, WA 98116
　　　　　　U.S.A.

or call:　　(800) 762-8383 (U.S.A. orders only)
　　　　　　(206) 938-1740 (customer service)
　　　　　　(206) 937-9335 (tech support)
　　　　　　(206) 935-7129 (FAX)

Please allow 2 to 3 weeks for delivery.

# Ordering Information

Licensing our products brings you wonderful benefits. Some of these benefits follow:

♦ Gets rid of that pesky reminder window that comes up when you start up the software

♦ Entitles you to one hour free phone support for 90 days (your dime)

♦ Ensures that you have the latest version of the product

♦ Encourages the authors of these programs to continue bringing you updated/better versions and new products

♦ Gets you on our mailing list so you are occasionally notified of spectacular updates and our other Windows products

♦ And, of course, our 90-day money-back guarantee

# The Barry Press Utilities

### Version 5-19-92
### Copyright © by Barry Press

*B*arry Press, a shareware author in California, has assembled an impressive array of utilities, each of which serves its own purpose. The utilities in this set are as follows:

Applet *gives you access to individual Control Panel dialog boxes.*

CalPop *is a pop-up calendar showing any month from 1980 to 2037.*

Flipper *switches your printer from portrait to landscape and back.*

Holder *enables you to start applications from buttons on your desktop.*

Match *compares any two text files in Windows or in DOS.*

Runner *provides a quick File Run box, without Program Manager.*

| | |
|---|---|
| **Type of Program:** | Utilities |
| **Requires:** | Windows 3.1 or later. (Do not run it under Windows 3.0.) |
| **Registration:** | Use the form at the end of this chapter to register with the shareware author. |
| **Technical Support:** | Barry Press provides registered users with technical support via mail and CompuServe. |
| **Similar Shareware:** | The Time utility in this set improves on the Windows Clock and has some similarities with ClockMan, a more elaborate alarm system found in *Windows 3.1 SECRETS,* published by IDG Books Worldwide. The other utilities fill their own unique niches. |

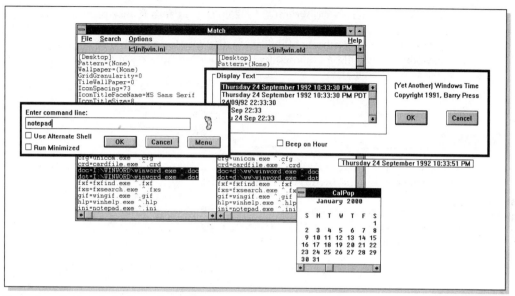

**Several applications in the Barry Press Utilities.**

# Installation

To install the Barry Press Utilities, run WSETUP on Diskette 1. After installation, all the separate Barry Press Utilities program files will be located in a directory you specified, such as C:\BPUTIL, and a group window in Program Manager will display icons for each utility.

It is not necessary for you to add the C:\BPUTIL directory to the PATH= statement in your AUTOEXEC.BAT file for these utilities to work properly. However, doing so is recommended because it makes it possible for you to run these utilities from a File Run command line in Program Manager or File Manager, without typing in the C:\BPUTIL directory name as part of the command.

If you want to move some files to different directories, the utilities will still work properly in most cases. However, executable files and their related help files, such as MATCH.EXE/MATCH.HLP and HOLDER.EXE/HOLDER.HLP, must be located in the same directory to function correctly.

Two files included with the Barry Press Utilities, MELTDOWN.AD and VHOLD.AD, are modules that work with the After Dark for Windows retail screen-saver utility. If you use After Dark, you may want to move these files to that directory, which is usually C:\AFTERDRK.

# Applet

Applet is designed to let you run Control Panel applications (or *applets*) without having to run (and tie up) the Control Panel.

Applets are found in Control Panel extension files, which generally have the CPL extension (for example, MAIN.CPL). Control Panel extension files are found in your \WINDOWS\SYSTEM directory.

To run an applet, you can use the command line from the Program Manager:

>   APPLET *filename index*

where *filename* is the Control Panel pathname (for example, C:\WINDOWS\SYSTEM\MAIN.CPL) and *index* is the title of the applet within the extension file you want to run.

Some extensions (for example, MAIN.CPL) contain more than one applet; *index* enables you to specify which one you want. If you don't know, omit the parameter. Applet will present a list box naming the applets in the extension file, along with the index for each.

Some of the Control Panel files you may find in Windows follow:

| | |
|---|---|
| MAIN.CPL | Contains the applets COLOR, DATE/TIME, DESKTOP, FONTS, INTERNATIONAL, KEYBOARD, MOUSE, PORTS, PRINTERS, and NETWORK (if you are currently attached to a network) |
| DRIVERS.CPL | Configures multimedia and other drivers |
| SND.CPL | Associates sounds with various Windows actions (such as launching a program), if you have a speaker driver and speakers |
| CPWIN386.CPL | Configures 386 Enhanced mode (if Windows is in enhanced mode) |

You can create an icon in Program Manager to run any of these applets. Click File New to create a new program item and then type the appropriate command line. For example, you can type the following:

>   **APPLET C:\WINDOWS\SYSTEM\MAIN.CPL COLOR**

*Warning:* Using the Windows Control Panel, you can run only one applet at a time in the entire system. Applet makes it possible for you to run several at once and makes it possible for you to run the same one several times at once. Although running multiple applets at the same time is not a problem, running multiple copies of the same applet is definitely a bad idea because the applets weren't designed for that.

So far, I haven't found a way to keep you from shooting yourself in the foot by running more than one instance of the same applet at the same time. So I'll simply post this warning:

*Don't run more than one copy of a Control Panel application at a time. And, to be as safe as possible, don't run more than one applet from a single file at the same time.*

It doesn't matter if one is under the real Control Panel and another is under Applet, both are under Applet, and so on. *Don't do it.* Even though it might work for specific applets, it's not a good idea.

I wrote Applet for a friend who wanted to keep open the applet that controls his SoundBlaster Pro sound board but not tie up the Control Panel.

# CalPop — A Simple Calendar for Microsoft Windows

CalPop is a small program for Microsoft Windows that displays any month between January 1980 and December 2037.

When you start CalPop, it displays the current month. The arrow buttons on the scroll bar at the bottom change the display by one month; the left arrow

```
┌─────────────────────────┐
│ ▬        CalPop          │
│      January 2000        │
│                          │
│   S  M  T  W  T  F  S    │
│                      1   │
│   2  3  4  5  6  7  8     │
│   9 10 11 12 13 14 15     │
│  16 17 18 19 20 21 22     │
│  23 24 25 26 27 28 29     │
│  30 31                   │
│ ◄───────┤   ├────────►   │
└─────────────────────────┘
```

**The CalPop utility displays a calendar for any month between 1980 and 2037.**

moves back one month, and the right arrow moves forward one month. The left and right scroll-bar ranges have similar effects, but the change is by one year. The scroll-bar thumb may also be moved to any point desired.

You may run more than one instance of CalPop to display several months.

CalPop responds to a keyboard interface for the scroll bar as well as the mouse. The arrow keys correspond to the arrow buttons, the PgUp and PgDn keys to the scroll ranges, and the Home and End keys to the first and last months.

I wrote CalPop when I couldn't find a Windows 3 version of a similar program I'd picked up long ago on CompuServe.

# Flipper — Simple Printer-Orientation Control for Microsoft Windows

Flipper runs only as an icon and displays the current orientation of the default printer. When double-clicked, it will change the printer's orientation, updating the icon in the process. Flipper notices when you change the printer orientation via the Windows Setup dialog box directly, as well as when you change the default printer.

Some printer drivers don't respond properly under Windows 3.0 to the software interface for determining and changing the paper orientation. For those drivers (most notably, Epson), Flipper will display a question-mark icon, indicating that it can't do its job. Many such drivers were upgraded in Windows 3.1 to use the UNIDRV.DLL Universal Printer Driver technology, correcting this problem in the process. You do not require a new version of Flipper to run with those drivers.

I wanted a dolphin for the icon (of course) but had no handy clip art, and I'm no artist. The icons for portrait and landscape in the earlier versions of Flipper

Know the current printer orientation by watching which way the dolphin jumps.

weren't exactly ready for the Museum of Modern Art. The dolphin icons in this release are wonderful, however, and are the work of Michael Lessa. (Thanks! Thanks also to Peter Montgomery for getting them to me.)

I wrote Flipper because I was tired of waiting around for one or another application to load the printer driver so I could change from portrait to landscape and vice versa. I keep it as the second item in my LOAD= line (under Windows 3.1, in my StartUp group), so it always ends up near the lower left corner of my display. Flipper has no Control menu and cannot be closed once started.

You can also change the orientation of your printer from within another application (such as a Word for Windows or an Excel macro). To do so, use PORTRAIT.EXE and LANDSCAP.EXE, which are described in the "Portland" section, which follows.

# Portland (PORTRAIT.EXE and LANDSCAP.EXE) — Direct Printer-Orientation Control for Microsoft Windows

Portland is a package of two programs — PORTRAIT.EXE and LANDSCAP.EXE — that provide direct printer-orientation control for Microsoft Windows. Running either of the programs sets the current default printer's orientation to portrait or landscape, respectively. The programs open no windows and terminate after doing the work. If you have Flipper running, the effects of the orientation change will be visible in the Flipper icon. The programs are useful from Windows batch files (for example, using the new Norton Desktop) and from macros in many Windows applications (for example, Excel and WinWord).

Some printer drivers don't respond properly under Windows 3.x to the software interface for determining and changing the paper orientation. For those drivers (most notably, Epson), Portland will not be capable of doing its job. Many drivers were upgraded for Windows 3.1, correcting this problem in the process. You will not require a new version of Portland to run with those drivers.

The dolphin icons stored in the program files (so they'll show up right with Program Manager) are the work of Michael Lessa.

I wrote Portland as a variant of the Flipper program in response to a user's request.

# Holder for Windows

Holder is a Windows application that launches other applications from icon-like buttons placed anywhere on the Windows desktop. Each instance of Holder appears as a button, with an icon displayed on the face and the title for the application displayed below the button. For example, a Holder button for Holder itself can look like this:

**The Holder button for the Holder program itself shows a holding hand as the icon.**

Double-clicking the button with the left mouse button (or pressing the Enter key when the button has the input focus) launches the corresponding application set up on the button. Double-clicking the title (below the icon) and holding down the left mouse button brings up the Holder system menu.

## Command-line parameters

Holder supports command line parameters to enhance its use in the StartUp group of the Windows 3.1 Program Manager, as shown in the following list:

| Command Line Parameters | Interpretation |
| --- | --- |
| None | Holder displays a list of known application tags, displaying a button for the selected one. |
| List of defined application tags | Holder displays a button for each tag. This may be mixed with undefined tags as desired. |
| List of undefined application tags | Holder displays an Options dialog box for each one and then displays a button for each. |
| * (asterisk) | Holder displays a button for all tags defined in the PRESS.INI file. |

## Using Holder in the Windows StartUp group

Holder is particularly effective when added to the Windows StartUp group in the Program Manager, using command-line parameters to specify the Holder buttons to be displayed. For example, placing a program item with the command line

```
HOLDER.EXE *
```

into the StartUp Group in the Program Manager will cause all defined buttons to be displayed when Windows starts.

You can select specific buttons by using their tags on the command line. For example, you can run Holder and define an icon called *control* that will start the Control Panel. The command line

HOLDER.EXE CONTROL

will then display a button like this:

**The Holder button for the Control Panel program shows the standard Control Panel icon.**

If you set up Program Manager with its Minimize on Use option checked (and don't run Holder minimized), when Windows starts, you'll end up with a clean desktop — with the Holder buttons displayed where you positioned them and the Program Manager neatly stowed as an icon at the bottom of the screen.

# System menu commands

The following menu items appear on the Holder system menu, in addition to the usual Windows system menu items:

Options

Font

New

Delete

Index

Using Help

About Holder

## Options

The Options command provides access to a dialog box with controls on the operation of Holder for launching a specific application. Options are available to control the Holder button title, the application launched, the launch working directory, start-up parameters, and the icon displayed on the Holder button for the application.

The Program Setup group of controls specifies how the application is to be launched, along with the title to appear below the Holder button for the application:

| Control | Function |
| --- | --- |
| Description | Specifies the title shown below the Holder button for this application. You may also change the title by making the specific button the active window and typing the new title. Complete the new title by pressing Enter; cancel the change by pressing Esc. |
| Command Line | Specifies the command line to be executed to launch the application, including any command-line parameters. |
| Working Directory | Specifies the directory to be changed to when the application is launched. |
| Browse | Opens a file browse dialog box to permit selection of the application's executable file. |
| Radio Buttons | Allows selection of how the window should appear when the application is launched: **Normal:** The application window is opened normally, as with File Run from Program Manager or File Manager. **Minimized:** The application window is opened as an icon at the bottom of the screen. **Maximized:** The application window is opened full screen. **Hidden:** The application window never appears. This option should not be used for Windows programs or for DOS applications that ever require user input; it is intended for applications that simply do some function invisibly and exit. |

The Icon Setup group of controls specifies the icon to appear on the face of the Holder button for the application:

| Control | Function |
| --- | --- |
| Current | Displays the icon currently displayed on the button face |
| Icon File | Specifies the full path of the file from which the icon is to be loaded |
| Choices | Displays the icons found in the specified file and allows selection of a specific one |
| Browse | Opens a file browse dialog box to allow selection of the file from which the icon is to be selected |

Options information is saved in the file PRESS.INI, stored in the Windows directory.

## Font

The Font command invokes a dialog box with which you can select the font and text size used in the Holder title area. The font change applies globally to all instances of Holder. Although the dialog box shows options for boldface or italic text, these selections are ignored.

Confirming the dialog box (by clicking OK) changes the font in all running instances of Holder, as well as sets the font choice for future invocations. Font selections are saved in the file PRESS.INI, which Windows places in your Windows directory.

## New

The New command invokes a dialog box you can use to enter the Holder tag for a new application launch setup. The list box below the edit field shows the existing tags. Each application setup requires a unique tag.

After a unique tag is entered, the Options dialog box appears and the setup for the application can be completed. After the dialog box is completed, the Holder button for the tag appears in the upper left corner of the display. You can move it by holding down the left mouse button in the title area and dragging the button to the desired location.

## Delete

The Delete command enables you to delete a previously defined application setup for Holder. A dialog box similar to that for New appears, listing the known applications' tags. A confirm dialog box appears to verify your selection before the delete is performed.

## Index

The Index command activates the Windows Help application and displays the help index for Holder.

## Using Help

The Help on Help command activates the Windows Help application and displays help information on using Windows Help.

## About Holder

The About Holder command displays a dialog box for Holder. The dialog box includes the version number of the program and the date the executable file (HOLDER.EXE) was created.

# Match — Text Comparison for Microsoft Windows and DOS

## Summary of operation

Match is a Windows application that compares the contents of two text files. The overall Match window is divided into two *child windows* below the menu bar, termed the *left-hand* and *right-hand* Match windows. Text files may be loaded into both of these child windows. Text loaded into the child windows is matched line by line, with the results of the comparison displayed in the windows. For any given line of text, there are three possibilities:

1. If the line matches a corresponding line in the opposite window, then the two lines are displayed alongside each other with the normal window text colors. These colors are user-selected via the Windows Control Panel.

2. If the line occurs in the left-hand window but not the right, or in the right-hand window but not the left, then the line is displayed in reverse video and a blank line is displayed alongside it in the opposite window.

3. If the line corresponds to a differing line in the opposite window, then the two lines are displayed alongside each other, both lines in reverse video.

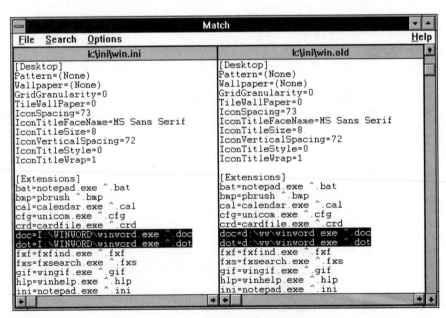

The Match utility compares text files from DOS or Windows and shows the result of the comparison in the two child windows.

Under Windows 3.1 and later, Match supports drag and drop. You can highlight two filenames in the Windows File Manager, drag them with your mouse, and drop them on the Match window (or the Match icon, if minimized). The filenames are opened in the Match window and compared.

Match will work correctly in any drive and directory as long as MATCH.EXE and its help file, MATCH.HLP, are located in the same directory.

Match also includes a DOS version. Every Windows program includes a module (called the *DOS stub*) that, when the program is run at the DOS command line, usually displays the message This program requires Microsoft Windows. The Match program, however, actually runs the DOS version of itself when started from the DOS command line in this way.

The DOS version requires two filenames, as follows:

MATCH *filename1 filename2*

The two filenames are the files to be compared. The filenames may include a complete path, such as a drive and directory.

When run from a DOS command line, Match writes a listing of the differences between the two files to a device called *standard output.* This device is usually your DOS text-mode screen. But you can redirect this output to a file or a printer by adding a greater-than sign (>) and a filename or printer port:

MATCH WIN.INI WIN.OLD>C:\TEMP\COMPARE.TXT

MATCH WIN.INI WIN.OLD>LPT1

The output from Match is formatted for a 132-column printer, such as a laser printer using its compressed type font. Before sending Match output to a printer, configure the printer for compressed printing using its front panel (or the formatting commands described in its manual).

# Match keyboard shortcuts

Match provides the following command-accelerator keys:

| | |
|---|---|
| Ctrl+F12 | Open a file into the left-hand Match window. |
| Alt+Ctrl+F2 | Open a file into the left-hand Match window. |
| Ctrl+Shift+F12 | Open a file into the right-hand Match window. |
| Alt+Ctrl+Shift+F2 | Open a file into the right-hand Match window. |

| F3 | Search Next |
|---|---|
| Shift+F3 | Search Next Compare |
| Ctrl+F3 | Search Next Difference |
| | |
| F4 | Search Previous |
| Shift+F4 | Search Previous Compare |
| Ctrl+F4 | Search Previous Difference |
| | |
| F5 | String Again |
| Shift+F5 | String Next |
| Ctrl+F5 | String Previous |
| | |
| Alt+F4 | Exit Match |

Match provides the following window scrolling keys (*scroll up* means toward the front of the files). Scrolling up or down applies to both Match windows. Scrolling left or right applies only to the specific Match window.

| Window Scrolling Keys | |
|---|---|
| ***Vertical Scrolling*** | |
| Home | Scroll to the first line in both files. |
| End | Scroll to the last line in both files. |
| PgUp | Scroll up one window in both files. |
| PgDn | Scroll down one window in both files. |
| Up arrow | Scroll up one line in both files. |
| Down arrow | Scroll down one line in both files. |
| ***Horizontal Scrolling — Left Match Window*** | |
| Ctrl+Home | Scroll right to the left edge of the file. |
| Ctrl+End | Scroll left to the right edge of the file. |
| Ctrl+PgUp | Scroll right the width of the window. |
| Ctrl+PgDn | Scroll left the width of the window. |
| Ctrl+up arrow | Scroll right one character. |
| Ctrl+down arrow | Scroll left one character. |
| ***Horizontal Scrolling — Right Match Window*** | |
| Ctrl+Shift+Home | Scroll right to the left edge of the file. |
| Ctrl+Shift+End | Scroll left to the right edge of the file. |

*(continued)*

| Window Scrolling Keys (continued) | |
|---|---|
| *Horizontal Scrolling — Right Match Window (continued)* | |
| Ctrl+Shift+PgUp | Scroll right the width of the window. |
| Ctrl+Shift+PgDn | Scroll left the width of the window. |
| Ctrl+Shift+up arrow | Scroll right one character. |
| Ctrl+Shift+down arrow | Scroll left one character. |

## Matching algorithm

Because text files may contain inserted or changed lines, simple character-by-character file comparison algorithms are inadequate for discovering the changes between two files in any useful way. Match incorporates a line-oriented algorithm designed to find inserted or changed lines and to display these changes in a useful form.

Match operates by scanning the two files from front to back. After a pair of lines that differ are found, Match looks for a changed section in the two files or an inserted section in one or the other file, after which the files once again are compared. A minimum number of lines must correspond exactly before Match decides that it has isolated the difference between the two files. The default value for this minimum number of lines is 3. The value may be changed via the Options menu item.

The matching algorithm used requires a large number of string comparisons if the changed sections in the files contain many lines, possibly leading to the conclusion that the program has stopped if processing a large change. Although bugs are *always* possible, I haven't yet seen the program fail to complete matching a set of files given enough time.

The matching process (after the second file is selected) goes in two steps. First, the file is read into memory in its entirety. Completion of this step is marked by the cessation of disk activity and the display of the full pathname of the file at the top of the appropriate child window. Second, Match proceeds to determine the matching and differing lines in the two files. This step proceeds with the Windows wait (hourglass) icon displayed for the mouse cursor, with completion marked by the display of the file data in the child window. Other programs can run while the comparison proceeds, and the window may be resized, iconized, or closed while the comparison is in process.

Finally, it is possible that a change will be larger than the tables used to track change information. If this situation happens, Match will display a message box indicating the situation and will not display data past the last point successfully matched.

## File menu commands

The File menu item provides commands for directing the loading of text files into the left and right windows for matching against one another. Separate File Open commands are provided for the left and right Match windows, with keyboard accelerators for each. The File menu item also provides a command for exiting Match altogether.

Under versions of Windows that support drag and drop for applications, one or two files may be dropped into the Match window from the File Manager. Match attempts to do the sensible thing with the files dropped:

◆ If two files are dropped, one is loaded into the left window and one into the right.

◆ If one file is dropped and the left window is empty, the file is loaded into the left window. Otherwise, the file is loaded into the right window.

### Open Left

The Open Left command of the File menu item directs that a file be loaded into the left-hand Match window. A File Open dialog box is displayed for selection of the file, which is then opened, read, and compared against the file in the right-hand window, if any. Lines of text that cannot be matched against lines in the right-hand window are displayed in reverse video.

You choose the file to be loaded into the left-hand window via a File Open dialog box. A check box entitled Clear is provided at the bottom of the dialog box; if checked, it causes the right-hand pane to be cleared before the selected file is loaded into the left-hand pane.

You may also invoke the Open Left command via the Ctrl+F12 or Alt+Ctrl+F2 key combination.

### Open Right

The Open Right command of the File menu item directs that a file be loaded into the right-hand Match window. A File Open dialog box is displayed for selection of the file, which is then opened, read, and compared against the file in the left-hand window, if any. Lines of text that cannot be matched against lines in the left-hand window are displayed in reverse video.

You choose the file to be loaded into the right-hand window via a File Open dialog box. A check box entitled Clear is provided at the bottom of the dialog box; if checked, it causes the left-hand pane to be cleared before the selected file is loaded into the right-hand pane.

You may also invoke the Open Right command via the Ctrl+Shift+F12 or Alt+Ctrl+Shift+F2 key combination.

## Exit

The Exit command terminates the Match application, removing it from the screen. The key combination Alt+F4 is equivalent to the Exit command.

# Search menu commands

The Search menu item provides commands for advancing forward or backward in the matched files, stepping from one set of changes to another or to a specified text string. Comparison search commands are provided for moving to the next set of differing lines, the next set of identical lines, or the next set of lines that are of the opposite sense (same/different) to the current set. Each of these three functions is provided for moving forward and backward in the file. String search commands are provided for searching backward or forward (using an exact, case-sensitive match) for a specified string.

All nine Search commands operate relative to the line(s) at the top of the Match window and move the top line to the requested point. The display control is such that a full window of text lines is maintained on the display at the end of the file, so the search may stop short in cases where reaching the requested destination would cause less than a full window to be displayed. In cases where no lines meeting the requested search can be found, a message box is displayed, indicating that the search failed.

## Next

The Next command moves the Match window display forward (toward the end of the files) to the next interesting point in the comparison. If the top line in the Match window is a pair of identical lines, the new top line will be the next pair of differing lines. If the top line is a pair of differing lines, the new top line will be the next pair of identical lines.

The search never goes farther than the last line in the file(s) so that a full window of text is displayed.

## Next Compare

The Next Compare command moves the Match window display forward (toward the end of the files) to the next pair of identical lines following the top line in the left and right windows. It does not matter whether the top lines are identical or not for the Next Compare search.

The search never goes farther than the last line in the file(s) so that a full window of text is displayed.

### Next Difference

The Next Difference command moves the Match window display forward (toward the end of the files) to the next pair of differing lines following the top line in the left and right windows. It does not matter whether the top lines are identical or not for the Next Difference search.

The search never goes farther than the last line in the file(s) so that a full window of text is displayed.

### Previous

The Previous command moves the Match window display backward (toward the beginning of the files) to the next interesting point in the comparison. If the top line in the Match window is a pair of identical lines, the new top line will be the next previous pair of differing lines. If the top line is a pair of differing lines, the new top line will be the next previous pair of identical lines.

### Previous Compare

The Previous Compare command moves the Match window display backward (toward the beginning of the files) to the next pair of identical lines preceding the top line in the left and right windows. It does not matter whether the top lines are identical or not for the Previous Compare search.

### Previous Difference

The Previous Difference command moves the Match window display backward (toward the beginning of the files) to the next pair of differing lines preceding the top line in the left and right windows. It does not matter whether the top lines are identical or not for the Previous Difference search.

### String Again

The String Again command repeats the previous string search, moving the Match window display to the next line in either window matching the last-entered search string. With the exception noted shortly, the line matching the search string is moved to the top of the display window. An error message is displayed if the string cannot be found. Wrap-around to the beginning or end of the files is not performed.

The search is case-sensitive and in the direction of the prior search. If there was no prior string search, the default search direction is forward and a prompt is displayed to permit a search string to be entered.

As with the other Search commands, the search never displays farther forward in the file than the point at which a full screen of text is displayed, even if this causes the line containing the matched string not to be at the top of the display window.

## String Next

The String Next command searches forward in the files for a specified search string, moving the Match window display to the next line in either window matching the string. With the exception noted shortly, the line matching the search string is moved to the top of the display window. The search is case-sensitive. An error message is displayed if the string cannot be found. Wrap-around to the beginning of the files is not performed.

As with the other Search commands, the search never displays farther forward in the file than the point at which a full screen of text is displayed, even if this causes the line containing the matched string not to be at the top of the display window.

## String Previous

The String Previous command searches backward in the files for a specified search string, moving the Match window display to the previous line in either window matching the string. The line matching the search string is moved to the top of the display window. The search is case-sensitive. An error message is displayed if the string cannot be found. Wrap-around to the end of the files is not performed.

# Options menu commands

The Options menu item provides access to controls on the operation of Match. Options are available for controlling the matching process, for setting up the window colors, and for selecting the font used for display. You can display information on each of these commands by selecting the appropriate item.

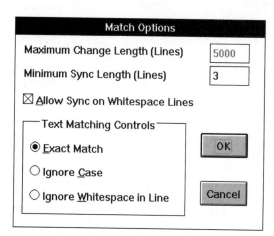

The Match Options dialog box enables you to control how matches are determined.

## Matching Options

When the Matching Options command is selected, the Match Options dialog box is displayed.

The elements of the dialog box have the following functions:

**Maximum Change Length (Lines):** This option is currently not changeable. The value controls the maximum number of lines of differing text that can be handled between regions of identical text. If more than this number of lines of differing text occurs, Match will display a dialog box indicating that the changes were too great to process.

**Minimum Sync Length (Lines):** This option controls the number of identical lines Match must find before it declares that a set of differences has ended and the following lines correspond to each other. The default value is 3. Increasing this value will eliminate certain false matches but can also increase the size of the blocks Match declares as being changed.

**Allow Sync on Whitespace Lines:** When checked, this option allows lines consisting entirely of whitespace characters to be included when looking for sequences of matching lines following a difference. Turning off this option can improve matching in files containing sequences of blank lines.

**Text Matching Controls:** In addition to doing exact, character-by-character comparisons of text lines, Match can relax the comparison to ignore case or to ignore whitespace characters within the line. Check the corresponding radio button to change the text comparison. Matching exactly and matching ignoring case are likely to be faster than matching ignoring whitespace within the line.

## Color

The Color commands support selecting a color for the text and background for both matched and differing text lines. The four commands that are available follow:

Matched Background

Matched Foreground

Different Background

Different Foreground

Each command invokes a color-selection dialog box. Although both solid and dithered colors may be displayed in the dialog box (depending on your video adapter), only solid colors are used by Match for text display. You may have to experiment some to find the colors that work best for you on your display.

The default colors for Match are taken from the Windows color selection made through the Windows Control Panel. Color selections made within Match are saved in the file PRESS.INI, which Windows places in your Windows directory.

### Font

The Font command invokes a dialog box in which you can select the font and text size used to display the matched files. The font selection is limited to fixed-pitch fonts available for your display. Although the option is present for bold or italic text, these selections are ignored.

Font selections made within Match are saved in the file PRESS.INI, which Windows places in your Windows directory.

## Help menu

The Help menu item provides access to Windows Help for the Match application. Commands are available for the Match help index, for the Match keyboard summary, and for help on the Windows Help application. A command is also available to show the About box for Match.

# Runner — A Simple Command Line for Microsoft Windows

Runner is a small program for Microsoft Windows that exists only as an icon. When activated by the mouse, Runner displays a command line equivalent to what the Windows Program Manager or File Manager File Run commands offer, but without the need for you to open either of those two windows. Runner accepts command lines that run PIF files or file associations. Pressing Enter or clicking OK will cause the command line to be executed. Both Windows and DOS programs may be executed with Runner.

Runner is also capable of running applications minimized (as icons) and of running DOS applications under control of an alternate shell (for example, to run full screen rather than in a window).

I wrote Runner when I tired of opening Program Manager just to run another program. I keep it as the first item in my Windows 3.1 StartUp group, so it always ends up in the lower left corner of my display.

Runner provides the following options and commands.

```
┌─────────────────────────────────────────────────────────┐
│  Enter command line:                                      │
│  ┌─────────────────────────────────────────────┐   ⌇    │
│  │ notepad|                                      │         │
│  └─────────────────────────────────────────────┘         │
│  ☐ Use Alternate Shell   ┌────────┐ ┌────────┐ ┌────────┐│
│                          │   OK   │ │ Cancel │ │  Menu  ││
│  ☐ Run Minimized         └────────┘ └────────┘ └────────┘│
└─────────────────────────────────────────────────────────┘
```

**When you activate the Runner program, you see a command line similar to the one displayed by the Program Manager or the File Manager File Run commands.**

## Use Alternate Shell

This option instructs Runner to run the command line using an alternate shell. This option is ignored when you're starting a Windows application.

Normally, Runner uses the shell specified by the %COMSPEC% environment variable — or COMMAND.COM if %COMSPEC% is undefined. The Alternate Shell option instructs Runner to ignore the setting of %COMSPEC% and use the shell specified with the Alternate Shell menu item.

This option is useful, for example, for selecting an alternative PIF file (perhaps one that runs full screen rather than in a window) or an alternative command-line interpreter (perhaps that from the Norton Utilities rather than that from DOS).

## Run Minimized

This option instructs Runner to run the application as an icon.

## Menu

This option pops up a menu of subcommands to Runner, including one to set up the alternative shell.

# Time — Yet Another Digital Clock for Microsoft Windows _____

Time is a digital clock for Windows. You can select the format of the display and can choose where the window sits on the screen. The window does not force itself to the front when covered, so it's compatible with all Windows screen blankers.

**┌ Thursday 24 September 1992 10:33:51 PM ┐**

**The Time program is a digital clock that you can move around the screen.**

Time is started by the command TIME.EXE. Depending on the program to which you issue the command, the shorter command TIME may be interpreted as the built-in DOS command TIME, which isn't what you want.

The first time the program starts on your machine, it will choose its location on the screen. You can position the window by holding down the left mouse button in the window and dragging it to the desired position.

The next time the program starts, it will place its upper left corner where you positioned it, with the exception that it will adjust the position if required to force the entire window on-screen. This means that if you want the window to always be positioned in the lower right corner, you can move the window as far right and down as possible and then terminate (press Alt+F4) and restart the program. The window will remain aligned with the edge no matter how long or short the date string becomes.

Time also gives you control over its format and whether or not it beeps every hour. To control these options, mouse-click the window and then press F1. A dialog box will appear. Choose the time format you want by clicking the corresponding model line in the dialog box. Select or deselect beeps on the hour by checking or unchecking the box for Beep on Hour. Install the new options by clicking OK; cancel all changes by pressing Cancel.

I wrote Time simply because none of the many I'd pulled off BBSs or other sources did things the way I wanted.

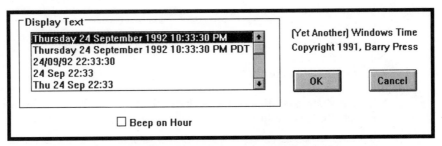

**Click on the Time display window and press F1 to display a dialog box that enables you to change the format of the time display and whether or not the clock beeps on the hour.**

# Registration

The entire set of programs and documentation is Copyright 1991-1992 by Barry Press and is released as shareware. If you use any of the utilities in the collection beyond a two-week evaluation period, you are obligated to send $20.00 (U.S. funds; cash, check, or money order) to Barry Press, 4201 Empress Ave., Encino, CA 91436-3504.

Registration licenses a specific user on as many machines as are used solely by that user or licenses a specific machine (not network servers) for an unlimited number of users. You may copy this software (subject to the $20.00 registration fee for each user or machine) freely as long as the entire collection is distributed without modification. Please accompany your registration with the following form so I can contact you regarding updates.

**Barry Press**
4201 Empress Avenue
Encino, CA 91436-3504
CompuServe: 72467,2353

Name: _____

Company: _____

Street/Apt: _____

City/State/ZIP: _____

Country: _____

Computer: _____

Preferred Disk Size: _____

Registered Version: May 19, 1992

Registration entitles you to notification of updates to the software plus a copy of the next utility added to the collection.

# Source Code Availability

Registered users may, for an additional $75.00 (U.S. funds), purchase a complete copy of the source code and related files for the entire set of utilities. The source was developed with the Microsoft 6.00a C compiler and Windows SDK, and later with Quick C/Windows plus the Windows 3.1 SDK. The source code, although it remains the copyrighted property of Barry Press, may be included by purchasers in other derivative programs that are distributed or sold as long as the copyrighted source code is itself neither given away nor sold and as long as the notice that portions are copyrighted by Barry Press appears clearly in the product.

# Disclaimer

No warranties are expressed or implied for this software, including merchantability or suitability for a particular purpose. No responsibility will be assumed by the author for any loss or damage due to its use.

# Checkers

## Version 1.3
### Copyright © by Gregory Thatcher, Berkland Software

*T*his is the classic two-player game of Checkers — in its own Windows version. It's so *classic, in fact, that it even enforces the rule that you* must *capture a piece if you can do so in your current move.*

*To move, you simply click on the piece you want to move and then on the square you want to move to. If you have no mouse, this chapter describes a way to use the arrow keys, spacebar, and Enter to move your pieces.*

*In the following documentation, Gregory Thatcher refers to the human player as* she, *to distinguish the player from the checker pieces, which are traditionally referred to as* men, kings, *and* he.

| | |
|---|---|
| **Type of Program:** | Game |
| **Requires:** | Windows 3.0 or later |
| **Registration:** | Contributions to support the further development of Windows shareware, and to obtain the source code, may be sent to the shareware author at the address at the end of this chapter. |
| **Technical Support:** | This game should require no technical support, but Berkland Software does reply to comments and questions by mail. |

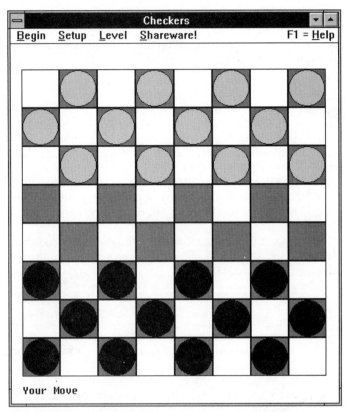

Checkers is the classic two-player game, now brought to Windows.

# Game Instructions

Checkers is played by two people, on the same board that is used for chess, with pieces in the form of disks. These pieces are called *checkers* or *draughts*. All the checkers are alike in form but come in one of two colors: red or black. (On a monochrome monitor, they appear as light and dark.) One player moves the black pieces, and the other moves the red.

All pieces stand and move solely on the black squares. Initially, all pieces are *single men* but may become *kings* as described later in this chapter.

Black moves first, and thereafter the players move alternately. A player loses the game when she cannot move in turn. Usually, the reason is that all her pieces have been captured, but this may also happen if all her pieces are immobilized. Many games are drawn by agreement, when few pieces remain and neither player has an advantage sufficient to win.

## Noncapturing move

A single man may only move forward on the dark diagonal, one square at a time, when not capturing.

## Capturing move

The capturing move is a jump. If a red piece sits forward and adjacent to a black piece — and the black square behind the red piece in the same line is empty — the black piece may jump over the red piece into the empty square and remove the red piece from the board. If a piece makes a capture, and lands on a square from which it can make another capture, it continues jumping in the same turn. It may change direction during jumps, but only forward if it is a single man.

If a player can make a capturing move, she *must* do so. She may not make a noncapturing move. If she has a choice between several captures in the same move, the player has a free choice.

## Crowning

The row of squares furthest from the player's starting rows is the king row. If one of her single men reaches this row, it becomes a *king*. The king has the same powers as a single man, but it can also move backward as well as forward. Moves in both directions may be combined in a series of jumps. However, if a single man reaches the king row through a capture, he may not continue to make jumps in that turn.

**When a piece is crowned, it looks like two concentric circles (representing a king).**

# Moving the Pieces

## Mouse instructions

To move the pieces with a mouse, click on the black checker you want to move. The selected square begins to flash. Then click on the square to which you want to move the piece. The checker moves from its original location to its new location.

## Keyboard instructions

Using the arrow keys, move the arrow cursor to a square that contains a black checker (if you use the numeric keypad arrow keys, make sure that Num Lock is off). Press the spacebar or Enter to select that checker for a move. The selected square begins to flash. Select the black square to which you want to move the piece by moving the arrow cursor to that square and pressing the spacebar. The checker moves from its original location to its new location.

## Captures

Follow the same procedure when making a capture. Remember that if you can make a capture, you *must* do so, particularly if one piece can make two or more captures in a single move.

## The computer's turn

After you have completed a move, the arrow changes into an hourglass while the program calculates its next move. The cursor then changes back into an arrow cursor, and the program makes its move.

# The Menus

## The Setup menu

Use the Setup menu to switch sides (from Black checkers to Red, and vice versa), observe the program play against itself with the AutoPlay option, or play against another human with the Two Player option.

```
Setup
√ One Player
  Two Player
  AutoPlay

√ Player is Black
  Player is Red

  Switch Sides
```

**Use the Setup menu to choose colors and the number of players who will play the game.**

## The Level menu

The Level menu enables you to increase or decrease the program's playing capability.

```
Level
  Beginner
  Novice
√ Intermediate
  Expert
  Master
```

**Use the Level menu to specify how proficient the computer is at the game.**

# Contributions and Source Code

Questions, comments, and criticisms are more than welcome. If you enjoy this game and would like to support further development of Windows shareware, please send $5.00 to

**Berkland Software**
P.O. Box 511
5337 College Ave.
Oakland, CA 94618

For a disk of copyrighted source code, send $20. Thanks.

# ClipMate *can't use*

## Version 1.54
## Copyright © by Thornton Software Solutions

*T*he Clipboard is one of Windows' greatest features because it enables you to cut or copy almost anything out of one application and paste it into another. But the Clipboard has a major limitation: It can hold only one thing at a time. As soon as you add an item, the previous contents of the Clipboard are lost forever.

*ClipMate gives you almost total control over any text you may want to copy to the Clipboard. You can see any of the last 50 text items in the Clipboard (you can change this number). And you can save any items to a permanent disk file. ClipMate only works on text — not graphics or other formats — but text is what most people need help with. (The Windows Paintbrush can save multiple graphics into the same file, if you need that feature.)*

| | |
|---|---|
| **Type of Program:** | Text Processing |
| **Requires:** | Windows 3.0 or later. A VGA display or better. Norton Desktop for Windows users must use NDW Version 2.0 or later. |
| **Registration:** | Use the form at the end of this chapter to register with the shareware author. Registered users receive a new copy of the program, a printed manual, and two additional programs. |
| **Technical Support:** | Thornton Software Solutions supports registered users by mail and CompuServe. |
| **Similar Shareware:** | PrintClip, a free program featured in *Windows 3.1 SECRETS,* published by IDG Books Worldwide, also enables you to print the text contents of the Clipboard. But ClipMate provides many more features. |

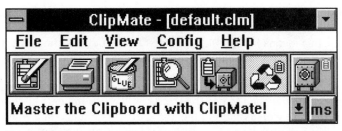

The ClipMate program enables you to copy more than one text item to
the Windows Clipboard.

# Installation Notes

To install ClipMate, run WSETUP on Diskette 1 and select CLIPMATE. WSETUP
decompresses the ClipMate files to a directory you specify and creates a group
window in Program Manager for ClipMate.

The ClipMate icon in the Program Manager has a command line that points to
ClipMate, which you can see if you highlight the icon and click File Properties.
Here is an example:

    C:\GIZMOS\CLIPMATE\CLIPMATE.EXE

If you want ClipMate to run every time you start Windows (instead of starting it
manually from Program Manager when you want to use it), you can add the
preceding command line to your WIN.INI file, on the LOAD= line or the RUN= line
(as described in the "Read This First" chapter). Users of Windows 3.1 can drag
the ClipMate icon into the StartUp group of the Program Manager to do the
same thing.

ClipMate doesn't need to be in the Path to work correctly, and there are no
funny environment variables to set.

## Using special filenames for data

If you want to use a filename other than ClipMate's DEFAULT.CLM filename for
data you save from the Clipboard, you can specify your preferred filename as a
parameter to ClipMate. In this case, for example, the command line in the
Program Manager can be

    C:\GIZMOS\CLIPMATE\CLIPMATE.EXE MYFILE.CLM

If you use a special filename, however, you must make sure that ClipMate loads this file rather than DEFAULT.CLM when you start ClipMate. In the Program Manager, this means that MYFILE.CLM must be included at the end of the command line that starts ClipMate.

The LOAD= and RUN= lines of WIN.INI, however, don't allow parameters to applications. If you need to use the LOAD= or RUN= statements in Windows 3.0 to load ClipMate with a different file, the correct command line would be simply MYFILE.CLM. You would then have to set up an association of CLM files to ClipMate. You could do this by adding the statement CLM=C:\GIZMOS\CLIPMATE\CLIPMATE.EXE ^.CLM to the [Extensions] section of WIN.INI.

It's easier just to let ClipMate use DEFAULT.CLM for most purposes.

## Looking at files ClipMate creates

The first time that you run ClipMate, it will create a file called *x:\windows*\CLIPMATE.INI. Your WIN.INI file is not altered in any way, nor are any of your other system files. For more information, see the "CLIPMATE.INI" section in this chapter.

ClipMate will save Clipboard data into DEFAULT.CLM or another CLM file that you specify.

# Overview

ClipMate is designed to enhance the operation of the native Clipboard capability of Windows. From a functional standpoint, the Windows Clipboard works exactly as it should: allowing the user to transfer an item of data within an application or between applications. In practice, however, the Clipboard falls short: It can hold only one item of data at a time. It can hold multiple formats of that item, yes, but it's still the same item of data. After you perform a Cut or Paste, the contents of the Clipboard are emptied, and your new piece of data is now the sole occupant of the Clipboard. There is no capability for you to append new data onto the existing Clipboard data, no Undo capability, and no long-term memory. That's where ClipMate steps in.

ClipMate adds several enhancements to the operation of the Windows Clipboard. It enables you to keep many generations of previous Clipboard occupants (called *Clip Items*) for later retrieval. If there is a particular piece of data that you use often, it can be stored indefinitely in ClipMate's Safe List. You can even append multiple Clip Items into one piece of data for pasting into an application through a process called *Gluing*.

Here's how ClipMate operates:

ClipMate sits idle most of the time, waiting for any activity in the Windows Clipboard.

Whenever you put anything on the Clipboard (by cutting or copying), ClipMate gets a message from Windows. ClipMate checks to see whether the Clipboard is holding an acceptable format (TEXT is the only format currently supported). If ClipMate can use the data on the Clipboard, it pastes the data into itself and dynamically allocates storage for it. It places the new data in one of its lists, creates a title from the first 50 characters in the text, and displays the title in the text window at the top of the Clip Item Selection List Box. If the Magnify window is active, the new Clip Item is displayed within it.

Access to the Clipboard data is easily obtained through the use of a drop-down list. After you make your selection, ClipMate automatically copies the item to the Clipboard. It is then ready for your use in any application that offers Clipboard support for text.

# Buttons of the Main Window

## Visual cues

ClipMate uses buttons to help you quickly access ClipMate's most commonly used features. Also, the buttons often will give you visual cues as to the state of ClipMate and the Windows Clipboard in general.

Depending on the current layout that you have selected, you will see some buttons and not others.

## Checking and graying

In some cases, buttons appearing on the screen will appear to be grayed or checked, thus assuming the behavior of standard Windows radio buttons or check boxes when they are disabled. This setup gives you visual cues as to the current state of ClipMate.

Here are the visual components of ClipMate:

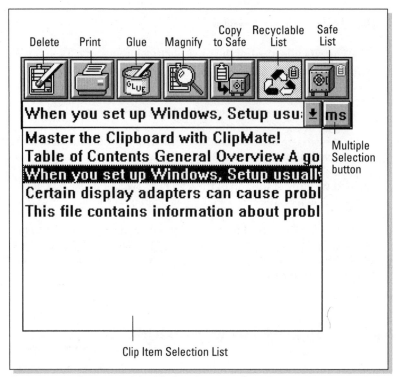

The buttons and sections of the ClipMate window give you control over the program.

These items are described later in this chapter in the section "Using the Main Window Buttons."

# Layout — Full Layout versus Brief Layout _____

ClipMate gives you the option of displaying all its graphical controls, along with the menu (Full Layout), or just showing some of the graphical controls, with no menu (Brief Layout).

Why would you want to use the Brief Layout?

The Full Layout gives you full functionality but may take up valuable screen space.

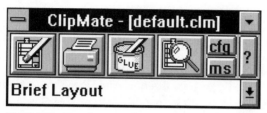

The Brief Layout gives you the most-used functions of ClipMate, saving you some screen space.

Sometimes, you don't need the full functionality of ClipMate and would gladly trade some functionality for valuable screen space. This is especially true when you are using the Keep Window On Top option, found in the Config dialog box. The Brief Layout was created to fill this need.

The Brief Layout gives you the Delete, Print, Glue, and Magnify buttons, along with the Config, Multi Select, and About buttons.

## How to change layouts

The layout is selected in the Config dialog box, which is accessed from either the Config menu (in the Full Layout view) or the CFG button (in the Brief Layout view). Make your choice in the box entitled Full Layout (See All Controls?). Select OK to close the window.

In this version of ClipMate, the layout can't be redefined on the fly. You will need to exit ClipMate and restart in order to see the new layout. The layout will be in effect indefinitely, until you switch layouts again (if ever).

## Limitations of Brief Layout

Unless you switch between the Recyclable List and the Safe List a lot, you probably won't miss the Full Layout. All menu options are also absent, but you have buttons that will access the Config dialog box and the About box. From the About box, you can also access the on-line Help system. Unless you want to work with different files, you won't be needing anything under the File menu, either. Find and Find Next can be accessed by their accelerator keys, Ctrl+F and Ctrl+N, respectively.

# Magnify Window

The Magnify window displays the Clip Item that is currently selected in the Clip Item Selection List Box. You use it to get a full look at what the Clip Item actually looks like rather than just a glimpse of the title. Also, you can edit either the Clip Item or the title. There is a powerful Flow Paragraph function that will reformat the Clip Item into paragraph format. This makes the text more usable by word processing applications.

## To open the Magnify window

You open the Magnify window by either selecting the Magnify option under the View menu or pressing the Magnify button. After you open it, the button will appear in its "pressed" state.

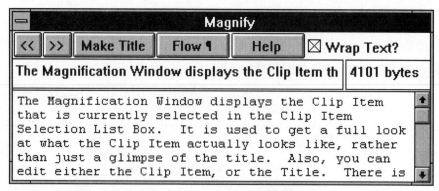

The Magnify window displays the entire currently selected Clip Item.

## To close the Magnify window

The Magnify window is closed in the same way that it is opened. Press the Magnify button, and you will see it pop back up from its checked state as the Magnify window closes.

Alternatively, you can double-click the control box in the upper left corner of the window.

## Editing

You may edit either the text of the Clip Item or its title. When you edit the title, it won't appear in the Clip Item Selection List immediately. The Clip Item Selection List will be updated when another Clip Item is selected. Editing the title has the same effect as Edit Title.

## The buttons

| Browse | Selects previous/next Clip Item |
| Make Title | Creates title from selected text |
| Flow Paragraph | Reflows paragraph |
| Help | Brings this help topic |
| Wrap Text check box | Turns word wrap on/off |

## Editor hot keys

The following standard Windows accelerator keys (also called *hot keys*) can be used in the Magnify window:

| Key(s) | | Function |
| --- | --- | --- |
| Backspace | | Deletes the character to the left of the insertion point (or deletes selected text) |
| Delete | | Deletes the character to the right of the insertion point or deletes selected text) |
| **Windows 3.0** | | |
| Shift+Delete* | Cut | Deletes the selected text and places it on the Clipboard |
| Shift+Insert* | Paste | Inserts text from the Clipboard to the active window |
| Ctrl+Insert* | Copy | Makes a copy of the selected text and places it on the Clipboard |

*(continued)*

| Key(s) | | Function (continued) |
|---|---|---|
| **Windows 3.1** | | |
| Ctrl+X* | Cut | Deletes the selected text and places it on the Clipboard |
| Ctrl+C* | Copy | Inserts text from the Clipboard to the active window |
| Ctrl+V* | Paste | Makes a copy of the selected text and places it on the Clipboard |

\* Actions with an asterisk cause a Clipboard update and therefore cause the Magnify window to display whatever you have just copied to or pasted from the Clipboard. To use this effectively, see the section "Power hints."

*Note:* The Magnify window remembers its size and location, even from one session to the next, by storing them in the CLIPMATE.INI file.

## Power hints

You can copy part or all of the Magnify window to the Clipboard and thus back into ClipMate by using the accelerator key for Copy: Ctrl+Insert. To do so, just select the text that you want to copy and then press Ctrl+Insert. You are then presented with only the text that you have selected.

Why is this? Your new text was copied to the Clipboard, so ClipMate made itself a copy. New Clip Items are always made the current selection because they reflect the current Clipboard contents (unless the Safe List is currently active).

*Windows 3.1 users:* You can use Ctrl+C, which is the new standard for Windows.

Here's an example of why you would want to use this feature:

Windows 3.0 Help enables you to copy any given help topic to the Clipboard but doesn't let you select the text that you want; you get the whole topic. Suppose that there is a help topic that has an example you want to include in a document you're writing. From Help, you can copy the topic to the Clipboard; from within ClipMate's Magnify window, you can do another copy on the specific chunk that you want.

## Clip Items

When any application places text on the Clipboard, ClipMate makes a copy for itself. This copy of the Clipboard contents is considered to be a Clip Item and is stored in a Clip Item List.

A Clip Item will have a Clip Item Title that is initially constructed from the first 50 characters of the Clip Item. You may edit this title in the Magnify window or by selecting Edit Title from the Edit menu.

Clip Items are dynamically sized on creation. They will typically consume a byte of memory for each character in the text, plus 50 characters for the title, and a few extra bytes to keep track of everything.

You can edit the Clip Item in the Magnify window.

New Clip Items will be placed on one of the Clip Item Lists, depending on which list is the Active List and on the option chosen in the Config screen.

# Clip Item Lists

As they are pasted from the Clipboard, Clip Items are stored in Clip Item Lists. ClipMate supports two Clip Item Lists.

## The Recyclable List

This list maintains a user-defined number of Clip Items. New Clip Items are at the top of the list and work their way down as newer items are added. When the number of Clip Items in the list exceeds the user-specified limit, Clip Items are deleted from the list, thus freeing up space in the system. Because the space is reusable, the list is known as the *Recyclable List*.

## The Safe List

This list stores as many Clip Items as you would ever want to keep. As with the Recyclable List, new Clip Items enter the Safe List at the top of the list and work their way down as newer items are added. But *you* are responsible for deleting obsolete Clip Items. This is a handy way to keep track of "boilerplate" items, such as letter templates, return addresses, or even often-used chunks of code, if you happen to be a programmer.

New Clip Items will be placed on one of the Clip Item Lists, depending on which list is the Active List and the option chosen in the Config screen.

# Using the Main Window Buttons

This section describes the operation of the buttons in the ClipMate window.

## Delete button

This button deletes the currently selected Clip Item or Items from the Active List. The next item in line is then copied to the Clipboard, and that item is shown in the Clip Item Selection List Box.

This button is available in both the Full Layout and the Brief Layout.

This operation works with single or Multiple Selections.

## Print button

This button prints the currently selected Clip Item or Items.

This button is available in both the Full Layout and the Brief Layout.

This operation works with single or Multiple Selections.

The shortcut is Ctrl+P.

Printer support is very generic. Output will appear in a font that is supported by your printer (such as Courier). There are no options for fonts, margins, or such. The purpose of this is so that ClipMate can give basic printer services to as many printers as possible. ClipMate users can print any text that they can get into the Clipboard — with only a mouse click! If you need more sophisticated printing, just copy your data into any application that meets your needs.

Item(s) will be printed to the default Windows printer, unless you have specified a printer by using the Print Setup option, found in the File menu. After you have chosen a printer with Print Setup, it stays that way until you change it to something else. It is not reset on shutdown. This makes it very convenient for users with more than one printer. There are several ClipMate users that direct their ClipMate output to their desktop (dot-matrix) printer, while leaving their shared network (laser) printer for other tasks such as word processing.

*Note:* The notion of retaining a printer selection from session to session is not typical practice in Windows. However, it makes sense in this case. If you use ClipMate to make 3270 emulation more bearable, I'm sure you'll agree. There is a potential pitfall that could arise if you were to delete the printer definition for the printer that you have chosen as ClipMate's printer. If you do this, just select another printer with the Print Setup option of the File menu.

# Glue button

 The Glue function concatenates (appends together) selected Clip Item(s) into one big Clip Item. The resulting item is then copied back onto the Clipboard for use by other applications.

This button is available in both the Full Layout and the Brief Layout.

There are two ways to use this feature. The first method is to turn the Glue mode on and then copy data to the Clipboard. As each item enters the Clipboard, ClipMate "glues" it to the previous occupant of the Clipboard. We'll call this method *Auto Glue*. The second method is to glue existing Clip Items together. We'll call this method *Manual Glue*.

## Auto Glue

Auto Glue is a special mode of operation, where ClipMate appends each new text item directly to the end of its predecessor instead of creating new Clip Items for each new piece of text. If you turn on the Glue mode and then copy ten paragraphs to the Clipboard from other applications, you will have *one* Clip Item that is ten paragraphs long. In addition, the resulting Clip Item will always be on the Clipboard and will be up to date. You won't even have to interact with ClipMate at all in order to use this new item.

To use, just click the Glue button or select Glue Together from the Edit menu. You should *not* perform a Multiple Selection prior to entering Glue mode. Doing so would invoke a Reactive Glue, discussed shortly.

When you enter Glue mode, a fresh, empty Clip Item will be created. It will initially have a title stating Glue In Process. As you copy text from other applications, the title will change to indicate the number of items that have been glued together. To finish, click the Glue button again. The title will change to Glue Finished, *X* Items, and ClipMate will exit Glue mode. At any time during the Glue operation, you can utilize the new item in its current state.

The Auto Glue mode will end automatically if you try to use other ClipMate functions while it is active. You may open or close the Magnify window but only to browse the data. Any other action will terminate the current Glue operation, as if you had pressed the Glue button to turn the Glue off. After it is stopped, you can't restart a Glue. However, you can perform a Multiple Selection and use the Manual Glue mode to put several Glues (or single items) together.

## Manual Glue

The Manual Glue operation requires you to have previously performed a Multiple Selection.

The Manual Glue is useful for making one large Clip Item out of several smaller items. You select the items that you want by performing a Multiple Selection and then pressing the Glue button (or Glue Together from the Edit menu).

One advantage that Manual Gluing has over Auto Gluing is that you don't have to plan it in advance. Another is that it is easy to change the order of the result because the Multiple Selection gives you the ability to select items in any order that you want.

Here's a real-life example of Manual Gluing in action:

Suppose that you need to buy a PC for your office at work. You sign on to the on-line corporate catalog and browse around to see what's out there. Whenever you see something that you want, copy it to the Clipboard. When you're done shopping, use the Multiple Selection List dialog box to select the components of your new computer system, in whatever order you want. Use the Glue button to combine your Multiple Selection into one big Clip Item that you can then paste into the order form or on-line order screen. Painless!

## Magnify button

This button opens or closes the Magnify window.

When the Magnify window is open, the Magnify button will appear to be checked. In this way, it functions like a standard Windows check box. When you press it again, it pops up, and the Magnify window closes.

This button is available in both the Full Layout and the Brief Layout.

It is also accessible from the View menu.

## Copy to Safe List button

This button copies selected Clip Item(s) to the Safe List.

This operation is only available when the Recyclable List is the Active List.

This operation works with single or Multiple Selections.

This button is *not* available in the Brief Layout.

## Activate Recyclable List button

 This button causes the Recyclable List to become the Active List.

This button is *not* available in the Brief Layout.

It is also accessible from the View menu.

The Recyclable button and Safe button are bound together and act like radio buttons. When you press one, it takes on a checked appearance and the Clipboard lights up. The other button pops out and is now ready to be pushed in again.

## Activate Safe List button

 This button causes the Safe List to become the Active List.

This button is *not* available in the Brief Layout.

It is also accessible from the View menu.

The Recyclable button and Safe button are bound together and act like radio buttons. When you press one, it takes on a checked appearance and the Clipboard lights up. The other button pops out and is now ready to be pushed in again.

## Clip Item Selection List combo box

You use the Clip Item Selection List to copy Clip Items from one of the Clip Item Lists back onto the Clipboard. You will accomplish this by simply selecting the title of a stored Clip Item from the Clip Item Selection List.

The Clip Item Selection List is a standard Windows combo box that incorporates a static text window with a drop-down list. By clicking the down-arrow icon to the right of the text window, you will see a scrolling list, by title, of the Clip Items in the active list. When you have made your selection, the list will go away, the title of the selected Clip Item will appear in the text window, and the item will be copied to the Clipboard.

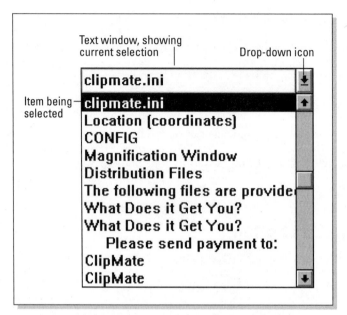

The Clip Item Selection List lets you copy Clip Items back to the
Clipboard so you can then paste them into other applications.

### Effect on the Magnify window

If the Magnify window is open, then it will also reflect the new selection.

### Keyboard use

Alternatively, you can use the up and down arrows on the keyboard to make
the selection. This sometimes has an advantage, such as when you are brows-
ing the list through the Magnify window. It is very easy to sequentially zip
through each Clip Item by pressing the down-arrow key. In order to use the
arrow keys, you must first give input focus to the list box or the text window at
the top of the list box. Just click the text window itself with the mouse; it will
appear in reverse video to indicate that it has the input focus. You should learn
to use both methods because each has advantages.

### Rules of thumb

1. Whenever either of the Clip Item Lists becomes active, the top entry of the
   active list will be shown in the text window and therefore will also be
   copied to the Clipboard. This includes the initial activation of the Recyclable List on start-up.

2. Whenever the Clipboard receives data that can't be represented as text, ClipMate's text window will become blank. This indicates that ClipMate doesn't own the contents of the Clipboard and doesn't know what is in it.

3. The Clipboard may contain formats other than TEXT. When multiple formats are placed on the Clipboard, ClipMate makes a copy of the TEXT item and ignores the rest. If you cause ClipMate to update the Clipboard, the other formats will be lost as your Clip Item moves into the Clipboard.

## Multiple Selection List button and dialog box

This button opens a dialog box that enables you to select more than one Clip Item at a time, as compared with the Clip Item Selection List Box, which enables you to select only one Clip Item. There are several operations that take advantage of the Multiple Selection, such as Delete, Print, Glue, and Copy to Safe List.

The Multiple Selection dialog box consists of two list boxes: The Selection List is on your left. This is where you make your selections. The Confirmation List is on your right. This shows you the order in which you made your selections. It is for your reference only and can't be manipulated.

Here's how to use the Multiple Selection dialog box:

1. If you will need to see the Magnify window, activate it before opening the Multiple Selection dialog box. Use of the Magnify window is highly recommended.

2. Press the MS button to bring up the dialog box. After the dialog box is up, you can't go back to the rest of ClipMate without selecting either OK or Cancel.

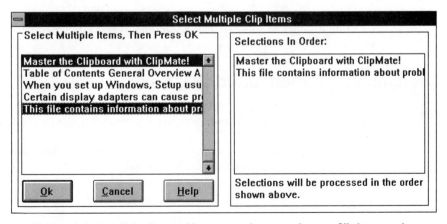

The Multiple Selection dialog box enables you to select more than one Clip Item at a time.

3. If necessary, move or resize the Magnify window.

4. The Selection List appears in the list box on the left. With the mouse or spacebar, select the titles of the Clip Items that you want to manipulate. As you make each selection, the Clip Item you select is displayed in the Magnify window. Because the Magnify window only holds one Clip Item at a time, only the most recent selection will be shown. To deselect, simply click again.

5. In the Confirmation List (on the right), your selections will appear in the order that you selected them. This *read-only* window provides visual confirmation that you have selected the items in the order that you intended. It is especially helpful when you're gluing Clip Items because it gives a "thumbnail sketch" of what you are composing. For the Copy to Safe List operation, the order also comes into play. The items will be copied to the Safe List in the order that you selected them and therefore in the order that they appear in the Confirmation List.

6. If you change your mind about a particular item, just click it again. It will be unhighlighted and disappear from the Confirmation List on the right. You can select and deselect as many times as you want.

7. When you are done with your selections, click OK.

8. The Delete, Print, Glue, and possibly Copy to Safe (depending on what list is currently active) buttons should now be enabled. You can now perform any of these functions by using the Multiple Selection.

Actions that are sensitive to Multiple Selections follow:

Delete

Print

Glue

Copy to Safe List (only if the Recyclable List is currently active)

## Configuration button and dialog box

 This button is accessible from the Config pull-down menu (when ClipMate is in the Full Layout) or the CFG button (when ClipMate is in the Brief Layout).

The Config dialog box lets you change various ClipMate settings. They are stored in the CLIPMATE.INI file for later retrieval.

```
┌─────────────────────────────────────────────┐
│ ─            ClipMate Configuration          │
│ ┌Automatically Save Current File When Shutting Down?┐
│   ◉ Always Save        ○ Ask User            │
│ └──────────────────────────────────────────┘ │
│ ┌Where to Put New Clipboard Items?──────────┐ │
│   ◉ Recyclable List    ○ Current Active List │
│ └──────────────────────────────────────────┘ │
│ ┌──────────────────────────────┬──────────┐ │
│ │ Length of Recyclable List:   │  25      │ │
│ ├──────────────────────────────┼──────────┤ │
│ │ Max size for clip Item:      │  4096    │ │
│ ├──────────────────────────────┴──────────┤ │
│ │ ┌Behavior and Appearance─┐    ┌───────┐ │ │
│ │ │ ☐ Keep Window On Top?  │    │ Help  │ │ │
│ │ │                        │    ├───────┤ │ │
│ │ │ ☒ Full Layout (See all Controls?) │ Ok │ │
│ └──────────────────────────────────────────┘ │
└─────────────────────────────────────────────┘
```

The Config dialog box enables you to change various ClipMate settings.

## Automatically Save Current File When Shutting Down?

When you close ClipMate, a check is made to see whether the current file needs saving. If so, then this value is checked to see whether you want to Always Save. If so, then ClipMate saves the file and you aren't bothered with confirmation. Otherwise, ClipMate will ask you whether you want to save the file.

The default is Always Save.

## Where to Put New Clipboard Items?

When ClipMate detects that there is a new Clip Item to retrieve from the Clipboard, it must decide in which list ClipMate should store it. If the Recyclable List is currently active, then the new item will always go there. If the Safe List is active, then it checks this value and places the item accordingly. This is useful in order to keep from cluttering up your Safe List with trivial items if you happen to have the Safe List active. On the other hand, you may want to turn on Current Active List if you want to collect some items that you want to keep for a long time.

The default is Recyclable List.

## Length of Recyclable List

This item enables you to control the length of the Recyclable List. ClipMate will accumulate Clip Items in the Recyclable List and allow the list to grow until this limit is reached. When the list is at its limit, an old item will drop off from the bottom for every new item added to the top.

Increasing this value will cause ClipMate to keep more Clip Items, but the trade-off is that it will use more memory.

The default is 25.

## Max size for clip item

This is a truncation threshold for new Clip Items in terms of bytes of storage. If the size of a new Clip Item exceeds this limit, then the Clip Item is truncated. This is useful in the event that you copy a large chunk of text — perhaps an entire document in your word processor. It prevents ClipMate from capturing and storing the entire item and saves both time and memory. If you want to be able to capture larger items (or lower the threshold), just adjust this number. It cannot exceed the system limit of 16384 and shouldn't be set lower than 1024.

This value only affects new Clip Items and doesn't affect glued Clip Items.

Increasing this value will allow ClipMate to capture larger items, but the trade-off is that it will use more memory.

The default is 4096.

## Keep Window On Top?

This item enables you to force ClipMate to "float" to the top of all other windows. It is especially helpful when you have a lot of windows open or if you are using an application that is running full screen, such as a word processor.

If you find that the Full Layout takes up too much of your screen space, try the Brief Layout.

If it still takes up too much screen space, try minimizing it to an icon, which will also "float" on the screen. You can position the icon anywhere that you want, even in the same place that you want the ClipMate window to occupy.

There is a trade-off. It will probably float above your screen saver. Also, if ClipMate and another application are both trying to stay on top, they may spend a lot of your CPU time bickering with each other and will create an annoying flickering effect. However, it is easy to turn the Keep Window On Top? option on and off.

The default is unchecked (no).

### Full Layout (See all Controls)?

ClipMate gives you the option of displaying all its graphical controls, along with the menu (Full Layout), or just showing some of the graphical controls, with no menu (Brief Layout). Here is where you make that choice.

For a full explanation, see "Layout — Full Layout versus Brief Layout."

The trade-off is that when you're in Brief Layout, not all features are accessible. In particular, you lose the ability to switch back and forth between the Recyclable List and the Safe List. In the Full Layout, you have access to all features, but ClipMate will take up more screen space.

The default is Full Layout.

## About button and dialog box

The About dialog box is accessible from the Help About pull-down menu (when ClipMate is in the Full Layout) or the ? button (when ClipMate is in the Brief Layout).

In addition to displaying the normal about information, this dialog box gives you the opportunity to register ClipMate and access the on-line help. The Help button is provided in order to give access to help when ClipMate is in the Brief Layout.

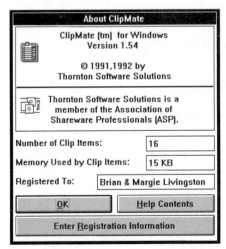

**The About dialog box provides information about ClipMate.**

*Help Info*

| | |
|---|---|
| Number of Clip Items: | Total of both Recyclable and Safe Lists |
| Memory Used by Clip Items: | Total memory used by both lists |
| Registered To: | Hopefully you! |

# Menus

Although ClipMate's most often used features are represented by buttons on the toolbar, there are still more functions to be found in the menus. Full descriptions follow for functions that are unique to the menus. Where a toolbar equivalent exists, a reference is made to that description.

*Note:* Menus are not available in the Brief Layout.

## File menu

The File menu includes commands that enable you to open and save ClipMate files.

For the most part, it will not be necessary for you to ever choose any of these. ClipMate will automatically open DEFAULT.CLM when it starts or a file that you specify on the command line (of the icon that launches ClipMate). On closing, ClipMate will attempt to save both of the Clip Item Lists into the current file. Depending on the option that you have selected in the Configuration screen, you may be prompted before the file is saved. Therefore, if you always use DEFAULT.CLM, you will never need to use the File menu.

| | |
|---|---|
| New | Clears storage, creates a new file. |
| Open | Opens existing file. |
| Save | Saves current file. |
| Save As | Saves with new name. |
| Print Setup | Sets printer. See "Print button." |
| Print Item(s) | Prints current item or multiple selection of items. See "Print button." |
| Exit | Ends ClipMate. Alternatively, you can double-click the Control Menu icon in the upper left corner of the main window to exit ClipMate. If Always Save is checked in the Configuration screen, then the current file (usually DEFAULT.CLM) will automatically be |

saved. Otherwise, you will be prompted to save
changes if either list has been added to or modified
in any way. The CLIPMATE.INI file in the Windows
directory will be updated on exiting from ClipMate.

# Edit menu

The Edit menu enables you to manually alter the contents of either of the two
lists. Most commands are also available on the icon bar.

| | |
|---|---|
| Edit Title | The Edit Title dialog box enables you to change the title of a Clip Item. Although the title is initially constructed from the first 50 characters of the Clip Item, changing the title will have no effect on the Clip Item. It is provided for your reference only. As an alternative to this dialog box, you can edit the title in the Magnify window. |
| Delete Item | Deletes the currently selected Clip Item(s) from the Active List. The next item in line is then copied to the Clipboard, and that item is shown in the Clip Item Selection List Box. See "Delete button." |
| Copy to Safe List | Copies selected Clip Item(s) to the Safe List. This operation is only available when the Recyclable List is active (that is, when the Recyclable List button is pressed). This operation works with single or Multiple Selections. See "Copy to Safe List button." |
| Glue | Glues Clip Items together. See "Glue button." |

# View menu

The View menu enables you to change the Active List, open or close the
Magnify window, or perform word searches with the Find or Find Next commands. Most commands are also available on the icon bar.

| | |
|---|---|
| Activate Recyclable List | Causes the Recyclable List to become the Active List (items put on the Clipboard are added to temporary memory). See "Activate Recyclable List button." |
| Activate Safe List | Causes the Safe List to become the Active List (items put on the Clipboard are added to the Safe List disk file). See "Activate Safe List button." |
| Magnify | Opens or closes the Magnify window. See "Magnify button." |

| Find | See description that follows. |
| Find Next | See description that follows. |

Here are some notes on the Find and Find Next menu items:

The Find command will prompt you for some text to search for and then search the Active List for the first occurrence of the specified text. It is *not* case sensitive.

If the string is found, the corresponding Clip Item is selected and displayed in the edit window of the Clip Item Selection List Box. If not, you will receive a notification message and the edit window will be blank.

If the Magnify window is active, then it will also reflect results of the search, in the same way that the edit window of the Clip Item Selection List box does.

These menu items are not available in the Brief Layout. However, you can still access the Find function by pressing Ctrl+F and the Find Next function by pressing Ctrl+N.

# CLIPMATE.INI

The CLIPMATE.INI file, written automatically by ClipMate, holds various settings and preferences. It is used rather than WIN.INI because this is considered to be proper programming practice these days. It relieves the system of having to load a lot of garbage into memory and makes it easy for you to remove an application.

The CLIPMATE.INI file is saved every time ClipMate is shut down, whether or not a change has actually taken place. It has nothing to do with the Ask User and Always Save options found in ClipMate's Configuration dialog box.

Here are the default settings for CLIPMATE.INI:

```
[ClipMate]
AlwaysSave=1
AskUser=0
RecyclableList=1
ActiveList=0
KeepOnTop=0
MaxView=1
RecyclableLength=25
MaxClipSize=4096
```

```
X=0
Y=0
magX=100
magY=100
magW=200
magH=400
Registered Name=Not Registered
Registered Number=
device=
```

# Additional Settings

There are some additional settings that are not configurable within ClipMate but will be used by ClipMate if they are present in this file. In normal situations, they would not be needed. They are provided in the event that someone has a problem that could be remedied by adjusting one of these settings:

HeapLimit=4096          Memory heap threshold

TimerTick=1000          Timer limit, in milliseconds, for Keep On Top

GlueDelayTime=1000      Delay for Glue Action when OwnerDraw format is present on the Clipboard

## Known problems

Norton Desktop for Windows users will need to upgrade to Version 2.0 of NDW in order to use ClipMate.

## Bug reports

Please send any bug reports, along with a description of your system (hardware and software), to CompuServe ID 70743,2546 or to

Thornton Software Solutions
P.O. Box 26263
Rochester, NY 14626

# Distribution Files _____

The following files are provided with ClipMate and constitute a complete ClipMate package:

CLIPMATE.EXE    The executable program — requires Windows 3.*x*.

CLIPMATE.HLP    Help file.

CLMICONS.DLL    Dynamic Link Library to support the icon ribbon. May be placed in Windows directory or kept in the same directory as CLIPMATE.EXE.

CLMREAD.TXT    Read Me file with any special considerations or installation notes.

CLMREG.TXT    Registration form.

VENDOR.DOC    Vendor description for shareware vendor or BBS sysop.

FILE_ID.DIZ    BBS Standard Description File.

ClipMate writes a file called CLIPMATE.INI to save your settings. If you share copies of ClipMate with others, do not distribute the CLIPMATE.INI file! The settings may not be correct for their systems.

# Deinstallation _____

These instructions are included in the event that you determine that ClipMate does not meet your needs, and therefore it should be removed from your system.

Before deleting ClipMate, you should review the contents of the Overview screen in the on-line help. If you have put ClipMate through a proper evaluation, everything on that screen should be familiar to you. If this is not the case, you may want to spend some more time evaluating ClipMate.

In the event that you want to remove ClipMate from your system, erase the following files:

*ClipMate distribution files (in* CLIPMATE *directory):*
CLIPMATE.EXE
CLIPMATE.HLP
CLMICONS.DLL
CLMREAD.TXT
CLMREG.TXT
VENDOR.DOC
FILE_ID.DIZ

*ClipMate data files:*

*.CLM
CLIPMATE.INI (found in your Windows directory)

*ClipMate group window in Program Manager:*

Minimize any ClipMate group window in Program Manager and then click File
Delete to remove it from Program Manager.

Please note that no changes were made to your WIN.INI, SYSTEM.INI, or any other
Windows system files. There are no hidden files.

# Registering ClipMate

## How much does it cost?

The registration fee for ClipMate is $25.00 in U.S. funds. U.S. and Canada
shipping is free. Outside the U.S. and Canada, add $2.00 for foreign shipping and
handling.

## What does it get you?

By registering ClipMate, you gain several things:

◆ A new diskette. I will send you the latest and greatest release of ClipMate on
your choice of either a 720K 3.5-inch (the default) or 360K 5.25-inch diskette.

◆ A printed manual.

◆ A registration number, which will remove the annoying SHAREWARE
NOTICE reminder screens from all 1.*x* versions of ClipMate.

◆ Peace of mind. You have fulfilled your obligation and have made the
shareware concept work. You are not breaking the law — at least in this
particular case!

◆ Access to support. If you have problems using ClipMate, either from a user
or a technical perspective, I am there to help you. You can reach me by U.S.
mail or by my CompuServe mailbox (70743,2546). Support is guaranteed for
90 days from the date of registration. If I can't resolve your problem to our
mutual satisfaction, I will refund your money as long as the problem is
brought to my attention within the 90-day window.

- A voice. Your completion of the User Survey (located in the file CLMREG.TXT) will help drive the future of ClipMate. The addition of Print and Glue are two features that were added at the request of users.

- A *bonus*. MDIBALL.EXE and PALDEMO.EXE, two colorful Windows programs, come free with registered copies.

## Bonus programs for registered users

Outside of expensive drawing software, there are not very many Windows programs that utilize the 256-color capabilities found in many of today's mainstream video boards and monitors. When I bought my system, I had no way to even prove to myself that it would show any more colors than a standard 16-color VGA system. My first attempts at Windows programming addressed this need: I wrote two Super VGA demo programs that show off the equipment. Although they have no real commercial value, they are very entertaining and are useful when demonstrating 256-color boards and monitors. Rather than let them just sit on my hard drive, I thought I'd share them with registered users of ClipMate.

PALDEMO.EXE is a Windows Palette demonstration utility that displays a custom palette of 236 colors (Windows reserves 20 for itself). If you have a standard VGA system, PALDEMO.EXE will just make you envious. It will dither most of the colors by mixing two colors together rather than displaying pure colors. It is a very easy way to demonstrate the 256-color capabilities of most SVGA or XGA systems.

MDIBALL.EXE is an animated bouncing ball that leaves a multicolored trail behind as it works its way through the 236 colors in its custom palette. This creates a strange 3D effect as the trails overlap. If you have a standard VGA system, it's still entertaining, although not as dramatic as on a 256-color SVGA or an XGA system.

All users who register will receive the MDIBALL.EXE and PALDEMO.EXE programs at no additional charge. Previously registered users who are interested should contact me by CompuServe or by mail.

Please note that these two programs are completely unrelated to the function of ClipMate, and the omission of them in the unregistered version does not cripple ClipMate in any way.

# License Agreement

This license gives the user the right to install and use one copy of ClipMate for Windows. If the user of a registered copy of ClipMate is the *primary user* of more than one machine (for example, one at work, one at home, and a laptop), a single license will cover all machines that are *used primarily* by the registered user.

Users of ClipMate must accept this disclaimer of warranty:

ClipMate is supplied as is. The author disclaims all warranties, expressed or implied, including, without limitation, the warranties of merchantability and of fitness for any purpose. The author assumes no liability for damages, direct or consequential, which may result from the use of ClipMate.

Service will be guaranteed for a period of at least 90 days of the date of registration. Support will be provided by U.S. mail or by electronic mail in CompuServe.

# How To Register

There are several ways to register ClipMate. Choose the one that best suits your needs.

## Ordering directly from Thornton Software Solutions

One of the ClipMate distribution files is CLMREG.TXT. This is the preferred method of registering ClipMate. I recommend that you edit it electronically, print it, and mail it to Thornton Software Solutions.

Or fill out the form that follows or send a letter (and a check or money order) including the information on the following page.

Name: _____

Address: _____

_____

_____

Phone: _____

CompuServe ID (if any): _____

Diskette Size (3.5" is default; otherwise, 5.25"): _____

Signature: _____

Please attach a check or money order for $25.00 (U.S.).

Shipping and handling is free in the U.S. and Canada (other locations please add $2.00). Mail to

**Thornton Software Solutions**
P.O. Box 26263
Rochester, NY 14626

Make check or money order payable to Chris Thornton.

Please note that volume discounts, site licenses, and bundling prices can be obtained by contacting the author directly.

## Foreign registrations

If you are outside the U.S. and can't get a check drawn on a U.S. bank, try a postal money order. Another alternative is to send cash by way of registered mail. Under no conditions should you send me a check drawn on a non-U.S. bank. It would likely cost me between $10 and $25 to get it cashed!

# Ordering through CompuServe

Through an arrangement with CompuServe, you can order a registered copy of ClipMate and charge it to your CompuServe account.

## Ordering Information

1. Sign on to CompuServe, type **GO SWREG,** and press Enter. (*SWREG* stands for Shareware Registration.)

2. Select Register Shareware from the main SWREG menu.

3. Select Registration ID from the SEARCH BY menu.

4. Enter **173** as the ID.

5. ClipMate's description should be on the screen. Press Y to register.

## User Feedback

Please note that although CompuServe will be taking your order, it will be filled by Thornton Software Solutions. You are not circumventing the developer-user relationship that makes the shareware system work so well. Thornton Software Solutions values your input and encourages you to complete the user survey that is at the end of the file CLMREG.TXT. Just delete the first portion of the file, which is the order form. Mention that you've registered through another channel and send it in. Of course, electronic mail is fine! This is by no means a requirement, but it will help direct the future of ClipMate and therefore serves both of our interests.

# Ordering from Software Excitement!

Through an arrangement with Software Excitement!, you can charge ClipMate to your Visa or MasterCard. You can call their 1-800 phone number or fax or mail your order with the form that appears shortly.

## Ordering Information

To order by phone, call 1-800-444-5457 (outside the U.S., call 503-826-6884) and ask to purchase a registered copy of ClipMate for Windows. The item number is V318.

To order by fax, complete this form and fax it to Software Excitement! at 503-826-8090.

To order by mail, complete, sign, and mail this form to

**Software Excitement!**
IBM Department
6475 Crater Lake Hwy.
Central Point, OR 97502

Name: _____

Address: _____

_____

_____

Phone: _____

Visa/MC #: _____

Exp. Date: _____

Signature: _____

Disk Size      [   ] 3.5"      [   ] 5.25"

ClipMate is SE! item number V318.

| ITEM | PRICE | QTY | TOTAL |
|------|-------|-----|-------|
| ClipMate for Windows Version 1.5 | $25.00 | _____ | _____ |
| Foreign Shipping (other than Canada) | $ 2.00 | _____ | _____ |

## User Feedback

Please note that although Software Excitement! will be taking your order, it will be filled by Thornton Software Solutions. You are not circumventing the developer-user relationship that makes the shareware system work so well. Thornton Software Solutions values your input and encourages you to complete the user survey that is at the end of the file CLMREG.TXT. Just delete the first portion of the file, which is the order form. Mention that you've registered through another channel and send it in. This is by no means a requirement, but it will help direct the future of ClipMate and therefore serves both of our interests.

# Code Breaker

## Version 1.01a
## Copyright © by Charles W. Haden

*C*ode Breaker is a memory game that is more difficult than it looks. The computer chooses five random numbers; you make a guess, and the computer gives you clues about how many of your guesses were correct and which were in the correct position.

The sample game shown on the facing page gives you an idea how the game is played. The first guess, in the bottom row, was 12345. After the Did I get it right? button was pressed, the computer gave the clue 0 0. These zeroes mean that two of the numbers in 12345 are correct, but neither is in the correct position.

The guess in the second row from the bottom, 67812, received a clue of 0 0 0. This clue, indicating three correct numbers, means that we have three correct numbers in our guess, but we still don't know which ones are correct.

By changing our guesses, we got clues like 1 1 0, indicating that three numbers were correct, but only two were in the correct position. The clues in the subsequent moves gradually led us to the conclusion that there must be a 6 and a 7 in the answer, plus a 1 or a 2. Finally, by a process of elimination (scribbled on a separate piece of paper), we found that we could rule out all numbers other than 3 from the last two buttons. Our final guess, 76133, was the correct one.

If you're a programmer and would like to modify Code Breaker's behavior, Charles Haden includes the full C-language source code on disk. But it's much more fun just to play the game. Enjoy!

| | |
|---|---|
| **Type of Program:** | Game |
| **Requires:** | Windows 3.0 or later |
| **Registration:** | Free. This program requires no registration. |
| **Technical Support:** | None |

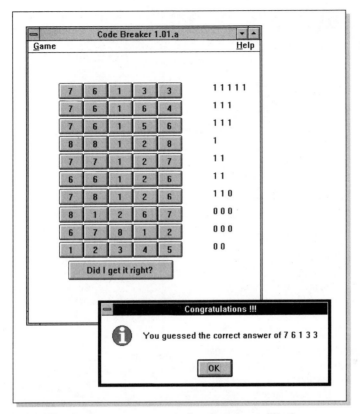

In Code Breaker, you try to guess a series of numbers while the
computer gives you clues about which numbers are correct.

# Playing Code Breaker

The goal of this game is to guess the same sequence of numbers as that of the
computer. The number sequence the computer generates is made up of five
digits in the range 1 to 8. As you make guesses, the computer gives you clues.

A clue of 1 means that a number you chose is correct *and* in the correct
position. A clue of 0 means that a number is correct but in the wrong position.
The position of the clues is not representative of the position of the buttons.

You change your guess by clicking on the buttons. The number on the button
increases by 1 each time you click the button until 8 is reached; clicking again
causes the number to start over at 1.

To test your guess, click on the Did I get it right? button. The computer tests
your guess and displays any clues.

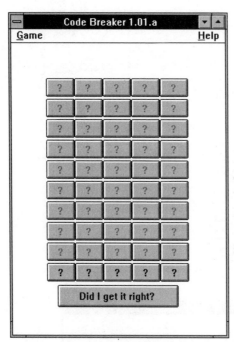

When you start Code Breaker, it displays rows of blank buttons; you make a guess by clicking on each button in the bottom row until it represents the correct number.

This program is my revision to Kenneth Fogel's free Code Breaker game. I made revisions to the program just to keep in practice and to further my Windows programming skills. The following is a list of a few changes I have made that I feel add to the enjoyment of this game:

♦ The number of buttons per row has been increased from 4 to 5.

♦ Hash defines have been used to specify the number of rows and columns. (There are still a few places to be fixed to work properly with these hash defines, primarily with the print statements.)

♦ A new menu structure is now used.

♦ The information previously displayed on the main page has been put in a dialog box displayed when the Help menu entry is clicked.

♦ The code has been cleaned up to use true ANSI-C for function parameters rather than K&R style.

♦ The size of the buttons has been increased. (This may cause odd-looking screens on an EGA monitor. The current setup was designed on a VGA monitor running at $800 \times 600$ resolution.)

- When a player has won or lost a game, all the number buttons are disabled and the guess button ignored, forcing the player to choose a new game if it is so desired.

- A general cleanup of the code (at least to my liking) was done. (The reason for this cleanup is that I learned my Windows programming from the Petzold book and have somewhat tailored my style after his.)

Because the original author of this program has hinted at the continuation of developing this program toward the color aspect, I am going to try and aim my efforts at making the game easier and friendlier to use. The following is a list of the ideas I am considering adding to this program, as time allows:

- Add a true help function that uses the Windows help utility.

- Add the capacity to change the number of columns and rows — and even the range of numbers — at run time.

- Further clean up the code (more streamlined and flexible).

- Possibly convert to a true C++ program (objects, classes, and so on).

As was intended by the original author, this is *freeware,* and the source code is included. Following is a list of files needed to re-create this program. (***Note:*** The MAKEFILE may need to be tailored to your specific system.)

```
CBREAK.C
CBREAK.DEF
CBREAK.H
CBREAK.ICO
CBREAK.RC
CBREAK2.ICO
MAKEFILE (optional)
```

Original author:

**Kenneth Fogel**
Omnibus Systems
8108 Norfolk Road
Cote St-Luc, Québec
Canada H4X 1A3
CIS: 74646,2157

Coauthor:

**Charles W. Haden**
Shoebox Software
699 Lantana Street, Apt. #54
Camarillo, CA 93010
U.S.A.
CIS: 71760,3557

Happy Programming!

# DirNotes for Windows

**WDN.EXE — Version 1.2 by Pat Beirne**
**Copyright © by Corel Systems Corp.**

*D*irNotes for Windows gives you the ability to break the 8-character filename limit of DOS by typing 38-character descriptions for each of your files. Although this will never substitute for having the same ability in the Windows File Manager (where it should be built in), it can be a big help when you have a lot of files and need some way to keep track of what they mean.

When you run DirNotes, it displays a list of filenames. Switch to the directory you want to annotate, type a description, and click on the file you want to describe. When you exit DirNotes (or click on File Exit/Update), your description is saved.

DirNotes stores the data you type in a text file called DIRN-ABC.DAT, where abc represents the first three letters of the directory name. You can print this text file if you want a permanent record of your filenames and their meanings. (Don't edit it with a word processor, though, because it's in a fixed-length format that might be altered by the application.)

Because DirNotes is a small and simple application, there's no way that it can force Windows applications to apply 38-character descriptions to every file you save. But, because DirNotes accepts filenames on its command line, you can program this capability into some applications that support macro languages. For example, you can redefine the File Save-As command in your word processor. Then, when you save a file called MYFILE.DOC, your word processor would automatically run a command such as the following:

    C:\DIRNOTES\WDN.EXE  MYFILE.DOC

This command runs DirNotes, with your just-created file highlighted in its dialog box, ready for you to type a 38-character description.

Under Windows 3.1, DirNotes also supports File Manager's drag-and-drop capability. If DirNotes is running as an icon or a window, you can drag a filename from File Manager and drop it on DirNotes. The DirNotes window switches to the directory containing that file and enables you to type your description.

*DirNotes works well with a free utility for DOS called DIRNOTES.COM. This utility writes and reads the same data file as DirNotes for Windows. So you can use either one, depending on whether you're in Windows or DOS. You can even create a disk full of files, annotate them with DirNotes, and send the disk (along with WDN.EXE and DIRNOTES.COM) to friends. Running either utility provides your associates with a description of each file.*

*DIRNOTES.COM was published in the September 1987 issue (Vol. 6 No. 15) of PC Magazine, a computer periodical. You can get this utility by accessing CompuServe, typing **GO ZIFFNET,** and then selecting the Software and Utility Library. Select the Download a Utility option and specify filename V6N15.ZIP to download. This file can be decompressed with ZIP Tools for Windows, described elsewhere in this book.*

*But, if you have Windows, you really don't need the DOS utility because you can do it all with DirNotes for Windows. Let's hope that the Windows File Manager supports some capability like this soon.*

| | |
|---|---|
| **Type of Program:** | File Management |
| **Requires:** | Windows 3.0 or later |
| **Registration:** | Free. This program requires no registration. |
| **Technical Support:** | None |

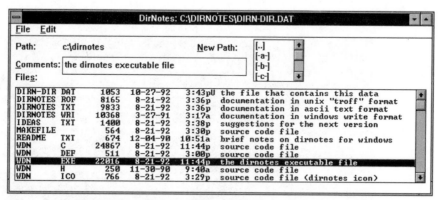

**When you start DirNotes, you see a list of filenames. Type a description and then click the filename you want that description to apply to.**

# Description _____

DirNotes is a tiny Windows application that enables the user to add annotation to directories. For compatibility with the DOS utility DIRNOTES.COM, this application enables the user to associate up to 38 characters with each file.

The notes are stored in a file called DIRN-*xxx*.DAT, where *xxx* is the first three letters of the directory name. If the name is less than three letters, a hyphen (-) is used. For example, for the root directory, the note file is called DIRN----.DAT. The format for this file is identical to that used by DIRNOTES.COM, a popular DOS program.

When the program is run, it first checks the command line for a filename. The name is split into disk and path and filename. The disk and path are used for locating the relevant notes file. If the notes file does not exist, it is created. The filename is used for searching within the notes for the relevant entry. The exception is filenames that match DIRN-???.DAT, which are not used for searching.

When the correct directory is known, a DIR is done, probably using the system (DIR) call. The result is WSPRINTed into the main list box and sorted as it's entered.

Each entry in the directory pool can have a capital *U* appended to it (at column 40). This stands for Update and signifies that a file has been changed since the last time the DirNotes database was updated.

```
┌─┬──────────────────────────── DOS Session ────────────────────┬─┬─┐
│ ─ │                                                            │ ▼ │ ↕ │
├───┴──────────────────────────────────────────────────────────┴───┤
│ C:\DIRNOTES>dirnotes                                               │
│                                                                    │
│     Directory of C:\DIRNOTES                                       │
│                                                                    │
│ DIRN-DIR DAT     1053   10-27-92    3:52pU the file that contains this data │
│ DIRNOTES ROF     8165    8-21-92    3:36p  documentation in unix "troff" format │
│ DIRNOTES TXT     9833    8-21-92    3:36p  documentation in ascii text format │
│ DIRNOTES WRI    10368    3-27-91    3:17a  documentation in windows write format │
│ IDEAS    TXT     1400    8-21-92    3:38p  suggestions for the next version │
│ MAKEFILE          564    8-21-92    3:30p  source code file │
│ README   TXT      674   12-04-90   10:51a  brief notes on dirnotes for windows │
│ WDN      C      24867    8-21-92   11:44p  source code file │
│ WDN      DEF      511    8-21-92    3:00p  source code file │
│ WDN      EXE    22016    8-21-92   11:44p  the dirnotes executable file │
│ WDN      H        250   11-30-90    9:40a  source code file │
│ WDN      ICO      766    8-21-92    3:29p  source code file <dirnotes icon> │
│ WDN      RC      2173    8-21-92    3:25p  source code file │
│                                                                    │
│                                                                    │
│          13 Files                         Press Esc to exit        │
│                                                                    │
└────────────────────────────────────────────────────────────────────┘
```

The note file for a directory keeps the typical size, date, and time information for each file in the directory but adds a 38-character field for annotations. This figure shows the DOS program, DIRNOTES.COM, running in a DOS session under Windows.

The relevant notes file is read into RAM and parsed on the fly into fixed-length records. As the records are read in, they're compared with the entries in the main list box. Nonmatching entries are discarded. Matching entries are checked for identical length and date. If the directory pool date/time is the same as the old pool date/time, the *U* is cleared to a blank. Any existing comments are moved from the input file into the list box.

When all the records are moved over, the windows are displayed showing the filename, extension, size, date, time, new-marker, and comments. If the program was started with a specific file, the list box is scrolled to that entry.

At the top of the screen is an edit box into which the comments are duplicated. The user can modify the 38 characters of the comments in this box. Any scroll activity in the list box takes away and saves the comments from the edit box.

# The DirNotes Menus

The menus for this application are simply as follows:

| <u>F</u>ile |
| --- |
| E<u>x</u>it/Update |
| <u>Q</u>uit/NoUpdate |
| <u>A</u>bout... |

The File menu provides options for quitting the application and saving your changes or for quitting and not saving your changes.

| <u>E</u>dit | |
| --- | --- |
| <u>U</u>ndo | AltBkSp |
| <u>C</u>opy | CtrlIns |
| Cu<u>t</u> | ShftDel |
| <u>P</u>aste | ShftIns |

The Edit menu provides options for cutting, copying, and pasting text, as well as undoing the last edit.

*Note:* The edit box has been subclassed so that the up-arrow, down-arrow, PgUp, and PgDn keys scroll the list box. The Directory list box has been subclassed so that the spacebar acts as if you double-clicked.

# Program Structure

Complete source code in the C language is included with DirNotes; the following information will be useful to programmers who want to tinker with DirNotes. Each section describes a different procedure in the source code.

## Start-up

♦ Register the windows class.

♦ Wake up the main and child windows.

♦ Fill them with data.

♦ Message loop.

The main window is created through CreateDialog(). This enables us to specify the shape of the child elements in the RC file. Because it should look and feel like a dialog box, the IsDialogMessage() is called in the message loop.

At exit time, the subclassing proc-instances are freed.

## Main WndProc

Because the program acts like a dialog box, we don't bother painting.

The only messages we pick up are these:

| | |
|---|---|
| WM_SIZE | To adjust the size of the list box |
| WM_DESTROY | To do autosave |
| WM_SETFOCUS | So that it wakes up "ready to type" |
| WM_INITMENU | To gray out certain entries |
| WM_COMMAND | To receive messages from the children and menus |
| WM_DROPFILES | To detect dropped files ← new in Version 1.2 |

## Wakeup

The WakeUp() code calls CreateDialog() to start up the main window and the three children. It then measures the system font and the fixed-space system font to adjust window sizes. It also configures the child boxes: the edit box (limits text entry to 38 characters) and the file list box (uses a fixed-space font); then it subclasses the edit box and the directory box.

## FillListBox

The file list box is filled as described previously: First read the disk for real files and then read and match the old comments file, throwing away entries that do not match. *Note:* In this program, directories are included in the listing where they are not in the DOS program DIRNOTES.COM.

## CopyComments

Every time the user scrolls the entry in the file list box, we move the comments from the edit box into the corresponding entry in the list box. The flag fLocalDirty indicates whether the comments have been modified. Note that when you replace an entry in a list box, you must WM_INSERTSTRING before you WM_DELETESTRING. Note also that we push and pop the global flag fDirty because the act of stuffing the edit box causes the fDirty flag to be set, which is not significant.

## NewDir

If the user changes directories, we first save the old comment file (if it has been touched: fDirty). Then we get the new directory, parse it for the comment-file-name, and then refill the list box.

The rest of the code is self-explanatory.

# Disk Copy for Windows

### DC.EXE — Version 1.11
### Copyright © by Terratech

*DOS provides a DISKCOPY command to make one copy of a floppy disk from another. But the DOS command is limited to using less than 640K of memory, meaning that you must insert and remove today's high-density disks several times to copy all of each one. Windows 3.1's File Manager has a simple Disk Copy command, but it is designed for single copies and totally freezes background processes while copying.*

*Disk Copy for Windows (DC.EXE) enables you to copy the contents of any floppy disk and make as many copies as you like — in the background. DC works from a Windows dialog box; if you make an icon in the Program Manager for it, DC works automatically without any further attention from you (except, of course, to insert new disks).*

*DC does have some limitations. Because of the failings built into the DOS and Windows architecture, you should not try to use two Disk Copy windows to make disk copies in two drives simultaneously (drives A and B, for example). PCs are simply not set up to handle this much disk activity at once. It's fine to leave two or more idle Disk Copy icons minimized on your desktop, faithfully waiting for you to use them when needed, however.*

| | |
|---|---|
| **Type of Program:** | Utility |
| **Requires:** | Windows 3.0 or later |
| **Registration:** | Use the form at the end of this chapter to register with the shareware author. |
| **Technical Support:** | Terratech provides technical support by mail to registered users of Disk Copy. |

## Overview

Disk Copy (DC) is a single-pass disk copier for use under Windows 3.*x*. DC is designed to alleviate floppy swapping when you're copying diskettes. Normally, DC will be capable of copying the entire diskette to memory. If there is not enough memory available for this, the remainder will be temporarily written to a hard drive or RAM disk. In case memory and disk space together are not sufficient, DC will attempt to do a multiple-pass copy.

# Command Line Syntax

The command line syntax for Disk Copy is as follows:

> DC {x:} {options}

where x: is a valid floppy drive letter and *options* is one or more of the options listed in the following section.

The DC.GRP group window file, provided for Program Manager (see the section "Installing the Program Manager Group Window" later in this chapter) includes icons for running Disk Copy on drives A and B with the most commonly used options (/e for execute and /i for iconize during execution). An example of this command line is as follows:

> DC A: /e /i

# Options

| | |
|---|---|
| +*number* | Number of copies desired (default is 1) |
| /0 or /1 | Icon style value (default is 0) |
| /a (**a**lways) | Always format destination diskette |
| /e (**e**xecute) | Run without any additional user input |
| /f (**f**ormat if needed) | Format destination diskette if needed (default) |
| /i (**i**con) | Minimize during execution |
| /n (**n**ever format) | Never format destination diskette |
| /p (**p**ause) | Do not close window on exit |
| /P (**P**ause) | Do not close window on exit and restore if iconic |
| /v (non**v**erbose) | Minimum display of progress |
| /V (**V**erbose) | Maximum display of progress |
| /r (verify **r**eadable) | Verify diskette is readable |

## Exit values

Disk Copy sets these DOS Errorlevel values when exiting. These values can be tested in a DOS batch file or by way of a Windows batch language such as WinBatch, a program featured in *Windows 3.1 SECRETS,* published by IDG Books Worldwide. Disk Copy also displays a Windows dialog box if an error occurs.

| | |
|---|---|
| 0 | No error |
| 1 | Command line error |
| 2 | Error during copy |
| 4 | User abort |
| 8 | DC PROGRAM NOT REGISTERED |
| 16 | DC program will not open |
| 32 | DC program corruption |

These values are additive. For example, if DC is not registered (8) and a command line error is detected (1), the DOS Errorlevel will be set to 9. If needed, you could test for all these error situations, but it's easier just to let Disk Copy inform you of errors if they occur.

# Disk Copy Dialog Box

When DC.EXE is run without a drive letter as a parameter, it displays a Windows dialog box.

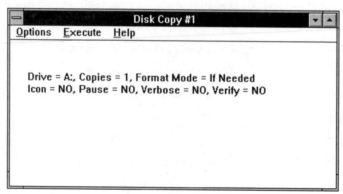

The Disk Copy program displays a dialog box if you issue the DC.EXE command without parameters.

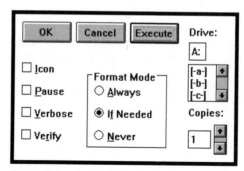

The configuration dialog box contains options
that you can also specify with command line
parameters.

Clicking the Options menu item opens the configuration dialog box. Each of the
options in the dialog box performs the same actions as the same options when
placed on the DC.EXE command line.

# Icon

When this option is selected, DC is reduced to an icon when disk copying is
underway. The DC window will be restored if an error is encountered.

# Pause

When this option is selected, DC will not close its window after the disk copying
is completed. DC will automatically pause and restore an iconic window if the
exit value, as described in the "Command Line Syntax" section, is not 0 or if the
pause and restore option is in effect.

# Verbose

When this option is selected, DC will post additional information when disk
copying is underway.

## Verify

When this option is selected, DC will verify that the diskette is readable after every write operation. *Selecting this option will result in a substantially slower disk copy.*

## Format Mode

### Always

The destination diskette is always formatted to the same specifications as the source diskette.

### If Needed

If the destination diskette is unformatted, it will be formatted to the same specifications as the source diskette. If the destination diskette is already formatted to different specifications than the source diskette, additional user input will be required.

### Never

Unless the destination diskette is already formatted to the same specifications as the source diskette, the disk copy will terminate.

## OK button

The parameters that were in effect before the configuration dialog box was selected are updated.

## Cancel button

The parameters that were in effect before the configuration dialog box was selected remain unchanged.

## Execute button

The disk copying will begin with the current options.

## Abort menu item

Clicking the Abort menu item (which is displayed on the DC menu in place of
Execute while disk copying is taking place) causes the disk copying to halt.

# Keyboard Shortcuts _____

F1 Gets Help and displays the Help Index for the application. If the Help
window is already open, pressing F1 displays the Using Windows Help
topics.

 Shift+F1 Changes the mouse pointer to a question-mark pointer so that you
can get Help on a specific command, screen region, or key. You can
then choose a command, click the screen region, or press a key or key
combination you want to know more about. (This feature is not available in all Windows applications.)

# Temporary File Location_____

If the SET TMP= environment variable (not SET TEMP=, as with some Windows
programs) is set to a valid directory in your AUTOEXEC.BAT file, DC will look to
write temporary files there; otherwise, the C:\ directory will be used.

# Recommended Usage _____

Although DC will allow multiple instances of itself, *it is strongly recommended that
you not write to more than one diskette drive at a time.* Having multiple instances
in the idle state is perfectly acceptable.

# Installing the Program Manager Group Window

The DC distribution disk comes with a DC.GRP group window file for use with
Windows' Program Manager. Install this group file and view the properties of the
various program items. To do this, follow these steps:

1. In the Program Manager, click File New.

2. In the dialog box that appears, click Program Group and then click OK.

3. In the Program Group dialog box, type **Disk Copy** for the Description and **C:\DISKCOPY\DC.GRP** as the group filename. (Substitute the correct filename if you installed Disk Copy into a different drive or directory.) Click OK. A new group window should appear. Drag its corners with your mouse to make the window an appropriate size for your display.

4. If the preceding steps were successful, you should see a group window in Program Manager that looks like the figure that follows. The icons in this group window run DC in a dialog box, automatically on drive A, and automatically on drive B.

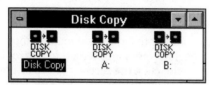

**When you install Disk Copy into the C:\DISKCOPY directory, the group window shows icons for running DC in a dialog box, automatically on drive A, and automatically on drive B.**

5. If you installed Disk Copy into a directory other than C:\DISKCOPY, you may see a group window with generic empty-window icons, like this:

**When you install Disk Copy into a different directory, the group window shows generic-window icons.**

6. If this is the case, you need to edit the icons' properties to include the correct directory name before they will work properly. To do this, highlight the first icon in the group and then click File Properties from the Program Manager's menu. In the dialog box that appears, replace the C:\DISKCOPY directory in the Command Line (as shown in the figure that follows) with the name of the actual directory where Disk Copy is installed. It is not necessary to change the icon; this will happen automatically when you click OK. If the generic icon turns into the correct Disk Copy icon, repeat this procedure on the other two icons in the group.

```
  ┌─────────────────────────────────────────────────────┐
  │ ▭           Program Item Properties                  │
  ├─────────────────────────────────────────────────────┤
  │ Description:      │ Disk Copy              │    ┌──────────┐ │
  │                   └────────────────────────┘    │   OK     │ │
  │ Command Line:     │ c:\gizmos\diskcopy\dc.exe │   └──────────┘ │
  │                                                 ┌──────────┐ │
  │ Working Directory:│                        │    │ Cancel   │ │
  │                                                 └──────────┘ │
  │ Shortcut Key:     │ None                   │                 │
  │                                                 ┌──────────┐ │
  │                                                 │ Browse...│ │
  │         ┌───┐                                   └──────────┘ │
  │         │   │       ☐ Run Minimized            ┌──────────┐ │
  │         └───┘                                   │Change Icon..│ │
  │                                                 └──────────┘ │
  │                                                 ┌──────────┐ │
  │                                                 │  Help    │ │
  │                                                 └──────────┘ │
  └─────────────────────────────────────────────────────┘
```

**To get rid of the generic-window icons, change the directory in the Windows Program Item Properties dialog box.**

# Why Register?

The main reason to purchase any program is because it is ethically correct. Not registering is an abuse of the shareware concept and in the long run will cause this method of distribution to disappear. DC represents a large investment of time and money, and as such the author expects compensation if you use DC beyond the trial period.

Although the unregistered version is not lacking any disk-copying features, it does not allow completely automatic operation.

┌─────────────────────────────────────────────────────────────┐
│ If you continue to use this program after the seven-day trial period, please │
│ remit $15 in U.S. funds (Washington state residents add $1.14 tax) to │
│ │
│ **Terratech** │
│ 19817 61st Ave. S.E. │
│ Snohomish, WA 98290 │
│ │
│ │
│ Name: _____ │
│ │
│ Address: _____ │
│ │
│ _____ │
│ │
│ _____ │
│ │
│ Format:    [ ] 3.5" diskette   [ ] 5.25" diskette │
└─────────────────────────────────────────────────────────────┘

A disk will be sent to you containing a registered version.

You are encouraged to copy this program as described next.

*Notice:* Users of this program are granted a limited license to make copies of this program for trial use by others on a private, noncommercial basis. This limited license does *not* include the following:

1. Distributing this program in connection with any other product

2. Making the program available for any consideration or "disk fee"

3. Distributing the program in modified form

TERRATECH DISCLAIMS ALL WARRANTIES, EITHER EXPRESS OR IMPLIED, INCLUDING, BUT NOT LIMITED TO, IMPLIED WARRANTIES OF MERCHANTABIL-ITY AND FITNESS FOR A PARTICULAR PURPOSE, WITH RESPECT TO THE PRODUCT. SHOULD THE PROGRAM PROVE DEFECTIVE, THE PURCHASER ASSUMES THE RISK OF PAYING THE ENTIRE COST OF ALL NECESSARY SERVIC-ING, REPAIR, OR CORRECTION AND ANY INCIDENTAL OR CONSEQUENTIAL DAMAGES. IN NO EVENT WILL TERRATECH BE LIABLE FOR ANY DAMAGES WHATSOEVER (INCLUDING WITHOUT LIMITATION DAMAGES FOR LOSS OF BUSINESS PROFITS, BUSINESS INTERRUPTION, LOSS OF BUSINESS INFORMA-TION, AND THE LIKE) ARISING OUT OF THE USE OR THE INABILITY TO USE THIS PRODUCT EVEN IF TERRATECH HAS BEEN ADVISED OF THE POSSIBILITY OF SUCH DAMAGES.

# Exclaim

!.EXE — Version 1.21
Copyright © by Terratech

*E*xclaim is one of the most ambitious programs (for its size) in this book. Exclaim emulates all the major DOS internal commands (DIR, COPY, and so on) in a graphical window that you can resize, scroll, and use like any other window. Yet Exclaim uses only 76K of memory, unlike ordinary 640K DOS sessions that actually use over 550K.

Therefore, you can put Exclaim on the LOAD= line of your WIN.INI file, or in the StartUp group of the Windows 3.1 Program Manager, and have a DOS prompt handy whenever you need one. Or, because Exclaim is really a Windows program named !.EXE, you can click on File Run in Program Manager and simply type *!*. As a genuine Windows application, you can feed *!* keystrokes from a Recorder macro, unlike with DOS sessions.

Remember when you run Exclaim that you are not running a copy of COMMAND.COM, the DOS command line interpreter. Exclaim does not support SET, FORMAT, and other DOS commands. And, when you start a batch file from Exclaim, the batch file actually starts running in a separate DOS window. (You can override this setup, however, by using the CALL command, as described in this chapter.)

Although Exclaim does not support every possible DOS command and feature, it offers many commands not available in DOS. You can MOVE files to a different location, change the COLOR of your command line window, and write IF...THEN...ENDIF statements unlike anything possible in DOS. You can even start Windows applications from the Exclaim command line. Type **NOTEPAD**, for example, and the Windows Notepad appears in its own window.

Because most of Exclaim's commands work the same way as their DOS counterparts (such as COPY), the best documentation for these commands is actually in your DOS manual. But, because Exclaim is not the DOS command line, be sure to test any commands you use to make sure that they work the same way you expect. We think that you'll find it worth the effort to learn Exclaim.

| | |
|---|---|
| **Type of Program:** | Utility |
| **Requires:** | Windows 3.0 or later |
| **Registration:** | Use the form at the end of this chapter to register with the shareware author. |
| **Technical Support:** | Terratech provides technical support to registered users by mail. Registered users also receive an enhanced version. |
| **Similar Shareware:** | WinCLI, a Windows command line processor featured in *Windows 3.1 SECRETS,* published by IDG Books Worldwide, provides some but not all of the commands supported in Exclaim. |

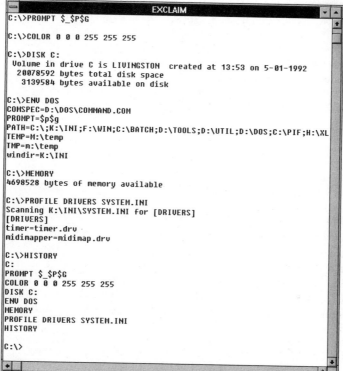

```
                          EXCLAIM
C:\>PROMPT $_$P$G

C:\>COLOR 0 0 0 255 255 255

C:\>DISK C:
 Volume in drive C is LIVINGSTON  created at 13:53 on 5-01-1992
  20078592 bytes total disk space
   3139584 bytes available on disk

C:\>ENV DOS
COMSPEC=D:\DOS\COMMAND.COM
PROMPT=$p$g
PATH=C:\;K:\INI;F:\WIN;C:\BATCH;D:\TOOLS;D:\UTIL;D:\DOS;C:\PIF;H:\XL
TEMP=M:\temp
TMP=m:\temp
windir=K:\INI

C:\>MEMORY
4698528 bytes of memory available

C:\>PROFILE DRIVERS SYSTEM.INI
Scanning K:\INI\SYSTEM.INI for [DRIVERS]
[DRIVERS]
timer=timer.drv
midimapper=midimap.drv

C:\>HISTORY
C:
PROMPT $_$P$G
COLOR 0 0 0 255 255 255
DISK C:
ENV DOS
MEMORY
PROFILE DRIVERS SYSTEM.INI
HISTORY

C:\>
```

**Exclaim gives you much more than a regular Windows command line window.**

# Overview _____

Exclaim (!.EXE) is a Windows application that minimizes, if not eliminates, the need to run a DOS shell such as COMMAND.COM. This is especially useful when you are running Windows in standard mode because you can run more than one Exclaim window but not more than one DOS session. But there is much to be gained by using Exclaim in enhanced mode, too. Because Exclaim is a Windows application, you can avoid the problems and inefficiencies associated with running DOS sessions under Windows.

# How To Start Exclaim _____

After you run WSETUP, an Exclaim (!) group window can be found in your Program Manager. To start Exclaim, double-click on the ! icon in Program Manager; alternatively, click on File Run, type !, and click on OK. The Exclaim window appears.

You can also follow the ! with any command. For example, if you want to reset the system time, you can type the following:

**! TIME**

The familiar DOS Enter new time: prompt appears in the Exclaim window.

If you want to run a series of commands from Program Manager's File Run dialog box, Exclaim can run a command file. It can be a text file with a ! extension or a DOS batch file with a BAT extension.

For example, you might create a file called CLEANUP.! for the purpose of deleting files with a BAK extension. CLEANUP.! might look as follows:

```
DEL C:\WP\*.BAK
DEL C:\DOCS\*.BAK
```

If both Exclaim and this command file are on your DOS path, you can run these commands from Program Manager by clicking on File Run and typing the following:

**! CLEANUP**

You can also use Exclaim's CALL command to execute a series of statements. See "CALL" later in this chapter.

# Exclaim Files and Uninstall

Exclaim must be on your DOS path for you to start it by simply typing ! in a File Run dialog box. WSETUP installs the following Exclaim files into your Windows directory where they are automatically on the path:

!.DOC, !.EXE, !.FRM, !.HLP, and !.HST

If you prefer to keep these files in their own directory, you can move them to a C:\EXCLAIM directory (or any directory name) and then put that directory on your path. To add a directory to your path, open your C:\AUTOEXEC.BAT file in Notepad or another plain-text editor. Find the line that begins PATH= and add your Exclaim directory, followed by a semicolon. For example, the PATH= line might read as follows:

PATH=C:\EXCLAIM;C:\DOS;C:\WINDOWS;C:\

To uninstall Exclaim, delete the five files named previously, plus the !.INI file if you created one. Then remove the Exclaim group window from Program Manager by minimizing it and clicking on File Delete.

# Exclaim (!.EXE) Quick Reference Card

The following chart summarizes the commands available in Exclaim. Commands that do not exist in MS-DOS are shown in **BOLD.** For commands with several options, see the "Command Reference" section later in this chapter.

## Commands Available in Exclaim

| Command | Function |
|---|---|
| ? | Displays the available commands in Exclaim. |
| command /? | Any command, plus /?, displays Windows help text. |
| **ABOUT** | Displays information concerning Exclaim. |
| ATTRIB {setting} filename | Displays and optionally changes file attributes. See "ATTRIB." |
| **BEEP** | Causes the system speaker to beep. |
| CALL filename {parameters} | Processes commands from the specified file. See "CALL." |
| CD directory | Changes the current directory. |
| **CDD** x:\directory | Changes the current drive and directory. See "CDD." |
| CHDIR directory | Same as CD. |
| CLS | Clears the screen. |
| **COLOR** text-rgb background-rgb | Sets screen colors, using RGB values. See "COLOR." |
| COPY sourcefile {targetfile} | Copies one or more files to another location. |
| DATE {mm-dd-yy} | Displays or sets the date. |
| DEL filename {filename2 ...} | Deletes one or more sets of files. |
| DIR {/A} {/W} {directory or filename} | Lists the files in a directory. Accepts multiple filenames. /A=all files (including hidden files); /W=wide format. |
| **DISK** {x:} | Displays the status of a disk. |
| **DISPLAY** {text}{$_} | Displays text and meta-characters. See "DISPLAY." |
| ECHO {text} | Displays the current echo setting or text. See "DISPLAY." |
| ECHO ON or OFF | Turns the status of echo on or off. |
| ERASE filename {filename2 ...} | Same as DEL. |
| **ENV** | Displays the Exclaim environment settings. |
| **ENV** ! SAVE | Saves the Exclaim environment settings. |
| **ENV** DOS | Displays the DOS environment. |
| EXIT {WINDOWS} | Closes Exclaim and optionally starts the Windows exit routine. |
| GOTO label | Jumps to the specified label in a called file. |
| HELP {command} | Opens the Windows Help engine and displays Exclaim help. |
| **HISTORY** | Displays the last ten commands. |
| IF condition THEN ... ENDIF | Tests errorlevel, file existence, or string matching. See "IF condition THEN...ENDIF." |
| **LOAD** filename {parameters} | Starts a Windows or DOS program minimized. |
| MD {x:\}directory | Makes a directory. |

*(continued)*

## Commands Available in Exclaim (continued)

| Command | Function |
|---|---|
| MKDIR {x:\\}directory | Same as MD. |
| **MEMORY** | Displays a report of the system memory. |
| **MOVE** sourcefile {targetfile} | Copies files and then deletes source files (if possible). See "MOVE." |
| PATH | Displays the current DOS path. |
| PAUSE | Halts processing of commands until a key is pressed. |
| **PROFILE** section {filename} | Displays a section of WIN.INI or any INI file. See "PROFILE." |
| PROMPT {text}{$character} | Changes prompt; supports meta-characters. See "PROMPT." |
| RD {x:\\}directory | Removes an empty directory. |
| RMDIR {x:\\}directory | Same as RD. |
| REM {comment} | Nondisplayed comments; used for documentation purposes. |
| REN filename newname {/D} | Renames files; with /D, renames directories. See "REN and RENAME." |
| RENAME filename newname {/D} | Same as REN. |
| **RETURN** {END} | Exits a called file; with END, exits all called files. See "RETURN." |
| **TASK** | Displays names and handles of running applications. See "TASK." |
| **TASK** {action}{handle} | Performs action, such as Maximize, on the program with the specified handle. See "TASK." |
| TIME {hh:mm:ss.xx} | Displays or sets the time, to hundredths of a second. |
| TYPE filename {filename2 ...} | Displays one or more files as text on-screen. |
| VER | Displays DOS, Windows, and Exclaim versions. |
| VERIFY | Displays current Verify setting (with Verify On, DOS checks for bad disk sectors during Copy operations). |
| VERIFY ON or OFF | Turns the Verify setting on or off. |
| VOL {x:} | Displays a disk drive's volume label (name). |
| **Key Combinations** | **Function** |
| Esc | Aborts the current command. |
| Ctrl+S | Pauses (stops) a command. Press any key to restart. |
| *The following history keys may be redefined in the !.INI file:* | |
| Ctrl+E | Retrieves commands, from newest to oldest. |
| Ctrl+X | Retrieves commands, from oldest to newest. |
| Tab or Ctrl+I | Retrieves the latest command that begins with the characters you typed before pressing Tab. |

## !.INI _____

!.INI is a text file that, to be read by Exclaim, must reside in the same directory as !.EXE. The settings supported by !.INI are of the following form:

```
[!]
Owner=                        ; encoded name of owner
AutoTracking=TRUE             ; panning window tracks cursor
CheckBreak=TRUE               ; check for <Ctrl+C> or <Ctrl+Break>
IconName=color                ; color, gray or mono icon
Prompt=$p$g                   ; default prompt
TextColor=192 192 192         ; RGB values of text color
BackgroundColor=0 0 0         ; RGB values of background color
ScreenWidth=80                ; virtual text screen width
ScreenHeight=100              ; virtual text screen height
WindowTitle=EXCLAIM           ; title of window
HistoryDownKey=24             ; ASCII decimal value for Ctrl+X
HistoryUpKey=5                ; ASCII decimal value for Ctrl+E
HistorySearchKey=9            ; ASCII decimal value for Tab
```

The values shown are the defaults. Registered users are given an encoded string for the Owner variable, which results in the suppression of the registration requests. None of the variables are required, nor does a !.INI file need to exist.

Exclaim maintains a command history. You may scroll up one command to display the previous action by pressing Ctrl+E (ASCII decimal value 5). You may scroll down one command to start at the top of the command history (the earliest command) by pressing Ctrl+X (ASCII decimal value 24).

These key combinations are part of the well-known WordStar diamond keys, which move cursors in the WordStar word processor. You can change these key combinations by adding other values to !.INI. For example, Ctrl+A has an ASCII decimal value of 1, Ctrl+B has a value of 2, and so on. Note that Ctrl+I (ASCII value 9) has the same meaning as the DOS Tab key. ASCII value 9 (Tab) is used by Exclaim to retrieve the latest command that begins with any letters you type.

## Running External Applications _____

Both Windows and DOS applications may be started from the Exclaim prompt. However, you should ensure that the PIF file for a given DOS application does *not* close its window on exit if there is output that you care to view after the DOS program has terminated.

Files with the extension BAT are run by the operating system command processor (COMMAND.COM) in a separate window, unless you start a BAT file with the Exclaim CALL command.

Exclaim will run a filename that has an association in the [Extensions] section of WIN.INI (starting MYFILE.DOC, for example, might load the document into WordPerfect for Windows or Word for Windows, if such an association exists). But, if a given file extension does not have an association, trying to execute it will usually cause unpredictable results.

Exclaim internal commands are given priority over MS-DOS commands. For example, if you type **HELP ATTRIB** in Exclaim, you get a Windows Help window with information on ATTRIB, not DOS help text.

If a filename is entered with no extension (such as CLEANUP), Exclaim will look on the path for files with the extensions !, COM, EXE, and BAT, in that order.

# Keeping a Batch File Window Open

When you start a batch file in Exclaim (without using the CALL command), the batch file starts running in a separate window controlled by COMMAND.COM. After running, your batch file may disappear from sight if the _DEFAULT.PIF file that runs DOS sessions is set to Close Window On Exit.

To keep batch file windows open, you must change this setting or place the line COMMAND at the end of your batch file. Doing so makes the window remain on-screen after the batch file commands are completed. (Type **EXIT** and press Enter to close this window.)

# Running DOS Commands in a Separate Window

To run DOS commands in a separate DOS session, which remains open as long as you like (until you type **EXIT** to close it), type **COMMAND** in Exclaim. This command starts a new copy of COMMAND.COM, which runs any commands you type in the new window that appears.

For example, to run the DOS FORMAT A: command and keep the window open to watch its error messages (if any), you can type **COMMAND** in Exclaim to open a permanent DOS session. Then type **FORMAT A:** in that window, which remains open and displays all messages.

# Pipes and Redirection

Exclaim does not support the DOS pipe symbol ( | ) or the redirection symbols (< and >). Therefore, a statement such as TYPE FILENAME.TXT | MORE, which pipes the output of TYPE into the MORE filter, cannot be used in Exclaim. You can use the Ctrl+S keystroke combination to stop scrolling instead of using MORE.

You also cannot redirect the output of a command into a file or a printer with a statement such as TYPE FILENAME.TXT > LPT1. You can, however, accomplish this task without the redirection symbol by using a statement like COPY FILENAME.TXT LPT1.

# Virus Protection

If !.EXE detects that it has been modified in any way (such as by a virus), it will refuse to run.

# Command Reference

All Exclaim commands are described in the "Exclaim (!.EXE) Quick Reference Card" section, earlier in this chapter. Those commands that support multiple options, or have additional details, are described in this section.

## ATTRIB

ATTRIB displays and optionally changes file attributes. The syntax is as follows:

ATTRIB {settings} filename

The file attributes are as follows:

| | |
|---|---|
| +A | Archive attribute on |
| -A | Archive attribute off |
| +S | System attribute on |
| -S | System attribute off |
| +H | Hidden attribute on |
| -H | Hidden attribute off |
| +R | Read-only attribute on |
| -R | Read-only attribute off |

For example, the following command makes MYFILE.TXT read-only (so that it cannot be accidentally erased) and turns off the Archive attribute, which is used by backup programs:

    ATTRIB +R-A MYFILE.TXT

You may display, but not change, the attributes on any file that Windows has open if SHARE.EXE is loaded.

# CALL

CALL processes commands from a specified batch file, which causes the batch file to execute within the Exclaim window instead of starting a new session of COMMAND.COM. The syntax is as follows:

    CALL *filename {parameters}*

Within the called file, its own name is substituted for the DOS %0 variable. The variables %1 to %9 are replaced sequentially with any parameters supplied on the command line. Any parameter that begins with a slash (/) belongs to the CALL statement. Commands prefaced with an at symbol (@) will not be displayed. Calls may be nested up to four levels deep, with up to nine parameters per call.

For example, the following command might start a backup batch file and feed it a date parameter:

    CALL C:\BATCH\BACKUP.BAT 1-1-93

***Note:*** There is no default extension for the called file. A file with the extension ! may be typed at the command line without its extension or the command CALL. If a ! file is started without its extension from within another file, control will not return to the original location after completion of the ! file.

# CDD

CDD changes the current drive *and* directory. The syntax is as follows:

    CDD *x:\directory*

Exclaim supports implicit drive and directory changing, making CDD less necessary. If you type a valid drive and directory at the Exclaim command line, Exclaim changes the current drive and directory accordingly.

# COLOR

COLOR changes the text and background colors. The syntax is as follows:

COLOR *text-rgb background-rgb*

The RGB values are three integers that specify the relative intensities of red, green, and blue, respectively. These settings can range from 0 (minimum intensity) to 255 (maximum intensity). Entering **COLOR** with no arguments sets the colors to the default values (light gray text on a black background).

Some combinations of the background RGB values result in a dithered rather than a pure color, causing an undesirable effect during window scrolling. By manually resizing the window height, you can avoid this condition.

You can determine the RGB values by opening the Windows Control Panel, double-clicking on the Color icon, and then clicking on Color Palette and Define Custom Colors. In this dialog box, Exclaim uses the same numbers to define colors as Windows does.

Some common colors and their RGB values follow:

| Color | Full Intensity | Half Intensity |
|---|---|---|
| Red | 255 0 0 | 128 0 0 |
| Yellow | 255 255 0 | 128 128 0 |
| Green | 0 255 0 | 0 128 0 |
| Cyan | 0 255 255 | 0 128 128 |
| Blue | 0 0 255 | 0 0 128 |
| Purple | 255 0 255 | 128 0 128 |
| White | 255 255 255 | 192 192 192 (Light Gray) |
| Black | 0 0 0 | 128 128 128 (Dark Gray) |

# DISPLAY

DISPLAY serves a similar function to the ECHO command in DOS. However, DISPLAY places text on-screen from a command file without assuming that you want a carriage return at the end of each line. DISPLAY also supports numerous meta-characters (such as $D for the current date). These meta-characters enable you to define messages that are not possible with ECHO.

The syntax is as follows:

DISPLAY {*text*}{$*character*}

The command DISPLAY $_ outputs a blank line. The dollar sign followed by an underscore outputs a carriage-return line-feed combination.

For example, to display a message with the date and time and the words *Remember to back up.* on a separate line, use this command:

DISPLAY $D $T$_$_Remember to back up.$_

See "PROMPT" later in this chapter for a full list of the meta-characters DISPLAY supports.

# ECHO

The use of DISPLAY is recommended over ECHO to output text to the screen in a command file. DISPLAY supports many more options than ECHO.

# IF *condition* THEN ... ENDIF

The IF structure provides conditional execution of statements in command files. An IF statement in Exclaim can execute several lines, as opposed to the IF statement in DOS, which can execute only one.

The syntax is as follows:

IF *condition* THEN
*statement1*
*statement2*
...
ENDIF

Valid conditions are as follows:

ERRORLEVEL *value*
EXIST *filename or directory*
*string1 operator string2*

Valid operators for string comparisons are as follows:

| | |
|---|---|
| EQ | strings are equal |
| NE | strings are not equal |
| LT | string1 is less than string2 (in ASCII value) |
| LE | string1 is less than or equal to string2 |
| GT | string1 is greater than string2 |
| GE | string1 is greater than or equal to string2 |

*Note:* Only Exclaim internal commands return an errorlevel to Exclaim. IF ERRORLEVEL *value* always tests whether the errorlevel is *equal to or greater than* the value specified.

Exclaim can perform string comparisons on DOS environmental variables or compare parameters with known strings. For example, you can determine whether a command file DOBAK.! was started with the parameter C:\BACKUP and, if it was, delete *.BAK files in that directory by using the following commands:

```
IF "%1" EQ "C:\BACKUP" THEN
DEL C:\BACKUP\*.BAK
ENDIF
```

Unlike those in DOS, Exclaim IF string comparisons are not case sensitive. Therefore, you need to test "%1" against "C:\BACKUP" only once — not against every possible combination of C:\BACKUP in uppercase and lowercase. The quotation marks (") are necessary in string comparisons in case a parameter is blank, which would cause an error.

# MOVE

MOVE copies one or more files to another location. The source files are deleted, if possible (for example, they might be read-only or on a write-protected diskette).

The syntax is as follows:

MOVE *sourcefile* {*targetfile*}

*Note:* To move files from one directory to another on the same drive, it's faster to use the REN or RENAME command, which can rename files into different directories (thereby moving them).

# PROFILE

PROFILE displays a section of an initialization (*.INI) file. The syntax is as follows:

PROFILE *section* {*filename*}

WIN.INI is searched if no filename is specified. The path is searched for any filename you specify, unless you override the path by including a drive or directory in the filename.

# PROMPT

PROMPT changes the Exclaim command line prompt. The syntax is as follows:

PROMPT {*text*}{$*character*}

PROMPT and DISPLAY support the following meta-characters:

| | |
|---|---|
| $$ | the literal $ character |
| $_ | carriage-return line-feed (new line) |
| $b | the vertical-bar ( | ) character |
| $! | the Exclaim version number |
| $d | the current date |
| $e | the Escape character |
| $g | the greater-than (>) character |
| $h | a backspace |
| $l | the less-than (<) character |
| $n | the current drive |
| $p | the current drive and directory (the current path) |
| $q | the equal-sign (=) character |
| $t | the current time |
| $v | the DOS version number |
| $w | the Windows version number |

For example, you can display the date, time, and current path in a prompt — and also hide the seconds and hundredths of seconds in the time by backspacing over them — as follows:

PROMPT $D, $T$H$H$H$H$H$H $P$G

The prompt would look like this:

Fri 1-1-93, 12:00 C:\>

Entering **PROMPT** with no arguments resets the prompt to $P$G (the current path and a greater-than symbol).

# REN and RENAME

REN and RENAME can rename files to another directory, as long as the old directory and the new directory are on the same drive. The syntax is as follows:

REN *filename newname*

For example, you can move all your old *.DOC document files from C:\DOCS to C:\SAVE with the following command:

REN C:\DOCS\*.DOC C:\SAVE\*.OLD

To move files to a different drive, use the MOVE command.

You may not rename any file that Windows has open if SHARE.EXE is loaded.

## RETURN

RETURN exits a called file. The syntax is as follows:

    RETURN {END}

If RETURN has no parameters, only the currently called file is terminated, not all files called from the original command file.

## TASK

TASK performs actions, such as Maximize, on a specified program. The syntax is as follows:

    TASK {*action*} {*handle*}

The possible actions are ACTIVATE, CLOSE, MAX, MIN, and RESTORE.

TASK performs the requested action on the task referenced with the specified handle as returned when you're running external applications (described in the "Running External Applications" section, earlier in this chapter) or using the LOAD command.

*Note:* If no parameters to TASK are given, the names and handles of all the currently loaded tasks are displayed. If no handle is given, the action is applied to the Exclaim window.

# Registration

## Why register?

The main reason you should purchase any program is that doing so is ethical: Not registering is an abuse of the shareware concept. In the long run, nonregistration will cause this method of distribution to disappear. Exclaim represents a big investment of the author's time and money; therefore, the author expects compensation if you use Exclaim beyond the trial period. You need to register only once for all 1.*x* versions of Exclaim.

# Shareware notice and disclaimer

! 1.21

# Order form

All lines of this form must be completed in full in order to process your order. *You must register each copy of ! that is used on your site. (One copy may not be used on multiple machines.)* Please make checks or money orders payable to Terratech and remit to

**Terratech**
19817 61st Ave. S.E.
Snohomish, WA 98290

! REGISTRATION FEE:

Registration with no disk
Quantity:_____ copies at $20.00 (U.S.) per copy: _____

Registration with 5 ¼-inch disk
Quantity:_____ copies at $25.00 (U.S.) per copy: _____

Registration with 3 ½-inch disk
Quantity:_____ copies at $25.00 (U.S.) per copy: _____

SUBTOTAL: _____

Washington State residents add 7.6% sales tax: _____

TOTAL: _____

Purchaser's name and shipping address:

_____

_____

_____

Authorized representative/contact and title (if business):

_____

Telephone (specify day and evening numbers):

_____

*continued*

Purchaser understands that ! is provided as is and without warranty of any kind, either express or implied. Purchaser warrants that each copy will be used on only one machine and that purchaser's copy will not be made available to any third parties.

Purchaser's printed name: _____

Signature: _____

Date: _____

A registered version will be sent to you on disk. You are encouraged to use the following guidelines for copying this program.

*NOTICE:* Users of this program are granted a limited license to make copies of this program for trial use by others on a private noncommercial basis. This limited license does *not* include

1. Distributing this program in connection with any other product without written permission from Terratech

2. Making the program available for any consideration other than a minimal "disk fee"

3. Distributing the program in modified form

TERRATECH DISCLAIMS ALL WARRANTIES, EITHER EXPRESS OR IMPLIED, INCLUDING BUT NOT LIMITED TO IMPLIED WARRANTIES OF MERCHANT ABILITY AND FITNESS FOR A PARTICULAR PURPOSE, WITH RESPECT TO THE PRODUCT. SHOULD THE PROGRAM PROVE DEFECTIVE, THE PURCHASER ASSUMES THE RISK OF PAYING THE ENTIRE COST OF ALL NECESSARY SERVIC-ING, REPAIR, OR CORRECTION AND ANY INCIDENTAL OR CONSEQUENTIAL DAMAGES. IN NO EVENT WILL TERRATECH BE LIABLE FOR ANY DAMAGES WHATSOEVER (INCLUDING WITHOUT LIMITATION DAMAGES FOR LOSS OF BUSINESS PROFITS, BUSINESS INTERRUPTION, LOSS OF BUSINESS INFORMA-TION, AND THE LIKE) ARISING OUT OF THE USE OR THE INABILITY TO USE THIS PRODUCT EVEN IF TERRATECH HAS BEEN ADVISED OF THE POSSIBILITY OF SUCH DAMAGES.

# File Garbage Can for Windows

Version 10/2/92
Copyright © by Denam Systems

*W*hen DOS or Windows deletes a file, it doesn't actually remove the contents of the file from your disk. Instead, the file is marked for deletion and disappears from your directory listings. But the data does not actually change until some other file is written to the same sector of the disk by coincidence.

This fact has spawned a widely available group of utilities that can "undelete" files on your disk. These utilities are helpful when you have accidentally deleted a file, but they also pose a risk: Anyone with an undelete utility can read disk files you thought were safely erased.

File Garbage Can gives you total peace of mind when you want to ensure that no one can find old, deleted versions of your confidential financial reports, personnel records, or whatever. Simply start File Garbage Can, select a filename, and erase it. The file is deleted and overwritten with a pattern of ones and zeros, making it impossible for anyone to delve into your private documents.

Because this type of erasure cannot be undone, File Garbage Can does not erase multiple files or directories; you must deliberately select the filename to erase. That's why it's called File Garbage Can.

File Garbage Can comes in two versions: GARBAGE0.EXE for Windows 3.0 and GARBAGE1.EXE for Windows 3.1. The only difference is that GARBAGE1.EXE enables you to drag a filename from File Manager and drop it on File Garbage Can's icon to delete it. If you don't want the possibility of accidentally dropping something on GARBAGE1.EXE's icon, run GARBAGE0.EXE under Windows 3.1 instead. (GARBAGE1.EXE won't run under Windows 3.0, however.)

Dennis Fischer, the author of the program, is a bit of a Latin buff. You may run into dialog boxes with OK buttons that say Ave Atque Vale *(Hail and Farewell)* or Finem Respice *(Consider The End)*.

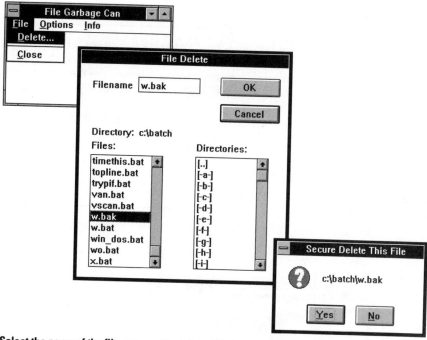

Select the name of the file you want to delete; File Garbage Can deletes the file and overwrites its space on the disk to make sure that it cannot be undeleted.

| | |
|---|---|
| **Type of Program:** | Utility |
| **Requires:** | Windows 3.0 or later (GARBAGE0.EXE). Windows 3.1 or later (GARBAGE1.EXE). Do not run GARBAGE1.EXE under Windows 3.0. |
| **Registration:** | Use the form at the end of this chapter to register with the shareware author. |
| **Technical Support:** | Denam Systems provides registered users with technical support by mail and CompuServe. |
| **Similar Shareware:** | For a utility that enables you to drag one or more files from the File Manager to a trash can icon — but does not securely erase them so they can't be undeleted — use Trash Can for Windows, a program featured in *Windows 3.1 SECRETS,* published by IDG Books Worldwide. |

# Overview

Ordinary DOS and Windows file-delete actions are *not* secure. The file is merely marked as deleted, but the data in the file is still sitting on the disk. Any undelete program or disk-scan program can read the data on the disk. The file remains insecure until another file happens to overwrite the disk area.

File Garbage Can takes care of the security problem that occurs with an ordinary file delete. We *guarantee* that the deleted file *cannot* be recovered.

# Options

You can select the program options from the menu or by using command line options. The options are as follows:

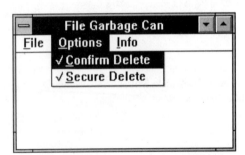

The Options menu provides a pair of options that control whether you are prompted to confirm the delete and whether the deleted file's disk location is overwritten.

## Confirm Delete (turned on by default)

A dialog box will appear before the file is deleted. You will be asked to confirm that you want the file deleted. When this option is turned off, the file will be deleted without confirmation.

## Secure Delete (turned on by default)

By default, File Garbage Can deletes a file and overwrites the file area on disk. When this option is turned off, an ordinary DOS file delete will be done. This can save a considerable amount of time in a large file, but, of course, you give up the security.

# Command Line Options

-C   Turns the Confirm Delete option off

-S   Turns the Secure Delete option off

-I   Starts the program minimized (as an icon)

You can add these options to the command line in any order or fashion. For example, GARBAGE -CS turns the Confirm Delete and Secure Delete options off.

# Shareware

File Garbage Can is distributed as shareware. As such, you have a chance to review the program to determine whether it fits your needs. This does *not* mean the program is free. You are expected to pay the small fee to register your program if you continue to use it.

## *Caveat emptor* (Let the buyer beware)

Neither Denam Systems nor the author(s) of this program are liable or responsible to the purchaser or user for loss or damage caused, or alleged to be caused, directly or indirectly by the software and its attendant documentation, including (but not limited to) loss of software, interruption of service, loss of business, or anticipatory profits.

## *Cetera desunt* (The rest is missing)

You're right. There are a number of things that could be added to this program. Why don't you send us your suggestions and ideas? We'll see whether we can add them. We can be contacted at

**Denam Systems**
1115 Madison St. NE, Suite 226
Salem, Oregon 97303
CompuServe: 70405,1422

## Order form

Name: _____

Address: _____

_____

_____

Contact Individual: _____

_____

| Quantity of Units | Unit Price |
|---|---|
| 1 – 5 | $5.00 |
| 6 – 10 | $4.75 |
| 11 – 15 | $4.50 |
| 16+ | $4.25 |
| Site License (SL) | Agreed price |

| Qty. | | Unit Price | Total |
|---|---|---|---|
| ____ Garbage Can Software | × | _____ | = _____ |

Note that File Garbage Can software has been delivered and accepted by the customer.

# GrpIcon 2.0

**GRPICON.EXE — Version 2.0**
**Copyright © by Inner-City Software**

---

*GrpIcon (Group Icon) solves a nagging problem in both Windows 3.0 and Windows 3.1. The Program Manager in both Windows versions supports numerous group windows. But, after you've minimized several of these group windows, their icons all look the same!*

*GrpIcon enables you to customize each of your Program Manager group windows. Doing so can help you remember the purpose of each one — or just entertain you when you need a smile. With GrpIcon, you can customize the icon, font, background color, and wallpaper used by group windows.*

*When you first run GrpIcon, you are presented with a dialog box that may be surprising: There is no OK or Cancel button. Simply click on the GO button to load GrpIcon temporarily so that you can see its effect in the Document Control icon of each Program Manager group window. To disable GrpIcon, run it again and click on Close from the System menu of the icon that appears.*

| | |
|---|---|
| **Type of Program:** | Utility |
| **Requires:** | Windows 3.0 or later |
| **Registration:** | Use the form at the end of this chapter to register with the shareware author. |
| **Technical Support:** | Inner-City Software provides technical support to registered users by mail, telephone, fax, and a bulletin board system. |

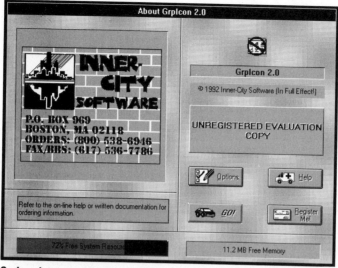

**GrpIcon lets you customize the Program Manager group windows so that there's a difference among them when they're minimized.**

# Overview

GrpIcon is a simple little utility for Microsoft Windows 3.x that enables you to visually customize your Windows Program Manager. GrpIcon associates icons with your program groups to replace the default Group Icon, which all groups otherwise display. The customized icons make the Windows Program Manager easier to use, especially if you have many Program Manager groups. GrpIcon reads icons from just about any Windows file that can contain icons, including files with the extensions ICO, EXE, DLL, DRV, IL, NIL, and ICL.

# Starting GrpIcon

To start GrpIcon, do one of the following:

- ♦ Double-click on the GrpIcon icon.
- ♦ Highlight the GrpIcon icon and press Enter.
- ♦ Select File Run and type *x:\directory\***GRPICON** in the dialog box.

GrpIcon is now active and running in hidden mode.

# Using GrpIcon 2.0

After successfully completing installation, you can start GrpIcon as previously described. Unless you change the visibility option, GrpIcon does not show an icon when it is running. You can change the visibility option by running a second instance of GrpIcon. To hide the visible GrpIcon icon, select Hide from the control menu. The dialog controls in GrpIcon are standard Windows 3.1 Common Dialog Controls, described in your *Windows User's Guide.* Please refer to it if you need assistance in navigating the dialog-box controls.

## Modifying options

To view or modify options, select About GrpIcon from the Group Properties menu. The dialog box contains various options that enable setup modification, as well as options to change icon size and fonts.

## Changing start-up configurations

To change start-up options, font, or icon size in the Group Properties menu, select the Options button on the dialog box by clicking on it with the mouse or by using the Tab key to select it and then pressing Enter. The dialog box now shows list boxes to select font style and size and check boxes to enable changes to the start-up configuration.

If you want to start GrpIcon on Windows start-up, check the start-up option box either by clicking on it with the mouse or by using Tab+spacebar to select it.

## Changing the Group Properties menu fonts

The option dialog box also features options to change the appearance of the font style and icon size in the Group Properties menu. (This changes the font and icons in this menu *only*; it has no effect on any other fonts or icons.)

To change font style or size, click on the Font button with the mouse or use Tab+spacebar to select the Font button.

A character dialog box will appear. View and select your font style and size from this box.

## Changing the Group Properties menu icon size

To change the icon size in the Group Properties menu, click on the icon list box or use Tab+spacebar to select it. You have a choice of large icons, small icons, or no icons.

## On-line Help

You can access on-line Help by selecting the Help button. If this button appears grayed after installation, check the path of the GRPICON.HLP file. It should be in the directory in which GrpIcon was installed.

## Registration

The registration button enables you to print the registration form. For registration information, refer to "Registering GrpIcon," later in this chapter.

## GO

The GO button enables you to run GrpIcon after installation. Changes immediately take place; there is no need for you to restart Windows. After the GO button is pressed, the option window closes.

# Customizing Program Manager Groups

## Assigning group icons

To customize your Program Manager Group icons, follow these steps:

1. Click once on the system box in the upper left corner of any Program Manager group window; alternatively, use the keyboard and press Alt+spacebar. This action will open the group's system menu.

2. Notice that a menu option called Group Properties… has been added to the system menu. Select the Group Properties… option.

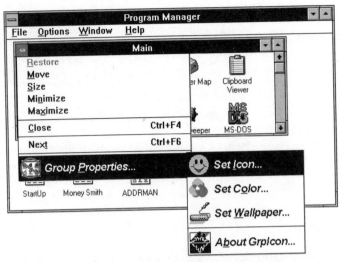

To use GrpIcon to customize Program Manager groups, click on the
system box in any group window and select the new Group Properties...
command; the Group Properties menu appears.

3. The options for the Group Properties menu are Set Icon..., Set Color..., Set
   Wallpaper..., and About GrpIcon.... Select Set Icon....

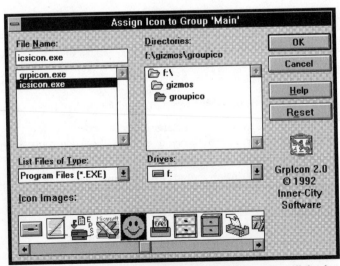

After you select Set Icon... from the Group Properties menu, a dialog box
appears that enables you to select the icon you want to assign to a group
window.

4. The Assign Icon to Group dialog box will appear. The list box entitled File Name lists files in the current directory. Use the mouse to navigate the directory structure in the Directories list box. (Use the Tab key to move within the dialog box if you are using the keyboard.)

   The Inner-City Icon Library (ICSICON.EXE), when opened, enables you to change the group icon of a minimized group by dragging and dropping.

5. When a file is highlighted in the Files list box, and the file contains icons, the icons appear in the icon viewer at the bottom of the dialog box. Some file formats may contain several icons. EXE and DLL files generally have icons embedded in them. GrpIcon comes with a library of icons stored in ICSICON.EXE (installed with GrpIcon).

6. Use the scroll bar on the icon viewer to search forward or backward for other icons, if necessary. When using the keyboard, use the Tab key to move within the dialog box and select icons by using the arrow keys, if necessary.

7. When a suitable icon is selected, close the dialog box by clicking on OK or pressing Enter. The selected icon is immediately assigned to the active Program Manager group. If you close the dialog box by pressing the Esc key or clicking on the Cancel button, no changes are made to the group. Do not press the Reset button.

8. Perform the preceding steps for each group whose icons you want to customize.

**The Main group is now represented by a smiley-face icon.**

## Setting wallpaper backgrounds

To set wallpaper backgrounds for Program Manager groups, follow these steps:

1. Select the group to which the wallpaper is to be assigned; from the system menu, select Group Properties…. (Press Alt+spacebar if you are using the keyboard.)

2. Select the Set Wallpaper… option; the Set Wallpaper dialog box appears.

3. To select the bitmap to be used, locate the bitmap filename in the File list box. (GrpIcon can install bitmaps from the Windows directory.) Using the mouse, click on the desired bitmap and then on OK. Or use Tab and the arrow keys to select the bitmap and then press Enter.

4. When a bitmap is highlighted in the Files list box, it also appears in the bitmap Images viewer at the bottom of the dialog box. The Tile bitmap option permits the bitmapped image to be tiled over the entire window background.

5. When a suitable bitmap is selected, click on OK or press Enter. This action immediately assigns the bitmap to the group and closes the dialog box.

6. Perform the preceding steps for each group you want to customize with a wallpaper.

To use GrpIcon to set wallpaper backgrounds, click on the system box in the group's window, select the Group Properties… command, and select Set Wallpaper….

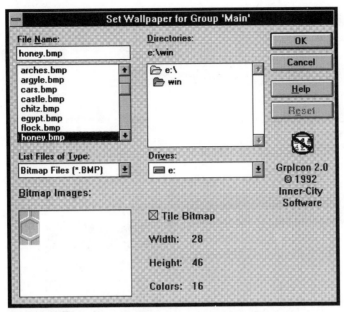

The Set Wallpaper dialog box lets you select bitmap files to use as wallpaper in group windows.

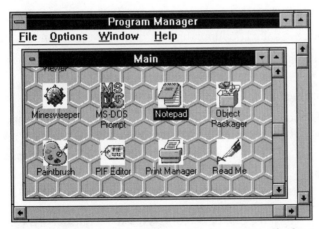

The wallpaper for the Main group window is now customized to a honeycomb pattern.

## Changing background colors in group windows

To assign background colors to Program Manager groups, follow these steps:

1. Select the group for which the background color is to be assigned; from the system menu, select Group Properties....

To use GrpIcon to set background colors, click on the system box in the group's window, select the Group Properties... command, and select Set Color....

2. Select the Set Color... option; the Set Color dialog box appears.

3. Select the background color for the group window. You may select a background color from the existing palette or create a custom color.

4. To create custom colors, do one of the following:

   Using the mouse, drag the color-refiner cursor in the color-definer box until the desired color appears in the Color/Solid box.

   Using the keyboard, type values in the Red, Green, and Blue boxes or in the Hue, Sat, and Lum boxes.

5. When you have the desired color, click on the Add to Custom Colors button. (If you are using the keyboard, press Tab+spacebar.) The new color will appear in one of the Custom Colors boxes at the bottom of the dialog box.

6. Select the color by clicking on its box or by pressing Tab to move to the box and then pressing the spacebar.

7. When the color is selected, click on OK or press Enter. This action immediately assigns the color to the group and closes the dialog box.

8. Perform the preceding steps for each group to which you want to assign background colors.

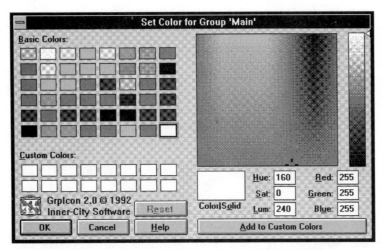

The **Set Color** dialog box lets you select an existing background color or create a customized color.

# Looking at the Inner-City Software Icon Library

The Inner-City Icon Library is a file containing a number of icons that can be used as program icons. When the icon library is open, it enables you to replace icons by using the Windows drag-and-drop function. This function can only be performed with the use of the mouse. The icon library is installed in the GrpIcon program group during installation.

To use the ICS Icon Library, follow these steps:

1. Open the Program Manager group for GrpIcon. Using the mouse, double-click on the ICS Icon Library icon.

2. Select the icon you want to use.

3. Click and hold the mouse button while dragging the icon over the program group you want to assign to it.

4. Release the mouse button; the icon is immediately assigned.

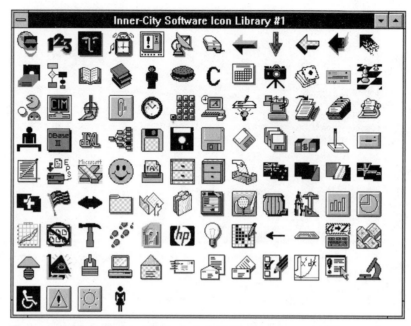

The Inner-City Software Icon Library, included with the program, provides many icons you can assign to Program Manager groups.

# Registering GrpIcon

## How to register

GrpIcon is distributed by way of BBSs and other channels in Demonstration mode. *Demonstration mode* enables you to evaluate the complete program without any limitation of features so that you can make an informed decision about whether or not you will purchase GrpIcon. If you purchase GrpIcon, you receive a registration number that places the program in *Operating mode.* The only difference between the two modes is that when GrpIcon is operating as a demo, it reminds you every now and then that it is running. (It was discovered during our Beta Test cycle that the enhancement GrpIcon provides is so natural and common-sense oriented that people tend to forget that GrpIcon is there!)

Purchasing and registering GrpIcon costs only $20.00 in U.S. currency. Checks and money orders should be sent to

**Inner-City Software**
P.O. Box 969
Boston, MA 02118-0969

Registration will entitle you to free technical support, upgrades, and discounts on other Inner-City Software products.

## GrpIcon 2.0 registration form

To register your copy of GrpIcon, print and fill out this form. Send this form and a check or money order for $20.00 (in U.S. funds) to Inner-City Software at this address:

**Inner-City Software**
P.O. Box 969
Boston, MA 02118-0969

Name: _____

Address: _____

City: _____ State: _____ ZIP: _____

Telephone(s): _____

Occupation: _____

Let us know where you got GrpIcon (please be specific):

_____

Let us know what you think of GrpIcon:

_____

# About Inner-City Software

## Who we are

Inner-City Software is a small-time outfit that wants to grow up into a large small-time outfit.

What we mean is that although we want to get big enough so everyone in the world will use our stuff someday, we don't want to lose the informality and fun style of the basement programmer's shop that we enjoy today. The name *Inner-City Software* is designed to let you know that this product came to you straight outta the 'hood. All the people who made this happen are products of various inner-city, predominantly Black neighborhoods throughout the U.S.A. The reason for making this type of statement is twofold: For those who do not live in the 'hood, we want you to know that there is a lot of positive creativity and downright genius in the 'hood. Just don't expect to read about it in your newspaper (positive news doesn't sell papers). For those who *are* in the 'hood, we want to be an inspiration and provide encouragement for continued learning and teaching and reaching, because it *is* true that you can do whatever you set your mind to. Don't believe the hype that tells you otherwise!

## Other Inner-City Software product offerings

As of the date of this release, GrpIcon is the only released product bearing the Inner-City Software name. Last year, we did NoDOS (the DOS Icon Eliminator), but we sold that product to someone else. Oh, yeah, we also have a couple of freebie programs out there, like the (I'll Be Back) Terminator that talks to you, the Windows 3.1 Control Panel Applet for After Dark, and PFBFix, a font utility we did last year. But GrpIcon is really it right now. We are about halfway through with a *wonderful* set of utilities that will complement GrpIcon and make life with Windows even more simple, fun, and useful. Stay tuned for further details.

## Product catalog

There ain't one yet. When there is, you'll get it in the mail if you are a registered user of any Inner-City Software product.

## Mailing list

Whenever a new product comes out, we will drop you a line if you have registered anything with us. It is not really economically feasible to send out letters for upgrades to $20 packages, but if we get our act together and put out some higher ticket stuff, then we can afford to send out letters for everything!

## Inner-City Software's mission and how U can help

Inner-City Software is committed to developing profitable, hi-tech, computer-based businesses within the inner-city communities of America. At this time, the development and marketing of computer software programs is our primary vehicle for achieving this mission. Our short-term game plan is to penetrate the market with our existing products and then to expand our operation to provide training in computer programming and literacy from the junior-high-school level on up. We believe in self-determination and are confident that people will do for themselves and break the vicious cycles of dependency that have developed in our inner-city communities if and only if the following things happen:

1. They are convinced that they do have a chance to be somebody.

2. They have access to role models of success with whom they can identify.

3. They are encouraged by persons they respect to work toward self-dependency.

4. They are given tools and techniques that they can use to become independent.

5. They have a support system to help keep them on track and counter-balance the negative society in which we live.

Our goal is to eventually provide all these benefits to whomever chooses to work with us.

To achieve our short-term goals, we need to complete the two dozen or so product ideas that are under development or still on the drawing board, and we need to get these ideas out as soon as possible. For this to happen, we need to be able to work on these projects 24 hours a day instead of just evenings and weekends, as is the present case. In other words, we need to secure adequate financing to support a couple of programmers and a clerical/marketing person. To that end, we are working on a formal business plan, targeted for completion by June 1993. For a first round of financing, we will be soliciting a relatively small amount of money to be used primarily to cover living expenses while we work on developing a market presence in the computer software industry. If you or someone you know is curious about the possibility of investing in Inner-City Software, please contact Kenny G. at 800-538-6946 anytime. Together, we can become part of the solution. Peace.

## Credits

The following persons contributed directly to the Inner-City Software product that you are using right now:

| Who | What |
| --- | --- |
| Kenny G. | Product concept and program coding and debugging |
| MC Darryl D | Coding assistance on several app and DLL routines |
| Isis | Clerical and moral support and good ideas |
| Michele Brooks & Kulaj Enterprises | Windows Help and the manual |
| Hi-Fi Rick, Howie, Patrick, Ted, and Jim | Beta testing and suggestions |

## Acknowledgments and thanks

I would like to thank the following persons and organizations that have been helpful in some way or another in making this product and Inner-City Software a reality:

| *Thanks To* | *For* |
|---|---|
| Blaise Computing | Providing the basis for the ICS Custom Controls; they are based on the Blaise Windows Control Palette library |
| Eric Granderson | Introducing me to the Science of Personal Achievement |
| Kappa Alpha Psi Fraternity | Yo |
| Marcus Garvey, The Honorable Elijah Muhammad, Napoleon Hill, Martin Luther King Jr., El-Hajj Malik El-Shabazz | Their lives' work |
| Microsoft Developer Support | Sample source code |
| Mike Neumann | Constant encouragement and negotiations with our first corporate client |
| Mom and Dad | Good raising and all the support and encouragement |
| The Captain | Positive energy, kindred spirit, and business-plan assistance |
| The Honorable Louis Farrakhan and the Nation of Islam | Continuous wake-up calls and reminders of the condition of the have-nots of America |

And, of course, I want to thank you for using this program, whether you register it or not. The mere fact that you like the program and continue to use it is an affirmation of the marketability of my ideas. If there was something missing in the program that caused you to decide not to register it, you thought it was not worth registering, or whatever, please feel free to call toll-free at 800-538-6946 with your comments or suggestions. Your feedback will help make the next Inner-City Software product better, and maybe I will get you to kick out the cash next time!

Peace.

*— Kenny G.*

# Software License

GrpIcon is not and has never been public-domain software, nor is it free software.

Nonlicensed users are granted a limited license to use GrpIcon on a 14-day trial basis for the purpose of determining whether GrpIcon is suitable for their needs. The use of GrpIcon, except for the initial 14-day trial, requires registration. The use of unlicensed copies of GrpIcon, outside of the initial 14-day trial, by any person, business, corporation, government agency, or any other entity is strictly prohibited.

A single-user license permits a user to use GrpIcon only on a single computer. Licensed users may use the program on different computers but may not use the program on more than one computer at the same time.

No one may modify or patch the GrpIcon executable files in any way, including but not limited to decompiling, disassembling, or otherwise reverse-engineering the program.

A limited license is granted to copy and distribute GrpIcon only for the trial use of others, subject to the preceding limitations and also the following:

1. GrpIcon must be copied in unmodified form, complete with the file containing this license information.

2. The full machine-readable GrpIcon documentation must be included with each copy.

3. GrpIcon may not be distributed in conjunction with any other product without a specific license to do so from Inner-City Software.

4. No fee, charge, or other compensation may be requested or accepted, except as authorized as follows:

5. Operators of electronic bulletin board systems (sysops) may make GrpIcon available for downloading only as long as the preceding conditions are met. An overall or time-dependent charge for the use of the bulletin board system is permitted as long as there is not a specific charge for the download of GrpIcon.

6. Software vendors may distribute GrpIcon but only after obtaining written permission from Inner-City Software. Such permission is usually granted. Please write for details (enclose your catalog). Vendors may charge a disk-duplication and handling fee, which may not exceed five dollars.

7. Nonprofit user groups may distribute copies of the GrpIcon files to their members, subject to the preceding conditions, without specific permission. Nonprofit groups may collect a disk-duplication fee not to exceed five dollars.

EXCEPT AS PROVIDED ABOVE, INNER-CITY SOFTWARE DISCLAIMS ALL WAR-RANTIES, EITHER EXPRESS OR IMPLIED, INCLUDING BUT NOT LIMITED TO IMPLIED WARRANTIES OF MERCHANTABILITY AND FITNESS FOR A PARTICU-LAR PURPOSE, WITH RESPECT TO THE PRODUCT. SHOULD THE PROGRAM PROVE DEFECTIVE, THE PURCHASER ASSUMES THE RISK OF PAYING THE EN-TIRE COST OF ALL NECESSARY SERVICING, REPAIR, OR CORRECTION AND ANY INCIDENTAL OR CONSEQUENTIAL DAMAGES. IN NO EVENT WILL INNER-CITY SOFTWARE BE LIABLE FOR ANY DAMAGES WHATSOEVER (INCLUDING WITHOUT LIMITATION DAMAGES FOR LOSS OF BUSINESS PROFITS, BUSINESS INTERRUPTION, LOSS OF BUSINESS INFORMATION, AND THE LIKE) ARISING OUT OF THE USE OR THE INABILITY TO USE THIS PRODUCT EVEN IF INNER-CITY SOFTWARE HAS BEEN ADVISED OF THE POSSIBILITY OF SUCH DAMAGES.

Use of this product for any period of time constitutes your acceptance of this agreement and subjects you to its contents.

### U.S. GOVERNMENT RESTRICTED RIGHTS

Use, duplication, or disclosure by the Government is subject to restrictions as set forth in subdivision (b)(3)(ii) of the Rights in Technical Data and Computer Software clause at 252.227-7013. Contractor/manufacturer is Inner-City Software, P.O. Box 969, Boston, MA 02118.

### TRADEMARKS

Windows is a trademark of Microsoft Corporation.

Grplcon is a trademark of Inner-City Software.

# Glossary of Terms _____

**Background Colors.** Colors displayed in window backgrounds or on the desktop.

**Custom Colors.** An option that enables you to modify colors to be used as background colors.

**Group Icon.** The icon that represents a group in Program Manager when the group window is minimized.

**Group Properties.** An option added to the Control menu by Grplcon. The Group Properties menu contains options for changing icons and setting colors and wallpaper, as well as modifying start-up configurations.

**Group Properties Menu Fonts.** The fonts that appear in the Group Properties menu can be modified with the use of the Font option in the Options dialog box.

**Group Properties Menu Icon Size.** The Options dialog box has an option that changes the size of icons or eliminates icons in the Group Properties menu.

**Icon Library.** This file contains a number of icons and enables the assignment of icons using the drag-and-drop function.

**Icon Viewer.** Enables you to view an icon before assigning it to a Program Manager group.

**Reset.** Reverts icons, background colors, and wallpaper to Program Manager defaults.

**Set Color.** A menu option that enables you to change the background colors of Program Manager group windows.

**Set Icon.** An option that enables you to set an icon for a Program Manager group.

**Set Wallpaper.** A menu option that enables you to display a background bitmapped image in Program Manager windows.

**Startup Configurations.** An option that enables you to select how and when GrpIcon will start.

**Test Drive.** An option that closes the About dialog box.

**Tile Option.** Enables bitmapped images to be tiled to cover the group window background.

**Visibility Option.** Enables you the option to have the GrpIcon icon visible while it is running.

**Wallpaper.** A bitmapped image displayed in the window or desktop background.

# Hearts for Windows

### Version 1.2
### Copyright © by Paul Pedriana

*We often play a round of Hearts with our niece, Aimeé, and we've always thought of it as a nice family game.*

*But there are card sharps who play Hearts for blood or even for money! In these games, we're told, it's considered part of the game to make rude comments on your opponents' latest blunder or misfortune.*

*Hearts for Windows should satisfy both kinds of players. You, the human, play against three opponents generated by the computer. These players are some tough competitors, and they sound off with some very personal rude comments. But you can adjust the strength of the other players and turn off the repartee, if you like.*

*Hearts is unusual among Windows programs in that it uses both the left and right mouse buttons. You select cards with the left mouse button (as when you are picking three cards to pass). You actually play a card with the right mouse button.*

*Hearts for Windows is another one of those addictive card games — but, unlike Solitaire, there's quite a bit of skill involved. Enjoy!*

| | |
|---|---|
| **Type of Program:** | Game |
| **Requires:** | Windows 3.0 or later |
| **Registration:** | Use the form at the end of this chapter to register with the shareware author. Registered users receive a version with additional features. |
| **Technical Support:** | Paul Pedriana supports registered users by mail, including new card-back designs on request. |

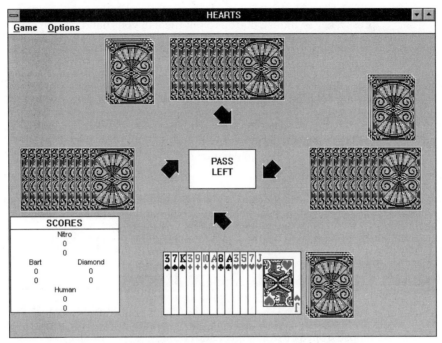

Hearts for Windows is an addictive card game that sharpens your skills and your wit.

# Brief Description of Hearts

Hearts for Windows is a four-player card game in which the goal is to get as few points as possible. Cards of the Heart suit are worth 1 point, and the Queen of Spades is worth 13 points. You want to avoid these 14 cards. The highest card of the lead suit takes the four cards in the trick, and the player that does this gets to lead for the next trick. You must play the suit that was led, if you have it; otherwise, you can play any card. After 13 tricks are played, the points are added up and cards are dealt again. The game is over when a player gets 100 points (he or she is the loser).

# Game Play

At the start of the game, the players must select three cards to pass. The cards are selected with the *left* mouse button and passed and played with the *right* mouse button. When all players have passed their three cards, the passes are completed with the three cards passed to you in the "up" position. You can press a key or mouse button to put them in your hand, or you can wait a few seconds for this to be done for you.

The player with the Two of Clubs must then play it. If you have it, you can play it (or any other card, when it's your turn) by selecting it with the left button and playing it with the right button, or by directly playing it with the right button.

The winner of the trick is shown by the cards sliding toward him or her after all cards are played. It's now the winner's turn to play the first card of the next trick. Scores are continually updated on the scorecard so that you can see who's winning.

If you play a card illegally, a box comes up that says why the card was illegal, with a beep. You must click on the box or press a key to make it go away.

# Game Options and Menu Items

After starting Hearts, you will be given a choice of whom to play against. You can choose the default players (good players but not the best), or you can choose from a custom-player selection.

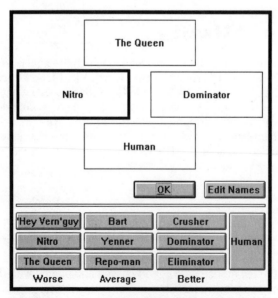

Hearts gives you a selection of opponents so that you can arrange the players to best suit you.

If you choose the custom players, the player-selection window expands to show many buttons with player names on them. The best players are on the right; the weakest players are on the left. Every time you select a player, the box goes to the next player for selection. You can keep selecting players in circles until you select the OK button.

Please note that if you want to play against the computer, you must make sure that at least one of the players is Human. Also note that any or all of the players may be human or computer players. So, if you want, you can have the computer play itself, or you can somehow tape cardboard to the screen or something and have two or more people play against the computer players at once.

You can receive on-line help by selecting the Options menu and selecting the How to Play item. This action will bring up a box that explains the exact rules of the game, how to select cards, and some hints for new players. The F1 key will also bring up the help box.

Card backings for Hearts are selected from the Options menu and can also be selected with the F2 through F5 keys (F2 through F9 in the registered version).

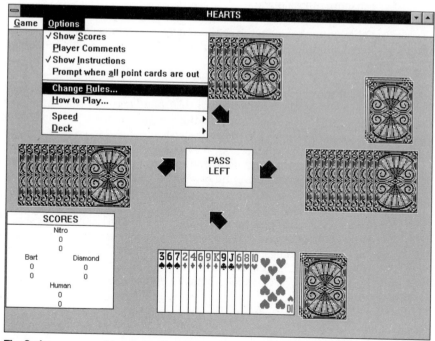

The Options menu enables you to change the rules, view instructions for the game, and other things.

```
┌─────────────────────────────────────────────────────┐
│                 Hearts Rules Options                  │
├─────────────────────────────────────────────────────┤
│ ☒ Jack of Diamonds worth -10 points.                  │
│ ☐ When Player Scores exactly 100 his score goes to zero. │
│ ☒ Shooting gives you -26 instead of giving others +26. │
│ ☐ You must dump the Queen of Spades at first chance.  │
│ ☐ You cannot play point cards on the first round.     │
│  ┌────┬──┬──┐ Score to      ┌──────┐  ┌────────┐      │
│  │100 │▲ │  │ End Game       │  OK  │  │ CANCEL │      │
│  └────┴──┴▼─┘               └──────┘  └────────┘      │
└─────────────────────────────────────────────────────┘
```

Selecting the Change Rules command on the Options menu enables
you to modify the rules of the game.

You can change the game speed by selecting Speed from the Options menu. You
also can change it by pressing the keys 1 to 5; 5 is the fastest (no delay).

Players will say things that appear in cartoon-like quote boxes. You can turn off
these comments with an Options item. Other menu items in the Options menu
are more or less obvious.

Other options exist in the registered version. Some of these options are hidden
in the nonregistered version through elaborate tricky key sequences that are
revealed when you register.

The scorecard is a window (which may be moved) that shows two things for
every player: his or her score for this round and his or her total score for the
game. You can get more information on a given player by clicking with the
mouse on that player in the scorecard.

You can select a new game with the Game menu item, or you can quit with the
Game Quit option. At the end of a game, you are prompted for whether to play
again.

There are a number of improvements in Version 1.2 over Versions 1.0 and 1.1.
Some of these improvements pertain to bug fixes, and others are new additions.
Among other things, there are new card backings (Gumby, for instance; the registered version has eight cool backings — all better than Solitaire). The option to
throw in all cards when all points are out is included, as well as new quotes and

new interesting actions by the game. With Version 1.2, you can change the names of your opponents. All changes in play setup are remembered from one play to the next.

# How To Run Hearts for Windows

Hearts requires Windows 3.0 or later and runs in any Windows mode — and in as little as about 45K of memory. However, it runs much faster if you have 300K or more of free memory. You must have a mouse to select and play the cards. If you cannot afford a mouse, you probably won't have enough money to give me any for all the trouble I went through to make this program, so I don't feel so bad about not having keyboard support for the cards in Version 1.2. Sorry.

Hearts also works on monochrome monitors, but because of the low resolution of many monochrome monitors, you may not be able to see the entire play space at one time. If this is the case, simply use the arrow keys to scroll around the play space if you want or need to see a different part of the play space. The Home key can bring you back to the center.

After running WSETUP to install Hearts on your system, you can use the Windows Program Manager's New Item menu function to install the program HEARTS.EXE as part of the games directory, if you want. (Or you can drag it with your mouse into that directory from the group window in which WSETUP installs it.) You can use the Browse button in the New Item dialog box to find the HEARTS.EXE program if you cannot find it.

It is best (very desirable for Hearts and all Windows programs) if you run HEARTS.EXE from your hard drive if it is not already there. Any Windows program will run very slowly if you run it from a floppy drive. Note that only the HEARTS.EXE file is truly needed to play the game. The files HEARTS.TXT and CARDS.AD are not needed, and you may not want them if you are low on disk space.

The CARDS.AD file is an After Dark screen-saver module that you may copy to your C:\AFTERDRK directory, if you have that program. Other screen savers are now capable of running After Dark AD files themselves. I will periodically change CARDS.AD to do different things and eventually play card games themselves. Different versions will have different names.

# The Author of Hearts

**Paul Pedriana**
P.O. Box 271551
Concord, CA 94527

CompuServe ID: 70541,3223

I am presently a poor biologist living in Northern California in Pleasant Hill, a city 20 miles east of Oakland (I got a bad case of poison oak in the Oakland hills the night of that bad fire in October 1991). I do this computer work on the side as a hobby and race bicycles in the spring and summer. (Cyclists in the Bay Area might recognize me as the guy on the bike with the stars and moons, like card design #1). I have a B.A. degree from U.C. Berkeley in Biochemistry (1989). I program in C/C++ and assembly when needed (I also have done FORTRAN).

The version of Hearts I am distributing has no eliminated parts or other demo traits. This is the complete, unprotected version. Why is this? Because I don't like those incomplete programs. If I really like a program, I pay the author for it, even if I already have a final version of it. I've even paid a couple authors $5 for programs that I never really used simply because I wanted to support them and encourage them to write more. But I can't expect everyone to be like this. Nevertheless, Hearts took considerable time to develop to its present state. I did the programming (C++ and ASM), and Brian Mallari and I (old Hearts buddies) worked together to create the playing styles of the different players you find here.

# Registration

The registered version of Hearts has a number of improvements over the unregistered version. It has twice as many card backings, more quotes, and better opponents. Also, it will not fool with your player's quote like the unregistered version. Also, the players (in general) won't nag you as much, although some people have said they like it.

If you send me, Paul Pedriana, $10, I will register you as a permanent owner of a copy of Hearts; this also will entitle you to future registered versions of Hearts free (see below) and future Windows programs as well. (I'm working on it!) I've done other programs for DOS and Windows, but they probably will not be of interest to you.

As a registered owner, you may ask to make changes to Hearts that are not completely unreasonable, free of charge (for example, you may want a player to have the comments that you supply or to play a way that you specify). You can send me any number of $71 \times 96$ 16-color bitmaps for your card-back designs. (The next version of Hearts will enable you to simply put the bitmap in the same directory as Hearts, and Hearts will pick it up itself.) Or else you may want different opponent names, background colors, or menu options. Also, please send suggestions for new Windows programs (games or not); I will do the ones that are most feasible and likely to generate interest. On the other hand, you may want to fool with the HEARTS.INI file to change the players' names that are the defaults.

Any suggestions and comments about found bugs are always welcome from anyone. *Very good* suggestions get free registration if they can be implemented for Hearts or any other similar game. All correspondence will be answered by me.

I am continuously working on new projects, with time as my only obstacle. It's hard to get anyone to commit the necessary time to help me with these things.

# Future Directions

Hearts Version 1.2 doesn't do everything anyone could ever want, so there will be a Version 2.0. Some of the new things to be in Version 2 will be tougher opponents, new card designs, and an option for programmers to create their own players by simply putting a PLR file in the same directory as Hearts.

Suggestions for new Windows programs are welcome, whether they pertain to Hearts or to any other ideas.

# Registration Form

Send $10 in U.S. funds to

**Paul Pedriana**
P.O. Box 271551
Concord, CA 94527

CompuServe ID: 70541,3223

Name: _____

Address: _____

_____

_____

Preferred Diskette Format: [ ] 3.5"   [ ] 5.25"

# Hyperoid

### Version 1.1
### Copyright © Edward Hutchins

*H*yperoid is a freeware blast 'em game that rivals commercial arcade games in intensity and excitement. It takes some skill to control your little spacecraft, but if it was easy to rack up a high score, what fun would it be?!

*Hyperoid is distributed under the terms of the GNU General Public License (found on disk in the file COPYING.TXT), which states that the program is free and may be modified. The source code (HYPEROID.C and so on) is provided for programmers who'd like to experiment with it. GNU (pronounced* new*) is a project of the Free Software Foundation, which is writing a royalty-free version of the UNIX operating system. GNU stands for GNU's Not UNIX.*

**Type of Program:**    Game

**Requires:**    Windows 3.0 or later

**Registration:**    Free. This program does not require registration.

**Technical Support:**    None

## Hello and Welcome to Hyperoid Version 1.1 ___

The object of the game is intuitive: Shoot everything! (Well, almost everything, heh heh!) If the keyboard buffer overflows in all the excitement, ignore the beeps you hear and they'll go away.

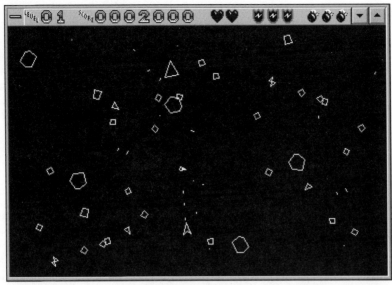

In Hyperoid, you're the little triangular ship, shooting at (almost) anything that moves.

# The Controls

The following keys control your ship:

| | |
|---|---|
| Left or right arrow | Spin left or right. |
| Down or up arrow | Forward or reverse thrust. |
| Spacebar | Fire! |
| Tab | Shields. |
| S | Smartbomb. |
| Esc | Pause or Boss key. |

## Rules

You have three lives, unlimited fuel and firepower, three shields, and three smartbombs. Your ship gets darker when you lose a life, but you keep on playing (unless you hit an asteroid). You get an extra life every 100,000 points. When you lose the game, you start over immediately and can finish off the current level (which should now be 0) before starting over at level 1 (there is no waiting around between games).

Hyperoid uses the Windows palette manager, so if you have a palette-capable color display (and you read the on-line help pages or the "HYPEROID.INI" section, which follows), you should be able to set up better colors than the Windows defaults. I have also tested Hyperoid on a monochrome 286, and it seems to work fine. If you want to remap the keys, look at the "Virtual Key Codes" section of this chapter (or in the Windows Software Development Kit) for some non-ASCII virtual key codes.

The source code is available on disk, as per the GNU General Public License. Please read the license if you have any questions or contact me at the addresses provided in this chapter (electronic mail preferred).

If you make modifications or bug fixes to Hyperoid, please use me as a clearing-house to prevent versions flooding out into the universe. (You don't have to, but I'd appreciate it.) If you write the world's greatest game using some of my source, please send me a note telling me what it is and where it's available.

## HYPEROID.INI

After you've run Hyperoid, you can modify the HYPEROID.INI file, which Hyperoid writes into your Windows directory. Hyperoid automatically keeps track of the window size and highest score played. Here are the items you can set:

```
[Hyperoid]
X=9              ; Distance in pixels from the left edge of screen.
Y=14             ; Distance in pixels from the top of screen.
W=552            ; Width of window in pixels.
H=467            ; Height of window in pixels.
Hi=n             ; Highest score played so far.
LicenseRead=1    ; 1 means you've seen the public license.
Max=0            ; Change to 1 to maximize the game window.
Mono=0           ; Change to 1 for a monochrome screen.
DrawDelay=n      ; Default is 50 microseconds delay per frame. This is the
                   minimimum. Increase in increments of 50 to slow down the
                   game on fast PCs.
```

```
[Palette]
Black=r g b              ; You can change the red-green-blue values, as
DkGrey=r g b             ; found in the Control Panel's Colors dialog box.
Grey=r g b
White=r g b
DkRed=r g b
Red=r g b
DkGreen=r g b
Green=r g b
DkBlue=r g b
Blue=r g b
DkYellow=r g b
Yellow=r g b
DkCyan=r g b
Cyan=r g b
DkMagenta=r g b
Magenta=r g b

[Keys]
Shield=keycode           ; You can change the keys for these functions.
Clockwise=keycode
CtrClockwise=keycode
Thrust=keycode
RevThrust=keycode
Fire=keycode
Bomb=keycode
```

***Note:*** Virtual key codes usually match the key's ASCII value (see the following section).

# Virtual Key Codes _____

Most of the keys in Hyperoid can be redefined using the numbers in the following table. For example, if you want to make the up-arrow key the forward thrust (rather than the reverse thrust) and vice versa, you could insert the lines Thrust=38 and RevThrust=40 into the [Keys] section of HYPEROID.INI.

| Virtual Key Name | Number | |
|---|---|---|
| VK_TAB | 9 | 9=default shields |
| VK_RETURN | 13 | |
| VK_SHIFT | 16 | |
| VK_CONTROL | 17 | |
| VK_CAPITAL | 20 | Fire=20 makes your Capslock into autofire! |
| VK_ESCAPE | 27 | 27=default boss key |
| VK_SPACE | 32 | 32=default fire key |
| VK_PRIOR | 33 | |
| VK_NEXT | 34 | |
| VK_END | 35 | |
| VK_HOME | 36 | |
| VK_LEFT | 37 | 37=default counter-clockwise key |
| VK_UP | 38 | 38=default reverse thrust key |
| VK_RIGHT | 39 | 39=default clockwise key |
| VK_DOWN | 40 | 40=default thrust key |
| VK_INSERT | 45 | |
| VK_DELETE | 46 | |
| VK_A-VK_Z | 64 - 90 | 83=default smartbomb key (ASCII S) |
| VK_NUMPAD0 | 96 | |
| VK_NUMPAD1 | 97 | |
| VK_NUMPAD2 | 98 | |
| VK_NUMPAD3 | 99 | |
| VK_NUMPAD4 | 100 | |
| VK_NUMPAD5 | 101 | |
| VK_NUMPAD6 | 102 | |
| VK_NUMPAD7 | 103 | |
| VK_NUMPAD8 | 104 | |
| VK_NUMPAD9 | 105 | |
| VK_MULTIPLY | 106 | |
| VK_ADD | 107 | |
| VK_SEPARATOR | 108 | |
| VK_SUBTRACT | 109 | |
| VK_DECIMAL | 110 | |
| VK_DIVIDE | 111 | |
| VK_F1-VK_F16 | 112 - 127 | |

# Hit the Stars!

You will occasionally see a five-pointed star wander across the playing area. If your ship touches a star, you are given extra lives, smartbombs, and so on, at random.

# Legal Junk

Hyperoid, a game for Microsoft Windows, is Copyright © 1991 by Edward Hutchins.

Internet:  eah1@gauguin.wustl.edu

U.S. mail:  **c/o Edward Hutchins**
6635 #1 W. Washington Ave.
St. Louis, MO 63130

This program is free software; you can redistribute it or modify it under the terms of the GNU General Public License as published by the Free Software Foundation — either Version 1 or (at your option) any later version.

This program is distributed in the hope that it will be useful, but WITHOUT ANY WARRANTY; without even the implied warranty of MERCHANTABILITY or FIT-NESS FOR A PARTICULAR PURPOSE. See the GNU General Public License for more details.

You should have received a copy of the GNU General Public License along with this program in the file COPYING.TXT; if not, write to the Free Software Foundation, Inc., 675 Mass. Ave., Cambridge, MA 02139, U.S.A.

*Note:* Windows is a trademark of Microsoft Corp.

# IconCalc

## Version 1.02
## Copyright © by David A. Feinleib

*I*conCalc is the neatest *little calculator we've ever seen. It fits into a single icon an entire six-function calculator (add, subtract, multiply, divide, change sign, and backspace). And you can make it float over all your other windows so that it's available whenever you need it. Simply drag its icon wherever you want it to appear on your screen.*

*You* must *use the* right *mouse button to click on the tiny buttons. The left mouse button (as it does with all minimized icons) brings up the System Menu. This menu enables you to access Help or to set the Preferences dialog box for your choice of colors and behavior. You can set IconCalc to beep when you click on a number, but because PC speakers are a varied lot, the beep doesn't work on every PC.*

*You can enter very large numbers into IconCalc. But, if the number exceeds six significant digits, IconCalc switches to scientific notation. The number 1,234,567,891,234, for example, might be shown in IconCalc as 1.23457E+012. The E stands for Exponent. You move the decimal point 12 places to the right to convert the number to standard notation. This is the same as $1.23457 \times 10^{12}$, approximately.*

*After you learn to hit those tiny buttons with your mouse, you'll find that IconCalc does more in less space than any other Windows application!*

| | |
|---|---|
| **Type of Program:** | Calculator |
| **Requires:** | Windows 3.0 or later |
| **Registration:** | Use the form at the end of this chapter to register with the shareware author. |
| **Technical Support:** | David Feinleib provides registered users with technical support by CompuServe, Byte Information Exchange (BIX), FidoNet, and mail. |

| Move | |
|------|------|
| Close | Alt+F4 |
| Switch To... | Ctrl+Esc |
| Help... | |
| Preferences... | |
| About... | |

The IconCalc icon itself *is* the application. Clicking on the icon with the left mouse button displays the System Menu. Clicking with the right button runs the calculator's functions.

# Introduction

- ◆ IconCalc is a full-function calculator in an icon for Microsoft Windows 3.0 or later.

- ◆ It can stay in front of other applications so that you can see it and use it as you work.

- ◆ It takes up little memory.

- ◆ It has context-sensitive help.

- ◆ It has a variety of color schemes from which to choose.

# Requirements for Running IconCalc

- ◆ Microsoft Windows 3.0 or later

- ◆ IconCalc (ICONCALC.EXE, ICONCALC.HLP, ICONCALC.DOC, DAFLIB.DLL, and DAFLIB.HLP)

# Entering Numbers _____

To enter a number, click the right mouse button on the number or operation you want. You *must* use the right mouse button; clicking the left mouse button brings up IconCalc's System Menu.

You can also use the numbers and operations on the keyboard and the numbers and operations on the numeric keypad. (Num Lock must be *on* for you to use the numeric keypad.)

IconCalc displays exponents if necessary. IconCalc displays Error if you attempt to divide by zero. Click on AC or press C on the keyboard to clear the error.

The following list describes the function of each button:

| *Press* | *or Click* | **To Do This** |
|---|---|---|
| 0 | 0 | 0 |
| 1 | 1 | 1 |
| 2 | 2 | 2 |
| 3 | 3 | 3 |
| 4 | 4 | 4 |
| 5 | 5 | 5 |
| 6 | 6 | 6 |
| 7 | 7 | 7 |
| 8 | 8 | 8 |
| 9 | 9 | 9 |
| Backspace | ← | Delete last number entered |
| * | * | Multiply |
| / | / | Divide |
| + | + | Add |
| − | − | Subtract |
| = or Enter | = | Do the calculation |
| C | AC | Clear |
| . | . | Decimal point |

# Moving IconCalc

To move IconCalc, click the IconCalc icon with the left mouse button and, while holding the mouse button down, move IconCalc.

# Closing IconCalc

Click on the IconCalc icon with the left mouse button and then click on Close.

# Understanding IconCalc Options

To bring up a list of options, click the IconCalc system box once.

## Help

The Help option brings up help about IconCalc and explains how to use context-sensitive help. It also displays an index of all help available for IconCalc.

## Preferences

The Preferences dialog box enables you to change your preferences for IconCalc.

### Stay In Front Of Other Applications

To have IconCalc stay in front of other applications, select Stay In Front Of Other Applications. This selection causes IconCalc to remain in front of an application, even if that application is covering IconCalc's icon.

### Screen Saver Compatibility

Selecting Screen Saver Compatibility causes IconCalc to be hidden when a screen saver becomes active. IconCalc reappears after the screen saver stops.

Use the Preferences dialog box to change the way the
application works or the colors it uses.

### Beep When An Operation Is Selected

To have IconCalc beep when an operation is selected (+, –, /, *, =), select Beep
When An Operation Is Selected.

### Beep When Any Button Is Selected

To have IconCalc beep when any button is selected, select Beep When Any
Button Is Selected.

## About

Select the About option to display information about IconCalc.

# Getting Help

IconCalc help can be accessed in three ways:

♦ Select Help from the IconCalc System Menu. An index of all help available for IconCalc is displayed. You also receive information on how to use IconCalc's context-sensitive help.

♦ Access context-sensitive help by clicking on one of the IconCalc System Menu items, holding down the mouse button, and pressing F1.

♦ Access context-sensitive help from IconCalc's Preferences dialog box by clicking on the Help button.

# How To Contact the Shareware Author

Comments and suggestions (and reports of problems) are greatly appreciated. You can contact me in the following ways:

♦ Write to

**David A. Feinleib**
1430 Mass. Ave.
Suite 306-42
Cambridge, MA 02138

♦ Send BIX mail to

pgm

♦ Send CompuServe mail to

76516,20

♦ Send mail on a BBS through FidoNet (IBM UG BBS, Boston MA.) to

Node: 1:101/310
David Feinleib

# How To Pay for and Register IconCalc

IconCalc is shareware. You may make copies of this program and give them to others as long as the documentation is provided with the program, both unaltered.

Please send $12 to register IconCalc. If you would like to receive IconCalc on disk, send an additional $3.00 for 5¼-inch disks or $4.00 for 3½-inch disks. As a registered user, you can receive support by BIX, CompuServe, FidoNet, or mail.

Shipping to Canada is an additional $1.50. Shipping outside of North America is an additional $2.00.

Please include your name, address, and current version number. (The version number can be found in the About dialog box.)

Site licenses, LAN licenses, and substantial quantity discounts are available.

Customization of IconCalc is available but is not included in the shareware registration fee. The fee charged for customization depends on the amount and significance of the customization.

Please contact me for more information regarding the preceding two items.

## Registration form

I cannot process checks not drawn on U.S. or Canadian banks. Traveler's checks and international money orders can be accepted. You can also send payment by bank transfer to account 560201 22878538 34 (please add an additional $6.00 for processing fees).

Send all registrations to

**David A. Feinleib**
1430 Mass. Ave.
Suite 306-42
Cambridge, MA 02138

IconCalc _____ @ $12.00 each  $ _____

5.25" Disk _____ @ $3.00 each   $ _____

3.5" Disk _____ @ $4.00 each   $ _____

Shipping and handling:

Add for shipping to Canada                          $1.50
Add for shipping outside U.S. and Canada    $2.00
Add for checks drawn on Canadian banks     $2.00
Add for bank transfers                                   $6.00
$ _____

TOTAL         $ _____

Check/Money Order #: _____

Name: _____ Date: _____

Company: _____

Address: _____

City, State, ZIP: _____

Country: _____

Phone: _____

Fax: _____

Electronic Mail: _____

Where did you obtain the program(s)? _____

Windows Version: _____ IconCalc Version: 1.02

Printer Type (make, model, cartridges): _____

Comments: _____

_____

## Thanks!

Thanks very much to Peter Kaminski for getting the icons "just right" and for coming up with the different color schemes.

## Other products by the same author

For a list of other shareware programs by the same author, see the "WinClock" chapter in this book.

## Disclaimer

IconCalc is supplied as is. The author disclaims all warranties expressed or implied, including, without limitation, the warranties of merchantability and of fitness for any purpose. The author assumes no liability for damages, direct or consequential, which may result from the use of IconCalc.

# Jewel Thief

**Version 1.3**
**Copyright © by ServantWare**

---

*J*ewel Thief is an enjoyable game that gets more difficult with each level you complete.

**Type of Program:**    Game

**Requires:**    Windows 3.0 or later

**Registration:**    Use the form at the end of this chapter to register with the shareware author.

**Technical Support:**    ServantWare provides technical support to registered users by mail, telephone, and CompuServe.

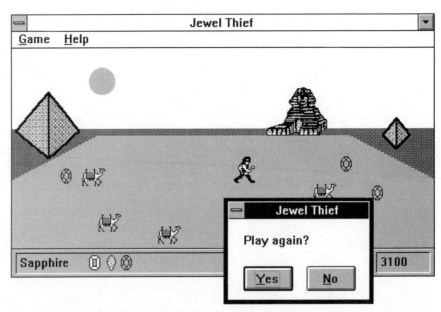

The object of Jewel Thief is to steal the jewels while avoiding the guards; there are 14 levels to move through before you learn about the jewel of great price.

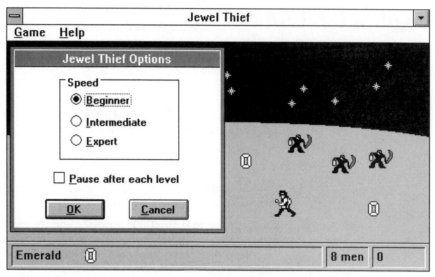

You can select the speed at which you — and the guards — move through the levels of the game.

# How To Play

Your goal is to steal as many jewels as you can by running over the jewels with your mouse while avoiding the guards. After you steal all the jewels on one level, a new set of guards will appear. The scene changes every two levels. You lose a man every time a guard touches you or you leave the playing field. After you steal the diamonds at the expert speed, you will find out about the jewel of great price.

# History and Humor

Jewel Thief is dedicated to my wife, Nancy, who enhanced my knowledge of jewels past that of an engagement ring. She also inspired the rainbow in the last scene. Jewel Thief is not crippled in any way — except that it can't sing. I figured that you didn't want the whole office to know that you are not getting your work done. For those of you who make it to the castle scene, yes, I know that gold is not a jewel, but I needed a 14th level to round out the game.

# Program Contents

| | |
|---|---|
| ASP.BMP | Logo for ASP. |
| JWLTHIEF.BMP | Logo for Jewel Thief. |
| JWLTHIEF.EXE | The game. |
| ORDERFRM.WRI | Order form, registration, license, usage, warranty information, and ASP ombudsman statement. |
| PACKING.LST | This list in text-file format. |
| README.WRI | Last-minute information and humorous tidbits. Also, information about shareware and the Association of Shareware Professionals (ASP). |
| VEND&BBS.WRI | Information and restrictions for disk vendors, individual distributors, computer clubs, user groups, and sysops. Also, recommended descriptions of Jewel Thief for catalogs and BBSs. |

# Author Information

ServantWare is a software company owned and operated by Paul Ligeski. At ServantWare, we strive to uphold the character quality that is part of our name: service. This concept is fundamental to our approach to product development, production, and marketing.

Please feel free to contact me (Paul Ligeski) at any time if you have any questions, comments, or suggestions:

**Paul Ligeski**
President and CEO
ServantWare
1426 Brookfield
Ann Arbor, MI 48103 U.S.A.
CompuServe: 76636,1166
Internet: 76636,1166@COMPUSERVE.COM

# Shareware

Jewel Thief is a *shareware* program. What does that mean? In short, Jewel Thief is a copyrighted program you may try and share with others; after 30 days, you must register Jewel Thief. Following is an explanation of the shareware concept.

## Some definitions

You've probably heard the terms *public domain, freeware, shareware,* and others like them. Your favorite BBS or disk vendor probably has many programs described by one or more of these words. There's a lot of confusion about and among these terms, but they actually have specific meanings and implications. After you understand them, you will have a much easier time navigating the maze of programs available to you and understanding what your obligations are, or aren't, with each type of program.

Let's start with some basic definitions:

*Public domain* has a very specific legal meaning. It means that the creator of a work (in this case, the software) who had legal ownership of that work has given up ownership and dedicated the work "to the public domain." After something is in the public domain, anyone can use it in any way he or she chooses, and the author has no control over the use and cannot demand payment for it.

*Copyrighted* is the opposite of public domain. A copyrighted program is one where the author has asserted his or her legal right to control the program's use and distribution by placing the legally required copyright notices in the program and documentation. The law gives copyright owners broad rights to restrict how their work is distributed and provides for penalties for those who violate these restrictions. When you find a program that is copyrighted, you must use it in accordance with the copyright owner's restrictions regarding distribution and payment.

*Shareware* is copyrighted software that is distributed by authors through bulletin boards, on-line services, disk vendors, and copies passed among friends. It is commercial software that you are allowed to use and evaluate before paying for it. This makes shareware the ultimate in money-back guarantees.

## The shareware concept

Most money-back guarantees work like this: You pay for the product and then have some period of time to try it out and see whether or not you like it. If you don't like it or find that it doesn't do what you need, you return it (undamaged); at some point — which may take months — you get your money back. Some software companies won't even let you try their product! In order for you to qualify for a refund, the diskette envelope must have an unbroken seal. With these "licensing" agreements, you only qualify for your money back if you haven't tried the product.

With shareware, you get to use the product for a limited time, without spending a penny. You are able to use the software on your own system(s), in your own special work environment, with no sales people looking over your shoulder. If you decide not to continue using it, you throw it away and forget all about it. No paperwork, phone calls, or correspondence to waste your valuable time. If you do continue using it, then — and only then — do you pay for it.

Shareware is a distribution method — *not* a type of software. Shareware is produced by accomplished programmers, just like retail software. There is good and bad shareware, just as there is good and bad retail software. The primary difference between shareware and retail software is that with shareware you know whether it's good or bad *before* you pay for it.

As a software user, you benefit because you get to use the software to determine whether it meets your needs before you pay for it; authors benefit because they are able to get their products into your hands without the hundreds of thousands of dollars in expenses it takes to launch a traditional retail software product. There are many programs on the market today that would never have become available without the shareware marketing method.

The shareware system and the continued availability of quality shareware products depend on your willingness to register and pay for the shareware you use. It's the registration fees you pay that enable us to support and continue to develop our products.

Please show your support for shareware by registering those programs you actually use and by passing them on to others.

Shareware is kept alive by *your* support!

# Jewel Thief Order Form

You can register Jewel Thief with your Visa or MasterCard by calling 1-800-444-5457 in the U.S.A. or by faxing the order form that follows to 503-826-8090.

You can also mail a check or money order for $10.00 to

**ServantWare**
1426 Brookfield
Ann Arbor, MI 48103
U.S.A.

Please make checks payable to ServantWare.

You will receive a registration code to remove the registration reminder screen.

Name: _____

Address: _____

City, State, ZIP: _____

Phone: _____

Program: _____ Jewel Thief v1.3 _____

Comments: _____

_____

_____

_____

(Comments can also be left on CompuServe at [76636,1166]).

# Trial Use License

Jewel Thief is *not* a public-domain program. It is Copyright © 1991 – 1992 by ServantWare. All rights reserved.

ServantWare hereby grants you a limited license to use this software for evaluation purposes for a period not to exceed thirty (30) days. If you intend to continue using this software (and/or its documentation) after the thirty (30) day evaluation period, you *must* make a registration payment to ServantWare. Using this software after the thirty (30) day evaluation period without registering the software is a violation of the terms of this limited license.

This software and accompanying documentation are protected by United States Copyright law and also by International Treaty provisions. Any use of this software in violation of Copyright law or the terms of this limited license will be prosecuted. The conditions under which you may copy this software and documentation are clearly outlined in VEND&BBS.WRI.

# Ombudsman Statement

This program is produced by ServantWare, a member of the Association of Shareware Professionals (ASP). ASP wants to make sure that the shareware principle works for you. If you are unable to resolve a shareware-related problem with an ASP member by contacting the member directly, ASP may be able to help. The ASP Ombudsman can help you resolve a dispute or problem with an ASP member but does not provide technical support for members' products. Please write to the ASP Ombudsman at 545 Grover Road, Muskegon, MI 49442-9427 or send a CompuServe message by CompuServe mail to ASP Ombudsman 70007,3536.

# Warranty Information

# MathGraf

**Version 2.4.1**
**Copyright © by Patrick Robin**

*M*athGraf *is a remarkable graph plotter that will amuse novices and enlighten expert number crunchers.*

*You can load any of more than a dozen* MGF *files that come with MathGraf. Or you can create your own math functions and watch MathGraf quickly plot them on an x-y axis.*

*You can type a wide variety of math functions into MathGraf's Function dialog box. As the value of* x *(the horizontal axis) changes, MathGraf calculates the effect on* y *(the vertical axis).*

*The tricky part about MathGraf is that it uses the same Postfix notation as many scientific calculators. Postfix notation differs from the symbols you are used to seeing in math equations. The benefit of Postfix is that it can represent complex functions without the use of parentheses to specify the order of calculation.*

*For example, conventional notation might specify the following function:*

$(3x + 2) / (4x - 5)$

*The same function can be represented in Postfix without parentheses because each math symbol appears* after *the numbers it operates on:*

$3 x * 2 + 4 x * 5 - /$

*The preceding line might be read as "3 and x are multiplied, and 2 is added to that; then 4 and x are multiplied, and 5 is subtracted from that; then the second result is divided into the first result."*

*It looks odd at first, but if you master Postfix notation, you can use MathGraf as a quick and powerful graphing tool for almost any mathematical function.*

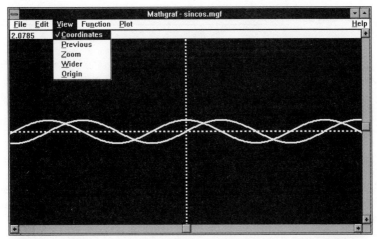

**MathGraf enables you to plot equations on an x-y graph; the program uses the Postfix notation.**

| | |
|---|---|
| **Type of Program:** | Math Graphing |
| **Requires:** | Windows 3.0 or later |
| **Registration:** | Use the form at the end of this chapter to register with the shareware author. |
| **Technical Support:** | Patrick Robin provides registered users with technical support through CompuServe and mail. |

# Running MathGraf

After installing with WSETUP, you can start MathGraf by double-clicking the MATHGRAF.EXE file in the File Manager. You can also start it by double-clicking the MathGraf icon in the Program Manager.

If you associate MGF files with MathGraf, you can also start MathGraf by double-clicking on any MGF file in the File Manager. To do this in Windows 3.1, first click once on any MGF file in File Manager. Then click on File Associate and associate MGF with *x:\directory*\MATHGRAF.EXE.

# The File Menu _____

## New, Open, Save, and Save As

These functions will start, load, or save a graphics definition file containing up to ten distinct curves.

## About

If you have a licensed copy of MathGraf and have entered your license key, the About box will display the owner of this copy and the number of users covered by the license. Otherwise, the licensing information will be displayed.

# The Edit Menu _____

## Copy

The Edit Copy option copies the current graphic window to the Clipboard. The contents of the Clipboard can then be pasted into other Windows graphics programs, such as Paintbrush, and printed. See the "Printing" section later in this chapter.

# The View Menu _____

## Coordinates

The current x,y coordinates of the mouse pointer are displayed on the screen when the Coordinates option is turned on.

## Zoom

The Zoom option permits you to restrict the graphic interval. Press the left mouse button and drag the mouse while holding the mouse button. You can move around the graph by clicking on the scroll bars with the mouse or by using the arrow, PgUp, and PgDn keys.

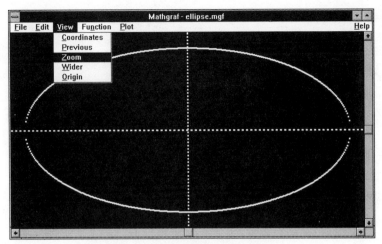

**Use the View Zoom command to restrict the graphic interval.**

## Wider

The Wider option enlarges the x and y range by a factor of two.

## Origin

This function redraws the current graphic without changing the interval size but centering it at the Origin.

# The Function Menu (How To Define Your Own Math Functions)

Functions for MathGraf to plot are defined in the dialog box that appears when you click on Function. The function must be in terms of $x$ only, as in f($x$).

The function can contain the following items:

♦ The variable $x$

♦ Any real or integer constant

♦ p (for pi — 3.14159 . . .)

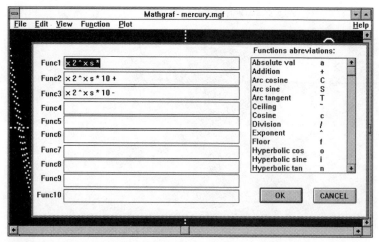

**When you click on Function, a dialog box appears to assist you in creating the functions you want MathGraf to plot.**

♦ e (for 2.7182818...)

♦ Any function abbreviation listed in the dialog box (also shown in the following chart)

| Function | Abbreviation |
|---|---|
| Absolute val | a |
| Addition | + |
| Arc cosine | C |
| Arc sine | S |
| Arc tangent | T |
| Ceiling | ~ |
| Cosine | c |
| Division | / |
| Exponent | ^ |
| Floor | f |
| Hyperbolic cos | o |
| Hyperbolic sine | i |
| Hyperbolic tan | n |
| Log base 10 | L |

*(continued)*

| Function | Abbreviation (continued) |
|----------|--------------------------|
| Modulo | m |
| Multiplication | * |
| Natural Log | l |
| Sine | s |
| Square root | r |
| Subtraction | − |
| Tangent | t |

The function must be entered in Postfix notation. That is, you can view the function as being evaluated from left to right. Each time a *number* or a *variable* is read, it is placed on top of a *memory stack*. Each time an *operator* (+ or * or ^, for example) is read, it is applied to the last one or two numbers placed on the stack. Then the *result* of the operation is placed on top of the stack. This method is identical to the one used in many scientific calculators.

There must be at least one space character between each element of the function. An error message is displayed when a syntax error is detected in one of the functions.

Here are some examples of functions you might want to display, in conventional (Infix) notation and the Postfix notation used in MathGraf:

| The Result You Want | Infix Notation | Postfix Notation |
|---------------------|----------------|------------------|
| 3 times *x*, plus 2 | $3x + 2$ | 3 x * 2 + |
| *x* raised to the power of 3 | $x^3$ | x 3 ^ |
| sine of *x* plus 2 | $\sin(x+2)$ | x 2 + s |
| absolute value of cosine 3*x* | $abs(\cos(3*x))$ | x 3 * c a |
| the modulo of *x* and 5 | *x* modulo 5 | x 5 m |
| the negative value of *x* | $-x$ | x −1 * |

Note that to obtain −x, you multiply x by −1.

# The Plot Menu

## Redraw

This command redraws the graphic screen.

## Interval

The Plot Interval command displays a dialog box showing four interval values. The values *xa, xb, ya,* and *yb* can be any real numbers, where *xa* < *xb* and *ya* < *yb*.

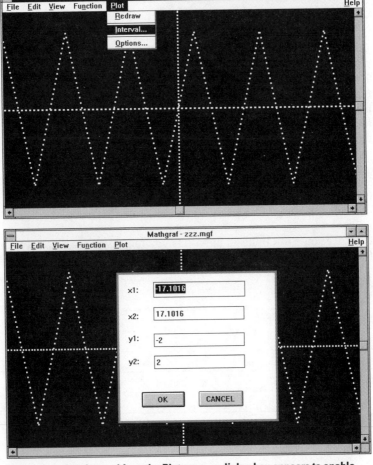

When you select Interval from the Plot menu, a dialog box appears to enable you to specify the four interval values x1, x2, y1, and y2.

The numbers you enter for the interval values can be in decimal or exponential notation. Following are some examples of valid numbers:

2

34.99875

2.1E-10

## Options

The Options command enables you to select one of nine combinations of pen widths and resolutions. Select a large pen on very high-resolution screens. Graphics will be displayed much faster if you select a small pen and low resolution.

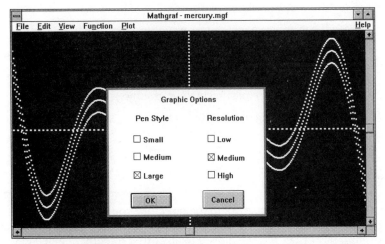

**When you select Options from the Plot menu, a dialog box appears to enable you to select pen widths and resolutions.**

Available pen widths follow:

| | |
|---|---|
| Small | 1 pixel |
| Medium | 2 pixels |
| Large | 3 pixels |

# The Help Menu

For help concerning MathGraf, click on the Help option from the MathGraf menu. The MATHGRAF.HLP file on the MathGraf disk is an ASCII file with the same information as the Help option. It is not necessary to have MATHGRAF.HLP on the disk to run Help.

You can also communicate any questions to me by CompuServe mail at address 70134,111.

# Printing

You can print a graphic by copying it to the Clipboard with the Copy option in the Edit menu and then pasting it into a graphics package, such as Micrografix Designer or Windows Paintbrush. From there, the graphic can be sent to the printer.

1. Draw your graph.

2. Select the Copy option in MathGraf.

3. Open the graphics package (for example, Paintbrush).

4. Select the Paste option in the Edit menu of Paintbrush. (If necessary, click on Options Image-Attributes to make Paintbrush's drawing area large enough for your graphic. Then click on View Zoom-Out to display the entire drawing area before pasting in your graphic.)

5. Modify the drawing or print it as it is.

# Installation Notes

WSETUP copies MATHGRAF.EXE to the directory you specify; it copies SELECT.DLL to your Windows directory (the directory where your Windows executables reside). SELECT.DLL may be moved to any other directory named in your DOS path.

The *.MGF files found in the MathGraf directory are demonstration functions. You can load them with the Open option in the File menu.

## License key

For registered users, enter the license key printed on your license certificate. It must be entered in the license dialog box, which you obtain by clicking on the License Info button that MathGraf displays when starting.

The key is case-sensitive. Please make sure that you type it exactly as it appears on your license certificate. The key is stored in the WIN.INI configuration file in your Windows directory. This file is part of the Windows software and is used by other applications to store configuration information. Keep your license certificate in a safe place because you must reenter the key if you reinstall Windows or if the WIN.INI file is erased or corrupted. If you lose your license key, write to us and we will promptly send a new one.

## Updates

Updated versions of MathGraf can be obtained on the CompuServe WINADV forum, by anonymous ftp on the Internet host clvax1.cl.msu.edu, or by mail from the address at the end of this chapter.

## Copyrights and warranty

MathGraf 2.4.1 is a shareware product. It can be copied freely in the unlicensed format and distributed for evaluation purposes on the condition that it is un-altered and accompanied by this documentation. In this case, *unlicensed* means *not accompanied by a license key.* You cannot be charged for an unlicensed copy of MathGraf except to cover copying charges of a maximum of $7.

MathGraf is provided "as is" without any warranty, expressed or implied, including but not limited to fitness for a particular purpose.

## Suggestions and bug reports

Your comments and suggestions are appreciated. They are needed to improve future releases by including features needed by users. We are also interested in hearing about new ideas for entirely different programs that can make use of the great graphical environment that is MS Windows.

Please send your comments to

**Patrick Robin**
99 Grove
Greenfield Park
Quebec, Canada J4V 2X2

or by CompuServe mail to 70134,111.

Please mention from what source you obtained the demonstration version of MathGraf.

## Registration Form

Remit to

**Patrick Robin**
99 Grove
Greenfield Park
Quebéc, Canada J4V 2X2

Name: _____

Address: _____

_____

_____

Contact individual:

_____

_____

Qty                          Unit Price        Total

_____ MathGraf 2.4.1 License (first user)      $35 U.S./Canada _____

_____ MathGraf 2.4.1 additional license(s)     $23 U.S./Canada _____

Do you want to receive a

disk _____          license key only _____

I use [ ] 5.25" disks   [ ] 3.5" disks

Note that MathGraf computer software has been delivered and accepted by the customer. Upon receipt of this paid invoice, a license key will be sent, as well as a disk containing MathGraf, if requested.

Please specify from what source you obtained the demo version:

_____

# Mega Edit

## Version 2.02
## Copyright © by Computer Witchcraft, Inc.

*T*he text editor that comes with Windows — Notepad — is severely limited. Notepad cannot open more than one file at a time, it cannot insert one file into another, and it can't even open a file larger than about 50K.

*Mega Edit solves all these problems and more. Mega Edit has almost no limitations on the size of files you can open (up to your entire Windows virtual memory). And, unlike with Notepad, you can easily configure Mega Edit for the number of spaces you want in Tabs, the number of characters per line, and so on.*

*When you run into problems with Notepad, you'll almost certainly find the cure in Mega Edit.*

**Type of Program:**    Text Processing

**Requires:**    Windows 3.0 or later, in standard or enhanced modes. Users of Norton Desktop for Windows must use NDW 2.0 or later.

**Registration:**    Use the form at the end of this chapter to register with the shareware author.

**Technical Support:**    Computer Witchcraft, Inc., provides technical support to registered users by telephone, fax, CompuServe, Internet, and mail.

**Similar Shareware:**    WinEdit, a program featured in *Windows 3.1 SECRETS,* published by IDG Books Worldwide, is a similar text editor optimized for programmers (for example, double-clicking a C language keyword brings up Microsoft C help files, if you have them).

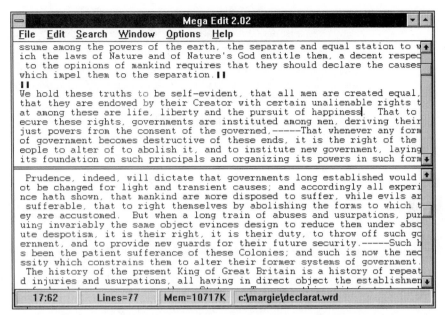

Mega Edit is a text editor that outperforms Windows Notepad on almost every level.

# Overview

Mega Edit is a powerful ASCII text editor. It is designed specifically to facilitate complex editing tasks involving multiple or large files. Such tasks would be difficult or impossible with most editors currently available for Microsoft Windows 3.x.

In addition to the usual capabilities of any Windows 3.x-compliant text editor, Mega Edit's features include the following:

♦ **Support for very large file editing.** Mega Edit can use up to the amount of available virtual memory on systems running in 386 enhanced mode. With 16 megabytes of RAM installed, this can be up to about 64 megabytes. (In general, when running in 386 enhanced mode, Windows will support about four times the amount of installed physical RAM.) Mega Edit has *no preset limits* for file size capability.

♦ **Support for multiple file handling.** You can load up to 25 files at once.

♦ **Support for multiplatform file formats**. The editor can automatically recognize and load Macintosh and UNIX text files, as well as standard DOS text files. It also has an Export/Conversion capability for outputting files loaded in any one of these formats to either of the others.

♦ **Binary file viewing.** The editor also allows loading of binary files for viewing. When a binary file is loaded, it is displayed in a clean, 72-character-per-line format.

♦ **A split-screen feature.** This feature enables you to scroll through and edit the same document at two places simultaneously, or to view and edit different documents simultaneously.

♦ **Support for variable, scalable fonts.**

♦ **Word wrap.**

# Editing Multiple Files _____

Please note that each time you load a file during an editing session, *that file remains in memory,* even when you open or create a new file.

After opening one or more files, you will observe that the names of these files are appended to the bottom of the File menu. You can switch from one file to another by selecting the desired filename from the File menu.

Note that multiple file handling is supported by the split window feature. After you have split the editing area, you can open or switch to a new file in the current pane and retain the original file in the other pane.

When you switch from one file to another, the line and column position of the caret is retained. When you switch back, you can resume editing where you left off.

It is not necessary for you to explicitly save a file when opening or creating a new one. You can save the file at any time by switching back to it and selecting the Save option from the File menu. If you exit the editor, you will be prompted to save any unsaved files in memory.

# Split Window Features _____

Mega Edit supports the splitting of the main edit window into two separate panes, each with the same number of lines. You can split the edit window by pressing Ctrl+S or by selecting the Split Window option from the Window menu.

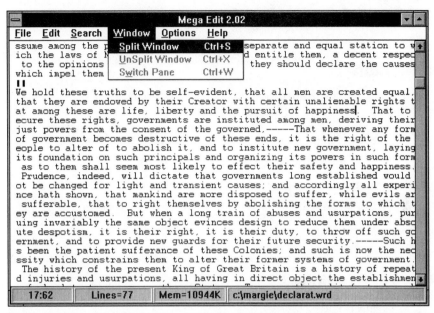

You can split the editing window by selecting the Split Window option from the Window menu.

Initially, when you split the edit window in two, the same file exists on both sides of the divider that appears. You can now scroll each window pane independently, using either the keyboard or one of the two scroll bars beside each pane. You can perform any editing function on either side of the divider.

You can also open, create, or switch to an additional file on either side of the divider so that more than one file is visible in the editing area at the same time.

After splitting the main editing area, you can switch between the two sides of the partition by clicking the mouse in the opposite partition or by selecting the Switch Pane option from the Window menu. The accelerator key for this operation is Ctrl+W.

Finally, you can resume editing in single-window mode by selecting the Unsplit Window option from the Window menu. The accelerator key for this operation is Ctrl+X. When you unsplit the window, the file that contained the caret just before you issued the unsplit command becomes the current file. The caret position is retained.

# Keyboard Commands _____

## Navigation

| | |
|---|---|
| Beginning of document | Ctrl+Home |
| End of document | Ctrl+End |
| Start of line | Home |
| First alphabetic character of line | Home, Home |
| End of line | End |
| One word right | Ctrl+right arrow |
| One word left | Ctrl+left arrow |

## General functions

| | |
|---|---|
| Insert line | Ctrl+N |
| Delete line | Ctrl+Y |
| Delete to end of line | Shift+Ctrl+Y |

## Extend highlighted selection

| | |
|---|---|
| Line up | Shift+up arrow |
| Line down | Shift+down arrow |
| Character right | Shift+right arrow |
| Character left | Shift+left arrow |
| Page up | Shift+PgUp |
| Page down | Shift+PgDn |
| To end of document | Shift+Ctrl+End |
| To start of document | Shift+Ctrl+Home |

## Accelerator keys (menu shortcut keys)

| | |
|---|---|
| Help | F1 |
| Save file | F2 |

| | |
|---|---|
| DOS shell | F12 or Alt+F2 |
| Exit application | Alt+F4 |

| | |
|---|---|
| Cut selected text | Shift+Delete |
| Copy selected text | Ctrl+Insert |
| Paste Clipboard contents at caret | Shift+Insert |
| Clear selected text | Ctrl+Delete |

| | |
|---|---|
| Find again | F3 |
| Go to line or percentage of document | Ctrl+G |

| | |
|---|---|
| Split window | Ctrl+S |
| Switch pane | Ctrl+W |
| Unsplit window | Ctrl+X |

*(Courier font only)*

| | |
|---|---|
| Enlarge text | Ctrl+numeric-keypad plus |
| Reduce text | Ctrl+numeric-keypad minus |

| | |
|---|---|
| Print current file | Ctrl+P |

# File Menu Commands

## New

The New option enables you to create a new, unnamed file for editing. Initially, the file is named NONAME. When you save the file, you will be allowed to rename it something more distinctive.

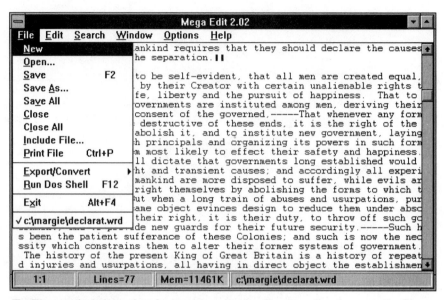

The File menu includes options for opening and saving files, as well as for converting files to other formats and running the DOS shell.

## Open...

Open enables you to load a preexisting disk file into memory for editing. Using various fonts available on the Options Change-Font menu, it is possible for you to view and edit files in any of the standard DOS text formats: plain ASCII, ANSI, or OEM (ASCII plus IBM graphics characters), as well as standard Macintosh and UNIX text files. When a Macintosh or UNIX file is loaded, edited, and subsequently saved, it retains its original Macintosh or UNIX file format, unless you specifically convert the file to another format by using the Export/Convert menu choice (described later).

Please see the description of the Options Change-Font menu for more information on getting the best match between file format and character font.

*Note:* Mega Edit also lets you load binary files for viewing only. When you load a binary file, the editor will automatically detect that it is in binary format and display the file with 72-character line lengths. This setup provides for a very clean, comprehensible display of data. If you try to save a binary file after it has been loaded, the editor prevents you from doing so. (To actually edit binary files, you must use a hexidecimal editor.)

# Save (F2)

Save causes the current file to be saved to disk. If the file is currently named NONAME, the default for files created with the Edit menu's New command, you will be prompted for a filename of your own devising.

*Note:* Files originally loaded with Macintosh or UNIX formats retain their native characteristics when saved with any of the Save commands. To modify the operating-system format of a text file, use the Export/Convert menu choice, described later.

# Save As...

Save As brings up a dialog box prompting you for a new name for the current file. After you supply the new name, the file is written to disk under the new filename. It is also known within the Mega Edit environment by the new name.

# Save All

Save All causes all files currently loaded into the editor to be saved to disk. A dialog box will come up, asking you to give your own name to any NONAME files created with the New command (see comments about the New command, earlier in this chapter).

# Close

Close causes the current file to be closed. If the file has been modified since it was last saved, you will be asked whether you want to save the file before closing it. *(The filename at the bottom of the screen is displayed in red whenever the file has unsaved modifications.)* If you say Yes, the file will be saved to disk before it is closed. This also enables you to rename files named NONAME.

# Close All

Close All enables you to close all currently open files with one command. If any open files have modifications, you will be prompted about saving them, as with the Close command.

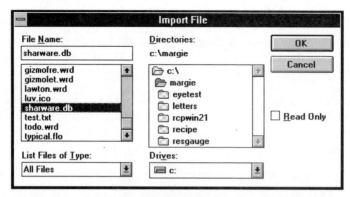

You can import a file into another file at the caret position by selecting
Include File from the File menu and providing the filename in this dialog
box.

## Include File...

Include File enables you to incorporate an existing disk file into the currently
open file at the caret. A dialog box will be presented; it is similar to the one that
appears when you select the Edit menu's Open command. When you have finished identifying a file with this dialog box, the file is immediately pulled into
the current document at the current position of the caret.

## Export/Convert

Export/Convert enables you to output the current file to a different operating
system's file format. This menu choice contains a submenu with three options:
As DOS Text..., As Macintosh Text..., and As Unix Text.... Choose the desired
output file format. Then respond to the File Save As dialog box to retain the
same filename or rename the file, according to your needs. Using the Export/
Convert facility, you can repeatedly convert a file between the three different
formats.

## Run DOS Shell (F12)

Choosing this option causes a copy of the DOS operating system to be
spawned, giving you access to the DOS prompt. If you are running in 386 enhanced mode, you can press Alt+Enter to window this process. In any mode,
you can press Ctrl+Esc to switch back to Windows. After you exit Mega Edit, the
DOS shell you spawn will continue until you explicitly close it. After it is started,
it is entirely independent of Mega Edit.

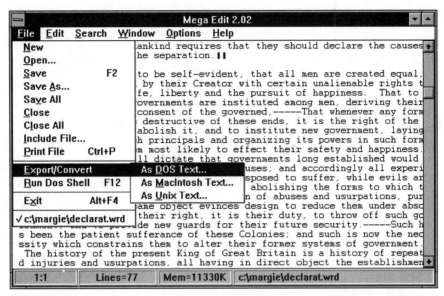

**The Export/Convert option enables you to convert files between three different formats.**

## Exit (Alt+F4)

Choosing Exit is the same as choosing Close from the system menu. It causes the Mega Edit application to shut down and exit. Before Mega Edit completely shuts down, you will be prompted about saving any unsaved, modified files.

# Edit Menu Commands

To use the Cut, Copy, or Clear commands on this menu, you must first select some text from the current document so that the command has an object to operate on.

## Cut (Shift+Delete)

Cut causes the selected text to be excised from the document. It is also placed in the Windows Clipboard. It is then available for subsequent pasting — to another location, another file loaded in Mega Edit, or another application altogether. (For example, you can paste text into your word processing application or a terminal-emulation program.)

## Copy (Ctrl+Insert)

Copy causes the selected text to be placed in the Windows Clipboard. It is then available for pasting into another location or file or into another application altogether. The selected text in its current location is not affected.

## Paste (Shift+Insert)

The Paste option can be selected from the Edit menu only when the Windows Clipboard contains contents compatible with Mega Edit (that is, the Clipboard contains some form of ASCII text). You may position the caret at any position within an open file and select Paste to insert the contents of the Clipboard at the location of the caret. The text will flow into place as though you had typed it yourself, leaving the caret at the end of the text that was pasted in.

## Clear (Ctrl+Delete)

Choosing Clear causes highlighted, selected text to be excised from the document. The text is *not* placed in the Clipboard. Use this option when the Clipboard contains data that you do not want to overwrite.

# Selecting Text

*Useful Tip:* You can select text with any of these methods. Notice that whole lines — including the invisible *newline characters* at the ends of the lines — are selected when the highlight extends all the way to the right edge of the editing area, next to the scroll bar. Conversely, newline characters at the ends of lines are *not* selected when the highlight does not extend all the way to the right. Selecting or not selecting whole lines, including the newline at the end of each line, subtly affects how various Edit menu operations behave. Experiment with this to get a good understanding of how cut-and-paste operations work.

You can select text with the mouse, the keyboard, or the scroll bar.

## Selecting with the mouse

Click the left mouse button at a point in the text that you want to serve as the origin point for the selection. Continue to hold the left mouse button as you drag the cursor in any direction. All text between the origin point and the current location of the cursor is selected, as indicated by the reverse-video highlighting of the selected region.

If you drag the cursor outside of the editing window, the editor will perform automatic scrolling to expand or contract the selection in any direction.

After you have highlighted the region you want to select, release the left mouse button. You may then continue to modify the currently selected region by using combinations of the Shift key and arrow keys, plus the Home, End, PgUp, and PgDn keys. Alternatively, use the scroll bar to scroll through your document and then Shift+click to extend the selection to a new position.

## Selecting with the keyboard

Position the caret at a point in the text that you want to serve as the origin point for the selection. You can position the caret either by left-clicking with the mouse or by navigating the caret to the desired position with the arrow keys.

To start selecting, hold the Shift key in combination with one of the various caret navigation keys, such as the arrow keys, the Home and End keys, or the PgUp and PgDn keys. Continue these techniques until the section of text that you want to select is highlighted in reverse video.

## Selecting with the scroll bar

Position the caret at a point in the text that you want to serve as the origin point for the selection. Next, using the scroll bar, scroll up or down through the document by clicking above or below the thumb, by dragging the thumb, or by clicking on the scroll bar's up and down arrows, until you reach the other end of your selection. (Notice that the caret remains "stuck" to the origin point of the selection. If you scroll a full window or more, the caret will no longer appear on the screen.) Finally, hold the Shift key while pointing the mouse at the end point for your selection and click the left mouse button. The caret will be placed where you clicked, and your selection will appear highlighted.

You can continue to modify or refine your selection, if you want, by holding the Shift key and using the keyboard, by continuing to hold the left mouse button and dragging, or by using the scroll bar again. As long as you use the scroll bar to move around your document, the selection remains "sticky" and you can Shift+click somewhere else to redefine the end point of your selection.

# Search Menu Commands

## Find

When you choose Find, a dialog box will prompt you for one or more characters or words to search for.

***Note:*** Instead of typing the search text directly into the dialog box, *you may preselect the search text by highlighting the text in the document* with the mouse or the keyboard before you select Find. If you do so, the text you selected in the document appears in the dialog box automatically.

Beneath the input box for the search text, there are several check boxes that enable you to tailor the specifics of how the search will be conducted:

If you check the Start at First Line box, the search commences from the first line of the current document. If you uncheck this box, the search commences from the current position of the caret.

If you check the Case Sensitive box, the search will match only with a case-exact match of the search text you supply. If this box is unchecked, uppercase and lowercase will be ignored for matching purposes.

If you check the Whole Words Only box, the search will ignore any text found that matches your search text but is surrounded on either side by alphabetic characters. This option can help you weed out matches that might result when you are looking for the word *super*, for example, but not words such as *supercalafragalisticexpialadochious*. If you leave this box unchecked, matches will be accepted when your search text is found as part of a larger group of characters.

```
┌─────────────────────────────────────────┐
│               Search                     │
├─────────────────────────────────────────┤
│  Find What:                              │
│  ┌────────────────────────────────────┐  │
│  │ pursuit of happiness               │  │
│  └────────────────────────────────────┘  │
│  ┌─ Search Criteria ─────┐   ┌─────────┐  │
│  │  ☒ Start at First Line│   │   OK    │  │
│  │  ☐ Case Sensitive     │   └─────────┘  │
│  │                       │   ┌─────────┐  │
│  │  ☐ Whole Words Only   │   │ Cancel  │  │
│  └───────────────────────┘   └─────────┘  │
└─────────────────────────────────────────┘
```

The Search dialog box provides three Search Criteria check boxes for the selected text.

After you supply the search text and the criteria for the search, a rapid, literal search will be conducted through the text of the current document. If a match is found, the line containing the matching text will be centered in the edit area. The caret will be placed immediately after the last character in the matching text.

# Again (F3)

Choosing Again repeats the most recent search, starting from the current position of the caret in the current document. The accelerator key for this action is F3. It is much more convenient to use the accelerator key for this operation instead of selecting it from the menu.

# Replace

Replace enables you to substitute one group of characters for another — at one, several, or *all* locations where the text occurs in the current document. As with the Find operation, a dialog box prompts you for search text.

*Note:* Instead of typing the search text directly into the dialog box, *you may preselect the search text by highlighting the text in the document* with the mouse or the keyboard before you select Replace. If you do so, the text you selected in the document appears in the dialog box automatically.

Additionally, you are prompted for the replacement text that will be substituted for the search text. It is acceptable not to list anything as the replacement text. This action tells the dialog box that you want to *delete* instances of the search text.

As with Find, you can also configure the check boxes located within the box labeled Criteria. These check boxes work the same as in Find (discussed earlier in the chapter), but there is an additional check box called Confirm Changes. If this box is checked, you will be prompted whenever a match is found for your search text to decide whether this particular instance should be replaced. This dialog box also includes a Cancel button, enabling you to halt the whole operation at any point. You should make sure that the Confirm Changes box is checked if certain instances of your search text should *not* be replaced. If you are certain that *all* instances should be replaced, it is best to leave this box unchecked. The operation proceeds much faster when it is not necessary to prompt about each instance.

## Goto

Goto brings up a dialog box prompting you for a number. Ordinarily, this number is interpreted by the Goto operation as the number of a line in the current document. Optionally, you can enter a *percentage* of the document rather than a line number. For example, if you enter 75 as the number and change the dialog's radio button to indicate a percentage, Mega Edit places in the center of the screen the line that occurs three-quarters of the way through the document. Otherwise, the editor will locate and center the line corresponding exactly to the number you entered in the Goto dialog box.

# Window Menu Commands

These commands control Mega Edit's split-screen features.

## Split Window (Ctrl+S)

Split Window subdivides the editing area into two equal sections, separated by a divider. Initially, the same file exists on each side of the divider, which enables you to scroll through and edit two parts of the file simultaneously. The split-screen feature is integrated with multiple file-handling features. After you have split the screen, you can load or create new files or switch to other currently loaded files on either side of the divider.

Current caret positions are retained in all loaded files. When you switch a file into one of the visible panes, your position within a given document remains where it was when you last worked with the file.

## Unsplit Window (Ctrl+X)

Unsplit Window causes the split editing area to revert back to a unitary window. The document currently containing the caret fills the entire area.

## Switch Pane (Ctrl+W)

Switch Pane causes the caret to move from one side of the divider separating the two editing areas to the other, which makes the file on that side the current file. You can also move the caret from one side of the divider to the other by clicking with the mouse.

# Options Menu Commands _____

## Word Wrap On/Off

Choosing this command toggles Mega Edit's word-wrap feature on and off. If word wrap is currently on, a check mark appears by this menu choice.

You can set the right margin (where wrapping occurs) with the Options Preferences dialog box. The Options Preferences dialog box also lets you set a default start-up behavior for word wrap. (More information on the Options Preference menu choice is presented shortly.)

## Set Tab

Choosing this option lets you set the value of tab stops in Mega Edit. Tab stops are positioned at intervals of $x$ columns across the editing area. The value you supply here sets this interval, the unit being the width of a character. You can set the default start-up Tab interval with the Options Preferences dialog box (discussed later in this chapter).

## Colors

Options on this pop-up menu let you choose between three different color sets for the editing area of Mega Edit.

Choosing Standard Colors causes the editing area colors to correspond to the colors set in your WIN.INI file. These colors can be controlled with the Windows Control Panel utility or any other utility that enables you to tailor Windows' various system colors. Standard Colors is the factory default; it enables you to customize colors for certain types of monitors that support color irregularly or that only have monochrome colors (such as laptops).

Choosing Metallic Colors causes text to appear as black on a silver background. Additionally, the reverse-video highlight colors will be white text on a dark gray background. This color combination is attractive and very easy on the eyes and is recommended for VGA monitors or better.

Choosing Maize and Blue causes text to appear as gold on a sky-blue background. Highlight colors will be red text on a powder-blue background — another attractive color set for VGA monitors.

## Change Font

This pop-up menu enables you to customize Mega Edit's text fonts to best suit your taste, viewing conditions, and text format.

Choosing Courier Font selects Mega Edit's most flexible font, the Courier font. This is the only font in which Mega Edit enables you to use the Enlarge Font and Reduce Font options to size the font for maximum visibility. The Courier font is an ANSI font. To view/edit files that have IBM Extended ASCII characters, you should select the OEM (IBM) font.

Choosing ANSI Font selects Windows' ANSI font.

Choosing OEM (IBM) Font selects a font that, before the widespread use of Microsoft Windows, served as the default text font for DOS applications. The Windows OEM (IBM) font supports most of the extended character set that is part of the OEM font. It is useful for viewing files produced with DOS applications that might have used these characters (mostly line- and box-drawing characters, along with a variety of special symbols for mathematics, and so on). If one of the other fonts is selected, OEM extended characters will appear as the corresponding characters from the ANSI character set, but these will probably not match the original symbols in the OEM font.

Choosing System Font selects the Windows fixed-width system font. This is the same font used by the Notepad utility supplied with the retail Windows product.

## Enlarge Font

This option can only be selected when you have set the default font to Courier in the Options Change Font pop-up menu. Selecting it will cause a magnification of the Courier text in your document. You can select this option repeatedly, until the maximum amount of magnification has been reached. It is easier to control this operation using the keyboard accelerator key, Ctrl+numeric-keypad plus.

*Note:* On some systems, eliciting this choice only once may not produce a change in the size of the font. Try pressing Ctrl+numeric-keypad plus repeatedly, until a change in the font size occurs.

# Reduce Font

This option can only be selected when you have set the default font to Courier in the Options Change Font pop-up menu. Selecting it will cause a decrease in the size of the Courier text in your document. You can select this option repeatedly, until the minimum display size of the font has been reached. It is easier for you to control this operation by using the keyboard accelerator key, Ctrl+numeric-keypad minus.

# Preferences

Preferences invokes a dialog box that enables you to set some default behaviors of Mega Edit to best suit your use of the product. When you modify values in the Preferences dialog box and click on OK to exit, your changes are retained from one editing session to the next — until you again invoke this dialog box and make changes.

## Tabs

**Default Setting:** The value you supply here becomes the default Tab interval when you start up a Mega Edit session. You can also change this value on the fly by modifying the value here or with the Options Set Tab menu option.

## Word Wrap

**Startup in Wordwrap Mode:** If this check box is checked, Mega Edit will start up assuming that you want the word-wrap feature turned on for all documents. You can override the default during a particular editing session by selecting Options Word Wrap On/Off to toggle the word-wrap feature to the desired state.

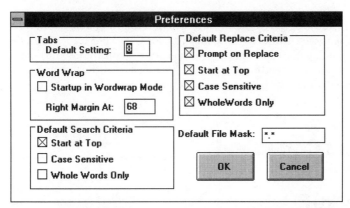

Use the Preferences dialog box to make changes to the way Mega Edit acts by default; changes are saved from session to session.

If you uncheck this box, Mega Edit will start up assuming that you do not want to use the word-wrap feature in each new document. Again, override the default at any time by toggling the feature with the Options Word Wrap On/Off menu option.

**Right Margin At:** The value you enter here indicates the character position where text should be wrapped to the next line (when the word-wrap feature is toggled on). This value is measured in character-width units. In effect, the value here represents the maximum line length in characters.

### Default Search Criteria

The states of these various check boxes determine the default configuration that appears preselected in the dialog box that appears when you select Find from the Search menu. Please see the section on the Search Find menu earlier in this chapter for specific details.

### Default Replace Criteria

The states of these various check boxes determine the default configuration that appears preselected in the dialog box that appears when you select Replace from the Search menu. Please see the section on the Search Replace menu earlier in this chapter for specific details.

### Default File Mask

The Default File Mask is the wildcard text that appears by default in all dialog boxes that open new files for loading or importing into Mega Edit. You can use this mask, or wildcard, to display a specific subset of files from the entire list of files that would appear in the Files list box of these dialog boxes. The factory default of *.* selects all files, without doing any filtering. A mask text of *.TXT would filter out all files in the current directory, except those with the extension TXT.

If you use Mega Edit to work with files that follow specific naming conventions, such as program source-code files (*.C for C or *.PAS for Pascal), or if you impose naming conventions on your files for organizational purposes, you may want to consider setting the default file mask to perform some filtering for you. Otherwise, just leave it set to the factory default of *.*.

# Print Menu Command

## Print File (Ctrl+P)

Choosing Print File causes the current file to be printed on the currently selected printer.

# Mega Edit Files

| | |
|---|---|
| MEGAEDIT.EXE | Application executable file. |
| MEGAEDIT.HLP | Application on-line help. |
| MEGAED.DLL | Mega Edit dynamic link library. |
| COMMDLG.DLL | Windows 3.1 Common Dialog library. This file is placed in your Windows directory if you are running Windows 3.0. If you delete Mega Edit, do not delete this file because another application may depend on it. Windows 3.1 comes with (and many Windows 3.1 applications require) a version of this file. |
| READ1ST.TXT | Product documentation. |
| README.TXT | Copyright and distribution guidelines. |
| REGISTER.TXT | Registration information. |
| REG_FORM.TXT | Registration form. |
| VENDOR.TXT | Application for limited distribution rights. |
| RELEASE.TXT | Release notes — improvements from release to release. |

*Note:* When you use Mega Edit and modify some of the defaults on the Options menu, Mega Edit creates two files in your Windows system directory called MEGAEDIT.BIN and MEGAINFO.BIN. These files are used for retaining your session preferences. You may delete these files at any time, but doing so will result in Mega Edit reverting to the factory settings.

Generally speaking, all Mega Edit distribution files should remain together in the same directory. However, you may copy the MEGAEDIT.HLP and MEGAED.DLL files to your Windows directory if Mega Edit generates errors concerning not finding these files (see "Troubleshooting," which follows).

# Troubleshooting

♦ **You don't like the default opening size of the Mega Edit screen.**

Mega Edit decides on its opening screen size by checking the Right Margin At value set in the Options Preferences dialog box for word wrap. The size selected will be just large enough to accommodate the margin. If you increase or decrease this value, Mega Edit will change its opening size accordingly. To modify this setting, select Preferences from the Options menu.

♦ **Problems with general protection fault when Mega Edit starts.**

We have had several reports of this, and all have been traced to the user launching Mega Edit from versions of the Norton Desktop for Windows before Version 2.0. Versions of Norton Desktop for Windows before 2.0 are incompatible with Mega Edit. If you have this problem, try running Mega Edit directly from the Program Manager or use the File Manager. In most cases, this action will eliminate the problem.

♦ **Problems with the application not finding the help file or not being able to load MEGAED.DLL.**

If you *do not* use the Windows Program Manager as your main Windows manager program, be sure to set up whatever manager you are using so that the initialization, or working, directory for starting up Mega Edit is the same as the directory that holds the Mega Edit program files. One of Program Manager's virtues is that it automatically handles this; some alternative Windows managers do not and have to be *configured* to start an application in its source directory. Alternatively, you can simply copy the two files MEGAED.DLL and MEGAEDIT.HLP to your Windows subdirectory, normally C:\WINDOWS.

Symptoms of a problem in this area might be error messages such as Can't find MEGAED.DLL, please insert in drive A: or problems finding the MEGAEDIT.HLP help file.

♦ **Problems retaining preference settings from session to session.**

If, for some reason, you do not have a standard Windows directory structure, with a directory called \WINDOWS\SYSTEM, you may have some problems operating Mega Edit. It is recommended that you create a subdirectory called \SYSTEM beneath whatever directory holds your main Windows executable files, which should resolve any problems.

# Tips on Using Mega Edit

Mega Edit includes an extensive on-line help system. Documentation contained in the on-line system explains every feature of the product. You can invoke on-line help by pressing the F1 function key at any time after you have started the editor.

The on-line help system is organized to be practical and concise. Using the browse feature, you can read every topic that it contains in 30 minutes or less. It is recommended strongly that you read through the topics in the main index entitled "Up and Running." These topics provide a good overview of Mega Edit features. Although reading the manual has become a lost art these days (generally with good reason!), you are encouraged to spend 30 minutes reading the on-line reference to the product. You shouldn't have any problem understanding the product or its features thereafter.

New users should note that Mega Edit has some special, extended features to support complex editing tasks that involve many or large files. Again, please have a good look at the "Up and Running" topics in the on-line help system. These topics are also covered in the sections "Overview," "Editing Multiple Files," and "Split Window Features" at the beginning of this chapter.

# Registration

We at Computer Witchcraft believe that Mega Edit is a product meeting the highest standards of excellence in design and software craftsmanship. We hope that you agree!

As an additional benefit to the consumer, Mega Edit has been released as shareware so that you can try out the software on your system to see whether it meets your needs before you buy. If you make the determination that you would like Mega Edit to become a part of your software library, you should take responsibility to pay for the product by registering it.

## Benefits of registration

♦ Latest version

♦ Manual in Write format

♦ Registration information on About screen

♦ No shareware registration screen

♦ Technical support by way of CompuServe and Internet

♦ On our mailing list

♦ Upgrade protection

♦ Total Customer Satisfaction guarantee

When you register Mega Edit, you will receive a disk containing the latest version of the product. We are continually improving Mega Edit and releasing new versions. So it is quite likely that your registered version will be a more recent version than the one you picked up through shareware channels.

You will receive a copy of the Mega Edit manual in Microsoft Write format. Your name or company name will appear on the About screen, but your copy of Mega Edit will otherwise be free from start-up screens or registration screens of any kind.

Registered users are eligible for technical support by CompuServe, Internet, mail, fax, or telephone.

We will put you on our company's mailing list so that you will receive materials describing the availability of upgraded editions of the software and other new products from Computer Witchcraft that may be of interest to you.

Upgrade protection: When you register Mega Edit, you will receive the most recent version of Mega Edit, but we are always improving the product. At some point in the future, you may find a newer (later) version of Mega Edit as shareware. Not to worry! Registered users can just install the newer shareware version with the registration file from the older version and consider the new version registered! The new software will display your name and company information on the About screen and will eliminate any registration screens. This feature will work for all new shareware versions — at least up to the next major release.

We strive for Total Customer Satisfaction and will happily refund your money, including shipping and handling charges, if for any reason you are unsatisfied with our product. You do not have to return the product.

## How to register

As of January 1, 1992, the registration fee for Mega Edit is $35.50 in U.S. dollars, *plus* a shipping and handling fee (see the table that follows).

Please send the *total,* which includes the appropriate shipping and handling fee, from the following table:

| Country | Registration | Shipping/handling | TOTAL |
| --- | --- | --- | --- |
| United States | $35.50 | $3.50 | $39.00 |
| Canada and Mexico | 35.50 | 5.00 | 40.50 |
| Other countries | 35.50 | 9.00 | 44.50 |

For your convenience, you may order/register using your credit card 24 hours a day by telephone, fax, or electronic mail. We accept MasterCard, Visa, Discover, American Express, JCB Cards, Carte Blanche, and Diners Club.

| Telephone: | (415) 752-2477 (If no answer, please leave your order on voice mail.) |

| Fax: | (415) 752-8971 |

Electronic mail:
  CompuServe:       76130,1463
  Usernet/Internet:  megaedit@witchcraft.com

If you're not registering by mail, please include essentially all the information on the registration form (REG_FORM.TXT). If you're registering by voice mail, please speak clearly and repeat all the important information: your name, address, credit-card information, and media on which to send you your copy of Mega Edit.

You may, of course, register by regular mail and use a check, money order, or credit card to pay. Please make all checks or money orders payable to COMPUTER WITCHCRAFT, INC., in U.S. dollar-denominated drafts drawn on a U.S. bank. The cost to us for non-U.S. checks is prohibitive.

If you're registering by mail, please enclose the registration form included with Mega Edit (REG_FORM.TXT) or the form that follows.

*Note:* If, for some reason, you cannot use the printed registration form, it's fine just to send a note with the registration information, along with your check, money order, or credit-card information. *Please allow up to four weeks for delivery.* (We will try to do better than that.)

Thanks for registering Mega Edit. Stay in touch!

## Product registration form

Mega Edit@™ Version 2.02

Name: _____

Company/Address: _____

_____

_____

Your Telephone Number: _____
(include area/country code)

Disk Media, check one:  [  ] 5.25"  [  ] 3.5"

Date Ordered:      Month _____ Day _____ Year _____

**Registration Name**  *(Capitalization and punctuation will be exactly as listed)*

Your Name (required): _____

Company/Org. (optional): _____

Credit-Card Orders
Please Check One:  [  ] MasterCard  [  ] Visa  [  ] JCB

[  ] American Express  [  ] Discover  [  ] Carte Blanche  [  ] Diners Club

Credit-Card Number: _____

Expiration Date:  Month _____      Year _____

Cardholder's Signature: _____
(for mail or fax orders)

**Price Calculation:**

Registration Fee:                        $35.50

California residents add Sales Tax:   _____

Shipping and Handling:               _____

   $3.50 United States
   $5.00 Canada & Mexico
   $9.00 Other countries

Total Cost:                          _____

Checks or money orders: Make payable in U.S. currency on a U.S. bank.
Credit-card payments may be sent by mail, e-mail, fax, or telephone.

**Computer Witchcraft, Inc.**  Internet: megaedit@witchcraft.com
P.O. Box 210441                    CompuServe: 76130,1463
San Francisco, CA 94121-0441             Fax: (415) 752-8971
U.S.A.                         Telephone: (415) 752-2477

Thanks!

How did you receive your copy of Mega Edit?

[ ] *Windows GIZMOS*

[ ] CompuServe [ ] BIX [ ] Genie [ ] AOL

[ ] Other BBS: _____

[ ] Catalog: _____

[ ] Other: _____

# Disclaimer of Warranty

This software and documentation are sold "as is" and without warranties as to performance of merchantability or any other warranties whether expressed or implied. Because of the various hardware and software environments into which this program may be put, no warranty of fitness for a particular purpose is offered.

Although we have made every effort to test the product in a wide variety of operating environments, good procedure dictates that any program be thoroughly tested with noncritical data before relying on it. The user must assume the entire risk of using the program. Any liability of the author will be limited exclusively to product replacement or refund of purchase price.

# μLathe (MicroLathe)

## Version 1.5.1
## Copyright © by Daniel S. Baker

*MicroLathe is a phenomenal display program that does what graphics applications costing hundreds of dollars can't. It converts virtually any free-form shape you draw into a three-dimensional wireframe model and then shades that model with realistic lighting and coloring.*

*The degree of control you get is impressive. Draw any random shape and then alter its rotation, texture, hue, and other qualities in the MicroLathe Control Panel.*

*It's so easy to draw a line and get an attractive result that you should have hours of fun with μLathe. (The Greek letter μ is pronounced* micro *and is often used to refer to microcomputers — hence, MicroLathe's name.)*

| | |
|---|---|
| **Type of Program:** | Graphics |
| **Requires:** | Windows 3.1 or later. (Do not run under Windows 3.0.) |
| **Registration:** | Use the form at the end of this chapter to register with the shareware author. |
| **Technical Support:** | Daniel Baker provides technical support to registered users by CompuServe and mail. |

## Overview

μLathe (MicroLathe) is an easy-to-use modeling tool that enables you to create three-dimensional objects using the metaphor of the carpenter's lathe.

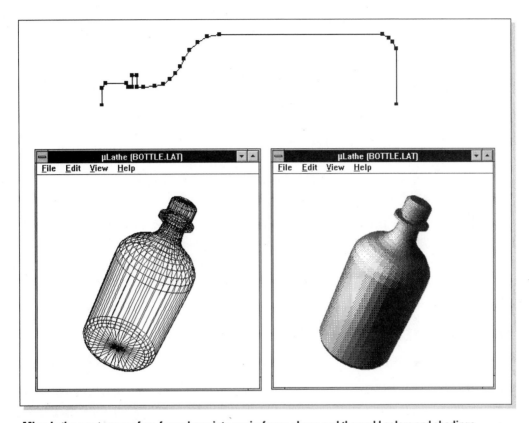

MicroLathe can turn any free-form shape into a wireframe shape and then add colors and shadings.

# Procedures

## Creating a 3D object

You use the Lathe view to create the outline of an object. This outline will be spun 360 degrees in lathe fashion about its axis to create a three-dimensional object.

Suppose that you want to model a bottle. Imagine the bottle lying on its side. The top half of the bottle's contour is the shape you enter into the μLathe window. Start at either the left or right side of the object and click the mouse at various points along the contour of the bottle. Each time you click, a new endpoint is added to the outline, and a line segment is drawn between the last two endpoints entered. Continue in this manner until your object attains the desired shape. The outline of your bottle might look something like this:

Creating the free-form shape in the μLathe window.

○ When you move the mouse directly over a handle, the cursor becomes a circle, indicating that the endpoint beneath the cursor can be moved if you press and hold the mouse button.

✚ The cross-hair cursor indicates that a new endpoint and line segment will be added if you click the mouse button.

*Note:* When you hold down the Ctrl key while you press the mouse button, the new or existing endpoint snaps to the nearest gridpoint.

## Viewing a 3D object

After creating the outline of an object in the Lathe view, select the 3D option from the View menu or click on the View button in the Control Panel. Your outline will be rotated 360 degrees about its axis to produce a 3D object. Using the Control Panel, you can change the position and appearance of your object.

The following graphic shows three views of an object:

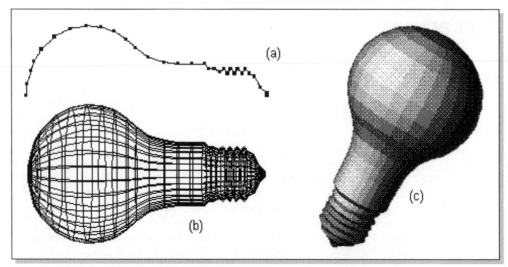

Three views of a graphic produced in μLathe.

**Object Outline (Lathe View):** Figure (a) shows a typical outline — in this case, a light bulb.

**Wire Frame Object (3D View):** Figure (b) shows the outline of the light bulb (a) rotated around its axis, creating a wireframe object.

**Shaded Object (3D View):** Figure (c) depicts the object after rotation and constant shading have been applied using the μLathe Control Panel.

# Using the μLathe Control Panel

The μLathe Control Panel enables you to change several parameters that govern the appearance of your 3D object. Click on any item in the Control Panel to view a description of its function.

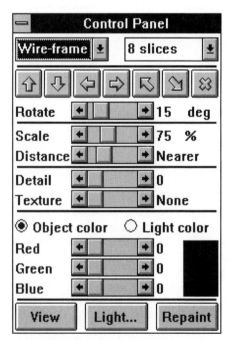

The μLathe Control Panel enables you to change the appearance of a 3D object.

_____

# File Menu Commands _____

## New

This option clears any existing object and prepares the program for the creation of a new object. If there is an unsaved object, you are given the opportunity to save your changes.

## Open

This option opens a lathe object saved on disk. If there is an unsaved object, you are given the opportunity to save your changes.

## Save

This option saves the current lathe object to disk.

## Save As

This option saves the current lathe object to disk under a new filename.

## Save Image

This option saves a bitmapped image of the 3D object to disk. Currently, two bitmap file types are supported: BMP (used with Windows Paintbrush) and TGA (used with Targa video boards). Using the list box at the right of the Save Image dialog box, you may specify the resolution of the bitmapped file in bits per pixel. The recommended setting will be highlighted.

*Note:* There is no advantage to saving a bitmapped file in a resolution higher than the recommended resolution; the image quality does not change, but the resulting file is considerably larger. Specifying a resolution lower than the one recommended results in a loss of color accuracy.

# Save Sequence

This option enables you to save multiple views of your 3D object in a single Windows DIB (Device Independent Bitmap) file. These bitmaps can be displayed in animated fashion by the Autodesk Animator Player for Windows or by the MiniMovie application bundled with μLathe.

When Save Sequence is selected, you are prompted for a DIB filename. In the X, Y, and Z rotate fields, enter the number of degrees you want your object to rotate around that axis per frame. Negative values are allowed. You must also specify the total number of frames for the sequence.

Here is an example: The graphic that follows depicts a sequence generated with the Save Sequence command. At the time the command was selected, the 3D object, a bottle, appeared as shown in frame 1. The sequence was created using a value of 60 for Y rotation (60 degrees positively about the Y axis), zero for X and Z rotation, and 6 for the number of frames. Note that because the bottle was rotated about a single axis, and because 60 degrees times 6 equals 360 degrees, the bottle makes one complete revolution about the Y axis.

*Note:* Even though the sequence operation has been greatly accelerated in this new version, the process can take a long time if your object is complex or if the number of frames you request is large. You can abort the sequence by clicking the mouse button in the μLathe window. The μLathe program must be in the foreground for sequencing; don't switch to another application while the sequence is in progress.

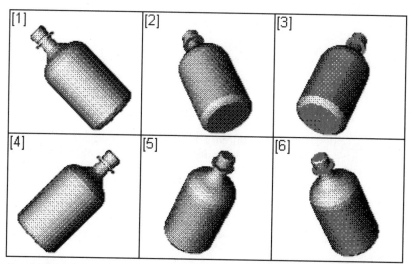

Use the Save Sequence command to specify how a 3D image will rotate around the X, Y, and Z axes and the number of frames in which you want the action to take place.

A 3D candle created in μLathe.

## Exit

This option exits the μLathe application.

# Edit Menu Commands

## Undo

This option revokes the previous endpoint insertion or endpoint move.

## Copy

This option copies the contents of the μLathe window to the Clipboard. On paletted video systems (generally all 256-color systems), the palette is copied as well. Note that when the "snapshot" is taken, the Control Panel window disappears momentarily if it covers any part of the μLathe window.

## Clear

This option erases all endpoints in the current lathe object but keeps the Control Panel settings and filename intact.

## Grid

This option enables you to create a grid of evenly spaced points in the Lathe view. Using the Ctrl key, you can force endpoints to be aligned (snapped) to the gridpoints.

## Light Source

The Light Source dialog box enables you to change the position and intensity of the light source. Click on a control in the dialog box to view a description of its function.

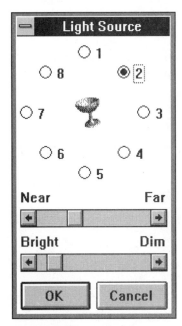

The Light Source dialog box enables you to direct the position and intensity of the light that affects the shading of the 3D object.

**This object is in the process of being repainted: the program first draws the wireframe and then applies shading to each of the surfaces.**

## Repaint

This command causes the 3D object to be completely rerendered. The Repaint command performs the same function as the Repaint button in the Control Panel.

# View Menu Commands

## Lathe

This option changes the current mode to the Lathe view, where objects are edited.

## 3D

This option changes the current mode to the 3D view, where 3D objects are rendered.

## Control Panel

This command hides the Control Panel if it is currently displayed or displays it if it is currently hidden.

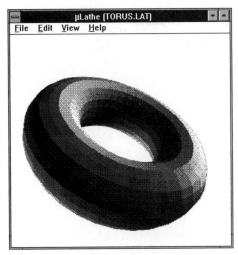

**A 3D view of a tire — or a doughnut.**

# MiniMovie 1.5.1

MiniMovie is a utility that plays DIB (Device Independent Bitmap) files. A single DIB file may contain any number of bitmap images. The images are displayed one after the other in the MiniMovie window to produce a simple form of animation.

## Creating movies

The easiest way to create a movie is to let a program generate it for you. The μLathe application generates movies (called *sequences*) that are compatible with the MiniMovie utility.

Another way to create a movie is to manually combine multiple BMP format bitmaps into a single DIB file. Use a program that supports the BMP file type (Paintbrush, for example) to create several bitmaps, one for each frame of your movie. Then use the COPY command to concatenate the BMP files into a DIB file.

For example, the following statement combines every BMP file in the current directory, in the directory order, into a single DIB file called ANIMATE.DIB:

    COPY /B *.BMP ANIMATE.DIB

The next few statements copy four bitmaps, BITMAP1.BMP, BITMAP2.BMP, BITMAP3.BMP, and BITMAP4.BMP — in that order — to a DIB file called MOVIE.DIB:

```
COPY /B BITMAP1.BMP MOVIE.DIB
COPY /B MOVIE.DIB+BITMAP2.BMP MOVIE.DIB
COPY /B MOVIE.DIB+BITMAP3.BMP MOVIE.DIB
COPY /B MOVIE.DIB+BITMAP4.BMP MOVIE.DIB
```

## Starting MiniMovie

MiniMovie can accept an optional command-line parameter. If given, the parameter must be the filename of a DIB file. If no parameter is supplied, the first thing you see is a dialog box that will enable you to select and load a DIB file.

Inside the dialog box is a Load Frames check box. If the Load Frames option is checked, all the frames in the movie are loaded into memory for optimum performance. This option may not be possible if the DIB contains a large number of frames or if it consists of very large bitmaps. If this option is not selected, each frame is loaded from the disk as needed.

## Notes

After the last frame of a movie has been displayed, the movie is repeated from the first frame in an endless loop.

The MiniMovie window's size is determined by the size of the first frame. The bitmaps of successive frames may be larger or smaller, but the size of the window remains fixed.

If the MiniMovie application posts an error message while trying to load a DIB file with the Load Frames option selected, try loading the DIB file again with the Load Frames option turned off.

When creating a movie, keep in mind that smaller movies (in terms of width and height, not file size) play more smoothly than large ones.

When you attempt to play an animation created in a different screen mode, be aware that the color-conversion process can cause movie load times to be exaggerated. Loading a 24-bit DIB file on a 256-color system, for example, can take quite awhile.

Running multiple instances of MiniMovie in a paletted video mode (generally, all 256-color systems are paletted) causes performance to be severely degraded.

# MiniMovie controls

The following controls appear in the MiniMovie window:

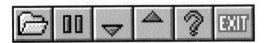

**The MiniMovie Control Panel enables you to control
the action of the movie.**

From left to right, these controls have the following functions.

## Open

The Open button enables you to select another DIB file for viewing. It displays
the same dialog box that appears when MiniMovie is first started.

## Pause

Selecting the Pause button stops the animation. Selecting it again resumes the
animation. (The button turns into a Play button when the animation is stopped.)

## Slower

When selected, the Slower button slows the speed of the animation by increasing the time delay between the display of successive frames.

## Faster

When selected, the Faster button increases the speed of the animation by de-
creasing the time delay between the display of successive frames.

## Help

The Help button causes the MiniMovie help system to appear.

## Exit

The Exit button shuts down the MiniMovie application.

# Registration Information

A $15 donation for the use of μLathe will be graciously accepted. You will re-
ceive an authorized copy of μLathe on diskette and will be entitled to free
upgrades and fixes as they are available.

If you are a Windows programmer, $30 will get you the aforementioned registration, plus the complete C-language source code to this program.

MiniMovie is installed with μLathe by WSETUP, but it is a separate product with separate registration. A $15 donation for the use of MiniMovie will be graciously accepted if this product is of use to you. Such a donation will entitle you to an authorized diskette version, free upgrades, and the complete C-language source code.

Send check or money order (U.S. funds only, please) to the author at this address:

**Daniel S. Baker**
5993 Slippery Rock Drive
Columbus, Ohio 43229

Feel free to contact me on CompuServe at 71551,2300.

[ ] $15 — MicroLathe license only

[ ] $30 — MicroLathe license and C source code

[ ] $15 — MiniMovie license and C source code

Name: _____

Address: _____

_____

_____

Preferred Diskette Size:     [ ] 3.5"  [ ] 5.25"

# Mile Bones

### MB.EXE — Version 2.1
### Copyright © by André Needham

*M*ile Bones *is a card game in which you and the computer race toward a goal. The object of the game is to be the first to reach 700 miles. Along the way, several things may occur. You can play your* Mileage cards *to increase your total mileage. However, the computer — your opponent — can play* Hazard cards *to frustrate you. You, in turn, can avoid the hazards by playing* Remedy cards *or Safeties.*

*Mile Bones is fun for all ages. You can just start playing it, without really knowing the names of the cards. But Mile Bones is one of those games in which it's most definitely a good idea to read the rules. That way, you can deliver to your opponent a devastating* Coup Fourré!

| | |
|---|---|
| **Type of Program:** | Game |
| **Requires:** | Windows 3.0 or later |
| **Registration:** | Use the form at the end of this chapter to register with the shareware author. |
| **Technical Support:** | It's hard to imagine this game requiring any technical support, but André Needham does encourage registered users to mail in suggestions, questions on strategy, and so on. |

## Overview

Mile Bones is a Windows card game that simulates a driving trip. The object of the game is to be the first to reach 700 miles. (You can lengthen the game to 1,000 miles under an *extension,* described later.)

The Mile Bones playing field is made up of three rows of cards. The middle row shows your cards. You must move cards to the Battle pile in the top row to gain mileage toward your goal. The bottom row shows the computer's cards.

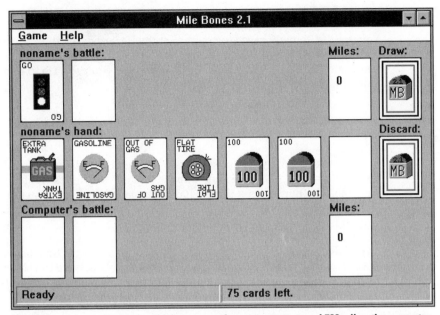

**Mile Bones is a card game in which you race the computer to travel 700 miles; the computer plays Hazard cards, and you can counter with Remedy cards.**

# The Cards

There are four types of cards that make up the 101-card deck:

## Mileage cards

Mileage cards come in five distances: 25, 50, 75, 100, and 200 miles. Playing these cards (when you can) increases your total mileage.

## Hazard cards (also called "dirt")

The five Hazard cards are Out of Gas, Flat Tire, Accident, Speed Limit, and Stop. You can play these cards on the computer (if you have them) to hinder the computer's progress toward the 700-mile or 1,000-mile goal.

Of course, the computer can do the same to you! To remove a Hazard card, you must play a Remedy or a Safety card.

## Remedy cards

You use the Remedy cards to counteract the Hazard cards the computer plays on you (or vice versa). The five cards are Gasoline, Spare Tire, Repairs, End of Limit, and Go. These cards are only temporary. If you use a Go to remove a Stop, the computer can play another Stop on you.

## Safeties

In contrast to Remedy cards, Safeties counteract Hazards permanently (well, at least until the current game ends). Unlike Remedies, Safeties can be played at any time, whether or not a Hazard has been played on you. If you are lucky enough to get and play all four Safeties (Extra Tank, Puncture Proof, Driving Ace, and Right of Way), you will be unstoppable!

If you have a Safety in your hand when the computer plays the corresponding Hazard on you, you can *Coup Fourré* by immediately playing the Safety — before drawing a card. This way, you pick up bonus points, as described later.

## *Coup Fourré*

Immediately playing the correct Safety card to counteract a Hazard that the computer played on you is called a *Coup Fourré* (pronounced *KOO for-AY* — *counterattack* in English).

If the computer plays a Hazard on you during its turn, you should not draw a card at the start of your turn. Instead, if you have the correct Safety (an Extra Tank card to counter an Out of Gas card, for example), play it on your Battle pile. This nets you 400 points (instead of the standard 100 for playing a normal Safety). You are automatically given two cards off the Draw Deck (if it isn't empty), and it is *still your turn.*

You see a red outline around the Safety card when it is displayed on the screen. The computer can also do a *Coup Fourré*, so be careful.

# How do the cards relate to each other?

Each Hazard card matches up with a Remedy *and* a Safety card. In other words, if the computer plays the Hazard Stop on you, you can either play the Remedy Go or the Safety Right of Way before you can play any more mileage cards. Here is how everything relates:

| Hazard Cards | Remedy Cards | Safety Cards |
|---|---|---|
| Stop | Go | Right of Way |
| Speed Limit | End of Limit | Right of Way |
| Accident | Repairs | Driving Ace |
| Flat Tire | Spare Tire | Puncture Proof |
| Out of Gas | Gasoline | Extra Tank |

**The Cards**

Hazard   Remedy   Safety

Each Hazard card can be countered by a corresponding Remedy card or a Safety card.

## How many of each card are there?

**Mileage:**

Ten 25-mile cards       Ten 50-mile cards

Ten 75-mile cards       Twelve 100-mile cards

Four 200-mile cards

**Hazards:**

Two Out of Gas cards       Two Flat Tire cards

Two Accident cards       Three Speed Limit cards

Four Stop cards

**Remedies:**

Six Gasoline cards       Six Spare Tire cards

Six Repairs cards       Six End of Limit cards

Fourteen Go cards

**Safeties:**

One Extra Tank card       One Puncture Proof card

One Driving Ace card       One Right of Way card

# Playing the Game _____

When you first start the game under Windows, you see three rows of rectangles. These are places where cards will be placed, picked up, or displayed.

The top two rows of rectangles are for the human player (that's you!). The bottom row of rectangles is the computer's row.

The leftmost rectangle in the top row is your Battle pile. This is where you play a Go card to start the game, where the computer plays Hazard cards, and where you play Remedy or Safety cards.

To the right of that is the Speed Limit rectangle. The computer plays a Speed Limit card here, and you play the End of Limit card (if you have one) to remove the Speed Limit.

The space to the right of this is where your Safeties, if any, are shown. (However, you play all Safety cards onto the Battle pile, not here.)

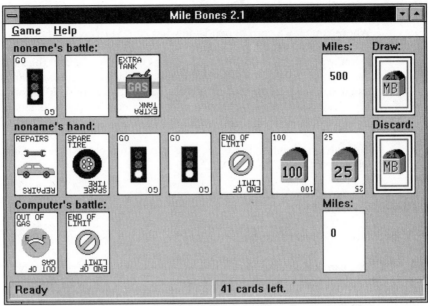

**You and the computer play cards on the various rectangles on the playing field.**

The next rectangle to the right contains the number of miles you have played. This is where you play Mileage cards.

Finally, the last rectangle in the top row is the Draw Deck. At the start of your turn, you can move the mouse cursor over this rectangle and click the left mouse button to add a card to your hand (assuming that the deck isn't empty). Those without a mouse can use the arrow keys to move the cursor and use the spacebar or the Enter key to select.

The first seven rectangles in the second row represent your hand. At the start of a turn, you have six cards. After you draw a card, you must either play or discard a card to end your turn. To play a card, move the cursor over the card and click the left mouse button. Now drag the card by moving the mouse (keep holding the left button); let go of the button to drop it on one of five other locations (described either previously or shortly) to play the card or on the Discard Deck to the right of your hand to throw the card away.

The last row of rectangles is identical to the first, but it shows the computer's piles for Battle, Speed Limit, Safeties, and Miles played.

## Where can a card be played?

Where you play a card depends on what card you have selected.

If you want to play a Hazard card on the computer, click on the card in your hand, drag it to either the computer's Battle or Speed Limit rectangle (the two squares on the left on the bottom row), and drop it there. You cannot do this if the computer is already stopped or has a Safety that protects against the Hazard you are trying to play on it.

You can play Safety and Remedy cards on either of the first two squares on the left side of the top row.

Mileage cards must be played on your Mileage pile (in the top row, below the word *Miles:*).

If you want to discard a card, drag the card to the Discard pile.

You can also double-click on any card in your hand to smart-play it. If playing the card is a valid move, it is played. Otherwise, it is discarded.

## When can a card be played?

When a card can be played is a bit more complex. At the start of the game, you must either play a Go or Right of Way card on your Battle pile before you can play any mileage. (This is true throughout the game: You can only play mileage if you have a Go or Right of Way.)

**Mileage cards:** You (and the computer) can play only two 200-mile cards in a single game. Also, if you are under a Speed Limit restriction, you must play mileage of 25 or 50 only. If you are very close to 700 points (or 1,000 if you extend the game), you can only play up to the exact mileage needed to finish the game. That is, if you have 650 points, you can only play a 25-mile or 50-mile card because larger mileage cards would put you over 700.

**Remedy cards:** Except for the Go card, Remedy cards can only be played when the computer has played a Hazard on you. After you play a Remedy, you then play a Go card on top of it to continue playing mileage. If you have previously played a Right of Way card, however, you can play mileage immediately because you don't need a Go card.

**Safety cards:** You can play a Safety card whenever you want. If you play one during your turn, you get another turn before the computer does.

In a special case, you can also play a Safety *before* you even draw a card. This is called a *Coup Fourré* (or *counterattack* in English). If the computer plays "dirt" (a Hazard card) on you during its turn, you should not draw a card at the start of your turn. Instead, select the correct Safety (an Extra Tank to counter an Out of Gas, for example) and play it on your Battle pile. This nets you 400 points rather than the standard 100 for playing a Safety normally. You automatically get two cards off the Draw Deck (if it isn't empty), and it is still your turn. You see a red outline around the Safety card when it is displayed on the screen. The computer can also do a *Coup Fourré*, so be careful.

## What is an extension?

When you have played exactly 700 miles (you cannot go over), the computer asks whether you want to extend the game to 1,000 miles. If you answer No, you win the game. If you answer Yes, you must play to exactly 1,000 miles before you win the game (and the computer might just beat you to it). Winning the game on an extension adds 200 points to your score.

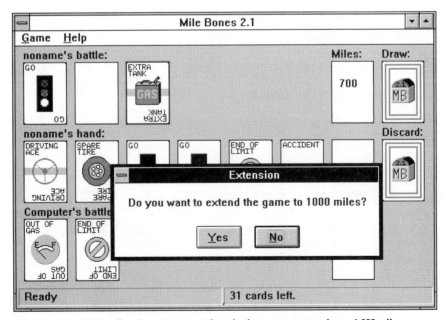

After you reach 700 miles, the computer asks whether you want to play to 1,000 miles.

## End of game

The game ends if either you or the computer reaches 700 or 1,000 miles. However, if neither player can finish, the Draw Deck runs out. You must then play whatever cards you can and discard the rest. When your hand is empty, the game is over. If you manage to reach 700 or 1,000 miles after the deck runs out, you earn 300 points for Delayed Action.

When the game is over, you see the scoring dialog box. Most of the items in this list are easy to understand or have already been explained, but here are some extra details:

*Trip Completed* means that you reached the 700 or 1,000 mile goal first (you won the game). *Shutout* means the computer (or maybe even you) played no Mileage cards during the game. The other player earns 500 points for this coup. If you win and did not play any 200-mile cards, you get 300 points for a *Safe Trip*.

The *Grand Total* shows the total score from previous games, until either you or the computer (yes, this does happen) reaches 5,000 or more points. Then the Grand Total resets to 0. If your score was high enough, your name is entered in the High Score table.

## High Score table

You qualify for the High Score table if the score you reach is one of the three highest over 5,000 points or if the difference between your score and the computer's score (the *spread*) is one of the three highest.

If you click on the Clear Scores button, you erase any high score records saved in the MB.INI file.

# Tips on Playing Mile Bones Version 2.1

You can press F1 in most dialog boxes to get help. Alternatively, press Shift+F1 and click the mouse on any area of the screen to find out what that area is used for.

Instead of clicking on the card you want to play — and then clicking where you want it to go — you can drag the card and drop it where you want to play it.

If you're allergic to drag and drop, there's an Options dialog box you can use to turn it off. You can also set whether or not Mile Bones sorts your hand for you.

If you double-click on a card, it is *smart-played*. If playing the card is a legal move, it is played. Otherwise, the card is discarded.

# Registration

If you have any questions, suggestions, or comments about this game, feel free to write me at the address that follows. Also, if you really enjoy the game and play it more than a few times, feel free to send money. $10 is the minimum suggested amount. This amount registers you as an owner of the program, and you will receive news of any new versions of the software, any bugs (not!), and so on.

Many thanks to the people who sent in $10 for the old version, 2.0. I know that there are many more of you out there playing Mile Bones who haven't registered. Now, with the new, improved version, how about it? You're probably just going to waste the $10 on lottery tickets or something. Send it to me instead — I'll put it to good use!

Thank you for supporting shareware!

**André Needham**
P.O. Box 2516
Renton, WA 98056

Name: _____

Address: _____

_____

_____

# Money Smith

## Version 2.0
### Copyright © by Bradley J. Smith

*Money Smith truly gives you value for your money! Money Smith is a complete, easy-to-use, double-entry bookkeeping system — plus a full-function financial calculator that rivals the expensive calculators that banks and brokers use.*

*Even if you don't need a bookkeeping system, reading Money Smith's documentation and using its calculator to check on your financial investments can be very rewarding. Try it!*

| | |
|---|---|
| **Type of Program:** | Personal Finance |
| **Requires:** | Windows 3.0 or later |
| **Registration:** | Use the form at the end of this chapter to register with the shareware author. |
| **Technical Support:** | Bradley Smith provides registered users with technical support through CompuServe, Prodigy, and mail. |

# Introduction to Money Smith

## Why use Money Smith?

Why use a tool like Money Smith? You may not need it. If you are already financially secure, are not worried about where your money is coming from or going to, and are not interested in establishing a budget or tracking investments, there is no reason to use this product. Unfortunately, the rest of us *do* need a tool like Money Smith to help us better manage our money and make financial decisions.

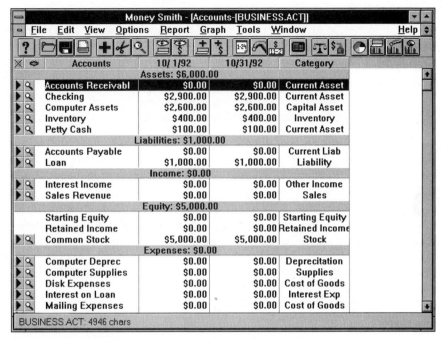

**Money Smith is a complete bookkeeping system made easy to use.**

## About the documentation

The documentation is essentially laid out on a need-to-know basis. Each topic is short and should take you about 5 to 10 minutes. To begin, you need only read steps 1 through 7 to start Money Smith, set up your accounts, and begin using most of its features. This will take you about an hour if you are a slow reader. The time is well spent because there are a number of timesaving features detailed along the way.

## About Money Smith

Money Smith is a full-featured tool for financial management. It is scalable. You are not forced to use features you don't want to use. If you don't want a budget, don't establish one. If you don't care about account categories, don't use them. If you'd rather track your investments using a spreadsheet, you are not forced to enter them here. We designed it to be simple, but we have the features to satisfy more-demanding users.

Money Smith is easy to learn. Unlike other money-management programs, Money Smith has a fully graphical interface. If you can use a mouse, you can learn Money Smith easily. Our press-and-point help system lets you point out the things you need help with. Just click on the ? icon and then click on the field, item, or menu command you need help with. What could be easier?

My advice? Start small and learn the advanced features as you go. The key is to start, and start soon. If you start now, you'll have a base of information to make decisions from. If you start later, you'll continue to make many of your financial decisions blindly.

## Help

Money Smith has comprehensive help features, including this entire documentation, on-line. Our original point-and-press ? (question mark) icon on the toolbar changes the mouse cursor into an arrow with a question mark. Press the menu selection or item you want help on, and help magically appears. The same help is available if you press Shift+F1. You can also press F1 at any time (even in dialog boxes) to get context-sensitive help. You won't find these features in just any piece of shareware!

# Step 1: Starting Money Smith

Double-click on the Money Smith icon after setting it up using the WSETUP program. Another method is to select the Run command from the Program Manager's File menu and then type the path to Money Smith, such as C:\GIZMOS\MONEY\SMITH.EXE.

## Licensing window

Money Smith brings up a licensing window the first time you run it. This window lets you type your name and read the license. It is very important that you type your name and read the license terms before selecting the I Agree button. If you don't type your name, the I Agree button is not enabled. If you agree to the license terms, choose I Agree and continue. If you have problems with the terms, you can disagree and exit the program. Please read the license and understand that the program is provided "as is." We will not be held liable for any losses of any kind that you might suffer as a result of using this program.

## Exiting Money Smith

To exit, you can double-click on the Money Smith system menu box, choose the System Close command from the system menu box, or choose the File Exit command.

# Step 2: Using Money Smith Files

All Money Smith data for a particular set of accounts is stored in a single file with an ACT extension. You might keep one Money Smith file for all your home accounts and another for a small business. You can name Money Smith files any way you choose, as long as you keep the ACT extension.

## For the beginner

The easiest way to establish accounts is to use one of the sample Money Smith ACT files distributed with Money Smith. Just open a file (HOME.ACT is a good starting point) using the File Open command and edit the accounts to reflect your own starting balances and budgets. The File Open command is represented as an open folder icon on the toolbar. Applications using the sample files are described in the section entitled "Looking at Examples Using Money Smith," later in this chapter.

## Creating a new Money Smith file

Creating an empty Money Smith file is easy. Just choose the File New command from the menu and add accounts and transactions as you please. Be sure to save the file when you exit from Money Smith, or your work will be lost.

## Saving a Money Smith file

Choose the File Save command from the menu or press the F3 key to save the currently active Money Smith file. The Save command is represented as a floppy disk on the toolbar. If you have not given this file a name, you are prompted to type one now. You don't need to type the ACT file extension because it is assumed. If you have the status bar on, you should see the name and size of the file on the status bar after you save the file.

## Opening an existing file

Choose the File Open command or select the file from the numbered list at the bottom of the File menu. Alternatively, you can access the File Open command by clicking on the open-file icon on the toolbar. The name and size of the file appear on the status bar after the file has been opened. The file is opened with the last active window views.

## Using passwords

Money Smith has a password feature to prevent unauthorized people from looking at your private files. You can enable this feature on any file using the Options Set-Password command. Just type a new password twice (so that they match), and the password is set. Anyone attempting to open the file is asked the password. If that person types the wrong password, he or she can't open the file. Don't forget your password, or you won't be able to open the file either! Refer to the Options Set-Password command for removing and altering existing passwords.

## Copying, backing up, and saving as another name

To copy, back up, or save your file to another filename, just open the file as described previously and then choose the File Save-As command. Select or type the directory desired and then type the new filename. Click on the OK button to save the file; click on the Cancel button to cancel the save. Alternatively, you can use the Windows File Manager or another disk-copying utility to copy your ACT file to another disk or directory.

# Step 3: Learning Interactive Windows

One of the most powerful features of Money Smith Version 2.0 is the graphical interface we call *Interactive Windows*. The interface enables you to intuitively access the functions you need without even touching the toolbar or menu. To edit an account or transaction, for example, just press the small magnifying glass next to the account or transaction. To zoom to an assets graph, just press the Assets bar. Like most true graphical interfaces, learning this takes time, but the ability to avoid menus and toolbars makes Money Smith much easier to use in the long run.

# About Interactive Windows

Interactive Windows are introduced at this point to eliminate confusion when windows start popping up all over the screen. They may seem confusing at first, but you will quickly come to appreciate the power they provide. Interactive Windows provide context-sensitive functions directly on the reports, graphs, and views you use most.

Press-and-point help works well with Interactive Windows and lets you easily navigate the windows. Just click on the ? icon on the toolbar and then click the field or icon you need help with.

# A summary of interactive fields

A number of features can be directly accessed from the main views and reports:

♦ **Close Box:** Click here to close the current window.

♦ **View (Eye) Icon:** Click here to toggle from account to transaction view.

♦ **Accounts:** Click here to create a new account.

♦ **Transaction:** Click here to add a new transaction.

♦ **Dates:** Click on a date to change the date.

♦ **Category:** Click here to define a new category.

♦ **Type Bars:** Click here to graph the accounts of this type.

♦ **Register Triangle:** Click here to see the register of transactions for this account.

♦ **Edit Magnifying Glass:** Click here to edit the account or transaction.

♦ **Investment Icon:** Click here to see the investment records for this account.

♦ **Mark/Unmark Transaction:** Press this button to toggle the cleared transaction flag.

# Investment report fields

The following are available only from the investment report:

♦ **Investment:** Add a new investment transaction.

♦ **Price:** Graph the price history of the investment.

♦ **Value:** Graph the value history of the investment.

♦ **Return:** Graph the return history of the investment.

## Other interactive functions

You can edit any account, transaction, or investment by simply double-clicking on it. Also, any menu function can be run from any of the Interactive Windows.

Editing menu functions are carried out in the context of the current window. For example, if you press the big "+" icon while your current window is an account report, you add an account. If you press the Cut (scissors) icon while your current window is an investment window, you end up cutting the current investment transaction.

File, Report, and other nonediting functions work in the context of the current accounting file. For example, if you press the Save icon from any active window, you save the currently active account file. If you press the Print icon, you print the current window. Other menu functions follow in this fashion.

## Interactive graphs

The graph legends are interactive. Again, the function depends on the context of the graph. If you click on an account legend, you see the transaction register report for the corresponding account. If you click on a category name, the category report pops up. If you click on an investment legend, the corresponding investment dialog box pops up.

# Step 4: Setting Up Your Accounts

Everything you want to track using Money Smith should be an account. Accounts represent actual accounts or property (called *assets*), real loans, liens or liabilities, your net worth — which in Money Smith is called *equity* — and your income and expenses. The key to tracking your finances is setting up a good set of accounts. If you have too many, your decisions will be clouded by trivial data. If you have too few, you won't be able to track what's really going on. In general, it's best to start with a few accounts and grow as you go. You can make up new accounts as you type transactions by just typing an account name that does not exist. So there is no reason to knock yourself out with accounts at the beginning.

## Using Account view

It's easiest to work on accounts from the Account view. Choose the View Account command, or press the button on the toolbar that shows an eye over a checkbook, to view accounts. Account view shows a list of all your accounts listed alphabetically by type, with their name, category, and starting and ending balances. Account view also displays totals for your assets, liabilities, equity, income, and expenses. Using Interactive Windows, you can perform a variety of functions from Account view.

# For the beginner

The easiest way to establish accounts is to use one of the sample ACT files distributed with Money Smith. Just open a file (HOME.ACT is a good starting point) using the File Open command and then edit the accounts to reflect your own starting balances and budgets. Delete the ones you don't need and add others as you go.

# Adding accounts

To add an account, choose the Edit Add command or press the big "+" toolbar button while in Account view. Fill out the Account dialog box as described next.

### Filling out the Account dialog box

At a minimum, fill in the Name, Type, and Start Balance or Budget fields in the Account dialog box. Use the Tab key to move from field to field. Other fields are optional and can be filled in later. The Name is any unique account name like

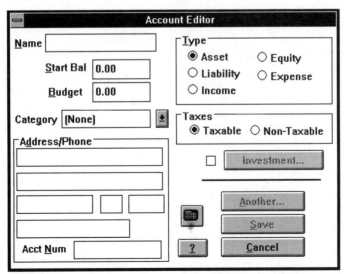

Use the Account dialog box to set up accounts: Specify a starting balance or monthly budget amount, the type of account, and account name.

*Checking* or *Savings.* The Type can be asset, liability, equity (net worth), income, or expense. The Start Bal (starting balance) represents the account balance at the beginning of the month you start using Money Smith. The Budget is a monthly expected income or expense for the account. Click on the Another button to save the account and bring up another. Click on the Cancel button to stop adding accounts.

## Editing accounts

Suppose that you've entered your accounts but messed up a few. Select the offending account by clicking on it with the mouse or use the arrow keys to highlight it while still in Account view. Choose the Edit Edit command or click on the magnifying glass icon (either the one next to the account or the one on the toolbar). Double-clicking on the account or pressing the Enter key from Account view also works. Any of these actions brings up the Account dialog box. Use the Tab key or mouse to move to the field you want to change and either type or select the new value. Click on the Save button or press the Enter key to save your changes. Click on the Cancel key to discard your changes.

## Deleting accounts

Suppose that you have an account that's no longer needed, or maybe you're just deleting an account from one of our examples. Before you can delete an account, you must make sure that there are no transactions against it. If there are, Money Smith will tell you. Select the account you want to delete from Account view using the mouse or arrow keys; then choose the Edit Cut command or click the scissors icon on the toolbar.

Money Smith will prompt you to confirm the deletion. If you still have transactions assigned to the account, Money Smith won't delete the account. To find these transactions, you can select the account and switch to Register view by choosing the Report Current Account Register command or clicking on the small register triangle next to the account you want to zoom to. You may have to change the date to view the transactions you are interested in. Delete or edit these transactions and assign them to another account.

## Limitations

You are currently limited to 200 accounts in a single Money Smith file.

# Step 5: Entering Transactions

Any flow of money from one account to another is called a *transaction*. You can find the most obvious examples of transactions by opening your checkbook. When you write a check to pay your electric bill, you are creating a transaction from your checkbook account to your *Electric* expense account. When you make a credit-card purchase, you create a transaction from your MasterCard account to the appropriate expense account. When you pay off that credit card, you create a transaction from your Checking account to your MasterCard account.

## Thinking transactions

It takes awhile to think in terms of transactions. The two primary questions are these:

*"Where's the money coming from?"*

*"Where's the money going to?"*

If you have answers to both of these questions, you are ready to enter transactions.

## Transaction view

Money Smith has lots of ways to look at transactions. You probably want to be in a transaction window when editing transactions. Transaction view shows you all your transactions for the current accounting dates. You can get to Transaction view by using the View Transaction command, by clicking on the icon with an eye over a dollar sign on the toolbar, or by pressing the eye button from the title bar of the Account View window.

## Current Register report

Another handy report is the Current Account Register report. The register report shows the transactions for only the current account (Checking, for example). This view is great if you're working from just one account. To get to Register view, just press the small register triangle next to the account you want to see on any account report or window. Alternatively, you can select the account using the mouse or keyboard and then choose the Report Current-Account-Register command.

## Account Reconciliation report

One last useful transaction report is the Reconcile Current Account report. This report enables you to easily compare your cleared and uncleared account balances. The report is particularly useful for clearing checks when you get an account report at the end of the month. To see this report, first select the account you want to see from any account window by using the mouse or keyboard and then select the Report Reconcile-Current-Account command.

## Dates

The current dates determine which transactions are viewable and what account balances you see. By default, Money Smith sets the accounting dates to reflect the beginning and end of the current month. You can alter the Money Smith defaults to Beginning of Year or Today using the Options Preferences command. If you want to see another month or several months, use the Options Date command to change the current dates. The small calendar-page icon on the desktop, as well as the date title on most Interactive Windows, also activates the Date command.

## Adding transactions

To add transactions, make sure that you are in Transaction view or reports; then choose the Edit Add command or click on the big "+" button on the toolbar. Fill in the Transaction dialog box as described shortly.

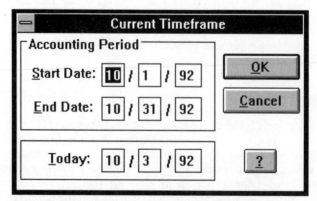

Select the Date command to change the accounting dates from the first and last days of the month to any starting and ending period you want.

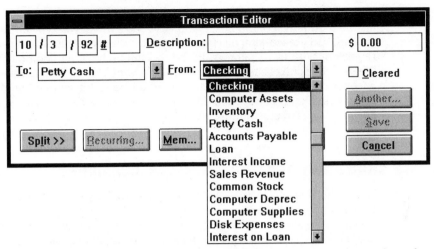

Enter transactions using the Transaction dialog box (this one is set up for transaction-style entries); select accounts from the drop-down combo box.

## Check-style versus transaction-style entry

There are two separate, but similar, transaction-entry formats available in Money Smith. You can set either using the Options Preferences command.

The default, called *check-style* transactions, has a familiar check-like format. You make deposits and withdrawals to a single account (the Use account in the dialog box). This format is very useful for entering a lot of transactions from a single account.

The other format, called *transaction-style* transactions, uses an accountant-style To and From entry system. Transaction-style entry is useful when you have a lot of different accounts involved.

People who have used other financial packages, or who use Money Smith just to balance their checkbooks, usually prefer the check-style entry. People running businesses, who are familiar with accounting, and people insulted by check-style entry will prefer transaction-style entry.

## Filling out the Transaction dialog box

To fill out the Transaction dialog box, enter the date and check number (if any) of the transaction. Enter the payee (for a check) or a description of the transaction. It is important that you fill in the Description or Payee field. Then enter the amount for the transaction in your local currency. For transaction-style entries, you can enter the To and From accounts by either typing the names or selecting them from the combo box. For check-style entries, you typically enter the account you are working on (Checking) in the Use combo box and select either Deposit or Withdrawal along with the account in the other combo box. The Cleared check box is used to help reconcile your account and is usually checked once the transaction has cleared the bank. Click on the Another button or press the Enter key to save this transaction and bring up another. Click on Save or Cancel to stop adding transactions.

## Using smart-number fields and the calculator

One of the powerful features in Money Smith is called *smart-number entry fields*. Basically, any field you can put a number into becomes a complete calculator. You can type a math expression, such as **29.5*4,** and Money Smith will automatically do the math for you and place the result in the field.

For more complex financial calculations, you can bring up the Money Smith financial calculator. Just click on the calculator icon on the toolbar or in most dialog boxes. The financial calculator has its own detailed on-line help and documentation files. Select the help index from within the calculator to see this documentation on-line.

## Making up accounts on the fly

A powerful feature of Money Smith is that it enables you to make up new accounts while entering transactions. Suppose that you have a new bill or expense that didn't exist before. In the Transaction dialog box, just type the new account name in either the To or From field. When you try to save this transaction, Money Smith asks whether you want to add the new account; if you do, the Account Editor dialog box appears to let you add it — all without skipping a beat.

## Performing recurring transactions on the fly

Money Smith lets you automate repetitive bills and transactions using recurring transactions. Clicking on the Recurring button lets you do this. The topic is fully covered later in this chapter in the section on recurring transactions.

# Performing split transactions

A feature added in Money Smith Version 2.0 enables you to split a transaction to or from a second account. To use this feature, enter the amount of the entire transaction in the amount field, fill out the remainder of the dialog box as described previously, and then press the Split button. Pressing the Split button brings up additional fields in the dialog box. You must first select whether you want to split the To amount or the From amount. Then you select an account to split the transaction to and enter the amount of the split. As you enter the split amount, you see the dollar amount going to each account displayed under the corresponding account name. Verify these amounts before saving the transaction.

For example, suppose that you want to split a transaction from your checking account to the principal and interest accounts for a loan payment. Suppose that the total payment is $1,000, with $900 going to principal and $100 going to interest. Enter the total $1,000 payment amount, specifying Checking as the From account and Loan Principal as the To account. Press the Split button and select the Split To radio button. Then enter the split account as Loan Interest and the split amount as $100. You should see the correct amounts under each account name.

# Editing transactions

From either Transaction or Register view, select the transaction you want to change with the arrow keys or mouse. Choose the Edit Edit command or press the Enter key to bring up the Transaction dialog box. Double-clicking on the

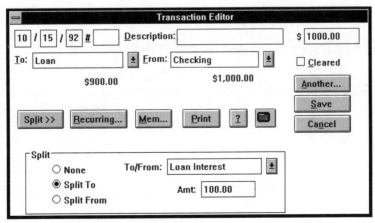

You can split a transaction: From a single payment, you can specify that a certain amount go to a second account.

transaction or pressing the magnifying button next to the account or on the toolbar also works. Use the Tab key or mouse to move to the field to which you want to make changes and press the Enter key or click on Save to save your changes.

## Deleting transactions

From Transaction or Register view, select the transaction you want to delete using the mouse or arrow keys. Choose the Edit Cut command or click on the scissors icon on the toolbar. Confirm your deletion by clicking on Yes. All your account balances are updated automatically.

## Printing transactions

You can print transactions from any of the Transaction views by using the File Print command. You can also print checks, if you have a capable printer and tractor-fed business checks of the right type. See "Printing Basics," later in this chapter, for more information.

## Limitations

The number of transactions is limited by the amount of memory Windows can allocate and by the program itself. Each transaction takes approximately 64 bytes, and Money Smith itself places a limitation of 32,767 transactions on your accounts. Typically, as you approach 1,000 transactions, performance degrades rapidly. It is wise to roll out your transactions at least yearly.

# Step 6: Using Money Smith Reports

Now that you have entered tons of financial trivia, what do you do with it? A great starting point is to print a few reports. Reports tell you lots of interesting things, like where your money is coming from and going to. They tell you your net worth. They help you balance your checkbook. Let's look at some Money Smith reports.

# Using reports

You create a report window using one of the commands under the Report menu. Report windows are documents of their own. One great thing about this is that they update automatically. If you add a transaction or change a balance, the report changes magically. You don't need to re-create it. The other great thing about Money Smith reports is that they are fully interactive. You can edit accounts, transactions, and investments, and perform virtually any operation while the report windows are active. You can even click on certain fields on the reports to jump to individual areas on the report. (See "Step 3: Learning Interactive Windows," earlier in this chapter.) Reports even have their own menu of commands for printing, copying, saving to a text file, and so on. Two important commands to know are the File Close command and the Window 1, 2, 3 command because they let you exit the report or just switch back to your Money Smith account window.

# Assessing your financial position

After you have the first month's data entered in Money Smith, it's a good time to evaluate your financial position. You typically do this task once a month.

First, set the accounting dates, using the Date command, to reflect a month you are interested in (typically the previous month). All your reports are now limited to that month. Start with the Balance statement. This statement shows your assets, liabilities, and net worth. The Balance statement is a snapshot of what you own, what you owe, and your net worth (equity). It's good to look at the percentages of your assets and liabilities. If you have too much tied up in one asset or liability, you may want to consider diversifying to other assets and liabilities. If your net worth (equity) is positive, you are probably in pretty good shape. Under Equity, you will see your retained earnings. If that number is positive, you had a good month because you took in more than you spent.

For a more detailed view of your income, try the Income report. This report shows your income and expenses for the month for each account. Take a look at the percentages. Where did all your money go? Click on the Expenses title bar to see a graph of your expenses. Which were the biggest? Why? Zoom in on some of your big expense accounts by clicking on the graph legend for the accounts. Look over the transactions before you close the windows. What can you do better next month?

A good start is to establish a budget. Every income and expense account can have a budget associated with it. Edit each account to establish a budget. You can view your budget versus actual income and expenses using the Budget report. After a few months, you can use the History graphs to view trends in your spending and refine your budget.

# Setting the report/graph title

Use the Options Report-Title command to change the title that appears at the top of all reports and graphs.

## The Balance (net worth) statement

The Balance statement gives you a snapshot of your current value or net worth. It shows you all your Assets (great!), all your Liabilities (not so great!), and your Equity (net worth). The percentages are nice because they show you where your money is really tied up. Equity is interesting because it shows both your starting equity (the sum of all your starting balances) from the beginning of the accounting period and your *retained income,* a fancy word for how much money you've earned and kept in one form or another for the accounting period.

## The Income (cash flow) statement

The Income statement shows you totals of all your income accounts and expense accounts for the current dates. Percentages show you where your money is coming from and going to. You'll probably be surprised by some of the expense percentages. The bottom line on this statement is your net income, which represents all your income minus all your expenses. If this is a positive value, you are in good shape. If it's negative, you may be in trouble because you are spending more dollars than you are taking in. Take a hard look at your expenses (the Graph Expense command might help) and the Budget report (described next) to try to get spending under control. Decide what you can do without and stick to it.

## The Budget report

The Budget report helps you compare your monthly budget against actual spending. It shows the difference between the budget you set for each income or expense account and the amount you actually spent. The difference is shown both in dollars and as a percent. By tightly monitoring this report, and modifying your budget to better reflect reality, you may be able to bring up that net-income figure from the Income report and live a little more financially secure.

## The Tax Summary report

If you have been vigilant all year long and entered data for a whole year, this report might help you fill out the old 1040 form. Basically, it just totals the income and expense accounts you marked as Taxable or Non-taxable and prints the totals. This might help remind you of the 10 bucks you gave to charity or the $100 you earned on that stock you forgot about. Money Smith will not do your taxes, however. It won't even attempt to estimate your taxes because tax laws change annually, and we're just not ready for that kind of litigation. Several commercial programs are out for this purpose, but a discount tax preparer probably costs no more than the software. You don't need to teach yourself how to use a tax preparer either!

## The Reconcile Account report

The monthly checking statement comes in, and, as usual, it doesn't match your account balance. You bring up Money Smith and switch to the Reconcile Current Account report. In a few minutes, you mark off the transactions that have cleared by pressing the little gray *X*s on the corresponding transactions. As you clear your transactions, the report changes to reflect new balances automatically. Why don't other financial programs give you interactive reports, you wonder? A quick press on the financial calculator icon lets you do a little math on the different balances, and in a few minutes your checkbook and statement are reconciled using Money Smith.

## The Category report

Categories are better covered in "Defining Account Categories," later in this chapter. Basically, a *category* is a collection of accounts you want to group together. It may be an investment portfolio, consumer debt, your entertainment expense accounts, or just about anything. This report shows you the current balances of all the accounts in your categories and totals them for you. Percentages let you see how much single accounts affect the category balance. This is a nice advanced-account feature. It is also very useful for tracking separate business or property expenses, as described in the section on sample applications.

## The Current Account Register report

This report simply shows all the transactions for a single account for the current accounting period. The running balance is kept on the right and updated as you enter, edit, and delete transactions. This command is commonly invoked by a click on the small triangle to the left of the account you want to view.

## The Investment report

Investments are better covered in "Understanding Investment Accounts," later in this chapter. Basically, an *investment* is a special account with separate investment transactions kept on it. Because investment information is kept separate from the account balances, you can track the value of a stock or mutual fund easily, without messing up the nice, neat double-entry accounting system that Money Smith uses for regular balances. The investment report shows all your investment transactions as well as the current values and return on a single investment account. Like all Money Smith reports, it is interactive, letting you add, edit, and delete investment transactions from an account.

# Limitations

You can only have a total of ten combined report and graph windows active on a single Money Smith file. This is not a problem for most users.

# Step 7: Using Money Smith Graphs

Another great way to look at your finances is by using Money Smith graphs. Graphs often let you see things that are not so obvious in the numbers. Money Smith graphs are fully interactive, so you can see the data as it's updated and even perform functions from graph windows.

## Using graphs

You create a graph window by using one of the commands under the Graph menu. Graph windows are documents of their own. One great thing about this is that they update automatically. If you add a transaction or change a balance, the graph changes as well. Another great thing is that they are interactive. You can switch graph types and zoom to other accounts at the press of a button. Two important commands to know are the File Close command and the Window 1, 2, 3 command because they let you exit the graph or just switch back to your Money Smith account window. You can also copy your graph to the Clipboard and read it into any graphical program like Paintbrush.

## Setting the report/graph title

Use the Options Report-Title command to change the title that appears at the top of all reports and graphs.

### The Assets, Liability, Equity, Income, and Expense graphs

All these graphs display a pie graph of accounts of the given type: assets, liability, equity (net worth), income, or expense. It's important to note that only accounts with positive balances are graphed. I don't have an easy method for graphing negative pie slices. These graphs have an interactive title bar that lets you switch to other types by pressing the corresponding button in the window. Similarly, you can zoom to a single account or category report by pressing on the corresponding graph legend.

### The One-Category graph

The Category graph enables you to select a category from your list of categories and shows the category composition in a pie graph. This is great for seeing how an investment portfolio is diversified, for example.

### The All-Category graph

The All-Category graph enables you to view the breakdown of all categories of a particular type. If you want to see how all the assets are distributed among the categories, just select this command. To see another type (like expenses), just click on the corresponding button on the window title bar.

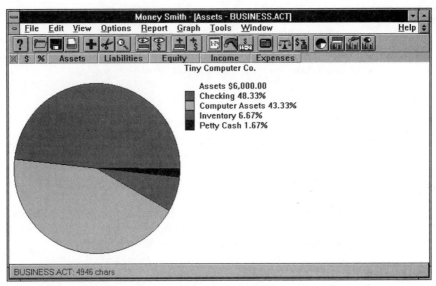

The All-Category graph shows you a pie graph of a particular group of categories.

## The History One Account, History One Category, and History Assets Etc... graphs

These graphs provide a monthly history of the end-of-month balance for the currently selected account, category, or type totals. They are very useful for observing long-term patterns in an account, a category, or overall balances. Note that these graphs show *all* data since the very first transaction recorded and do not limit the display to the current accounting dates. It is interesting to note how seasonal many expenses are, after you have collected a year's worth of data.

## The Current Investment graph

The Graph Current-Investment command enables you to see bar graphs of the price, value, or return history for a selected investment account. Just make sure that you first select the account you want to graph from Account view, or you get an error when you try to graph a noninvestment. The bar graphs show all your investment history and might help in deciding what to do with a stock or mutual fund.

***Note:*** Returns are calculated as total value over total investment and are not annualized or otherwise convoluted, so be careful when making decisions based on these values.

## Limitations

You can only have a total of ten combined report and graph windows active on a single Money Smith file. This is not a problem for most users, but you get an error when you open the eleventh window.

# Printing Basics

## What can I print?

You can print any graph, report, or view on virtually any Windows-compatible printer. If you have the right printer and order the proper checks, as described shortly, you can also print checks using Money Smith.

## General printing tips

Make sure that your printer is properly set up before using it. If you do not have the correct Windows driver installed for your printer, the printout does not work correctly. For graphs, reports, and views, the File Print command prints the currently active window. This command is also available from the toolbar as a printer icon. A Print dialog box shows the current document and page. You can click on the Cancel button in the Print dialog box to cancel a printout in progress or use the Windows Print Manager to manage the printing process.

## Printing windows

Printing any Money Smith window is easy. Select the window you want to print and choose the File Print command or click on the printer icon on the toolbar. Your current window — view, report, or graph — is printed on the printer.

## Adjusting print options

You can adjust printer options from the dialog box that comes up when you select the print command. The number of copies can be entered, a font selected, and grid or title box lines added to enable easy viewing of your report or graph. Fonts default to a 10-point size, but some fixed-pitch printer fonts may be too large to print a complete report. Most printers also print slower when the Print Grid or Print Title boxes are selected.

# Printing graphs

You first need to create a graph using the Graph commands; you can activate a previously created graph by clicking on it with the mouse. You can use two methods to print a graph: One is to print by using the File Print command, which you access from either the menu or by clicking on the print icon on the toolbar, to produce a full-page graph. If you want a smaller graph, use the Edit Copy command to copy the graph to the Clipboard and then import it into Windows Write, Paintbrush, or a similar application and print it from there.

# Ordering checks

Before you can print any checks, you need to order some. Before you order checks, I recommend that you perform a little test to make sure that your printer supports check-size paper. Money Smith supports general-purpose, tractor-fed, business-size checks of 8½ inches by 3½ inches and prints them in landscape mode. If your Windows tractor-fed printer driver does not support the 8½ by 3½-inch paper size in landscape mode, odds are the checks won't work. Money Smith also supports standard laser-printed checks in the 8½ by 11-inch cut-sheet form. You can check this by using the Printer Setup command: Press the Setup button in the dialog box and look at the list of paper sizes. You can also press the Print button from the Transaction dialog box, which forces you to set your printer paper size if it is not set correctly. I recommend printing a few checks on plain paper before you order real checks.

***Warning:*** If you have a tractor-fed printer, make sure that you *test* your printer for the 8½ by 3½-inch paper size, using actual paper. Some printer drivers do not support 3½-inch forms.

Check styles follow:

Tractor feed: 091013 and 091004 (Business size)

Laser checks: 081013 and 081004 (Business size)

Sample checks may be obtained from

**Deluxe Business and Computer Forms**
3660 Victoria Street North
P. O. Box 64046
St. Paul, MN 54164-0046
Phone: 1-800-328-0304

This organization has been cooperative and will usually send you a catalog and a few samples if you call. Money Smith works with most of the dual-purpose (one check and one blank page with check number for records) tractor checks with a little vertical adjustment. Deluxe Business and Computer Forms is not the only organization that prints checks; it just happens to be the one I got my samples from. Many other reputable companies make checks that work. Just use discretion and common sense before sinking a bundle into custom-printed checks.

## Printing tractor-fed checks

You print checks directly from your transactions. First, make sure that your printer is set up with the checks in it and that the form size is set to 8½ inches wide by 3½ inches high, in landscape mode. Next, bring up the Transaction dialog box to enter or edit a check and click on the Print button in the dialog box.

If your paper size is wrong, change it by using the File Printer-Setup command. Otherwise, your check is printed twice — once on the check and once on the receipt page. The transaction Description field is printed on the *Pay to the Order of* line. The To Account Address, if any, is printed below that, and the Transaction Date and Amount are printed in the appropriate columns. You may need to adjust your printer alignment to match the checks exactly.

If you switch back to normal printer paper after printing checks, be sure to adjust your printer page size accordingly.

## Printing laser checks

Laser checks are printed with the same procedure as tractor-fed checks. Select the Print button from the Transaction dialog box. For laser printers, you do not need to worry about adjusting the page size. Simply put the preprinted checks into your paper bin. Consult your printer manual to determine whether the checks should go face up or face down in the bin.

# Setting Up Recurring Transactions

## What's a recurring transaction?

Another great feature of Money Smith is its capacity to automate transactions so that you don't go crazy every month entering transactions. These are called recurring transactions. A *recurring transaction* is a transaction that happens with some regular frequency. A check box lets you either totally automate the transaction (so that you don't even know it was added) or have Money Smith bring the transaction up when you open the file so that you can edit it or cancel it. Don't use recurring transactions for investments. "Understanding Investment Accounts," later in this chapter, describes an investment reminder service that is better for this purpose.

# Creating recurring transactions the easy way

The easy way to create a recurring transaction is to bring up an existing transaction for editing by using the Edit Edit command from the Transaction or Register view. Then click on the Recurring button in the Transaction dialog box to bring up the Recurring Transactions dialog box.

## Filling out the Recurring Transactions dialog box

Fill out the dialog box as you normally would. The date field is the starting date of the transaction, which should be sometime in the future. Check or uncheck the confirm check box, depending on whether you want to confirm this transaction or have it be fully automatic. Generally, if a transaction is for the same amount each month and you're not interested in putting a check number in, make it fully automatic. Otherwise, make sure that you check the confirm box. Check the frequency as appropriate. Click on Save to save or click on Cancel to cancel this addition.

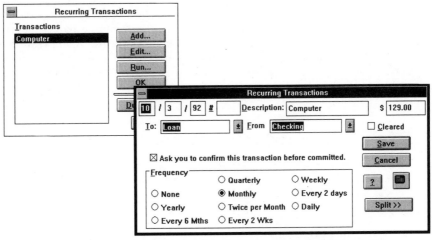

Use the Recurring Transactions dialog box to set up a transaction that occurs with some regularity.

### Specifying recurring transaction dates

When you enter your recurring transactions, you generally want them to start at some future date. Entering a date in the past can be done but generates a dialog box asking whether you want the transaction run now. If you run it now, each transaction necessary to bring the recurring transaction up to today's date is also run at this time. If you don't run it now, the transactions are deferred until the next time you open the file.

## Editing recurring transactions

The Tools Recurring-Transactions command and the icon with the dollar sign over the date on the toolbar both bring up a list of recurring transactions. You can add to, edit, or delete from the list. The basic procedure is to select the transaction you want to work with from the list box and then press the Add, Edit, or Delete button to bring up the transaction editor or a delete confirmation dialog box. The Run button forces an out-of-cycle transaction to be created but does nothing to the regular schedule of recurring transactions. The Quit button leaves the recurring transaction editor.

## Running recurring transactions

Ordinarily, you don't do anything to run recurring transactions. It automatically happens when you open the file. Just make sure that your system clock is correctly set before you run Money Smith. You can force an out-of-cycle recurring transaction by pressing the Run button from the Recurring Transactions dialog box, as described in the preceding paragraph. The Run button enables you to run a transaction with no recurring date or just run a transaction outside its normal cycle.

## Running memorized transactions

If you want a recurring transaction to run at a random period, you can set it up as a recurring transaction and specify None for the transaction frequency. This action creates a recurring transaction that never runs, unless you manually select the Run command from the Tools Recurring-Transactions dialog box. When you receive the bill or notice corresponding to this transaction, just go to the Tools Recurring-Transactions command and select the Run button for this transaction.

## Mixing transaction periods: nonstandard frequencies

How do you automatically handle nonstandard transactions? For example, suppose that you make a payment twice a month on the 5th and 23rd. Treating this as a twice-a-month payment does not work. The solution is simply to enter two recurring transactions — one that runs monthly on the 5th and one that runs monthly on the 23rd. By combining sets of standard transactions, you can form virtually any nonstandard transaction frequency.

## Limitations

Money Smith has a limitation of 40 recurring transactions active on one Money Smith file. This is not a problem for most home users.

# Defining Account Categories

## What's an account category?

An *account category* is nothing more than a group of accounts you want to occasionally see together. Examples include investment portfolios, your IRA accounts, and expense groupings like living expenses, entertainment expenses, and the like. The Report Category command and Graph Category command let you analyze these categories after you set them up.

## Creating categories the easy way (on the fly)

The easy way to create categories is to assign them as you build or edit your accounts. From Account view, select an account you want in the category and edit it by double-clicking on it with the mouse or by pressing the Enter key. This action brings up the Account dialog box, which has a field called Category. The Category field, by default, has a value of (None). Use the Tab key or mouse to move the cursor to this field and type the name of your new category. Press the Enter key or click on the Save button to save the transaction, and Money Smith asks whether you want to add this new category. Press Yes. Now edit the other accounts you want in the category; for these subsequent accounts, you can use the drop-down list of categories to select the newly added category instead of typing it.

## Editing categories

You can add, edit, and delete categories using the Tools Category command. The basic process is to select the category you want to act on and then click the Add, Edit, or Delete button. It is important to note that you will get an error if you delete a category with accounts defined in it.

## Viewing category data

You can look at your categories with the Report Category command. This command shows accounts in each category, sorted by type, with sums and percentages computed. This is great for tracking separate properties or business units. Categories can also be graphed. You can view either the history or composition of various categories with commands under the Graph menu.

## Looking at sample applications

Categories have many uses. They are useful for abstracting accounts to get a broad view of things. If you look at the categories set up in the sample accounts HOME.ACT and RENTER.ACT, you will see samples of this use. Broad categories like Living Expenses let you better see how the money is coming and going, for example.

Businesses, too, can take advantage of categories. The sample file BUSINESS.ACT shows how you can use categories to generate sums that correspond closely to summary balance and income statements.

You might also use a category to separately track small business or property expenses within your personal accounts. For example, if you own a property that you rent, you might want to assign all the accounts associated with that property to one category. Then, by simply using the Category report, you can get a quick summary of assets, income, and expenses associated with that property. If you have several properties, you can establish a separate category for each.

## Limitations

Currently, an account can be assigned to only one category at a time. You can only have 30 categories defined for one Money Smith file.

# Understanding Investment Accounts _____

## What's an investment account?

An *investment account* is a normal Money Smith account with an added investment history. The investment history keeps track of the price, value, and money invested in a security like a stock or mutual fund. The reason for keeping it separate from regular account balances and transactions is to maintain the sanity of the standard double-entry accounting system used by Money Smith. Automatic transaction features help you to keep your investment balance and account balance in sync. The advantage of an investment account is that it helps you track the value of your investments without destroying the simplicity of a standard cost-accounting system.

## Establishing an investment account

Some small investment examples are included in the sample account files that come with Money Smith. To add your own investment account, create an account as you normally would; then edit it by double-clicking on the account or pressing the Enter key in Account view. From the Account Editor dialog box, click on the Investment button to bring up the Investment Editor dialog box. Click on the Add button to add a new investment transaction.

## Looking at investment records

The easiest way to look at your investment records is to use the Current Investment report: select the command from the Report menu or press the investment icon (the small rainbow) next to the investment account you want to look at. The Investment report is fully interactive; you can easily edit investment records or jump to graphs by clicking on fields on the report.

## Filling in an investment history record

To create an investment record from the Investment report, press the Add icon (the large "+") on the toolbar. Enter a description, dollar amount invested, and price for the security. The number of shares are computed from the dollar amount and price. When you save your record, a corresponding regular transaction is displayed with the same information to update the underlying account with the new investment. Fill this in and save it if you want. This double-entry system maintains the balance of the underlying account without having its value fluctuate with the price of the security. This feature is enabled and disabled with the Auto Tx button in the Investment Editor dialog box.

## Editing history records

To change a history record, select the record in the Investment report and press the Edit icon (the magnifying glass). Change fields as you want; click on the OK button to make them permanent or the Cancel button to cancel the changes.

## Deleting investment history records

To delete an investment history record, select the record from the Investment report and then press the Cut icon (the scissors) on the toolbar. Unlike with transactions and accounts, you cannot paste investment records after they have been cut.

## Viewing history records

To view past performance, all you need to do is select the Rainbow investment icon next to the investment account in any Account view or report. This action brings up the investment report with all the investment, price, value, and performance information listed in an interactive format. Alternatively, you can use the Tools Investment command to bring up the Investment Editor dialog box, which has similar information in a slightly different format. You can also see these records graphically by using the Graph Current-Investment command.

## Removing investments from an account

You can remove the investment history from an account by pressing the Remove button in the Investment Editor dialog box for a given account. You generally do this by first editing the account. Click on the Investment button from the Account Editor dialog box and then click on the Remove button from within the Investment Editor dialog box. This action wipes out all investment records associated with this account completely, so be careful.

## Using another way to edit investments

You can also access the Investment Editor dialog box by using the Tools Investment command. This command lists all accounts defined as investment accounts and enables you to select and edit them.

## Using the investment reminder service

The *investment reminder service* is analogous to recurring transactions for investment accounts. The main difference is that the investment history record editor is always displayed for confirmation because it is assumed that you always need to enter a new security price. To set up the investment reminder, click on the Reminder button on the Investment Editor dialog box. Fill in the starting date, history record amount and description, and the frequency for the reminder. The From account indicates which account to transfer money from for regular transactions generated, if the Auto Tx check box is enabled. Click on OK to enable the reminder or click on Cancel to cancel the reminder. Reminders come up automatically when you open the file on or after the assigned date.

## Limitations

Money Smith keeps the last 20 investment history records and automatically rolls over into a starting investment balance for the investment.

# Performing End-of-Year Processing

## Why roll out transactions?

You could go on indefinitely writing transactions against the same set of accounts, but I recommend that you roll out your accounts at least once (sometimes more times) a year. Why? For one thing, Money Smith has to walk through all the transactions to get a good balance when you load the accounts or change the dates. After awhile, this process gets time-consuming. Another reason is that Money Smith quickly becomes a memory pig when you have files with thousands of transactions. It's also good to make a fresh start each year because that's what the IRS wants from you.

## What really happens?

After making a backup copy of your transactions, Money Smith rolls the dollar amounts from all your transactions before the cutoff date into the respective account balances and then deletes those transactions. The result is that you have the same asset, liability, and equity account balances but no more transactions. You start the year fresh.

## Running the end-of-year process

Select the Options End-of-Year command from the menu. If you want a closeout, or ending, date other than the one shown, click on Yes and enter another close-out date. Click on Yes if you want your investment history records rolled out with the regular transactions. Otherwise, your investment histories of any investment accounts will remain intact. If you want a backup copy (and I highly recommend this), click on Yes and enter a new name like HOME92 to save a backup of this file. If you choose to back up, you are also prompted about removing recurring transactions from the backup. I also highly recommend that you remove recurring transactions from the backup. Otherwise, you will be hit with a flurry of recurring transactions when you later want to access your backup file. Finally, you get one more chance to bail out: If you click on Yes (indicating that you *don't* want to bail out), the work is done and everything before the closeout date is rolled out.

# Looking at Examples Using Money Smith _____

In response to a number of you who wanted to use Money Smith in new ways, we wrote this section on real-world examples of using Money Smith. Using this section, you can tailor Money Smith's features to your particular application, be it home or business.

## Sample files

As described in "Step 2: Using Money Smith Files," earlier in this chapter, several sample files or "accounting templates" are included with Money Smith to make setting up accounts as painless as possible. To use one of these sample files, just open the file using the File Open command and edit the accounts to reflect your own starting balances and budgets. I strongly recommend that you use the File Save-As command to save your file as a name other than the name of the sample file so that your file is not overwritten if you ever need to reload Money Smith.

## Homeowners and renters

Files called HOME.ACT and RENTER.ACT are included for the homeowner and renter. These files have typical home accounts set up with names like *Checking, Paycheck,* and *Gas & Electric.* To better reflect your own financial position, you will need to edit, add to, and delete some of the sample accounts. Follow the instructions in "Step 4: Setting Up Your Accounts," earlier in this chapter, to alter the list of accounts. It is important that you set up your asset and liability accounts to reflect the starting balances of your actual assets and liabilities for the month you begin using Money Smith.

For example, suppose that you don't have a boat. Just select the Boat account and then click on the Cut command (the scissors icon) to delete the Boat account. If your mortgage is not the amount shown, just change the starting balance for the loan and the property to get what you want. If you have additional accounts you want to track, like your country-club expenses, just add a new expense account called *Country Club*. It will probably take a few iterations to get everything as you want it, but that's OK. Remember that you can always add new accounts on the fly, so there is no need to pull out all your hair right now.

## Real property: to add or not to add?

One item most people neglect is the value of their real property (furniture, cars, boats, computers, and so on). The choice to include them or not include them is yours. If you want a genuine idea of your overall net worth, you probably want to estimate the value of your furniture and other major items and put it in. You enter such items as *Asset* accounts. I personally only keep track of assets I might sell at some future point, like cars and boats. One gentlemen who wrote us actually keeps track of the value of every item he owns, right down to the last T-shirt, pencil, and pen. Like tracking expenses, it is an individual choice as to how much detail you want. More-detailed accounts require more work; less-detailed accounts mean less work but, inevitably, less information available for making real decisions.

## Tracking a small business

Money Smith is perfectly suited to a small business because it is a true double-entry accounting system. We track our entire business on Money Smith, using accounts very similar to those distributed in the sample file BUSINESS.ACT. In BUSINESS.ACT, accounts and categories are set up for a small shareware business. The mission is to use computers to produce software, so that explains why the accounts have names like *Computer Assets* and *Disk Expenses*. If you print out the account listing from BUSINESS.ACT and put it in terms of your own business, you should have little trouble. A small-business or accounting book would also help.

## Using **BUSINESS.ACT** for your business

Converting the sample file over to your own business is not as hard as it might seem. Just walk through the major account groupings and edit them as you please. We'll walk through a quick example here using a home sewing business. This business uses cloth and patterns to create clothing that it sells.

First, what are your assets? Clearly, you will need many of the accounts already there. You might use Accounts Receivable to keep track of items you have delivered but not yet been paid for. You might need the Checking and Petty Cash accounts to keep track of money. You may want separate Inventory accounts to keep track of patterns and cloth you have in stock and have not used. Your capital (production) assets for this business are probably not Computer Assets, so you can change that account to be *Sewing Machine* for this example.

Second, what are your liabilities? Here, include any business loans, business credit-card accounts, or Accounts Payable to include things you may have ordered but not yet paid for.

Third, what is your income? You can broadly establish one sales account, as we did in BUSINESS.ACT, or establish separate accounts for different major customer categories instead. For example, you might want to separate cash sales from those made with credit cards, to more easily balance your credit-card and cash accounts at the end of the month.

Fourth, what kind of equity do you have in your business? If you are not incorporated, you probably don't have common stock. A proprietorship might enter the initial investment in the business in place of the Common Stock account. A partnership could enter each partner's initial investment as a separate account.

Finally, what are your major expenses? It is important that you distinguish the cost of goods sold from other overhead expenses because the IRS typically wants to know how much you sold and how much the goods you sold cost you. For the sewing business, we might have cloth and patterns as cost-of-goods-sold expenses, and pins, needles, and other small items might go in a general supplies account. Depreciation expenses on the sewing machine replace the computer depreciation account. Other expenses, like marketing, might replace the printing and mailing expense accounts.

When you have a good set of accounts established, accounting is simply a matter of tracking where every single penny is coming from and going to. You must use discipline and keep up with your business to get any meaningful results. Save every receipt after you enter it for tax purposes. After a few months, you will find that the monthly income, balance, and history reports are invaluable for running your business.

## Tracking real estate

A common application of Money Smith is in managing real estate. My example assumes that you are a landlord tracking multiple rental properties. You can use the same principles to track a single property from your home or business account.

The secret to tracking multiple properties is to use the category feature of Money Smith. Simply define a category name (see the section on categories) for each property you want to track. Then define Asset, Liability, Income, Equity, and Expense accounts for each property and assign those accounts to the corresponding category. If you want to see all the income and expense data associated with one particular property, just use the Report Category-Summary command. The summary shows each property and the totals of all the accounts assigned to each, sorted by type. The various category graphs enable you to graphically see which properties account for the bulk of income and expenses, as well as to zoom in on individual properties to see various accounts.

This same technique can be used for tracking multiple business units or for separating business information from within your home account.

# Using the Money Smith Financial Calculator ___

You can use the Money Smith calculator just like a regular calculator. It performs the basic functions shown shortly, using either Infix or Postfix notation. The algebraic expression is shown on the top left, and the intermediate result is shown to the right. The number of digits shown correspond to the current currency settings. (Set currencies from the Windows Control Panel, International area.)

To start a calculation, just clear the calculator by using the C button and then type an expression as you would on most any calculator. The Backspace key lets you back up if you make a mistake.

| Button | Function |
| --- | --- |
| C | Clear expression |
| <- | Backspace |
| ^ | Raise to power |
| *, / | Multiply, Divide |
| +, − | Add, Subtract |
| ( ) | Group Infix expression |
| = | Evaluate expression |
| Enter | Enter Postfix number |

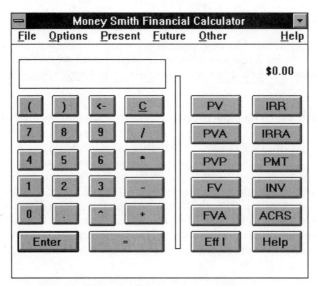

You can use the Money Smith calculator just like a regular
calculator, with either Infix or Postfix notation.

## Using financial functions

To perform a financial function, just press the button corresponding to the
desired function. (PV is present value, for example.) Type the required information, and the result is displayed at the bottom of the dialog box. Click on the OK
button to save the result to the calculator or click on the Cancel button to discard the result and return to the calculator.

## Performing compound financial calculations

You can use financial calculations in series to perform more complicated functions. For example, suppose that you want to compute the value of the $10,000
you have in an IRA if you continue to add $2,000 a year to it for ten years. First,
click on the FV button to calculate what your initial $10,000 will be worth in ten
years. When you have filled out that dialog box, click on the OK button. Click on
the "+" button on the calculator to indicate that you want to add something to
the current value. Next, click on the FVA button to calculate the value of your
additional $2,000-per-year deposit for ten years. When this dialog box is filled
out, click on the OK button. You will see the FV and FVA values added together.
Click on the "=" button to finish off the calculation. You can chain any of the
financial functions together in this way to get more complicated results. Just
remember to click on an operator like "+" between major financial functions so
that your results are added together rather than overwritten.

| Examples: Infix (Normal) Algebra | |
|---|---|
| *Expression* | *Result* |
| 100+3*2= | $106.00 |
| (5+4)*9 | $81.00 |
| 80.8/(2^3) | $10.10 |

| Examples: Postfix (Reverse Polish) Algebra | |
|---|---|
| *Expression* | *Result* |
| 100 3 + 2*= | $106.00 |
| 5 4 + 9 * = | $81.00 |
| 80.8 2 3 ^ / | $10.10 |

## Using the smart-number entry fields

A *smart-number entry field* is a numeric field that you can enter expressions into as well as numbers. All the financial function dialog boxes use Money Smith's original smart-number entry fields to make life easier on you. This means that you don't have to go back to the calculator to perform simple calculations. Just type your calculation directly into the field.

Five operators are supported: plus (+), minus (–), divide (/), multiply (*), and exponent (^). Parentheses are supported for Infix notation. Both Postfix and Infix expressions are accepted, depending on the current algebra setting.

Following is the basic procedure for using smart-number fields:

1. Select any numeric field in the dialog box.

2. Type an algebraic expression. When you press the Tab key to go to the next field, the result is displayed.

Here are some sample uses (assuming Infix algebra):

♦ To calculate a monthly interest rate for a 10 percent annual rate: 10/12

♦ To calculate the number of years to IRA eligibility assuming that you are 35 years old: 59.5 – 35

♦ To perform simple math: 254.32 – 73.44

## Using the Infix Algebra command

This command sets the calculator mode to Infix algebra. This is the "normal" form of algebra most people are familiar with. Infix algebra is generally of the form number, operator, number.

Expressions are evaluated with the exponent operator having the highest precedence, the divide and multiply operators the next highest precedence, and the plus and minus operators the lowest precedence.

Following is the basic procedure for using Infix algebra:

1. Choose the Options Infix-Algebra command from the menu.

2. Clear the calculator and type an algebraic expression.

| Examples: Infix (Normal) Algebra | |
|---|---|
| *Expression* | *Result* |
| 100+3*2= | $106.00 |
| (5+4)*9 | $81.00 |
| 80.8/(2^3) | $10.10 |

## Using the Postfix Algebra command

This command sets the calculator mode to Postfix algebra. This is the Reverse Polish notation used by scientists and engineers, and popularized by the Hewlett-Packard line of calculators. Numbers are placed on a numeric stack, with most operators working on the top number or the top two numbers on the stack. Note that the Enter key pushes numeric values on the stack, and the equal (=) key forces evaluation of the current expression. Note also that all smart-number entry fields work in Postfix mode, when Postfix is chosen.

Following is the basic procedure for using Postfix algebra:

1. Choose the Options Postfix-Algebra command from the menu.

2. Clear the calculator and type in a Postfix expression.

| Examples: Postfix (Reverse Polish) Algebra | |
|---|---|
| *Expression* | *Result* |
| 100 3 2 * + | $106.00 |
| 5 4 + 9 * | $81.00 |
| 80.8 2 3 ^ / | $10.10 |

# Using the Present Value (PV) function

The PV function performs simple present value calculations, based on a future value and a fixed interest rate.

Here is the procedure:

1. Choose the PV button or select the Present Value function from the menu.

2. Enter the future value, interest rate per period, and number of periods. The display is automatically updated with the calculated present value.

3. Click on OK to have the result entered in the calculator; click on Cancel to discard the result.

Here are some examples of Present Value:

**Q: How much money do I need to invest at an annual rate of 10 percent to get $10,000 in 15 years?**

**A:** Enter Future Value=10,000, Interest=10, and Num of Periods=15 to get a result of $2,393.92.

**Q: How much do I need to invest now at an annual rate of 8 percent to get $100,000 in 10 years, if interest is compounded monthly? (Use the smart-number feature based on 12 months.)**

**A:** Enter FV=100000, Interest=8/12, and Num of Periods=12*10 to get a result of $52,841.35.

# Using the Present Value of an Annuity (PVA) function

The PVA function performs simple present value calculations based on a fixed periodic investment.

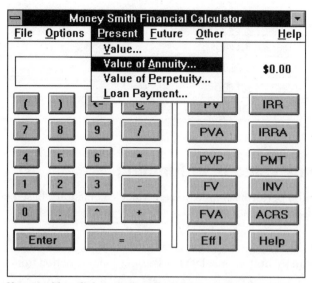

You can either click on the function buttons or select functions
from the menu bar to invoke common financial functions.

Here is the procedure:

1. Choose the PVA button or select the Present Value of an Annuity function
from the menu.

2. Enter the payment amount, interest rate per period, and number of periods.
The display is automatically updated with the calculated present value of
the annuity.

3. Click on OK to have the result entered in the calculator; click on Cancel to
discard the result.

Here are some examples of Present Value of an Annuity:

Q: **What's the present value of an annuity of $5,000 per year for ten years,
assuming a 7 percent interest rate?**

A: Enter Payment=5000, Interest=7, and Num of Periods=10 to get a result of
$35,117.91.

Q: **A retailer is selling a video camera financed at a price of $30 per month
for 48 months at 10 percent interest (compounded monthly). How much
am I paying for the camera, including financing, in today's dollars?**

A: Enter Payment=30, Interest=10/12, and Num of Periods=48 to get a result of
$1,182.84.

```
┌─────────────────────────────────────────────────────┐
│ ═   │       Present Value of an Annuity              │
├─────────────────────────────────────────────────────┤
│                                                       │
│      Payment        │100.00│        ┌──────────┐      │
│                                     │    OK    │      │
│  Interest per Period │10.000│   %   └──────────┘      │
│                                     ┌──────────┐      │
│  Number of Periods  │10.00 │        │  Cancel  │      │
│                                     └──────────┘      │
│                                     ┌──────┐          │
│                                     │  ?   │          │
│      Present Value        $614.46   └──────┘          │
│                                                       │
└─────────────────────────────────────────────────────┘
```

**After you select a financial function, a dialog box appears and asks you for the information that the function requires.**

# Using the Present Value of a Perpetuity (PVP) function

The PVP function performs a simple present value calculation of the value of a perpetual payment. Examples of perpetuities are fixed-income preferred stock and lifetime fixed payments like pensions or lifetime annuities. (**Note:** A true perpetuity pays forever, but pensions and the like can often be thought of as perpetuities because you are not particularly concerned with the value of the pension after your death.)

Here is the procedure:

1. Choose the PVP button or choose the Present Value of a Perpetuity function from the menu.

2. Enter the payment amount and the effective interest rate per payment period. The display is automatically updated with the calculated present value of the perpetuity.

3. Click on OK to have the result entered in the calculator; click on Cancel to discard the result.

Here are some examples of Present Value of a Perpetuity:

**Q: What's the present value of a perpetuity that pays $1,000 per year indefinitely, if you discount inflation at 7 percent per year?**

**A:** Enter Payment=1000 and Interest=7 to get a result of $14,285.71.

**Q: What's the value of my $3,000-per-month fixed lifetime pension, if I expect a 5 percent inflation rate per year?**

**A:** Enter Payment=3000 and Interest=5/12 to get a result of $720,000.

## Using the Present Loan Payment (PMT) function

The PMT function calculates the payment for a loan, given the present value, interest rate, and number of periods. It can be used for calculating your loan payment for your car, house, and so on.

Here is the procedure:

1. Choose the PMT button or select the Present Loan Payment function from the menu.

2. Enter the loan amount (in present dollars), effective interest rate per payment period, and number of periods. The display is automatically updated with the calculated payment per period for the loan.

3. Click on OK to have the result entered in the calculator; click on Cancel to discard the result.

Here are some examples of Present Loan Payment:

**Q: What's the monthly loan payment on a car that has a total cost of $14,000, assuming 8 percent annual interest and a 48-month loan?**

A: Enter Loan Amount=14000, Interest=8/12, and Num of Periods=48 to get a result of $341.78.

**Q: What's the yearly payment on a house costing $100,000 at an interest rate of 10 percent financed for 30 years?**

A: Enter Loan Amount=100000, Interest=10, and Num of Periods=30 to get a result of $10,607.92.

## Using the Future Value (FV) function

The FV function performs simple future value calculations based on a present value and fixed interest rate.

Here is the procedure:

1. Choose the FV button or select the Future Value function from the menu.

2. Enter the present value, interest rate per period, and number of periods. The display is automatically updated with the calculated future value.

3. Click on OK to have the result entered in the calculator; click on Cancel to discard the result.

Here are some examples of Future Value:

**Q: If I invest $10,000 now at a fixed interest rate of 10 percent, how much will I have in 15 years?**

**A:** Enter Present Value=10,000, Interest=10, and Num of Periods=15 to get a result of $41,772.48.

**Q: If I put $1,000 in a savings account paying 5 percent compounded quarterly, how much will it be worth in five years? (Use the smart-number feature based on four quarters/year.)**

**A:** Enter Present Value=1000, Interest=5/4, and Num of Periods=4*5 to get a result of $1,282.84.

# Using the Future Value of an Annuity (FVA) function

The FVA function performs a simple future-value calculation, based on a fixed payment and fixed interest rate. It can be used for calculating the future value of fixed periodic investments.

Here is the procedure:

1. Choose the FVA button or select the Future Value of Annuity function from the menu.

2. Enter the payment value, interest rate per period, and number of periods. The display is automatically updated with the calculated future value of the annuity.

3. Click on OK to have the result entered in the calculator; click on Cancel to discard the result.

Here are some examples of Future Value of Annuity:

**Q: If I invest $2,000 per year in an IRA at a fixed interest rate of 10 percent, how much will I have in 15 years?**

**A:** Enter Payment=2000, Interest=10, and Num of Periods=15 to get a result of $63,544.96.

**Q: If I invest $100 per month in an investment paying 7 percent (compounded monthly), how much will I have in eight years?**

**A:** Enter Present Value=100, Interest=7/12, and Num of Periods=8*12 to get a result of $12,819.88.

# Using the Investment Required for a Future Value (INV) function

The INV function calculates the fixed payment needed to reach a certain investment goal in a fixed number of years, at a fixed interest rate.

Here is the procedure:

1. Choose the INV button or select the Future Investment for a Future Value function from the menu.

2. Enter the Future Value, interest rate per period, and number of periods. The display is automatically updated with the calculated investment required.

3. Click on OK to have the result entered in the calculator; click on Cancel to discard the result.

Here are some examples of Investment Required for Future Value:

**Q: I want to be a millionaire in 30 years; how much do I need to invest yearly at a fixed interest rate of 10 percent to get my first million?**

**A:** Enter Future Value=1000000, Interest=10, and Num of Periods=30 to give the rather modest result of $6,079.35 per year! Start saving!

**Q: I want to save for my child's college education. I estimate the total cost of her college 15 years from now to be $400,000 in future dollars. How much do I need to invest each month at a rate of 9 percent (compounded monthly) to send her to school?**

**A:** Enter Future Value=400000, Interest=9/12, and Num of Periods=15*12 to get a result of $1,057.07.

# Using the Effective Annual Interest (EffI) function

The EffI function calculates an effective interest rate based on a fixed interest rate and the number of periods the interest is compounded over yearly. For example, a 10 percent fixed interest rate compounded monthly gives an effective annual rate of 10.47 percent.

Here is the procedure:

1. Choose the EffI button or select the Other Effective Annual Interest function from the menu.

2. Enter the interest rate per year and number of periods the interest rate is compounded over per year. The display is automatically updated with the calculated effective annual rate of interest.

3. Click on OK to have the result entered in the calculator; click on Cancel to discard the result.

Here are some examples of Effective Annual Interest:

**Q: My bank offers 5 percent on savings, with dividends compounded quarterly. What's the effective annual rate?**

**A:** Enter 5 percent annual interest with 4 periods per year to get an annual rate of 5.09 percent.

**Q: A money-market fund offers 7.2 percent compounded daily. What's the annual rate assuming that the fund holds a 7.2 percent yield for the year?**

**A:** Enter Interest=7.2 and 365 periods per year to get an effective rate of 7.46 percent.

# Using the Internal Rate of Return (IRR) function

The IRR function calculates the effective rate of interest for an investment given a present value, future value, and number of periods. Note that for sales of held items, the Present Value may be the purchase price of the investment and the Future Value may be the sales price of the investment.

Here is the procedure:

1. Choose the IRR button or select the Other Internal Rate of Return function from the menu.

2. Enter the Future Value, Present Value, and number of periods in the dialog box. The display is automatically updated with the calculated effective rate of interest per period.

3. Click on OK to have the result entered in the calculator; click on Cancel to discard the result.

Here are some examples of Internal Rate of Return:

**Q: A zero-coupon bond sells for $800, with a face value of $1,000, maturing in four years. What's the rate of return for the bond?**

**A:** Enter Present Value=$800, Future Value=$1000, and 4 periods to get a returned rate of 5.74 percent.

**Q: I sold my house that I held for ten years. My purchase price was $50,000, and the sales price was $100,000. What return did I get on my real-estate investment?**

**A:** Enter Present Value=$50,000, Future Value=$100,000, and Num of Periods=10 to get an effective rate of 7.18 percent.

## Using the Internal Rate of Return for an Annuity (IRRA) function

The IRRA function calculates the effective rate of interest for a regular investment given a payment, future value, and number of periods.

Here is the procedure:

1. Choose the IRRA button or select the Other Internal Rate of Return for Annuity function from the menu.

2. Enter the Payment, Future Value, and number of periods in the dialog box. The display is automatically updated with the calculated effective rate of interest per period.

3. Click on OK to have the result entered in the calculator; click on Cancel to discard the result.

Here are some examples of Internal Rate of Return for Annuity:

**Q: I have invested $100 per month over five years in a fund now worth $8,000. What's my effective annual return?**

**A:** Enter Payment=100*12, Future Value=$8000, and 5 periods to get a returned rate of 14.43 percent.

**Q: I put $2,000 per year in my IRA accounts for the last ten years. They now have a total value of $40,000. What's my overall annual rate of return?**

**A:** Enter Payment=2000, Future Value=40000, and Num of Periods=10 to get an effective rate of 14.74 percent.

## Using the ACRS Depreciation (ACRS) function

The ACRS function calculates the depreciation for a given year based on the 1986 version of the ACRS depreciation tables. You enter the purchase price, select the class of property, and enter the year.

1986 act classes are listed in this section. Note that regulations change yearly; please consult a tax publication before using!

Note that 27.5 and 31.5 Year property is not supported by this tool because it is depreciated on a straight-line basis, prorated from the month placed in service.

| Class | Type of Property |
|---|---|
| 3 Year | Research Equipment |
| 5 Year | Autos, Tractors, Trucks, Computers |
| 7 Year | Industrial Equipment, Office Furniture |
| 10 Year | Long Lived Equipment |
| 27.5 and 31.5 Year | Real Estate, Buildings |

Here is the procedure:

1. Choose the ACRS button or select the Other ACRS Depreciation function from the menu.

2. Enter the purchase price of the property, choose the correct property class, and enter the year you want depreciation calculated for.

3. Click on OK to have the result entered in the calculator; click on Cancel to discard the result.

Here are some examples of ACRS Depreciation:

**Q: I bought a new computer for $3,000 for my business. What's my first year ACRS depreciation?**

**A:** Enter Price=3000, Class=5-Year, and Year=1 to get a depreciation of $600.

**Q: I purchased a truck for my business use for $20,000. I am in the third year of writing it off. What's my depreciation for the third year?**

**A:** Enter Price=20000, Class=5-Year, and Year=3 to get a depreciation of $3,800.

# Licensing Terms

## Obtaining registered licensed versions

You can obtain a registered, licensed version of Money Smith from Money Smith Systems by remitting payment as described in the following sections and as described in the REGISTER.TXT file. You can look at and print REGISTER.TXT by using the Windows Notepad application. Site licenses are available; write for details.

## License

Money Smith is marketed as shareware, but it is not free. You are given a 30-day trial period to decide whether you want to purchase the software. The full license is described in the "General terms" section. Basically, it says we're not responsible for any damages whatsoever that result from using this product and that you agree to register the product if you use it outside the 30-day trial period. The Association of Shareware Professionals Ombudsman statement is at the end of the license. The ASP is a professional organization to help mediate problems between us and the public. The ASP does not provide technical support.

## Definition of shareware

Shareware distribution gives users a chance to try software before buying it. If you try a shareware program and continue using it, you are expected to register. Individual programs differ on details: Some request registration and others require it; some specify a maximum trial period. With registration, you get the simple right to continue using the software and an updated program.

Copyright laws apply to both shareware and retail software, and the copyright holder retains all rights, with a few specific exceptions as stated shortly. Shareware authors are accomplished programmers, just like retail authors, and the programs are of comparable quality. (In both cases, there are good programs and bad ones!) The main difference is in the method of distribution. The author specifically grants the right to copy and distribute the software, either to all and sundry or to a specific group. For example, some authors require written permission before a commercial disk vendor may copy their shareware.

Shareware is a distribution method, not a type of software. You should find software that suits your needs and pocketbook, whether it's retail or shareware. The shareware system makes fitting your needs easier because you can try before you buy. And because the overhead is low, prices are low also. Shareware has the ultimate money-back guarantee: If you don't use the product, you don't pay for it.

## Registering

We're not going to do any arm-twisting about registering. We distribute full working copies of Money Smith, with the understanding that you are a responsible person who recognizes a software value. The only difference between the version you have in your hands and the registered version is the reminder dialog boxes that come up when you start Money Smith. Registering gets rid of those dialog boxes and also gets you the very latest version, not to mention heavy discounts on upgrades. To register, use the form at the end of this chapter or print the REGISTER.TXT file to the printer (using either the Windows Notepad utility or the DOS PRINT command). Fill out the form and send it in with payment.

## Benefits of registration

♦ A disk (720K or 360K) including the latest version of Money Smith with documentation and examples

♦ A professionally bound and printed manual of complete documentation

♦ A 90-day limited warranty with mail support (see license for details)

♦ All the reminder dialog boxes removed from the software

♦ Notification of and nice discounts for later versions

## Phone-ordering services

Call 1-800-242-4775 and ask for product #10441.

To make it easy to register, we have arranged for the Public (software) Library (PsL) to take orders by MasterCard, American Express, Visa, or Discover.

You can call 1-800-242-4775 or 713-524-6394 or fax to 713-524-6398, or you can order through CompuServe at 71355,470 or through the mail (no group discounts/site licenses) at PsL, P.O. Box 35705, Houston, TX 77235-5705. These numbers are for *ordering only*.

PsL does not provide technical support, site licenses, or discounts and does not handle returns or give you any technical information. PsL only takes orders! Contact Money Smith Systems at P.O. Box 333, Converse, TX 78109 if you want to order in quantity or do anything but order.

*Second Phone Ordering Service:* 1-800-444-5457; product number V303.

We have an arrangement with Software Excitement! to take registrations as well. You can call them toll free at the preceding number or fax to 503-826-8090; for foreign orders, call 503-826-8082. The mailing address is Software Excitement, 6475 Crater Lake Hwy., Central Point, OR 97502.

## CompuServe electronic mall

You can order your copy through the CompuServe Mall: type **GO SE.**

## Direct international registration

(Price is U.S. $29.95 plus $6 shipping.)

Credit-card orders can be made at the voice or fax phone number provided earlier. For mail orders, checks/money orders should be in U.S. dollars drawn on U.S. banks. Many post offices offer International Money orders, which are also acceptable.

## Eurosoft Registration Service in foreign currency

For the convenience of European users, we have signed with Eurosoft Registration Service. Mail orders can be made in foreign currency to the following:

United Kingdom and Scandinavia: Mail 19.97 pounds sterling to

**Hillfoots Data Services**
Mains House
Tillcoultry
Clackmannanshire
FK13 6PQ, UK

*Remainder of Europe:* Mail DM 59,92 or equivalent to

**Abegglen, Heinz**
0367-206054-50
Credit Suisse
CH-3800 Interlaken
Switzerland

(Currencies are OK.)

*Other Services:*

The following groups offer currency-conversion services to aid in international registrations. Terms vary, but these services generally charge a small fee to take your order in local currency and write a check in U.S. dollars drawn on a U.S. bank to us. I have no affiliation with any of these services; I offer their addresses as a convenience here.

UK: PC Independent User Group
87 Higland St, TONBRIDGE, Kent TN9 1RX, ENGLAND
Phone: 0732 771512
International: +44 732 771512; FAX +44 732 771513

Australia: BrightsPark Computers
  P.O. Box 253, Morley, WA 6062
  Phone: (09)375-1178 or 018 917-877; FAX (09) 375-1668
  Accepts Visa, MasterCard, AMEX, Diners Club, Bankcard

# Registration form for Version 2.0

Money Smith Copyright © 1991-1992 by Bradley J. Smith
All Rights Reserved. CompuServe [70324,1077]; Prodigy [VTDW36A]
***Instructions:*** *Fill out the form completely.* Print clearly. Send completed form
with U.S. check or money order payable to

**Money Smith Systems,** P.O. Box 333, Converse, TX 78109

| DESCRIPTION | QTY | PRICE(US$) | TOTAL |
|---|---|---|---|
| 1 Copy Money Smith with manual _____ copies | | x $29.95 | $ _____ |

***\* Site License Discounts:*** *Includes 1 disk, 1 copy of manual, plus site license*
*agreement — only by mail.*

| | | | |
|---|---|---|---|
| 2-4 computers at $25.00 each | _____ computers | x $25.00 | $ _____ |
| 5-9 computers at $23.00 each | _____ computers | x $23.00 | $ _____ |
| 10-24 computers at $20.00 each | _____ computers | x $20.00 | $ _____ |
| 25-49 computers at $18.00 each | _____ computers | x $18.00 | $ _____ |
| 50-74 computers at $16.00 each | _____ computers | x $16.00 | $ _____ |
| 75 and up $1200 one-time fee per site. | | | |
| | | | |
| Financial Calculator only | _____ copies | x $15.00 | $ _____ |
| Additional printed manuals | _____ copies | x $ 6.00 | $ _____ |

| | | |
|---|---|---|
| **SUBTOTAL** | | $ *4.00* |
| Shipping and Handling | | $ _____ |
| Texas residents **only:** add 8¼% sales tax | | $ _____ |
| $2 extra for overseas shipping & handling | | $ _____ |
| **GRAND TOTAL** | | $ _____ |

***\* International orders:*** See details in README.TXT!

DISK SIZE: 3½" (720K) ☐      5¼" (360K) ☐

REGISTER TO: _____

COMPANY: _____

SHIP TO: _____

CITY: _____ STATE: _____ ZIP: _____

COUNTRY: _____

PHONE: (Optional) _____ DATE: _____

# License agreement

This is a legal agreement between you (either individual or entity) and Money Smith Systems. If you have purchased a registered version and do not agree to the terms of this agreement, promptly return the disk and accompanying items within 90 days for a full refund.

### Limited distribution rights

A limited license is granted to copy and distribute the unregistered shareware version of Money Smith subject to the conditions below and the following:

1. No fee, charge, or compensation may be accepted for distribution of Money Smith except

   A. Time-related usage fees for electronic bulletin boards not directly related to the downloading of this program.

   B. Association of Shareware Professionals (ASP) member distributors may charge a nominal fee of no more than $7 to distribute this shareware version.

   C. Others wishing to charge a fee not provided for above can do so only with the express written consent of Money Smith Systems or Bradley J. Smith.

2. No one may modify Money Smith files, documentation, or executables in any way, including reverse-engineering the program.

3. The full machine-readable documentation, help files, executable file, and examples must be included with each copy.

# Single-user license

A single-user license permits users to use Money Smith only on a single computer. Licensed users may use the program on different computers as long as the program is not used on more than one computer at a time. Site license or network use requires a separate license. No one may copy or distribute any portion of the registered documentation, files, or executables, except for registered users with the express purpose of backing up these files for personal use on a single computer.

# Notice

Money Smith is not and has never been public-domain software, nor is it free software. Unregistered users are granted a limited single-user license to use the shareware version of Money Smith on a 30-day trial basis for the purpose of determining whether Money Smith is suitable for their needs. Use of Money

Smith beyond the initial 30-day trial period requires registration. The use of unlicensed copies of Money Smith outside of the initial 30-day trial by any person, business, corporation, government agency, or any other entity is strictly prohibited.

## Limited warranty for registered users

Money Smith Systems warrants that the disks provided with the registered version of Money Smith are free from defects for a period of 90 days from the purchase date. You may return defective disks to us for replacement or a full refund. For refunds, the complete package including documentation must be returned in a saleable state. Money Smith Systems also agrees to provide mail software support for a period of 90 days from the original purchase date. Direct questions to Money Smith Systems, P.O. Box 333, Converse, TX 78109.

## Limitation of liability

MONEY SMITH SYSTEMS AND BRADLEY J. SMITH HEREBY LIMIT THEIR LIABILITY TO, AT MONEY SMITH SYSTEMS SOLE DISCRETION, 1) THE ORIGINAL PURCHASE PRICE OF THE SOFTWARE OR 2) REPLACEMENT OF A DEFECTIVE DISK. PURCHASER OF SOFTWARE AGREES NOT TO HOLD MONEY SMITH SYSTEMS OR BRADLEY J. SMITH LIABLE FOR ANY DAMAGES WHATSOEVER BEYOND ONE OF THE TWO REMEDIES DESCRIBED ABOVE.

## Assign to successor clause

Purchaser of this software hereby agrees that Money Smith Systems may at any time without notice or consent of purchaser assign this license to a successor corporation, business, or heir. Any rights, liabilities, and warranties may be transferred at Money Smith Systems' sole discretion along with this license to the successor corporation, business, or heir.

## General terms

Use of this program for any period of time equates to agreement to all terms of this license. Money Smith is only one possible tool for financial management. You should make *no financial decisions whatsoever* based on the feedback Money Smith provides. This software is provided as is.

EXCEPT AS PROVIDED ABOVE, MONEY SMITH SYSTEMS AND BRADLEY J. SMITH DISCLAIM ALL WARRANTIES WITH RESPECT TO THIS PRODUCT, EITHER EXPRESS OR IMPLIED, INCLUDING, BUT NOT LIMITED TO, IMPLIED WARRANTIES OF MERCHANTABILITY AND FITNESS FOR A PARTICULAR PURPOSE. SHOULD THE PRODUCT PROVE DEFECTIVE IN ANY WAY, THE PURCHASER ASSUMES THE RISK OF SERVICING, REPAIR, CORRECTION, INCIDENTAL, OR CONSEQUENTIAL DAMAGES (INCLUDING BUT NOT LIMITED TO DAMAGES RESULTING FROM INVESTMENT DECISIONS MADE, BUSINESS PROFITS LOST, INTERRUPTION OF BUSINESS, LOSS OF INFORMATION, AND THE LIKE) FROM USING THIS SOFTWARE.

This agreement is governed by the laws of the state of Texas and shall inure to the benefit of Money Smith Systems and any successors, administrators, heirs, and assigns. Any action or proceeding brought by either party against the other arising out of or related to this agreement shall be brought only in a STATE or FEDERAL court of competent jurisdiction located in Bexar County, Texas. The parties hereby consent to personal jurisdiction of said courts.

Association of Shareware Professionals (ASP) Ombudsman Statement:

"Bradley J. Smith is a member of the Association of Shareware Professionals (ASP). ASP wants to make sure that the shareware principle works for you. If you are unable to resolve a shareware-related problem with an ASP member by contacting the member directly, ASP may be able to help. The ASP Ombudsman can help you resolve a dispute or problem with an ASP member but does not provide technical support for members' products. Please write to the ASP Ombudsman at 545 Grover Road, Muskegon, MI 49442 or send a CompuServe message through CompuServe Mail to ASP Ombudsman 70007,3536."

## Acknowledgments

Money Smith is a trademark of Bradley J. Smith.

IBM is a trademark of International Business Machines.

Microsoft, Windows, Paintbrush, Notepad, DOS, Word, and Excel are all trademarks of Microsoft Corp.

Borland C++ is a trademark of Borland International.

The Association of Shareware Professionals (ASP) is a nonprofit group dedicated to the shareware profession.

PKZIP, PKUNZIP, and PKSFX are all trademarks of PKWARE, INC.

Many thanks to Charles Petzold and Jeffrey Richter for their fine books and examples of Windows programming.

If I missed any other credits, it was unintentional, so please write and I'll be sure to include them in future versions.

# Parents

Version 2.3
Copyright © by NickleWare

---

*P*arents is a simple Windows program that helps you chart a family tree for yourself or anyone. This is a great way to preserve memories at family reunions, record births in the family, or just enlighten yourself about your kin.

**Type of Program:** Database

**Requires:** Windows 3.0 or later

**Registration:** Use the form at the end of this chapter to register with the shareware author.

**Technical Support:** NickleWare provides registered users with technical support through CompuServe and mail.

## Introduction

Parents is an application designed to help make collecting and organizing your genealogy easier. With the help of Parents, you can more easily gather, store, and view information about all your ancestors, your children, and your children's children.

Parents enables you to enter and store vital information such as names; birth, marriage, and death dates and places; and more. All this information can then be easily organized and related together to form your family tree. You also can print detailed information about any one of your ancestors, as well as print your immediate family tree.

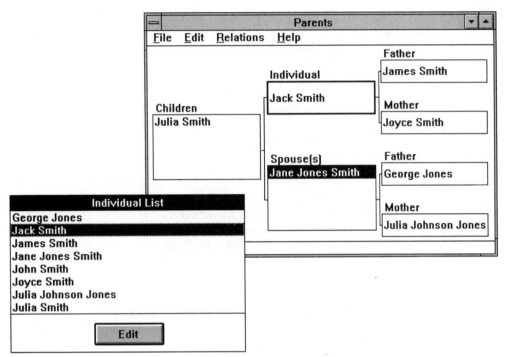

**Parents is a program that helps you chart a family tree.**

# Getting Started

When you run WSETUP to install Parents, a Parents group window is added to your Program Manager. Double-click on the Parents icon to start the program. Parents then creates all the data files it needs to run and places them on the same drive and path where the software was installed.

When Parents is started for the first time, the following entry is placed in your WIN.INI file:

```
[PARENTS]
DBPath=x:\directory\
```

This entry tells Parents where to find the data files. The key word DBPATH is set equal to the drive and full path (*including* the trailing backslash) where the Parents data files reside. Here is an example:

```
[PARENTS]
DBPath=C:\PARENTS\
```

You can change where Parents looks for its data files by simply altering the value for DBPATH. Then move the data files from the directory where they were created to the new directory you specified in the DBPATH= line.

# The Individual Work Sheet _____

The main window for data collection is called the Individual Work Sheet. All the genealogical information about any individual can be entered in this window. It contains fields for the individual's name, birth date and place, christening date and place, marriage date and place, where and when the individual died, and when and where the individual was buried. In addition to these fields are a miscellaneous Notes field, which can be used for storing any additional information, and a place for indicating the sex of the individual. The information entered into the date and place fields does not have to be in any specific format.

## Menu selections for the Individual Work Sheet

### New

The New selection, from the File pull-down menu, displays a blank Individual Work Sheet. After all the information has been entered into the worksheet, click on the Save pushbutton. This action adds a new record to the database, storing all the information that was entered.

Use the **Individual Work Sheet** to enter specific information about the major events in an individual's life.

### Open

The Open selection, from the File pull-down menu, displays a list of all the individual names that have been entered into the database. You can select an individual name from this list by highlighting the name and clicking on the Select pushbutton or by double-clicking on the selection. All the information that was previously stored in the database about this individual is displayed in the worksheet. This information can be updated or added to, and then saved.

### Print

The Print selection prints the worksheet information for the currently selected individual name.

## Pushbutton actions for the Individual Work Sheet

### Save

This action saves the information entered into the Individual Work Sheet. If you click on Save after entering a new individual record, the information is added to the database. If you click on Save after updating the information for an existing individual record, the updates are saved in the database.

### Delete

The information in an existing individual record can be deleted from the database if that individual's name is not currently being used in the Family Tree. After you click on the Delete pushbutton, a message prompt appears, requesting a confirmation of the action. If the individual's name exists in the Family Tree, a message prompt appears, indicating that the individual record cannot be deleted.

### Close

This action closes the Individual Work Sheet. If you opened the Individual Work Sheet by selecting Open from the File menu, the Individual List reappears.

### Next

This action displays the data for the next individual record in the database.

### Previous

This action displays the data for the previous individual record in the database.

# The Immediate Family Tree

The Immediate Family Tree displays, and enables you to update, a selected individual's family tree. The Family Tree's center box has a thicker border than the other boxes in the tree. Placing any individual name in this box causes the names of the individual's immediate family to appear in the other boxes of the tree.

An individual name can be placed in the Family Tree's center box in one of two ways. The first way is by dragging and dropping the name from the Individual List. To drag and drop, you click on a name to highlight it and, while holding the mouse button, move the mouse pointer over the center box. When you release the mouse button, the selected name appears in the center box, and the rest of the tree is automatically filled in. The second method is to highlight an individual name in the Individual List, pull down the Relations menu, and select Individual. The selected name appears in the center box, and the rest of the tree is filled in.

You can also use the Immediate Family Tree to create a family tree: First make a selection from the Individual List and place that selection in the center box. Then, in the same manner as described previously, place the name of each member of the immediate family in the appropriate box. As each selection is placed in the tree, that selection is related to the individual named in the center box, according to the position in which it is placed.

To the left of the center box is the Children List. Each child of an individual named in the center box should be placed in the Children List.

Directly below the center box is the Spouse List. The individual's current spouse and each previous spouse (if any) should be placed in this list.

At the top right of the center box is the Father box. The Father of the named individual should be placed in this box. Directly below the Father box is the Mother box.

There are also two other boxes that are tied to the Spouse List. These two boxes display the names of the parents of the currently highlighted spouse name in the Spouse List. You cannot use these two boxes to relate a Father or a Mother to a Spouse.

There are several special features of the Immediate Family Tree. The first feature is that the tree can be shifted in any direction to show the extended family tree. You can accomplish this shift by dragging and dropping an individual name from any of the other family tree boxes to the center box. For example, suppose that the current individual name in the center box is John

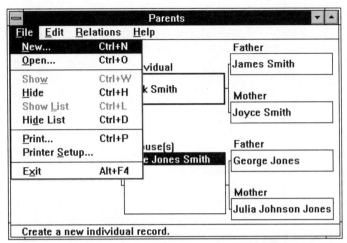

From the Immediate Family Tree, you can create new individual records
to add to specific locations on that tree.

Smith, and his father is Jack Smith; if you drag and drop *Jack Smith* from the
Father box to the center box, the family tree instantly reorganizes to show Jack
Smith's immediate family. In the process, *John Smith* moves from the center box
to the Children box, which indicates that John Smith is a child of Jack Smith; the
name that appears in the Father box is John Smith's Grandfather.

The second special feature of the family tree is the capacity for you to edit the
information about an individual. You can do this editing by highlighting a name
in the Individual List and clicking on the Edit pushbutton below the list, or by
double-clicking on a name in the list or in the Family Tree. The Individual Work
Sheet appears that contains all the information previously stored in the database. The information on this worksheet, except for the individual's name, can
be updated and saved. After editing the information, click on the Close
pushbutton to return to the Immediate Family Tree.

# Menu selections for the Immediate Family Tree

## Show

The Show menu selection shows an empty Immediate Family Tree. You can use
this tree to display or update an individual's family tree.

## Hide

The Hide menu selection hides the Immediate Family Tree and Individual List
(and Individual Work Sheet, if shown).

## Show List

The Show List menu selection shows the Individual List. You can use this list to build an Immediate Family Tree.

## Hide List

The Hide List menu selection hides the Individual List.

## Print

The Print menu selection prints the currently displayed Immediate Family Tree or Individual Ancestral Tree.

## Clear

The Clear menu selection can be found on the Edit pull-down menu. You use it to clear the family tree or remove a relationship between two individuals, depending on which family tree box is currently selected. You can select a family tree box by clicking on it with the mouse. Then a dotted rectangle appears around the individual's name contained in the box. If the center box is cleared, the entire family tree is cleared. If the Father or Mother box is selected, the box is cleared and the relationship is removed. If one of the children or spouses is highlighted, that child or spouse is cleared from the list and the relationship is removed. The two boxes tied to the spouse box cannot be cleared.

## Relations

The Relations pull-down menu is only available when the Immediate Family Tree is shown. It can be used as an alternative way of placing a name in a family

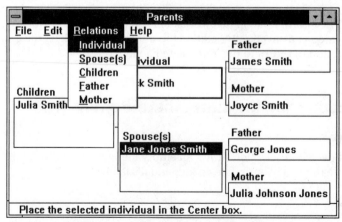

You can use the Relations menu to place individual names in the Immediate Family Tree.

tree box. If you highlight a name in the Individual List and then choose one of the selections in the Relations pull-down menu, that individual's name is placed in the corresponding family tree box.

# Special Features

## Drag and drop

When an item is being transferred from one list to another, it may be dragged and dropped. To drag and drop, you can point to an item with the mouse pointer, click on it, and, while still holding the mouse button down, position the mouse pointer on top of the destination entry field. When the mouse button is released, the selected item appears in the entry field. For example, to place an individual name in the family tree, drag and drop that name from the Individual List to the appropriate box in the tree.

## Clipboard

The Clipboard is a convenient way of transferring data between Parents and other Windows applications or between different Parents windows. To use the Clipboard functions, simply highlight any text displayed in an entry field, pull down the Edit menu, and choose Copy or Cut. The Copy function places a copy of the highlighted text in the Windows Clipboard. The Cut function also places the highlighted text in the Clipboard but removes it from the entry field as well.

To retrieve text from the Clipboard, first place the cursor at the position inside an entry field where the Clipboard text should be inserted or appended. Then pull down the Edit menu and choose Paste. The Clipboard text is placed in the entry field at the cursor position.

## Printing

When the Print selection is chosen from the File pull-down menu, the user has the option of printing either the Immediate Family Tree or an Individual Ancestral Tree. When the selection has been made, a dialog box appears that prompts the user for a report title, type of report, and whether to include the date and time the report was printed. If the user selects the Individual Ancestral Tree, he or she also has the choice of printing the entire tree or just part of it.

```
┌─────────────────────────────────────────────┐
│                 Chart Setup                   │
├───────────────────────────────────────────────┤
│  Title: │The Jack Smith Family│                │
│                                                │
│  ┌─Chart Type──────────┐ ┌─Generations───────┐ │
│  │ ◉ Individual         │ │ ◉ All             │ │
│  │ ○ Immediate Family   │ │ ○ Part  Level: [ ] │ │
│  └──────────────────────┘ └───────────────────┘ │
│                                                │
│      ☐ Include Date          ☐ Include Time     │
│          ┌──────┐        ┌────────┐            │
│          │  OK  │        │ Cancel │            │
│          └──────┘        └────────┘            │
└───────────────────────────────────────────────┘
```

**When you select the Print command, the Chart Setup dialog box appears.**

# Exiting _____

When you finish using Parents, you should exit the program with the Exit selection from the File pull-down menu. If you forget and turn your computer off before exiting, Parents cannot guarantee that your ancestors' records have been saved correctly. It is very important that you always exit Parents with the Exit selection.

# Registration _____

Parents is not public domain, nor is it free software. You are granted a limited license to use this product on a trial basis. You are also granted a license to copy Parents, along with the documentation, for trial use by other users. Parents has not been intentionally crippled or limited in its functionality in any way.

If you want to continue using Parents, you must send $25 to

**NickleWare**
P.O. Box 393
Orem, UT 84059 U.S.A.

If you would like an original disk copy or an update to the latest release of the software, please add $5 for shipping and handling.

Name: _____

Address: _____

_____

_____

[  ]   Parents registration:   $25

[  ]   Disk with latest version:        $5

Amount enclosed:  $ _____

Preferred disk size:[   ] 3.5" [   ] 5.25"

We encourage you to copy Parents and share it with those who may be interested in tracking down their roots and learning where they came from. The on-line documentation must accompany the Parents software.

NickleWare or Bradley Nicholes shall not be liable for any damages, whether direct, indirect, special, or consequential, arising from the use or failure of this program to operate in the manner desired by the user.

NickleWare CompuServe ID: 72730,1002

# PixFolio

### Version 1.04.15
### Copyright © Allen C. Kempe

*Graphics files in Windows can become very large and hard to manage. And no two programs use the same graphics file format (or so it seems). PixFolio aims to solve these problems in several ways.*

*PixFolio makes catalogs of your graphics; you can search through the catalogs to find just the graphic you want. You can search on typed descriptions, or you can search for special criteria — graphics with 16 colors or fewer, files saved after a particular date, and many other options.*

*To help you save disk space, PixFolio can maintain the location of your graphics across several different disks. You can store infrequently used graphics on floppy disks, for example. PixFolio can help you identify the exact disk when you need a certain graphic months from now.*

*PixFolio excels at converting graphics files from one format to another. You can convert over a dozen different formats into BMP or PCX files, for example, and then edit them in Windows Paintbrush.*

*Graphics can be quite complicated, so PixFolio includes many options for manipulating and managing them. Read this chapter to learn about all of PixFolio's capabilities to enhance the graphics on your Windows PC.*

| | |
|---|---|
| **Type of Program:** | Graphics |
| **Requires:** | Windows 3.0 or later |
| **Registration:** | Use the form at the end of this chapter to register with the shareware author. |
| **Technical Support:** | ACK Software, the publisher of PixFolio, provides registered users with technical support by telephone and mail. |
| **Similar Shareware:** | Paint Shop and WinGIF, programs featured in *Windows 3.1 SECRETS,* published by IDG Books Worldwide, also convert graphics files but don't necessarily support the same formats and cataloging options that PixFolio does. |

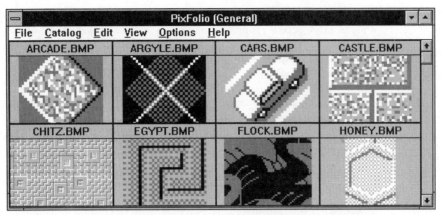

**PixFolio can catalog your graphics files, keep track of them across several disks, and make retrieval of a particular graphic a snap.**

# Overview

PixFolio is designed to assist the user in managing a collection of graphics images so that they can be readily retrieved when needed.

Central to the purpose of PixFolio is the capacity to read a variety of different graphics formats produced by many popular programs. Also of major value to users is the capacity to convert images from one format to another.

The central theme of PixFolio is the concept of the *catalog*. A catalog is like a disk-file directory in that it is an index to a file. But PixFolio catalogs go beyond being just a simple index. PixFolio enables the user to annotate catalog entries with comments. The user can supply keywords to a catalog entry so that searches can be made to select images meeting the search criteria.

With graphics images taking up vast amounts of valuable and expensive disk space, it becomes necessary to keep them on removable floppy disk media. In many cases, only one or two images fit on a floppy disk, resulting in a modest-sized graphics collection occupying dozens of disks. PixFolio can keep track of these *off-line* copies (they are referred to as *backup* copies even though, in many cases, the floppy-disk copy is the only storage location). When the user desires to view one of these copies, PixFolio makes it easy to locate the right disk.

Many programs are available that allow extensive editing of images using sophisticated techniques. Although PixFolio possesses a number of editing tools that can be used to manipulate images in various ways, its main purpose remains that of cataloging and keeping track of images. Even so, PixFolio possesses a basic set of editing tools that may satisfy most of the needs of users. Images can be rotated, resized, flipped about an axis, cropped, and expanded. In addition,

PixFolio offers the capacity to dither images. *Dithering* is a means of displaying images whose color resolution exceeds your video system's capacity.

PixFolio also supports the Windows Clipboard; graphics formats not directly supported by PixFolio can be imported through the Clipboard. PixFolio also can export an image through the Clipboard to another application.

# Understanding Catalogs and Their Uses _____

Catalogs are, in simplest terms, a list of images. The content and scope of a catalog is left to the user to define. For example, you may want to catalog images by project or usage. Or you may want to catalog images by size, color resolution, graphics format, content, and so on. PixFolio can easily handle whichever way you choose.

Catalog content does not necessarily have to be exclusive. A given image need not be represented in only one catalog; it can be located in more than one catalog at a time.

# Creating a Catalog _____

PixFolio always maintains at least one catalog. However, the user can add as many catalogs as the system's disk storage permits.

Before delving into the details of creating a catalog, it is worthwhile to explain a couple attributes associated with a catalog. These attributes are entered in the Catalog Select Catalog dialog box, an example of which follows:

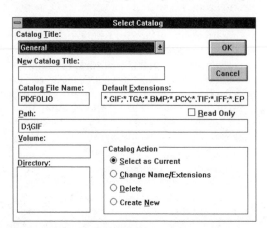

**You use the Select Catalog dialog box to define some of the attributes of the catalog.**

# Using the Select Catalog dialog box

## Name

Each catalog defined in PixFolio has a name. The initial catalog created the first time that PixFolio is run has the name Default. The name can be anything meaningful to the user. For example, you can name a catalog *GIF Images, 640x480, Ajax Contract,* or *Nature*, relating to the content, format, or use of the images that the catalog will maintain. The name of a catalog can be changed at any time by the user.

## Catalog File Name

The filename of a catalog also is user defined. Any filename recognizable by DOS can be used. PixFolio catalogs have filename extensions of CAT and CIX, which cannot be changed by the user. Also defined as part of the filename is the *path* — the disk drive and subdirectory where the catalog and its associated index reside. It is suggested that the location of a catalog be in the same directory as the majority of the images contained in the catalog because the catalog's path also becomes the default path for accessing the images.

## Default Extensions

If a given catalog is to contain only certain graphics formats, the default file extensions for files displayed in the File Open dialog box can be defined for each catalog.

## Volume

A volume name can optionally be specified for a catalog. If present, the volume name of the drive containing the catalog is checked before a catalog is opened. This option is useful when a catalog exists on a removable drive such as a Bernoulli box. If the correct volume is not mounted, you are prompted to insert the proper volume.

Each catalog defined in PixFolio is represented by a Catalog$x$= entry in the WIN.INI file. These entries are automatically maintained by PixFolio. The one case where the user might have to manually modify the WIN.INI file entry is if he or she wants to move or rename a catalog filename.

The actual creation of a catalog is done with the Catalog Select Catalog command. When creating a new catalog, the user must supply a name for the catalog, a filename, a path, and a list of default file extensions. The volume ID is optional.

## Read Only

A catalog may be opened as Read Only. In this case, you cannot perform any actions (such as Catalog Build) that modify the catalog.

## Changing catalog attributes

The name of a previously defined catalog can be changed along with the default file extensions by the use of the Catalog Select command. Also, the optional volume ID may be changed.

## Deleting a catalog

A catalog can be deleted by the use of the Catalog Select command. Deleting a catalog has no effect on the images contained in the catalog.

# Cataloging an Image

There are two methods you can use to catalog an image. The first is the manual way: selecting the Catalog Catalog command when an image is displayed. The second is to automatically update a catalog from a list of image filenames with the Catalog Build command.

## Cataloging manually

The first method is probably more convenient for cataloging images one at a time. Where many images must be cataloged, the second method, using the Catalog Build command, is preferred. The second method is useful in initially establishing a catalog.

An example of a catalog entry follows:

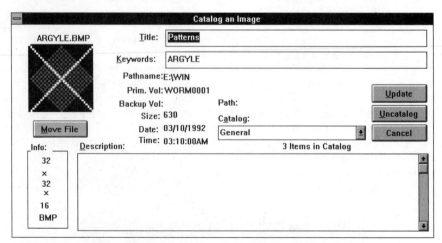

**When you select the Catalog Catalog command, the Catalog an Image dialog box appears; use this dialog box to catalog an individual graphics file.**

The preceding illustration is an example of the Catalog Catalog command. It brings up a dialog box with a number of fields that you can fill in. Other fields are updated by the program.

## User fields

**Title:** This is the title of the image. If a GIF89a image has a title, it is filled in automatically. The maximum number of characters that can be entered is 59, including carriage returns and line feeds.

**Keywords:** This field can contain a number of keywords, up to the length of the entry box, that you can use when searching. These keywords also can be used for selecting a list of files meeting requested search criteria. The maximum number of characters that can be entered is 87.

**Description:** This field can be used for entering any descriptive data concerning the file, up to 1,200 characters. This field can be scrolled and edited with standard Windows editing commands. If a GIF89a image has text data included with it, it is placed here.

**Catalog:** This field is a drop-down combo list box, used for selecting the catalog to be updated.

## Program fields

**Filename:** The name of the graphics file.

**Pathname:** The primary location (hard disk) pathname and volume label are displayed, as well as the backup (floppy disk) location. Therefore, there can be two access paths for the file.

**Primary Vol:** The volume name of the primary location.

**Backup Vol & Path:** The volume name and path of the backup floppy disk.

**Size:** File size in bytes.

**Date & Time:** Creation date and time of the file.

**Info:** The height, width, number of colors, and file format are displayed in a box in the lower left corner of the dialog box.

You can perform several functions by pressing the following buttons:

**Catalog/Update:** Updates the catalog entry; when the button reads *Catalog*, this is a new entry. If desired, the target catalog can be changed beforehand.

**Uncatalog:** Deletes the catalog entry. This button is grayed if there is no catalog entry to delete. This option does not delete the file itself.

**Cancel:** Cancels the dialog box and returns you to the application.

**Move File:** Moves or copies the file to some other location.

**(Image):** The *thumbnail image* is itself a button. When the original image is displayed, clicking on it causes it to be regenerated. This is useful if you previously cataloged the original image and then made a change to it like brightening or cropping it. In Browse mode, clicking on the image has no effect.

*Note:* These buttons are redefined if the dialog box is entered with the Catalog Build command: The Catalog or Update button becomes Next, the Uncatalog button becomes Previous, and the Move File button becomes View.

# Cataloging with the Catalog Build function

The second method of cataloging images is more suited to making multiple updates to a catalog.

## Using the Catalog Build dialog box

The list box in the Select Items to Catalog dialog box contains files you can select to add to the catalog. When a file (or files) is selected and the Build button is pressed, the image is read in and cataloged. The Auto Update option, if off, enables fully automatic updating of the selected files; otherwise, the user must press the Catalog button for each file after updating the keywords, description, and title information.

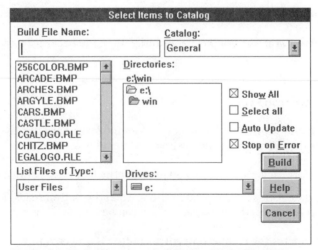

Use the Catalog Build command to display a dialog box that you can use to make more than one update to a catalog at a time.

If the Show All option is off, the list box only displays those files *not* cataloged in the selected catalog. The Select all option can be used for selecting all files at once; it toggles on and off the selection status of all files displayed.

You can turn off the Stop on Error option to bypass prompts for error or warning messages, such as when large 24-bit files are read.

A feature of the Catalog Build command is that images already cataloged are not read to create a thumbnail. However, the catalog entry is updated with backup volume and path information for files on floppy disk.

Another feature of the Catalog Build command is that if a floppy disk containing images is processed, and the floppy disk is not labeled, PixFolio prompts you and labels the disk for you so that the catalog entry can indicate the volume ID.

# Maintaining catalog information

There are two broad categories of information kept in the catalog entry for an image. First is file-attribute information, such as file size, date created, format, and so on. This data cannot be changed directly by the user. Also included in this category is a thumbnail representation of the image, used in various types of displays of catalog information.

The second category of information maintained for a catalog entry consists of entries for title, description, and keywords. All these elements can be directly modified by the user. In most cases, this data must be supplied by the user. In a few cases, such as for GIF89a images, the title and description are obtained from the image but can be edited by the user.

## Accessing catalog information

There are four means by which the user can access and change catalog information:

♦ **With the Catalog Catalog command.** Using this command, a catalog record can be created or updated for the currently displayed image.

♦ **With the Catalog Browse command.** This command lets you view, sequentially, the contents of a catalog. User-supplied information, such as title, description, and keywords, can be changed. An important option that also can be accessed is the Search function. The scope of entries displayed in a catalog can be modified by setting search criteria. In addition to searching on keywords defined for each entry, a search can take into account such attributes as file size, format, number of colors, or date.

♦ **With the Catalog Build command.** This command provides a convenient means of updating a catalog with a large number of entries. This can be done automatically, or the function can pause for each image to enable the user to update title, description, or keyword information.

♦ **With the View Thumbnails command.** This command causes a display of as many thumbnail images of cataloged items as can be displayed in the current window. Scrolling commands, either from the keyboard or mouse, enable the user to scroll through all the entries in the catalog. Clicking on a thumbnail image displays a menu. One of the options on this menu displays the current catalog entry. By this means, the user can update the title, description, or keywords.

Information other than user-supplied title, description, and keywords is automatically updated when exercising the Catalog Catalog or Catalog Build command. The Catalog Build command is particularly useful for updating a catalog with the location of files. For example, if you copied images to floppy disks, the Catalog Build command can be used for updating the catalog with the "backup" locations of the files.

## Multicatalog updating

Users will undoubtedly find it occasionally necessary to move an image from one catalog to another. This is very easy with PixFolio. There are two ways that this can be done, short of simply cataloging an image from scratch in another directory.

♦ Assuming that an image is already cataloged, use the Catalog Catalog command to display the catalog entry. Then simply select a new catalog, using the Catalog combo list box to pick the catalog in which you want the image, and then press the Catalog button. This method has its drawbacks, however; the original catalog entry in the original catalog is still present and must be manually deleted if it is no longer desired. Secondly, the original catalog is no longer selected; to continue working in that catalog, you must reselect the original catalog.

♦ A superior way of moving images from one catalog to another is through the View Thumbnails command. Individual thumbnail images are "marked" for some future action. Then the Process Thumbnails command is used to Move, Copy, or Delete all the marked thumbnails. Moving or copying thumbnails to another catalog does not entail replacing the current catalog selection so that operation can continue uninterrupted in the current catalog.

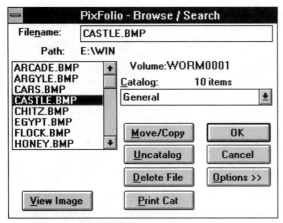

Use the Catalog Browse command to specify the criteria with which you want to limit the display of images within a catalog.

## Restricting the display of catalog entries

When dealing with large catalogs consisting of hundreds of images, it may be desirable to restrict the display of catalog entries to those meeting certain criteria. You can do this by using the Catalog Browse command to apply search criteria to the catalog list. Alternatively, individual catalog entries can be marked and hidden from the Thumbnail View screen.

The Catalog Browse command provides a dialog box listing the entries in a catalog. You can change the target catalog by selecting another catalog from the Catalog combo list box.

This dialog box provides a number of functions that can be applied to a catalog entry:

**Move/Copy:** The file can be moved or copied to another location.

**Delete File:** The file can be deleted from the hard disk. The file is also deleted from the catalog.

**View Image:** The file can be opened and viewed.

**OK:** The catalog entry for the file can be viewed and updated. Double-clicking on the filename is the same as pressing the OK button. When the catalog entry dialog box is displayed, the OK, Delete, and Move buttons are replaced by Prev, Next, and View, respectively.

```
┌─────────────────────────────────────────────────────────────────────────┐
│ ─                    PixFolio - Browse / Search                           │
├─────────────────────────────────────────────────────────────────────────┤
│ Filename:  ┌─────────────────────────┐                                    │
│            │ CHITZ.BMP               │      ■ Backup Exists on Floppy Disk │
│   Path:    E:\WIN                                                          │
│ ┌─────────────┐   Volume:                  Format:                        │
│ │ CHITZ.BMP   │                            ┌──────────────────────────┐   │
│ │ EGYPT.BMP   │   Catalog:      10 items   │ BMP                      │   │
│ │ FLOCK.BMP   │   ┌──────────────────┬─┐                              │   │
│ │ HONEY.BMP   │   │ General          │▼│   Special Conditions:         │   │
│ │ THATCH.BMP  │   └──────────────────┴─┘   ┌──────────────────────────┐   │
│ │ ZIGZAG.BMP  │                            │ @D<01/01/92              │   │
│ │             │   ┌──────────┐ ┌──────────┐                              │ │
│ │             │   │ Move/Copy│ │    OK    │  Search Keywords:            │ │
│ │             │   └──────────┘ └──────────┘  ┌─────────────────────────┐  │
│ └─────────────┘   ┌──────────┐ ┌──────────┐  │ PATTERN                 │  │
│                   │ Uncatalog│ │  Cancel  │  └─────────────────────────┘  │
│                   └──────────┘ └──────────┘                               │
│                   ┌──────────┐ ┌──────────┐ ┌──────────┐  ┌────────────┐  │
│ ┌─────────────┐   │Delete File│ │Options >>│ │  Search  │  │  Show All  │  │
│ │ View Image  │   └──────────┘ └──────────┘ └──────────┘  └────────────┘  │
│ └─────────────┘   ┌──────────┐              6 items selected               │
│                   │ Print Cat│                                            │
│                   └──────────┘                                            │
└─────────────────────────────────────────────────────────────────────────┘
```

**After entering criteria for which you want to search and clicking on the Options>> button, the list of graphics files is limited to those files that match the specified criteria.**

**Cancel:** Cancels the dialog box, returning you to the main viewing window.

**Uncatalog:** Deletes the file from the catalog only.

**Print Cat:** Prints the selected catalog entry.

## Searching for files

Four different search criteria can be applied to a catalog to restrict the catalog list to a subset. The four categories that can be used for the search are as follows:

♦ Whether a backup copy exists.

♦ File format — for example, GIF87a, TIFF, PCX, and so on — as they appear in the Info box on the catalog display.

♦ Match on one or more keywords.

♦ Match on special conditions — for example, file size, width, height, number of colors, or backup volume name.

You access the Search function by pressing the Options>> button.

To search, enter the desired search value(s) in the Format edit box (29 characters maximum), the Special Conditions edit box (87 characters maximum), or the Search Keywords edit box (87 characters maximum). If nothing is entered in a box, that box is not used in the search.

The Backup Exists on Floppy Disk check box is a three-state control. If the box is gray, it has no effect on the search. If one of the edit boxes is blank, then all catalog records that do not have a backup location are selected. If the Backup check box is checked, only those catalog records with a backup file location are selected. The search criteria are ANDed to select a record. That is, if search criteria 1 (Backup) is satisfied *and* search criteria 2 (File Format) *and* search criteria 3 (Special Conditions) *and* search criteria 4 (keywords) are satisfied, the record is selected.

Wildcard characters (* and ?) can be used in search arguments. For example, to select all GIF files, use the search argument GIF* to select both GIF87a and GIF89a formats. You can use either spaces or commas to separate search arguments. The underscore character (_) may be used in place of a space in a search argument, if that space is significant. For example the entry *STAR_TREK* searches for the string *Star Trek*; the entry *STAR TREK* matches either *Star* or *Trek*. Case is not significant in searches.

In order to include special conditions in the search, such as file size, image width, and so on, PixFolio has five special search arguments that can be used in the Format and Special Conditions edit boxes. *Do not use these special codes in the Keywords box.* The special codes all start with an @ sign and are followed by the code letter for the particular value to be tested for, an operator (< -- less than; = -- equal, # -- not equal, or > -- greater than), and the value to be tested for.

The valid codes are as follows:

@B      Backup volume name

@C      Number of colors: 2, 16, 256

@D      Date, in the format mm/dd/yyyy

@H      Height of image

@P      Primary pathname

@S      File size in bytes

@W      Width of image

Some examples follow:

@W=320              Select images whose width is 320 pixels.

@D>01/01/1991       Select all dates later than January 1, 1991.

@B=GIF0020          Select all images residing on backup volume GIF020.

@C>16               Select all images with more than 16 colors.

@P=C:\PIXFOLIO      Select all images in subdirectory C:\PIXFOLIO.

When the Search button is pressed, the catalog is searched for records meeting the desired criteria. At the completion of the search, the new catalog list is displayed in the list box. To change the search criteria, enter new search values and click on Search again.

The modified catalog list is in force until the Show All button is pressed, a new catalog is selected, or another search operation is performed. The View Thumbnail View command only displays the currently selected catalog entries.

# Viewing Images _____

The method used for viewing an image depends on whether or not the image is cataloged. If an image is not cataloged, the only way to view it is to use the File Open command to locate the file and then read and display the image. Once displayed, the file can be edited or cataloged in the catalog of choice.

After an image is cataloged, however, it can be viewed in several ways:

♦ From the Catalog Browse dialog box, you can display the image by pressing the View button.

♦ From the View Catalog Entry dialog box, you can display the image by pressing the View button. You activate the View Catalog Entry dialog box by double-clicking on a filename in the Catalog Browse dialog box or by clicking on OK.

♦ From the View Thumbnails display, use the mouse to click on the desired image. Then, while holding the left mouse button down, select the View option from the pop-up menu. An image displayed in this manner cannot be edited or modified unless it is displayed in the main window. However, the Display Main menu option enables you to do this.

# Looking at Supported Formats _____

Graphic formats supported by PixFolio are as follows:

| | |
|---|---|
| BMP | Windows bitmap format. |
| CLP | Windows Clipboard file. |
| DRW, GRF | Micrografx vector file formats (read-only). |
| EPS | Encapsulated PostScript embedded TIFF preview images (read-only). |
| FLI, FLC, CEL | Autodesk Animator FLI/FLC animation files (read-only). |
| GIF | CompuServe Graphics Interchange Format. PixFolio supports both the GIF87a and GIF89a standards. (The Graphics Interchange Format is the copyright property of CompuServe Incorporated. GIF is a Service Mark property of CompuServe.) |

| | |
|---|---|
| ICO | Windows icon. |
| IFF, LBM, CE | Deluxe Paint II LBM and IFF files. The file extension CE is created by Digital Vision's Computer Eyes video-capture product. |
| IMG | GEM/IMG (Digital Research) format (read-only). |
| MAC | Macintosh Macpaint files (read-only). |
| PCX | Z-Soft Paintbrush files. |
| RLE | Windows Run Length Encoded file format. |
| TGA | Targa (TrueVision Advanced Raster Graphics Array) file format. |
| TIF | Tagged Image File Format. |
| WMF | Windows Metafile (read-only). |
| WPG | WordPerfect Graphics WPG files (read-only). |

PixFolio can also support additional graphics formats if an application uses Aldus-standard graphics import filters. Two such applications are Word for Windows and Aldus Pagemaker. To use these additional graphics formats, you must list them in the [MS Graphic Import Filters] section of WIN.INI. A sample of this section of the file follows:

[MS Graphic Import Filters]

Windows Metafile(.WMF)=d:\windows\msapps\grphflt\wmfimp.flt,WMF

DrawPerfect(.WPG)=d:\windows\msapps\grphflt\wpgimp.flt,WPG

Micrografx Designer/Draw(.DRW)=d:\windows\msapps\grphflt\drwimp.flt,DRW

AutoCAD Format 2-D(.DXF)=d:\windows\msapps\grphflt\dxfimp.flt,DXF

HP Graphic Language(.HGL)=d:\windows\msapps\grphflt\hpglimp.flt,HGL

Computer Graphics Metafile(.CGM)=d:\windows\msapps\grphflt\cgmimp.flt,CGM

Encapsulated Postscript(.EPS)=d:\windows\msapps\grphflt\epsimp.flt,EPS

Tagged Image Format(.TIF)=d:\windows\msapps\grphflt\tiffimp.flt,TIF

PC Paintbrush(.PCX)=d:\windows\msapps\grphflt\pcximp.flt,PCX

Lotus 1-2-3 Graphics(.PIC)=d:\windows\msapps\grphflt\lotusimp.flt,PIC

AutoCAD Plot File(.PLT)=d:\windows\msapps\grphflt\adimport.flt,PLT

Excel Chart(.XLC)=d:\aldus\usenglsh\filters\chartimp.flt,XLC

The preceding section of the WIN.INI file was created by the Word for Windows setup program. Other applications, such as Pagemaker, provide additional filters, but they must be added to the WIN.INI file manually before PixFolio recognizes them. Also note that PixFolio does not use one of the preceding graphics filters for formats it supports directly, such as PCS, TIF, DRW, EPS, and WPG.

## Color resolution formats

Images can be read in several resolutions:

| | |
|---|---|
| 1 BPP | 1 bit per pixel, or 2 colors: black and white. |
| 4 BPP | 4 bits per pixel, or 16 colors. |
| 8 BPP | 8 bits per pixel, or 256 colors. |
| 24 BPP | 24 bits per pixel, or 16 million colors. |

The number of colors displayed is determined by the maximum number of colors that your video display and driver software can handle. PixFolio retains all color information in an image, even if it cannot be displayed properly.

For example, if you are using the standard VGA driver that comes with Windows, you can display only the 16 colors that Windows uses. If you read an image that uses 256 colors, most of the colors are displayed using the "nearest" color. The result in most cases can be described as awful.

PixFolio offers a workaround for this situation with its Auto Dither option. Dithering is a way of simulating the display of many colors by substituting various combinations of the 16 colors. This fools your eyes so that the image appears to have more shades of color than are actually displayed. Turning Auto Dither on forces PixFolio to automatically dither images for display if the images have more colors than the display can support.

## Thumbnail view

PixFolio offers a graphical way of viewing the contents of a catalog: the Thumbnail View option. Selecting View Thumbnails results in a display of the thumbnail pictures created for each catalog entry. PixFolio displays as many thumbnails as fit in the current window dimensions. For best results, it is suggested that the window be expanded to a full screen.

Only those items in the current catalog that have been selected and that have not been hidden are displayed, unless the Catalog Display Hidden option is active. Catalog entries are normally displayed in alphabetical sequence, but the user can define another sequence by moving the individual thumbnails around to suit.

## View Thumbnail View

The content of the display depends on the selection criteria currently in effect. Use the Catalog Browse command to restrict the items displayed. Additional options available through a pop-up menu enable you to hide selected thumbnails from view.

You can browse the selected contents of a catalog by using the PgUp and PgDn keys or the up and down arrows to scroll up or down a page or line, respectively.

You can display a pop-up menu by holding the left mouse button over a thumbnail image. This menu offers the following commands:

```
Information
Hide Thumbnail
Mark Thumbnail
View
Process Thumbnails
Launch Application
Slide Show
```

**When you hold down the left mouse button over a thumbnail image, a pop-up menu of commands appears for the thumbnail image.**

**Information:** Displays the catalog entry for the image. User-supplied data, such as description, keywords, and title, can be changed if desired.

**Hide Thumbnail:** If this command is selected, the thumbnail is removed from the display.

**Mark Thumbnail:** This command marks or unmarks the thumbnail for some further action (applied using the Process Thumbnails command explained shortly). Marked thumbnails are checked and have an asterisk (*) next to the filename in the title bar.

**View:** This command causes a full-size view of the image to be displayed.

**Add Thumbnail:** This command is only present when the Catalog Display Hidden option is on. Its intended purpose is to enable you to "unhide" a thumbnail that was previously hidden or that was not selected by the Catalog Browse command.

**Process Thumbnails:** This command enables the user to perform one of the following actions on all previously marked thumbnails:

♦ *Move* the catalog entries to another catalog.

♦ *Copy* the catalog entries to another catalog.

♦ *Delete* the catalog entries.

♦ *Hide* the catalog entries.

♦ *Print* the marked catalog entries.

♦ *Mark* all catalog entries.

♦ *Unmark* all catalog entries.

♦ *Move/copy* marked files to some other drive or directory. The determination of whether to move or copy is made in the dialog box presented to select the target catalog. You can select a check box option if you do not want to be prompted for each marked file. In this case, subsequent files are all moved or copied to the same target location.

♦ Another option can be set to *not* update the catalog with the new location of the files. This option is intended to be invoked when you are making copies of files for some external use. For example, when you want to copy a list of marked files to a floppy disk to give to another user.

♦ *Add* marked entries back to the display. (This option is present only when the Catalog Display Hidden option is in effect.)

*Note:* You have to select a target catalog only for the Move and Copy options; all other options operate on the currently selected catalog. For the Move, Copy, and Print options, you can select a check box if you want PixFolio to retain the marks on the items. This is useful if you want to perform multiple operations on the marked images, such as copying items to another directory and then printing the same entries.

**Launch Application:** This command can be used for starting up another application using the selected image. You are prompted for the program and pathname and for any additional parameters.

PixFolio appends the filename and parameters to the contents of the Program box to be used as the command line for starting up the application.

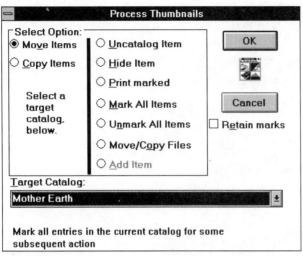

The Process Thumbnails command displays a dialog box in which you select the action to be performed on the marked thumbnail images.

When you select the Launch Application command, a dialog box appears; use it to specify which program you want to launch.

A default for the Program edit box can be established for a particular file type, such as GIF or PCX, by adding an entry to the PixFolio section of WIN.INI as follows:

*xxx=c:\directory\program,*{parameters}

where *xxx* is the file type: GIF, PCX, BMP, and so on.

You can use Windows Notepad or SYSEDIT.EXE to edit WIN.INI.

**Slide Show:** This command causes all the marked slides in the current catalog to be displayed sequentially, in full-screen mode. Files to be displayed must exist on a nonremovable drive.

# Editing Images _____

PixFolio possesses a modest set of tools that enable you to edit and manipulate images. Using these tools, you can perform the following actions.

## Cropping or trimming an image

To trim off excess portions of an image, use one of the following techniques:

♦ Using the mouse, hold the left mouse button down at the point that is to become the upper left corner of the resulting image. Drag the mouse to the opposite corner of the desired portion of the image. A rectangle, called a *marquee,* is drawn on the screen. If the marquee is not in the desired location, you can repeat the operation to draw the marquee until you are satisfied. When the marquee is stretched out to its desired extent, release the left mouse button and then select Edit Crop. The image is trimmed to contain only that area encompassed by the marquee.

♦ If you want to trim the image only on the right side or the bottom, move the window borders by using the mouse to drag the borders to the desired positions. Then select the Edit Expand option to crop the image.

## Expanding an image

You may want to expand the size of an image so that the borders are extended without otherwise changing the size of the image. There are several ways to do this:

♦ If you only want to add to the right side and bottom of the image, simply drag the window borders out to the desired location and then select the Edit Expand option.

♦ If you want to add area evenly all around the image, first select the Options Center-Image command. Next, drag the window borders to make the window the desired size. The image is now centered in the middle of the new window. Finally, select Edit Expand to expand the image. The area added to the window is set to the currently defined background color. (See "Background Color," described in "Using the Options Menu," later in this chapter, for information on how to set the background color.)

♦ To add area to an image, but not necessarily evenly on all sides, first select the Options Center-Image command. Next, drag the window borders to make the window larger than the desired size. The image is now centered in the middle of the new window. Using the mouse, enclose the area desired in the image with a marquee rectangle. Finally, select the Edit Crop command. As in the preceding example, the area added to the image is painted the current background color.

# Resizing an image

In the preceding discussion on cropping and expanding images, the image itself did not change size; only the overall size of the window in which the image is displayed was changed. You also can stretch or shrink the size of the image itself. If desired, this can be done independently for each axis (left-right or top-bottom). This may be desirable to achieve some artistic effect or to compensate for distortion caused by conversion from another graphics format.

One important point to keep in mind when resizing an image is that resizing is done by replicating or eliminating pixels. The best results are obtained when the shrink or stretch factor is some integer-multiple of the original image, such as times 2 or divided by 2. Using a fractional factor results in distortion of the image, although this effect can vary, depending on the details of the image. It can be particularly noticeable if the image contains a repeated pattern.

There are two methods that you can use to resize an image:

♦ Select the Edit Resize command and enter the desired dimensions. Resizing can be done independently on either the X or Y axis. The resizing factor can be specified either as a percentage or in terms of absolute pixel dimensions.

♦ Use the mouse and the left mouse button to draw a marquee encompassing the area to be resized. Then, in a similar fashion, draw a marquee to delineate the new dimensions of the selected region using the *right* mouse button. When you release the right mouse button, the image is overlaid with the stretched or shrunken region. The resulting image can then be cropped as desired.

To stretch to dimensions larger than those of the current image, first expand the image so that there will be sufficient room for the stretched image.

## Rotating and flipping an image

The suite of PixFolio's image-editing tools is rounded out by several additional features. These are the ability to rotate an image in 90-degree increments and the ability to flip or mirror the image about its X (horizontal) axis or Y (vertical) axis. These features are available through the Edit Resize command.

## Using Clipboard operations

All the editing commands described in the preceding sections primarily affect an entire image. Additional editing operations using the Windows Clipboard can be used to cut or copy all or part of an image to the Clipboard. The data in the Clipboard can then be pasted to another application. Likewise, you can copy information from other applications to the Clipboard and then paste the data into PixFolio.

PixFolio copies both DIBs (device-independent bitmaps) and DBBs (device-dependent bitmaps) to the Clipboard. PixFolio can also accept these two formats — as well as the Windows Metafile format — from the Clipboard.

PixFolio automatically converts an image's palette and color resolution so that, for example, a 16-color image can be pasted onto a 256-color image without corrupting the colors. If the Clipboard image being pasted has a different color resolution than that of the current image, you can either convert the current image to the higher resolution or dither the Clipboard image to the lower resolution.

One possible action that can be performed using the Clipboard is to combine several images into one image. See "Creating a New Image," later in this chapter.

## Using palette operations

Each image displayed possesses a *palette*. This palette is a list of colors used to display the image. In most cases, the palette is limited to some particular value that is directly proportional to the color resolution of the image. This is generally 2, 16, or 256 colors. If your video display supports 24-bit color, the palette can contain more than 16 million colors.

The majority of video displays can display only 256 colors or fewer at a time. Nevertheless, these 256 colors are not fixed; they can be any one of 256,000 different colors. The purpose of the palette is to tell the video display which 256 of the possible 256,000 colors will be used.

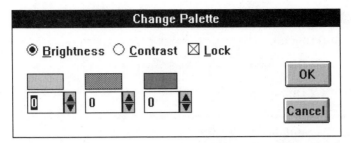

When you select the View Change-Palette command, a dialog box appears
that enables you to change the brightness or contrast of a color image.

The palette makes it possible for you to change the colors in the image. Two of
the most common palette operations are adjusting the contrast and brightness
of an image. By making all the colors more intense, the brightness of the image
can be adjusted. Likewise, by adjusting the darker colors unequally, the
contrast of the image can be adjusted. Many scanned images contain a wider
range of color than can be effectively displayed by many video displays. If an
image is too dark, brightening it or adjusting the contrast may bring out details
that otherwise are not seen. PixFolio can easily handle such adjustments with
the View Change-Palette command. A complementary command is the View
Gray-Scale command, which can be used for converting a color image to shades
of gray.

# Creating a New Image

PixFolio provides for the creation of a completely new blank image, which can
then be edited. For example, suppose that you want to combine several images
into a composite image. The way to do this is as follows:

1. Create a blank image of the desired size by utilizing the File New command.

   a. The default dimensions shown in the X Dimension and Y Dimension
      boxes are those of the current window size before you select File New. If
      you know what size you want the new image to be, manually enter the
      desired X and Y dimensions. The Set to Window and Set to Clipboard
      buttons set or reset the X and Y values to those of the current window
      or Clipboard image (if any). Select Set to Clipboard if you want the new
      image to be sized the same as the image in the Clipboard.

```
┌─────────────────────────────────────────────┐
│              Create New Image                 │
│ ┌─Window Dimensions─────────────────────────┐ │
│ │ ┌────┐                                     │ │
│ │ │320 │  X Dimension   [ Set to Window   ]  │ │
│ │ └────┘                                     │ │
│ │ ┌────┐                                     │ │
│ │ │200 │  Y Dimension   [ Set to Clipboard ] │ │
│ │ └────┘                                     │ │
│ └───────────────────────────────────────────┘ │
│ ┌─Color Resolution──────┐ ┌─Palette─────────┐ │
│ │ ○ 1bpp, 2 colors      │ │ ○ Default 16/20 colors│
│ │ ○ 4bpp, 16 colors     │ │ ◉ 256 colors    │ │
│ │ ◉ 8bpp, 256 colors    │ │ ○ Clipboard     │ │
│ │ ○ 24bpp, >256 colors  │ │                 │ │
│ │                       │ │ [ OK ] [Cancel] │ │
│ └───────────────────────┘ └─────────────────┘ │
└─────────────────────────────────────────────┘
```

Use the File New command to display a dialog box and create a
new image with specific attributes.

b. The color resolution of the new image defaults to 1 bit per pixel. If you
want more than two colors, select some other value. The value selected
is the maximum number of colors that the image can contain.

c. The initial palette of the new image defaults to the Windows default
palette. This palette contains 16 colors, unless you have a Super VGA or
better resolution video driver, in which case it contains 20 colors. You
can select a 256-color palette that contains a default set of colors. If there
is a palette stored in the Clipboard, you can select it as the palette for the
new image. It is recommended that you use the palette from the Clipboard if it is available; using the Clipboard palette eliminates the need to
convert the image from the Clipboard when you paste it to the new
image.

2. After filling out the Create New Image dialog box, paste the contents of the
Clipboard to the new image.

3. Switch to another instance of PixFolio, or some other application, to copy to
the Clipboard the remaining images you want to combine.

4. Repeat steps 2 and 3 as often as necessary; select File Save to save the new
composite image.

# Saving Images

The user must save images displayed by PixFolio if the user has edited or changed the image in some way and wants to save the resulting image. The user may also want to change the format or color resolution of the image, as stored on disk, to some graphics format other than the original. All these needs can be satisfied with the File Save command.

In contrast to the Move and Copy options, File Save creates a disk file from the currently displayed image — as it is currently displayed. Move and Copy, on the other hand, do not interpret the image data stored on disk.

The format of a saved image can be established in several ways. First, the extension provided for the output file can be used by PixFolio to determine the desired format. Second, the File Save dialog box offers a number of graphics-format selections.

## Format conversions

You can use PixFolio to change the format of an image from one format to another. This is useful when you have an image that you want to input to another program that doesn't support a particular format. In this case, read the image into PixFolio and then save it to the desired format. PixFolio images may be saved in the following formats:

| | |
|---|---|
| GIF87A | CompuServe Graphics Interchange Format |
| TIF | Tagged Image File Format |
| PCX | Windows Paintbrush format |
| TGA | Targa |
| BMP | Windows bitmap format |
| RLE | Windows Run Length Encoded |
| IFF | Amiga IFF (also Computer Eyes CE format) |

## Color resolution

Normally, the user does not want to change the color resolution of an image. In some cases, however, there may be good reasons for doing so. It is safe to say that the most efficient storage of an image takes place when the number of colors used in the image is fewer than the color resolution and is greater than the next lowest color-resolution value. Generally images are stored as 1 bit (2 colors), 4 bits (16 colors), 8 bits (256 colors), or 24 bits (16.8 million colors).

Little is gained by reducing the color resolution of an image: This results in a loss of color information. Likewise, increasing the color resolution increases the storage-space requirements, while providing no additional color information.

The most rational exception to this rule is converting 24-bit images to 8-bit images. If you don't have a 24-bit video display, there is little need to retain the extensive color information contained in 24-bit images (unless the end use, such as for commercial printing applications, requires it). The display of 24-bit images on the usual VGA, Super VGA, or even 8514 video display is very time-consuming. For that reason, you may want to convert a 24-bit color image to 8 bits to facilitate viewing it at a later time. PixFolio can easily handle this conversion through the File Save command.

Sometimes images are written in 256-color format but contain only 16 colors or fewer. In this case, the disk space taken up by the image is substantially reduced by reducing the color resolution to 16 colors (4 bits).

## Dithering

Another option that can be utilized to convert, for example, a 24-bit image to an 8-bit image is the View Dither-Color command. Although this operation can take a considerable length of time, the results can be quite good. Dithering initiated by the View Dither-Color command — as opposed to dithering initiated with the Auto Dither option — permanently changes the color resolution of the file. The Auto Dither option, on the other hand, only dithers the image for display on a device that cannot display all the colors in the image.

Images also can be dithered to black and white. This may be desirable in preparation for printing because many printers (except for color printers) can print only black or white and don't know what to do with shades of gray.

PixFolio uses the Burkes Filter algorithm for dithering to black and white and the Stucki Filter algorithm for dithering color images.

# Printing

## Selecting a printer

Before printing images or catalog entries, you must select a printer. This can be done with either the Program Manager Control Panel or the File Select-Printer command. A dialog box appears, enabling you to select a printer, perform any necessary setup on it, and select options that control how PixFolio prints images and catalog entries.

```
┌─────────────────────────────────────────────────┐
│                  Printer Setup                    │
├─────────────────────────────────────────────────┤
│  Select Printer:                                  │
│ ┌Generic / Text Only on LPT1:      ┐  ┌────────┐ │
│ │ HP LaserJet III on LPT1:         │  │   OK   │ │
│ │ HP PaintJet on LPT1:             │  └────────┘ │
│ │                                  │  ┌────────┐ │
│ │                                  │  │ Cancel │ │
│ │                                  │  └────────┘ │
│ └──────────────────────────────────┘  ┌────────┐ │
│                                        │ Setup..│ │
│  □ Print Catalog using Thumbnails      └────────┘ │
│  ⊠ Dither when Printing             ┌──────────┐ │
│  □ Alt Cat Prt Format   ⊠ Use Low Mem Option     │
└─────────────────────────────────────────────────┘
```

Use the Printer Setup dialog box to select a printer and specify any special options.

The Print Catalog using Thumbnails option, if turned on, forces PixFolio to use the thumbnail image that is part of the catalog entry. Otherwise, the image is read from disk before printing. If this option is turned off, a far superior picture resolution results, at the expense of the time necessary to read the images in. It also may be less convenient because you may have to repeatedly swap disks to read images that do not reside on your hard disk.

Turn the Dither when Printing option on if the printer cannot print color or convert to gray scale. In that case, PixFolio performs the necessary dithering. This option affects the printing of whole images as well as of catalog entries.

The Use Low Mem Option check box applies to printing full-size images. If turned on, the image is first dithered and then resized, resulting in lower print resolution but faster execution and less memory use. This option determines the default for the like-named option on the Resize Print dialog box.

The Print Catalog using Thumbnails, the Dither when Printing, and the Use Low Mem Option selections are saved in the WIN.INI file, by printer. When a new printer is selected, its options are established automatically.

The Alt Cat Prt Format check box enables you to select an alternative *dense* print format when printing a catalog. When this format is selected, only the thumbnails and their filenames are printed. On 8½ by 11-inch paper, you can print 20 thumbnails per page.

Pressing the Fonts>> button enables you to select a typeface and type size for the catalog print functions. Separate font information can be established for each printer and is used the next time the printer is selected.

```
┌─────────────────────────────────────────────┐
│ ─              Print Image                    │
├─────────────────────────────────────────────┤
│ Ready to print to HP PaintJet on LPT1:        │
│                                               │
│                 Percent:    Pixels:           │
│  Resize X %:   │ 100  │    │ 32  │   0.18in    │
│                                               │
│  Resize Y %:   │ 100  │    │ 32  │   0.18in    │
│                                               │
│  ☐ Low Mem    ┌────────┐  ┌────────┐          │
│               │   OK   │  │ Cancel │          │
│  ☒ Dither     └────────┘  └────────┘          │
└─────────────────────────────────────────────┘
```

**Use the File Print option to display a dialog box that enables you to
specify how a particular image is to be printed.**

Please note that selecting a font style other than Regular does not result in that
style being used. PixFolio itself determines whether to print portions of the
catalog printout in bold or underlined text.

## Printing images

An image or a selected portion of it may be printed with the File Print command. To print just a portion of an image, use the mouse to draw a marquee
around the portion you want to print. Then select the File Print option.

The Print Image dialog box enables you to scale the picture to the desired size.
To aid in selecting the correct size, the size of the image can be expressed as a
percentage of the original or in pixels. The resulting size, in inches or centi-
meters, also is displayed. If the printer horizontal and vertical resolutions are
not the same, PixFolio assumes that the image is composed of square pixels
and automatically scales the image accordingly to avoid distortion.

Selecting the Low Mem option results in a reduced-memory requirement to
print the image. This is accomplished by dithering the image (if dithering is
selected or appropriate) before the image is scaled for printing. With Low Mem
turned off, the image is scaled and then dithered. This results in better print
quality at the expense of speed. Your PC may not have enough available
memory to print successfully with Low Mem turned off. In this case, you will
have to turn it on.

Because many printers cannot print color (or convert the colors to gray scale),
it may be necessary to dither the image in preparation for printing. PixFolio can

perform the necessary dithering. To dither, select the Dither option. Of course, if your printer can print color images or can handle gray scale, this is not necessary. The Dither option's initial state is determined by the Dither when Printing option in the Select Printer dialog box.

## Printing catalog entries

There are three ways to print a catalog entry:

♦ Select Print Catalog from the Catalog Browse dialog box. Only one entry, the currently selected item, can be printed at a time.

♦ Select the Catalog Print command from the Catalog menu. This prints all the selected entries in the current catalog. You can use the Catalog Browse search commands to narrow the scope of the request to those catalog entries meeting requested criteria. Up to four catalog items are printed per page.

♦ Select the Print option from the Process Thumbnails dialog box, accessed from the pop-up menu in Thumbnail View. This command prints only marked catalog entries. It is the best way to print specific items. Up to four items are printed per page.

*Note:* There are two catalog print formats supported by PixFolio. The default format prints two to four entries per page. This format prints all keywords, the title, description, and path information for each entry. The Alternate print format prints about 20 thumbnail entries per page. This option can be selected with the File Select-Printer command.

Before selecting any of these options, however, you should first select a printer and the desired typeface and size to be used.

# Using the Options Menu

PixFolio offers several options that you can use to alter the operation of PixFolio to suit the user.

## Display Warnings

In some cases, it is necessary for PixFolio to issue warning messages to the user. These messages, when the user becomes familiar with PixFolio, may be more of an irritation than a help. Therefore, the user can suppress all but the most serious errors and warnings by selecting this option.

√ Display Warnings
√ Center Image

√ DIB to Screen
√ Auto Dither
  Verify Catalog
√ Fix TIFF

  Background Color...
  Default Options...

The Options menu provides several options you can use to change the operation of PixFolio to suit you.

## Center Image

If a window is expanded, or a full-screen view is selected, the image being displayed is located in the upper left corner of the window. Selecting the Center Image option causes all images smaller than the size of the current window to be centered, both vertically and horizontally, in that window.

## DIB to Screen

PixFolio attempts to maintain both a device-independent bitmap (DIB) and a device-dependent bitmap (DDB) for any image being displayed. Display of DIBs is slow — particularly 24-bit color images. For this reason, it is best to allow PixFolio to create a DDB. However, in situations where memory is low, there may not be enough memory to create a DDB. By selecting the DIB to Screen option, the user forgoes creation of a DDB, and the DIB is displayed directly to the screen.

## Auto Dither

If your display driver is not capable of displaying 256 colors — for example, the standard VGA driver can display only 16 colors — you can turn the Auto Dither option on, to cause images that contain more than 16 colors to be automatically dithered *for display only*. The original image data, containing 256 colors, is not modified; if the file is saved, none of the colors are lost.

If you want to dither an image and save it as a dithered image, you must select one of the View Dither options to dither the image — even if it has been displayed as dithered — if the Auto Dither option is on.

Dithering is slow, so you may want to keep this option turned off until you specifically want to view a dithered image. If you have a 256-color driver, the Auto Dither option causes 24-bit color images to be dithered. But you should be warned that this may take a very long time — perhaps as much as an hour.

## Verify Catalog

If you suspect that the catalog index has been corrupted, turning this option on temporarily forces the catalog index entries to be verified with the matching catalog record. Invalid indexes are then removed.

## Fix TIFF

This option relaxes the TIFF standard a certain amount for certain types of TIFF files that do not have the correct values for the Strip Byte Counts tag.

## Background Color

When the size of an image is increased, the additional area of the image is painted the background color, specified by Set Background Color. The background color is also used for painting the surface of an image created with the File New command.

A dialog box is presented, which enables the user to set the background to the desired color. An option (Color Solid) in the dialog box determines whether backgrounds are painted with solid colors or dithered colors. The dithering option may give a wider apparent range of colors, particularly if the palette is limited to, say, 16 colors by the video display.

You also can define custom colors that are saved for the next execution of PixFolio.

# Setting the Play Rate

PixFolio can display GIF animation sequences from GIF87a files. However, because the GIF file is not decoded in real time — which in many cases is used to "pace" the display — a Set Play Rate option is provided to the user (on the View menu) to set the time delay between successive frames of the animation.

# Setting Default Options

Default options, which go into effect whenever PixFolio is started, can be specified through the Options menu. Some of these options are as follows:

```
┌─────────────────────────────────────────────────────────┐
│                      PixFolio Options                     │
│  Default Catalog                                          │
│  ┌──────────────────────────────┐ ┌─┐   ┌──────────┐     │
│  │ General                      │ │↓│   │    OK     │     │
│  └──────────────────────────────┘ └─┘   └──────────┘     │
│  Default Extensions:                                      │
│  ┌────────────────────────────────────────┐              │
│  │ *.BMP; *.DIB; *.RLE; *.GIF; *.PCX; *.   │              │
│  └────────────────────────────────────────┘              │
│  Default Directory:                                       │
│  ┌────────────────────────────────────────┐ ┌──────────┐ │
│  │                                         │ │  Cancel  │ │
│  └────────────────────────────────────────┘ └──────────┘ │
│                                                           │
│  ☐ Center Image          ☐ DIB to Screen                  │
│  ☒ Display Warnings      ☐ Fix TIFF                       │
│  ☒ Solid Background      ☐ Auto Dither                    │
└─────────────────────────────────────────────────────────┘
```

**If you select the Default Options command from the Options menu, a dialog box of options appears.**

## Default Catalog

This option specifies which catalog is initially selected.

## Default Extensions

This option specifies the file extensions of all files that should be displayed on a file-selection list. The value of this option is used, in turn, as the default for establishing a similar option whenever a new catalog is created.

## Default Directory

If this option is used, it specifies the current path displayed whenever the File Open dialog box is accessed. Otherwise, the path of the default catalog is used.

## Center Image

This option determines whether or not images are displayed centered.

## DIB to Screen

This option turns on the DIB-to-screen feature. When this option is on, PixFolio does not attempt to create a device-dependent bitmap for display but instead paints directly to the screen. This may be helpful if memory is limited and there is not enough memory to create a separate device-dependent bitmap.

## Solid Background

This option determines whether backgrounds are solid or dithered.

## Fix TIFF

This option determines whether the special rules for TIFF files are put into effect.

## Display Warnings

This option determines whether warning messages are suppressed.

## Auto Dither

This option determines whether images are automatically dithered if their color resolution is greater than that of the display.

All these options can be set with the Options Default-Options command.

# Using Removable Media _____

PixFolio normally considers fixed media such as hard drives and network drives as primary storage media and "removable" drives such as floppy disks as backup locations. In some cases (for example, when using a Bernoulli box, which DOS considers removable), you may want to change the way PixFolio treats such drives.

If you want to consider a particular drive as a primary storage location, add the following option to the [PixFolio] section of your WIN.INI file with Notepad or some other text editor:

Primary Drives=$x\{,y,...\}$

where $x$ is the drive letter of a drive to be considered fixed. More than one drive can be thus overridden. You do not need a comma after the last drive letter.

If you want PixFolio to treat a drive as removable (for example, if you want to store backup copies on a network drive), add the following option to your WIN.INI file:

Backup drives=$j\{,k,...\}$

As in the preceding example, you do not need a comma after the last drive letter.

Here is an example: Bernoulli drives E and F are to be considered primary storage, even though DOS thinks that they are removable. Network drives J and K are to be considered backup drives:

```
[PixFolio]
Primary Drives=E,F
Backup Drives=J,K
```

The Catalog Select-Catalog command provides for specification of a volume ID for a catalog. If present, the volume ID is checked before opening the catalog.

You can disable the internal logic for handling the graphics formats DRW, TIF, and WPG by using the following line:

Disable {DRW} {TIF} {WPG}=Yes *or* No

Note that EPS is also turned off by turning TIF off. When the internal logic for handling these formats is turned off, PixFolio then uses graphics filters, such as the ones provided with Word for Windows or Pagemaker. For more information, see "Looking at Supported Formats," earlier in this chapter.

For example, to disable PixFolio's WPG code, insert the following line into the [PixFolio] section of the WIN.INI file:

```
[PixFolio]
Disable WPG=Yes
```

# Understanding Profile Options

PixFolio normally keeps its configuration options in the [PixFolio] section of your WIN.INI file. In some cases, this may not be desirable (for example, in a network environment where several different users are using PixFolio).

As an option, PixFolio may be configured to keep its options in an alternative location. If a file named PIXFOLIO.INI exists in the same directory as PixFolio, or in a directory on the path, PixFolio maintains its options there and ignores WIN.INI. In this case, references to WIN.INI mentioned in this documentation also apply to PIXFOLIO.INI.

# Disclaimer Agreement

Users of PixFolio must accept this disclaimer of warranty:

PixFolio is supplied as is. The author disclaims all warranties, expressed or implied, including, without limitation, the warranties of merchantability and of fitness for any purpose. The author assumes no liability for damages, direct or consequential, which may result from the use of PixFolio.

PixFolio is a "shareware program" and is provided at no charge to the user for evaluation. Feel free to share it with your friends but please do not give it away altered or as part of another system. The essence of "user supported" software is to provide personal computer users with quality software without high prices and yet to provide incentive for programmers to continue to develop new products. If you find this program useful and find that you are using PixFolio and continue to use PixFolio after a reasonable trial period, you must make a registration payment of $35 to Allen C. Kempe (d/b/a ACK Software). The $35 registration fee licenses one copy for use on any one computer at any one time. You must treat this software just like a book. An example is that this software may be used by any number of people and may be freely moved from one computer location to another, as long as there is no possibility of it being used at one location at the same time it's being used at another — just as a book cannot be read by two different persons at the same time.

Commercial users of PixFolio must register and pay for their copies of PixFolio within 30 days of first use, or their license is withdrawn. Site-license arrangements may be made by contacting Allen C. Kempe (d/b/a ACK Software).

Anyone distributing PixFolio for any kind of remuneration must first contact Allen C. Kempe (d/b/a ACK Software), at the address provided in this chapter, for authorization. This authorization will be automatically granted to distributors recognized by the ASP as adhering to its guidelines for shareware distributors, and such distributors may begin offering PixFolio immediately. (However, Allen C. Kempe [d/b/a ACK Software] must still be advised so that the distributor can be kept up to date with the latest version of PixFolio.)

You are encouraged to pass a copy of PixFolio along to your friends for evaluation. Please encourage them to register their copy if they find that they can use it. All registered users receive a copy of the latest version of the PixFolio system.

## Registration Form

Name: _____

Company: _____

Address: _____

_____

_____

Country: _____

CompuServe/Internet, etc., electronic-mail address:

_____

Where did you obtain your copy of PixFolio?

_____

Which version do you have? (This can be obtained by viewing the About menu command.)

[ ] 1.04    [ ] _____

Are there any features you would like to see added to PixFolio?

_____

_____

Do you think PixFolio would benefit by support of additional graphics formats? If so, which ones?

_____

_____

Any other comments would be appreciated.

_____

*continued*

Distribution disk size desired:

[ ] 3.5" (720K)

[ ] 3.5" (1.44MB)

[ ] 5¼ (360K)

[ ] 5¼" (1.2MB)

If you do not specify a disk size, distribution will be on 3.5-inch (1.44MB) disks.

Include your $35 registration fee, plus $4 shipping and handling ($7 outside the U.S. and Canada), and mail to

**Allen C. Kempe**
ACK Software
298 W. Audubon Drive
Shepherdsville, KY 40165
U.S.A.

In Europe, send DM 70, plus DM 8 for COD, to

**Softwarevertrieb D & T Little**
Grillparzerstrasse 40
D-8000 Munich 80
Germany
Tel: 089/470 63 38

You can also order directly from ACK Software or from the Public (software) Library with your MasterCard, Visa, American Express, or Discover Card.

By Phone:          800-2424-PsL or 713-524-6394

By Fax:             713-524-6398

By CompuServe:  71355,470

By Mail:            PsL, P.O. Box 35705, Houston, TX 77235-5705

These numbers are for ordering only. For information about dealer pricing, volume discounts, site licensing, shipping of product, returns, latest version number, or other technical information, call 502-955-7527, write ACK Software, or send electronic mail through CompuServe to 71220,23.

When you register, you receive a disk with the latest version. This entitles you to phone and mail support. In addition, you will receive update notices and bug reports. The serialized disk you receive is not copy protected, but it is for your own personal use (and is not to be distributed to others). Your registration also entitles you to one additional free update when a new version comes out.

# Recipe Maker

**Version 2.13**
**Copyright © by Nickleware**

*W*hen people talk about home computers, *experts who doubt the existence of this market say, "What would people need computers at home for? To save recipes? Ha, ha."*

*In fact, surveys of PC packages bought for home use show recipe-planning programs consistently selling right up there in the top ten. Most families spend a considerable amount of time planning and shopping for a week's meals. Now there is a shareware program that helps you get this task accomplished with as little fuss as possible.*

*Recipe Maker automates most meal planning and prints shopping lists for you. You must first, of course, type the recipes you commonly use. Recipe Maker makes this task easier, however, by enabling you to drag items from your Ingredients List and drop them into your Recipe Cards (instead of typing everything). And, after you've accomplished that, you should find your weekly shopping chores considerably lighter.*

*Both the homemaker who cooks three meals a day for a family and the institutional cook who prepares cafeteria-style meals for hundreds will find Recipe Maker useful. The homemaker can give measurements to Recipe Maker in either U.S.-style teaspoons and pints or international-style milliliters and liters. And, because institutional kitchens often measure huge quantities of ingredients by weight rather than volume, Recipe Maker just as easily accepts pounds and kilograms.*

*When your weekly meal schedule is ready, Recipe Maker prints your shopping list sorted by the department where you would find each item in a supermarket: Bakery, Produce, Canned Goods, and so on. Recipe Maker isn't psychic; it can't determine whether you have enough of an ingredient in stock or need to buy more. If your recipes call for baking soda, for example, it just prints* baking soda *on your shopping list; you have to determine for yourself whether or not to purchase another box. But, with all the things that Recipe Maker* does *do for you, you'll spend less time making your shopping lists than ever before.*

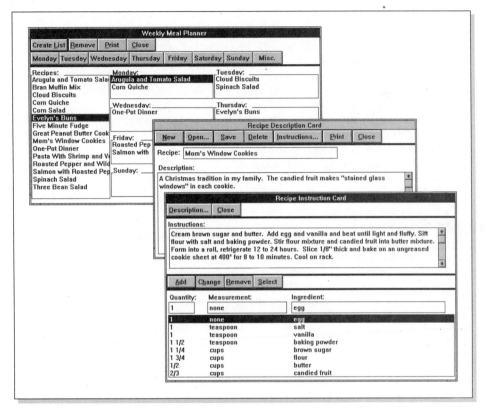

**Recipe Maker simplifies the logical connections between using recipes, planning meals, and creating shopping lists.**

| | |
|---|---|
| **Type of Program:** | Database |
| **Requires:** | Windows 3.0 or later |
| **Registration:** | Use the form at the end of this chapter to register with the shareware author. |
| **Technical Support:** | NickleWare provides registered users with technical support through CompuServe and mail. |

# Introduction

Recipe Maker is an application designed to help make weekly grocery shopping, meal planning, and recipe organization easier. With the help of Recipe Maker, you can plan each meal for an entire week and in just minutes have a complete shopping list of items needed to make those meals come together.

Recipe Maker enables you to enter and store all your recipes. After your recipes have been stored, you can recall and print any of them in just seconds. Recipe Maker also stores and alphabetizes all the different ingredients and measurements necessary to make your meals.

# Getting Started

After installing Recipe Maker with WSETUP, you can start RECIPE.EXE from the File Run menu selection of the Windows Program Manager or from the Recipe icon in the Program Manager. Recipe Maker then creates all the data files it needs to run and places them on the same drive and path where the software was installed.

When Recipe Maker is started for the first time, the following entry is placed in your WIN.INI file:

```
[RECIPE]
DBPath=x:\directory\
```

This entry tells Recipe Maker where to find the data files. The key word DBPATH is set equal to the drive and directory (*including* the trailing backslash) where the Recipe Maker data files reside. Here is an example:

```
[RECIPE]
DBPath=C:\RECIPE\
```

You can change where Recipe Maker looks for the data files by simply altering the DBPATH line. Then move the Recipe Maker database files (*.DB files) and index files (*.IDX files) from the directory where they were created to the new directory you specified in the DBPATH= statement. Save WIN.INI and restart Recipe Maker for this change to take effect.

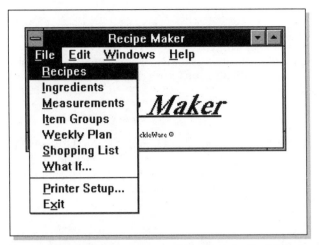

The Ingredients, Measurements, and Item Group (or Food Group)
lists are available from the File menu.

# What Are Lists?

The Measurements, Ingredients, and Item Group (Food Group) lists are really
the heart of the Recipe Maker database. These lists act as three separate
buckets that hold all the information necessary to put your recipes together.
Each time you enter a measurement, ingredient, or food group into a recipe,
that information is pulled out of the corresponding bucket. This concept makes
for much easier and faster recipe entry — and much less effort on your part.
Each of these three lists can be selected from the main window File menu.

## List window actions

There are several pushbutton actions available from each of the three list
windows: the Measurements List, the Ingredients List, and the Item Group List
windows.

### Add

After a new item has been entered, you can click on the Add pushbutton.
Recipe Maker then quickly checks the list to make sure that the new item is
unique. If it is, Recipe Maker adds the item to the database. Otherwise, Recipe
Maker tells you that you have entered a duplicate item.

## Change

To change an item, highlight the item and click on the Select pushbutton, or double-click on the item with your mouse. The selected item appears in the edit box above the list. Edit the item and then click on the Change pushbutton. Recipe Maker checks the list to make sure that the changed item is unique and stores it in the database.

## Remove

To remove an item from a list, highlight it and click on the Select pushbutton, or double-click on the item with your mouse. Then click on the Remove push-button. Recipe Maker asks you to confirm the action. Depending on your response, the action is completed or canceled.

# Measurements List

Some of the first entries that must be made — before you begin to enter your recipes — are the measurements. These are the different measurements that you use in your recipes. For example, *Cup, Tablespoon,* and *Gallon* are some of the measurements that might be used.

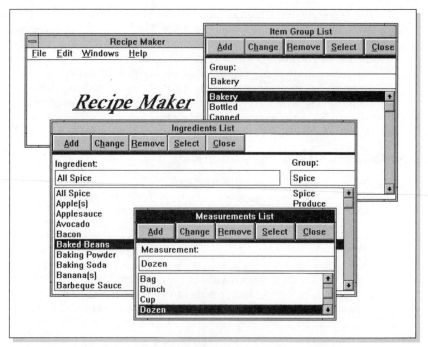

**The Measurements, Ingredients, and Item Group (or Food Group) lists are the heart of Recipe Maker's database.**

## Item Group List

The Item Group List (Food Group List) is a simple list of the different types of ingredients entered into Recipe Maker's Ingredients List. These groups have such names as *Dairy, Meats,* or *Dry Goods.* By entering these food groups, Recipe Maker can keep track of all your ingredients and categorize your shopping lists, which ultimately helps make your grocery shopping much easier and quicker.

## Ingredients List

The Ingredients List is a list of all the ingredients needed to make your recipes. Before a recipe can be entered, all the necessary ingredients must be put into the Ingredients List. A Food Group (Item Group) must also be entered along with the ingredient name.

# Recipe and Instruction Cards

When Recipe Card is chosen from the main window File menu, Recipe Maker displays blank Recipe and Instruction Cards. The Recipe Card consists of the recipe name and description; the Instruction Card contains the instructions, quantities, measurements, and ingredients. The Recipe and Description fields on the Recipe Card and the Instructions field on the Recipe Instruction Card are text-entry fields; you can type data directly into these fields. Quantities, measurements, and ingredients are entered in the same way as for a list.

Before a measurement or ingredient can be entered into a recipe, it must first exist in a corresponding list. As the cursor is moved between the Measurement and Ingredient fields, Recipe Maker looks up the entry in the database and displays the closest match if it cannot match the entry exactly.

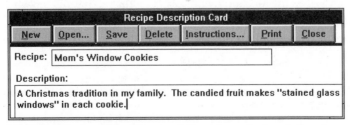

The Recipe Card contains the name of the recipe and a description of the recipe.

---

**Recipe Description Card**

| New | Open... | Save | Delete | Instructions... | Print | Close |

Recipe: Mom's Window Cookies

Description:

A Christmas tradition in my family. The candied fruit makes "stained glass windows" in each cookie.

**Recipe Instruction Card**

| Description... | Close |

Instructions:

Cream brown sugar and butter. Add egg and vanilla and beat until light and fluffy. Sift flour with salt and baking powder. Stir flour mixture and candied fruit into butter mixture. Form into a roll, refrigerate 12 to 24 hours. Slice 1/8" thick and bake on an ungreased cookie sheet at 400° for 8 to 10 minutes. Cool on rack.

| Add | Change | Remove | Select |

| Quantity: | Measurement: | Ingredient: |
|-----------|--------------|-------------|
| 1 | none | egg |

| Quantity | Measurement | Ingredient |
|----------|-------------|------------|
| 1 | none | egg |
| 1 | teaspoon | salt |
| 1 | teaspoon | vanilla |
| 1 1/2 | teaspoon | baking powder |
| 1 1/4 | cups | brown sugar |
| 1 3/4 | cups | flour |
| 1/2 | cups | butter |
| 2/3 | cups | candied fruit |

**The Recipe Instruction Card uses the Measurements and Ingredients lists to help complete the recipe entries.**

Before an entry is added to the list, each of the three fields must contain values. There may be times when a measurement does not apply. For example, the ingredient *eggs* usually has a quantity but not a measurement. In this case, the word *NONE* (or something similar) should be entered into the Measurement field (as well as the Measurements List) to indicate that the measurement does not apply. The resulting recipe entry looks like this:

| Quantity: | Measurement: | Ingredient: |
|-----------|--------------|-------------|
| 2 | none | eggs |

After a recipe has been completely entered, you can add it to the database by clicking on the Save pushbutton on the Recipe Card window.

Updating a recipe is similar to adding a new one, but all the recipe information already exists on the screen. When the Recipe Card window is displayed, click on the Open pushbutton. Recipe Maker displays a list of all the recipes that

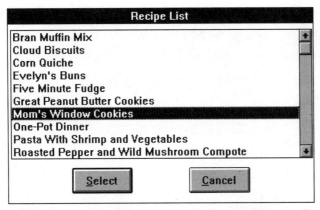

From the Recipe Card window, click on the Open pushbutton to display a
list of all the recipes you have entered; highlight one and click on the
Select button to read or edit that recipe.

currently exist in the database. To select a recipe, simply highlight it and click
on the Select pushbutton or double-click on the item. After a recipe has been
selected, all the data is displayed on the Recipe and Instruction Cards. The
recipe can then be changed and saved in the same manner as described
previously.

To delete a recipe, click on the Open pushbutton from the Recipe Card window,
select a recipe, and then click on the Delete pushbutton. Recipe Maker deletes
the recipe from the database.

To print a recipe, click on the Open pushbutton from the Recipe Card window,
select a recipe, and then click on the Print pushbutton. Recipe Maker formats
the recipe information and prints it.

# Weekly Plan and Shopping List

The Weekly Plan window enables you to plan an entire week of meals and have
Recipe Maker compile a shopping list to match your plan. After this selection
has been made, Recipe Maker displays a window containing a list for each day
of the week — plus a miscellaneous list and a list of all the recipes in the
database. The way to plan a week is to highlight a recipe in the Recipe List and
then click on one of the weekday pushbuttons. Recipe Maker places the name
of the selected recipe in that day's list. When you finish planning the week, click
on the Create List pushbutton. Recipe Maker compiles a list of all the ingredients needed to make the selected recipes.

```
┌─────────────────────────────────────────────────────────────────────────────┐
│                           Weekly Meal Planner                                 │
├─────────────────────────────────────────────────────────────────────────────┤
│  Create List │ Remove │ Print │ Close                                         │
├─────────────────────────────────────────────────────────────────────────────┤
│ Monday │ Tuesday │ Wednesday │ Thursday │ Friday │ Saturday │ Sunday │ Misc.  │
├─────────────────────────────────────────────────────────────────────────────┤
│ Recipes:                  │ Monday:               │ Tuesday:                  │
│ Arugula and Tomato Sala   │ Arugula and Tomato Salad │ Cloud Biscuits          │
│ Bran Muffin Mix           │ Corn Quiche           │ Spinach Salad             │
│ Cloud Biscuits            │                       │                           │
│ Corn Quiche               ├───────────────────────┼───────────────────────────┤
│ Corn Salad                │ Wednesday:            │ Thursday:                 │
│ Evelyn's Buns             │ One-Pot Dinner        │ Evelyn's Buns             │
│ Five Minute Fudge         │                       │ Pasta With Shrimp and Vegetable │
│ Great Peanut Butter Cook  │                       │                           │
│ Mom's Window Cookies      ├───────────────────────┼───────────────────────────┤
│ One-Pot Dinner            │ Friday:               │ Saturday:                 │
│ Pasta With Shrimp and V   │ Roasted Pepper and Wild Mushro │                  │
│ Roasted Pepper and Wild   │ Salmon with Roasted Pepper Com │                  │
│ Salmon with Roasted Pep   ├───────────────────────┼───────────────────────────┤
│ Spinach Salad             │ Sunday:               │ Misc.:                    │
│ Three Bean Salad          │                       │                           │
│                           │                       │                           │
└─────────────────────────────────────────────────────────────────────────────┘
```

**The Weekly Plan helps you plan your week's menu: Click on a recipe in the first column and then click on the pushbutton corresponding to the day you want to serve that recipe. Then click on Create List to create a shopping list.**

If you have just created the shopping list from the Weekly Plan window, you may want to edit it or add to it. After you select the Shopping List window, Recipe Maker displays the shopping list and gives you the option to add, change, or remove any item or print the list. You also have the option to indicate the quantity to buy. When the shopping list has been edited completely, it is then ready to be printed. Turn your printer on and click on the Print pushbutton. Recipe Maker categorizes the list by food group and prints out your shopping list.

# What If

The What If... window enables you to have Recipe Maker make recipe suggestions based on selected ingredients. For example, suppose that you have chicken and rice and want some recipe suggestions that contain those ingredients. Recipe Maker quickly searches through the recipe database and shows you a list of all the recipes that contain one or both of these ingredients.

When the What If... window appears, you see two list boxes. The first one contains all the ingredients currently defined in the Ingredients List. The second is the What If list box. You can move ingredients from the Ingredients list box to the What If list box by either highlighting a selection and clicking on the Move pushbutton or dragging and dropping an ingredient from one list to

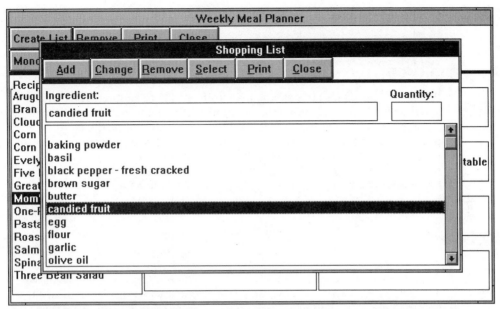

You can preview the shopping list Recipe Maker creates and add or delete items as well as specify quantities.

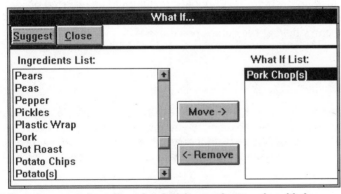

If you have some ingredients but don't know what to make with them, Recipe Maker can make some recipe suggestions for you.

the other. Ingredients can be removed from the What If list box in the same manner. When all your selections have been moved from the Ingredients list box to the What If list box, click on the Suggest pushbutton. Recipe Maker searches the recipe database and displays a list of all the matching recipes. A recipe can then be selected in the same manner as described in the "Recipe and Instruction Cards" section, earlier in this chapter.

# Special Features _____

## Drag and drop

Whenever you want to transfer an item from one list to another, you can *drag and drop the item*. This means that you can select an item with the mouse pointer and (while still holding down the mouse button) drag the mouse pointer over to the destination entry field. When you release the mouse button, the selected item appears in the entry field. For example, if an ingredient is being added to a recipe, the ingredient can be dragged and dropped from the Ingredients List to the Ingredient field on the Instruction Card.

## Clipboard

The Clipboard is a convenient way of transferring data between Recipe Maker and other Windows applications or between different Recipe Maker windows. To use the Clipboard functions, simply highlight any text displayed in an entry field, pull down the Edit menu, and choose Copy or Cut. The Copy function places a copy of the highlighted text in the Windows Clipboard. The Cut function also places the highlighted text in the Clipboard but also removes it from the entry field. To retrieve text from the Clipboard, place the cursor at the position in an entry field where the Clipboard text should be inserted or appended. Then pull down the Edit menu and choose Paste. The Clipboard text is placed in the entry field at the cursor position.

## Exiting

When you finish using Recipe Maker, you should exit the program by using the Exit item from the main window's File menu. If you forget and turn your computer off before exiting, Recipe Maker cannot guarantee that your recipes have been saved completely. It is very important that you always exit Recipe Maker with the Exit command.

*Good luck and easy shopping!*

# Registration

Recipe Maker is not public domain, nor is it free software. You are granted a limited license to use this product on a trial basis. You are also granted a license to copy Recipe Maker, along with the documentation, for trial use by other users. If you want to continue using the product, you must send $25 to

**NickleWare**
P.O. Box 393
Orem, UT 84059 U.S.A.

If you want an original disk containing the latest release of Recipe Maker, please add $5 for shipping and handling.

Name: _____

Address: _____

_____

_____

[ ] Recipe Maker registration:     $25

[ ] Disk with latest version:       $ 5

Amount enclosed:                    $_____

Preferred disk size:   [ ] 3.5"     [ ] 5.25"

We encourage you to copy Recipe Maker and share it with anyone who might be interested in making grocery shopping, meal planning, and recipe organization easier. The on-line documentation must accompany the Recipe Maker software.

NickleWare or Bradley Nicholes shall not be liable for any damages, whether direct, indirect, special, or consequential arising from the use or failure of this program to operate in the manner desired by the user.

NickleWare CompuServe ID: 72730,1002

RS232
COM

# RS232 Serial Monitor

**UARTMON.EXE — Version 1.2**
**Copyright © by Unitech Associates, Inc.**

*R*S232 *Serial Monitor is a highly technical utility designed for PC professionals who need to see what is happening on serial ports (RS-232 ports) as they use a modem.*

*We've included this program because, to monitor serial ports in this way, you usually have to buy a separate piece of hardware called a* breakout box. *These expensive little boxes display the signals sent from your PC's Universal Asynchronous Receiver/ Transmitter (UART) chip. This chip converts the data inside your computer into pulses going out the serial ports. Using UARTMON.EXE, you can examine the workings of these ports right inside Windows — and it's free.*

*By itself, UARTMON.EXE does nothing. Only when a communications program is using a serial port does UARTMON.EXE display any useful information. You first start UARTMON.EXE and then start your communications program in Windows and watch the settings change.*

*Because it's a freebie designed for use by support professionals, RS232 Serial Monitor has little documentation or on-line help regarding serial-communications concepts. The use of UARTMON.EXE is self-evident to PC professionals but may be confusing to users who are new to communications principles. These topics are beyond the scope of this book. But you can find an in-depth explanation of Windows' use of serial ports in the "Modems and Communications" chapter of* Windows 3.1 SECRETS, *published by IDG Books Worldwide.*

| | |
|---|---|
| **Type of Program:** | Utility |
| **Requires:** | Windows 3.0 or later |
| **Registration:** | Free. This program does not require registration. |
| **Technical Support:** | None |

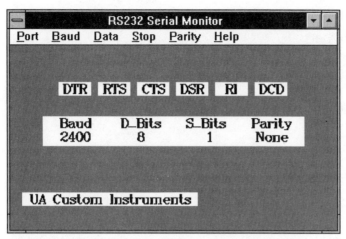

**RS232 Serial Monitor enables you to watch what's going on in the computer's serial ports without buying an expensive breakout box.**

# Description

The RS232 Serial Monitor is designed to monitor the UARTs associated with serial ports (COM1 through COM4). It is intended to be used simultaneously with an application that uses the UART. It should not interfere in the monitoring mode, although the menus enable the user to change the baud rate, data bits, stop bits, and parity. Certain combinations of data bits, stop bits, and parity are not valid and are inhibited in the menus. Because the intended use is to *monitor* the serial port, the serial ports are not opened and the interrupts are not modified, tested, or chained. If no application is using the UART, the monitor does not reflect valid information. (In other words, the UART must be initialized by an application other than the monitor.)

# Principle

In the BIOS data area of system memory is a list of serial-port addresses in the four words beginning at 0000:0400. Most systems use the default 3F8 for COM1 and 2F8 for COM2. There is no standard for COM3 and COM4, so make sure that the BIOS data area correctly reflects the right addresses for COM3 and COM4 if your machine has these ports. Windows uses the default addresses listed shortly, but these can be altered using the COM*x*Base=*xxx*h statement in the [386Enh] section of SYSTEM.INI. (For more information, see the SYSINI2.TXT file in your Windows 3.0 directory or the *Windows Resource Kit* for Windows 3.1, available for $19.95 from Microsoft if you call 206-882-8080.)

**Default Windows 3.0:**

| | |
|---|---|
| COM1=3F8h | |
| COM2=2F8h | |
| COM3=2E8h | ;should be 3E8h fo rmost applications |
| COM4=2E0h | ;should be 2E8h fo rmost applications |

**Default Windows 3.1:**

COM1=3F8h
COM2=2F8h
COM3=3E8h
COM4=2E8h

**Change using:**

[386Enh]
COM1Base=*xxx*h
COM2Base=*xxx*h
COM3Base=*xxx*h
COM4Base=*xxx*h

If you encounter any problems accessing serial ports, it is a good idea to verify the addresses stored in the BIOS data area. You can accomplish this by using the Ports menu. There is an option called IO_Address, which shows the IO_Address as determined from Windows' default setting or the values read from the BIOS. If a COM*x* address shows Default as the source, the BIOS does not know the address. It is still possible that software (including a Windows application) can function if it is written to bypass the BIOS data-area values for the UART IO address. If a COM*x* address shows the source as BIOS, the value for that port was determined from a read of the BIOS data area.

When the IO address is known for a given UART, it is a simple task to investigate the UART registers to determine the status of the various RS-232 lines. The monitor gets a WM_TIMER message every 200 milliseconds and updates the screen with any changes in the UART status.

As a utility, this can be very useful when you're first connecting a new serial device. Basically, the program is a Windows *breakout box.*

# Distribution

UARTMON.EXE and the on-line documentation are provided free by Unitech Associates, Inc., Newark, Delaware. They may be copied and distributed, provided that no money is charged for them and they are not modified. Although the program has been extensively tested, Unitech Associates, Inc., provides no warranty concerning its usefulness on all systems, and UA, Inc., accepts no responsibility or liability for any mishap resulting from its use.

Questions or comments can be answered by

Dale S. Hoover, CompuServe ID 73300,3712

or sent to the following address:

**Dale S. Hoover**
Vice President
Unitech Associates, Inc.
P.O. Box 566
Newark, DE 19715

# SideBar Lite

## Version 2/11/92
## Copyright © 1992 Paper Software, Inc.

*T*he separation of the Windows Program Manager from the File Manager is an irritation to many Windows users. SideBar Lite combines many functions of both applications. And, with a brilliantly simple design, SideBar Lite manages to do all this in a tool bar that takes up less than one-eighth of your screen!

*You can access most of SideBar Lite's functions by clicking its System Menu icon — the rectangle at the left edge of SideBar Lite's title bar. You can make this drop-down menu display all the groups and applications in your Program Manager. Then you can make SideBar Lite your Windows* shell *— the program that runs automatically when you start Windows and from which you run other programs.*

*Using SideBar Lite as your shell, however, has one restriction. You cannot start another program from the Windows command line in DOS. You cannot, for example, use the following command:*

    C:> WIN CLOCK

*This feature will be added in a future version of SideBar.*

*If you like SideBar Lite, we highly recommend the registered, retail version of the program, called SideBar. SideBar adds a few disk-management functions, such as the capacity to copy and move files. Those functions that only exist in SideBar show up "grayed out" in SideBar Lite, so you know that they're there. But SideBar Lite is not crippled in any way. Those features it supports are fully functional and give you an excellent way to evaluate both versions of the program.*

| | |
|---|---|
| **Type of Program:** | Windows Shell |
| **Requires:** | Windows 3.0 or later |
| **Registration:** | Use the form at the end of this chapter to register with the shareware author. |
| **Technical Support:** | Paper Software provides registered users with technical support by telephone, fax, and mail. |

# Overview

shape clay into a vessel
it is the emptiness
that makes it useful

so we are helped by
what is not
to use
what is

— Lao-tsu,
    *Tao Te Ching*

## The SideBar Lite concept

SideBar Lite is a high-performance shell for Microsoft Windows. SideBar Lite's sleek iconbar design makes it the fastest and most practical way to organize the Windows desktop and open your applications. SideBar's optimized memory usage and small footprint enable it to be kept constantly available on the side of the screen, without getting in the way or slowing down system performance. However, you can slightly boost Windows performance by closing SideBar Lite, even when it is the shell.

**SideBar Lite combines functions from both the Windows Program Manager and the File Manager.**

## The anatomy of SideBar Lite

SideBar Lite consists of a main menu, six "arrange" buttons, a DOS-compatible command line, and two types of views which contain objects that can be opened or worked with. The Side-Bar view can contain active tasks (applications that are currently running) and disk drives. It can also contain any directories and files you place on SideBar Lite for quick access. From the SideBar view, you can switch between active tasks, open directories and files, or switch to a disk view. Disk views contain the directories and files for a given disk. From the disk view, you can navigate through directories and open files.

## Organizing your Windows desktop

SideBar Lite makes it easy for you to organize your Windows desktop. You can tile, size, optimize, minimize, or hide windows quickly by pressing one of the six "arrange" buttons at the top of SideBar Lite. You can also turn on the

Include Active Tasks option in the Iconbar menu to move all the icons from the bottom of the screen onto SideBar Lite. This effectively eliminates window and icon clutter and makes it easier for you to access your active tasks.

# Organizing and opening your applications

Two features make SideBar Lite excellent for organizing and opening your applications.

## Using the Applications menu

The Applications menu lets you open the programs and files in your Program Manager groups quickly. To access this menu, select it from the SideBar Lite main menu.

## Placing applications on SideBar Lite

Applications, associated files, and even directories can be placed on SideBar Lite for quick reference. After you have placed an object on SideBar Lite, you can open it by double-clicking on it.

# Boosting Windows performance

By turning on the Start As Windows Shell and Replace Task Manager preferences, you can dedicate all system resources to a specific application by closing SideBar Lite and running Windows *without* a shell. When you want to open another application, double-clicking on the Windows desktop or pressing Ctrl+Esc opens SideBar Lite again.

# Requirements

SideBar Lite requires the same hardware and software as Microsoft Windows with two exceptions:

♦ You must have at least 1MB of RAM (SideBar Lite cannot run in Windows 3.0 real mode).

♦ Your display must support a resolution higher than CGA (that is, EGA, VGA, SVGA, XGA, and so on).

A mouse is helpful when you're using SideBar Lite, but it's not required. Be sure to read "SideBar Lite and the Keyboard," later in this chapter, if you do not use a mouse with Windows.

## The SideBar Lite files

SideBar Lite includes the following files:

SIDEBAR.EXE        The SideBar Lite program file

SBLITE.WRI        The SideBar Lite user guide

The first time you run SideBar Lite, it creates (in the same directory) the files SIDEBAR.INI and SIDEBAR.FLR to store user preferences and SBDOS.BAT to run DOS commands.

These files can be moved to any directory and do not need to be on the DOS path. If you do move them, and you use Program Manager to start SideBar Lite, check the File Properties of the SideBar Lite icon to make sure that the icon's command line includes the new directory name.

## Opening SideBar Lite

After you have installed SideBar Lite, it can be opened the same way you open any other Windows application. This includes double-clicking on SIDEBAR.EXE in the File Manager or on the Sidebar icon in a Program Manager group.

The first time you open SideBar Lite, it displays the Preferences panel so that you can select your preferences and enter the directory SideBar Lite is installed in (such as C:\SIDEBAR).

# SideBar Lite Notes

SideBar Lite consists of the following components:

- ♦ System box
- ♦ Title bar
- ♦ Arrange buttons
- ♦ Command line
- ♦ View titles
- ♦ SideBar view
- ♦ Disk view

## System box

Clicking on the system box displays the SideBar Lite main menu.

## Title bar

You can move SideBar Lite around the screen by dragging the title bar. Double-clicking on the title bar moves SideBar Lite back to the side of the screen.

## Arrange buttons

Functions in the following list are listed left to right, top row first:

- ♦ Button 1 cascades windows.
- ♦ Button 2 tiles windows side by side.
- ♦ Button 3 tiles windows vertically.
- ♦ Button 4 sizes windows, leaving visible the icon row at the bottom of the screen.
- ♦ Button 5 sizes windows, leaving visible SideBar Lite on the side of the screen.
- ♦ Button 6 minimizes all windows and arranges their icons at the bottom of the screen. If the Include Active Tasks option is on, SideBar Lite hides all windows instead of minimizing them.

## Command line

You can enter standard DOS commands here. Note that pressing the F2 key immediately places the cursor on the command line. Read "The Command Line," later in this chapter, for examples of valid commands.

## View Titles

View Titles are located between the command line and the first view. If two views are open, a second View Title appears between the views. You can open, close, or size views by dragging the View Titles with the mouse. Double-clicking on a View Title switches between top/bottom and left/right view layouts. Right-double-clicking on a View Title switches between single and left/right view layouts.

## SideBar view

The SideBar view contains active tasks (applications that are currently running), disk drives, and directories or files you place on SideBar Lite for quick access. Using the SideBar view, you can do the following:

♦ Switch to an active task by double-clicking on it.

♦ View the contents of a directory or open a file you have placed on SideBar Lite by double-clicking on it.

♦ Work with objects you select (for example, removing them from SideBar Lite, changing their description, and so on).

♦ Open a Disk view by double-clicking on a disk drive.

## Disk view

The Disk view contains the directories and files for a specific disk. Using the Disk view, you can do the following:

♦ Open files or directories by double-clicking on them.

♦ Open the SideBar view by double-clicking on the words *SideBar view*.

# The Main Menu

To access the SideBar Lite main menu, click once on the SideBar Lite System Menu icon or press Alt+spacebar.

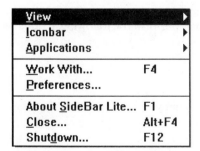

**Access the SideBar Lite main menu by clicking on the SideBar Lite System Menu icon or pressing Alt+spacebar.**

# View

The View menu controls how objects are presented in the *current view* (the view currently containing a cursor). Using it, you can do the following:

- ♦ Sort objects.
- ♦ Change the appearance of objects.
- ♦ Refresh the current view.

# Iconbar

The Iconbar menu controls the appearance and properties of SideBar Lite itself. Using it, you can do the following:

- ♦ Select a layout for SideBar Lite's views.
- ♦ Select SideBar Lite's font.
- ♦ Select the side of the screen SideBar Lite appears on.
- ♦ Include active tasks in the SideBar view.
- ♦ Keep SideBar Lite on top of all other windows on the screen.

# Applications

This menu corresponds to your Program Manager groups. Clicking on a selection opens a submenu or launches an application.

# Work With

The Work With panel enables you to perform the following actions on the objects you have selected in a view:

- ♦ Place the object on SideBar.
- ♦ Remove the object from SideBar.
- ♦ Change the description of an object you have placed on SideBar.

# Preferences

The Preferences panel enables you to customize SideBar Lite. This includes making SideBar Lite the Windows shell, replacing the Windows Task Manager with SideBar Lite, selecting confirmation preferences, and customizing the SideBar Lite fonts.

## About SideBar Lite

The About SideBar Lite menu item displays information regarding SideBar Lite, SideBar 1.0, and our company.

## Close

This option closes SideBar Lite.

## Shutdown

This option closes SideBar Lite and ends your Windows session.

# The View Menu

The View menu controls how objects are presented in the current view (the view containing a cursor). Using it, you can do the following:

♦ Sort objects.

♦ Change the appearance of objects.

♦ Refresh the current view.

| √ By Description | | View | ▶ |
|---|---|---|---|
| By Type | | Iconbar | ▶ |
| By Date | | Applications | ▶ |
| By Size | | | |
| √ As Icons | F7 | Work With... | F4 |
| As Descriptions | Shift+F7 | Preferences... | |
| As Details | Ctrl+F7 | About SideBar Lite... | F1 |
| | | Close... | Alt+F4 |
| Refresh | F5 | Shutdown... | F12 |

**The View menu controls how objects are presented in the current view.**

Select one of the following four items to sort the objects in the current view (note that you can only sort objects in a Disk view):

| | |
|---|---|
| **By Description** | Sorts objects alphabetically |
| **By Type** | Sorts objects by file extension |
| **By Date** | Sorts objects by date |
| **By Size** | Sorts objects by size |

Select one of the following three items to change the appearance of objects in the current view:

| | |
|---|---|
| **As Icons** | Displays the SideBar view icons |
| **As Descriptions** | Displays the current view as descriptions |
| **As Details** | Displays a Disk view with all file attributes |

## Refresh

The Refresh option lets you manually refresh the contents of the current view. Normally this is not necessary because SideBar Lite automatically performs a refresh after you use the Work With panel. This ensures that all open views remain accurate. There are, however, two cases in which you might want to refresh manually:

♦ The Refresh Views After Working With Objects preference has been turned off.

♦ You are returning to SideBar Lite after using another application that has changed the contents of the current view.

# The Iconbar Menu

The Iconbar menu controls the appearance and properties of SideBar Lite itself. Using it, you can do the following:

♦ Select a layout for SideBar Lite's views.

♦ Select SideBar Lite's font.

♦ Select the side of the screen SideBar Lite appears on.

♦ Include active tasks in the SideBar view.

♦ Keep SideBar Lite on top of all other windows on the screen.

| | | | | |
|---|---|---|---|---|
| | | View | ▶ | |
| √ Single View | F6 | Iconbar | ▶ | |
| Top/Bottom Views | Shift+F6 | Applications | ▶ | |
| Left/Right Views | Ctrl+F6 | Work With... | F4 | |
| Small Font | | Preferences... | | |
| √ Medium Font | | About SideBar Lite... | F1 | |
| Large Font | | Close... | Alt+F4 | |
| Left Side of Screen | | Shutdown... | F12 | |
| √ Right Side of Screen | | | | |
| Include Active Tasks | | | | |
| Keep on Top | | | | |
| √ Show Status Bar | | | | |

**Use the Iconbar menu to control the appearance and properties of SideBar Lite itself.**

## Views

There are three possible view layouts available in SideBar Lite:

**Single View**       Displays a single SideBar Lite or Disk view.

**Top/Bottom Views**  Displays two views, one above the other. The View Titles can be dragged to size or close either view.

**Left/Right Views**  Displays two views side by side.

Note that double-clicking on the View Title switches between the top/bottom and left/right view layouts.

## Fonts

SideBar Lite uses the font you select here when displaying the command line and views. To customize these fonts, use the Preferences panel.

## Left/Right Side of Screen

Select one of these two items to place SideBar Lite on the left or right side of the screen.

## Include Active Tasks

This option controls whether or not SideBar Lite lists all currently running applications in the SideBar view. Turning this option on eliminates the clutter caused by icons at the bottom of the screen by organizing them neatly in the SideBar view.

Note that most Windows applications function normally when the Include Active Tasks option has been turned on. However, applications that do not conform to Windows standards may become unstable. If you notice that a particular application experiences problems when switching to or from it, turn off the Include Active Tasks option before opening the problem application.

## Keep on Top

Select this option if you want SideBar Lite to continuously float to the top of all other windows on the screen. This can be helpful when you need SideBar Lite visible at all times.

## Show Status Bar

Select this option to display a status bar at the bottom of SideBar Lite.

# The Applications Menu

The Applications menu lets you open your applications quickly. Simply click on a menu item to open a submenu or launch an application.

SideBar Lite allows up to 20 submenus in the Applications menu. To refresh the menu, choose Refresh Menu... from the Applications menu.

# The Work With Panel

The Work With panel can be opened in four ways:

♦ By dragging and dropping selected objects with the right mouse button

♦ By selecting Work With from the SideBar Lite main menu

♦ By pressing F4

♦ By right-double-clicking on either the SideBar view or Disk view

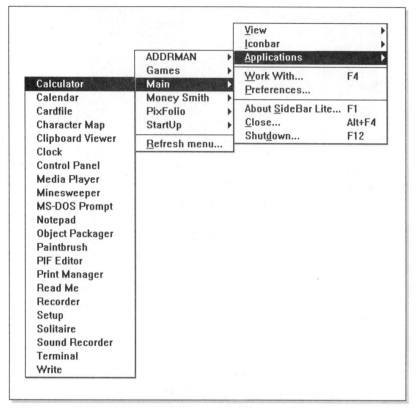

**Use the Applications menu to store up to 20 application names that you can then click on to open a submenu or launch the application.**

The Work With (source) field enables you to indicate the objects you are working with. If you have any objects selected when you display the Work With panel, this field is set to Selection. However, you can change the contents of this field at any time by typing a DOS pathname.

The list of actions lets you select the way you want to work with the objects you have indicated in the source field. If you display the Work With panel by dragging and dropping selected objects, the action is automatically selected for you.

A Destination field appears when an action that requires a destination is selected. If you display the Work With panel by dragging and dropping selected objects, this field is automatically filled in for you.

```
┌─────────────────────────────────────────────────┐
│ ▬              Work With Objects                  │
├─────────────────────────────────────────────────┤
│ Work With: │Selection                           │ │
│                                                   │
│        By:  ○ Copying                             │
│             ○ Moving                              │
│             ○ Deleting                            │
│             ○ Renaming                            │
│             ○ Changing attributes                 │
│             ○ Associating                         │
│             ○ Placing on SideBar                  │
│             ◉ Removing from SideBar               │
│             ○ Changing description on SideBar     │
│                                                   │
│                                                   │
│                                                   │
│                           ┌─────┐  ┌────────┐     │
│                           │ Go  │  │ Cancel │     │
│                           └─────┘  └────────┘     │
└─────────────────────────────────────────────────┘
```

You can use the Work With panel to arrange or delete objects from
the SideBar or to change the description of an object.

## Placing an object on SideBar Lite

You can use the Work With panel to place a file or directory on SideBar Lite for
quick reference. There are two ways to do this:

♦ By dragging and dropping the selected object from the source view to the
SideBar view by holding down the right mouse button

♦ By selecting the object you want to place on SideBar Lite and then pressing
F4 to display the Work With panel

To use either of these two procedures, first open a Disk view containing the
object you want to place and then select the object.

### Dragging and dropping

Hold down the right mouse button to drag the selected object from the source
view and drop it (by releasing the mouse button) on the SideBar view. The
Work With panel is then displayed with its fields automatically filled in.

### Pressing F4

Press F4 and enter the pathname of the file you want to place on SideBar Lite in the source field. Wildcards are not accepted. If you want to place an object selected in the current view, leave the key word Selection in this field and then select the Placing On SideBar Lite action.

### Placing the object

Enter in the Destination field the description you want this object to have. When all the fields on the Work With panel are set correctly, press the Go button to place the object on SideBar Lite.

## Removing an object from SideBar Lite

You can use the Work With panel to remove a file or directory you have placed on SideBar Lite or to close an active task. There are two ways to do this:

♦ By dragging and dropping the selected object from the SideBar view to the Windows desktop by holding down the right mouse button

♦ By selecting the object you want to remove and then pressing F4 to display the Work With panel

### Dragging and dropping

If you want to remove an object by dragging and dropping, select the object on the SideBar view that you want to remove. Then hold the right mouse button to drag the selected object from the SideBar view and drop it (by releasing the mouse button) on the desktop. The Work With panel is then displayed with its field automatically filled in.

### Pressing F4

The source field should always indicate Selection. Select the Removing From SideBar Lite action.

### Removing the object

When all the fields on the Work With panel are set correctly, press the Go button to remove the object.

## Changing the description of an object on SideBar Lite

You can use the Work With panel to change the description of a file or directory you have placed on SideBar Lite. You can do this by selecting the object you want to change the description of and pressing F4 to display the Work With panel.

The source field should always indicate Selection. Select the Changing Description on SideBar Lite action and then enter the new description for the selected object in the destination field.

When all the fields on the Work With panel are set correctly, press the Go button to change the object's description.

# The Preferences Panel

The Preferences panel enables you to customize SideBar Lite. This includes making SideBar Lite the Windows shell, replacing the Windows Task Manager with SideBar Lite, selecting confirmation preferences, and customizing the SideBar Lite fonts.

## SideBar Lite directory

The name of the directory where SideBar Lite is located is indicated in the top field.

**SideBar Lite Preferences**

SideBar directory: F:\GIZMOS\SIDEBAR

☐ Replace task manager
☐ Start as Windows shell
☒ Refresh views after working with objects
☐ Minimize upon opening object
☒ Popup application menu when right clicking on desktop
☐ Show hidden and system files in disk views
☐ Confirm when replacing during copy or move
☒ Confirm on first delete
☐ Confirm on each delete
☒ Confirm on directory delete
☒ Confirm when closing SideBar
☒ Confirm when shutting down system

| Small Font | Helv | 8 pt. | Normal |
| Medium Font | Helv | 8 pt. | Bold |
| Large Font | Tms Rmn | 16 pt. | Bold |

Save   Cancel

Use the Preferences panel to customize SideBar Lite.

## Replace task manager

SideBar Lite can function as a complete replacement for the Microsoft Windows Task Manager. If you turn this preference on, you can open SideBar Lite by double-clicking on the Windows desktop or by pressing Ctrl+Esc.

## Start as Windows shell

SideBar Lite uses less memory and is more flexible than the Microsoft Windows Program Manager. Because of this, you might want to make SideBar Lite your Windows shell. When you do so, SideBar Lite functions as your Windows shell in much the same way that Program Manager does, with one exception: You can close SideBar Lite without terminating your Windows session. This enables other applications to use the memory that SideBar Lite was using.

Note that if you replace the Program Manager with SideBar Lite, you should also replace the Windows Task Manager with SideBar Lite so that you can open SideBar Lite again by double-clicking on the Windows desktop or by pressing Ctrl+Esc.

## Minimize upon opening object

If you want SideBar Lite to minimize itself whenever you open or switch to an application, select this preference.

## Confirm when closing SideBar Lite and Confirm when shutting down system

Select either of these preferences to control whether a confirmation prompt appears before you can close SideBar Lite or exit Windows.

## Font selection

The fields at the bottom of the Preferences panel are used for customizing the SideBar Lite fonts. The three fields to the left enable you to enter the names of your new fonts. The remaining fields are drop-down boxes containing the possible type faces, point sizes, and styles.

## Cancel

If you don't want to save the changes you made, click on the Cancel button.

## Save

Press the Save button to save any changes you made.

# The Command Line

You can use the command line to enter several DOS commands. Following are some examples, showing how the command line can be used in SideBar Lite.

Note that in the retail version of SideBar, the commands COPY, MOVE, DEL, and RENAME are supported. When one of these commands is entered, the Work With panel is automatically displayed with its fields set according to the command you entered.

| Using the Command Line in SibeBar Lite | |
|---|---|
| *Command* | *Result* |
| c:> **MD directory** | Creates a new directory in the current view's directory |
| c:> **RD directory** | Removes a directory (NEWDIR) from the current view's directory |
| c:> **CD\EXCEL** | Changes the current view's directory to C:\EXCEL |
| c:> **DIR *.XLS** | Fills the current view with all files matching *.XLS |
| c:> ***.XLS** | Fills the current view with all files matching *.XLS |
| c:> **FORMAT A:** | Formats a disk in drive A, using the DOS FORMAT command |
| c:> **EDLIN README.TXT** | Opens the DOS Edlin editor with the file README.TXT loaded |
| c:> **README.TXT** | Opens the file README.TXT by checking the association for TXT files (usually Windows Notepad) and then opening that program |
| c:> **NOTEPAD** | Opens Windows Notepad |
| c:> **NOTEPAD README.TXT** | Opens Notepad with the README.TXT file loaded |
| c:> **COMMAND** | Opens a DOS session |

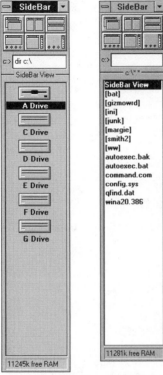

Use the SideBar Lite command line to enter DOS commands; the view area is replaced by a view of the results of the DOS command.

# SideBar Lite and the Mouse

Most of SideBar Lite's features can be accessed with the mouse.

Clicking on the System Menu icon displays the main menu. Double-clicking on the System Menu icon closes SideBar Lite.

You can move SideBar Lite by dragging the title bar. Double-clicking on the title bar returns SideBar Lite to its usual place on the side of the screen.

You can open a second view by dragging the View Title down. (The View Title is located between the command line and the SideBar view.) Double-clicking on the View Title switches between left/right and top/bottom view layouts. Right-double-clicking on the View Title switches between single and left/right view layouts.

You can open a second view by dragging the View Title down with the mouse.

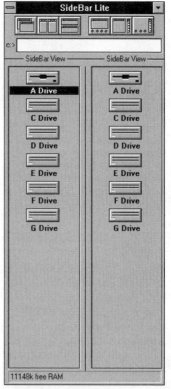

Right-double-clicking on the second View Title switches between single and left/right view layouts.

Clicking on an object selects it. Dragging selects multiple objects. Double-clicking on an object opens it.

Dragging the second View Title (located between two top and bottom views) resizes the views. Dragging it all the way to the top or bottom of SideBar Lite closes the top or bottom view. Double-clicking on the second View Title switches between left/right and top/bottom view layouts. Right-double-clicking on the second View Title switches between single and left/right view layouts.

Dragging a selection with the right mouse button from a Disk view to the SideBar view places the selection on SideBar Lite.

Dragging a selection with the right mouse button from the SideBar view to the desktop removes the selection from SideBar Lite.

Right-double-clicking on either the SideBar view or Disk view displays the Work With panel.

# SideBar Lite and the Keyboard

In addition to supporting the mouse, SideBar Lite provides exceptional keyboard support.

| Using the Keyboard in SideBar Lite | |
|---|---|
| **Key** | **Function** |
| Alt+spacebar | Displays the main menu. |
| Alt+F4 | Closes SideBar Lite. |
| F12 | Closes Windows. |
| Shift+F1 | Cascades windows. |
| Shift+F2 | Tiles windows side by side. |
| Shift+F3 | Tiles windows vertically. |
| Ctrl+F1 | Sizes windows, leaving the icon row visible at the bottom of the screen. |
| Ctrl+F2 | Sizes windows, leaving SideBar Lite visible on the side of the screen. |
| Ctrl+F3 | Minimizes all windows and arranges their icons at the bottom of the screen. If the Include Active Tasks option is on, SideBar Lite hides all windows instead of minimizing them. |
| F1 | Displays the About SideBar Lite panel. |
| F2 | Places a cursor on the command line. |
| F4 | Displays the Work With panel. |
| F5 | Refreshes the current view. |
| F6 | Switches to a single view. |
| Shift+F6 | Switches to a top/bottom view layout. |
| Ctrl+F6 | Switches to a left/right view layout. |
| F7 | Displays the contents of the SideBar view as icons. |
| Shift+F7 | Displays the contents of the current view as descriptions. |
| Ctrl+F7 | Displays the contents of the current Disk view as details. |

If you have no mouse, use your arrow keys to select an object. To select multiple objects, hold Shift while using the arrow keys. To open or run an object, press the Enter key when that object is selected.

Note that if you do not have a mouse, you must use the Enter key for actions whenever this documentation says to double-click the mouse.

# Key Terms _____

| | |
|---|---|
| Active task | Any application currently open, minimized, or hidden on the desktop. |
| Application | A program used to accomplish a specific task — for example, a word processor. |
| Arrange buttons | Six buttons, located under SideBar Lite's title bar, that arrange windows on the screen. |
| Command line | A field, located under SideBar Lite's arrange buttons, that enables you to enter standard DOS commands. |
| Current view | The view currently containing the cursor. |
| Desktop | The Windows background on which windows and icons are displayed. |
| Disk view | The type of view that lists the directories and files for a given disk drive. |
| Object | Any item displayed in a view. The objects in a view can be active tasks, disk drives, directories, files, and the SideBar Lite object. |
| Pathname | The name of a file, including the drive and directory it is located in. For example, C:\WORD\DOCUMENT\RESUME.DOC. |
| Selection | Any objects that have been selected in a view. |
| SideBar view | The type of view that lists active tasks, disk drives, and directories or files you place on SideBar Lite for quick reference. |

| | |
|---|---|
| System Menu icon | The box in the upper left corner of each window. The SideBar Lite System Menu icon contains SideBar Lite's main menu. |
| View | An area on SideBar Lite that displays the contents of the SideBar view or a disk drive. See also *SideBar view*. |
| View Title | The line directly above a view, summarizing its contents. |
| Windows shell | The application that automatically opens when Windows is first started. The default Windows shell is Program Manager. SideBar Lite can optionally become the Windows shell. |

# SideBar Lite Tips

## Using the Include Active Tasks option

One of the really cool things you can do with SideBar Lite is move the active task icons that are normally at the bottom of your screen onto the iconbar itself. To do this, turn on the Include Active Tasks option in the Iconbar menu.

Most applications do not have a problem with being included on SideBar Lite, but there are a few exceptions. If SideBar Lite detects that an application does not conform to standard Windows programming practices, it leaves it as an icon at the bottom of the screen instead of including it on the iconbar.

Note also that SideBar Lite does not support animated icons at this time. Applications that have animated icons are also left at the bottom of the screen so that you can continue to see the animation.

Although SideBar Lite is intelligent in many ways, it's not omniscient. It sometimes includes a nonstandard active task; this can result in unreliable operation. If you notice that a particular application has trouble being included on SideBar Lite, turn the Include Active Tasks option off in the Iconbar menu when using the problem application.

## Turning off Include Active Tasks before running Microsoft tutorials

Before using a tutorial in a Microsoft application like Excel or Word for Windows, you must turn off the Include Active Tasks option in the Iconbar menu. Otherwise, Windows may become unstable.

## Limiting the drives shown on Sidebar Lite

If you want to limit which disk drives are shown in the SideBar view, add the following line to your SIDEBAR.INI file:

IncludeDrives=*drive-list*

where *drive-list* indicates the drives you want to see. Here is an example:

IncludeDrives=ABCFZ

The preceding line shows only drives A, B, C, F, and Z, even if more drives are recognized by Windows. Note that if one of the drives in the list is not available, SideBar Lite does not show it.

## Creating and removing directories with SideBar Lite

To create a directory with SideBar Lite, use the standard DOS MKDIR command. For example, to create a directory called ARTISTS, you can enter the following command in the SideBar Lite command line:

**MKDIR ARTISTS**

If you later want to remove the directory, you can either use the Work With panel to delete it or enter the DOS RMDIR command in the command line, as follows:

**RMDIR ARTISTS**

Note that you can use the standard DOS abbreviations for these commands (MD and RD).

# Registration Information

"Truly cool system management"

— *Computer Currents,* Nov. '91

"Functional simplicity for windows"

— *Byte,* Dec. '91

"SideBar has a spare elegance and purity that will appeal to many Windows users"

— *PC Magazine,* Jan. 28, '92

"Four stars"

— *Associated Press*

once the whole is divided
the parts need names

wise is the one
who embraces
the whole

— Lao-tsu,
*Tao Te Ching*

# Thank you

We at Paper Software would like to thank you for your interest in SideBar Lite, the intensely simple, high-performance shell for Microsoft Windows. SideBar Lite represents the first step toward our goal of simplifying technology for the individual. We sincerely hope that our product inspires you, while enhancing your graphical computing experience.

# Intensely simple

When we were branded as minimalists on the front page of the Wall Street Journal last November, we had to agree. You see, we believe a Windows shell should provide only the most important features in the most practical way. That's why SideBar Lite is intensely simple. *Intense* because of what it offers. *Simple* because of how it's offered.

SideBar Lite's sleek iconbar design makes it the fastest and most practical way to organize the Windows desktop and open your applications. Its optimized memory usage and small footprint enable it to be kept constantly available on the side of the screen without getting in the way or slowing down system performance. In fact, because SideBar Lite is the first *closeable* Windows shell, it can be closed so that *100 percent of your system's resources are dedicated to the task at hand.*

SideBar Lite's real value comes from balance. We spent many long nights deciding what features to include and what features to throw out. What we came up with is, we believe, the best possible combination of features for a Windows shell. We are confident that you'll agree with the balance we chose. However, if you have suggestions for improvement, please contact us. We love to incorporate customer ideas in future products.

## SideBar versus SideBar Lite

SideBar 1.0 was released as a retail product on October 3, 1991. Since then, it has received rave reviews from our customers and the press. SideBar Lite is our special shareware release of the retail product. It is not "crippleware." SideBar Lite is a fully functional Windows shell, *sans* file management.

If you like SideBar Lite, you'll absolutely flip over the retail release of SideBar. It provides comprehensive, high-performance directory and file management through drag and drop or the command line. Also included is a floating application menu that pops up when you right-click on the Windows desktop. Best of all, these potent extras are packed into a single 200K SIDEBAR.EXE file you simply copy to your hard drive and run.

## Ordering SideBar or SideBar Lite

The version of SideBar Lite included with this documentation is for evaluation purposes only. Any other use requires the purchase of a license.

You can own the full-scale, retail release of SideBar for only $39.99. This price includes our famous album-cover packaging, with a Jump Start card, the latest version of SideBar, and the award-winning SideBar Notebook.

If you like SideBar Lite and would like to use it, you can purchase the latest version for $29.99. This price includes a 3.5-inch or 5.25-inch disk with a cool little manual.

Both products include free upgrades to the next version, along with incredible, unlimited, free customer support. In fact, you can even call our customer support hotline and ask our technicians to take you on a tour of the product over the phone so that you don't miss a single feature. Both products also come with a 60-day, money-back guarantee.

To order either SideBar or SideBar Lite, call us at 800-551-5187. We accept MasterCard, Visa, COD, personal checks; and most purchase orders. If you have questions or would like to receive a brochure, you can reach us at 914-255-0056. You can also fax us at 914-255-7572.

By the way, you can also order SideBar from Egghead Discount Software by calling 800-EGGHEAD.

## Be a part of the dream

When it comes right down to it, Paper Software exists to make great products — not necessarily great profits. This is evident in our packaging and the way we conduct business. Our dream is to make technology as simple and as practical as a sheet of paper. In order to pursue this dream, we at least need to cover our expenses so that we can continue to bring intensely simple software to the masses. So please, invest in the dream and pay for SideBar Lite if you like it.

Do not use SideBar Lite without paying for it. We decided to eliminate "nag screens" so that it is easier for you to evaluate the software — not so that it is easier for you to keep SideBar Lite without paying for it. Our developers, writers, artists, and packaging folks put in a massive amount of work on this project. When you pay for either SideBar or SideBar Lite, these people breathe easier because they can pay their bills. More important, they also become anxious to turn out new products you'll love.

## Paper Software and the environment

The individuals who comprise Paper Software (based in the heart of New York's Catskill Mountains) have a perpetual love affair with the planet Earth. For example, instead of packaging the commercial version of SideBar in a bulky box, we decided to use an album cover. It uses far less cardboard and ships in a recycled envelope rather than yet another bulky box stuffed with toxic Styrofoam shells. The distributors didn't appreciate this very much (they sell packaging, not software), but we're sure that some trees did.

The SideBar Notebook was also designed with the environment in mind. We used a more intuitive graphical layout, with labeled pictures, instead of trying to explain visual information by using text. This format enables you to make an immediate correlation between what you are seeing on the screen and what you are reading about. It also reduces the amount of paper needed for the document by one-third.

Combined, these steps save tons of paper annually. Of course, all our printing is done on recycled paper using a soy-based (nonpetroleum) ink.

## Things you should know

This document assumes a working knowledge of Microsoft Windows. Windows terms such as the *desktop, drag and drop, selecting,* and so on, are used often. If you are comfortable with these terms, you can proceed with confidence. If not, you will find the "Basic Skills" chapter of the *Microsoft Windows User's Guide* helpful.

The information in this document is subject to change without notice and does not represent a commitment on the part of Paper Software, Inc. The software described in this document is furnished for *evaluation purposes* only. Any other use requires the purchase of a license.

© Copyright 1992 Paper Software, Inc.

All rights reserved.

Version date: February 11, 1992

Paper Software, the Paper Software logo, SideBar, and SideBar Lite are trademarks of Paper Software, Inc. Microsoft is a registered trademark and Windows is a trademark of Microsoft Corporation.

SideBar Lite is dedicated to artists everywhere.

SideBar Lite was created by Mike McCue. Lite Write was written by Leonard Giannotti and Mike McCue.

The following individuals made SideBar Lite intensely simple:

Mike Weber, Mario Mercado, Bob Crofton, Diana Campanella, Kristine Farrell, Erica Swerdlow, Craig Miller, Joyce Klein, Karl Stantial, the cool individuals of Rainbow Diskette Services, the folks at Computer Metropolis, Igor the Boston cab driver, and Lao-tsu.

Thanks also to our beta testers who kept reality distortion to a minimum.

# Registration Form

If you have comments about SideBar, SideBar Lite, or Lite Write, write or call us:

**Paper Software, Inc.**
Route 467
New Paltz, NY 12561
914-255-0056

Name: _____

Address: _____

_____

_____

[  ] Retail version of SideBar:           $ 39.95

[  ] Registration of SideBar Lite:        $ 29.99

Total Enclosed: _____

# Super Resource Monitor

### SUPERRM.EXE — Version 1.2
### Copyright © by Softblox Incorporated

*S*uper Resource Monitor is a free utility that keeps track of your System Resources. System Resources *is Windows jargon for the memory it sets aside to load menus, icons, and other graphical objects.*

*Knowing about your Free System Resources (FSR) is important because Windows usually cannot start any additional applications after FSR falls below about 15 percent. Windows users are often confused when they receive messages such as* No memory is available — close some windows, *even when the Help About dialog box for Program Manager shows more than 1 megabyte of RAM free. You may be out of FSR even if you have plenty of RAM.*

*Super Resource Monitor is a handy way to manage your memory. It can be configured to pop up a dialog box to warn you when Free System Resources falls below, say, 25 percent. You can then close some windows before attempting to start a new application.*

*You can also use Super Resource Monitor to compact your Windows memory. Sometimes, Windows applications don't completely free the memory they use. This leaves "islands" in memory that Windows can't use until some application claims and frees (compacts) that memory. This is the reason that the performance of your Windows environment sometimes gets noticeably slower during the day as you open and close various applications. Super Resource Monitor automatically checks your memory every second and compacts it every ten seconds. You can reduce the frequency of these checks to reduce the monitor's impact, if any, on other applications' performance.*

*Super Resource Monitor consists of only two files: SUPERRM.EXE and SBICTLW.DLL, a library of customized window objects (which are visible in the Super Resource Monitor itself). As a free utility, Super Resource Monitor has no on-line documentation or technical support. Softblox Incorporated wrote it for its own diagnostic use and as an advertisement for its other programming services. The company also produces a retail product, SmartPad for Windows, that enables you to create floating button bars for any Windows application. For more information, contact the company at the address shown in the About dialog box of Super Resource Monitor.*

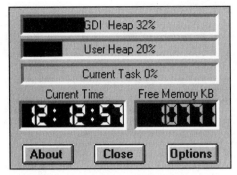

**Super Resource Monitor is just that: a system resource monitor that keeps track of what memory is being used.**

*In the remainder of this chapter, we describe each of the features of Super Resource Monitor.*

| | |
|---|---|
| **Type of Program:** | Utility |
| **Requires:** | Windows 3.0 or later |
| **Registration:** | Free. This program requires no registration. |
| **Technical Support:** | None |

# Overview

Super Resource Monitor is a utility that enables you to display and manage your Free System Resources in Windows.

# The Main Window

When you start Super Resource Monitor (SUPERRM.EXE), it displays a small window with three *meters* (similar to gas gauges), a digital clock, and a numerical display of free Windows memory. The meters indicate the percentage of three different types of Windows System Resources: the GDI Heap, the User Heap, and the Current Task Heap. These terms are described in the following sections.

## What are Free System Resources?

Windows sets aside certain areas of memory to load menus, icons, and other graphical objects. One of these areas is used by GDI.EXE, the Graphic Device Interface, which draws pixels on your display. The other area is used by USER.EXE, which responds to mouse clicks, key presses, and other user actions. Whichever memory area has a *lower* percentage of its memory unused is reported by Windows as the percentage of Free System Resources. For example, if 40 percent of the GDI memory area is unused, and 30 percent of the User memory area is unused, the Windows Program Manager reports 30 percent Free System Resources in its Help About dialog box.

## GDI Heap, User Heap, and Current Task Heap

A *heap* is an area of memory that Windows or a Windows application can use. The *GDI Heap* and *User Heap* are areas set aside for two of Windows' most important programs: GDI.EXE and USER.EXE. The *Current Task Heap* is an area of memory set aside for a Windows application. This is often called the *local heap* because it is used only by one application and is not available to other applications.

Different applications use their local heap in different ways. Even if an application uses 100 percent of its local heap, it can usually allocate more memory, so this is not a cause for concern.

The total amount of memory available to Windows, from which it allocates all the local heaps, is often called the *global heap.* This number is usually reported by utilities (such as Super Resource Monitor) that display statistics such as Total Memory Available and Free Memory Available.

## Configuring Meter Colors and Alarms

Double-clicking on the GDI Heap, User Heap, or Current Task meter displays a small dialog box that enables you to set colors and alarms for that meter.

Click on a color in the left side of the dialog box to indicate the memory *used*; click on a color in the right side of the dialog box to indicate the memory *free*. Then click on the OK button to close the dialog box.

You can also set an alarm to display a message when the percentage used in a certain heap exceeds the level you specify. For example, you might want to set an alarm to go off when the GDI Heap or User Heap is more than 70 percent

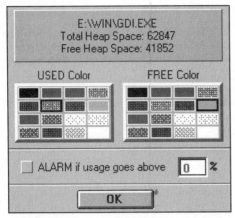

E:\WIN\GDI.EXE
Total Heap Space: 62847
Free Heap Space: 41852

USED Color          FREE Color

☐ ALARM if usage goes above  [0]  %

OK

**Double-clicking on a meter displays a dialog box
from which you can select colors and set alarms
for that meter.**

used (less than 30 percent free). Because Windows cannot open another application after Free System Resources falls below about 15 percent, this alarm gives you an opportunity to close some unused windows before trying to start a major application or process (such as printing).

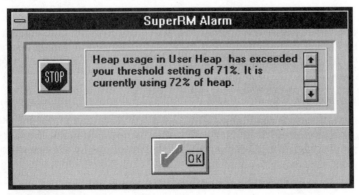

SuperRM Alarm

Heap usage in User Heap  has exceeded
your threshold setting of 71%. It is
currently using 72% of heap.

STOP

✓ OK

**When a specific heap exceeds an amount you specify, Super Resource
Monitor displays an alarm box.**

**Double-click on the Current Time or Free Memory area to display a dialog box from which you can select a color for that area.**

## Configuring the Time and Free Memory Windows

Double-clicking on the Time and Free Memory windows in the main window displays a small dialog box that enables you to specify colors for these windows. Click on Yellow, Green, Red, or Gray and watch the window change color. Click on OK to save your preferred color.

## The About Button

Clicking on the About button on Super Resource Monitor's main window displays an informative dialog box. The dialog box indicates the current Windows mode (Standard or Enhanced), the type of processor and math coprocessor (if any), the total memory available to Windows, and the largest block of free memory.

The largest block of free memory is important because, despite the total amount of memory available to Windows, Windows cannot load another application into memory that is larger than the largest free block. If you try to load a larger program, Windows may swap some programs from memory to disk or it may display a warning message for you to close some windows.

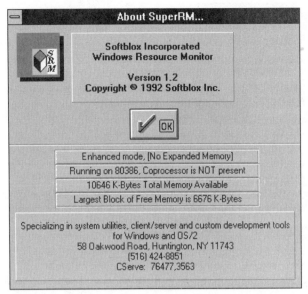

**The About dialog box provides important information about Windows and the Super Resource Monitor.**

# The Close Button

Clicking on the Close button exits Super Resource Monitor.

# The Options Button

Clicking on the Options button enlarges the Super Resource Monitor main window so that it displays several additional choices. These choices enable you to determine when Super Resource Monitor samples available memory and compacts memory and whether the main window should float over other applications. These concepts are described in the following sections.

## Sample Every *x* Second

By default, Super Resource Monitor queries Windows for the amount of memory available every 1 second. You can change this value to up to 999 seconds (more than 16 minutes) to improve the performance of other applications. However, querying Windows requires very little time (fractions of a millisecond), so you shouldn't need to change this value.

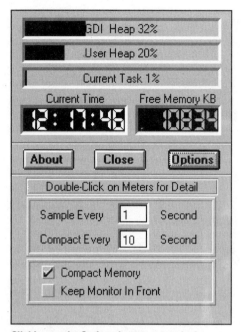

Clicking on the Options button expands the
main window so that it includes additional
options you can control.

## Compact Every x Second

By default, Super Resource Monitor compacts memory every 10 seconds. This
eliminates "islands" in memory that sometimes occur when an application you
exit does not or cannot free all the memory it used. Compacting memory can
make more memory available to other applications you start later.

You can change this value to up to 999 seconds, but (like sampling memory)
compacting memory detracts very little from the performance of applications,
so you shouldn't need to change this value.

## The Compact Memory check box

Click on the Compact Memory box to turn on and off Super Resource Monitor's
capability to compact memory. When a check mark appears in the box, Super
Resource Monitor checks memory and (if necessary) asks Windows to compact
its memory.

## The Keep Monitor In Front check box

When the Keep Monitor In Front check box is checked, the Super Resource Monitor main window floats on top of most other Windows applications. This is useful when you want to see the effect on memory of using a particular Windows application. You might want to turn this option off if Super Resource Monitor remains visible when a screen-saver utility tries to blank your screen.

# SmartPad for Windows

SmartPad for Windows is a retail Windows program from Softblox Incorporated. It enables you to define floating button bars for Windows applications. SmartPad features include the following:

♦ You can create customizable tool boxes for *any* Windows application, including those that you write yourself.

♦ You can use common tool boxes, which are available in all applications, or associate tool boxes with specific applications and have those tool boxes come up only when you start those applications.

♦ You can automate operations using sophisticated macro recording and playback features for your keyboard and mouse activity.

♦ You can use buttons to launch programs (with full support for drag and drop), prompt for filenames and strings, execute macros, or send DDE commands.

♦ You can create global or application-specific keyboard shortcuts for your common operations, as well as pop-up "balloon help" for buttons within a pad.

♦ SmartPad is fully compatible with Windows 3.0 and 3.1, as well as Norton Desktop for Windows.

At this writing, the list price for SmartPad is $59.95. For more information on SmartPad for Windows, contact Softblox Incorporated at 58 Oakwood Road, Huntington, NY 11743, U.S.A. The telephone number is 516-424-8851. The CompuServe ID is 76477,3563.

# Widget

### Version 1.1
### Copyright © by Metz Software

*Widget is a free utility designed for PC support people who need to know how much time various applications use in the Windows environment.*

*Windows enables several applications to run at the same time. However, some applications take a long time for their own processing. When this happens, you spend a lot of time looking at the Hourglass icon, the Windows wait symbol.*

*If a person is using a PC that is too slow for the work to be done, he or she can look at the Hourglass icon for several minutes each day. Depending on that person's hourly wage, it might be more cost-effective for the company to buy that person a faster PC instead of wasting that person's time waiting for the computer to catch up.*

*Widget enables you to measure precisely how many seconds per minute a Windows user simply sits there waiting for the computer. This information can help make a case to upgrade certain computers from 386-class machines to 486-class machines, for example.*

*Widget can also help diagnose problems with background applications that seem to be starved for time. If you start a communications program, for example, and try to download a file in the background, that background process may abort if the communications application does not get a certain percentage of computer time. If such programs often lose characters or drop the transmission line, you can use Widget to find out which other programs take 100 percent of the computer's time when they load, open a file, sort, and so on. Spreadsheet programs often grab all available processor time when they open large files, for example.*

*Metz Software also produces retail programs, including the excellent File F/X file manager and the award-winning Metz Task Manager. Look for these products at any retail software store near you or contact Metz Software at the address at the end of this chapter.*

| | |
|---|---|
| **Type of Program:** | Utility |
| **Requires:** | Windows 3.0 or later |
| **Registration:** | Free. This program requires no registration. |
| **Technical Support:** | None |
| **Similar Shareware:** | Other Metz Software shareware programs, Desktop Navigator (a file manager) and Task Manager, are featured in *Windows 3.1 SECRETS,* published by IDG Books Worldwide. See the end of this chapter for additional descriptions. |

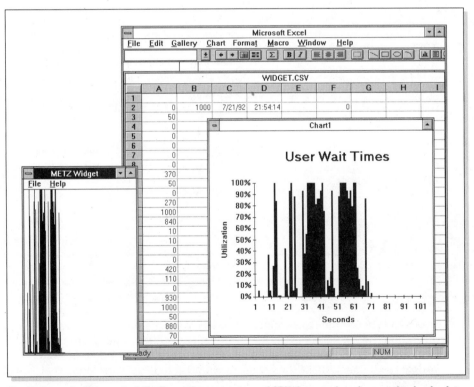

The Widget window, on the left, shows the percentage of CPU time used each second to load a data file into Excel; the resulting data file was opened in the Excel window, on the right, and charted.

# Introduction

Metz Widget measures how long you wait for CPU processing. If applications yield frequently — that is, if they release CPU time for use by other applications — the wait time is small. If one or more applications take a long time to yield, the wait time is large. Long yield times can be caused by heavy use of memory, an underpowered machine, or a combination of both. If you're waiting a lot, you should probably consider upgrading your system.

# How Metz Widget Works

The main Widget window displays a histogram of the wait periods. Each vertical bar is one pixel wide. The height of each bar ranges from two pixels high to the height of the window area. Each bar represents the accumulative amount of waiting during one time interval. The initial time interval is 1 second, but this can be changed in the Preferences dialog box. For example, if Metz Widget waits a total of 0.75 second during a given second, the vertical bar for that second is three-quarters of the window's client area in height. The bar heights are relative. In other words, the bar is three-quarters high regardless of the window's size. If there are too many bars, bars scroll off the left of the application window.

If you like, you can store the wait time values in a comma-separated-values (CSV) file. This file can be imported into Microsoft Excel or another application for further analysis.

# The File Menu

## Pause command

When you choose the Pause command, Metz Widget stops calculating wait times, and the histogram in the Metz Widget application window stops scrolling. When Metz Widget is paused, you see a Resume command in the Metz Widget File menu. Choose the Resume command to begin calculating wait times again.

## Clear Window command

When you choose the Clear Window command, the histogram is erased from the Metz Widget application window. The histogram graph begins again at the far left of the display.

## Reset File command

The Reset File command deletes the output filename specified in the Preferences dialog box. When additional file output is generated, the file is re-created.

## Preferences command

When you choose the Preferences command, the Preferences dialog box is displayed so that you can set up Widget.

# The Preferences Dialog Box

When you choose the Preferences command, the Preferences dialog box is displayed. Use the Preferences dialog box to configure Metz Widget.

## Window check box

Check the Window check box to display the histogram in the scrolling application window.

```
┌──────────────────── METZ Widget ────────────────────┐
│ ┌─Preferences──────────────────────────────────┐    │
│ │ ⊠ Window                                      │    │
│ │ ⊠ File, Filename:   c:\widget\widget.csv      │    │
│ │ Time interval (seconds):   1                  │    │
│ │ Minimum time (milliseconds):  0               │    │
│ │ User:                                         │    │
│ │ □ Hide window                                 │    │
│ │ □ Pause on startup                            │    │
│ └───────────────────────────────────────────────┘    │
│            [ OK ]        [ Cancel ]                   │
└───────────────────────────────────────────────────────┘
```

**Use the Preferences dialog box to configure Widget.**

## File check box

Check the File check box to record wait times in an output file. This file is a comma-separated-values (CSV) file suitable for importing into a spreadsheet program. The accumulated wait time for each time period is written to the file.

Before and after each session, the file is stamped with a zero wait time, the time interval, the current date and time, and the user name, if you have entered one. The file is also stamped before and after each pause, before and after the preferences are set, when Widget is exited or closed, and when Windows is exited. Wait times and time intervals are given in milliseconds. (One thousand milliseconds equal one second.)

## Filename box

If you check the File check box, you can store the wait time data in the file you specify in this box. Choose the path and filename of the comma-separated-values (CSV) file in which you want to store the accumulated wait times.

## Time interval box

Specify the interval (in seconds) between measurements of wait times.

## User box

Enter a user name to record in the file you have specified. The User box enables you to assess wait times for different users on the same system.

## Hide window check box

Check the Hide window check box to hide the Metz Widget application window. If you want to display the application window again, run Widget again.

## Pause on startup check box

Check the Pause on startup check box to start Metz Widget paused. You must choose the Resume command to start it again.

# Other Programs from Metz Software

The following Microsoft Windows applications are currently available from Metz Software.

## Metz File F/X

Metz File F/X incorporates Desktop Navigator and Task Manager and adds three powerful new utilities: Text Search, File Find, and Undelete. "Among the Windows-specific file managers, File F/X stands out for its relatively clean design and its ease of use..." — Michael Miller, *InfoWorld,* 4/22/91.

## Metz Task Manager

Metz Task Manager is a replacement for the Microsoft Task List application. Task Manager expands on the Task List functions, providing a comprehensive set of utilities such as a screen blanker, file manager, customizable tools menu, and more.

## Metz Desktop Manager

Metz Desktop Manager is designed to provide you with a friendly menuing system plus several utilities. With Desktop Manager, you can easily create menus and submenus that directly access your applications and data (across directories and drives). Additional features such as a customizable screen blanker, windows-arrangement functions, a directory-tree display, a file finder, point-and-shoot file management, and an automatic menu generator are also included.

## Metz Desktop Navigator

Metz Desktop Navigator is designed to provide fast access to your drives, directories, and files. File and directory management functions are included as well. Additional features such as a customizable screen blanker, windows-arrangement functions, and a file finder are also included.

## Metz Phones

Metz Phones is a Microsoft Windows application designed for maintaining lists of names, phone numbers, and addresses. If you have a Hayes-compatible modem, Phones can dial the phone for you.

## Metz Dialer

Metz Dialer is a pop-up speed dialer that, when coupled with a Hayes-compatible modem, provides a quick and convenient method of dialing phone numbers. A customizable pull-down menu enables you to add names and numbers you frequently call.

## Metz Lock

Metz Lock is a security application for Microsoft Windows. Lock can be used for preventing unauthorized use of your system while it is unattended.

## Metz Runner

Metz Runner is a utility that provides a quick method for running applications and files.

## Metz Time

Metz Time is a digital pop-up date-and-time display that can be placed anywhere on the screen.

## Metz Freemem

Metz Freemem is a moveable digital display of free conventional and free expanded memory.

# For More Information

For more information, contact Metz Software, P.O. Box 6699, Bellevue, WA 98008-0699. Telephone: 206-641-4525. Fax: 206-644-6026.

11:27

# WinClock

**Version 3.21**
**Copyright © David A. Feinleib**

*W*ith all of Windows' multitasking features — which enable you to run two or more programs simultaneously — nothing in Windows enables you to make a program run at a certain time. Such a feature would let you tell your communications program to call another computer at night when telephone rates are cheap, for example.

*With WinClock, you can not only run programs at specified times, but you can also set alarms for yourself or set stopwatches to measure elapsed time.*

*If you don't need these features, WinClock simply provides you with a window that shows you the correct date and time. This window can be configured for a wide variety of international date and time formats and can be made to float over all other windows to keep it visible.*

| | |
|---|---|
| **Type of Program:** | Alarm Clock/Scheduler |
| **Requires:** | Windows 3.0 or later |
| **Registration:** | Use the form at the end of this chapter to register with the shareware author. |
| **Technical Support:** | David Feinleib provides registered users with technical support through CompuServe, FidoNet, the Byte Information Exchange (BIX), and mail. |
| **Similar Shareware:** | ClockMan, a program featured in *Windows 3.1 SECRETS,* published by IDG Books Worldwide, also sets alarms and timers. |

**16:28  18-Oct-92**

**At its simplest, WinClock displays a small time-and-date window; it also can run applications at specified times.**

# Introduction

WinClock is a digital clock for Microsoft Windows 3.x that has the following features:

- ◆ Displays the time and date in many different formats
- ◆ Supports ten alarms (that can be set to go off daily or only on a specified date)
- ◆ Has an optional hourly beep
- ◆ Enables alarms and beeps to be set to return you to Windows or leave you in a DOS session (if a DOS session is active)
- ◆ Has a Run-Program timer (gives you the ability to run programs at specified times)
- ◆ Enables you to set the date and time easily
- ◆ Stays optionally in front of other applications
- ◆ "Remembers" its position on the screen
- ◆ Supports two stopwatches and two countdown timers
- ◆ Has a colon separating the hours and minutes that can be set to blink
- ◆ Has context-sensitive help
- ◆ Has direct screen-saver compatibility (automatically detects active screen savers)
- ◆ Has Cascade and Tile compatibility
- ◆ Works with monitors of all resolutions

```
 ▬  11:30 am  10-17-92
   Move
   Close           Alt+F4
   Switch To...    Ctrl+Esc
   Help...
   Set Time/Date...
   Alarms...
   Timers...
   Hourly beep
   Preferences...
   About...
```

The WinClock system menu provides a list of
options that customize the program.

# Using the WinClock Options

To bring up a list of options, click the WinClock system box once.

## Help

The Help option brings up help about WinClock and explains how to use
context-sensitive help. It also displays an index of all help topics available for
WinClock.

## Set Time/Date

The Set Time/Date option enables you to easily enter the time and date. When
the window pops up, enter the correct time and date. Click on AM or PM to set
the time in 12-hour format or click on 24-hr and enter the time in 24-hour
format. WinClock automatically converts 24-hour format to 12-hour format if
you click on PM after 24-hr was selected. WinClock also converts from PM to
24-hour format.

The current time and date are shown in the edit boxes when the window
originally appears. To update the time and date displayed in the edit boxes to
the current time and date, click on the Time or Date pushbutton, depending on
which you want to update.

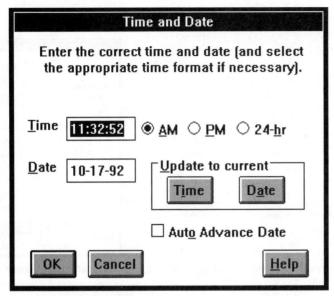

Use the Time and Date dialog box to enter the correct time and date;
you can easily switch from 24-hour format to 12-hour format and vice
versa.

When you have made all your choices, click on OK or press Enter. If you want to
leave the old time and date, click on Cancel.

You should select Auto Advance Date only if you are using a version of DOS that
does not advance the date correctly at midnight.

# Alarms

The Alarms option enables you to configure WinClock's alarms. To set an alarm,
first click on the alarm you want to set (Alarm 1, 2, and so on). When you have
made your choice, click on OK. If you want to leave the alarms the way they
were, click on Cancel.

## Enabled

If you want the alarm to be on, select Enabled (so that there is an X in the box).
If you do not want the alarm to be on now (you only want to set it for use at a
later time), click on Enabled until there is no X in the box.

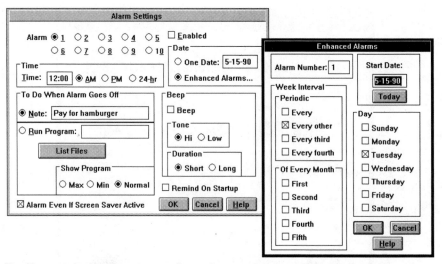

The Alarms option enables you to configure alarms; you can specify the date and time and what you want to happen when the alarm goes off.

## Time

Enter in the Time edit box the time you want the alarm to go off. If you select AM or PM, enter the time in 12-hour format. If you select 24-hr, enter the time in 24-hour format.

## Date

**One Date:** Select One Date to have the alarm go off on a single date. Type the date in the edit box.

**Enhanced Alarms:** Click on Enhanced Alarms to open a dialog box with advanced options for alarms. See "Enhanced alarms," later in this chapter.

## Beep

To have the alarm beep when it goes off, select Beep (so that there is an X in the box). Select Hi or Low pitch. Select the duration of the beep. Short is about 8 seconds; Long is about 30 seconds. You may stop both beeps by clicking on OK when the box alerting you about the alarm appears.

## Note

If you want, type a note for WinClock to display when the alarm goes off.

## Run Program

Select Run Program to run a program at the time you've set for the alarm. Type the full pathname of the program you want to run. Select Max if you want the program to be maximized when it runs. Select Min to have the program minimized. Select Normal to have the program shown in its normal size.

If you type the name of a program that does not exist on your hard disk, a warning message appears when you click on OK. You can then choose to edit the name of the program or to leave it unedited.

# Enhanced alarms

Clicking on Enhanced Alarms in the Alarm Settings dialog box displays a more advanced dialog box with the following options.

### Start Date

Enter the start date in the edit box. The *start date* is the date from which the alarm specified in the rest of the dialog box starts. The start date causes the alarm to go off beginning with that date.

### Week Interval

**Periodic:** The periodic selection causes alarms to go off on dates such as every Thursday, every other Wednesday, and so on. Select the period you want and then choose the days with which they should be combined.

**Of Every Month:** This selection causes alarms to go off on dates such as the first Thursday of every month, the second Wednesday of every month, and so on.

### Day

This selection you make in the Day section of the dialog box is combined with the Periodic and Of Every Month options you select in the Week Interval section.

### Examples

**Periodic:** To have an alarm go off every other Tuesday, select Every Other in the Periodic section of the dialog box and Tuesday in the Day section.

Suppose that you entered **5-15-90** in the Start Date edit box and selected Every and Tuesday; because 5-15-90 was a Tuesday, the alarm goes off on 5-15-90, 5-22-90, 5-29-90, 6-04-90, and so on.

**Of Every Month:** To have an alarm go off on the second Wednesday of every month, select Second in the Of Every Month section of the dialog box and Wednesday in the Day section.

Suppose that you entered **5-15-90** in the Start Date edit box, selected Third in the Of Every Month section, and Monday in the Day section; the alarm goes off on 6-17-90 because that date was the third Monday of the month.

## Timers

WinClock has two stopwatches and two countdown timers. By selecting different options, you can have WinClock display some or all of the timers — as well as the time and date. To use a countdown timer, you must type a number from which to count down in the Countdown From edit box. This number must be in the form HH:MM (hours:minutes). If it is not in this form, any number found (that is before nonnumeric characters, excluding the colon) is used as the minutes.

Select Display Timer individually for each timer you want to display (or not display). Select Display Date or Display Time if you want to display the date or time while one or more of the timers are running. The display of the date and time does not depend on the timer that is currently selected.

Use the Timers option to set either of the two stopwatches or the two countdown timers.

Display Seconds is selected by default. If you do not want to display the seconds, click on this option so that there is no X in the box. You can choose to display the seconds individually for each timer. The seconds are displayed only if Display Timer has been selected.

The settings you make in the Timer dialog box only affect the WinClock display while one or more timers are running. The settings are saved while WinClock is running but are reset to the default when WinClock is restarted.

When you have selected to display a timer, it is displayed as follows:

The first stopwatch appears as S1 00:00:00.

The second stopwatch appears as S2 00:00:00.

The first countdown timer appears as C1 00:00:00.

The second countdown timer appears as C2 00:00:00.

The current count (time elapsed) of the selected timer appears in the Current Count box when the Timers dialog box is displayed.

When a timer is stopped, its current count is displayed in the Current Count box until you switch to another timer. The stopped timer then resets itself to zero.

The Start/Stop button reflects whether the currently selected timer is running. If the current timer is running, the button shows the word *Stop* so that you can stop the timer. If the current timer is not running, the button shows the word *Start* so that you can start it.

Each countdown timer can be set to beep or not to beep. Select Beep (so that there is an X in the box) if you want the countdown timer to beep when it finishes. Select the pitch and the duration of the beep. The Short beep lasts about 8 seconds; the Long beep lasts about 30 seconds. You can stop both beeps by clicking on OK when the timer window appears, alerting you that the timer has finished.

# Hourly Beep

Select the Hourly Beep option if you want WinClock to sound a short beep and flash on the hour. A check mark appears next to Hourly Beep in the system menu if it is selected. To turn off the hourly beep, click on Hourly Beep again. The check mark disappears.

*Special note for 386 enhanced mode:* If a DOS session is active and hourly beep is enabled, WinClock by default returns you to Windows and beeps. You must then double-click on the DOS icon to return to the DOS session. If you do not want to be returned to Windows when an hourly beep occurs, deselect the For Hourly Beep check box in the Preferences dialog box.

# Preferences

The Preferences dialog box enables you to change how the date and time are displayed. Select the options you want, as described in the following sections, and click on OK.

## Time formats

**24-hour and 12-hour formats:** WinClock supports 24-hour format, 12-hour format with AM and PM, and 12-hour format without AM and PM. Select your preferred style.

**Display Seconds:** WinClock includes seconds in its time display when this option is turned on.

```
┌─────────────────────────── Preferences ───────────────────────────┐
│                                                                     │
│ ┌Time Format─┐ ┌Day────┐ ┌Month────┐ ┌Day─────┐ ┌Year──────┐        │
│ │ ◉ 3:00 PM  │ │○ Mon  │ │◉ 1     │ │◉ 3     │ │◉ 90      │        │
│ │ ○ 15:00    │ │○ Monday│ │○ 01    │ │○ 03    │ │○ 1990    │        │
│ │ ○ 3:00     │ │◉ No Day│ │○ Jan   │ │○ No Day│ │○ No Year │        │
│ │ ☐ Display Seconds     │ │○ January│                               │
│ │ ☐ Blink Colon         │ │○ No Month│                              │
│ │                       ┌Date Format──────────────────────┐         │
│ │ ○ PM  ◉ pm           │◉ MDY  ○ DMY  ○ YMD  Separator [-]│         │
│ └───────────────────────┘                                 │         │
│ ┌Remember Screen Location────┐                                      │
│ │                   ☐ Lock Location    ┌Display──────────┐          │
│ │ ◉ One Location                       │☒ System Box     │          │
│ │ ○ Return To Lower Right Corner On Startup│☒ Stay In Front│         │
│ │                                      │☒ Anti-Cascade   │          │
│ ┌Screen Saver Compatibility──┐         └─────────────────┘          │
│ │◉ Auto  ○ Delay [4:56] MM:SS  ○ None │                             │
│ ┌Return To Windows If DOS Box Active:─┐ ┌OK┐ ┌Cancel┐ ┌Help┐        │
│ │☒ For Alarms    ☒ For Hourly Beep    │                             │
│ └─────────────────────────────────────┘                             │
└─────────────────────────────────────────────────────────────────────┘
```

**Use the Preferences option to change how the date and time are displayed and specify the particulars of other aspects of WinClock.**

**Blink Colon:** If you want the colon that separates the hours and minutes of the time to blink on the second (when the seconds are not displayed), select Blink Colon (so that there is an X in the box).

**PM or pm:** When WinClock displays time in the 12-hour format with AM and PM, it displays the suffixes AM and PM in uppercase when PM is selected and in lowercase when pm is selected.

## Date formats

**Options:** You can choose to display the date in any combination of day of the week, month, day of the month, and year.

**Date Format:** Select the date format you prefer: month first (MDY), day first (DMY), or year first (YMD).

**Separator:** You can change the character that separates the parts of the date by typing a different character in the Separator edit box. For example, you can use a slash (/), period (.), or hyphen (-) between numbers in a date. Although it is possible to type into the Separator box more than one character, only the first character you type is used.

## Remember Screen Location

**One Location:** WinClock remembers one screen location by default. This means that when you move WinClock, it remembers its position on the screen. The next time you run WinClock, it goes to the position where it was when it was last closed.

**Return To Lower Right Corner on Startup:** If you want to move WinClock to a certain location temporarily, but then revert to its default screen position in the lower right corner of your screen, select Return To Lower Right Corner on Startup. The next time you run WinClock, it reverts to its default location.

**Lock Location:** This option locks WinClock's location on the screen so that you can't move it accidentally.

## Screen Saver Compatibility

WinClock is compatible with most available screen savers. Note that WinClock itself is *not* a screen saver.

**Auto:** Setting this option causes WinClock to be hidden (not displayed on the screen) when a screen saver saves the screen. This option is compatible with most screen savers. It is recommended that you try this option first if you want screen-saver compatibility.

**Delay:** Setting this option causes WinClock to be hidden when the mouse and keyboard have not been activated for the amount of time that you specify in the edit box.

You must set the delay in the form MM:SS (minutes:seconds). If it is not in this form, any number found (before nonnumeric characters, excluding the colon) is used as the seconds.

Use this option if the Auto option (discussed earlier) does not work correctly with your screen saver. Set the delay to a few seconds *less* than your screen saver's delay. This setup prevents WinClock from appearing on-screen after your screen saver blanks the screen.

**None:** This option turns off screen-saver compatibility, which means that WinClock is not hidden if you have a screen saver, and it activates before WinClock hides itself.

## Return To Windows If DOS Box Active

The following information only applies when Windows is running in 386 enhanced mode.

**For Alarms:** If a DOS box is active and an alarm is enabled and set to go off, WinClock by default returns you to Windows and (1) displays the message, (2) beeps, and/or (3) runs a specified program. You must then double-click on the minimized DOS icon to return to your DOS session. If you do not want to return to Windows when an alarm occurs, deselect the For Alarms check box in the Preferences dialog box.

**For Hourly Beep:** If a DOS box is active and hourly beep is enabled, WinClock by default returns you to Windows and beeps. You must then double-click on the DOS icon to return to the DOS box. If you do not want to return to Windows when an hourly beep occurs, deselect the For Hourly Beep check box in the Preferences dialog box.

## Display

**System Box:** If you want WinClock to display a system box on its window, select System Box. Hiding the system box reduces the area that WinClock takes up on the screen. For more information, see "Displaying or Hiding the System Box" later in this chapter.

**Stay In Front:** If you want WinClock to always appear over other applications, select Stay In Front.

**Anti-Cascade:** Select Anti-Cascade if you do not want WinClock to be cascaded when you cascade applications with the Windows Task List.

## About

Select About from the system menu to display information about WinClock.

# Getting Help

WinClock Help can be accessed in three ways:

♦ Select Help from the WinClock system menu. This action displays an index of all help available for WinClock. It also explains how to use WinClock's context-sensitive help.

♦ Access context-sensitive help by clicking on one of the WinClock system menu items, holding down the mouse button, and pressing F1.

♦ Access context-sensitive help from most of WinClock's dialog boxes by clicking on the Help button, if one is displayed.

# Displaying or Hiding the System Box

You can display or hide the system box in the following ways:

♦ Open the Preferences dialog box and select System Box (so that there is an X in the box). This setup displays the system box. To hide the system box, open the Preferences dialog box and deselect System Box (so that there is no X in the box).

♦ Double-click on the WinClock *client area* (the area in which the time and date are displayed). If the system box is hidden, it becomes visible. If it is displayed, it becomes hidden.

# Cascading or Tiling with WinClock

The Windows Task List (which you access by pressing Ctrl+Esc or by double-clicking on an empty spot on the Windows desktop) has buttons to cascade (overlap) or tile (not overlap) all open applications. The WinClock window does not cascade or tile because it always remains the same size. But the Task List counts WinClock as one of the applications it cascades or tiles. This can cause the other applications not to use the full screen when the Task List cascades or tiles all open windows. You can prevent this in the following ways.

## Cascading

If you want to cascade open windows, it is useful to select the Anti-Cascade option in the Preferences dialog box. This option causes WinClock to be ignored by Task List when it cascades applications.

To turn the Anti-Cascade option on, select Preferences from WinClock's system menu. In the Preferences dialog box, select Anti-Cascade (so that there is an X in the box).

## Tiling

If you want to tile open windows, you should first click once with the right mouse button on the WinClock *client area* (the area where the time and date are displayed). This action causes WinClock to be hidden for about seven seconds, during which time you can tile the other open windows correctly.

# Moving WinClock

To move WinClock, click on WinClock and, while holding the mouse button, move WinClock.

# Closing WinClock

To close WinClock, do one of the following:

♦ Double-click on the WinClock system box.

♦ Click on the WinClock system box once and then click on Close.

# Using the WinClock Files

The following files are included with WinClock, and you can delete them to deinstall WinClock:

WINCLOCK.EXE
WINCLOCK.DOC
WINCLOCK.HLP

DAFLIB.HLP
REGISTER.DOC
DAFLIB.DLL
DATEFUNC.DLL
WCHOOK.DLL
WSAVER.DLL
PRODLIST.TXT
READ.ME

The following files are created by WinClock in your Windows directory:

WINCLOCK.INI
WINCLOCK.CFG

# How To Contact the Shareware Author

Comments and suggestions (and reports of problems) are greatly appreciated.
You can contact me in the following ways:

♦ Write to David A. Feinleib, 1430 Mass. Ave., Suite 306-42, Cambridge, MA
  02138.

♦ Send Byte Information Exchange (BIX) mail to pgm.

♦ Send CompuServe mail to 76516,20.

♦ Send mail on a BBS through FidoNet (IBM UG BBS, Boston, MA) to Node
  1:101/310 David Feinleib.

♦ Send Internet mail to 76516.20@compuserve.com.

# How To Pay For and Register WinClock

WinClock is shareware. You can make copies of this program and give them to
others as long as the on-line documentation is provided with the program and
all files are unaltered.

Please refer to the About dialog box for information on registering the program.
From the About dialog box, you can print a registration form. Alternatively, you
can print the file REGISTER.DOC or use the form at the end of this chapter.

# Thanks!

My thanks to those BIX users who, by downloading WinClock, inspired me to write this version. Credit is due to John Ogren for suggesting the addition of international date formats. Thanks to Guy J. Gallo for his suggestions (most of which were implemented) on the alarms. Thanks to Steve Garcia, Ernest Karhu, Mark Lutton, and William Saito for their suggestions, which greatly influenced this version of WinClock. Special thanks to Peter Kaminski for his help with the icons, his numerous comments and suggestions, and his support from the beginning and through the testing stages, all of which resulted in many of the changes in this version. My thanks to Peter W. Meek for his encouragement, sense of humor, testing, and suggestions for the new alarm options. Thanks to Steve Moshier for help with the algorithms used in the new alarm options. Thanks to Bruce Wheelock for his extensive testing. Thanks to Arlan Fuller for his sense of humor and help with various parts of WinClock.

# Other products by the same author

## For Microsoft Windows 3.x

*Utilities:*

**RunProg:** RunProg, a program featured in *Windows 3.1 SECRETS,* published by IDG Books Worldwide, enables you to run a program (from the Program Manager or from your WIN.INI file) at a size that you specify: maximized, minimized, normal, hidden, or at specified coordinates.

**Pos:** Pos displays the mouse cursor position in relation to the screen (screen coordinates) and in relation to the window that has the input focus. Pos makes a good addition to the Windows Software Development Kit and is also useful when selecting monitor resolutions. It was originally developed to enable the user to move the mouse cursor to screen positions ahead of time. In addition, Pos can display the dimensions of a window.

**PrintSwitch:** Easily switch between HPPCL and PostScript modes on a Hewlett-Packard laser printer with a PostScript cartridge installed.

**IconCalc:** A full-function calculator in an icon (see elsewhere in this book).

**Mem:** Mem can display the amount of memory free, the largest block of memory free, the percent of system resources free, and the amount of disk space free on drives you select. Mem can sound an alarm when the disk space, free memory, or percent of system resources free goes below amounts you specify (a different amount can be specified for each disk drive).

**ChCursor:** If you find that you sometimes lose track of the mouse cursor on the screen, ChangeCursor enables you to press the right mouse button to highlight the cursor. Other features include the capacity to position the cursor in the center of the screen with a click of the right mouse button and the capacity to hide the cursor when you start typing and then display it again when you move the mouse.

**Lock:** Lock is a keyboard lock and screen saver. It automatically locks the keyboard after a certain time.

**SaveSet:** SaveSet enables you to cause the Save Settings check box that appears when you exit Windows to be automatically checked or unchecked.

**Click:** Click produces a keyboard *click*. This is especially useful for those users who have used a keyboard click for DOS but have been unable to find one for Microsoft Windows. The duration and pitch of the click can be easily changed by the user.

### *Games:*

**Hop:** The only computer Hop-Over puzzle. Hop is a short form of Chinese checkers. (Hop can undo moves and solve the puzzle automatically if you want it to.)

**Magic Squares:** The only magic squares game for Windows 3.x. (A *magic square* is a square array of numbers in which each row, column, and diagonal adds up to the same number.) Magic Squares can save and retrieve games and includes several solutions on disk. You can specify different size puzzles, from 3 by 3 to 9 by 9.

**Slide:** Slide is the classic sliding-block puzzle. Features: Saves and retrieves games, can undo moves one at a time, saves the last game automatically, has a 3-by-3 to 9-by-9 puzzle size.

## For DOS

**DskNum:** DskNum estimates the number of disks needed for a DOS backup. It estimates for 360K, 720K, 1.2MB, and 1.44MB disks.

**DlFile (with DirSrch):** DlFile goes through your disk directories looking for the filespec you specify. If found, it prompts you to delete it. This is very convenient for finding and deleting *.BAK files.

**ShowDirs:** ShowDirs displays directories on your system that match the one specified. It can search a single drive or an entire system.

**Mem:** Mem displays the amount of conventional memory in your computer and the amount free. It also displays information about extended memory if you have it in your computer.

These programs are available on BIX, CompuServe, and the Boston Computer Society's IBM BBS, and from other shareware libraries. If you want more information, contact me as described in "How To Contact the Shareware Author," earlier in this chapter.

# Error Messages and Solutions

W1000 — No system timers available

WinClock must use one of the Windows Timers to update the time. You should try closing another application, closing WinClock, and running WinClock again.

W1010 — Unable to save WinClock configuration file

WinClock was unable to save the information you entered in the Preferences box.

W1020 — Invalid time entered

You entered an invalid time. Enter a valid time.

W1021 — Invalid date entered

You entered an invalid date. Enter a valid date.

# Disclaimer

WinClock is supplied as is. The author disclaims all warranties expressed or implied, including, without limitation, the warranties of merchantability and of fitness for any purpose. The author assumes no liability for damages, direct or consequential, which may result from the use of WinClock.

# Registration Form

On registering, you receive a registration number and a disk with the latest version of the program. Future upgrades are available for a small fee.

I cannot process checks unless they are drawn on U.S. or Canadian banks. Traveler's checks and international money orders are accepted. You can also send payment by bank trans-fer to account 560201 22878538 34 (please add an additional $6.00 for processing fees).

Send all registrations to **David A. Feinleib,** 1430 Mass. Ave., Suite 306-42, Cambridge, MA 02138

| Program | Quantity | | Amount | Current Version |
|---|---|---|---|---|
| WinClock | _____ | $16.00 each | $_____ | 3.21 |
| RunProg | _____ | $12.00 each | $_____ | |
| PrintSwitch | _____ | $16.00 each | $_____ | |
| Mem | _____ | $12.00 each | $_____ | |
| IconCalc | _____ | $12.00 each | $_____ | |
| Other_____ | _____ | $16.00 each | $_____ | |

***Shipping and handling:***

| | | |
|---|---|---|
| Add for shipping inside U.S. | $ 4.00 | $_____ |
| Add for shipping outside U.S. | $ 6.00 | $_____ |
| Add for checks drawn on Canadian banks | $ 2.00 | $_____ |
| Add for bank transfers | $ 6.00 | $_____ |
| | TOTAL | $_____ |

Check/Money Order #:_____

Name: _____ Date: _____

Company: _____

Address: _____

City, State, ZIP: _____

Country: _____

Phone: _____ Fax: _____

Electronic Mail: _____

Where did you obtain the program(s)? _____

Windows Version: _____

Printer Type (make, model, cartridges): _____

Comments:

# WinEZ

### Version 3.0
### Copyright © by New Generation Software Ltd.

*WinEZ (pronounced win-easy) solves one of the little time-wasting features of Windows. If you want to start a new program, you must leave the program you are using and find the Windows Program Manager. Then, if you want to switch to another running program, you must find an empty spot on the desktop to double-click (or press Ctrl+Esc), to bring up the Windows Task List.*

*WinEZ provides you with both of these functions. You can start any program that has an icon in Program Manager, or switch to any running program, by pulling down WinEZ menus represented by two buttons that appear on the title bar of every Windows application.*

*You'll find WinEZ a simple yet powerful way to run all your Windows applications. After you use it, you'll wonder why no one ever thought of it before.*

| | |
|---|---|
| **Type of Program:** | Program Management |
| **Requires:** | Windows 3.0 or later |
| **Registration:** | Use the form at the end of this chapter to register with the shareware author. |
| **Technical Support:** | New Generation Software provides technical support to registered users through fax, CompuServe, and mail. |
| **Similar Shareware:** | Launch, a program featured in *Windows 3.1 SECRETS*, published by IDG Books Worldwide, provides a customizable menu to start applications using the right mouse button. |

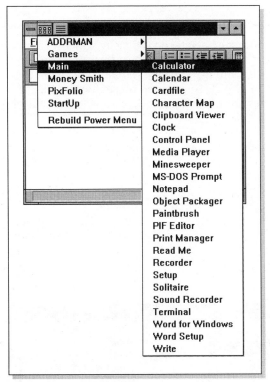

**WinEZ provides you with easy access to the Program Manager and the Task List from any application.**

# Introduction

WinEZ is a Windows utility that provides a fast and easy way to do the following:

♦ Start new applications (defined in your Program Manager or Norton Desktop groups) from within the application you are using.

♦ Close and end applications.

♦ Switch directly to any other active application (no more need to use Ctrl+Esc).

♦ Navigate directories to start applications using WinEZ's enhanced version of the Program Manager's Run facility.

All these tasks are accomplished with easy-to-use, pull-down menus attached directly to the active application's title bar.

## Overview _____

Have you ever found yourself opening up too many Windows applications, only to find that you get lost searching for that one application you need? Or have you ever found yourself wanting to quickly start an application from *within* the application you are using? Well, New Generation Software Ltd. has the solution for you! WinEZ provides one of the easiest ways to switch among and start applications under Windows.

When WinEZ is installed and running, it places two new icons on the title bar of the active application. The left icon, or Fast Path icon, enables you to quickly start any application in the Windows Program Manager; you can configure it to jump directly to the Program Manager (or any add-in Windows shell you define). The right icon, or Task Switch icon, provides you with a list of all active applications. Similar to the Windows Task List, WinEZ goes one step further and provides task switching without the need for you to use Ctrl+Esc or double-click on the desktop.

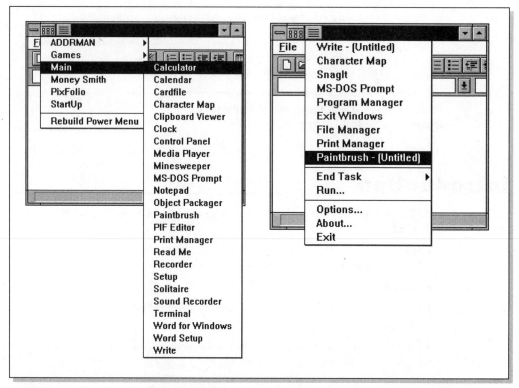

**The left button enables you to start any application in the Windows Program Manager; the right button provides you with a list of all active applications.**

WinEZ also provides an enhanced Run facility, which offers you an easy way to navigate directories and start applications. It remembers the last five programs you executed as well as the last directory path.

# Installing and Getting Started

After you install WinEZ with WSETUP, you have two choices to get WinEZ up and running:

♦ To run WinEZ automatically every time you start Windows, modify the WIN.INI file, found in the Windows subdirectory. Using Notepad, edit the line containing the LOAD keyword and append the program name WINEZ.EXE. Here is an example:

        LOAD=C:\WINEZ\WINEZ.EXE

The next time you start Windows, WinEZ starts for you automatically.

In Windows 3.1, you can accomplish the same thing by dragging the WinEZ icon from its group in Program Manager into the StartUp group.

♦ If you want to start WinEZ manually, run C:\WINEZ\WINEZ.EXE from a group window of the Program Manager or the File Run menu of File Manager.

# Features

WinEZ attaches two icons to the title bar: a Fast Path icon and a Task Switch icon. These icons provide you with one of the fastest ways to switch between and start applications under Windows.

## The Fast Path icon (left icon)

The Fast Path icon (the left icon) enables a user to start another application without ever leaving the current application. The Fast Path icon can be configured two ways — to display a pull-down Power menu or to switch to the Program Manager window — with three possible actions:

**1. WinEZ's Power menu.**

With WinEZ's Power menu feature, you can start any application you've defined in group windows of the Program Manager (or Norton's Desktop for Windows). The Power menu is a drop-down menu that displays a list of all the group windows in the Program Manager. Each group has a submenu that contains all the applications in that group. Instead of leaving your current application to activate the Program Manager, just bring up the Power menu and, *voilà!*, your group applications are just a click away.

**2. Switch directly to the Program Manager (or *any* add-in Windows shell).**

You can also configure WinEZ's Fast Path icon to enable a user to jump directly to any active application. By default, WinEZ jumps directly to the Program Manager. However, WinEZ can be configured to activate any add-in Windows shell (see "Setting WinEZ's Options," later in this chapter).

**3. Clicking the right mouse button on the Fast Path icon.**

By clicking the right mouse button on the Fast Path icon when in Power menu mode, you can jump directly to the Program Manager (or any add-in shell specified in the Options menu).

## The Task Switch icon (right icon)

The Task Switch icon (the right icon) enables you to quickly switch to *any* active application. There is no need for you to hunt down that one particular window or press Ctrl+Esc to bring up the Task List. From the current application, WinEZ's Task Switch icon provides a pull-down menu of all active applications.

The Task Switch icon also presents the user with other features of WinEZ. Along with the active applications, other items in the menu are as follows:

**End Task:** This item further expands into a submenu of active tasks. It provides the user with a fast and easy way to end other active applications. Select an item from the list, and WinEZ ends the program.

**Run...:** This item starts the enhanced Run facility. A dialog box appears, enabling you to type the name of an application to execute or to select an application from a list box. See "Run dialog box facility," later in this chapter.

**Options...:** This item displays a dialog box that enables you to configure WinEZ. You can configure the action performed by the Fast Path icon and the behavior of the windows when switching between applications (see "Setting WinEZ's Options," later in this chapter, for more details).

**About...:** This item brings up WinEZ's About dialog box.

**Exit:** This item ends WinEZ and removes it from memory.

*Note:* The Exit selection item is unavailable (grayed out) on nonstandard windows (such as dialog boxes).

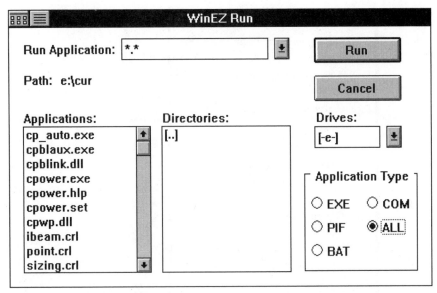

Use the Run dialog box to start applications not defined by a Program Manager group.

## Run dialog box facility

When Run is selected from the Task Switch icon menu, a dialog box appears that enables a user to start applications not defined by a Program Manager group.

Included in this dialog box is a list box that contains files found in the current directory. The Run dialog box is similar to the File Open dialog box found in many Windows applications. A user can change directories or drives by selecting the appropriate items in the directories list box.

A filter is available to enable certain file types to be included in the list box. Current filters include EXE, COM, PIF, BAT, and all files. Use these filters to quickly locate the file that you want to execute. An additional feature of the Run dialog box is its capacity to keep track of the last five commands executed.

## Setting WinEZ's Options

You can configure WinEZ by selecting the Options item from the Task Switch icon menu. The Options dialog box is where WinEZ's switching behavior can be set and the Fast Path icon actions configured.

```
                WinEZ Options
 ┌ Switching Options ──────────────────┐
 │   ⦿ Default                          │
 │   ○ Always Minimize on Switch        │
 └──────────────────────────────────────┘
 ┌ Fast Path (Left) Icon Invokes ──────┐
 │   ⦿ Power Menu                       │
 │      ⊠ Always Rebuild on Startup     │
 │   ○ Title of Window:                 │
 │     ┌────────────────────────────┐   │
 │     │ Program Manager            │   │
 │     └────────────────────────────┘   │
 └──────────────────────────────────────┘
 ┌ WinEZ Icon Position ────────────────┐
 │   ⦿ Left                             │
 │   ○ Right                            │
 │   ○ Pels from the Left:  [0]  ▲▼     │
 └──────────────────────────────────────┘

      [   OK   ]        [ Cancel ]
```

Use the Options dialog box to configure WinEZ's switching behavior and the Fast Path icon's actions.

## Switching behavior

When you're using WinEZ to switch between applications, WinEZ attempts to return the application to the state in which it was found (assuming that all switching was done with WinEZ). You can also configure WinEZ to always minimize applications when switching to other applications. Choose the switching behavior from the Options dialog box by selecting the radio button corresponding to the preferred option:

♦ **Default:** With this option, WinEZ attempts to return the application back to the state in which it was found (if all switching was done with WinEZ).

♦ **Always Minimize on Switch:** With this option, WinEZ always minimizes the application before switching to another.

*Note:* WinEZ only minimizes windows that support being minimized.

## Fast Path icon actions

You can configure the Fast Path icon to perform one of two functions. The icon can be configured for WinEZ's Power menu or to switch a user directly to the Program Manager (or any specified active application). These two options are available for your selection. Choose the Fast Path function by selecting the radio button corresponding to the preferred option:

♦ **Power Menu:** If this option is chosen, the Power menu is displayed when you click on the Fast Path icon (see "The Fast Path icon," earlier in this chapter, for information on how to use the Power menu).

Selecting Always Rebuild on Startup causes WinEZ to rebuild the Power menu when it is invoked. If this option is not set, you may have to select the Rebuild Power Menu option to list the most current groups in the Power pull-down menu.

♦ **Title of Window:** If this option is chosen, the application specified in the entry field is activated when the Fast Path icon is clicked on. To specify the application you want to switch to, enter the text found in the title bar of that application.

This is *also* the name of the window that the *right* mouse button invokes from Power menu mode.

## WinEZ icon position

The WinEZ icons can be positioned anywhere on the title bar:

♦ **Left** left-justifies the WinEZ icons.

♦ **Right** right-justifies the WinEZ icons.

♦ **Pels from the Left** places the WinEZ icons the specified number of pixels (pels) from the left side of the title bar.

*Note:* Use this option to adjust WinEZ's icons if there is an icon conflict or if WinEZ looks out of place (for example, in Super VGA mode, WinEZ is sometimes off by a pixel).

# Using WinEZ with Norton Desktop

WinEZ automatically detects whether you have the Norton Desktop loaded as your shell when using Windows. WinEZ searches the Shell= line in your SYSTEM.INI file for the character string NDW.EXE, as shown here:

```
Shell=C:\NORTON\NDW.EXE
```

All Norton groups and subgroups are listed on the WinEZ Power menu. Subgroups are not nested.

*Note:* All group and subgroup filenames *must* end in the QAG extension. This is done automatically by Norton if, when creating a group, no extension is specified.

If you have a group named *Norton Desktop* (which Norton creates on installation), it is recommended that you rename it something else (for example, *Norton Utilities*). This prevents WinEZ from getting confused between the Norton Desktop application and the Norton Desktop group file.

Because passwords are not part of the DOS operating system, WinEZ bypasses all Norton Desktop passwords set when executing an application. Also, Norton groups (just *groups*, not *applications*) created with a password are not part of the WinEZ Power menu.

*Note:* Norton also bypasses its own passwords if you execute a program from the File Manager utility. True security really has to be done at an operating-system level.

When you select Rebuild Power Menu, WinEZ automatically saves your Norton configuration. This is necessary to perform the rebuild of the menus.

# General WinEZ Notes and Information

♦ If you are having trouble entering the registration information, make sure that you are entering *both* the registration name and number *exactly* as specified on the mailed invoice thank-you letter (this is the name and number we processed your order by).

♦ To get the WinEZ Power menu to stay up without having to hold the left mouse button, drag the cursor to the first application group on the list. The Power menu stays up, and you can then pick and choose application groups.

♦ WinEZ supports up to 25 application groups and 40 applications per group. If you have more groups or applications per group (which is hard to imagine), WinEZ truncates.

♦ You may not be able to create menus under low memory conditions.

♦ To make the dragging of the mouse more responsive when using the Power menu, add the following lines to the [Windows] section of your WIN.INI file, found in your Windows subdirectory:

```
[Windows]
MenuShowDelay=0
MenuHideDelay=0
```

♦ Sometimes in Super VGA mode, WinEZ's icon placement is off by a pixel. Use the Options dialog box to move the icon. (Use the Options menu item to resolve icon conflicts, also.)

♦ WinEZ creates two files during execution. These files are placed in your Windows subdirectory:

WINEZ.INI    File created by WinEZ to save its option settings.

WINEZ.DAT    File created by WinEZ that contains data from the Program Manager for the Power menu. This file should not be edited.

♦ WinEZ returns the following error codes from the Run dialog box or Power menu:

| Return Code | Meaning |
| --- | --- |
| 0 | Out of memory |
| 2 | File not found |
| 3 | Path not found |
| 11 | Invalid EXE file |
| 14 | Unknown EXE type |

♦ Norton group filenames must end in the QAG extension (this is the default extension). Password groups are not supported.

♦ If you are having problems executing Version 3.0, delete the files WINEZ.DAT and WINEZ.INI from your Windows subdirectory (remember to first write down your registration number, if any) and then restart WinEZ.

# Disk Contents

| | |
| --- | --- |
| WINEZ.EXE | Main program |
| WINEZRUN.EXE | Called by WinEZ to process the Run dialog box |
| WINEZGRP.EXE | Called by WinEZ to process the group files |
| REGISTER.EXE | Called by WinEZ to perform registration |
| WINEZ3.TXT | WinEZ documentation |

# Licensing and Distribution

WinEZ is copyrighted and has been released for distribution as shareware. Please note that a great deal of effort and time has been invested in the development of this program. You are granted a license to try WinEZ for a reasonable trial period without risk. If, after this time, you find this program useful and intend to use it, you are expected to register. The base registration fee is $29.95.

You will find a registration form at the end of this chapter. It outlines the procedures for registering your copy of the program. Please keep in mind that NGS must have a registration form on file for you before any product support can be offered.

Operators of electronic bulletin board systems (sysops) are encouraged to post WinEZ for downloading by their users.

WinEZ can be uploaded to and downloaded from commercial systems, such as CompuServe, the Source, and BIX. The only charge paid by the subscriber is for on-line time, and there is no charge for the program. Those copying, sharing, or electronically transmitting the program are required not to delete or modify the copyright notice and restrictive notices from the program or documentation; anyone doing so will be treated as a contributory copyright violator.

If you are passing this program on to others, uploading it to a bulletin board system, or including it in a user's group library, do not separate the files contained in the distribution archive; pass the entire archive on to the intended party. This ensures that those who receive the program have all the correct configuration utilities and documentation necessary to get WinEZ up and running quickly. A listing of the files you should have and a description of each is listed earlier in this chapter.

The WinEZ on-line documentation cannot be modified by users. The program cannot be separated from the on-line documentation when distributed. Printed or photocopied (xeroxed) copies of the WinEZ documentation (that is, *this* documentation) cannot be distributed or sold without the written permission of New Generation Software Ltd.

No other person, other than NGS, may accept payment or royalties for this program.

This license to use WinEZ does *not* include the right to distribute or sell WinEZ. Distribution terms are detailed in the on-line file WINEZ3.TXT.

## ASP

WinEZ is a shareware program conforming to standards established by the Association of Shareware Professionals (ASP).

## Trademarks

The following trademarks and service marks appear in this product:

Microsoft is a registered trademark and Windows is a trademark of Microsoft Corporation.

PKUNZIP is a registered trademark of PKWARE, Inc.

Norton Desktop is a registered trademark of Symantec Corporation.

IBM is a registered trademark of International Business Machines.

## Limited warranty

This program and the accompanying documentation are provided "as is" without warranty of any kind, either expressed or implied, including but not limited to the implied warranties of merchantability and fitness for a particular purpose with respect to defects in the program or documentation. New Generation Software assumes no risk as to the quality and performance of the program. Should the program prove defective, you assume the entire cost of any loss of profit or any other commercial damage. Some states do not allow the exclusion of implied warranties, so the preceding exclusion may not apply to you. This statement shall be construed, interpreted, and governed by the laws of the state of Texas.

# Registration and Order Information_____

WinEZ is a shareware product and is available to you, free, for an evaluation period of 30 days. If you like what you see, and feel that it will be useful, you are encouraged to register with us. The base registration fee is $29.95.

*Note:* Registered users of previous versions of WinEZ can upgrade for free. You are not required to reregister. The registration number from the previous versions works with this later version.

What does registering give you? Well, by registering WinEZ, you

♦ Receive a registration number that removes that annoying About dialog box that appears every time you start WinEZ

♦ Receive a published *User's Guide* when you request that a disk be sent out with your order (see the order form at the end of this chapter)

♦ Receive *free* or discounted upgrades to future versions of WinEZ

♦ Encourage New Generation Software to continue producing new high-quality Windows utilities

## How do I register?

The quickest way to register is by credit card (Visa or MasterCard). Call our toll-free number, 1-800-964-7638 (or call 512-795-8587).

You also can register by sending the registration form (found at the end of this chapter) to NGS by doing one of the following:

♦ Sending the form by fax to 512-388-4053.

♦ Mailing the form to this address:

**New Generation Software Ltd.**
P.O. Box 9700, Dept. 271
Austin, TX 78766

♦ Sending the form electronically (through electronic mail) to NGS on CompuServe. Our CompuServe user ID is 70312,127.

After we process your order, you are given a registration name and number that you type in the Registration dialog box. Make sure that you type *both* the name and number *exactly* the way you received the information.

# WinEZ registration form

Name: _____

Company: _____

Address: _____

_____

City: _____ State: _____ ZIP: _____

Phone: (_____)_____ Country: _____

Registration Fee(s) _____ @ $29.95 each: _____.___

*All* customers are sent a disk and *printed* User's Guide. This guarantees the user that he or she will receive the most current version of the product. There is a $5.00 (outside the U.S., $7.50) shipping and handling charge.

Specify Disk Size: ____ 3.5" ____ 5.25"

Shipping and handling ($5.00; $7.50 outside U.S.): _____.___

Texas Residents add 8% sales tax: _____.___

Total: _____.___

Please enclose a check payable to New Generation Software or enter your credit card (Visa or MasterCard) information below. You can also place a credit-card order by calling the phone number below.

Card #: __ __ __ __ - __ __ __ __ - __ __ __ __ - __ __ __ __

Expiration date: ____/____

Signature: _____

Where did you get your copy of WinEZ?

_____

CompuServe User ID (if applicable): _____

SEND TO OR CALL

**New Generation Software Ltd.**
P.O. Box 9700
Dept. 271
Austin, TX 78766
Orders: 800-964-7638 or 512-795-8587
Fax: 512-388-4053
Or send to us through CompuServe (70312,127).
Please allow three weeks for delivery. Prices subject to change.

# WinKey

### Version 1.0
### Copyright © by DataGem Corp.

*W*hen the first IBM PC was designed, its keyboard closely followed the layout of the highly successful IBM Selectric typewriter. The PC's designers made one glaring mistake, however.

*On a Selectric, you could press the Caps Lock key to type a line in all capital letters. When you held down the Shift key to type the first letter of the next normal sentence, the Caps Lock key was disengaged because you didn't need it any more.*

*The IBM PC-1 didn't have a mechanical roller to shift up and down; the PC's Shift key was designed simply to reverse the current state of capitalization. When Caps Lock was off, pressing Shift resulted in capital letters, as you would expect. In the rush to get the PC-1 to market, no one tested the Shift key when Caps Lock was on. On a PC, therefore, typing **To Whom It May Concern** with Caps Lock on looks like **tO wHOM iT mAY cONCERN.***

*Microsoft could easily have fixed this in Windows. But, inexplicably, the company did not. WinKey remedies this and other keyboard problems. First of all, it restores the Shift key to its original role of capitalizing letters and disengaging Caps Lock. Additionally, it enables you to control Num Lock and Scroll Lock and reverse the Caps Lock and Ctrl keys (for keyboards that don't place the Ctrl key near the A key). You can, of course, customize all these behaviors in WinKey's control panel.*

*DataGem Corp. is already working on WinKey Version 2.0, which will enable you to redefine any key combination as any other key combination. Registered users will be the first to hear about the release of this new utility — another good reason to register with the author.*

| | |
|---|---|
| **Type of Program:** | Utility |
| **Requires:** | Windows 3.0 or later |
| **Registration:** | Use the form at the end of this chapter to register with the shareware author. |
| **Technical Support:** | DataGem Corp. provides registered users with technical support through CompuServe and mail. |

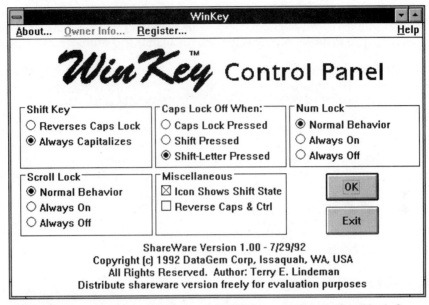

WinKey enables you to control the action of the Shift key as well as the Scroll Lock, Caps Lock, and Num Lock keys.

# Overview

WinKey is a Windows utility that solves several nagging problems related to keyboard entry. First, WinKey can force your keyboard Shift and Caps Lock keys to operate much like they would on a standard typewriter keyboard. When you attempt to type

**Pain in the Neck**

but forget that your Caps Lock key is on, you end up typing

**pAIN IN THE nECK**

On a typewriter keyboard, you do not experience this shift-reversal problem. Pressing the Shift key releases the Caps Lock key. This means that the first character is uppercase, no matter what, and that all other characters are their correct case. WinKey forces a Windows keyboard to act like a typewriter keyboard, eliminating the shift-reversal problem.

For Windows users trained on ten-key keypads, the Num Lock key poses a second problem. The numeric keypad has a way of getting unlocked through inadvertent contact with the Num Lock key. This causes a string of spurious cursor-movement, Home, End, Delete, PgUp, and PgDn keystrokes, sometimes with disastrous consequences. WinKey enables you to permanently lock the numbers on your ten-key keypad, eliminating this problem.

Some programs, such as Microsoft Excel and Terminal, have actions that vary based on the status of the Scroll Lock key. WinKey enables you to permanently set the Scroll Lock key to the value that works best for you.

Many users of notebook computers find that the Caps and Control (Ctrl) keys on their keyboards are placed opposite the way they are on a desktop PC keyboard. WinKey enables you to reverse the function of these two keys to simplify your transition back and forth between notebook and desktop PCs.

This version of WinKey does not change the behavior of DOS applications run under Windows.

# Installation

WinKey is copied by WSETUP to its own directory on your hard drive and to its own group window in Program Manager.

## How to run WinKey one time only

To test WinKey, double-click on the WinKey icon in Program Manager. Alternatively, click on File Run in the Program Manager or File Manager and type *x:*\**WINKEY\WINKEY.EXE** (substitute the correct drive and directory where you installed WinKey on your hard drive). When the WinKey control panel appears, select the settings you desire and click on OK. This minimizes WinKey to an icon on your icon line, where it now controls the behavior of the Shift key and the "toggle" keys: Caps Lock, Num Lock, and Scroll Lock.

## How to run WinKey every time you start Windows

**Windows 3.1 and later.** In the Windows 3.1 Program Manager, hold the Ctrl key as you drag the WinKey icon from the WinKey group to the StartUp group. This makes a copy of the icon in the StartUp group. (Remember that WinKey may be reversing your Ctrl and Caps Lock keys if it is running!) Highlight the icon by clicking on it once and then click on File Properties on the Program Manager menu. Click the Run Minimized box to place an X in the check box. This action makes WinKey load as an icon and start controlling the shift keys the next time you start Windows.

**Windows 3.0.** In Windows 3.0, use Notepad to open the file WIN.INI, which is usually located in your Windows directory. Find the line that begins LOAD=. Add the correct drive and directory for WinKey to this line. For example, if the line looks like

```
LOAD=CLOCK.EXE
```

add *x:*\WINKEY\WINKEY.EXE to the end of the line so that it looks like

```
LOAD=CLOCK.EXE C:\WINKEY\WINKEY.EXE
```

Make sure that the LOAD= and RUN= lines of WIN.INI do not exceed 127 characters. Windows cannot read these lines after 127 characters. If you are near this limit, remove all EXE extensions from these lines because Windows does not need the EXE extension to load programs. (The StartUp group in Windows 3.1 does not have the 127-character limitation.)

# Disabling WinKey

If WinKey is running, you can temporarily disable it by double-clicking on the WinKey icon and then clicking on the Exit button on the WinKey control panel.

# Deinstallation

To deinstall WinKey, use the following procedure:

**Windows 3.1 and later.** In Program Manager, minimize the WinKey group window and then click on File Delete to delete it. Remove the WinKey icon from the StartUp group. Finally, delete the *x:*\WINKEY directory.

**Windows 3.0.** Remove WINKEY.EXE from the LOAD= line of your WIN.INI file. In Program Manager, minimize the WinKey group window and then click on File Delete to delete it. Finally, delete the *x:*\WINKEY directory.

# Settings

You may want to skip this section and rely on the default WinKey settings. They should work well for most users.

If you want to modify the default keyboard settings, you can invoke the WinKey control panel by double-clicking on the WinKey icon or by running WinKey from the Windows File Run menu. You are presented with four groups of radio buttons. (In the following list, the asterisk [*] designates the default settings.)

**Shift Key**

> Reverses Caps Lock (Normal)
>
> Always Capitalizes*

**Caps Lock Off When:**

> Caps Lock Pressed (Normal)
>
> Shift Pressed
>
> Shift-Letter Pressed*

**Num Lock**

> Normal Behavior
>
> Always On*
>
> Always Off

**Scroll Lock**

> Normal Behavior*
>
> Always On
>
> Always Off

If you select the Reverses Caps Lock setting for the Shift key, you produce an uppercase character when Caps Lock is off and a lowercase character when Caps Lock is on. That is, the Shift key reverses the Caps Lock state. The Always Capitalizes setting causes an uppercase character to be generated, even if Caps Lock is on.

The Caps Lock Off When group specifies the circumstances that turn Caps Lock off. The Caps Lock Pressed setting enables you to toggle Caps Lock on and off by pressing the Caps Lock key. This is the normal setting for a PC keyboard.

The Shift Pressed setting for the Caps Lock group causes Caps Lock to always be turned off when the Shift key is pressed. You generate uppercase characters when the Shift key is pressed and lowercase characters after it is released. This setting emulates a standard typewriter.

The Shift-Letter Pressed option for the Caps Lock group is for Windows programmers. When you type such statements as **WM_COMMAND** you do not want Caps Lock to be released when you press the Shift key to generate the underscore character. You do, however, want caps unlocked when you press the Shift key concurrently with an alphabetic key.

The Num Lock group specifies how the Num Lock key and indicator are to operate. If you select the Normal Behavior option, the Num Lock key toggles the Num Lock light on and off. If you select Always On, the numbers are permanently locked on. The alternative functions of the keypad keys (Home, PgUp, and so on) are disabled. If you select Always Off, the numeric values of these keys are disabled and the cursor-movement, Home, and other functions are permanently enabled.

The Scroll Lock group of radio buttons enables you to permanently set the Scroll Lock key on or off or to use the normal toggle on/off behavior. Scroll Lock enables cursor keys to scroll the screen in Excel and invokes DEC-style VT-100 function keys in Windows Terminal.

Two check boxes are provided in a Miscellaneous group of settings:

**Miscellaneous**

> Icon Shows Shift State (default: checked)

> Reverse Caps Lock & Ctrl (default: not checked)

The Icon Shows Shift State check box is described in the "The WinKey icon," section.

Computer users who check the Reverse Caps Lock & Ctrl check box find the functions of the Caps Lock and Ctrl keys reversed. This reversal is useful for making your keyboard more closely conform to a regular 101-key keyboard.

When you finish making your selections, click on OK to minimize WinKey. The selected behavior is now in effect for all Windows applications.

When you choose options from the control panel, a file named WINKEY.INI is created in the WinKey directory to save your selections.

# The WinKey icon

By default, the WinKey icon displays a CAPS indicator that lights when alphabetical keystrokes will result in uppercase characters. This is not quite the same as the Caps Lock light, which remains on even when you press the Shift key to produce a lowercase character. The icon's CAPS light always tells you what case to expect.

If this flashing icon bothers you, you can disable it by unchecking the Icon Shows Shift State check box in the Miscellaneous group of the WinKey control panel.

## Owner information

After you install the registered version of this software and start WinKey for the first time, you are asked to enter your user name and company. You can change this information by clicking on the Owner Info menu bar item in the WinKey control panel. This menu item is grayed out in the shareware version of the program.

## Let's hear from you!

This program is intended to relieve pain, not inflict it. If you have problems, please let us know. Also, if you can think of related features you would like to see in WinKey, you can type a description up to 1,000 characters in the comments box of the registration form. If you are the first to suggest a new feature, you receive a free update of WinKey if that feature is incorporated. Send electronic mail to CompuServe 75540,762.

## The WinKey Files

| | |
|---|---|
| WINKEY.EXE | Main program |
| WINKEY2.DLL | Dynamic Link Library required by WinKey |
| WINKEY.WRI | Program documentation (Write format) |
| ORDER.TXT | Order form (ASCII text) |
| PACKING.TXT | List of files (ASCII text) |
| README.TXT | Introductory information (ASCII text) |
| SITELIC.WRI | Site License form (Write format) |
| VENDOR.WRI | Vendor terms and conditions (Write format) |
| FILE_ID.DIZ | Identification used by bulletin boards |

# Registration Information

This version of the program is for demonstration purposes only. You can distribute it freely, but it is not to be sold except by authorized distributors. End use for purposes other than evaluation requires payment of the registration fee. When you register, you receive the latest registered version of this product. An evaluation period of up to 30 days is authorized.

## How to register

You can register by selecting Register from the WinKey menu bar or by clicking on the Register button in the About box. You can then enter information into the Registration dialog box and then click on the Print Reg. Form button to print the filled-in registration form. If you have not yet decided to register, click on the button labeled Don't Register Yet.

Alternatively, use the blank registration form ORDER.TXT to register. You can print it from Notepad or any other ASCII text editor, or you can copy the file to your printer in DOS with the following command:

    COPY x:\WINKEY\ORDER.TXT lpt1

If you prefer, you can phone in your registration to the telephone order line listed shortly.

Please register to ensure continued support and upgrades for this product.

Standard registration is for a single computer. See the Windows Write document SITELIC.WRI in the WinKey directory for site-license information.

## Technical support

Forward your support requests to the address listed shortly or to CompuServe ID 75540,762. Please provide detailed information. The telephone order line is not available for technical support.

## Disclaimer

DATAGEM CORP. DISCLAIMS ALL WARRANTIES RELATING TO THIS SOFT-
WARE, WHETHER EXPRESSED OR IMPLIED, INCLUDING BUT NOT LIMITED TO
ANY IMPLIED WARRANTIES OF MERCHANTABILITY AND FITNESS FOR A PAR-
TICULAR PURPOSE, AND ALL SUCH WARRANTIES ARE EXPRESSLY AND
SPECIFICALLY DISCLAIMED. NEITHER DATAGEM CORP. NOR ANYONE ELSE
WHO HAS BEEN INVOLVED IN THE CREATION, PRODUCTION, OR DELIVERY OF
THIS SOFTWARE SHALL BE LIABLE FOR ANY INDIRECT, CONSEQUENTIAL, OR
INCIDENTAL DAMAGES ARISING OUT OF THE USE OR INABILITY TO USE SUCH
SOFTWARE EVEN IF DATAGEM CORP. HAS BEEN ADVISED OF THE POSSIBILITY
OF DAMAGES OR CLAIMS. IN NO EVENT SHALL DATAGEM CORP.'S LIABILITY
EXCEED THE PRICE PAID FOR THE LICENSE TO USE THE SOFTWARE, REGARD-
LESS OF THE FORM OF CLAIM. THE PERSON USING THE SOFTWARE BEARS ALL
RISKS AS TO THE QUALITY AND PERFORMANCE OF THE SOFTWARE.

Some states do not allow the exclusion of the limit of liability for consequential
or incidental damages, so the preceding limitation may not apply to you.

This agreement shall be governed by the laws of the State of Washington and
shall inure to the benefit of DataGem Corp. and any successors, administrators,
heirs, and assigns. Any action or proceeding brought by either party against the
other arising out of or related to this agreement shall be brought only in a State
or Federal Court of competent jurisdiction located in King County, Washington
State. The parties hereby consent to in personam jurisdiction of said courts.

## Registration form

**DataGem Corp.**
1420 NW Gilman # 2859
Issaquah, WA 98027, U.S.A.
Tech Support: CompuServe 75540,762
Phone Orders: 206-391-4415

Name: _____

Company: _____

Address: _____

_____

City/State/ZIP: _____

Country: _____

Daytime telephone: _____

Current WinKey Version: 1.0

Date: _____

Medium: _____3½-inch diskette _____5¼-inch diskette

Payment (U.S. funds only):

Check or money order     ____$15.00

COD                                 ____$20.00

MasterCard                       ____$15.00

Visa                                  ____$15.00

Credit-card number: _____ Expires: _____

Credit-card signature: _____

Purchase price from above: _____ copies @ _____ = _____

Washington residents add 8.2% (or _____ %) sales tax: _____

Total: _____

Comments/Requests: _____

_____

_____

# WinPoker

### Version 2.0
### Copyright © by Dean Zamzow

*One of the most popular games of all time is poker. Video Poker games have become very successful at separating people from their money in modern-day casinos. Now there is WinPoker; you can have all the fun of Video Poker without actually losing the money!*

**Type of Program:**   Game

**Requires:**   Windows 3.0 or later and a VGA display or better (not recommended for EGA displays).

**Registration:**   Use the form at the end of this chapter to register with the shareware author.

**Technical Support:**   Dean Zamzow provides registered users with technical support through CompuServe and mail.

## Overview of Video Poker

WinPoker is a duplicate of the popular casino game Video Poker. Two versions of Video Poker are supported in WinPoker. The shareware version of WinPoker plays the standard Video Poker game known as Jacks or Better. The registered version also plays Jokers Wild, which expands on the basic game by adding one Joker to the deck (the Joker can be used as any card). In addition, the registered version also has a Double Up option, which can be used with either of the two games.

In any casino game, of course, the object is to maximize the wins and minimize the losses. How do you win at this game? The object is to create the best possible poker hand so that you can be paid off with the highest possible winnings.

WinPoker gives you all the fun of Video Poker, and you don't actually lose any money!

The hierarchy of winning hands is basically the same as it is in conventional poker. A Royal Flush is the highest and the hardest hand (statistically) to get. Therefore, it receives the best odds for payoff. In the standard Jacks or Better game, you must have a pair of Jacks or better to receive any payoff at all.

Odds vary for Video Poker games, depending on where you play — Vegas, Reno, or Tahoe, for example — and what type of Video Poker you play: Jacks or Better, Jokers Wild, or Double Up. The odds in WinPoker replicate (as closely as possible) the odds of Las Vegas Video Poker games.

Initially, you are dealt five cards. You can hold any (or none) of those five cards. You are dealt replacement cards for any cards not held. This final hand is your winning (or losing) hand. Of course, this is a very general overview of the game. For detailed information on the game, choose the appropriate help item from the WinPoker Help menu.

Have fun and good luck!

# Playing the Game

For the standard option (Jacks or Better), you are dealt five cards from a standard 52-card deck.

For the Jokers Wild option (only available in the registered version), you are dealt five cards from a 53-card deck (a standard 52-card deck plus one Joker).

The cards are shuffled before each play. (This shuffle includes the Double Up option.) Your bet is immediately subtracted from your credits, just as if you were in a casino. If you are lucky enough to be dealt a winning hand, the hand you have won is highlighted in the odds window. You then decide which (if any) of the cards to hold or keep; deal again to get your replacement cards (if any). If you fail to have a winning hand, your credits stand; your bet is lost. If you do win, your credits increase according to bet size and odds for the hand you've won. Win Paid shows how much you won on that hand.

## Playing the game using a mouse

### Betting

Click the Bet menu and select the number you want to bet. This bet remains in effect until you change the bet. A check mark appears next to the current bet setting. The default bet is 5.

### Dealing

Click the right mouse button to deal cards.

### Holding cards

Point to the card you want to keep and click the left mouse button.

### Releasing cards

Point to the held card you want to release and click the left mouse button.

### Sizing the game

The game window cannot be resized because of the way the cards are stored.

### Minimizing the game to its icon

Point to the down-arrow button at the upper right corner of the screen and click the left button.

## Playing the game using the keyboard

### Choosing game options

Hold the Alt key and press the underlined letter of the option you want.

## Betting

Press Alt+B and then move the cursor down to the desired bet; press Enter. Alternatively, you can use the hot keys F1 (to bet 1) through F5 (to bet 5).

The bet remains in effect until changed. A check mark appears next to the current bet setting. The default is 5.

## Dealing

Press Enter or Alt+D to deal cards.

## Holding cards

Type the numbers 1 through 5, where 1 is the left-most card and 5 is the right-most card you want to hold.

## Releasing cards

Type the numbers 1 through 5, where 1 is the left-most card and 5 is the right-most card you want to release.

## Sizing the game

The game window cannot be resized because of the way the cards are stored.

## Minimizing the game to its icon

Press Alt+spacebar, release both keys, and press N (for miNimize).

# The Winning Hands of Video Poker

There are four suits: Spades, Hearts, Diamonds, and Clubs. There are 13 ranks: 2 through 10, Jack, Queen, King, and Ace. The hands are listed in their relative ease-to-get sequence (from easiest to hardest) and therefore their relative pay-offs (smallest to largest). The low-to-high sequence of the cards is as follows: 2, 3, 4, 5, 6, 7, 8, 9, 10, Jack, Queen, King, and Ace.

| Hands | Standard Game |
|---|---|
| One Pair of Jacks or Better | 1 for 1 |
| Two Pair | 2 for 1 |
| Three of a Kind | 3 for 1 |
| Straight | 4 for 1 |
| Flush | 6 for 1 |
| Full House | 9 for 1 |
| Four of a Kind | 25 for 1 |
| Straight Flush | 50 for 1 |
| Royal Flush | 300 for 1 (4,000 if 5 bet) |

# Video Poker Strategy

The strategy behind Video Poker is simple: You want to try to get the best winning hand possible out of the cards you are dealt. This is where Video Poker is different from slot machines. With a slot machine, it's all luck. In Video Poker, there is a certain amount of skill involved in deciding what cards to keep and what cards to throw away. Unlike regular poker, the "pots" are predetermined. The odds are always the same. The payoffs differ only in how much you originally bet. Each option has its own best strategy. The next release of WinPoker will include a built-in Hints option to help teach the best strategy for each of the options.

# The Menu Commands

## Game

Press Alt+G or click on Game to activate the Game menu option.

### New

The New option starts a new poker game. The following playing options are set to their defaults: Bet=5, Credits=0, and all the statistics are reset to zero.

### Open

If you have played a game previously and saved it, you must open that game with the Open command. The Open dialog box comes up, showing all files in the current directory that have the extension POK. You can either type the name of the game you want to open or choose the game from the list with the mouse. All defaults are as they were when you last saved that game.

## Save

The Save command saves the game as is if the game has an existing title. If it is a new game and untitled, the Save command takes you to the Save As command. The extension POK is automatically appended to the name you give. The items saved are

The bet

The bankroll

All the statistics

The status of the double up, jokers wild, and sound switches

## Save As

The Save As command enables you to give a name to the game you are saving. You can change the name of a previously saved game or give a name to a new game by using this option.

## Exit

The Exit command enables you to exit the WinPoker game and return to the Windows environment.

# Options

Press Alt+O or click Options with the left mouse button to access the Options commands. There are four Options commands.

## Set Colors

The Set Colors command brings up a dialog box that enables you to change the background and foreground colors WinPoker uses. The colors are based on an

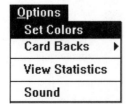

**The Options menu lists four commands you can use to customize the way WinPoker looks and plays.**

RGB (Red, Green, Blue) value, the same as is used in the Windows Control Panel Colors dialog box. You can set intensity values for each of the colors from 0 to 255. The preview bar in the dialog box shows you what the colors look like before you click on OK to change them.

### Card Backs

The Card Backs command enables you to change the card backs from the default (Star) to one of four other choices.

### View Statistics

The Statistics screen shows the various types of poker hands you can get. It counts the number of times you get each hand and gives the percentage of total hands played for each hand.

### Sound

The Sound command turns the sound for the game on or off.

## Bet

To change your bet, press Alt+B or click on Bet with the left mouse button. You can choose a bet of 1 to 5. You can change your bet at the beginning of each hand. After a bet is chosen, it remains at that amount until you change it again.

| HAND | COUNT | PERCENT |
|------|-------|---------|
| Royal Flush | – | – |
| Five of a Kind | – | – |
| Straight Flush | – | – |
| Four of a Kind | – | – |
| Full House | – | – |
| Flush | – | – |
| Straight | 1 | 1.96% |
| Three of a Kind | 4 | 7.84% |
| Two Pair | 5 | 9.80% |
| Jacks or Better | 17 | 33.33% |
| Non Winners | 24 | 47.06% |
| Total Hands | 51 | |

RESUME GAME        RESET TOTALS

The Statistics screen keeps track of how many times you've been dealt each hand and the percentage of times you've been dealt each hand.

Bet
1 F1
2 F2
3 F3
4 F4
√ 5 F5

The Bet menu offers five betting options; alternatively, use the F1 through F5 keys to place bets.

The hot keys you can use to change your bet, without going into the Bet menu, are the F1 (to bet 1) to F5 (to bet 5) keys.

## Deal

To deal new cards (either as a new hand or as replacement cards) with the keyboard, press Alt+D or Enter. With the mouse, left-click the Deal menu item or right-click anywhere in the WinPoker playing area.

# The WinPoker Files

Here are the files that should be with this package:

| | |
|---|---|
| README.1ST | This is the documentation. |
| WINPOKER.EXE | This is the executable for WinPoker 2.0. This file needs the CARDDLL.DLL file to run. |
| WINPOKER.HLP | This is the WinPoker on-line help file. |
| CARDDLL.DLL | This is a file of common routines required by WINPOKER.EXE. |
| WINPOKER.ORD | This is the WinPoker order form you can print and mail to me for your registered version of the program. |

The documentation is now in on-line Windows Help format. Just start up WinPoker and go to the Help menu item.

# Miscellaneous Information

This game is a Windows 3.0 application. It does not run in previous versions of Windows.

WinPoker was designed for a VGA or better display. Users of EGA displays do not see the bottom of the cards.

If there are problems, I would like to know about them. Leave me a note on CompuServe or send me mail, and I will try to respond as soon as I can.

# Registration Information

WinPoker is not and has never been public-domain software, nor is it free software.

Nonregistered users are granted a limited license to use WinPoker on a trial basis, for the purpose of determining whether it suits their needs.

No one may modify or patch the WinPoker executable files in any way, including but not limited to decompiling, disassembling, or otherwise reverse-engineering the program.

A limited license is granted for copying and distributing WinPoker, only for the trial use of others, subject to the preceding limitations and also the following: WinPoker must be copied in unmodified form, complete with all the included files.

Remember, registered users get an upgraded program that has the pester screen removed *and* that includes the Double Up and Jokers Wild options.

Once again, thank you for supporting shareware.

## The fine print

This software is for entertainment purposes only and is sold "as is," without any warranty as to performance or any other warranties, whether expressed or implied. Because of the many hardware and software environments in which this program may be used, no warranty of fitness for a particular purpose is offered. The user must assume the entire risk of using the program. Any liability of the seller will be limited exclusively to product replacement or the refund of the registration fee.

## A special thanks to. . .

James and Linda Tibbetts for their *outstanding* work beta-testing WinPoker 2.0. They were phenomenal.

All the people who register WinPoker as shareware. You guys keep me going, and I appreciate each and every one of you.

And last, but certainly not least, thanks to Sara. She spent extra hours designing the face cards and doing some heavy-duty testing of her own. She also puts up with me, takes care of me, and inspires me.

Thank you for trying WinPoker 2.0. I hope you find it enjoyable.

## WinPoker Registration Form

From WinPoker Help, you can click on File and print this topic to get a registration form similar to the one that follows. Send the form, along with $15.00, to

**Dean Zamzow**
P.O. Box 55761
Phoenix, AZ 85078

Technical Support: CompuServe ID 73500,3156

---

Enclosed please find $15.00 U.S. dollars to register WinPoker and receive the latest version on disk. I understand that the registered version does not have the pester screen and includes the Double Up and Jokers Wild options.

Please check one:

[ ] 3 ½ Disk

[ ] 5 ¼ Disk

Name: _____

Address: _____

_____

_____

Where did you acquire WinPoker 2.0? _____

Comments, Suggestions:

_____

_____

_____

# WinStart

### Version 1.1
### Copyright © by Briarwood Consulting

*WinStart is a simple DOS utility that does one thing and does it well: WinStart displays a text-mode message that enables you to press a letter to start Windows in real mode (for Windows 3.0 only), standard mode, or 386 enhanced mode.*

*Why would you want to use WinStart? After all, you can type **WIN /S** or **WIN /3** to start Windows in standard mode or enhanced mode.*

*WinStart is useful if you are testing Windows software and frequently want to switch between standard and enhanced modes. Or you might use it for any reason that causes you to switch between Windows modes, if you don't use the mode that automatically comes up when you start Windows.*

*The source code is included on disk for programmers who want to add features to this little program. If you only use Windows 3.1, for example, you could remove the real mode option from WinStart. Or you could add other options.*

| | |
|---|---|
| **Type of Program:** | DOS utility. Do not run under Windows |
| **Requires:** | Windows 3.0 or later |
| **Registration:** | Free. This program does not require registration. |
| **Technical Support:** | None |

## Overview

WinStart is a program, written in C, that performs start-up functions for Windows 3.*x*. I used a batch file to do the job previously, but I needed a project for a course in C programming (grin).

```
┌Windows 3.x Startup Utility════════════
│    Available modes:
│
│      R)   Real Mode (Windows 3.0 only)
│
│      S)   Standard Mode
│
│      3)   386 Enhanced Mode
│
│   Press the letter of your choice,
│      or any other key for DOS...
│
└════════════(c) 1992 Briarwood Consulting┘
```

Use WinStart to start Windows in whatever mode you want.

## Installation

Put WINSTART.EXE in a directory in your path (for example, C:\UTIL) and put a line at the end of your AUTOEXEC.BAT file that reads, simply, WINSTART. When you run WINSTART, a text-mode window that lists choices appears. Press the key for your desired choice.

## Program notes

The source code is supplied if you want (or need) to make any changes. The source code requires the Window Boss libraries to be compiled. These libraries are available on CompuServe or many BBSs in your area. One good source for the Window Boss is an SDN (Shareware Distribution Network) affiliated BBS in your area.

This software is hereby released as copyrighted freeware. No fees, except for disk duplication fees, may be charged for this program. Charles Puffe (the author) makes no warranty of any kind, expressed or implied, with respect to this software. In no event shall the author be liable for any damages, including losses of monetary or other value, or any other incidental or consequential damages arising out of the use of or inability to use this program, or for any claim by any other party. Portions copyright 1990 by Philip Mongelluzzo.

Please use this program and give me feedback on how I can improve it. Thanks for trying it!

**Charles Puffe**
Briarwood Consulting
268 Old Stagecoach Rd.
Meriden, CT 06450

# ZiPaper

## Version 1.3c
## Copyright © by Daniel Thomas

*W*indows *wallpaper is an attractive way to dress up your background screen. The problem is that looking at the same wallpaper image gets monotonous, and it's irritating to have to open the Control Panel every time you want to change your scenery.*

*ZiPaper (pronounced* zip paper*) solves both the disk-space and the monotony problems. ZiPaper chooses a wallpaper image at random (or in an order you specify) every time you start your PC or Windows. Although many utilities are capable of doing this, ZiPaper excels because it enables you to store all your large wallpaper files in a single, compressed file.*

*ZiPaper is one of the few DOS programs we've seen that really improves Windows. It has to be a DOS program, of course, because it must extract each wallpaper file before Windows loads the image. ZiPaper is also one of the few shareware programs that requires another shareware program to work. You must shrink your wallpaper into one of two formats: ZIP or LZH. You can use the ZIP Tools program, featured elsewhere in this book, to create ZIP files.*

*As a DOS program, ZiPaper has many command-line switches. These can be difficult to configure. This is one program that definitely requires you to read through the documentation before you can use it effectively. You should have a good knowledge of DOS batch files before you experiment. But, if you commonly edit your own AUTOEXEC.BAT file, you should be able to master ZiPaper.*

| | |
|---|---|
| **Type of Program:** | DOS Utility. Do not run under Windows. |
| **Requires:** | Windows 3.0 or later. Also requires a PC compression program, such as ZIP Tools, PKZip, or LHArc (as described later in this chapter), and experience with DOS batch files. |
| **Registration:** | Use the form at the end of this chapter to register with the shareware author. |
| **Technical Support:** | Daniel Thomas provides registered users with technical support through CompuServe, Prodigy, telephone, and mail. |

# Introduction and a Quick Tour

ZiPaper (that's *Zip Paper*) is a program that chooses one of your BMP files at random for use as your Windows wallpaper. Although there are several programs that do that, ZiPaper is different: It enables you to place all your BMP wallpaper files in a ZIP file (or an LHArc-format LZH file), reducing disk space dramatically.

You run ZiPaper *before* you start Windows each time (start ZiPaper from your AUTOEXEC.BAT file, for example).

You tell ZiPaper the name of the ZIP or LZH file that contains your BMP files for use as wallpaper. ZiPaper extracts a BMP file randomly, changes its name to WALPAPER.BMP, and places it in your Windows directory.

You make a one-time change to Windows, telling it to use the file WALPAPER.BMP as its wallpaper.

That's it (aside from the advanced options, discussed later).

# Installation

## Requirements for running ZiPaper

ZiPaper is a DOS program and therefore does not require Windows. However, it is designed to select Windows BMP files for use as Wallpaper, so if you don't have Windows, you don't need this program.

You need PKZIP.EXE and PKUNZIP.EXE from the following vendor:

**PKWare, Inc.**
9025 N. Deerwood Dr.
Brown Deer, WI 53223
Telephone: 414-354-8699
Bulletin Board: 414-354-8670

These two programs are available on the PKWare bulletin board and many other bulletin board systems as shareware. ZiPaper needs PKUNZIP.EXE to decompress wallpaper files from your ZIP file. You also need PKZIP.EXE to create your ZIP file.

If you prefer, you can use the LHArc program to create LZH files. LHArc is available on many bulletin board systems as well as from shareware vendors.

## Preparing wallpaper files

1. Compress all the BMP files you want to use as wallpaper into a ZIP or an LZH file. See PKZip's or LHArc's instructions on how to do this. Place the ZIP or LZH file in any directory you want.

2. Run Windows and then open the Control Panel's Desktop dialog box. In the area entitled Wallpaper, click the box labeled File. Delete the filename that is there (if any) and type **WALLPAPER.BMP.** If you have any Wallpaper that you want centered, please read "Advanced Options," later in this chapter. For now, click on Tile. Then click on OK to close the Control Panel.

3. If you have a wallpaper file named WALPAPER.BMP, rename it to some other name. ZiPaper uses the name WALPAPER.BMP for the current wallpaper file.

4. Make sure that the file ZIPAPER.EXE is in a directory on your path. You can place ZiPaper anywhere on your hard disk if you specify the path on the command line when you run the program, such as *x:*\ZIPAPER\ZIPAPER.EXE.

5. Because ZiPaper should be run each time *before* you run Windows, I suggest that you place the line that runs ZiPaper in your AUTOEXEC.BAT file or in a batch file that you use to run Windows. ZiPaper is a DOS program. *Do not* place ZiPaper in the LOAD= or RUN= line of your WIN.INI file. Doing so produces unpredictable results.

Here's the syntax for running ZiPaper:

ZIPAPER *filename* {*program*} {*options*}

where

ZIPAPER is the ZiPaper executable program

*filename* is the full name of your compressed file

*program* is the name of your decompression program

*options* represents parameters described in "Advanced Options," later in this chapter

If your compressed file is in ZIP format and PKUNZIP.EXE is on your path, you do not need to specify any *program* for your decompression program. ZiPaper runs PKUNZIP.EXE automatically.

If your compressed file is in ZIP format but PKUNZIP.EXE is *not* on your path, you must specify the full path to PKUNZIP.EXE, such as

ZIPAPER c:\graphics\images.zip c:\utility\PKUNZIP.EXE

If your compressed file is in LZH format, you must add an /LHA switch. If the LHA.EXE program is not on your path, you must also specify the full filename for the program. This would look as follows:

ZIPAPER c:\graphics\images.lzh c:\utility\LHA.EXE /LHA

6. If you've added the appropriate command line to your AUTOEXEC.BAT file, ZiPaper selects a wallpaper image at random from your compressed file the next time you start your computer.

# Advanced Options

ZiPaper supports the following options on its command line:

| | |
|---|---|
| /S | Runs Setup to configure wallpaper images |
| /1 | Uses configuration 1 (this is the default) |
| /2 | Uses configuration 2 |
| /3 | Uses configuration 3 |
| /4 | Uses configuration 4 |
| /W | Updates WIN.INI for your current Setup choice |
| /W /T | Tiles images configured as Default |
| /W /C | Centers images configured as Default |
| /F | Displays filenames for you to choose from |
| /F? | Prompts whether you want to select a filename |
| /F=*filename*.BMP | Forces ZiPaper to use one specific image |
| /NR | Not Random; ZiPaper selects images in the order you placed them in the ZIP or LZH file |

*Note:* ZiPaper can function just fine without these advanced options. They are available to enhance ZiPaper's operation, but you certainly don't have to use them.

ZiPaper creates a data file for each ZIP or LZH file you use. The file is given the same filename as the ZIP or LZH file, but it has the extension ZPA (for ZiPAper). This file stores Setup information about each wallpaper image in your ZIP or LZH file. (Don't worry if you add or remove wallpaper files from your ZIP or LZH file; ZiPaper adjusts its file accordingly.)

# Setup Screen: /S

If you run ZiPaper with the /S option, ZiPaper brings up a Setup screen. This screen enables you to tell ZiPaper a few things about each wallpaper file.

If you use PKUNZIP.EXE, and it is on your path, the command line might look like this:

ZIPAPER c:\bitmaps\images.zip /S

If you use LHA.EXE, and it is on your path, the command line might look like this:

ZIPAPER c:\bitmaps\images.lzh /LHA /S

Here are the things you can tell ZiPaper about each wallpaper file:

♦ **Positioning**. You can specify Tile, Center, or Default for each image. Usually, ZiPaper uses whichever setting (Tile or Center) you specify for your wallpaper in the Windows Control Panel. Specifying Tile or Center enables you to override the Control Panel setting with the /W switch. The Default setting enables you to specify Tiled or Centered using the switches /W /T and /W /C. These /W switches are explained in "Tiling options: /W, /W /T, and /W /C," later in this chapter. All files are initialized to Default at the start of ZiPaper.

♦ **Enabled or Disabled.** You can specify Enabled or Disabled for each wallpaper image, in each of four different configurations, in the Setup screen. This action enables you to control which images appear under different circumstances. All files are initialized to Enabled at the start of ZiPaper.

## Using the four configurations

You can specify the preceding options in *up to four different configurations* for each wallpaper. Why would you want to do that? Here are a couple of scenarios (although these are simple, you can devise more complex ones):

```
                          Configuration Screen

             -------1-------  -------2-------  -------3-------  -------4-------
 File Name   Tile   Select   Tile   Select   Tile   Select   Tile   Select
256COLOR.BMP Tile   Enabled  Def.   Enabled  Def.   Enabled  Def.   Enabled
ARCADE.BMP   Tile   Enabled  Def.   Enabled  Def.   Enabled  Def.   Enabled
ARCHES.BMP   Center Enabled  Def.   Enabled  Def.   Enabled  Def.   Enabled
ARGYLE.BMP   Def.   Disabled Def.   Enabled  Def.   Enabled  Def.   Enabled
CARS.BMP     Def.   Disabled Def.   Enabled  Def.   Enabled  Def.   Enabled
CASTLE.BMP   Def.   Enabled  Def.   Enabled  Def.   Enabled  Def.   Enabled
CHITZ.BMP    Def.   Enabled  Def.   Enabled  Def.   Enabled  Def.   Enabled

<Pg Dn> for more files   <Pg Up> for prior files   <Esc> to exit this screen

Instructions:   <Run ZiPaper with no parameters for more instructions>

Under "Tile", enter a D for default, C for center, or T for tile.
   ("Default" is Tile, unless the parameter "/C" is used)

Under "Select", enter a E for enabled, or D for disabled.
             Last File Extracted: ARCADE.BMP
```

**Use the Setup screen to configure each wallpaper file for each of four groups.**

**Scenario 1:** You run Windows in 640 x 480 mode and 800 x 600 mode. You have some wallpaper files that you want centered in 640 x 480 mode and tiled in 800 x 600 mode. You set one configuration to specify Centered and another to specify Tiled. Before you start Windows in 640 x 480 mode, you run ZiPaper with the /1 switch. Before you start Windows in 800 x 600 mode, you run ZiPaper with the /2 switch.

**Scenario 2:** You have some wallpaper files not appropriate for working hours, but you want to use them after hours. You set one configuration to Disable certain wallpaper files and run ZiPaper with the /1 switch during working hours. You set another configuration to Enabled and run ZiPaper with the /2 switch after hours.

Run ZiPaper with the /S option and look at the screen. It's pretty self-explanatory, when you understand the four option groups.

### Using the Setup screen

Use the Tab key and the arrow keys to move around the screen. Use PgUp and PgDn to scroll through all your files (if you have more than will fit on one screen).

Change an option by typing the first letter.

Press Esc when you're done. Before exiting, ZiPaper asks whether you want to save the options you just changed.

## Configurations: /1, /2, /3, and /4

Using the /1, /2, /3, or /4 switch tells ZiPaper which configuration to use. If you don't specify any of these, /1 is assumed.

## Tiling options: /W, /W /T, and /W /C

The tiling options enable you to override the Tile or Center setting for wallpaper in the Windows Control Panel.

### /W

The /W option means *Update the WIN.INI file*. Use this option when you want ZiPaper to look at the Tile/Center option you specified for each image in the Setup screen (see earlier). ZiPaper changes your WIN.INI setting to Tile or Center the current wallpaper accordingly. If an image is specified in the Setup screen as Default and you use the /W switch, ZiPaper changes your WIN.INI to Tiled for that image. ZiPaper saves the old version of WIN.INI as WININI.BAK.

*Note:* When you use the /W switch, the Windows directory must be the *current directory* if ZiPaper is to find your WIN.INI file. For example, if your WIN.INI file is in your C:\WINDOWS directory, you might use the following lines in a batch file to accomplish this:

```
C:
CD \WINDOWS
ZIPAPER c:\bitmaps\images.zip /W
```

## /W /T or /W /C

If you set up the Tile/Center option for an image to Default, the /W /T switch tells ZiPaper to force the default to Tile. The /W /C switch forces the default to Center.

### Command-line examples

The following examples show the /W switch updating WIN.INI to override the Tile or Center settings in the Windows Control Panel:

ZIPAPER D:\GRAPHICS\WALPAPER.ZIP /W

This runs ZiPaper and selects an image at random from D:\GRAPHICS\WALPAPER.ZIP (choosing from configuration 1). ZiPaper updates your WIN.INI file for the Tile/Center preference you specified in the Setup screen.

ZIPAPER D:\GRAPHICS\WALPAPER.ZIP /W /C /2

This runs ZiPaper and selects an image at random from D:\GRAPHICS\WALPAPER.ZIP (choosing from configuration 2). If the file's Tile/Center option is set to Default, it is Centered. Otherwise, ZiPaper updates your WIN.INI file for the Tile or Center preference you specified in the Setup screen.

## File Selection: /F, /F?, and /F=*filename*.BMP

At times, you may want to use a particular wallpaper file. Perhaps you are going to show off your Windows setup and you have a really eye-catching wallpaper. A new option (with three variations) has been added to facilitate this:

| | |
|---|---|
| ZIPAPER *filename* /F | You can select a filename. |
| ZIPAPER *filename* /F? | Asks whether you want to select. |
| ZIPAPER *filename* /F=*filename*.BMP | Selects a specific image. |

## /F

The /F option runs the ZiPaper Setup screen, just like the /S option does (the /S switch was described earlier). But the /F option lets you choose which wallpaper file you want ZiPaper to extract. Just highlight the file you want with the arrow keys and press F10.

## /F?

The /F? option is just like the /F option, but it asks you whether you want to select a file manually. You have three seconds in which to press Y. If you press Y, the Setup screen is brought up and you can select a file. If you answer N or the three seconds elapse, ZiPaper acts as though the /F option had never been specified. It extracts a wallpaper file randomly.

If you find yourself using the /F option frequently, run ZiPaper with the /F? option *all the time*.

## /F=*filename*.BMP

The /F=*filename*.BMP option enables you to force ZiPaper to extract a specified wallpaper file. You might use this option with a special batch file for those times that you know you want to use a specific wallpaper file.

# Not Random: /NR

The /NR (Not Random) option causes ZiPaper to extract wallpaper files in the order they appear in the ZIP file. This enables *you* to choose the order in which you see the wallpaper files.

# Life with ZiPaper

After you've done the installation steps, you need never bother with ZiPaper again — except to use the Advanced Options or maybe to send in a shareware fee (*grin*). You may add and remove BMP files from your ZIP or LZH file with no fear of upsetting ZiPaper.

ZiPaper creates a file with the same name as your ZIP or LZH file but with the extension ZPA (for ZiPAper) in the directory that contains your ZIP or LZH file. This file keeps track of what BMP files ZiPaper has chosen so that you get a more even distribution of wallpaper choices. It also holds your Advanced Options setup choices. If you have any problems, you can delete this file. It is re-created the next time ZiPaper runs. (Remember, though, that if you delete this file, you have to set up your Advanced Options again if you use them.)

# Installing Over Older Versions _____

## Users of ZiPaper Version 1.3a, 1.3, 1.2a, 1.2

Replace the ZIPAPER.EXE file with the new ZIPAPER.EXE. Delete the associated data files for each ZIP file. For example, if your ZIP file was named WALPAPER.ZIP, delete the file WALPAPER.ZPA.

If you have entered any Tile/Center options or Enable/Disable settings, you must reenter them (sorry).

## Users of ZiPaper Version 1.1

Replace the ZIPAPER.EXE file for Version 1.1 with the new ZIPAPER.EXE file.

Delete the file ZIPAPER.DAT, which is in the same directory as your wallpaper ZIP file. If you have entered any Tile/Center options or Enable/Disable settings, you must reenter them (sorry).

Because the wallpaper file is now extracted into the \WINDOWS directory, make sure that ZiPaper is run from that directory.

You may have to change the WIN.INI file to look for the file WALPAPER.BMP in the Windows directory. The easiest way to do this is to run the new version of ZiPaper and then run Windows. Double-click on the Control Panel icon in Program Manager and then the Desktop icon. Click on the down arrow next to the wallpaper filename and select the file WALPAPER.BMP from the list. Click on OK, and you're done!

## Users of ZiPaper Version 1.0

Replace the ZIPAPER.EXE file for Version 1.0 with the new ZIPAPER.EXE file.

Delete the ZIPAPER.DAT file in the same directory as your wallpaper ZIP file. If you don't delete this file, you *will* get unexpected results or errors.

# If You Have Problems

You can contact me on CompuServe at 72301,2164 and on Prodigy at CWRF01A.

Telephone support: Registered owners may call me.

# The Association of Shareware Professionals Ombudsman Information

This program is produced by a member of the Association of Shareware Professionals (ASP). ASP wants to make sure that the shareware principle works for you. If you are unable to resolve a shareware-related problem with an ASP member by contacting the member directly, ASP may be able to help. The ASP Ombudsman can help you resolve a dispute or problem with an ASP member but does not provide technical support for members' products. Please write to the ASP Ombudsman at 545 Grover Road, Muskegon, MI 49442 or send a CompuServe message through CompuServe mail to ASP Ombudsman, 70007,3536.

# How To Pay For and Register ZiPaper

Print the text file ZIPAPER.REG and fill it out. If you are missing that file, the registration form is reproduced at the end of this chapter, or you can contact me:

**Daniel Thomas**
2301 North Huron Circle
Placentia, CA 92670
CompuServe: 72301,2164
Prodigy: CWRF01A

I didn't make ZiPaper nagware. It doesn't bug you with a pop-up screen asking for money. All the same, please remember that this program is the result of much hard work and time spent on CompuServe, and all registrations help. If you think $15 is too much for this program, then don't use it!

Registration gets you the following:

♦ The right to continue to use this program

♦ The latest version on disk

♦ A small printed manual

♦ An assortment of wallpaper files

Enjoy!

— *Dan Thomas*

## ZiPaper V1.3c Registration Form

Send to **Daniel Thomas**
2301 N. Huron Circle
Placentia, CA 92670
CompuServe: 72301,2164
Prodigy: CWRF01A

Name: _____

Company: _____

Address: _____

_____

City: _____ State: _____ ZIP: _____

Phone: ( ___ ) _____ Country: _____

Electronic Mail (CompuServe and so on): _____

Where did you get your copy of ZiPaper?

_____

ZiPaper registration: $15.00 _____          $ $15.00

Disk Size (check one):

____    5.25 High Density ← best!

____    5.25 Low Density

____    3.5 High Density ← best!

____    3.5 Low Density

*FREE!* Wallpaper Files
compressed with PKZip (check one):

____    16 color, 24 files (mostly 640 x 480),
         totalling over 3.3 megs (decompressed) _____ $ FREE

____    256 color, 6 files (all 640 x 480),
         totalling over 1.8 megs (decompressed) _____ $ FREE

(Optional) Want both 16 and 256 color? add $4.00:     $ _____

Shipping and handling ($3 U.S. & Canada, $6 elsewhere):  $ _____

Total (U.S. Funds):                                   $ _____

Checks must be drawn on a U.S. bank and payable in U.S. funds. Canadian
customers may use a Canadian Post Office Money Order; make sure that
it is in U.S. funds.

Please make checks payable to Daniel Thomas.

# ZIP Tools for Windows

### Release 1.10
### FlashPoint ZIP, ZIPX, and WIZiper — Versions 3.10.01.10
### Copyright © by Richard S. Patterson, FlashPoint Development

*If you'd like some extra disk space, you'll love ZIP Tools. It compresses and decompresses files on command in Windows. You can shrink those old files you hardly ever use and get back 50 percent to 70 percent of the disk space they formerly occupied.*

*This has long been possible with PKZip and PKUnzip, which are very popular shareware utilities for the DOS operating system. But ZIP Tools handles ZIP-compatible files right in the Windows environment.*

***Important:*** *You must place the ZIP Tools directory on your DOS path or move the files into a directory on your path for ZIP Tools to work for you properly. There are other important instructions in this chapter; read it to get the most benefit from ZIP Tools.*

*After you've done this, simply double-click WIZiper's WIZ.EXE filename in the File Manager or double-click the Wiz icon in Program Manager to start compressing and decompressing your files.*

*For those who prefer a command-line interface, ZIP Tools includes FPZIP.EXE and FPZIPX.EXE. These little applications compress and extract ZIP files under your control. They have numerous options and parameters, exactly like PKZip and PKUnzip. For example, if you have a file called MYFILES.ZIP highlighted in the current directory in File Manager, you can click File Run and type the following command:*

**FPZIPX MYFILES**

*ZIP Tools then extracts the contents of MYFILES.ZIP into the current directory.*

*For even more power, you can associate ZIP files with WIZ.EXE or FPZIPX.EXE. Then you can simply double-click ZIP files or drag them from File Manager and drop them on WIZiper or FPZIPX to extract them. To associate ZIP files with WIZ.EXE, add the following line to the [Extensions] section of your WIN.INI file (and restart Windows):*

```
[Extensions]
ZIP=WIZ.EXE ^.ZIP
```

*A new versipn of PKZip, Version 2.0, was scheduled to be released after the publication of this book. PKZip 2.0 produces ZIP files that cannot be decompressed by PKZip 1.x or ZIP Tools for Windows 1.1. Contact the author of ZIP Tools for a later version that will support PKZip 2.0.*

*ZIP Tools is a long-awaited and welcome addition to our Windows tool kit.*

| | |
|---|---|
| **Type of Program:** | File Compression and Decompression |
| **Requires:** | Windows 3.0 or later |
| **Registration:** | Use the form at the end of this chapter to register with the shareware author. |
| **Technical Support:** | Registered users receive a fully illustrated manual and on-line Help files. FlashPoint Development provides registered users with technical support by telephone, CompuServe, and mail. |
| **Similar Shareware:** | Windows UnArchive, a program featured in *Windows 3.1 SECRETS,* published by IDG Books Worldwide, can also decompress ZIP files in Windows but doesn't compress them, as ZIP Tools can. |

# Welcome

Welcome to FlashPoint Development's ZIP Tools for Windows — the first, if not the only, full 100 percent Windows implementation of ZIP archive, file-compression, management, and expansion utilities to be distributed as shareware.

These software tools are essential to every Windows user who does the following:

♦ Uses a modem for communications

♦ Accesses bulletin board systems (BBSs) or mainframe services such as CompuServe or GEnie

♦ Believes free disk space is and will continue to be a valuable resource

A ZIP-compressed file is often 50 percent to 70 percent smaller than the aggregate size of its original member files. Thus, the major benefit is that ZIP file compression can save significant disk space; however, there are also several not-so-obvious benefits.

ZIP archives can also reduce the number of individual files stored on a disk drive by combining groups of related files in a single library or archive file. This can result in faster system response by DOS-based and Windows-based applications that otherwise experience noticeable slowdowns when forced to access directories containing large numbers of individual files. Fewer and faster disk accesses also prolong the life of a system's drives, which in turn may result in lower repair and replacement costs.

Those who transfer files to and from remote systems will see immediate savings in long-distance tolls and on-line service charges. These charges should be proportionately related to time saved by transferring a single, smaller, compressed ZIP file rather than several large, uncompressed, individual files.

No matter whether you are new to ZIP file compression or have been using the old reliable DOS ZIP utilities since their introduction by Phil Katz and PKWare, Inc., if you use Windows, you will certainly find additional benefits to be derived in upgrading to FlashPoint's ZIP Tools for Windows.

FlashPoint ZIP Tools are compatible with the PKZip 1.1 ZIP file format and support all PKZip 1.1 compression methods. Any file created or modified with ZIP Tools for Windows remains fully compatible with PKWare's DOS ZIP utilities.

## Using this documentation

How much a user knows about Windows, DOS, files and file compression, and general computer software and hardware determines how to best use this documentation.

This documentation has been organized into parts that hopefully enable FlashPoint ZIP Tools users to locate those sections they need to review and to avoid having to read or reread topics with which they are already familiar.

For example, persons who are already familiar with shareware, file compression, and what ZIP files are, probably do not need to read the first part of this guide, "Fundamental Concepts," and may prefer to skip to the second part, "Getting Started." Users who only use FlashPoint ZIP/ZIPX applications (FPZIP.EXE and FPZIPX.EXE) do not need to review the "Using FlashPoint ZIP" and "Using FlashPoint ZIPX" sections. Those who use WIZiper as an interface to FPZIP.EXE and FPZIPX.EXE may not be interested in the command line syntax or other technical details of FPZIP.EXE and FPZIPX.EXE and can ignore those sections.

# Preface

This version is the first full release of FlashPoint ZIP Tools for Windows, although the FlashPoint ZIP/ZIPX command modules have been distributed as shareware since late 1991.

The FlashPoint ZIP/ZIPX modules have undergone significant revisions and enhancements since their first release. Previous users should note several changes in their command line switches and parameters, additional features, improvements in speed, and modifications to their user interface.

A major addition to the tool sets, as a result of user feedback and requests, is the WIZiper (pronounced *wiz-per*) user interface. This graphical interface supports each and every feature of ZIP/ZIPX and adds several other features to boot. It also provides Windows 3.1-compatible drag-and-drop support (even under Windows 3.0), which enables simultaneous expansion of multiple ZIP archives, a ZIP file-member listing tool, file and directory browsers, setup features for itself and the ZIP/ZIPX modules, customized user-defined file masks — which are saved between sessions — and the capacity to virtually eliminate all keyboard input.

Other major enhancements to all modules and the addition of other tools are under development. As each new feature is completed, it will be added to those copies provided to registered users; however, because of the time and expense involved, we will not be releasing new shareware evaluation copies each time a new function is added, absent a major update or bug fix.

References to FlashPoint WinNAV or Windows Navigator and certain of its features — such as Windows 3.1 drag-and-drop compatibility — refer to a version of WinNAV released in the third quarter of 1992. This was the first official release of the Windows 3.1 version of WinNAV and is distributed as shareware through various on-line services in the file NAV310.EXE. The previous release, distributed as shareware through various on-line services in the file NAV062.EXE, is compatible with Windows 3.1 but does not support its drag-and-drop features.

As always, we hope your use of FlashPoint Development's applications and utilities make your day-to-day use of Windows a little more productive and, of course, a lot more fun.

# Acknowledgments and Legal Notices _____

FlashPoint, FlashPoint WindowWare, "It's FlashPoint WindowWare!," ZIP Tools for Windows, WIZiper, WIZ, FPZIP, FPZIPX, ZIPX, WinQPrt, and other WinQ and Flash tools and utilities, The Navigator and Windows Navigator, WinNAV, WinNie, Launch, Pack, Alias Directories, and other names, marks, logos, and derivatives thereof are trademarks and servicemarks of Richard S. Patterson and/or FlashPoint Development.

All others trade and service marks belong to their respective owners.

FlashPoint Development and its products are not affiliated with either David B. Gordon or FlashPoint of Austin, Texas.

Information in this document is subject to change without notice and does not represent a commitment on the part of either the author or copyright holder. The software described in this document is furnished under various license or nondisclosure agreements. The software may be used or copied only in accordance with the terms of the applicable agreements. Generally, unless otherwise noted, the purchaser may make one copy of the software for backup purposes. Subject to the provisions concerning distribution of unregistered evaluation copies, no part of this manual or product may be reproduced or transmitted in any form or by any means, electronic or mechanical, including photocopying and recording, for any purpose other than the purchaser's personal use without the written permission of the author and copyright holder.

The software described in this documentation, together with this documentation and related files, are part of a copyrighted unregistered release that may be distributed through shareware channels for evaluation purposes only, provided same are distributed as a single package and without modification.

The software, documentation, and files are subject to change without notice. The author and copyright holder retains all rights with respect to these materials and is not obligated to develop or distribute future releases, if any, of same through this or any other channel.

Notwithstanding the foregoing, those using these materials agree to and are bound by the terms and conditions contained herein, including all applicable license and nondisclosure agreements, and accept same "as is" and without warranty.

For further information, please refer to the applicable sections of the documentation distributed with this product.

# Fundamental Concepts

## Shareware distribution

Please note that these files and application programs are distributed through shareware channels for evaluation or demonstration purposes only. They are not free.

The term *shareware* simply refers to a method of software distribution or marketing, which is designed to let users try an application before they buy it. The software, however, still must be purchased or licensed by the user, just like other software sold in retail stores.

Continued use of copies of any shareware application, beyond the evaluation period, requires the users to purchase and register their copies with the software developer or copyright holder. Failure to do so, simply put, is theft.

For example, anyone who elects to use WIZiper, FPZIP, or FPZIPX beyond the thirty (30) day evaluation period is required to purchase a license for each copy of the application in use from FlashPoint Development. Information on purchasing licensed copies of FlashPoint Development's applications is covered in detail in other parts of this documentation; also refer to the FlashPoint License Agreements, order forms, and the applications' About boxes for more information.

Upon registration of FlashPoint Development's ZIP Tools for Windows, licensed users are provided with the current registered users disk, which contains the latest release of the applicable FlashPoint ZIP Tools and a complete, illustrated Users Guide in Microsoft Windows Write and Microsoft Word for Windows formats (FPZIP.WRI and FPZIP.DOC). In addition, the registered user disk may contain additional files and utilities.

## File compression and archives

Often terms such as *compression, archives, libraries,* and *compacting* are used interchangeably when referring to file and media utilities. However, the terms are far from identical.

### File compression

Generally, the term *file compression* refers to any method of reducing a single file's physical size, by varying degrees, and enabling it to be uncompressed at a later time without losing any of its essential characteristics.

The most obvious benefit is that a compressed file occupies less space on a hard drive, disk, tape, or other storage media. Another benefit is that compressed files can be transmitted over wire, telephone, or satellite in a shorter period of time than uncompressed files.

Many utilities and applications employ compression. For example, many software development companies now employ proprietary methods of compressing distribution files to reduce the costs of distribution disks; their setup programs uncompress the files at installation. Most popular graphics file formats are actually compressed data files.

The bottom-line benefit is that using compressed files can directly or indirectly result in substantial savings of time and money.

## Compacted and compressed files

Although the concept of *compacting files* might include compression, it also might include methods of permanently converting or modifying a file's essential characteristics. That is to say, compacting also includes techniques for reducing a file's size without providing any means for the compacted file later to be restored to a mirror image of the original file.

This technique is common to graphics files that do not require restoration to their original resolution. For instance, there is little need to store files in a 600-dots-per-inch (dpi) format when they will only be reproduced, displayed, or printed at 300 dpi. Thus, by converting the original files to more compact, lower-resolution files, significant savings in storage space can result.

For purposes of this documentation, we are not concerned with permanently converting files; we are concerned with temporarily storing files in a compressed form for later retrieval. Therefore, any references herein to *compacting* refers to the latter and not the former definition.

## Library and archive files

The terms *libraries* and *archives* refer to file formats that combine groups of files in a single file; that is to say, groups of files are contained within a single library or archive file.

Library files, at least when the term first became popular in personal computing with the advent of *.LBR files, referred to groups of uncompressed files; however, it was common for files to be compressed or *squeezed* by a stand-alone utility before being stored in a *.LBR file with a separate stand-alone library utility.

On the other hand, the term *archive files* tended to refer to groups of compressed files after the advent of the once-popular *.ARC file format. Thus, a single program was used to both compress and store multiple files in a single archive.

FlashPoint's ZIP tools (as do most third-party ZIP tools) create "zipped" files, which are another form of archive files. Thus, these applications can be considered archive programs in that a single utility program first determines the optimum method, if any, for compressing a file, compresses it, and finally stores or appends it to the archive or *.ZIP file.

ZIP file compression can save significant disk space on most systems and enable faster data transfer to other systems (for example, using a modem). A compressed file is often 50 percent to 70 percent smaller than its original size.

When this documentation refers to a ZIP file or zipfile, it refers to the main archive file. References to *member files* are to the group of files stored within a ZIP archive. Hopefully, this distinction will avoid confusion in trying to distinguish files that are zipped within an archive file that has the ZIP file extension.

# Archive and compression formats: a history

Over the years, numerous archive and compression formats have been employed in IBM-compatible personal computing and for non-DOS operating systems.

In the early days of CP/M, one popular compression method was squeezing files to create a file with the SQZ format; these files were then stored in a library file with the LBR extension. Later developers came up with other, more efficient, compression and storage formats, some of which are still occasionally used today.

Users with a modem who access a computer bulletin board system (BBS) or an on-line service such as CompuServe or GEnie, or who purchase shareware disks from various software vendors, may still occasionally come across archive files with extensions such as LBR, LZH, LSH, LSZ, ARC, and ARJ. However, they are more likely to find files with the ZIP file extension.

The most significant format before the ZIP format standard, created by Phil Katz of PKWare, Inc., was ARC, developed by System Enhancement Associates, Inc. (SEA). However, the ARC format was abandoned by the BBS and on-line community almost overnight.

In an attempt to zealously protect its ARC utilities market and to keep the ARC file format, the file extension ARC, and even the term *archive* itself proprietary, SEA made a fatal mistake and sued Phil Katz and PKWare, Inc., who had become SEA's biggest competitor after developing a set of more efficient ARC utilities.

Phil Katz and PKWare, Inc., having apparently decided that they could not afford to defend against the SEA lawsuit, were forced into a settlement agreement that required them to abandon their ARC utilities and code to SEA. But what appeared to be a major victory for SEA soon proved to be SEA's worst nightmare: Phil Katz and company didn't go away.

The BBS and on-line user community, justly or unjustly, became outraged at SEA, viewing it as the villain and Phil Katz as the underdog, and began to revolt. When Phil Katz chose to develop a new, improved, better-than-ARC set of DOS file compression and archive utilities (that is, PKZip), the ZIP standard was born. Within a few months, after some of the most heated on-line debates in the history of BBS and on-line computing, system operators (sysops) across the country began converting all ARC files on their systems to the ZIP format, and the ARC file format began to fade into history.

So much for history and legends. The ZIP Version 1.1 compression format is the most popular file compression format in use today; without question, it is the industry standard.

# Getting Started

FlashPoint Development's ZIP Tools for Windows are a set of integrated file compression and extraction applications that provide full file compression, testing, listing, and expansion support for ZIP compressed file formats.

## FlashPoint ZIP/ZIPX (FPZIP.EXE and FPZIPX.EXE)

FPZIP and FPZIPX are compatible with PKWare's PKZip Version 1.1 file formats and support both implosion and shrinking compression methods.

Files created under DOS by PKZip can be tested, modified, listed, or expanded by FPZIP and FPZIPX; files created by FlashPoint ZIP Tools for Windows can be manipulated under DOS, OS/2, UNIX, Amiga, and other operating systems by PKWare's ZIP utilities and those of various third parties.

Like the DOS PKZip and PKUnzip utilities, FPZIP and FPZIPX for Windows are strictly command line applications and have an optional parameter and switch syntax similar to their DOS counterparts. This arrangement enables third-party developers to incorporate support for FPZIP and FPZIPX into their own Windows applications.

FPZIP for Windows is the compression utility, used to create and modify existing ZIP files. It compresses one or more files, file directories, and directory branches into a single ZIP archive. Within a ZIP archive, a copy of each original file, referred to as a *member file,* is compressed or stored with its name, an optional relative path, its size, the date and time last modified, an optional file comment, and other important information.

FPZIPX for Windows is the extraction or expansion utility. It lists or extracts member files contained in a ZIP archive file and tests the compressed files' integrity. It even re-creates or builds directories stored within a ZIP file and expands member files to the appropriate directory.

## FlashPoint WIZiper (WIZ.EXE)

As indicated, FPZIP and FPZIPX are command line applications like their DOS counterparts. This means that, unlike most Window applications, users cannot run the programs and then enter the filename; the FPZIP or FPZIPX program must be started with all filenames, switches, and parameters specified in the DOS command line form. Obviously, this doesn't impress most Windows users who have invested a lot of time and money in Windows just to avoid command lines.

WIZiper (pronounced *wiz-per*) provides the ZIP capabilities most Windows users will want. It's a full Windows point-and-click, drag-and-drop, pop-up and pull-down user interface for both FPZIP and FPZIPX. No more command line and almost no keyboard input are required.

## Packing list

The following listing identifies the minimum files for ZIP Tools; additional files may also be included:

| | |
|---|---|
| WIZ.EXE | WIZiper User Interface for FPZIP and FPZIPX |
| FPZIP.EXE | ZIP compression/modification program |
| FPZIPX.EXE | ZIP extraction, test, and list program |
| README.TXT | *Really important* information on this release! |
| FLASHDOC.WRI | FlashPoint ZIP Tools Evaluation Users Guide |
| FPZXX.EXE | An executable file used by ZIP Tools |
| FPRES.DLL | A dynamic link library (DLL) used by ZIP Tools |
| FPSTR.DLL | A dynamic link library used by ZIP Tools |

If you are running Windows 3.0, the following files are also installed if you do not already have them:

| | |
|---|---|
| COMMDLG.DLL | Common Dialog Box dynamic link library |
| SHELL.DLL | New "shell" executable for Windows |
| TOOLHELP.DLL | Provides Windows 3.1 functions for Windows 3.0 |

Microsoft provides these files to enable Windows 3.1-specific applications to run unchanged under Windows 3.0.

# Installing FlashPoint ZIP Tools

## Quick installation

The WSETUP program on Disk 1 of the *Windows GIZMOS* disks installs ZIP Tools to a hard disk directory you specify.

The application files (those ending with the file extension EXE) can be copied to any directory on your DOS path setting; alternatively, the directory containing ZIP Tools can be placed on your path.

WSETUP installs the ZIP Tools resource files (those ending with the file extension DLL) into the Windows directory. You can move FPRES.DLL and FPSTR.DLL to any directory designated in your DOS path setting. Note, however, that some systems and Windows configurations may produce error messages about not being able to locate a file or dynamic link if these files are not in the Windows directory.

## Windows 3.0 installation

In addition to the "Quick installation" instructions just described, users who have not upgraded from Windows 3.0 also must ensure that the following dynamic link libraries (DLLs) are present or have been installed by WSETUP in their Windows subdirectory before attempting to run WIZ.EXE:

    COMMDLG.DLL
    SHELL.DLL
    TOOLHELP.DLL

These files are required to run WIZ.EXE because WIZiper is designed to take advantage of several new Windows 3.1 features such as drag and drop and common dialog boxes.

These files are required to be installed in the Windows directory (where the Windows GDI.EXE file and other DLLs are located).

## Advanced configuration

### Application setup dialog boxes

Further installation and user customization can be performed from each application's Setup and Options dialog panels.

When you are running an application, its Setup or Options dialog panel can be invoked through its System menu or, in the case of WIZiper, by selecting the main window's Options pushbutton control.

The Setup and Options dialog panels enable you to install default configuration settings so that you don't have to enter command switches and parameters each time the applications are run.

## Windows system configuration

Either WIZ.EXE or FPZIPX.EXE can be associated with all files having the ZIP extension. Most users find it more productive to associate ZIP files with WIZ.EXE rather than with FPZIPX.EXE.

When ZIP files are associated with either WIZ.EXE or FPZIPX.EXE, a simple double-click with the mouse — or pressing the Enter key while a ZIP filename is highlighted in FlashPoint's WinNAV or Windows File Manager shell — executes the associated program and loads the selected ZIP file for processing.

Refer to the applicable shell or file-manager application's user manual or to the *Microsoft Windows User Guide* for information on how to associate files.

## Drag-and-drop support for WIZiper

The user can set the default "Do on Drop" ZIP file action by editing or adding the DoOnDrop= keyword and the applicable Keyword Setting number to the FPZIP.INI file's [WIZ] section. The FPZIP.INI file should be located in your Windows directory.

For example, the user may open the FPZIP.INI file for editing with Windows Notepad and add or edit the following section keyword:

```
[WIZ]
DoOnDrop=5
```

In this example, the keyword DoOnDrop is set to 5. This sets the default drop action to Extract; when the user drops a ZIP file or group of ZIP files on WIZiper, each file is automatically extracted to the current or Set Options Destination directory.

WIZiper supports the following DoOnDrop actions and keyword settings:

| DoOnDrop Action | Supports Multiple Files | Keyword Setting |
| --- | --- | --- |
| Add/Replace | NO | 1 |
| Update | NO | 2 |
| Freshen | NO | 3 |
| Extract | YES | 5 |
| Test | YES | 6 |
| View | NO | 7 |

# Using FlashPoint Development's WIZiper (WIZ.EXE)

## What is WIZiper?

WIZiper (pronounced *wiz-per* and often referred to as *WIZ*) provides the ZIP capabilities most users want and need in a Windows application.

It is the user interface for both FPZIP and FPZIPX, and its window and dialog controls provide access to every function and command each utility is capable of performing.

## Windows, dialog panels, and controls

The easiest and quickest way to master FlashPoint's ZIP Tools is through WIZiper; the easiest way to master WIZiper is by becoming familiar with its windows, dialog panels, and controls.

### Main window

As can be seen in the following figure, WIZiper's main dialog panel or control window presents the user with a much less intimidating user interface than PKWare's DOS PKZip and PKUnzip utilities (which rely solely on the DOS command line) and most of their Windows shells.

The WIZiper main window is a graphical interface that helps you forget about the DOS command line.

The main window controls are logically ordered and consist of four control groups:

♦ Archive File group

♦ Command group

♦ File Selection group

♦ Execution group

## Archive File group

The Archive File group contains four user controls:

♦ Archive File Name edit box

♦ File Browse pushbutton

♦ List pushbutton

♦ Members drop-down list box

### The Archive File Name edit control

The Archive file edit control contains the name of an archive file to be created or modified. The archive name can be entered with one of the following methods:

♦ Manually typing the name in the edit box.

♦ Using a mouse to drop a selected archive file from another file utility. Note that the external application must support the Windows 3.1 drag-and-drop protocol — for example, Windows 3.1's File Manager or FlashPoint's WinNAV.

♦ Selecting an archive from the File Browser dialog panel.

♦ Selecting an active file from the List dialog panel.

### The File Browser pushbutton

The Browse button to the right of the Archive edit box activates the File Browser dialog panel.

**Use the Archive File group section of the main window to specify which archive file you want to work with.**

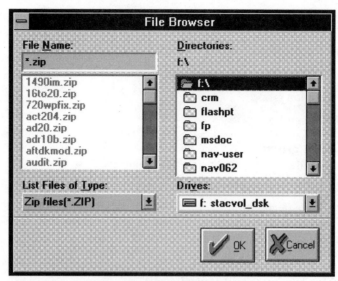

The File Browser dialog panel enables you to select an archive file from any drive or directory.

The File Browser dialog panel enables the user to scroll through all files, on any drive or directory on the system, to locate the desired file to be entered into the Archive edit box. When the appropriate ZIP file appears in the File Name edit box in the File Browser dialog panel, click the OK pushbutton; the selected filename (with applicable drive and path appended) is entered into the Archive edit box. To quit or close the File Browser without changing the original edit box, click the Cancel pushbutton or press the Esc key.

### The List dialog pushbutton

The List button activates the List dialog panel, which can be used to select an archive filename in addition to viewing a list of the archive's member files and various technical information for each member file and the archive itself.

The selected archive filename can be changed without exiting the List dialog panel. You do this by manually typing a new ZIP filename into the Archive edit box or by using the Browse button to the right of the edit box. The Browse button is used to display the File Browser dialog panel.

The File Browser enables the user to scroll through all files, on any drive or directory on the system, to locate the desired file to be entered into the Archive edit box. When the appropriate ZIP file appears in the File Name edit box in the File Browser dialog panel, click the OK pushbutton; the selected filename (with applicable drive and path appended) is entered into the Archive edit box in the

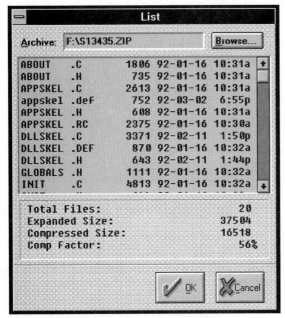

| List | | | | |
|---|---|---|---|---|
| Archive: | F:\S13435.ZIP | | | Browse... |

| ABOUT | .C | 1806 | 92-01-16 | 10:31a |
|---|---|---|---|---|
| ABOUT | .H | 735 | 92-01-16 | 10:31a |
| APPSKEL | .C | 2613 | 92-01-16 | 10:31a |
| appskel | .def | 752 | 92-03-02 | 6:55p |
| APPSKEL | .H | 608 | 92-01-16 | 10:31a |
| APPSKEL | .RC | 2375 | 92-01-16 | 10:30a |
| DLLSKEL | .C | 3371 | 92-02-11 | 1:50p |
| DLLSKEL | .DEF | 870 | 92-01-16 | 10:32a |
| DLLSKEL | .H | 643 | 92-02-11 | 1:44p |
| GLOBALS | .H | 1111 | 92-01-16 | 10:32a |
| INIT | .C | 4813 | 92-01-16 | 10:32a |

| Total Files: | 20 |
|---|---|
| Expanded Size: | 37504 |
| Compressed Size: | 16518 |
| Comp Factor: | 56% |

✓ OK    ✗ Cancel

**Use the List dialog panel to select an archive file and view its member files as well as technical information about each file.**

List dialog panel. To quit or close the File Browser without changing the original edit box, click the Cancel pushbutton or press the Esc key.

If the user selects the OK button to close the List dialog panel, the main window's Archive edit box is updated to reflect the last filename selected in the List dialog panel. If the user selects the Cancel pushbutton or presses the Esc key to close the List dialog panel, the main window Archive edit box remains unchanged.

### The Members drop-down list box

When a valid archive name is entered for an existing file, a listing of its member files will be loaded into the Members drop-down list box. This listing can be scrolled up or down to display all member files together with their uncompressed size and the date and time of creation or last modification.

### Command group

The Command group contains only two user controls:

♦ Command drop-down list box

♦ Set Options dialog pushbutton

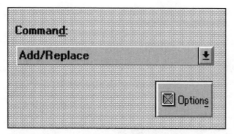

**Command:**

**Add/Replace** ▼

☒ Options

**Use the Command group section of the main
window to specify the file operation to be
performed on the archive file.**

### The Command drop-down list box

The Command drop-down list box is used to select the file operation to be performed on the specified ZIP file. The available commands include the following:

> Add/Replace
> Delete
> Extract
> Freshen
> Help - FPZip
> Help - FPZipX
> License - FPZip
> License - FPZipX
> Test
> Update
> View List

The Add/Replace command is used to add member files to either a new or existing ZIP file. All files that match the specified file mask are added to the ZIP file.
Added files overwrite existing member entries in the ZIP file if the new file's
name is identical to an existing member file's name.

The Delete command is used to delete specified member files from the ZIP
archive.

The Extract command is used to extract all or specified member files from a ZIP
archive (that is, when a copy of the member file is re-created or expanded to its
original size and date). The compressed member file within the ZIP remains
intact, until such time as the user removes it with the Delete command.

The Freshen command is used to replace existing ZIP file members with newer files having identical filenames. This option does not add files not already in the specified ZIP file.

The Help - FPZip command is used to start FlashPoint ZIP (FPZIP.EXE) and display its Help dialog panel. No other functions are performed.

The Help - FPZipX command is used to start FlashPoint ZIPX (FPZIPX.EXE) and display its Help dialog panel. No other functions are performed.

The License - FPZip command is used to start FlashPoint ZIP (FPZIP.EXE) and display information about the application, including version, release date, copyright and trademark notices, FlashPoint Development's address and telephone number, and software registration, license, and ordering information.

The License - FPZipX command is used to start FlashPoint ZIPX (FPZIPX.EXE) and display information about the application, including version, release date, copyright and trademark notices, FlashPoint Development's address and telephone number, and software registration, license, and ordering information.

The Test command is used to test the integrity of the specified ZIP file and its members.

The Update command is used to add only new member files to a ZIP file. This option only overwrites an existing member entry if a matching specified member file has a more recent date than an existing ZIP file member.

The View List command is used to display a listing of the ZIP file members, including descriptive and technical information.

**The Set Options dialog pushbutton**

The Command group's Options pushbutton displays the Set Options dialog panel.

The Set Options dialog panel is used to further refine the command function selected by the user.

The combined dialog controls enable the user to preset all options that can be performed by FPZIP or FPZIPX in conjunction with a selected command. These functions can also be invoked by executing either FPZIP or FPZIPX from a command line prompt and manually appending various switches and parameters to the command line.

```
┌─────────────────────────────────────────────────┐
│ ─                    Set Options                  │
├───────────────────────────────────────────────────┤
│ Destination:    d:\games              [ Browse... ]│
│ Work Directory: J:\tmp\               [ Browse... ]│
│ Exclude:        [                  ]   ☐ Activate  │
│ No Comp Ext:    ZIP,.LZH,.ARC,.PAK,.ZOO ☐ Activate │
│ ┌Compression Method┐┌Implode Factor┐┌Default Association┐│
│ │ ◉ 1. Best Type   ││              ││ ◉ Extract       ││
│ │ ○ 2. Implode Only││   5    ↨     ││ ○ Test          ││
│ │ ○ 3. Shrink Only ││              ││ ○ View          ││
│ └──────────────────┘└──────────────┘└─────────────────┘│
│ ☐ Recurse Subdirs  ☐ Expand Stored Dirs ☒ Echo Cmd Line│
│ ☐ Store Recur Dirs ☐ Overwrite          ☐ Auto Close  │
│ ☐ Comment ZIP                           ☒ Sound Beep  │
│ ☐ Comment Files                         ☒ Show Tech Info│
│ ☐ ZIP Date to Files                     ☒ Inform User │
│ ☐ Move to archive                       ☒ Warn User   │
│ ☐ From (mmddyy): 052492                 ☒ Alert User  │
│        [PUSH Reset] [ Save] [✓ OK] [✗ Cancel]         │
└───────────────────────────────────────────────────┘
```

**The Set Options dialog panel further refines the command specified in the Command edit box.**

The first group of dialog controls enables the user to predefine the Destination and Work Directory drive and path.

The Destination directory identifies the default drive and path that a ZIP file member is expanded to when the Extract command is executed. If the Destination is not specified by the user, the member files are extracted to the system's current directory.

The Work Directory identifies the default drive and path that FlashPoint ZIP (FPZIP.EXE) uses for its temporary build files needed to create or modify a ZIP archive file. Temporary build files are created when the Add/Replace, Delete, Freshen, or Update command is executed. If the Work Directory is not specified by the user, FPZIP uses the system's current directory for its temporary build files.

If FlashPoint ZIP does not have sufficient free work space to create temporary build files, the executed command fails.

To select the default Destination or Work Directory, the user has the option of typing the drive and path spec directly into the appropriate edit box or using the Browse pushbuttons in the upper right corner. If the user elects to use the Browse buttons, the Directory Browser dialog panel is displayed.

**If you click one of the Browse buttons in the Set Options dialog panel, the Directory Browser helps you select drives and directories.**

The Directory Browser enables the user to scroll through all drives and directories on the system to locate the desired path for either the Destination or Work Directory edit box. When the appropriate drive and path is selected in the Directory Browser, click the OK pushbutton; the selected path is entered into the appropriate Set Options edit box. To quit or close the Directory Browser without changing the original edit box, either click the Cancel pushbutton or press the Esc key.

The Exclude edit box control enables the user to designate a list of files or file types to be excluded from the ZIP archive. If activated, the excluded files are not added as members of the ZIP file.

The Activate check box control, near the right edge of the Exclude edit box, if checked, activates the Exclude files switch and excludes those files specified in the Exclude edit box.

The No Comp Ext edit box control is used in conjunction with the Do Not Compress Files with Special Extensions switch. The edit box control is used to designate a list of files having special file extensions that should not be compressed but merely stored in the ZIP archive. If activated, FPZIP makes no attempt to compress the designated file types. Compressed files, such as those having a ZIP, an ARC, or an LZH file extension, generally cannot be compressed further; therefore, it saves significant time to tell FPZIP not to waste time testing whether or not these file types can be compressed.

The Activate check box control, near the right edge of the No Comp Ext edit box, if checked, activates the Do Not Compress Files with Special Extensions switch.

The next control group, identified by the Compression Method group box, is composed of the following radio buttons:

♦ Best Type

♦ Implode Only

♦ Shrink Only

These buttons are used to set or limit the compression methods that FPZIP can use when adding files to a ZIP archive. They are used as follows:

♦ Select the Best Type radio button to enable FPZIP to automatically determine the most efficient compression method to use on a particular file. FPZIP uses the maximum compression method to achieve the smallest member file size. However, in some rare instances, a small file (for example, a one-line or two-line batch file) cannot be effectively compressed by either imploding or shrinking; in that case, the file is simply stored uncompressed.

♦ Select the Implode Only radio button to force exclusive use of the implode method of compression; shrink compression is not used. Files that cannot be compressed by imploding are stored uncompressed.

♦ Select the Shrink Only radio button to force exclusive use of the shrink method of compression; implode compression is not used. Files that cannot be compressed by shrinking are stored uncompressed.

The Implode Factor group box contains a single drop-down list box. It enables the user to set an implosion factor (that is, to optimize implode compression either for speed or maximum compression size). This affects imploding only, not shrinking. The user can select any number on a scale between 0 and 9, where 0 represents the fastest mode but the poorest compression size, and 9 represents the best compression size but the slowest mode. The default is 5.

The next control group, identified by the Default Association group box, is composed of the following radio buttons:

♦ Extract

♦ Test

♦ View

These buttons are used to set the default action for FPZIPX. If FPZIPX is executed without any action switch being specified in its command line, the Default Association is performed on the specified ZIP file.

The remaining group consists of three columns of check box controls. The first column is used to set FlashPoint ZIP (FPZIP.EXE) defaults, the second column sets FlashPoint ZIPX (FPZIPX.EXE) defaults, and the third column sets defaults for both FlashPoint ZIP and ZIPX.

The Recurse Subdirs check box sets the Recurse Subdirectories switch. If checked, FPZIP recurses through an entire directory structure (that is, the specified or current directory and each of its subdirectories or branches), searching for files to add to the ZIP archive.

The Store Recur Dirs check box sets the Store Path Name switch. If checked, both the filename and its relative path are stored in its ZIP file entry.

The Comment ZIP check box sets the Add ZIP File Comment switch. If checked, FPZIP prompts and enables the user to add comments for the ZIP file being created or modified.

The Comment Files check box sets the Add File Member Comments switch. If checked, FPZIP prompts and enables the user to add file comments for each individual member entry within the ZIP file being created or modified.

The Zip Date to Files check box sets the Set ZIP File Date to Latest Entry switch. If checked, the ZIP file's date and time are set to the date and time of its latest, or more recently created or modified, member-file entry.

The Move to archive check box sets the Move to Archive switch. If checked, the original unarchived member files, together with any specified directories (to the extent possible), are deleted after the ZIP file has been successfully created or modified.

The From (mmddyy) check box sets the Compress Files After Specified Date switch. If checked, FPZIP's compression commands only add files created or modified on or after the specified date. The date is entered in the edit box next to the From (mmddyy) check box in month-day-year format.

The Expand Stored Dirs check box sets the Restore Directory Structure switch. If checked, member files are expanded and copied on extraction to their original directories, if any, whose names are stored in the ZIP file; a stored path is rebuilt if it does not exist. Stored paths are relative to the target path. If the path does not exist on the user's system, FPZIPX creates it.

The Overwrite check box sets the Overwrite Exiting Files switch; this switch affects only FPZIPX during processing of the Extract command. If checked, the user prompt, which queries whether or not an existing file should be overwritten by the member file being expanded, is disabled; existing files automatically are overwritten by extracted files that have identical names.

If the Overwrite Existing File switch is not set (that is, the Overwrite box is not checked), a user dialog panel is displayed before a member file is extracted. This dialog panel provides several new extraction options not found in other DOS or Windows ZIP expansion utilities.

If the user selects the Cancel pushbutton, the existing file is not overwritten by the member file being extracted and FPZIPX terminates processing the Extract command.

If the user selects the Yes pushbutton, the existing file is overwritten by the member file being extracted. FPZIPX continues processing the Extract command and continues to prompt before overwriting other existing files.

If the user selects the All pushbutton, the existing file is overwritten by the member file being extracted, and all subsequent prompts to overwrite other existing files are disabled (just as if the Overwrite box had been checked on the Set Options dialog panel). FPZIPX continues processing the Extract command.

If the user selects the Skip pushbutton, the existing file is not overwritten, the member file is not extracted, and FPZIPX continues processing the Extract command.

If the user selects the Rename pushbutton, a dialog panel appears. This dialog panel enables the user to rename the member file to be extracted, thus avoiding overwriting the existing file and still enabling the member file to be extracted; FPZIPX continues processing the Extract command and continues prompting before overwriting other existing files. This avoids the common dilemma presented by other ZIP expansion utilities: either (1) having to terminate the extraction processing, renaming or moving the existing file, and then restarting the extraction process from scratch or (2) overwriting the existing file — a common dilemma for ZIP archives that contain README member files.

The Echo Cmd Line check box sets the Display Module and Command Line switch. If checked, both FPZIP and FPZIPX on execution display the full filespec for the current command module and echo the full command line entered by WIZiper or the user on start-up.

The Auto Close check box sets the Close Window on Completion switch. If checked, after completion of processing, both FPZIP and FPZIPX automatically close the application's main window and terminate.

The Sound Beep check box sets the Sound On switch. If checked, both FPZIP and FPZIPX make an audible beep when certain events occur (for example, when a user prompt or message box is displayed).

The Show Tech Info check box sets the Display Technical Information switch. If checked, both FPZIP and FPZIPX on execution display technical and debugging information during processing of a ZIP file and its members. Generally, this feature is of little use in everyday operations.

The Inform User check box sets the Display General Information switch. If checked, both FPZIP and FPZIPX on execution display general information on its progress and status.

The Warn User check box sets the Display Warning Information switch. If checked, both FPZIP and FPZIPX on execution display user warning information during processing of the ZIP file and its members. Generally, these warnings are not fatal, and the user can elect to continue processing.

The Alert User check box sets the Display Error Information switch. If checked, both FPZIP and FPZIPX on execution display all error information before terminating processing.

The last set of dialog controls consist of four pushbuttons, grouped along the bottom of the Set Options dialog panel. They function as follows:

♦ The OK pushbutton sets WIZiper's options to those selected in the Set Options dialog panel and returns to the main window. The new option settings are in effect only for the current WIZiper session or until the user updates them with the Set Options dialog panel. WIZiper does not save the new settings or update its Windows INI file.

♦ The Save pushbutton sets WIZiper's options to those selected in the Set Options dialog panel, writes them to or updates its Windows INI file, and returns to the main window. The new option settings are in effect, even between sessions, until the user updates them with the Set Options dialog panel.

♦ The Reset pushbutton is used to restore all dialog-panel controls to their last saved state. This forces WIZiper to reread the previous saved settings from its Windows INI file.

♦ The Cancel pushbutton (as well as the Esc key) enables the user to close the Set Options dialog panel without making any changes to the current options (that is, without changing options that were in effect before calling up the Set Options dialog panel).

### File Selection group
The File Selection group contains five user controls:

♦ File Mask edit box

♦ File Mask list box

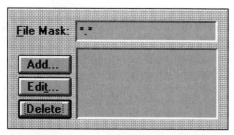

**Use the File Selection group section of the main window to specify the file specifications or parameters you want to use with the Execute command line.**

♦ Add List Item pushbutton

♦ Edit List Item pushbutton

♦ Delete List Item pushbutton

These controls are used to create, modify, or remove user-defined file specifications or parameters appended to the Execute command line. This makes it easier for users to select common filenames, types, or groups to be extracted, added, or otherwise manipulated on a repetitive basis.

Basically, this group's essential function is to add or append any text appearing in the File Mask edit window to the command line appearing in the Execute edit box.

The user can manually enter file specifications into the File Mask edit box or, once the user has configured his or her predefined file types using the Add, Edit, and Delete pushbuttons, can select a descriptive item from the File Mask list box. For example, the user can set up a File Mask list box item called Paintbrush Files which, when selected, inserts *.BMP *.PCX into the File Mask edit box.

To create a new list box item, the user selects the Add pushbutton; to modify an existing list box item, the user first selects (highlights) the list box item to be modified and then selects the Edit pushbutton. Selecting either button displays the Set Mask dialog panel.

The Set Mask dialog panel enables the user to enter a Description to be displayed in the File Mask list box and associated File Patterns that are inserted into the File Mask edit box when the list box item is selected. The file patterns can be full filenames or can include wildcards (? or *). Press the OK pushbutton to save the information to WIZiper's INI file; press the Cancel button to return to the main window without saving the information.

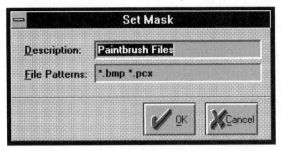

Use the Set Mask dialog panel to add File Mask list box
items that you then can select.

To delete or remove an existing list box item, the user first selects (highlights) the list box item to be removed from the File Mask list box and then selects the Delete pushbutton.

### Execution group

The Execution group contains six user controls:

Execute edit box

OK pushbutton          Executes command in normal window

Min pushbutton         Executes command in iconic window

Max pushbutton         Executes command in maximized window

Cancel pushbutton

Help pushbutton

The Execute edit box displays the actual command line to be executed when the user selects the OK, Max, or Min pushbutton. This edit box is updated each time the user changes any of the other main window controls (for example,

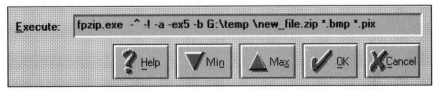

The Execution group shows the actual command to be executed and provides several
options for executing the command.

when the Command drop-down list changes from Add/Replace to Extract). The Execute command line can also be manually edited by the user.

The OK pushbutton control executes the command line application in a standard window.

The Max pushbutton control executes the command line application in a maximized window: full screen.

The Min pushbutton control executes the command line application in a minimized or iconic window: as a desktop icon.

The Help pushbutton control executes the Windows Help application and loads the FPZIP.HLP file. *Note:* At the time of this release, the FPZIP.HLP file was still under development but will be provided to registered users when it is completed.

An additional benefit is provided by the WIZiper's Execution group. WIZiper can function as an application launcher. It can be used to execute any command line or launch any DOS or Windows application, full screen, in a standard window, or as an icon. For this reason, many users will prefer to add WIZiper to their WIN.INI files' LOAD= statements or Program Managers' start-up groups.

## Other user controls

Other main window controls include a Minimize box and the System menu.

### The Minimize box

The Minimize box, in the upper right corner of the title bar, is a graphic box containing a down arrow. When the user clicks the box, the application is reduced or minimized to a desktop icon.

### The System menu

The System menu contains the following user items:

> Restore
> Move
> Minimize
> Close
> Switch To...
> List...
> Options...
> Help...
> About...

A System menu is invoked by one of the following methods:

♦ Clicking on the graphic box containing the dash symbol, located in the upper left corner of the application's noniconic window (to the left of the title bar)

♦ Clicking on the application's icon when minimized

♦ Pressing the Alt+spacebar key combination when the application has the active focus

The first five System menu items are the same as in other Windows applications: Restore resizes the application window to its normal state, Move enables the application to be repositioned on the desktop, Minimize reduces the application to a desktop icon, Close terminates the application, and Switch To displays the Windows Task Manager (or a user-substituted application or utility).

The next three system menu items, List, Options, and Help, perform the same function as the main window pushbuttons identified by the same names. They are duplicated in the System menu to provide access to these functions when the application is minimized as a desktop icon.

The final system menu item, About, invokes the application's About dialog panel.

### The Help system
The Help pushbutton control executes the Windows Help application and loads the FPZIP.HLP file. *Note:* At the time of this release, the FPZIP.HLP file was still under development but will be provided to registered users when it is completed.

### The Registration dialog panel
The Register pushbutton displays the User Registration dialog panel, which enables registered users who have licensed the application to enter their Registered User and Authorization Code information.

When a registered user enters the correct information and selects the Register pushbutton, all start-up, signon, and signoff dialog screens are disabled.

### Order info panels
The Order Info pushbutton provides the user with access to on-line information screens that display basic information on how to order, register, and license FlashPoint Development applications.

More detailed information on licensing FlashPoint Development applications are set forth in this and other documentation provided with the evaluation distribution packages.

# Using Windows Drag-and-Drop Functions

Windows 3.1 introduces a host of new functions to the Windows environment; one of the most notable is its shell drag-and-drop (DND) capabilities. The DND functions are also supported in Windows 3.0 through the use of SHELL.DLL, included in the WIZiper distribution package (and installed by WSETUP if you are running Windows 3.0).

DND enables WIZiper to act as a client for any windows file management shell, such as the Windows File Manager or FlashPoint WinNAV, that supports the

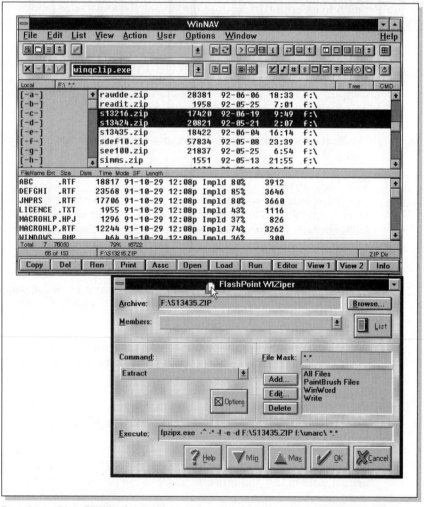

**Dragging multiple ZIP files (notice the mouse pointer) from FlashPoint WinNAV to WIZiper for simultaneous unzipping.**

DND server functions. This enables a user to select a file or group of files in the shell and drag them to and drop them on WIZiper; WIZiper then performs its default Do On Drop action.

# Dropping ZIP files

When a user drops a ZIP file on WIZiper, the main window's File Mask edit box control is set to *.* (the wildcard "all files" file specification), and WIZiper attempts to perform the user's preset, default Do On Drop action, if any. WIZiper assumes that a file having a ZIP file extension is in fact a ZIP archive.

The user can set the default Do On Drop ZIP file action by editing or adding the DoOnDrop= keyword, together with the applicable Keyword Setting number, to the FPZIP.INI file's [WIZ] section. The FPZIP.INI file should be located in your Windows directory.

For example, the user can open the FPZIP.INI file for editing with Windows Notepad and add or edit the following section keyword:

```
[WIZ]
DoOnDrop=5
```

In this example, the keyword DoOnDrop is set to 5. This sets the default drop action to Extract. When the user drops a ZIP file or group of ZIP files on WIZiper, each file is automatically extracted to the current or Set Options Destination directory.

WIZiper supports the following Do On Drop actions and keyword settings:

| DoOnDrop Action | Supports Multiple Files | Keyword Setting |
| --- | --- | --- |
| Add/Replace | NO | 1 |
| Update | NO | 2 |
| Freshen | NO | 3 |
| Extract | YES | 5 |
| Test | YES | 6 |
| View | NO | 7 |

As noted, some Do On Drop actions accept multiple dropped files, and some do not. If the user default function is set to either Extract or Test, and the user drags and drops a group of ZIP archives on WIZiper, multiple instances of FPZIPX are launched — one for each ZIP filename. After each FPZIPX module in the drop group has loaded, WIZiper automatically tiles the Windows desktop to enable the user to monitor each file's processing; this could seem somewhat confusing if you drop 20 or 30 ZIP archives on WIZiper.

## Dropping non-ZIP files

If the user drops any file on WIZiper other than a file ending with the ZIP file extension, the file is treated as a source file to be added to a ZIP archive. Such a file's name is added to WIZiper's main window File Mask edit box control.

In this release, if the user attempts to drop a group of non-ZIP files on WIZiper, only the last filename appears in the File Mask edit box. This may be changed in future releases of WIZiper.

If the user somehow manages to send a Windows drop-file message to WIZiper from an external application, but no files were selected by the external application, WIZiper sets the main window Archive edit box control to the default filename \NEW_FILE.ZIP and the File Mask edit box control to *.* (the wildcard "all files" file specification).

# Using FlashPoint ZIP (FPZIP.EXE) _____

FlashPoint's ZIP for Windows (FPZIP.EXE) is designed to be invoked or launched by other applications, and its functions are controlled by means of command line parameters and switches, similar to the PKWare DOS PKZip utility.

Thus, the application may be invoked by the standard Run or Launch command prompts available in most Windows shells, such as FlashPoint's WinNAV and Windows File Manager, or by more elaborate means, through the use of FlashPoint Development's WIZiper application.

## Command line format

The basic command line format for FPZIP can be broken down as follows:

FPZIP {-*switches*} *zipname* {*filenames*} {-X *filenames*}

The application name (FPZIP.EXE) can be used without the full drive and path specifications if it is on the path; use the full drive and path specifications if it is not on the path.

The –*switches* are either action or option commands. They are always preceded by a minus sign (–) and with one exception are always located in the command line before the *zipfile* name. The exception is the Exclude file switch (–X *filenames*), which always follows the *zipfile* name.

The *zipname* is a filename, including drive and path specifications, for the compressed ZIP file to be created, modified, or operated on. The extension ZIP is added if no file extension is specified.

The *filenames* are generally path or filename specifications for directories and files to be included in or excluded from the ZIP file operation and may include DOS wildcard characters. The Exclude file switch (–X *filenames*) can be considered as a parameter of sorts because it is the last item that appears on the command line for the FPZIP.EXE application.

A more detailed description of the actual command line syntax, parameters, and switches follows.

# Command line parameters and switches

## Syntax

FPZIP {–ADFHLU} {–^!*#CJMOPQRWZ} {–B *path*} {–E{INSX#}} {–T *date*} *zipfile*{.ZIP} {*filenames*} {–X *filenames*}

## Command switches and parameters

Command switches are preceded by a minus sign (–) and can be grouped. These switches can contain a single "action" command and one or more "options," which modify the action to be performed. All command switches for FPZIP precede the ZIP *filename,* with the single exception of the Exclude switch (–X), which should end the command line.

Files are added to the ZIP file if no action command appears on the command line and the user has not modified the Default Action switch in the Setup dialog panel. The action command switches are as follows:

| | |
|---|---|
| –A | Add files (default action). |
| –D | Delete files. |
| –F | Freshen files. |
| –H | Display help. |
| –L | Display about (license information). |
| –U | Update files command. |

The option command switches and parameters are as follows:

| | |
|---|---|
| –^ | Display current module and command line. |
| –* | Display technical information. |
| –! | Display warning and other trivial information (verbose mode). |

| | |
|---|---|
| –# | Optimize compression or speed (where # can be from 0 to 9). |
| –B *path* | Set work path for temporary build files. |
| –C | Add file-member comments. |
| –E{I,N,S,X,#} | Specify extra compression options: |

                –EI     Implode only.

                –EN   Normal or auto (default: FPZIP picks best).

                –ES   Shrink only.

                –EX  Normal or auto (same as N).

                –E#  Optimize compression or speed (where # can be from 0 to 9).

| | |
|---|---|
| –J | Junk/ignore directory names (do not store). |
| –M | Move files. |
| –N | Do not compress files with special extensions. |
| –O | Set ZIP file date to that of latest member entry. |
| –P | Store paths with member names. |
| –Q | Quiet mode. |
| –R | Recurse subdirectories. |
| –T *mmddyy* | Compress files after date *month-day-year*. |
| –W | Automatically close window on completion. |
| –X *filenames* | Exclude listed files. |
| –Z | Add ZIP file comment. |

## Action switch descriptions

### Add files command (–A)

Use the –A option to add files to either a new or existing ZIP file. This is the default action if no other option is specified. Added files overwrite entries in an existing ZIP file if their filenames are identical.

### Delete files command (–D)

Use the –D option to delete entries from a ZIP file.

### Freshen files command (–F)

Use the –F option to replace existing ZIP file entries with newer files having identical filenames. This option does not add files not already in the specified ZIP file.

### Display help (–H)
Use the –H option to display the FlashPoint Help dialog panel.

### Display about license information (–L)
Use the –L option to display information about this application, including version, release date, copyright, address, and license information.

### Update files command (–U)
Use the –U option to add new files to a ZIP file. This option only overwrites an existing entry if a specified file has a more recent date than an existing ZIP file entry.

## Option switch descriptions

### Display module and command line (–^)
Use the –^ option to display the full filespec for the current module and to echo the full command line entered.

### Display technical information (–*)
Use the –* option to display technical and debugging information during processing of the ZIP file and its members; this is the verbose mode and is generally of little use in everyday operations.

### Display warning and other trivial information: verbose mode (–!)
Use the –! option to display user warnings and information about irregularities detected during processing of the ZIP file and its members. Generally, these are not fatal, and the user can elect to continue.

### Optimize compression speed or size (–0 through –9)
Use a number between –0 and –9 to optimize the implode compression speed and size where 0 represents the fastest mode but the poorest compression size and 9 represents the best compression size but the slowest mode. The internal default setting is 5. See also "Specify extra compression options," later in this chapter.

### Alternative path for temporary build files (–B *path*)
Use the –B *path* option to force all temporary files to be created at an alternative location or on an alternative drive.

### Add file-member comments (–C)
Use the –C option to add file comments for individual entries within a ZIP file.

### Specify extra compression options (–E[I,N,S,X,#])
Use the –E{I,N,S,X,#} switches to specify extra or enhanced compression options.

If the Extra Compression switches are omitted, or if –E alone or –EN or –EX (normal or auto) is specified in the command line, FPZIP automatically chooses the best compression method to use. This version uses either the shrink or implode compression method or stores the file — whichever results in the smallest file size. This is the default.

If the –EI compression switch is used, FPZIP only uses the implode compression method or stores the file, whichever results in the smaller file size. When the –EI option is used to force exclusive use of the implode method of compression only, shrink compression is not used. Files that cannot be compressed by imploding are stored uncompressed.

If the –ES compression switch is used, FPZIP only uses the shrink compression method or stores the file, whichever results in the smaller file size. When the –ES option is used to force exclusive use of the shrink method of compression only, implode compression is not used. Files that cannot be compressed by shrinking are stored uncompressed.

The Extra Compression option switch can also include a number from 0 to 9 (for example, –E5 or –EI9 can be used). Also note that the number alone is also acceptable (for example, –5). This permits further optimization of the implode compression method: 0 indicates optimize for speed and not compression size; 9 provides a higher compression at a lower speed. The internal default is 5, which is the same as using –E5 as a switch setting.

### Junk path name: do not store (–J)
Use the –J option to prohibit paths from being stored with the filename in its ZIP file entry.

### Move files (–M)
Use the –M option to move files to a ZIP file. This option first adds a file to the ZIP file and then automatically removes the original or source file.

### Do not compress files with special extensions (–N)
Use the –N option to disable compression of files having certain extensions. These files are stored without compression. The file extensions can be set or modified using the System menu's Setup dialog panel; the default file types are *.ZIP, *.LZH, *.ARC, *.PAK, and *.ZOO. They can also be specified in a DOS environment SET NOCOMP= setting.

### Set ZIP file date to latest member entry (–O)
Use the –O option to set the ZIP file's date and time to the date and time of the latest file entry contained by the ZIP file.

### Store paths with member names (–P)
Use the –P option to store both the filename and its relative path in its ZIP file entry.

### Quiet mode (–Q)

Use the –Q option to force the application to run in a quiet mode. This switch disables most message switches (for example, technical and warning information) and enables the automatic close window switch; therefore, do not follow –Q by any switch that may alter these settings.

### Recurse subdirectories (–R)

Use the –R option to recurse through a directory structure (that is, the specified or current directory and each of its subdirectories or branches).

### Compress files after date (–T *mmddyy*)

Use the –T *mmddyy* option to add only files created or modified on or after the specified date. The date is entered in the *month-day-year* format.

### Automatically close window on completion (–W)

Use the –W option to automatically close the application window on completion of processing.

### Exclude listed files (–X *filename1 filename2...*)

Use the –X *filename1 filename2...* option to exclude the listed file specifications from being added to the ZIP file. This should be the last switch and parameter in the command line.

### Add ZIP file comment (–Z)

Use the –Z option to add a ZIP comment for the ZIP file.

## Parameters

### zipfile{.ZIP}

This parameter identifies the command line location of the full filename specification for the desired ZIP file to be created or modified. The extension ZIP is added if no file extension is specified.

### filename1 filename2...

This parameter identifies the paths or filename specifications of all files to be operated on. Multiple filenames and wildcards are permitted.

All files in a specified directory are processed unless a filename specification is provided to specify a subset of the files within the directory. The filename specification is similar to the standard DOS file expression and can contain wildcards.

Expressions can be used to match multiple members. There are two wildcards that can be substituted for a name or extension:

\*   An asterisk represents a whole word or a group of characters.

?   A question mark represents a single character.

## The Setup dialog panel

Selecting the Setup item from FPZIP's System menu displays the Setup dialog panel. This dialog panel enables the user to select from various groups of controls to set the default switches FPZIP uses if they are omitted from the command line.

The Temp Build File Dir item identifies the default drive and path that Flash-Point ZIP (FPZIP.EXE) uses for the temporary build files needed to create or modify a ZIP archive file. Temporary build files are created when the Add/Replace, Delete, Freshen, or Update command is executed. If the Work Directory is not specified by the user, FPZIP uses the system's current directory for its temporary build files. If FlashPoint ZIP does not have sufficient free work space to create temporary build files, the executed command fails. To select the default Temp Build File Dir, the user types the drive and path spec directly into the edit box.

The Exclude Filespecs edit box control enables the user to designate a list of files or file types to be excluded from the ZIP archive. If activated, the excluded files are not added as members of the ZIP file.

The No Compression Extensions edit box control is used in conjunction with the Do Not Compress Files With Special Extensions switch. The edit box control is used to designate a list of files having special file extensions that should not be compressed but merely stored in the ZIP archive. If activated, FPZIP makes no attempt to compress the designated file types. Compressed files, such as those having a ZIP, ARC, or LZH file extension, generally cannot be compressed further; therefore, it saves significant time to tell FPZIP not to waste time testing whether or not these file types can be compressed.

The On check box control to the right of the No Compression Extensions edit box, if checked, activates the Do Not Compress Files With Special Extensions switch.

The Implode Factor (0 to 9) edit box control enables the user to set an implosion factor (that is, to optimize implode compression either for speed or maximum compression size). This affects imploding only, not shrinking. The user can select any number on a scale between 0 and 9, where 0 represents the fastest mode but the poorest compression size and 9 represents the best compression size but the slowest mode. The default is 5.

The Compression Method group box is composed of the following radio buttons:

♦ Best Type

♦ Implode Only

♦ Shrink Only

These buttons are used to set or limit the compression methods that FPZIP can use when adding files to a ZIP archive. They are used as follows:

♦ Select the Best Type radio button to enable FPZIP to automatically determine the most efficient compression method to use on a particular file. FPZIP uses the maximum compression method to achieve the smallest member file size. However, in some rare instances, a small file (for example, a one-line or two-line batch file) cannot be effectively compressed by either imploding or shrinking; in that case, the file is simply stored uncompressed.

♦ Select the Implode Only radio button to force exclusive use of the implode method of compression; shrink compression is not used. Files that cannot be compressed by imploding are stored uncompressed.

♦ Select the Shrink Only radio button to force exclusive use of the shrink method of compression; implode compression is not used. Files that cannot be compressed by shrinking are stored uncompressed.

The Optional Commands group consists of two columns of check box controls. These controls are used to set various FlashPoint ZIP (FPZIP.EXE) default switches.

The Comment Files check box sets the Add File Member Comments switch. If checked, FPZIP prompts and enables the user to add file comments for each individual member entry within the ZIP file being created or modified.

The Comment ZIP check box sets the Add ZIP File Comment switch. If checked, FPZIP prompts and enables the user to add comments for the ZIP file being created or modified.

The Date to Entry check box sets the Set ZIP File Date to Latest Entry switch. If checked, the ZIP file's date and time are set to the date and time of its latest, or more recently created or modified, member-file entry.

The Auto Close check box sets the Close Window on Completion switch. If checked, on completion of processing, FPZIP automatically closes the application's main window and terminates.

The Recurse Dirs check box sets the Recurse Subdirectories switch. If checked, FPZIP recurses through an entire directory structure (that is, the specified or current directory and each of its subdirectories or branches), searching for files to add to the ZIP archive.

The Store Paths check box sets the Store Path Name switch. If checked, both the filename and its relative path are stored in its ZIP file entry.

The Move to ZIP check box sets the Move to Archive switch. If checked, the original unarchived member files, together with any specified directories (to the extent possible), are deleted after the ZIP file has been successfully created or modified.

The Sound Beep check box sets the Sound On switch. If checked, FPZIP makes an audible beep when certain events occur (for example, when a user prompt or message box is displayed).

The Verbose check box sets the Display Technical Information switch. If checked, FPZIP on execution displays technical and debugging information during processing of a ZIP file and its members. Generally, this feature is of little use in everyday operations.

The Inform User check box sets the Display General Information switch. If checked, FPZIP on execution displays general information on its progress and status.

The Warn User check box sets the Display Warning Information switch. If checked, FPZIP on execution displays user warning information during processing of the ZIP file and its members. Generally, these warnings are not fatal, and the user can elect to continue processing.

The Alert User check box sets the Display Error Information switch. If checked, FPZIP on execution displays all error information before terminating processing.

The last set of dialog controls consists of two pushbuttons, grouped along the bottom of the Setup dialog panel. They function as follows:

♦ The Save pushbutton sets FPZIP's default options to those selected in the Setup dialog panel, writes them to or updates its Windows INI file, and returns to the main window. The new option settings are in effect, even between sessions, until the user later modifies them with the Setup dialog panel.

♦ The Cancel pushbutton (as well as the Esc key) enables the user to close the Setup dialog panel without making any changes to FPZIP's default options (that is, the options that were in effect before calling up the Setup dialog panel remain unchanged).

# Using FlashPoint ZIPX (FPZIPX.EXE)

FlashPoint's ZIPX for Windows (FPZIPX.EXE) is designed to be invoked or launched by other applications, and its functions are controlled by means of command line parameters and switches, similar to the PKWare DOS PKUnzip utility.

Thus, the application can be invoked by the standard Run or Launch command prompts available in most Windows shells, such as FlashPoint's WinNAV and Windows File Manager, or by more elaborate means through the use of FlashPoint Development's WIZiper application.

## Command line format

The basic command line format for FPZIPX can be broken down as follows:

FPZIPX {–switches} zipname {x:\directory} {filenames}

The application name (FPZIPX.EXE) can be used without the full drive and path specifications if it is on the path; use the full drive and path specifications if it is not on the path.

The –switches are either action or option commands. They are always preceded by a minus sign (–) and are always located in the command line before the zipfile name.

The zipname is a filename, including drive and path specifications, for the compressed ZIP file to be created, modified, or operated on. The extension ZIP is assumed if no file extension is specified.

The x:\directory specification, if used, specifies the target directory to which the ZIP file members are to be expanded.

The filenames specification, if used, is generally path or filename specifications to be included in the ZIP file expansion operation.

A more detailed description of the actual command line syntax, parameters, and switches follows.

## Command line parameters and switches

### Syntax
FPZIPX {–EHLTVX} {–^*!DJOW} zipfile{.ZIP} {x:\directory\} {filenames}

## Command switches and parameters

Command switches are preceded by a minus sign (–) and can be grouped. These switches can contain a single action command and one or more options, which modify the action to be performed. All command switches in FPZIPX precede the ZIP *filename*.

ZIP archive file members are extracted if no action command appears on the command line and the user has not modified the Default Action switch in the Setup dialog panel. The action command switches are as follows:

–E    Expand (extract) archive members.

–H    Display help.

–L    Display license information.

–T    Test archive contents for validity.

–V    View (that is, list) archive contents.

–X    Expand (extract) archive members.

The option command switches and parameters are as follows:

–^    Display current module and command line.

–*    Display technical information.

–!    Display warning and other trivial information (verbose mode).

–D    Restore directory structure.

–J    Junk/ignore stored paths; do not re-create stored paths.

–O    Overwrite existing files.

–W    Close window on completion of processing.

## Action switch descriptions

### Expand member files (–E)
Use the –E option to expand a ZIP file or extract the specified members. Same as the –X switch in this release.

### Display help (–H)
Use the –H option to display the FlashPoint Help dialog panel.

### Display license (–L)
Use the –L option to display the FlashPoint license, registration, and information panels.

### Test integrity (–T)
Use the –T option to test the integrity of the ZIP file and its members.

### View member file listing (–V)
Use the –V option to display a listing of the ZIP file members, including descriptive and technical information.

### Expand member files (–X)
Use the –X option to expand a ZIP file or extract the specified members. Same as the –E switch in this release.

## Option switch descriptions

### Display module and command line (–^)
Use the –^ option to display the full filespec for the current module and to echo the full command line entered.

### Display technical information (–*)
Use the –* option to display technical and debugging information during processing of the ZIP file and its members. Generally, this switch is of little use in everyday operations.

### Display warning and other trivial information: verbose mode (–!)
Use the –! option to display user warning information during processing of the ZIP file and its members. Generally, these are not fatal, and the user can elect to continue.

### Restore directory structure (–D)
Use the –D option to expand files to the original directories stored in the ZIP file; a stored path is rebuilt if it does not exist. Stored paths are relative to the target path.

### Junk/ignore stored paths: do not extract (–J)
Use the –J option to ignore any directories stored in the ZIP file. All file members are extracted to the target directory, if designated, or to the current drive.

### Overwrite existing file (–O)
Use the –O option to disable the user prompt that queries whether or not an existing file should be overwritten by the member file being expanded.

If the Overwrite Existing File switch is not used and the INI default settings have not been modified, a user prompt is displayed before a member file is extracted. This dialog box provides several new extraction options not found in other ZIP expansion utilities.

If the user selects the Cancel pushbutton, the existing file is not overwritten by the member file being extracted, and FPZIPX terminates processing the Extract command.

If the user selects the Yes pushbutton, the existing file is overwritten by the member file being extracted. FPZIPX continues processing the Extract command and continues to prompt before overwriting other existing files.

If the user selects the All pushbutton, the existing file is overwritten by the member file being extracted, and all subsequent prompts to overwrite other existing files are disabled (just as if the Overwrite box had been checked on the Set Options dialog panel, which was discussed earlier in the section "Command group"). FPZIPX continues processing the Extract command.

If the user selects the Skip pushbutton, the existing file is not overwritten, the member file is not extracted, and FPZIPX continues processing the Extract command.

If the user selects the Rename pushbutton, a dialog panel is displayed. This dialog panel enables the user to rename the member file to be extracted, thus avoiding overwriting the existing file and still enables the member file to be extracted. FPZIPX continues processing the Extract command and continues to prompt before overwriting other existing files. The Rename option avoids the common dilemma presented by other ZIP expansion utilities of either (1) having to terminate the extraction process, renaming or moving the existing file, and then restarting the extraction process from scratch or (2) overwriting the existing file — a common dilemma for ZIP archives that contain README member files.

### Close window on completion (-W)

Use the -W option to automatically close the application window on completion of processing.

## Parameters

### *zipfile[.ZIP]*

This parameter identifies the command line location of the full filespec for the desired ZIP file to be expanded, tested, or viewed. The ZIP extension is added if no file extension is specified.

### *x:\directory\*

This parameter identifies the target directory where the ZIP file members are to be expanded.

### filename1 filename2...

This parameter identifies the filename specifications of all members within the ZIP file to be operated on; multiple filespecs and wildcards are permitted.

All ZIP file members are processed unless a filename specification is provided to specify a subset of the archive members. The filename specification is similar to the standard DOS file expression and can contain wildcards.

There are two wildcards that can be substituted for a name or extension:

\*     An asterisk represents a whole word or a group of characters.

?     A question mark represents a single character.

# The Setup dialog panel

Selecting the Setup item from the FPZIPX System menu displays the Setup dialog panel. This dialog panel enables the user to select from various groups of controls to set the default switches FPZIPX uses if the switches are omitted from the command line.

The Target Pathspec identifies the default drive and path to which a ZIP file member is expanded when the Extract command is executed. If the Target Pathspec is not specified by the user, the member files are extracted to the

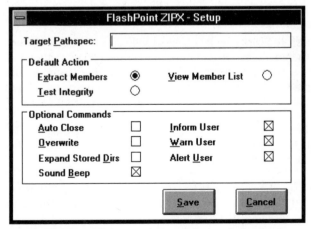

**Use the ZIPX Setup dialog panel to set default switches for the operation of the ZIPX application.**

system's current directory. To select the default Target Pathspec, type the drive and path specification in the Target Pathspec edit box.

The next control group, identified by the Default Action group box, is composed of the following radio buttons:

♦ Extract Members

♦ Test Integrity

♦ View Member List

These buttons are used to set the default action for FPZIPX. If FPZIPX is executed without any action switch being specified in its command line, then the Default Action is performed on the specified ZIP file.

The Optional Commands group consists of two columns of check box controls. These controls are used to set various FlashPoint ZIPX (FPZIPX.EXE) default switches.

The Auto Close check box sets the Close Window on Completion switch. If checked, on completion of processing, FPZIPX automatically closes the application's main window and terminates.

The Overwrite check box sets the Overwrite Exiting Files switch; this switch only affects FPZIPX during processing of the Extract command. If checked, the user prompt (which queries whether or not an existing file should be overwritten by the member file being expanded) is disabled and existing files are automatically overwritten by extracted files that have identical names. See the switch description in "Overwrite existing file (–O)," earlier in this chapter, for more information.

The Expand Stored Dirs check box sets the Restore Directory Structure switch. If checked, member files are expanded and copied on extraction to their original directories, whose names are stored in the ZIP file, if any; a stored path is rebuilt if it does not exist. Stored paths are relative to the target path. If the path does not exist on the user's system, FPZIPX creates it.

The Sound Beep check box sets the Sound On switch. If checked, FPZIPX makes an audible beep when certain events occur (for example, when a user prompt or message box is displayed).

The Inform User check box sets the Display General Information switch. If checked, FPZIPX on execution displays general information on its progress and status.

The Warn User check box sets the Display Warning Information switch. If checked, FPZIPX on execution displays user warning information during processing of the ZIP file and its members. Generally, these warnings are not fatal, and the user can elect to continue processing.

The Alert User check box sets the Display Error Information switch. If checked, FPZIPX on execution displays all error information before terminating processing.

The last set of dialog controls consists of two pushbuttons, grouped along the bottom of the Setup dialog panel. They function as follows:

♦ The Save pushbutton sets FPZIPX's default options to those selected in the Setup dialog panel, writes them to or updates its Windows INI file, and returns to the main window. The new option settings are in effect, even between sessions, until the user later modifies them with the Setup dialog panel.

♦ The Cancel pushbutton (as well as the Esc key) enables the user to close the Setup dialog panel without making any changes to FPZIPX's default options (that is, those options that were in effect before calling up the Setup dialog panel remain unchanged).

# Getting More Help

FlashPoint's ZIP Tools for Windows provides several forms of help for the user.

The most important source of help is the registered Users Guide, which provides the most detailed description of WIZiper, FPZIP, and FPZIPX, and their functions. It consists of more than 70 pages of text and graphics, including a detailed Table of Contents.

The simplest and fastest source of help is provided in FlashPoint ZIP and ZIPX's built-in Flash Card Help dialog panels. Each one provides a sample of the respective application's command line syntax and enables the user to select a topic from a drop-down list box for quick instructions about the usage of a particular command or parameter.

For more detailed on-line information, registered users will be able to invoke the Windows Help application and load the FlashPoint ZIP Tools HLP files. An update disk will be provided to registered users; this disk will contain the FPZIP.HLP file, together with the current version of FlashPoint Developments ZIP Tools for Windows and a complete registered Users Guide (in Windows Write and Word for Windows formats).

# Registered User Support and Feedback

Registered users who contribute will be notified when major updates and new products are available. Anyone wishing to offer advice and suggestions is most welcome to do so.

Those of you who have registered your copy of ZIP/ZIPX, and want to receive an updated copy of the latest shareware version, can always obtain a registered copy by mail; include the current disk fee ($15.00 in the U.S. and Canada, as of the date of this release) to cover materials, and postage and handling costs.

FlashPoint Development is a very small operation that aspires to provide quality Windows software at low prices; therefore, our user support resources are limited. Should you need assistance, we will try our best to help. If you do have a question, a bug report, or suggestions for future versions, please drop us a note and include the following:

♦ A self-addressed stamped envelope (if a reply is required)

♦ The version and software product you are using, which appears on the application's About dialog panel

♦ The versions of DOS and Windows you are using

♦ Your hardware configuration (model, memory size, printer, and so on)

♦ Any Windows or standard DOS applications that you may be running or have loaded under Windows at the time you are running WinNAV

This information will hopefully help us track any problems and suggest reasonable solutions to your problems.

Please address all inquiries and requests to

**Richard S. Patterson**
FlashPoint Development
P.O. Box 270492
Houston, Texas 77277

In addition, I can be reached on The Fox Micro BBS in Houston, Texas, where unregistered copies of the most recent release of FlashPoint applications are first posted. Fox Micro's BBS, in Houston, Texas, can be accessed by calling (713) 859-9105 (Public Node) and (713) 859-9108 (Private Node). Please note that access to the Private Node generally requires payment of a membership fee; information on obtaining membership is available on the Public Node. Those interested in Microsoft Windows may find the Windows conference and file area on this board to be one of the best in the Houston area. Please remember that this is an independent board, not run or operated by anyone affiliated with FlashPoint Development; we are the guests of the systems' operator: Please respect his rules and regulations.

In order to continue to provide quality software at reasonable rates, we generally are unable to return long-distance telephone calls unless you specifically advise us in advance that we may place the call collect.

# How To Register and Get License Applications _

FlashPoint's ZIP Tools for Windows, as with all commercial shareware applications, must be registered and licensed to be used. Simply put, this means that each user must purchase the right to continue using the applications beyond the initial 30-day evaluation period.

## License fees

Current single-user and per-copy license fees (revised October 27, 1992) are as follows:

|  | U.S. | Canada | Overseas |
|---|---|---|---|
| Single-User/Machine/Copy Registration Fee | $49.50 | $49.50 | $49.50 |
| Evaluation Disk Charge | 10.00 | 10.00 | 17.00 |
| Shipping & Handling | 5.00 | 5.00 | 7.00 |
| Purchase Order Proc. Fee | 20.00 | 20.00 | N/A |
| Fee for Non-U.S. Bank Check or Money Order | 15.00 | 15.00 | 25.00 |

## Required deposits — quantity and purchase orders

Purchase orders and quantity orders for single user/copy disk sets generally require a minimum deposit in accordance with the following schedule:

| Quantity | Deposit On P.O. |
|---|---|
| 1 to 9 | 0% |
| 10 or more | 10% |

These charges may not apply to some government agencies and major U.S. corporations; please contact FlashPoint Development to determine whether your agency or corporation qualifies for such deposit waivers.

## Fees and charges are subject to change

Please note that the scheduled rates and charges are current as of the date of this release; however, all fees and charges are subject to change without notice.

# Order Information

## Prepaid (non-credit card) orders

Prepaid orders require advance payment in U.S. funds, by cash, money orders, postal money orders, and personal and business checks subject to clearance of funds. The instrument must be payable to Richard S. Patterson.

For non-credit card, mail-order purchases, enclose the following items in an envelope:

♦ A fully completed copy of the registration or order form that appears at the end of this documentation.

♦ Full payment by cash, check, or money order made payable to Richard S. Patterson. For your own protection, do not send cash through the mail; we will not be responsible for cash that gets "lost."

Address the envelope to

**Richard S. Patterson**
FlashPoint Development
P.O. Box 270492
Houston, Texas 77277

Licensing materials will generally be sent to you on clearance of funds (that is, check or money order or receipt of cash). Media sets are often forwarded separately, depending on whether the disk order is for the current or next release, or whether a new version will be available within 30 days. Please allow two to four weeks for delivery.

# Site license orders

Site license orders must be placed directly with FlashPoint Development and require either (1) advance payment in U.S. funds by cash, money order, postal money order, or check, subject to clearance of funds or (2) purchase orders, together with any required deposit, subject to acceptance or preapproval by FlashPoint Development. All payment by check, money order, or other instrument must be payable to Richard S. Patterson.

For site license orders, enclose the following items in an envelope:

♦ A fully completed copy of the registration or order form that appears in this documentation or in the ORDERFRM.WRI file

♦ Two fully completed and executed copies of the Site License Agreement that appears in this documentation

Also include one of the following:

♦ Full payment by cash, check, or money order made payable to Richard S. Patterson. (For your own protection, do not send cash through the mail; we cannot be responsible for cash that gets "lost.")

♦ A preapproved purchase order, together with any required deposits, which provides for full payment by cash, check, or money order made payable to Richard S. Patterson, of the net balance due, within 30 days of receipt of all software materials.

The envelope must be addressed to

**Richard S. Patterson**
FlashPoint Development
P.O. Box 270492
Houston, Texas 77277

Licensing materials will generally be sent to you on clearance of funds (that is, check or money order or receipt of cash) and acceptance and approval by FlashPoint of the Site License Agreement and any purchase order. Media sets are often forwarded separately, depending on whether the disk order is for the current or next release, or whether a new version will be available within 30 days. Please allow two to four weeks for delivery.

# Credit-card, telephone, fax, and modem orders

FlashPoint Development does not accept orders by phone or credit card; however, several third-party shareware disk vendors are approved to accept registrations and orders for FlashPoint products. Contact your favorite shareware vendor or FlashPoint Development for a vendor in your area or for confirmation of specific vendors' authorization.

Please do not send credit-card orders directly to FlashPoint Development; they will be returned to you. Credit-card companies require that the shareware vendor receive such orders directly from the cardholder.

## Purchase orders and billing

Purchase orders are subject to acceptance and may require an advance deposit on large orders. Generally, purchase orders are rejected for orders of less than nine registrations, even if they are from a major national corporation or governmental agency; we are sorry, but we cannot justify spending hours reading the often cryptic language of multipage purchase orders for relatively small orders or single registrations.

Furthermore, purchase orders are not accepted if they purport to obligate us to your company's terms and conditions, which are contrary to those of our licensing agreements or disclaimer of warranties.

As stated herein, there are no warranties whatsoever associated with the software product and documentation, and FlashPoint Development and its suppliers are not responsible for its performance on a particular system. You are the sole judge of the product's effectiveness and suitability for your particular purposes and are given an opportunity to preevaluate same by using shareware distribution.

To order or register products by purchase orders, enclose the following items in an envelope:

♦ A fully completed copy of the order form that appears in the distribution package

♦ A purchase order stating, in clear and obvious type, the items and number of copies to be registered or purchased, together with your shipping and billing address

♦ Name, address, and phone number of a knowledgeable individual whom we may contact should any question about this order arise

Address the envelope to

**Richard S. Patterson**
FlashPoint Development
P.O. Box 270492
Houston, Texas 77277

# International orders

We recognize the difficulties our international customers face in presenting payment for our products. These difficulties include excessive fees charged for international money orders, postal delays, and currency-conversion problems of various types.

However, we can only accept drafts, checks, international and postal money orders, or travelers' checks payable in U.S. dollars. Drafts drawn on non-U.S. banks require an additional handling charge (Canada $15.00, other International $25.00). You must perform any necessary currency conversions on your end of the transaction and take any necessary steps to eliminate the possibility of the loss of the funds by the postal services.

All checks, drafts, and money orders must be made payable to Richard S. Patterson and *not* to FlashPoint Development.

Please do not pay by American Express or EuroChecks.

Although FlashPoint Development does not accept credit-card orders, registration and disk orders can be paid by credit card, Visa or MasterCard, through authorized U.S. shareware vendors.

It is strongly recommended that international orders be paid by Postal Money Orders because these appear to be honored by most U.S. post offices or by drafts drawn on U.S. banks with preprinted U.S. bank-routing numbers.

An additional charge to cover postal fees and handling is required on all international orders and is included in the scheduled charges section of this manual. All materials will be mailed airmail whenever possible, thus avoiding many unnecessary delays.

# License and Agreements

The following constitutes a legal agreement between you (either an individual or an entity), the end user, and FlashPoint Development. If you do not agree to the terms of this Agreement, promptly destroy or return to FlashPoint Development all copies of the software, any disks or media, and any accompanying items (including written materials or binders and other containers or media).

# FlashPoint Development license agreement

(Evaluation License)

1. **Grant of License.** FlashPoint Development grants you the nontransferable right to make a copy of the accompanying program (the "software"), together with any accompanying documentation ("documentation"), herein referred to as the "software application product," solely for use at one location for evaluation purposes only; the period of evaluation shall not exceed thirty (30) days from the date of its original installation and use. The software and documentation shall not be copied or used for any other purpose. Furthermore, you agree to destroy or erase all unregistered copies of the software and documentation upon the expiration of the thirty (30) day evaluation period or upon request of FlashPoint Development, whichever occurs first. You may not reverse-engineer, decompile, or disassemble the software.

2. **Use and Transfer.** You may not rent, lease, sell, sublicense, outsource, assign, or otherwise transfer this software or documentation. Notwithstanding the foregoing, you may distribute complete unregistered evaluation copies of the original software and documentation to third parties for the sole purpose of evaluation by them, provided such parties shall agree to be bound by the terms of this Agreement. You may not charge more than a minimal fee, not to exceed $10.00, to cover the costs of media, distribution, and handling of evaluation copies of the software and documentation, nor may you distribute same without clearly informing such third parties that the software and documentation are provided for the limited purpose of evaluation in accordance with the terms of this Agreement. Under no circumstances will you use or distribute a portion of the software nor will you use all or part of same in the distribution of other software, without providing a full and complete copy of the original software and documentation package. In the event that you elect to use or distribute the software application product, pursuant to or in violation of the terms of this Agreement, you agree to compensate, indemnify, hold harmless, and defend FlashPoint Development for, from, and against any claims or lawsuits, including attorneys' fees, that arise or result from the use and distribution of the software application product.

3. **Copyright.** The software and documentation are owned by FlashPoint Development or its copyright holders or suppliers and is protected by United States copyright laws and international treaty provisions. Therefore, you must treat the software and documentation like any other copyrighted material (for example, a book or musical recording) except that you may copy the software and documentation as provided in this Agreement.

4. **Disclaimer of Warranty.** THIS SOFTWARE AND DOCUMENTATION ARE PROVIDED "AS IS" WITHOUT WARRANTY OF ANY KIND. FLASHPOINT

DEVELOPMENT FURTHER DISCLAIMS ALL IMPLIED WARRANTIES, INCLUD-
ING, WITHOUT LIMITATION, ANY IMPLIED WARRANTIES OF MERCHANT-
ABILITY, FITNESS FOR A PARTICULAR PURPOSE, OR AGAINST INFRINGE-
MENT. THE ENTIRE RISK ARISING OUT OF USE, DISTRIBUTION, OR
PERFORMANCE OF THE SOFTWARE AND DOCUMENTATION REMAINS WITH
YOU. IN NO EVENT SHALL FLASHPOINT DEVELOPMENT OR ITS SUPPLIERS
BE LIABLE FOR ANY DAMAGES WHATSOEVER (INCLUDING, WITHOUT LIMI-
TATION, DAMAGES FOR LOSS OF BUSINESS PROFITS, BUSINESS INTERRUP-
TION, LOSS OF BUSINESS INFORMATION, OR OTHER PECUNIARY LOSS)
ARISING OUT OF THE USE OF OR INABILITY TO USE THE SOFTWARE OR
DOCUMENTATION, EVEN IF FLASHPOINT DEVELOPMENT HAS BEEN AD-
VISED OF THE POSSIBILITY OF SUCH DAMAGES. BECAUSE SOME STATES
DO NOT ALLOW THE EXCLUSION OR LIMITATION OF LIABILITY FOR CON-
SEQUENTIAL OR INCIDENTAL DAMAGES, THE ABOVE LIMITATION MAY
NOT APPLY TO YOU.

5. **U.S. Government Restricted and Limited Rights.** The software and documentation are provided with *restricted and limited rights.* Use, duplication, or
disclosure by the Government is subject to restrictions and limitations as
set forth in subparagraph (c)(1)(ii) of The Rights in Technical Data and Computer Software clause at DFARS 252.227-7013 of subparagraphs (c)(i) and (2)
of Commercial Computer Software — Restricted Rights at 48 CFR 52.227-19,
as applicable, and under other applicable law. Manufacturer is FlashPoint
Development, P.O. Box 270492, Houston, Texas 77277.

6. **Governing Law.** This Agreement is governed by the laws of the State of
Texas.

Should you have any questions concerning this Agreement, or if you desire to
contact FlashPoint Development for any reason, please write to FlashPoint
Development, P.O. Box 270492, Houston, Texas 77277.

## Order Form

**FlashPoint Development**
Attn: Richard S. Patterson
P.O. Box 270492
Houston, Texas 77277

Checks, money orders, and drafts must be made payable to Richard S.
Patterson.

|  | U.S. | Canada | Overseas | Enclosed |
|---|---|---|---|---|
| Single-User/Machine/Copy Registration Fee | $49.50 | $49.50 | $49.50 | _____ |
| Evaluation Disk Charge | 10.00 | 10.00 | 17.00 | _____ |
| Shipping & Handling | 5.00 | 5.00 | 7.00 | _____ |
| Purchase Order Proc. Fee | 20.00 | 20.00 | N/A | _____ |
| Fee for Non-U.S. Bank Check or Money Order | 15.00 | 15.00 | 25.00 | _____ |

TOTAL PAYMENT DUE (U.S. FUNDS)                                    $ _____

Registered Users' Names and Addresses (attach additional sheets
if necessary):

Purchaser's Name and Shipping Address (Physical and Mailing):

Purchaser's Authorized Representative/Contact Person and Title:

Telephone Number(s) (specify day and evening):

Current Version of Application Registering:

Payment Method: Cash [ ]   Money Order [ ]   Check [ ]   Credit Card [ ]
Purchase Order [ ]   P.O. No. _____

Where or how did you learn of this product: _____

Purchaser acknowledges that purchaser or purchaser's representative has read the
terms and conditions contained in the application's distribution/evaluation package,
as well as the applications About dialog panel, and agrees to be bound thereby and by
any other license agreements contained with any product registered, purchased, or
shipped. Furthermore, as indicated in the application's distribution/evaluation package, purchaser understands the software and documentation are provided "as is" and
without warranty of any kind, either express or implied. Purchaser warrants and
represents that the software and documentation will only be used in accordance with
the aforementioned license agreements.

Printed Name: _____

Signature: _____

Date: _____

# Site License Agreement

For all site license orders, purchaser must include, in addition to the Order Form for FlashPoint ZIP Tools for Windows, two complete and fully executed copies of the Site License Agreement, which follows.

Upon acceptance of the Site License Agreement by FlashPoint Development, a fully executed copy shall be returned to purchaser, together with all software materials and applicable FlashPoint License Agreements.

FlashPoint Development ("Licensor") for good and valuable consideration hereby grants to the following company or organization ("Licensee"), whose name, physical and mailing address are

_____

_____

_____

a site license for the use of _____ copies of ZIP Tools for Windows, subject to the terms and conditions of all applicable FlashPoint License Agreements and amendments thereof, which are delivered with or contained in the software product and incorporated herein by reference.

This is a perpetual license, for the sole use by Licensee, of the above designated FlashPoint software packages; such software is limited to use by the company and its employees at their regular place of business or in the course and scope of their employment. This license is not transferable and is limited to internal use and copying of the software by not more than the number of contracted copies — that is, the maximum users or machines as above indicated. Distribution, repackaging, outsourcing, reverse engineering, decompiling, sublicensing, assignment, leasing, or reselling of the software shall not be permitted under this agreement.

Licensor warrants that it is the sole owner of the software and has full and exclusive power and authority to grant this license.

Licensee hereby acknowledges and agrees that the software and documentation are provided "as is," without warranty of any kind. FlashPoint Development further disclaims all warranties, whether express or implied, including without limitation any implied warranties of merchantability, fitness for a particular purpose or against infringement. The entire risk arising out of use, distribution, or performance of the software and documentation remains with Licensee. In no event shall FlashPoint Development or its suppliers be liable for any damages whatsoever (including,

*continued*

without limitation, damages for loss of business profits, business interruption, loss of business information, loss of data, or other pecuniary loss) arising out of the use of or inability to use the software or documentation, even if FlashPoint Development has been advised of the possibility of such damages. Because some states may not allow the exclusion or limitation of liability for consequential or incidental damages, the above limitation may or may not be applicable. In no event, however, shall Licensor's aggregate liability for damages ever exceed the actual price paid for the license to use the above designated software package, regardless of the form of any claim.

This agreement shall be construed and enforced in accordance with the laws of the State of Texas, and in any action arising under the terms or conditions of this license agreement, jurisdiction and venue shall be proper as to all parties, in any State or Federal court located in Harris County, Texas.

LICENSOR:                              LICENSEE:

FlashPoint Development
P.O. Box 270492                        _____
Houston, Texas 77277                   _____
(713) 660-7240                         _____
                                       _____

By: _____           By: _____

Dated: _____, 199 ___       Dated: _____, 199 ___

# Index

## —A—

Address Manager
  * button, 28, 56
  + (add new address), 29
  - (delete address), 29
  "1 Required", phone information, 50
  About Address, 39
  active list, 57
  ADD file extension, 24
  Add mode, 25
  Add Names to All Addresses dialog box, 25
    More button, 25
  Addresses, 28
  Address Form, 40
  Address Manager About dialog box, 39
  Address Manager Help, F1 keyboard shortcut, 29
  address selection, 26–27
  All Addresses, 39
  All Important Dates, 27, 37
  Anniversary, 25, 32
  Another button, 26, 34
  Area Code Required, phone information, 50–51
  arrow keys, 29, 34, 56
  Association of Shareware Professionals (ASP)
    Ombudsman, 60
  Auto Area Code box, 34
  BACKUP.ADD file, 55
  backup file, 55
  BBS for Registered users, 60
  Best Fit Columns, 35–36, 48
  Cancel button, Found Strings dialog box, 35
  change
    existing forms, 56
    information, 34
  Change button, Edit User List Names..., 38
  color customization, 33
  column width controls, 56
  Commands, 39
  commands
    Alt+i (Dialer! menu), 30
    Alt+V (View menu), 30
    Alt+L (Lists menu), 30
    Alt+E (Edit menu), 30
    Alt+H (Help menu), 30
  Comments, 25, 32
  CompuServe ID, 60
  Control bar, * button, 28
  Control bar, 27–29
  copy name(s)
    to a list, 38
    to other Windows applications, 56–57
  Copy option, Windows Clipboard, 34
  create new field(s), 41
  Create User List..., 37, 51–52
    Add new name, 52
    New button, 52
  customize, 23–24
  Custom View Form Designer, 40–42
  Custom View Forms, 40–42
    Delete button, Modify/Delete edit box, 34
  delete field(s), 41–42
  Delete from User List..., 38–39, 52
  Delete Highlighted Names, 35, 38, 52

Delete key, 29
delete name(s)
  data file, 34–35
  User List, 35, 38–39, 52
delete selected address, - keyboard shortcut, 29
Delete User List..., 37
Design Custom View Forms..., 40–42
Dialer, 31
  *See also* Address Manager, Smart Dialer
    Settings...
Dialer! menu, 36
  Alt+i key command, 30
  Dialer button, 36
  Phone # edit box, 36
Disable Label Warning, 47–48
disclaimer, 58
Display Phone, 49
distance between labels in chars, print layout,
  43
Dot-Matrix Labels
  Avery, 42
  Disable Label Warning, 47–48, 53
  non-Avery, 42–43
  printing, 32, 42
Down arrow key, 29, 34
Edit Box
  Add Names to All Addresses, 25
  Modify/Delete, 27
Edit menu
  Add option, 34
  Alt+E key command, 30
  Copy option, 34
  Delete Highlighted Names, 35, 38, 52
  Modify/Delete edit box, 34
  Save Heading Columns, 35, 37
  Search..., 35
  Set Address Form..., 34
Edit/Modify dialog box, 40
Edit User List Names..., 38
  Change button, 38
Envelope(s)
  change format, 47
  Copies, 47
  feeder support, 47
  font information support, 46
  HP LaserJet III, 57
  Laser printing, 46–47
  name selection, 47
  Next button, 47
  Print All button, 46
  printing, 33, 42
  Print this One button, 46
  Return Address Info box, 46
  Send to Address Info box, 46
  Set Fonts..., 46
  sizes, 46
European Forms, 42
Exit
  Quit Address Manager, 34
  Smart Dialer Settings..., 50–51
export, 24
  names to other Windows applications, 56–57
Export..., 31
F1 keyboard shortcut, Address Manager Help, 29
F5 keyboard shortcut, invoke telephone Dialer,
  29, 36

F6 keyboard shortcut, select all names, 29
field
  create new, 41
  delete, 41–42
  names, 41
  position, 42
  sizes, 54
  text, 41
file extension, ADD, 24
file management, 55
File menu
  Alt+F key command, 30
  Colors, 33
  Design Custom View Forms..., 40
  Disable Label Warning, 47–48
  Export..., 31
  Fonts, 33
  Import..., 31
  Load Form..., 40
  Merge, 30–31
  New, 24, 30
  Open, 24, 30
  Print Laser Labels..., 44
  Print options, 32–33
  Quit, 34
  Save As..., 30
  Settings..., 31
  Smart Dialer Settings..., 31
  Windows Printer Setup..., 31
file name, valid, 24
filenames, 49
Filter mode, * button, 56
Filter mode, 27–28
Fonts, 33
forms
  create custom, 40
  existing, 40
Found Strings dialog box, 35
Full Book, phone number display type, 36
Full Book mode, 27, 35–7
Group 1, 39
Group 2, 39
guarantee, 90-day money back, 65
Help on Help, Microsoft Windows Index to Using
  Help, 39
Help menu
  About Address, 39
  Alt+H key command, 30
  Commands, 39
  Help on Help, 39
  Index, 39
  Keyboard, 39
  Overview, 39
Her Birthday, 25, 32
His Birthday, 25, 32
HP LaserJet III, 57
import, 24
  data, 53
  file format, 53
  Input File specifications, 54
Import..., 31
Index, on-line help, 39
Input File Specifications, 54
InsertAddress macro, 26
insertion, local area code, 34
Insert key, 29

Keyboard, 39
label(s), 42–43
  sizes, 55
Labels Across, printing, 42
Language box
  English, 49
  other than English, 49–50
languages, 23
Laser Label configuration screen, 44
Laser Labels, 32
  Avery, 44–45
  font selection, 44–45
  margin settings, 45
  non-Avery, 45
  START label, 44
Laser Label Settings dialog box, 44–45
layout control, 42
lettered buttons, 27–28
licensing agreement, 60–61
limited license, 61
Lines Between Labels, print layout, 43
Lines Per Label, print layout, 42
list limits, 23
List option, 28
Lists menu
  Add to User List..., 52
  All Addresses, 39
  Alt+L key command, 30
  Create User List..., 37, 51–52
  Delete from User List..., 38–39
  Delete User List..., 37
  Edit User List Names..., 38
  Group 1, 39
  Group 2, 39
Load Form..., 40
Local Area Code, 48
local area code insertion, 34
MACRO2.DOC file, 26
MACRO.DOC file, 26
margin settings
  Dot Matrix Labels, 43
  Laser Labels, 45
Menu command key combinations
  Alt+i (Dialer!), 30
  Alt+V (View), 30
  Alt+L (Lists), 30
  Alt+E (Edit), 30
  Alt+F (File), 30
  Alt+H (Help), 30
Merge, 30–31
Microsoft Windows Index to Using Help, 39
Mode, 28
Modem Settings
  initialization string selection, 49
  Prefix, 49
modify address, 27
Modify/Delete dialog box, 27
Modify/Delete edit box
  Delete button, 34
  Next button, 34
  Prev button, 34
More button, 25
move name(s) to another list, 52, 54
multiple labels for same name, printing, 43
New button, Create User List..., 51–52
New file, 24, 30
Next button
  Envelope(s), 47
  Modify/Delete edit box, 34
OK button
  Add option, 34
  Set Fonts..., 46
Open, 24, 30
Order Form, 64
Overview, 39
Page Mode, 27–29
  * button, 56

Phone # edit box, 36
phone information
  "1 Required", 50
  Area Code Required, 50–51
  entries, 51
  number display type, 36
  Wild Characters, 50–51
Prev button, Modify/Delete edit box, 34
print
  all names, 43
  Disable Label Warning, 47–48
  Distance between labels in chars, 43
  Dot-Matrix labels (Avery), 42
  Dot-Matrix labels (non-Avery), 42–43
  envelopes, 46–47
  F6 keyboard shortcut, 43
  fields, 42
  font selection, 54
  formatting for Laser labels, 55
  Labels Across, 42
  Laser-Printer labels, 44–45
  Lines Between Labels, 43
  Lines Per label, 42
  multiple labels for same name, 43
  options, 23
  Print All button (Envelopes), 46
  Print Double Column, 33
  Print Envelope dialog box/Save Changes, 47
  Print List, 32
  Print Preview, 32
  Print Single Column, 33
  Print this One button (Envelopes), 46
  selected names only, 43
  START label, 44
  Width of label in chars, 43
printer
  dot-matrix labels warning, 53
  driver, 31
Quick Look mode, 27, 35, 37
Quit, 34
recall last 3 entries, 34
registration, 22, 57, 65
Reminder information manager, 25
remove names from User list, 30, 35, 39, 52
Return Address Info box, 46
Rolodex Cards, 32
Save, Smart Dialer Settings..., 50–51
Save As..., 30
Save Changes, Print Envelope dialog box, 47
Save Heading Columns, 35, 37
saving data, 53, 55
search, 24
  parameters, 35
Search..., 35
  Cancel button, 35
  exiting Found Strings dialog box, 35
Send to Address Info box, 46
Set Address Form..., 34
Set Fonts...
  Envelope(s), 46
  OK button, 46
Settings..., 31
  Best Fit Columns, 35–36, 48
  Display Phone, 49
  Language box, 49–50
  Local Area Code, 48
  Modem Settings, 49
  phone number display type, 36
  Show Last Name First, 48
shipping charges, 58
Show Last Name First, 48
similar shareware, 22
Smart Dialer Settings..., 31
  "1 Required" option, 50
  3 digit prefixes, 50
  Exit, 50–51
  Save, 50–51
  Wild Characters option, 50

sort, 24
Sort By mode
  City, 29, 37
  First Name, Last Name, 29, 37
  Last Name, First Name, 29, 37
  State, 29, 37
  ZIP Code, 29, 37
START label, 44
status bar, 27–28, 56
  list type on screen, 52
STRINGS.USA file, 49
system requirements, 22
technical support, 22, 60, 65
Telephone Dialer, 24
To Reminder button, 25–26
U.S. Government Restricted Rights, 62
unlicensed copies, 57
Up arrow key, 29, 34
updates, 58–59
User-Defined Lists, 51–52
User List, add existing name, 52
View Form, 34, 56
View menu
  Add to User List, 38
  All Important Dates, 27, 37
  Alt+V key command, 30
  Full Book, 27, 36
  Quick Look, 27, 37
  Sort By, 29, 37
view options, 24
warranty, limited, 62
width of label in chars, print layout, 43
Wild Characters, 50
  phone information, 51
Wilson WindowWare, 22–65
Windows Clipboard, copy information to, 34
Windows Control Panel, printer driver activation, 31
Windows Printer Setup..., 31
Windows Print Manager, 53
WordBASIC macros, 26
Word for Windows 1.x, 26
Word for Windows, 2.0, 26
adventure game, 214–221
alarm clock/scheduler, 444–461
Applet
  cautions, 69
  Control Panel extension files, 68
  Control Panel files, Windows, 68
  CPL file extension, 68
  CPWIN386.CPL file, 68
  DRIVERS.CPL file, 68
  File New, 68
  icon, Program Manager, 68
  MAIN.CPL file, 68
  multiple
    applets, 69
    copies of a single, 69
  Program Manager run command line, 68
  SND.CPL file, 68
  Windows Control Panel
    multiple applets, 69
    multiple copies of a single, 69
application launcher utility, 66, 68–69, 72
ASP Ombudsman. See Association of Shareware
    Professionals (ASP) Ombudsman
ASP. See Association of Shareware Professionals
    (ASP)
Association of Shareware Professionals (ASP)
  General License Agreement, 13
  Money Smith, 2.0, 334
  *Windows GIZMOS*, 12–13
  WinEZ, 3.0, 473
Association of Shareware Professionals (ASP)
    Ombudsman
  Address Manager, 60
  Jewel Thief, 220

*Windows GIZMOS*, 12–13
ZiPaper, 1.3c, 507
Autodesk Animator Player for Windows, µLathe
   (MicroLathe v. 1.5.1), 265

# —B—

Baker, Daniel S., µLathe (MicroLathe v. 1.5.1),
   260–272
Barry Press, Barry Press Utilities, 66–89
Barry Press Utilities
   After Dark, 67
   Applet. *See* Applet
   CalPop. *See* CalPop
   disclaimer, 68, 89
   Flipper. *See* Flipper
   Holder for Windows. *See* Holder for Windows
   installation, 67
   license agreement, 88
   Match. *See* Match
   PATH=statement, AUTOEXEC.BAT file, 67
   registration, 66, 88
      form, 88
   Runner. *See* Runner
   similar shareware, 66
   source code, 89
   system requirements, 66
   technical support, 66
   Time. *See* Time
   updates, 88
   *Windows 3.1 SECRETS*, ClockMan, 18, 66
Berkland Software, Checkers, 90–95

# —C—

calculator, 204–213
calendar, utilities, 66, 69–70
CalPop
   display, 69
   limits, year, 69
   month, 69
   running several windows at once, 70
   scroll bar
      arrow buttons, 69
      ranges, 69
   scroll-bar thumb, 70
   user interface, 70
   year, 69–70
card game, 190–197, 486–495
Checkers
   Berkland Software, 90–95
   captures, 93
   capturing move, 92
   contributions, 95
   crowning, 92
   game pieces, 91
   keyboard instructions, 93
   Level menu
      Beginner, 94
      Expert, 94
      Intermedite, 94
      Master, 94
      Novice, 94
   mouse instructions, 93
   moves, 91–92
   noncapturing move, 92
   player identification, 90
   players, 91
   registrations, 90
   rules, 91
   Setup menu
      AutoPlay, 94
      One Player, 94
      Player is Black, 94
         Player is Red, 94
      Switch Sides, 94
      Two Players, 94
   source code, 95
   system requirements, 90
   technical support, 90
   Thatcher, Gregory, Berkland Software, 90
   turn sequence, 93
ClipMate
   ? button, Brief layout, 115
   About box, 102
   About button, 115
   About dialog box, 115
   accelerator keys
      Backspace (delete character to left of
         insertion point), 103
      Ctrl+F (Find), 102
      Ctrl+N (Find Next), 102
      Ctrl+P (Print), 106
      Delete (delete character to right of insertion
         point), 103
      Windows 3.0 Ctrl+Insert (copy selected text to
         Clipboard), 103
      Windows 3.0 Shift+Delete (cut to Clipboard),
         103
      Windows 3.0 Shift+Insert (Paste selected text
         from Clipboard to active window), 103
      Windows 3.1 Ctrl+V (Paste selected text from
         Clipboard to active window), 104
      Windows 3.1 Ctrl+X (Cut selected text to
         Clipboard), 104
      Windows 3.1 Ctrl+C (Copy selected text to
         Clipboard), 104
   Active List
      Activate Recyclable List button, 109, 117
      Activate Safe List button, 109, 117
   Always Save, 113
   Auto Glue method, 107
   Auto Glue mode
      exiting, 107
      Magnify window, 107
   Backspace key, delete character to left of
      insertion point, 103
   blank text window, 111
   bonus programs, registration, 122
   Brief Layout, 100–102
      ? button, 115
   Browse button, 103
   bug reports, 119
   CFG (Configuration) button, 101, 112–113
   change
      GlueDelayTime, 119
      Memory heap threshold, 119
      Timer limit, 119
   checked buttons, 99
   Clipboard contents
      current, 104
      multiple formats, 111
   Clipboard data
      CLM file customized, 98
      DEFAULT.CLM, 98
   Clip Item(s), 98–99
      append together, 107
      Config screen, 105
      edit, 102
      size, 105, 114
      storage, 113
   Clip Item Lists, 104
      Active List, 105
      Clipboard, 110–111
      delete obsolete items, 105
      item size, 105
      list maintenance, 105
      placement of items, 105
      Recyclable List, 105, 110
      Safe List, 105
   Clip Item Selection List, update, 103
   Clip Item Selection List Box, 99, 102, 109–110
      arrow keys, 110
      Magnify window, 110
   Clip Item Title, 105
   CLIPMATE.EXE file, 120
   CLIPMATE.HLP file, 120
   CLIPMATE.INI file, 98, 118–120
      ClipMate Settings, 112
   CLMICONS.DLL file, 120
   CLMREAD.TXT file, 120
   CLMREG.TXT file, 120
   CompuServe ID, 119, 121
   Config dialog box, 101–102, 112–115
   Config menu, 101, 112–113
   Configuration (CFG) button, 101, 112–113
   Control menu, Exit, 116
   Copy from Magnify Window, 104
   Copy to Clipboard
      Windows 3.0, Ctrl+Insert, 103–104
      Windows 3.1, Ctrl+C, 104
   Copy to Safe List, 117
      Multiple Selection, 112
      button, 108
   Ctrl+F, Find, 102
   Ctrl+N, Find Next, 102
   Ctrl+X (Windows 3.1), Cut selected text to
      Clipboard, 104
   Cut to Clipboard
      Windows 3.0, Shift+Delete, 103
      Windows 3.1, Ctrl+X, 104
   delete
      ClipMate, 120–121
      Delete key, 103
   Delete
      button, 106
      Item, 117
      Multiple Selection, 112
   disclaimer, 123
   edit, text, 103
   Edit menu
      Copy to Safe List, 117
      Delete Item, 117
      Edit Title, 103, 117
      Glue, 117
      Glue Together, 107–108
   Edit Title, 103, 117
   Exit
      Auto Glue, 107
      save changes, 116–117
   FILE_ID.DIZ file, 120
   File menu, 102
      Exit, 116–117
      New, 116
      Open, 116
      Print Item(s), 116
      Print Setup, 106, 116
      Save, 116
      Save As, 116
   filenames, 97–98, 118, 120
      customized, 97–98
      default, 97
   Find
      Ctrl+F (Brief Layout), 102
      View menu, 118
   Find Next
      Ctrl+N (Brief Layout), 102
      View menu, 118
   float window to top, 114
   Flow Paragraph, 102–103
   Full Layout, 100–101
   Full Layout, 101, 113, 115
   Glue
      Edit menu, 117
      Multiple Selection, 107, 112
   Glue button
      Auto Glue method, 107
      Manual Glue method, 107

Glue Together, Edit menu, 107–108
Gluing, 99
grayed buttons, 99
hardware requirements, 96
help, on-line, 115
Help About menu, About button, 115
Help button, 103
hot keys. *See* ClipMate, accelerator keys
installation, 97
Keep Window On Top option, 101
keyboard shortcuts. *See* ClipMate, accelerator keys
layout selection, 101
license agreement, 123
Magnify
  View menu, 117
  button, 108
Magnify Window, 99, 102, 110
  close, 103
  copying from, 104
  display, 102
  open, 102
Make Title button, 103
Manual Glue method, 107–108
Manual Glue mode, Multiple Selection, 108
MDIBALL.EXE file, bonus program, 122
MS button, 111
Multiple Selection
  Copy to Safe List, 112
  Delete, 112
  Glue, 112
  Glue mode, 107–108
  Manual Glue mode, 108
  Print, 112
Multiple Selection List dialog box, 111
  Confirmation List button, 111–112
  exiting, 111
  Selection List, 111–112
New, 116
Norton Desktop for Windows, 119
on-line help, 115
Open, 116
PALDEMO.EXE file, bonus program, 122
Paste from Clipboard to active window
  Windows 3.0, Shift+Insert, 103
  Windows 3.1, Ctrl+V, 104
pressed button, 102
Print
  button (Ctrl+P), 106
  Item(s), 116
  Multiple Selection, 112
  Setup, 106, 116
printer support, 106
  3270 emulation, 106
Recyclable button/Safe button, 109
Recyclable List
  Config dialog box, 113
  Copy to Safe List button, 108
  length limits, 114
Registration, 96, 115, 121
  bonus programs, 122
registration methods
  CLMREG.TXT file, 123
  CompuServe ID, 125
  foreign, 124
  order direct, 123–124
  Software Excitement!, 125–126
removal of ClipMate, 120–121
Safe button/Recyclable button, 109
Safe List, 98
  Config dialog box, 113
Save, 116
Save As, 116
similar shareware, 96
start up program, 97
Survey, User, 122, 126
system requirements, 96

technical support, 96, 121
Thornton Software Solutions, 96–127
title
  creation, 99
  display, 99
  edit, 102
  Glue Finished, 107
  Glue In Process, 107
user
  input, 119
  manual, 121
User Survey, 122, 126
VENDOR.DOC file, 120
View menu
  Activate Recyclable List, 109, 117
  Activate Safe List, 109
  Find (Ctrl+F), 118
  Find Next (Ctrl+N), 118
  Magnify, 108, 117
visual components, 100
Windows StartUp group, 97
WIN.INI statement, 96
Wrap Text check box button, 103
Code Breaker
  CBREAK2.ICO file, 131
  CBREAK.C file, 131
  CBREAK.DEF file, 131
  CBREAK.H file, 131
  CBREAK.ICO file, 131
  CBREAK.RC file, 131
  clues, 129
  coauthor, 131
  Did I get it right? button, 129
  EGA monitor appearance, 130
  filenames, 131
  freeware, 128
  future enhancements, 131
  game, Kenneth Fogel's Code Breaker, 130
  goal, 129
  guess buttons, 129–131
  Haden, Charles W., 128–131
  Help menu, 130
  menu structure, 130
  number buttons, 129–131
  original author, 131
  source code, 128
  system requirements, 128
  technical support, 128
command line processor, utilities, 148
Control Panel dialog box, utilities, 66
Copyrighted, definition, 217
CPU processing timer, utility, 436
Crippleware, definition, 11

## —D—

database
  Address Manager, 22–65
  genealogy, 338–347
  recipe file management, 385–395
DataGem Corp, WinKey, 1.0, 476–485
DC.EXE. *See* Disk Copy for Windows
definition
  Copyrighted, 9, 217
  Crippleware, 11
  Freeware, 9
  Public domain, 9, 217
  rolling demo, 11
  Shareware, 9–11, 217–218
Denan Systems, File Garbage Can for Windows, 166–171
DIRNOTES.COM DOS utility
  CompuServe GO ZIFNET, 133
  ZIP Tools for Windows, 133

DirNotes for Windows (WDN.EXE-v. 1.2)
  About, File menu, 135
  Beirne, Pat, Corel Systems Corp, 132–137
  command sequence, 134–135
  comment modification, 135
  Copy (Ctrllns), Edit menu, 135
  Cut (ShftDel), Edit menu, 135
  Directory list box, spacebar action=double click, 135
  DIRNOTES.COM DOS utility, 133
  edit box, scroll keys, 135
  Edit menu
    Copy (Ctrllns), 135
    Cut (ShftDel), 135
    Paste (Shftlns), 135
    Undo (AltBkSp) last edit, 135
  Exit/Update, File menu, 135
  File menu
    About, 135
    Exit/Update, 135
    Quit/NoUpdate, 135
  filename conventions, 134
  freeware, 133
  Paste (Shftlns), Edit menu, 135
  Quit/NoUpdate, Edit menu, 135
  source, CopyComments, 137
  source code
    filenames, 136
    FillListBox, 137
    Main WndProc, 136
    NewDir, 137
    Start-up, 136
    Wakeup, 136
  system requirements, 133
  Undo (AltBkSp) last edit, Edit menu, 135
  update markers, 134–135
  Windows 3.1, drag and drop, 132
  Windows GIZMOS], 132–137
Disk Copy for Windows (DC.EXE)
  ? pointer (cursor shape), Shift+F1, 143
  Abort menu item, configuration dialog box, 143
  always, /a, 139
  AUTOEXEC.BAT file, 143
  Cancel button, configuration dialog box, 142
  command line syntax, 139
  disclaimer, 146
  Disk Copy dialog box, DC.EXE command without parameters, 140–141
  DOS Errorlevel values, exiting, 140
  execute, /e, 139
  Execute button, configuration dialog box, 142
  F1, Help Index, 143
  Format Always, configuration dialog box, 142
  Format If Needed
    /f, 139
    configuration dialog box, 142
  Format Never, configuration dialog box, 142
  Help Index, F1, 143
  icon, /i, 139
  Icon, configuration dialog box, 141
  icon style value, /0 or /1, 139
  installation
    Disk Copy Program Group in C:\DISKCOPY\DC.GROUP, 143–144
    Disk Copy Program Group not in C:\DISKCOPY\DC.GRP, 144–145
  keyboard shortcuts
    F1 (Help Index if Help Window closed), 143
    F1 (Using Windows Help if Help window open), 143
    Shift+F1 (? pointer), 143
  license agreement, 146
  multiple drives, 143
  never format, /n, 139
  nonverbose, /v, 139
  Number of copies option, +number, 139
  OK button, configuration dialog box, 142

Options
/0 or /1 (icon style value), 139
always (/a), 139
execute (/e), 139
format if needed (/f), 139
icon (/i), 139
never format (/n), 139
nonverbose (/v), 139
number of copies (+number), 139
pause (/p), 139
Pause (/P), 139
verbose (/V), 139
verify readable (/r), 139
Options menu, configuration dialog box, 141
pause, /p, 139
Pause,
/P, 139
configuration dialog box, 141
Registration, 138, 145
system requirements, 138
technical support, 138
temporary file location, 143
Terratech, 138–147
unregistered limitations, 145
verbose, /V, 139
Verbose, configuration dialog box, 141
Verify, configuration dialog box, 142
verify readable, /r, 139
WinBatch, 140
DOS Shareware
Match. See Match
Runner. See Runner
DOS utility
starting up Windows, 496
Windows wallpaper, 498–508

**—E—**

Exclaim (!.EXE)
!.DOC file, 151
!.EXE file, 151
!.FRM file, 151
!.HLP file, 151
! icon, 150
!.INI file, 154
!.LST file, 151
ATTRIB command syntax, 156
batch file window, 155
CALL command syntax, 157
CDD command syntax, 157
COLOR command syntax, 158
command documentation, DOS manual, 148
command history
Ctrl+X (scroll down one command), 154
Ctrl+E (scroll up one command), 154
command priority, 155
delete Exclaim, 151
disclaimer, 163–164
DISPLAY command syntax, 158–159
DOS manual, command documentation, 148
DOS session, separate, 155
DOS symbol support, 156
ECHO command syntax, 159
Exclaim window, 149
external applications, 154–155
filename, 151
File Run, Program Manager, 148
history keys, Quick Reference Card, 153
IF [condition] THEN ... ENDIF command syntax, 159–160
installation
Exclaim Files, 151
WSETUP file, 150
key combinations, Quick Reference Card, 153
license agreement, 164

MOVE command syntax, 160
Order form, 163–164
PROFILE command syntax, 160
PROMPT command syntax, 161
Quick Reference Card
Commands, 151–153
history keys, 153
key combinations, 153
Registration, 149, 162–163
remove Exclaim, 151
RENAME command syntax, 161
REN command syntax, 161
RETURN command syntax, 162
similar shareware, 149
start
! icon, 150
File Run, 150
StartUp group, 148
system requirements, 149
TASK command syntax, 162
technical support, 149
uninstall Exclaim, 151
virus protection, 156
WIN.INI file, 148
LOAD= line, 148
WordStar diamond keys, 154
customizing, 154

**—F—**

Feinleib, David A.
DOS utility
DlFile (with DirSrch), 459
DskNum, 459
Mem, 460
ShowDirs, 459
IconCalc, 204–213, 458
ordering information, 460
WinClock, 3.21, 444–461
Windows 3.1 utility
ChCursor, 459
Click, 459
Hop, 459
Lock, 459
Magic Squares, 459
Mem, 458
Pos, 458
PrintSwitch, 458
RunProg, 458
SaveSet, 459
Slide, 459
file
compression for Windows, 510–566
decompression for Windows, 510–566
deletion utility, 166–171
manager, 132–137
File Garbage Can for Windows
Command Line Options
Confirm Delete off (-C), 169
Secure Delete off (-S), 169
Start program as an icon (-I), 169
CompuServe ID, 169
Confirm Delete
off (-C), 169
Options menu, 168
Denan Systems, 166
disclaimer, 169
file recovery, 168
Fischer, Dennis, 166
OK button
Ave Atque Vale, 166
Finem Respice, 166
Options menu
Confirm Delete, 168
Secure Delete, 168

Order Form, 170
Registration, 167
Secure Delete
off (-S), 169
Options menu, 168
security guarantee, 168
similar shareware, 167
Start program as an icon, -I, 169
system requirements, 167
technical support, 167
user input, 169
Windows 3.0, GARBAGE0.EXE file, 166
Windows 3.1, GARBAGE1.EXE file, 166
*Windows 3.1 SECRETS*, Trash Can for Windows, 167
File Run, utilities, 66
financial management, personal finance, 284–336
Fischer, Dennis, File Garbage Can, 166–169
FlashPoint Development
Patterson, Richard S., 510–566
ZIP Tools for Windows, 510–566
FlashPoint WinNAV, 513
FlashPoint WIZiper. See WIZiper; ZIP Tools for Windows
FlashPoint ZIP. See ZIP; ZIP Tools for Windows
FlashPoint ZIPX. See ZIP Tools for Windows; ZIPX
Flipper
icon, 70–71
Lessa, Michael, 71
Montgomery, Peter, 71
operating, 70
Portland (PORTRAIT.EXE and LANDSCAP.EXE), 71
question-mark icon, 70
UNIDRV.DLL Universal Printer Driver technology, 70
Windows, 3.0, 70
freeware
Code Breaker, 128–131
definition, 9
DirNotes for Windows (WDN.EXE-v. 1.2), 132–137
GNU General Public License, 198, 203
Hyperoid v., 1.1, 198–203
Super Resource Monitor (SUPERRM.EXE 1.2), 428–435
UARTMON.EXE (1.2), 396–399
Widget, 1.1, 437
WinStart, 1.1, 496–497

**—G—**

games
adventure, 214–221
board, 90–95
card, 190–197, 486–495
memory, 128–131
skill
arcade, 198–203
driving, 274–283
genealogy database, 338–347
General License Agreement, Association of Shareware Professionals (ASP), 13
graphics
image cataloger, 348–383
modeling tool, 260–272
graphing, 222–232
group windows customization utility, 172–189
GrpIcon 2.0 (GRPICON.EXE)
About Inner-City Software, 183–184
acknowledgments, 186
Add to Custom Colors button, 180
Assign Icon to Group dialog box, 177
Background Colors, 188
Color/Solid box, Set color, 180
creators, 185
Custom Colors, 188
Custom Colors Box, 180

demonstration mode, 182
dialog controls, *Windows User's Guide*, 174
disclaimer, 188
fonts, Group Properties menu, 174
GO button, 175
Group icon, 188
Group icon customization, 175–177
Group Properties, 188
Group Properties menu
  About GrpIcon, 176
  background colors, 179–180
  fonts, 174
  icon size, 175
  Select Set Icon, 176
  Set Color, 176, 179–180
  Set Icon, 176
  Set Wallpaper, 176, 178–179
Group Properties Menu Fonts, 189
Group Properties Menu Icon Size, 189
Group Properties... option, 175–182
Help button, 175
Icon Library, 189
icon size, Group Properties menu, 175
Icon Viewer, 189
icon visibility, 174
Inner-City Icon Library, 181–182
  ICSICON.EXE file, 177
Inner-City Software, 172, 182
  other products, 184
licensing agreement, 187–188
modify option, About GrpIcon, 174
on-line Help, 175
operating mode, 182
Registration, 172, 182–183
registration, form, 183
Registration button, 175
Reset, 189
saving changes, 177
search for other icons, 177
Set Color, 189
  Add to Custom Colors button, 180
  Color/Solid box, 180
Set Icon, 189
Set Wallpaper, 189
Set Wallpaper... option, 178–179
start GrpIcon, 173
Startup configurations, 174, 189
system requirements, 172
technical support, 172
Test Drive, 189
Tile Option, 189
toll free phone number, 186
view option, About GrpIcon, 174
Visibility Option, 189
Wallpaper, 189
  options, 178–179

## —H—

Haden, Charles W., Code Breaker, 128–131
Hearts for Windows 1.2
  After Dark, CARDS.AD file, 195
  bug reports, 197
  card backing customization, 190, 196–197
  CARDS.AD file, After Dark, 195
  F1 key, Help box, 193
  future enhancements, 197
  Game menu
    Game Quit, 194
    New Game, 194
  games directory, 195
  goal, 191
  hardware requirements, 195
  installation
    games directory, 195
    WSETUP file, 195

Mallari, Brian, 196
mouse usage, 190–191
New Game, Game menu, 194
Options menu
  Card backings, 193
  How to Play, 193
  player comments, 194
  registered version, 194
  speed controls, 194
Pedriana, Paul, 190, 196
players
  choices, 192–195
  human requirement, 193
  naming, 195
Quit, Game menu, 194
registration, 190, 196–197
  form, 197
rules, 192
scorecard, 194
scoring, 191
start game, 191–192
system requirements, 190, 195
technical support, 190
user input, 197
Versions 1.0 and, 1.1, 194
Holder for Windows
  About Holder command, 75
  command line parameter(s)
    * (asterisk), 72
    List of defined application tags, 72
    List of undefined application tags, 72
    None, 72
  controls
    Icon Setup group, 74
    Program Setup group, 74
  Delete command, 75
  Font command, 75
  Help command, Windows Help, 75
  Help Index for Holder, 75
  Holder button(s), 72
    select specific buttons on command line, 73
    set screen location, 73
  Holder icon, 72
  Holder system menu, 72
  Holder tag, 75
  Icon Setup group of controls, 74
  Index command, 75
  launching applications, 72
  New command, 75
  Options command, 73–74
  Program Manager
    Minimize Use option, 73
    screen location, 73
  Program Setup group of controls, 74
  Windows StartUp group, 72–73
Hutchins, Edward, Hyperoid v., 1.1, 198–203
Hyperoid v. 1.1
  bug fixes, 200
  color display, 200
  control keys, 199
  disclaimer, 203
  five pointed star, 203
  Free Software Foundation, GNU General Public
    License, 203
  freeware, 198–203
  GNU General Public License, 200, 203
  Hutchins, Edward, 198–203
  HYPEROID.INI file, 200–201
  Internet, 203
  key codes, 202
  mail address, 203
  monochrome monitor, 200
  player symbols, 199
  redefine keys, 202
  rules, 200
  source code, 198, 200
  system requirements, 198
  user modifications, 200
  virtual key codes, 202

## —I—

IconCalc
  About option, 208
  BBS through FidoNet, 209
  BIX mail, 209
  bug reports, 209
  button functions, 206
  close icon, 207
  CompuServe, 209
  customization, 210
  DAFLIB.DLL file, 205
  DAFLIB.HLP file, 205
  disclaimer, 212
  enter numbers
    keyboard, 206
    numeric keypad, 206
    Num Lock, 206
  Error message, 206
  exponent display, 206
  Feinleib, David, 204, 209
  filename, 205
  Help option, 207
  icon, 205
  ICONCALC.DOC file, 205
  ICONCALC.EXE file, 205
  ICONCALC.HLP file, 205
  Kaminski, Peter, 212
  LAN licenses, 210
  mouse use, 204
  move icon, 207
  other products, 444–461
  payment restrictions, 210
  Preferences dialog box
    Beep When An Operation Is Selected, 208
    Beep When Any Button Is Selected, 208
    Help button, 209
    Screen Saver Compatibility, 207
    Stay in Front of Other Applications, 207
  Preferences option, Preferences dialog box, 207
  registration, 204, 209–210
    form, 211
  scientific notation, 204
  site licenses, 210
  System menu
    context-sensitive help (mouse button+F1), 209
    Help, 209
  system requirements, 204–205
  technical support, 204
Inner-City Software
  (I'll Be Back) Terminator, 184
  GrpIcon 2.0 (GRPICON.EXE), 172, 182
  investment opportunity, 185
  mailing list, 184
  mission, 184–185
  NoDOS (DOS Icon Eliminator), 184
  PFBFix (font utility), 184
  Windows 3.1 Control Panel Applet for After Dark,
    184

## —J—

Jewel Thief
  application file names, 216
  Asociaton of Shareware Professionals
    Ombudsman, 220
  ASP.BMP file, 216
  Association of Shareware Professionals (ASP)
    Ombudsman, 220
  CompuServe ID, 214
  filename, 216
  goal, 215
  JWLTHIEF.BMP file, 216
  JWLTHIEF.EXE file, 216

license, limited, 220
limitations, 215
Order Form, 219
ORDERFRM.WRI file, 216
PACKING.LST file, 216
README.WRI file, 216
Registration, 214, 219
ServantWare, 214–221
speed, 215
system requirements, 214
technical support, 214
VEND&BBS.WRI file, 216
Warranty, 220

## —K—

Kempe, Allen C., PixFolio (1.04.15), 348–383
key combination definition, utility, 476–485

## —L—

μLathe (MicroLathe v. 1.5.1), 1.5.1
3D, View menu, 268
3D View
Shaded Object, 263
Wire Frame Object, 263
abort, Save Sequence, 265
Autodesk Animator Player for Windows, 265
Baker, Daniel S., 260
Control Panel, 263
View menu, 268
cursor shapes, 262
Edit menu
Clear, 267
Copy, 266
Grid, 267
Light Source, 267
Repaint, 268
Undo, 266
File menu
Exit, 266
New, 264
Open, 264
Save, 264
Save As, 264
Save Image, 264
Save Sequence, 265
Order form, 272
registration, 260, 271–272
Save Sequence
abort, 265
File menu, 265
Windows DIB (Device Independent Bitmap)
file, 265
source code, 272
system registration, 260
technical support, 260
View menu, 3D, 262, 268
View menu, 261–262
Control Panel, 268
μLathe, 268
Object Outline, 263
Windows DIB (Device Independent Bitmap) file,
animated, 265
*See also* MiniMovie
Lessa, Michael
Flipper, 71
Portland (PORTRAIT.EXE and LANDSCAP.EXE), 71
Ligeski, Paul, ServantWare, 216

## —M—

McAfee Associates, Virus Scan utilities, 16
Mallari, Brian, Hearts for Windows, 1.2, 196
Match
About box, 85
Allow Sync on Whitespace Lines, 84
change too large to display, 79
child windows, 76
Clear check box, 80
Color commands, 84–85
directory file location, 77
DOS filename requirements, 77
DOS output device selection, 77
DOS stub module, Windows, 77
DOS version, 77
Exit command, 81
Exit Match, Alt+F4 keyboard shortcut, 78, 81
File menu
Exit, 81
Open Left, 80
Open Right, 80
filenames, 77
File Open dialog box, 80
Clear check box, 80
Font command, 85
Help menu, Help for the Match application, 85
laser printer configuration, 77
left-hand window, 76
MATCH.EXE file, 77
Match help index, 85
MATCH.HLP file, 77
matching
algorithm, 79
background operation, 79
lines not in same location, 76
lines in same location, 76
Match keyboard summary, 85
Match Options, 83–85
Allow Sync on Whitespace Lines, 84
Font command, 85
Maximum Change Length (Lines), 84
Minimum Sync Length (Lines), 84
Text Matching Controls, 84
Maximum Change Length (Lines), 84
Minimum Sync Length (Lines), 84
Next command, 81
Next Compare command, 81
Next Difference command, 82
no match, 76
open file into left-hand Match window
Alt+Ctrl+F2 keyboard shortcut, 77, 80
Ctrl+F12 keyboard shortcut, 77, 80
open file into right-hand Match window,
Alt+Ctrl+Shift+F2 keyboard shortcut, 77, 80
Open Left command, 80
Open Right command, 80
Options command, 84
Previous command, 82
right-hand window, 76
Search menu
Next, 81
Next Compare, 81
Next Difference, 82
Previous command, 82
Previous Compare, 82
Previous Difference, 82
String Again, 82
String Next, 83
String Previous, 83
Search Next Compare, Shift+F3 keyboard
shortcut, 78
Search Next Difference, Ctrl+F3 keyboard
shortcut, 78

Search Previous Compare, Shift+F4 keyboard
shortcut, 78
Search Previous Difference, Ctrl+F4 keyboard
shortcut, 78
String Again, Ctrl+F5 keyboard shortcut, 78
String Next, 83
Shift+F5 keyboard shortcut, 78
String Previous, 83
Text Matching Controls, 84
Windows 3.1, drop and drag, 77
Windows, DOS stub, 77
window scrolling keys
horizontal for left window, 78
horizontal for right window, 78–79
vertical, 78
MathGraf
CompuServe ID, 229
conventional notation, 222
vs. Postfix notation, 227
Copy, Clipboard, 224
Edit menu, Copy, 224
file extension, MGF, 222
File Manager
starting with MATHGRAF.EXE file, 223
starting with MFG files, 223
File menu
About, 224
New, 224
Open, 224
Save, 224
Save As, 224
filenames, 223, 229
function abbreviations, 226–227
function dialog box, statements, 225–226
function evaluation
memory stack, 227
number or variable, 227
operator, 227
result, 227
syntax errors, 227
Function Menu, 225
function statements, 225–227
Postfix notation, 227
Help option, 229
installation
notes, 230
WSETUP file, 223
Interval
interval values, 228
Plot menu, 228
license key, 230
MATHGRAF.EXE file, 223, 230
MATHGRAF.HLP file, 229
MGF files, 222
notation of mathematical functions, 222
Open, File menu, 224
Options command, 229
Origin, View menu, 225
Patrick Robin, 222, 231
Plot menu
Interval, 228
Redraw, 227
Postfix notation, 222
vs. conventional notation, 227
printing, copy to Clipboard, 230
Redraw, Plot menu, 227
Registration, 223, 230
Order Form, 232
Save, File menu, 224
Save As, File menu, 224
SELECT.DLL file, 230
syntax errors, 227
system requirements, 223
technical support, 223, 229
unlicensed copy, 231
updates
CompuServe, 231
Internet, 231

user input, 231
View menu
  Coordinates, 224
  Origin, 225
  Wider, 225
  Zoom, 224
warranty, 231
Wider, View menu, 225
WSETUP file, 223
Zoom, View menu, 224
Mega Edit 2.02
  Again (F3), Find menu, 247
  binary files, 240
  Case Sensitive box, 246
  Change Font, 250
  Clear (Ctrl+Delete), 244
  Close, 241
  Close All, 241
  Colors, 249
  COMMDLG.DLL file, 253
  CompuServe ID, 257
  Computer Witchcraft, Inc., 234–259
  Copy (Ctrl+Insert), 244
  Cut (Shift+Delete), 243
  Default File Mask, 252
  Default Replace Criteria, 252
  Default Search Criteria, 252
  disclaimer, 259
  DOS text files, 242
  Edit menu
    Clear (Ctrl+Delete), 244
    Copy (Ctrl+Insert), 244
    Cut (Shift+Delete), 243
    Paste (Shift+Insert), 244
  Enlarge Font, 250
    Ctrl+numeric-keypad plus sign, 250
  Exit (Alt+F4), 243
  Export/Convert, 242
  fax number, 257
  features, 235–236
  File menu
    Close, 241
    Close All, 241
    Exit (Alt+F4), 243
    Export/Convert, 242
    Include File..., 242
    New, 239
    Open, 240
    Run DOS Shell (F12), 242
    Save All, 241
    Save As..., 241
    Save (F2), 241
  filename, 253
  Find menu
    Again (F3), 247
    Case Sensitive box, 246
    Goto, 248
    Replace, 247
    Start at First Line box, 246
    Whole Words Only box, 246–247
  Goto, Find menu, 248
  Help, Up and Running, 254–255
  Include File..., 242
  Internet/Usenet, 257
  Macintosh files, 240–242
  MEGAED.DLL file, 253
  MEGAEDIT.BIN file, 253
  MEGAEDIT.EXE file, 253
  MEGAEDIT.HLP file, 253
  Mega Edit manual, 255–256
  MEGAINFO.BIN file, 253
  multiple files, 236
  New, 239
  NONAME file, 239, 241
  Norton Desktop for Windows, 234
  on-line help system (F1), 254
  Open, 240

Options menu
  Change Font, 250
  Colors, 249
  Enlarge Font (Ctrl+numeric-keypad plus), 250
  Preferences, 251
  Reduce Font (Ctrl+numeric-keypad minus), 251
  Set Tab, 249
  Word Wrap On/Off, 249
Paste (Shift+Insert), 244
Preferences
  Default File Mask, 252
  Default Replace Criteria, 252
  Default Search Criteria, 252
  Options menu, 251
  Tabs Default Setting, 251
  Word Wrap, 251–252
Print File (Ctrl+P), 252
READ1ST.TXT file, 253
README.TXT file, 253
Reduce Font (Ctrl+numeric-keypad minus), 251
REG_FORM.TXT file, 253
REGISTER.TXT file, 253
registration, 234, 255–259
registration form, 258–259
RELEASE.TXT file, 253
Replace, 247
Right Margin At, Word Wrap, 252
Run DOS Shell (F12), 242
Save All, 241
Save As..., 241
Save (f2), 241
saving files, 236
selecting text
  keyboard, 245
  mouse, 244–245
  scroll bar, 245
Set Tab, 249
similar shareware, 234
Split Window (Ctrl+S), 236–237, 239, 248
Start at First Line, 246
Startup in Wordwrap Mode, Word Wrap, 251–252
switch files, 236
Switch Pane (Ctrl+W), 237, 239, 248
system requirements, 234
Tabs Default Setting, 251
technical support, 234, 256
telephone number, 257
text formats, file formats read, 240
troubleshooting
  default screen size, 253
  finding help file, 254
  general protection fault, 254
  loading MEGAED.DLL file, 254
  preference settings, 254
UNIX files, 240–242
Unsplit Window (Ctrl+X), 237, 239, 248
updates, 255–256
upgrade protection, 256
Up and Running, on-line help, 254–255
Usenet/Internet, 257
VENDOR.TXT file, 253
viewing multiple files, 237
warranty, 259
Whole Words Only, 246–247
wildcard text, 252
window display, 235
Window menu
  Split Window (Ctrl+S), 236–237, 239, 248
  Switch Pane (Ctrl+W), 237, 239, 248
  Unsplit Window (Ctrl+X), 237, 239, 248
*Windows 3.1 SECRETS*, WinEdit, 17, 234
window scrolling, 237
Word Wrap
  Right Margin at box, 252
  Startup in Wordwrap Mode box, 251–252
Word Wrap On/Off, 249

memory game, 128–131
Metz Software
  address, 442
  Metz Desktop Manager, 441
  Metz Desktop Navigator, 437, 441
  Metz Dialer, 442
  Metz File F/X, 436, 441
  Metz Freemem, 442
  Metz Lock, 442
  Metz Phones, 442
  Metz Runner, 442
  Metz Task Manager, 436–437
  Metz Time, 442
  Widget, 1.1, 436–442
Metz Widget 1.1. *See* Widget 1.1
*Microsoft Windows User's Guide*, Basic Skills, 426
Mile Bones (MB.EXE V 2.1)
  Battle pile, 278
  Clear Scores button, 282
  counterattack, 276, 281
  Coupe Fourre, 276, 281
  Delayed Action, 282
  dirt, 275
  Discard Deck, 279
  drag and drop, 282
  Draw Deck, 279
  end of Game, 282
  extended play, 281
  gameboard, 278–280
    cursor actions, 279
    Draw Deck, 279
    Speed Limit rectangle, 278
  Grand Total, 282
  Grip Completed, 282
  Help (F1), 282
  High Score table, 282
  keyboard shortcuts, Shift+F1+click on screen (Help), 282
  keyboard use, 279
  mouse use, 279
  Needham, Andre, 274–283
  Options dialog box, preferences, 282
  Playing Cards
    distribution, 278
    Hazard Cards, 275, 278
    Mileage Cards, 275, 278, 280
    relationships, 277
    Remedy Cards, 276, 278, 280
    Safeties, 276, 278, 280
  registration, 274, 282
  rules of play, 278–282
  scoring, 276, 280–282
  Shutout, 282
  smart-play, 282
  Speed Limit rectangle, 278
  system requirements, 274
  technical support, 274
MiniMovie 1.5.1
  application, 265
  color, 270
  command-line parameters, 270
  Control Panel
    Exit, 271
    Faster, 271
    Help, 271
    Open, 271
    Pause, 271
    Slower, 271
  display, 270
  error message, 270
  µLathe (MicroLathe v. 1.5.1), 265, 269–271
  movie creation, 269
  multiple instances, simultaneous, 270
  registration, 272
  Save Sequence, 265
  size, 270
  source code, 272
  window size, 270

Money Smith 2.0
  Account dialog box, 291
    Category, 309
    error message, 310
    Tools Category command, 310
  Account Editor dialog box, Investment button, 311–312
account(s)
  assets, 290
  categories, 309–310
  category, 301
  category limits, 310
  equity, 290
  establish, 287, 291
  expenses, 290
  groupings, 309–310
  income, 290
  investment, 301
  liabilities, 290
  liens, 290
  limits, 292
  loans, 290
  *See also* Money Smith 2.0, investment accounts
Account view, 290–292
  + toolbar button, 291
  Account dialog box, 309
  Cancel, 292
  Edit Add, 292
  Graph Current-Investment command, 303
  Report Category command, 310
  Save, 292
acknowledgements, 336
ACRS Depreciation (ACRS) function, financial calculator, 328–329
add an account, 291–292
add new account, Transactions dialog box, 296
All-Category graph, 302
back up, 288
Balance Statement, 299–300
BUSINESS.ACT file, 315–316
calculator, financial, 296
cash-flow report, 299–300
category, 301
Category graph, 302
checks
  ordering, 305–306
  printing, 306
CompuServe, 331–332
copy files, 288
Current Investment graph, 303
Current Register report, transactions, 293
Dates
  Beginning of Year, 294
  Today, 294
delete account, Edit Cut, 292
disclaimer, 286, 335–336
distribution rights, Association of Shareware Professionals (ASP) members, 334
documentation, 285
Edit Add, add an account, 291
Edit Cut, delete account, 292
Edit Edit, 292, 297–298
  Recurring Transactions dialog box, 307
Effective Annual Interest (EffI) function, financial calculator, 326–327
end-of-year processing, 313–314
File menu
  Exit, 287
  New, 287
  Open, 287
  Print, 298, 304
  Save As, 288
  Save (F3), 287
filenames, 314–316, 329
financial calculator, 296, 317–319
  ACRS Depreciation (ACRS) function, 328–329
  button functions, 317–318

compound financial calculations, 318–319
Effective Annual Interest (EffI) function, 326–327
financial functions, 318
Future Value of an Annuity (FVA) function, 325
Future Value (FV) function, 324–325
Infix notation, 317, 320
Internal Rate of Return for an Annuity (IRRA), 328
Internal Rate of Return (IRR) function, 327
Investment Required for a Future Value (INV) function, 325–326
Postfix notation, 317, 320–321
Present Loan Payment (PMT) function, 324
Present Value of an Annuity (PVA function), 321–323
Present Value of a Perpetuity (PVP) function, 323
Present Value (PV) function, 321
financial position, 299
Future Value of an Annuity (FVA) function, financial calculator, 325
Future Value (FV) function, financial calculator, 324–325
Graph Current-Investment command, Account view, 303
graphs, 302–304
  all categories, 302–303
  Assets, 302
  Current Investment, 303
  equity, 302
  expense, 302
  History Assets, 303
  History One Account, 303
  History One Category, 303
  income, 302
  Liability, 302
  one-category, 302
  Options Report-Title command, 302
  title change, 302
  types, 302
  windows limits, 301, 304
Help, 286
History Assets graph, 303
History One Account graph, 303
History One Category graph, 303
HOME.ACT file, 314–315
Infix notation, 317, 320
installation, 286
  WSETUP file, 286
interactive fields
  Accounts, 289
  Category, 289
  Close Box, 289
  Dates, 289
  Edit Magnifying Glass, 289
  Investment Icon, 289
  Mark/Unmark Transaction, 289
  Register Triangle, 289
  Transaction, 289
  Type Bars, 289
  View (Eye) Icon, 289
interactive functions
  Editing menu, 290
  File menu, 290
  Report menu, 290
interactive graphs, 290
Interactive Windows, 288
  date title, 294
Internal Rate of Return for an Annuity (IRRA), financial calculator, 328
Internal Rate of Return (IRR) function, financial calculator, 327
investment, 301
investment accounts, 311–313
  Account Editor dialog box, 311
  Account view, 312

Current Investment report, 311
double-entry, 311
Graph Current-Investment command, 312
history records, 311
Investment Editor dialog box, 311
investment reminder service, 313
limits, 313
Tools Investment command, 312
Investment Editor dialog box
  Auto Tx button, 311
  Reminder button, 313
  Remove button, 312
investment icon, 311–312
Investment report
  + button on toolbar, 311
  Add icon, 311
  Cut icon, 312
  Edit icon, 312
  Investment field, 289
  magnifying glass, 312
  Price field, 289
  Rainbow investment icon, 311–312
  Return field, 289
  scissors icon, 312
  Value field, 289
Investment Required for a Future Value (INV) function, financial calculator, 325–326
license, 329–330
  agreement, 330, 334
  single-user, 334
  unregistered users, 334–335
Licensing window, I Agree button, 286
limits
  account categories, 310
  accounts, 292
  graph windows, 301, 304
  investment accounts, 313
  recurring transactions, 309
  report windows, 301
  transactions, 298
magnifying glass icon, 292, 312
naming files, Save (F3), 287
Options End-of-Year, 314
Options Preferences, Dates, 294
Options Report-Title, 300
Options Set-Password, 288
ordering services
  CompuServe, 331
  Public Library (PsL), 331
passwords, 288
Postfix notation, 317, 320–321
Present Loan Payment (PMT) function, financial calculator, 324
Present Value of an Annuity (PVA function), financial calculator, 321–323
Present Value of a Perpetuity (PVP) function, financial calculator, 323
Present Value (PV) function, financial calculator, 321
print
  current window, 304
  graphs, 305
  laser checks, 306
  tractor-fed checks, 306
printer set up, 304
print options, 304
  Print Grid box, 304
  Print title box, 304
Rainbow investment icon, 311–312
Reconcile Current Account report, 294
Recurring button, 296, 307
recurring transactions, 296, 306–309
  create, 307–308
  dates, 308
  edit, 308
  limits, 309
  memorized transactions, 308

mixed periods, 309
out-of-cycle, 308
Run button, 308
Tools Recurring-Transactions, 308
undated, 308
Recurring Transactions dialog box, 307–308
None option, 308
Run button, 308
registered version, 329
register triangle, 293
REGISTER.TXT file, 329
Register view, 293
Edit Cut, 298
Edit Edit, 297–298
registration, 284, 330–331
Eurosoft Registration Service, 332–3
international, 332–333
order form, 333
RENTER.ACT file, 314–315
Report
Balance Statement, 299–300
Budget, 299–300
Category, 301, 310
Current Account Register, 293, 301
Current Investment, 311
History graph, 299–300
Income, 299–300
Investment, 301
Reconcile Account report, 301
Tax Summary, 300
report(s), 298–299
account reconciliation, 301
budget trends, 299
budget vs. actual income, 299–300
cash flow, 299–300
net worth, 299–300
non-taxable items, 300
spending trends, 299
taxable items, 300
window limits, 301
sample files
homeowners, 314–315
real estate management, 317
real property, 315
renters, 314–315
small business, 315–316
scissors icon, 292, 312
shareware, 330
small calendar page icon, 294
smart-number entry fields, 296, 319
Smith, Bradley J., 284–336
Software Excitement!, 331
technical support, 284, 330–331
tool bar
+ button, 291, 311
scissors icon, 292, 312
Tools Investment, Investment Editor dialog box,
312
Tools Recurring-Transactions dialog box, 308
Transaction dialog box, 295–296
add new account, 296
Split button, 297
transactions, 293
add new account, 296
check-style entry format, 295
Current Register report, 293
delete, 298
end-of-year processing, 313–314
limits, 298
printing, 298
Reconcile Current Account report, 294
transaction-style entry format, 295
See also Money Smith 2.0, recurring
transactions
Transaction View, 293
+ button on toolbar, 294
Edit Add, 294

Edit Cut, 298
Edit Edit, 297–298
warranty, 335
Windows File Manager, 288
Windows Notepad, 329
Montgomery, Peter, Flipper, 71

—N—

Needham, Andre, Mile Bones (MB.EXE V 2.1), 274–283
New Generation Software Ltd., WinEZ, 3.0, 462–475
Nicholes, Bradley
Parents 2.3, 388–347
Recipe Maker 2.13, 384–395
NickleWare, Parents 2.3, 338–347
Nickleware, Recipe Maker 2.13, 384–395
Norton Desktop for Windows
ClipMate, 119
Mega Edit, 2.02, 234
WinEZ, 3.0, 469–471

—P—

Paper Software, Inc.
Side Bar, 424–427
SideBar Lite, 2/11/92, 400–427
SideBar Notebook, 425–426
Parents 2.3
Children List, Immediate Family Tree, 342
Clipboard, 345
Close pushbutton, Individual Work Sheet, 341
CompuServe ID, 347
Delete pushbutton, Individual Work Sheet, 341
disclaimer, 347
drag and drop, 345
Exit, File menu, 346
Father box, Immediate Family Tree, 342
Immediate Family Tree
Children List, 342
Edit menu/Clear selection, 344
extended family tree, 342–343
Father box, 342
Hide List selection, 344
Hide menu selection, 343
Individual List, 342
Individual Work Sheet, 343
Mother box, 342
Relations menu, 344–345
remove relationship, 344
Show List selection, 344
Show menu selection, 343
Spouse List, 342
Individual List, 342
Individual Work Sheet, 340
Close pushbutton, 341
File menu/New, 340
File menu/Open, 341
File menu/Print, 341
Next pushbutton, 341
Previous pushbutton, 341
Save pushbutton, 341
installation, 339
WSETUP file, 339
Mother box, Immediate Family Tree, 342
New, File menu, 340
NickleWare, 338–347
Open, File menu, 340
Parents icon, 339
Previous pushbutton, Individual Work Sheet, 341
Print
File menu, 341, 345–346
Immediate Family Tree, 344
Individual Ancestral Tree, 344

pushbuttons
Close, 341
Next, 341
Previous, 341
Save, 341
registration, 338, 346
form, 347
Save pushbutton, Individual Work Sheet, 341
saving data, 346
Spouse List, Immediate Family Tree, 342
system requirements, 338
technical support, 338
WIN.INI file, 339–340
Patterson, Richard S., FlashPoint Development,
510–566
Pedriana, Paul, Hearts for Windows, 1.2, 190, 196
personal finance, financial management, 284–336
PixFolio 1.04.15
Auth Dither, 372
backup
copies, 349
removable media, 380–381
Burkes Filter algorithm, 372
Catalog an Image dialog box, 352–354
Backup Vol & Path, 353
Cancel, 354
Catalog, 353
Catalog/Update, 353
Date & Time, 353
delete catalog entry, 353
Description, 353
Filename, 353
Info, 353
Keywords, 353
Move File, 354
Pathname, 353
Primary Vol, 353
Size, 353
thumbnail image button, 354
Title, 353
Uncatalog, 353
Catalog Browse
entry display, 357
Print Catalog, 375
View button, 360
Catalog Browse/Search dialog box
Backup Exists on Floppy Disk check box,
358–359
Cancel, 358
Delete File, 357
Format edit box, 358
Keywords box, 359
Move/Copy, 357
OK, 357
Print Cat, 358
Search button, 359–360
search criteria, 358
Search Keywords edit box, 358
special codes, 359
Special Conditions edit box, 358
Uncatalog, 358
View Image, 357
Wildcard characters, 359
Catalog Build
backup files, 356
disk identification, 355
entry update, 355
Select Items to Catalog, 354
Catalog Print, 375
Clipboard operations, 368
color
resolution, 371–372
support, 368–369
Create New Image
Set to Clipboard button, 369–370
Set to Window button, 369–370
crop image, 366

Default options
    Auto Dither, 379
    Center Image, 379
    Default Catalog, 378
    Default Directory, 379
    Default Extensions, 378
    DIB to screen, 379
    Display Warnings, 379
    Fix tiff, 379
    Solid Background, 379
delete catalog, 352
disclaimer, 381–382
distribution, 381–382
dithering, 372
    Burkes Filter algorithm, 372
    Stucki Filter algorithm, 372
Edit Crop, 366–367
Edit Expand, 366
    Options-Center Image, 367
Edit Resize, 367–368
entry update, 355
expand image, 366–367
File
    New, 369
    Save, 370–371
    Select Printer, 372–374
file-attribute information, 355
file configuration, WIN.INI file, 381
filename extension
    CIX, 351
    CAT, 351
format, conversions, 371
formats
    color resolution, 362
    supported graphics, 360–362
image
    palette, 368–369
    resize, 367
    rotate, 368
    view, 366
information access
    Catalog Browse command, 355
    Catalog Build command, 356
    Catalog Catalog command, 355
    View Thumbnails command, 356
Kempe, Allen C., 348–383
move image to another catalog, 356
Options menu
    Auto Dither, 376–377
    Background color, 377
    Center Image, 376
    DIB to Screen, 376
    Display Warnings, 375–376
    Fix TIFF, 377
    Verify Catalog, 377
PixFolio (General) dialog box, 349
print
    formats, 375
    options, 372–375
Printer Setup, 373
    Alt Cat Prt Format, 373
    Dither when Printing, 373
    Fonts>>button, 373–374
    Print Catalog using Thumbnails, 373
    Use Low Mem Option, 373
Print Image dialog box
    Dither, 374–375
    Low Mem option, 374
    scaling graphic, 374
Process Thumbnails
    Add, 364
    Copy, 356, 364
    Delete, 356, 364
    don't update, 364
    Hide, 364
    Mark, 364
    Move, 356, 364

move/copy to another drive or directory, 364
    Print, 364
    Print option, 375
    Unmark, 364
reading capacity, 349
registration, 348
    CompuServe ID, 383
    Europe, 383
    form, 382–383
    order direct, 383
    Public (software) Library, 383
    U.S., 383
Select Catalog dialog box
    Catalog File Name, 350–351
    default file extensions, 351
    delete catalog, 352
    Name, 351–352
    read only box, 351
    volume name, 351
Select Items to Catalog dialog box
    Auto Update option, 354
    Build button, 354
    Select all option, 355
    Show All option, 355
    Stop on Error option, 355
similar shareware, 348
Stucki Filter algorithm, 372
system requirements, 348
technical support, 348
Thumbnail View, entry display, 357
trim image, 366
View Catalog Entry dialog box, View button, 360
View Change-Palette, 369
View Dither-Color, 372
View Gray-Scale, 369
view images
    Display Main menu option, 360
    uncataloged, 360
View menu, Set Play Rate, 378
View Thumbnails, 356, 362–366
    Add Thumbnail, 364
    browse contents, 363
    Hide Thumbnail, 363
    Information, 363
    Launch Application, 364–366
    Mark Thumbnail, 363
    move image to another catalog, 356
    Process Thumbnails, 364–365
    restrict display, 363
    Slide Show, 366
    View, 364
    View option, 360
Windows 3.1 SECRETS
    PaintShop, 348
    WinGIF, 348
Portland (PORTRAIT.EXE and LANDSCAP.EXE)
    Flipper, 71
    Lessa, Michael, 71
    printer control limitations, 71
    printer orientation default, 71
    Windows 3.x, 71
    Windows batch files, 71
printer orientation control utility, 66, 70–71
program management utility, 462–475
Public domain, definition, 217

—R—

real mode, Windows, 3.0, 13–14
recipe file management, database, 385–395
Recipe Maker 2.13
    Add pushbutton, 387
    add recipe, 389–390
    Change pushbutton, 388
    Clipboard, 394

CompuServe ID, 395
Copy, Edit menu, 394
Cut, Edit menu, 394
Delete pushbutton, 391
delete recipe, 391
disclaimer, 395
drag and drop, 394
File menu
    Exit, 394
    Recipe Description Card, 389
    Recipe Instruction Card, 389–390
filenames, 386
Ingredients List, 389–390
installation, 386
    WSETUP file, 386
Item Group List, 389
Measurements List, 388–390
Nicholes, Bradley, 384–395
Nickleware, 384–395
on-line documentation, 395
Open pushbutton, 390
Print pushbutton, 391
print recipe, 391
Recipe Card window, 391
Recipe Description Card, 389
RECIPE.EXE file, 386
Recipe icon, Program Manager, 386
Recipe List, 391
recipe suggestions, 392
registration, 385
    form, 395
Remove pushbutton, 388
Save pushbutton, 390
search for ingredients, 392–393
Select pushbutton, 391
Shopping List, 392–393
system requirements, 385
technical support, 385
update recipe, 390–391
Weekly Meal Planner window, 391–392
Weekly Plan, Create List, 391
What If... window, 392–393
Windows Program Manager, File Run menu, 386
registration notices, Shareware, 12
Robin, Patrick, MathGraf, 222
RS232 Serial Monitor utility, 396–399
Runner
    command line execution, 85
    DOS programs, 85
    Enter, 85
    Menu, 86
    OK button, 85
    Run Minimized, 86
    Runner icon, 85
    Use Alternate Shell option, 86
    Windows programs, 85

—S—

scheduler/alarm clock, 444–461
serial port monitor utility, 396–399
ServantWare, 216
    CompuServe ID, 216
    Internet address, 216
    Jewel Thief, 214–221
    Ligeski, Paul, 216
Shareware
    definition, 10–11, 217–218
    registration notices, 12
    registration from outside U.S., 11
SideBar Lite 2/11/92
    acknowledgements, 426
    active task, 420
    application, 420
    Applications menu, 410–411
    Arrange buttons, 404, 420

change description of file/directory, 413–414
Command Line, 404, 420
    DOS commands, 416–417
create directory, DOS command, 422
current view, 420
Desktop, 420
directory location, 403
Disk view, 405, 420
drive limits, 422
Enter key, 420
filenames, 403
hardware requirements, 402
Iconbar menu
    Fonts, 409
    Include Active Tasks, 410
    Include Active Tasks option, 421
    Keep on Top, 410
    Left/Right Side of Screen, 409
    Show Status Bar, 410
    View Layout Options, 409
keyboard equivalents
    Alt+4 (close SideBar Lite), 419
    Alt+spacebar (display main menu), 419
    Ctrl+F1 (size windows, icon row at bottom of screen), 419
    Ctrl+F2 (size windows, SideBar Lite visible on side of screen), 419
    Ctrl+F3 (minimize windows, arrange icons at bottom of screen), 419
    Ctrl+F6 (switch to left/right view layout), 419
    Ctrl+F7 (display contents of current Disk view as details), 419
    F1 (display About SideBar Lite panel), 419
    F2 (place cursor on command line), 419
    F4 (display Work With panel), 419
    F5 (refresh current view), 419
    F6 (switch to single view), 419
    F7 (display contents as icons), 419
    F12 (close Windows), 419
    Shift+F1 (Cascade windows), 419
    Shift+F2 (Tile windows side by side), 419
    Shift+F3 (Tile windows vertically), 419
    Shift+F6 (switch to top/bottom view layout), 419
    Shift+F7 (display contents of current view as descriptions), 419
licensing, 426–427
limitations, 421
Main menu
    About SideBar Lite, 407
    Applications, 402, 406
    Close, 407
    Iconbar, 406
    Preferences, 406–407
    Shutdown, 407
    View, 406
    Work With, 406
Microsoft applications, 421
*Microsoft Windows User's Guide*, Basic Skills, 426
mouse use
    close view, 418
    display main menu, 417
    display WorkWith panel, 419
    move SideBar Lite, 417
    open second view, 417
    place selection on SideBar Lite, 418
    remove selection from SideBar Lite, 418
    resize views, 418
    select object, 418
    switch view layouts, 418
object, 420
open
    Ctrl+Esc, 402
    SIDEBAR.EXE file, 403
    Sidebar icon, 403
    Windows desktop, 402
ordering SideBar or SideBar Lite, 424–425
    Egghead Discount Software, 425

overview, 401
Paper Software, Inc., 400–427
Pathname, 420
place file/directory on SideBar Lite, 412–413
Preferences, 403, 414–416
    Cancel, 416
    confirm when closing SideBar Lite, 415
    confirm when shutting down system, 415
    fonts, 415
    minimize opening object, 415
    replace task manager, 415
    Save, 416
    SideBar directory, 414
    start as Windows shell, 415
quit Windows, 407
registration, 400, 422–424
registration form, 427
remove directory, DOS command, 422
remove file/directory from SideBar Lite, 413
Replace Task Manager, 402, 415
restrictions, 400
SBLITE.WRI file, 403
screen placement, 409
selecting objects, 420
selection, 420
SIDEBAR.EXE file, 403
SideBar view, 405
SideBar vs. SideBar Lite, 424
Start As Windows Shell, 402, 415
System box, 404
System Menu icon, 421
system requirements, 400
technical support, 400
Title bar, 404
View, 421
    appearance options, 408
    Refresh, 408
    sort options, 408
    Title, 404, 421
Windows shell, 421
Work With panel
    Changing description on SideBar Lite, 413–414
    Destination field, 411
    Go button, 413–414
    open, 410
    Placing On SideBar Lite action, 412–413
    remove directory, 413, 422
    Remove From SideBar Lite action, 413
    Selection, 411
    source field, 411
Smith, Bradley J., Money Smith, 2.0, 284–336
Softblox Incorporated
    SmartPad for Windows, 428, 435
    Super Resource Monitor (SUPERRM.EXE 1.2), 428–435
Software Excitement!, Money Smith, 2.0, 331
Super Resource Monitor (SUPERRM.EXE 1.2)
    About button, 432
    Close button, 433
    Compact Every [x] Second, 434
    Compact Memory check box, 434
    Current Task Heap, 430
    Current Task Heap meter, 429
    desktop image, 429
    digital clock, 429
    filenames, 428
    Free Memory window, 432
    Free System Resources (FSR), 428, 430
    freeware, 429
    GDI.EXE file, Graphic Device Interface file, 430
    GDI Heap, 430
    GDI Heap meter, 429
    global heap, 430
    heaps, 429–430
    Keep Monitor in Front check box, 435
    meter alarms, 430–431
    meter colors, 430, 432

Options button, 433
    Sample Every [x] Second, 433
    SBICTLW.DLL file, 428
    size window display, 433
    SmartPad for Windows, 400, 435
    Softblox Incorporated, 428–435
    SuperRM Alarm box, 431
    SUPERRM.EXE file, 428
    system requirements, 429
    Time window, 432
    USER.EXE file, user actions information file, 430
    User Heap, 430
    User Heap meter, 429
    Windows free memory numerical display, 429
system resource monitor, utility, 428–435

—T—

technical requirements, *Windows GIZMOS*, 13–14
technical support
    CompuServe, 14–15
    *Windows GIZMOS*, 14–15
Terratech, Disk Copy for Windows (DC.EXE), 138–147
text file comparison, utilities, 66
text processor, 96–127, 234–259
Thatcher, Gregory, Checkers, 90–95
Thomas, Daniel, ZiPaper, 1.3c, 498–508
Thornton Software Solutions, ClipMate, 96–127
Time
    Beep on Hour, 87
    DOS TIME command, 87
    F1 command, 87
    format control, 87
    format control dialog box, Cancel, 87
    install new options, 87
    screen location, 87
    sound control, 87
    start command, 87
    Windows compatibility, 86

—U—

UARTMON.EXE (1.2)
    BIOS data area, 397–398
    CompuServe ID, 399
    COMx address, 398
    Default Windows, 3.0, 3.1, 398
    disclaimer, 399
    distribution, 399
    freeware, 396–399
    IO_Address option, 398
    operation, 399
    Ports menu, 398
    serial port access, 398
    system requirements, 396
    UART, serial ports, 397–398
    UART IO address, 398
    UART (Universal Asynchronous Receiver/Transmitter), 396–397
    Unitech Associates, Inc., 396–399
    Universal Asynchronous Receiver/Transmitter (UART), 396–397
    Windows default addresses, 397
Unitech Associates, Inc., UARTMON.EXE (1.2), 396–399
utilities
    application launcher, 66, 68–69, 72–75
    Barry Press Utilities, 66–89
    calendar, 66, 69–70
    command line equivalent, 66, 85–86
    command line processor, 148–169
    Control Panel dialog box access, 66, 68–69
    CPU processing timer, 436–443
    diskette copier, 138–147

DOS for starting up Windows, 496–497
DOS for Windows wallpaper, 498–508
file deletion, 166–170
group windows customization, 172–189
key combination definition, 476–485
printer orientation control, 66, 70–71
program management, 462–475
serial port monitor, 396–399
system resource monitor, 428–435
text file comparison, 66, 77–85
Windows break-out box, 396–399

## — V —

virus protection, *Windows GIZMOS*, 15–16
Virus Scan utilities, McAfee Associates, 16

## — W —

wallpaper, DOS utility for Windows, 498–508
Widget 1.1
    export file, 438
    File
        Clear Window, 438
        Pause, 438
        Preferences, 439
        Reset File, 439
    freeware, 437
    main window display, 438
    Metz Software, 436–442
    Microsoft Excel, importing files, 438
    operation, 438
    Preferences dialog box
        File check box, 440
        Filename box, 440
        Hide window check box, 440
        Pause on startup check box, 440
        Time interval box, 440
        User box, 440
        Window check box, 439
    similar shareware, 437
    system requirements, 437
    *Windows 3.1 SECRETS*
        Task Manager, 437
Wilson WindowWare Products
    Address Manager, 22–65
    Command Post, 63
    File Commander, 63
    Order Form, 64
    Reminder, 63
    WinBatch, 63
    WinBatch COMPILER!, 63
    WinCheck, 63
    WinEdit, 63
WinClock 3.21
    386 enhanced mode, 452, 454
    About, 455
    acknowledgements, 458
    Alarms
        Beep, 448
        Date, 448
        Enabled, 447
        Note, 448
        Run Program, 449
        Time, 448
    author contact, 457
    BIX mail, 457
    Cascading with, 455–456
    Close, 456
    CompuServe ID, 457
    DAFLIB.DLL file, 457
    DAFLIB.HLP file, 457
    DATEFUNC.DLL file, 457
    disclaimer, 460

Enhanced Alarms
    Day, 449
    Start Date, 449
    Week Interval, 449
error messages, 460
Feinleib, David A., 444–461
filenames, 456–457
Help
    getting, 455
    option, 446
Hourly Beep option, 451
Internet, 457
move, 456
overview, 445
payment, 457
Preferences
    Anti-Cascade, 456
    Date formats, 453
    Display, 454
    Remember Screen Location, 453
    Return to Windows If DOS Box Active, 454
    Screen Saver compatibility, 453–454
    System Box, 455
    Time formats, 452–453
PRODLIST.TXT file, 457
READ.ME file, 457
REGISTER.DOC file, 457
registration, 444, 457
    form, 461
Set Time/Date, 446–447
similar shareware, 444
System box, display/hide, 455
system requirements, 444
technical support, 444
Tiling with, 455–456
Timers, 450–451
    Beep, 451
    Countdown From, 450
    Current Count, 451
    Display Date, 450
    Display Seconds, 451
    Display Time, 450
    Display Timer, 450
    Start/Stop button, 451
WCHOOK.DLL file, 457
WINCLOCK.CFG file, 457
WINCLOCK.DOC file, 456
WINCLOCK.EXE file, 456
WINCLOCK.HLP file, 456
WINCLOCK.INI file, 457
*Windows 3.1 SECRETS*
    ClockMan, 444
    RunProg, 458
WSAVER.DLL file, 457
Windows 3.0, real mode, 13–14
[Windows 3.1 SECRETS]
    Big Cursor, 18
    BizWiz, 18
    Chess, 18
    Clean-Up, 17
    ComReset, 17
    Desktop Navigator, 17
    EDOS, 18
    File Commander, 17
    Graphic Viewer, 18
    Hunter, 17
    Icon Manager, 17
    Klotz, 18
    Lander, 18
    Launch, 17
    MetaPlay, 17
    Paint Shop, 17
    PrintClip, 18, 96
    Puzzle, 18
    RecRun, 17
    RunProg, 17
    Simon, 18

SnagIt, 18
Superload, 18
Task Manager, 17
Trash Can, 18
Unicom, 17
Viruscan, 17
W.BAT, 18
Whiskers, 18
WinBatch, 18, 140
WinCLI, 18, 149
WindBase, 17, 22
Windows Unarchive, 18
WinExit, 18
WinGIF, 17
WinPost, 17
WordBasic Macros, 18
X World Clock, 18
Windows
    shell, 400–427
    user interface, 510–566
    break-out box utility, 396–399
*Windows GIZMOS*
    Association of Shareware Professionals (ASP), 12–13
    Association of Shareware Professionals (ASP) Ombudsman, 12–13
    command explanations, 6–8
    crippleware, 11
    disclaimer, 13
    File Run command, 6
    freeware
        copyrighted, 9
        public domain, 9
    installation
        diskettes, 568
        instructions, 2
        program configuration, 569
        Windows shell group limitations, 569
        WSETUP file, 568
    key, commands, 7–8
    key labels, 7
    Livingston, Brian and Margie, 13
    registration, updates, 569
    registration benefits, 10–11
    rolling demo, 11
    shareware, 9–11
        registration notices, 12
    start command syntax, 6–8
    technical
        requirements, 13–14
        support, 14–15
    user interface
        keyboard, 8
        mouse, 8
    user levels, 1
        DOS beginner (How to Put an Application on the Path), 4
        DOS beginner (The Least You Need to Know about DOS), 3
        new Windows user (How Commands Are Explained), 6–8
        new Windows user (How to Load an Application at Startup), 5–6
    virus protection, 15–16
    WSETUP file, 2
        drive selection, 568
        File/Run, 568
        Norton Desktop for Windows, 568
        Windows GIZMOS dialog box/Add, 568
        Windows GIZMOS dialog box/Add All, 569
        Windows GIZMOS dialog box/Install, 569
WinEZ 3.0
    Association of Shareware Professionals (ASP), 473
    CompuServe ID, 474
    distribution limitations, 472
    error codes, 471

Fast Path icon, 464–466
  Power menu, 465–466, 469
  Program Manager, 466
  right mouse button, 466
  Title of Window, 469
filename, 471
install
  WIN.INI file, 465
  WSETUP file, 465
left icon, 464–466
licensing agreement, 472
New Generation Software Ltd., 462–475
Norton Desktop, 469–471
Options...
  Fast Path icon actions, 469
  Switching behavior, 468
  WinEZ icon position, 469
order information, 473–474
overview, 463–465
Power menu, Norton Desktop, 3.0, 469–470
REGISTER.EXE file, 471
registration, 462, 472–475
  form, 475
right icon, 464, 466
Run dialog box, 467
Run facility, 465
similar shareware, 462
startup, WINEZ.EXE file, 465
system requirements, 462
Task Switch icon, 464, 466
  About..., 466
  End Task, 466
  Exit, 466
  Options..., 466–469
  Run..., 466
technical support, 462
troubleshooting
  application group limits, 470
  drag response slow, 470
  icon placement, 471
  menu creation, 470
  registration form completion, 470
  WinEZ Power menu, 470
*Windows 3.1 SECRETS*, Launch, 462
WINEZ3.TXT file, 471
WINEZ.DAT file, 471
WINEZ.EXE file, 471
WINEZGRP.EXE file, 471
WINEZ.INI file, 471
WINEZRUN.EXE file, 471
WinKey 1.0
Caps Lock Off When
  Caps Lock Pressed, 480
  Shift Letter Pressed, 480–481
  Shift Pressed, 480
CompuServe ID, 483
DataGem Corp., 476–485
disable, 479
disclaimer, 484
distribution, 483
FILE_ID.DIZ file, 482
filenames, 482
install, WSETUP file, 478
Miscellaneous group
  Icon Shoft Shift State, 481
  Reverse Caps Lock & Ctrl, 481
Num Lock group
  Always Off, 480–481
  Always On, 480–481
  Normal Behavior, 480–481
ORDER.TXT file, 482
PACKING.TXT file, 482
README.TXT file, 482
registered version, owner information, 482
registration, 476
  form, 484–485, 495
  information, 483

run one time only, 478
Scroll Lock group
  Always Off, 480–481
  Always On, 480–481
  Normal Behavior, 480–481
settings, default, 480
Shift Key group
  Always Capitalizes, 480
  Reverses Caps Lock (Normal), 480
SITELIC.WRI file, 482
system requirements, 476
technical support, 476, 483
VENDOR.WRI file, 482
Windows 3.0, deinstall, 479
Windows 3.1 and later, StartUp group, 478
Windows 3.0, StartUp group, 479
Windows 3.1 and later
  deinstall, 479
  StartUp group, 478
WINKEY2.DLL file, 482
WinKey dialog box, 477
WINKEY.EXE file, 482
WinKey icon, CAPS light, 481–482
WINKEY.WRI file, 482
WinPoker 2.0
acknowledgements, 494
Bet menu
  Alt+B or left click on Bet, 492
  hot keys (1 through 5), 492–493
card deck, 487–488
CARDDLL.DLL file, 493
Deal menu, Alt+D or Enter, or left click Deal menu
  item, or right click WinPoker playing area,
  493
disclaimer, 494
distribution, 494
Double Up, registered version, 486
filenames, 493
Game menu
  Alt+G or click on Game, 490
  Exit, 491
  New, 490
  Open, 490–491
  Save, 491
  Save As, 491
hardware requirements, 486
Help menu, 493
Jacks or Better, shareware version, 486
Jokers Wild, registered version, 486
keyboard use
  Bet menu (Alt+B), 489
  bet placement (F1 through F5), 489
  dealing cards (Alt+D), 489
  holding cards (1 through 5), 489
  reduce window to icon (Alt+spacebar, release
    keys and press N), 489
  releasing cards, (1 through 5), 489
  sizing window, 489
mouse use
  Bet menu, 488
  dealing cards, 488
  holding cards, 488
  reduce window to icon, 488
  releasing cards, 488
  sizing window, 488
objective, 486–487
Options
  Alt+O or left click Options, 491
  Card Backs, 492
  Set Colors, 491–492
  Sound, 492
  View Statistics, 492
play rules, 487
README.1ST file, 493
registered version
  Double Up, 486
  Jokers Wild, 486

registration, 486
  limited license, 494
scoring, 487–488, 492
  winning hands, 489–490
shareware version, Jacks or Better, 486
software requirements, 493
system requirements, 486
technical support, 486
upgrade policy, 494
Video Poker, 486
  strategy, 490
WINPOKER.EXE file, 493
WINPOKER.HLP file, 493
WINPOKER.ORD file, 493
Zamzow, Dean, 486–495
WinStart 1.1
Briarwood Consulting, 496–497
disclaimer, 497
filenames, 497
freeware, 496–497
installation
  AUTOEXEC.BAT statement, 497
  WINSTART.EXE file, 497
source code, 496–497
system requirements, 496
Window Boss
  BBS, 497
  CompuServe, 497
  SDN (Shareware Distribution Network), 497
Window Boss Libraries, 497
*Windows GIZMOS*, 496–497
WINSTART.EXE file, 497
WIZiper, 522–537
application launcher, Execution group, 536
Archive File group
  Archive File Name edit control, 523
  File Browser pushbutton, 523–524
  List dialog pushbutton, 524–525
  Members drop-down list box, 525
Authorization Code, Registered User information,
  537
Command drop-down list box
  Command group, 525–533
  ZIP Delete, 526
  ZIP Extract, 526
  ZIP file Add/Replace, 526
  ZIP Freshen, 527
  ZIP Help - FPZip, 527
  ZIP License - FPZip, 527
  ZIP Test, 527
  ZIP Update, 527
  ZIP View List, 527
  ZIPX Help - FPZipX, 527
  ZIPX License - FPZipX, 527
Command group
  Command drop-down list box, 525–527
  Set Options dialog pushbutton, 527
Drop On Drop action
  non-ZIP files, 540
  ZIP files, 539
Execution group
  application launcher, 536
  Cancel pushbutton, 535–536
  Execute edit box, 535–536
  Help pushbutton, 535–536
  Max pushbutton, 535–536
  Min pushbutton, 535–536
  OK pushbutton, 535–536
File Browser pushbutton, Archive File group,
  523–524
File Mask list box
  Add List Item pushbutton, 534
  Delete List Item pushbutton, 534
  Delete pushbutton, 535
  Edit pushbutton, 534
  Set Mask dialog panel, 534

filenames, 519
File Selection group
  File Mask edit box, 533–534
  File Mask list box, 534
List dialog pushbutton, Archive File group, 524–525
Main window
  Archive File group, 523–525
  Command group, 525–533
  Execution group, 535
  File Selection group, 533–535
  Help pushbutton, 537
  Minimize box, 536
  Order Info pushbutton, 537
  Register, 537
  System menu, 536–537
Members drop-down list box, Archive File group, 525
Register, User Registration dialog panel, 537
Registered User information
  Authorization Code, 537
  User Registration dialog panel, 537
Set Mask dialog panel
  Cancel pushbutton, 534
  Description, 534
  File Patterns, 534
  OK pushbutton, 534
Set Options dialog panel
  close with Esc key, 533
  WIZiper Cancel pushbutton, 533
  WIZiper OK pushbutton, 533
  WIZiper Reset pushbutton, 533
  WIZiper Save pushbutton, 533
  ZIP Activate Do Not Compress Files with Special Extensions switch, 530
  ZIP Activate Exclude files, 529
  ZIP Comment Files (sets Add File Member Comments switch), 531
  ZIP Comment ZIP (sets Add ZIP File Comment switch), 531
  ZIP Compression Method Best Type, 530
  ZIP Compression Method Implode Only, 530
  ZIP Compression Method Shrink Only, 530
  ZIP Destination directory, 528
  ZIP Directory Browser, 529
  ZIP Exclude edit box, 529
  ZIP From (mmddyy) (sets Compress Files After Specified Date switch), 531
  ZIP Implode Factor group box, 530
  ZIP Move to archive (sets Move to Archive switch), 531
  ZIP No Comp Ext edit box, 529
  ZIP Recurse Subdirs (sets Recurse Subdirectories switch), 531
  ZIP Store Recur Dirs (sets Store Path Name switch), 531
  ZIP Work Directory, 528
  ZIPX Default Association Extract radio button, 530
  ZIPX Default Association Test radio button, 530
  ZIPX Default Association View radio button, 530
  ZIPX Expand Stored Dirs (sets Restore Directory Structure switch), 531
  ZIPX Overwrite (sets Overwrite Exiting Files switch), 531–532
  ZIP Zip Date to Files (sets Set ZIP File Date to Latest Entry switch), 531
  ZIP/ZIPX Alert User (sets Display Error Information switch), 533
  ZIP/ZIPX Auto Close (sets Close Window on Completion switch), 532
  ZIP/ZIPX Echo Cmd Line (Display Module and Command Line switch), 532
  ZIP/ZIPX Inform User (sets Display General Information switch), 533

ZIP/ZIPX Show Tech Info (sets Display Technical Information switch), 533
ZIP/ZIPX Sound Beep (sets Sound On switch), 532
ZIP/ZIPX Warn User (sets Display Warning Information switch), 533
System menu
  About, 537
  Close, 537
  Help, 537
  List, 537
  Minimize, 537
  Move, 537
  Options, 537
  Restore, 537
  Switch to, 537
user interface for Windows, 519
User Registration dialog panel, Registered User information, 537
Windows 3.1 drag-and-drop (DND) functions, 538
WIZ.EXE file, 519

— Z —

Zamzow, Dean, WinPoker, 2.0, 486–495
ZIP
  action command switches
    Add files: -A, 541–542
    Delete files: -D, 541–542
    Display about (license information): -L, 541, 544
    Display help: -H, 541, 543
    Freshen files: -F, 541–542
    Update files: -U, 541, 544
  command parameters
    [filename1 filename2...], 545
    [zipfile].ZIP, 545
  command(s)
    Add/Replace, 526
    command line format, 540
    Delete, 526
    Extract, 526
    Freshen, 527
    Help-FPZip, 527
    License - FPZip, 527
    syntax, 541–546
    Test, 527
    Update, 527
    View List, 527
  compatibility
    DOS PKUnzip, 518–519
    DOS PKZip, 518
  filenames, 519
  option command switches
    Add file-member comments: -C, 542–543
    Add ZIP file comment: -Z, 542, 545
    Alternative path for temporary build files: -B [path], 542–543
    Automatically close window on completion: -W, 542, 545
    Compress files after date month-day-year: -T mmddyy, 542, 545
    Display module and command line: -^, 541, 543
    Display technical information: -*, 541, 543
    Display warning and other trivial information (verbose mode), 541, 543
    Do not compress with special extensions: -N, 542, 544
    Exclude listed files: -X filenames, 542, 545
    Extra Compression: implode only: -EI, 542–544
    Extra Compression: normal or auto: -EN, 542–544
    Extra Compression: normal or auto: -EX, 542–544

Extra Compression: Optimize compression or speed: -E#, 542–544
Extra Compression: shrink only: -ES, 542–544
Junk/ignore directory names: -J, 542, 544
Move files: -M, 542, 544
Optimize compression/speed: -#, 542–543
Quiet mode: -Q, 542, 545
Recurse subdirectories: -R, 542, 545
Set ZIP file date to that of latest entry: -O, 542, 544
Store paths with member names: -P, 542, 544
Setup dialog panel
  Cancel, 548
  close with Esc key, 548
  Comment Files (sets Add File Member Comments switch), 547
  Comment ZIP (sets Add ZIP File Comment switch), 547
  Compression Method Best Type, 547
  Compression Method Implode Only, 547
  Compression Method Shrink Only, 547
  Do Not Compress Files With Special Extensions, 546
  Exclude Filespecs edit box, 546
  Implode Factor, 546
  No Compression Extensions: On check box, 546
  No Compression Extensions, 546
  Optional Commands group, 547–548
  Save, 548
  Temp Build File Dir, 546
Setup Options
  Activate Do Not Compress Files with Special Extensions switch, 530
  Activate Exclude files, 529
  Alert User (sets Display Error Information switch), 533, 548
  Auto Close (sets Close Window on Completion switch), 532, 547
  Comment Files (sets Add File Member Comments switch), 531, 547
  Comment ZIP (sets Add ZIP File Comment switch), 531, 547
  Compression Method Best Type radio button, 530
  Compression Method Implode Only radio button, 530
  Compression Method Shrink Only radio button, 530
  Date to Entry (sets Set ZIP File Date to Latest Entry switch), 547
  Destination directory, 528
  Directory Browser, 529
  Echo Cmd Line (sets Display Module and Command Line switch), 532
  Exclude edit box, 529
  From (mmddyy) (sets Compress Files After Specified Date switch), 531
  Implode Factor, 530
  Inform User (sets Display General Information switch), 533; 548
  Move to archive (sets Move to Archive switch), 531
  Move to ZIP (sets Move to Archive switch), 548
  No Comp Ext edit box, 529
  Recurse Dirs (sets Recurse Subdirectories switch), 547
  Recurse Subdirs (sets Recurse Subdirectories switch), 531
  Show Tech Info (sets Display Technical Information switch), 533
  Sound Beep (sets Sound On switch), 532, 548
  Store Paths (sets Store Path Name switch), 548
  Store Recur Dirs (sets Store Path Name switch), 531

Verbose (sets Display Technical Information switch), 548
Warn User (sets Display Warning Information switch), 533, 548
Zip Date to Files (sets Set ZIP File Date to Latest Entry switch), 531
ZiPaper 1.3c
Advanced Options
Center: /W /C statement, 501–502, 504
filename /F=filename.BMP statement, 501, 504–505
filename /F? statement, 501, 504–505
filename /F statement, 501, 504–505
Not Random: /NR statement, 501, 505
Setup Screen: /S statement, 501–502
Tile: /W /T statement, 501–502, 504
Update WIN.INI file: /W statement, 501–504
Associaton of Shareware Professionals (ASP) Ombudsman, 507
Configurations
Scenario 1: /1, 502–503
Scenario 2: /2, 502–503
Scenario 3: /3, 502–503
Scenario 4: /4, 502–503
Configuration screen, Enable/Disable, 502
experience, DOS batch files, 498
file extension, ZPA, 505
filenames, 506
installation
AUTOEXEC.BAT statement, 500
Control Panel dialog box, 500
directory location, 500
file preparation, 500
LHArc, 498
acquisition, 499
PKZip, 498
acquisition, 499
quick tour, 499
registration, 498, 507–508
form, 508
shareware requirements, PC compression program, 498
system requirements, 498–499
technical support, 498
CompuServe ID, 507
Thomas, Daniel, 498–508
updates, 507
updating,
ZIPaper v. 1.0, 506
ZIPaper v. 1.1, 506
ZIPaper v. 1.3a, 1.3, 1.2a, 1.2, 506
user manual, 507
wallpaper files, 507
ZIPAPER.DAT file, 506
ZIPAPER.EXE file, 506
ZIP Tools, 498
ZPA, file extension, 505
ZIP Tools for Windows
archive(s), 515–516
files, 516–517
formats, 517–518
COMMDLG.DLL file, 519
compacted vs. compressed files, 516
compacting, 515–516
compatibility, PKWare's DOS ZIP utilities, 512
compression formats, 517–518
disclaimer, 514, 562–563

documentation, organization, 512
file compression, 515–516
filenames, 519
Flash Card Help dialog panels, 555
FLASHDOC.WRI, 519
FlashPoint Development, 510–566
FPRES.DLL file, 519
FPSTR.DLL file, 519
FPZIP.EXE file, 519
FPZIPX.EXE file, 519
FPZXX.EXE file, 519
Help, 555
installation
advanced configuration, 520–521
application setup dialog boxes, 520
directory location, 520
Windows, 3.0, 520
Windows system configuration, 521
WIZiper drag-and-drop support, 521
WSETUP file, 520
libraries, 515
library files, 516–517
license agreement, 514, 561–563
site license, 565–566
license fees, 557–558
order information
billing, 560
form, 564
international orders, 561
prepaid orders, 558
purchase orders, 560
site license, 559
third party, 559–560
README.TXT file, 519
registered users, 555
registered Users Guide, 555
registration, 511
shareware distribution, 515
SHELL.DLL file, 519
similar shareware, 511
site license agreement, 565–566
system requirements, 511
technical support, 511, 556
Fox Mico's BBS, 556–557
TOOLHELP.DLL file, 519
updates, 556
Windows 3.0 files, 519
Windows Navigator, 513
*Windows 3.1 SECRETS*, Windows UnArchive, 511
WinNAV, 513
WIZ.EXE file, 519
*See also* WIZiper; ZIP; ZIPX
ZIPX
action command switches
Display help: -H, 550
Display license: -L, 550
Expand archive members: -E, 550
Expand member files: -X, 550–551
Test integrity: -T, 550–551
View member file listing: -V, 550–551
command line
format, 549
syntax, 549
command parameters
[x]:\directory\ 552
[filename1 filename2...], 553
[zipfile].ZIP, 552

command(s)
Help - FPZipX, 527
License - FPZip command, 527
compatibility
DOS PKUnzip, 518–519
DOS PKZip, 518
filenames, 519
format, command line, 549
option command switches
Close window on completion: -W, 550, 552
Display module and command line: -^, 550–551
Display technical information: -*, 550–551
Display warning and other trivial information: verbose mode: -!, 550–551
Junk/ignore stored paths: do not extract (-J), 550–551
Overwrite existing file: -O, 550–552
Restore directory structure: -D, 550–551
Setup dialog panel
Cancel, 555
close with Esc key, 555
Default Action Extract Members, 554
Default Action Test Integrity, 554
Default Action View Member List, 554
Save, 555
Target Pathspec, 553
Setup Options
Alert User (sets Display Error Information switch), 533, 554
Auto Close (sets Close Window on Completion switch), 532, 554
Default Association Extract radio button, 530
Default Association Test radio button, 530
Default Association View radio button, 530
Echo Cmd Line (sets Display Module and Command Line switch), 532
Expand Stored Dirs (sets Restore Directory Structure switch), 531, 554
Inform User (sets Display General Information switch), 533, 554
Overwrite Exiting Files All pushbutton, 532, 552
Overwrite Exiting Files Cancel pushbutton, 532, 552
Overwrite Exiting Files Rename pushbutton, 532, 552
Overwrite Exiting Files Skip pushbutton, 532, 552
Overwrite Exiting Files Yes pushbutton, 532, 552
Overwrite (sets Overwrite Exiting Files switch), 531–532, 552, 554
Show Tech Info (sets Display Technical Information switch), 533
Sound Beep (sets Sound On switch), 532, 554
Warn User (sets Display Warning Information switch), 533, 554
syntax, command line, 549
System menu, Setup, 553

# IDG Books Worldwide Registration Card
## *Windows GIZMOS*

Fill this out — and hear about updates to this book and other IDG Books Worldwide products!

Name _____

Company/Title _____

Address _____

City/State/Zip _____

What is the single most important reason you bought this book? _____

_____

Where did you buy this book?
- ❏ Bookstore (Name: _____ )
- ❏ Electronics/Software store (Name: _____ )
- ❏ Advertisement (If magazine, which? _____ )
- ❏ Mail order (Name of catalog/mail order house: _____ )
- ❏ Other: _____

How did you hear about this book?
- ❏ Book review in: _____
- ❏ Advertisement in: _____
- ❏ Catalog
- ❏ Found in store
- ❏ Other: _____

How would you rate the overall content of this book?
- ❏ Very good      ❏ Satisfactory
- ❏ Good           ❏ Poor
- Why? _____

| How many computer books do you purchase a year? |
| --- |
| ❏ 1       ❏ 6-10 |
| ❏ 2-5     ❏ More than 10 |

| What are your primary software applications? |
| --- |
| _____ |
| _____ |
| _____ |

| What size floppy disks do you prefer? |
| --- |
| ❏ 5 1/4"     ❏ 3 1/2" |

What chapters did you find most valuable? _____

What chapters did you find least valuable? _____

What kind of chapter or topic would you add to future editions of this book? _____

_____

Please give us any additional comments. _____

_____

Thank you for your help!

❏ I liked this book! By checking this box, I give you permission to use my name and quote me in future IDG Books Worldwide promotional materials. Daytime phone number_____ .

❏ FREE! Send me a copy of your computer book and book/disk catalog.

- - - - - - - - - - - - - - - - - - - - - - - - - - - - - - - - - -

Fold Here

Place
stamp
here

IDG Books Worldwide, Inc.
155 Bovet Road
Suite 610
San Mateo, CA 94402

Attn: Reader Response / Windows GIZMOS

# Complete Installation Instructions for the *Windows GIZMOS* Diskettes

T he programs on the *Windows GIZMOS* diskettes are stored in a compressed form in order to bring you more than 8 megabytes of programs. You cannot simply copy these diskettes to your hard drive; you must use the WSETUP program located on Diskette #1. The system requirements are the same as for Windows 3.0 or 3.1. You must be running in standard or enhanced mode, however; you cannot use real mode.

## STEPS: Installing Your *Windows GIZMOS* Programs

**Step 1. Insert Diskette #1.** Place Diskette #1 into your computer's floppy drive A: or B:, whichever drive is the correct size.

**Step 2. Run the WSETUP program.** Start Windows 3.1 or 3.0. Using the Windows Program Manager, pull down the File menu and select Run. Then type **A:\WSETUP** or **B:\WSETUP** and click OK. You can also use Norton Desktop for Windows as your program manager, but you must use NDW Version 2.0 or later.

**Step 3. Tell WSETUP which drive to use.** The default drive and directory under which the *Windows GIZMOS* directories are installed is C:\. You can select another drive or directory as the destination for the programs by editing the default value. During installation, WSETUP creates an additional subdirectory for each program you select, under the default or edited drive and directory. For example, if you type **C:\GIZMOS** and then install the program ClipMate, the ClipMate files will install into C:\GIZMOS\CLIPMATE.

**Step 4. Install the programs you want.** After you start WSETUP, you will see a dialog box with the names of all the *Windows GIZMOS* programs. In the file list on the left, click the mouse once on the name of the program you want to install and then click Add (see the following note on the Add All option). You can select more than one program to install at a time. When you have finished adding the programs you want, the complete list will appear in the box on the right. Click the Install button. WSETUP installs the programs you selected into their own separate directories. Make sure that you have at least as much free disk space as WSETUP says is necessary.

WSETUP also creates a group in Program Manager for each program, opens the group window, and installs the program icons into that group window. If you like, you can move the program icons to a different group by using the drag-and-drop method.

*Note:* If you have sufficient disk space, you will be able to use the Add All button, which will select all the programs from the disks for installation. Be aware, however, that the maximum number of program groups is only 45 or fewer, depending on the number of existing program groups and your system's available memory. If you install more programs than Program Manager can make new groups for, additional programs will install into the last group successfully created. If you're using Program Manager as your Windows "shell," we advise against installing all programs at once. However, some other Windows shell programs do not have this group limitation.

**Step 5.** **Configure the programs you installed.** Look at the first page of the chapter in this book that describes each program you selected. It may be necessary for you to take one or more additional steps to configure a program for the best performance on your system. For example, you may need to add a program to your path. If you need help, see the "Read This First" chapter for more details.

**Step 6.** **Register for updates.** If you like a program, register it with the author. Doing so may bring you a newer, improved version of the program or other benefits, as described at the end of each program's chapter.

_____

That's it! We hope you enjoy running these programs.